Progressive in Property

From Beginners To Winners

The Secrets Within The Stories

Published 2012

Printed by BookPrintingUK.com

Table of Contents

Why write a book like this?

Good question. I don't know about you, but I like reading about ordinary people achieving extraordinary things. It makes me want to go and do it; it inspires me and motivates me into action.

You'd have to be without a pulse not to be inspired by the humble yet transformational true stories in this book. They'll make you feel alive, they'll give you hope and faith, and even more than that they will help you to realise that you can do it too.

So who is the book for?

Primarily, I had three types of people in mind when writing the book.

1. Those who are new to Property investing, and are wanting more money, more free time and a better lifestyle
2. Those who have had Property investing education but struggled to put the training into action
3. Those who are already investors and need help with motivation, inspiration and need a gentle push [or kick up the backside if it is from Rob!]

Whether you're new to Property investing and not sure how and where to start, or if you're already an experienced investor, there are strategies and solutions in this book that you will greatly benefit from. These are practical, real life case studies of ordinary people who had little experience just a few short months or years previously. They have gone from beginners to winners, and in quick time too. In fact for many of them, the only one regret they still hold is that they wished they had started sooner.

Credit crunch, global turbulence, crashes & recessions

Without doubt, the Property market has changed dramatically in recent times. It's harder to get finance and mortgages to buy Properties, and to be honest, investors using 2-3 year old strategies are getting left behind. It has forced investors to find new solutions to new problems.

Most people have never experienced these conditions in their lifetime. They are unprecedented. Yet, there are a pioneering few that have been determined to not only find these solutions, but to utilise a huge 'contrarian' opportunity to shift wealth faster than ever before from big corporates to everyday entrepreneurs.

The intention is that at least one story will resonate with you and inspire you into immediate action. And if so, we will have humbly achieved our mission.

It is often said that there are more millionaires created in a recession than in an expanding economy. Necessity is the mother of invention.

Think, get educated, take action and enjoy the rewards.

"Once you make a decision, the universe *conspires* to make it happen."

Ralph Waldo Emerson

About the Author Robin Shaw

My first experience of Property was when I lived in Aberdeen in the 1990s. I was getting married to my then girlfriend and we were looking for a bigger place to move into. I was working in Dundee at the time and commuting back each night, frustrated at the lack of information available on this new thing called the Internet. As a Property buyer I wanted to find all the Property for sale in a specific area. Back then that meant talking to every solicitor (Scotland doesn't have many estate agents) and finding out the information yourself. Fortunately, in Scotland, each solicitor Property centres collated all the Property in its catchment area into a magazine, making the job a little easier for the Property buyer than it is in England.

Internet property centre

This was the time when the Internet was starting to be talked about in the mainstream press, and was about to skyrocket. I was working in IT and just waking up to the possibilities the Internet was opening up in my business, and in the world in general.

Building on the concept of the solicitor Property centre model in Scotland, I thought it was a natural extension for the Internet to sit above these centres to provide an overview of the Scottish Property market, and so the Internet Property Centre was born to make Property buyers' lives easier.

However, after extensive focus group testing, the solicitors just weren't ready for such a leap from quills to the world wide web, and after a year we made the company dormant and I went back to freelance IT. Shortly after that, a company called Rightmove appeared and took the internet Property market by storm. For me, this was a big lesson/mistake showing that just having the idea isn't enough. Sales, marketing, persistence, and who you know are just as important.

Life continued apace and we rented our flat in Aberdeen whilst we worked in London for a year. We decided to move to London but sold the Property for a profit (almost accidentally). It planted a seed in my head that Property was a good place to make money.

We then bought our flat in Wimbledon in 1998 after getting married at what we thought was the peak of the Property market. Little did we realise it was about to go through the roof.

We had our first child and decided to leave London and move to York to have more of a family life. I wanted to rent out our flat in Wimbledon and buy a house in York but didn't know how. My wife wasn't keen because of the "risk". She had given up work and we all relied on my income and didn't like the idea of paying two mortgages "If" no one rented our flat. Because I didn't know how (and not wanting to upset a new mother) I didn't push the issue and we sold. This is a decision I later came to regret as house prices rocketed the following year! I'm sure this story is a familiar one. Another mistake that I came to learn from. So often you learn what you want from what you don't want. I didn't want to repeat that mistake ever again!

Rich dad poor dad

For a long time, I'd had a feeling there was more to life than freelance IT work and started reading wealth creation books. I read a book that was to become an epiphany for me. It was such a powerful book because it laid out for the first time the answers I'd been looking for but didn't know to ask. As you will see many of the people in this book have read it and I recommend it to anyone embarking on wealth creation to read it. It put me onto Property which led to me reading the Property Investing books written by Rob & Mark. I recommend you go check them out right away.

(And no, I don't get a commission from them) ☺

The importance of income producing assets

Life ticked along quite nicely but I was restless after reading Rich Dad Poor Dad. It resonated so much with me that I became frustrated with my job. I thought as a freelance contractor that I had a company. In reality I just had a highly paid job. I owned a job, not a business. When I stopped working so did the money!

My wife had gone back to part-time work after having our second child (Rob will learn about that when he has a second child ☺). She did the book keeping for a letting agent. Shortly after, the owner offered to sell it to us. We were very excited by the possibilities it opened up to us as a family. She could be her own boss and drop and pick up the kids from school, but we didn't know how we were going to afford it.

However, I was now armed with a new mind-set. Instead of saying "I can't afford it", as the poor mind-set does, I asked instead "How can I afford it?"

This was driven home to me by my eldest son, Ben. Don't ask me why, but I used to put the "Rich Kid, Smart Kid" CD on when the boys went to sleep at night in the hope this knowledge would "seep" into their psyche from an early age. When it was my turn to put the boys to bed I'd take out the Thomas the Tank Engine CD and swap it.

One of the key phrases on there is "Poor Dad says 'I can't afford that!'" and Rich Dad says "How can I afford that?". It is in the subtlety of language that the mind's thoughts are revealed. I was discussing the cost of buying the letting agency with my wife when I came out with the Poor Dad's "We can't afford that!".

This must have triggered something in Ben because I heard the voice of a 7 year old say "Poor Dad says 'I can't afford it.' Rich Dad says 'How can I afford it?'" in true Dustin Hoffman "Rain Man" style. So there it was. My 7 year old was now reminding me of some of the key principles of the rich mind-set.

The answer was very simple and was provided by the owner of the letting agency. Buy the company over 10 years and pay for it out of the profits each month! Without realising it ,we had managed to acquire control of an income producing asset with none of our own money!

We also bought the building that the business was in so the business paid the rent, which in turn covered the mortgage. So, a business and a Property was now putting money in our pockets each month.

The importance of getting educated

I recognised that we'd fumbled our way through this deal. We had parked money in the deposit for the Property even though we bought slightly below market value. I now know we should have refinanced as soon as possible to pull more of our deposit back out, but this was at a time when the credit crunch was about to hit.

As a freelance IT consultant I appreciated the value of continuous improvement and maintaining marketable skills through training, so when a short time later an advert in the local paper advertised a 2-hour taster to learn how to invest in Property, I booked on.

That 2-hour taster led to a 3-day workshop at which I finally met people I connected with. I'd found my tribe. Like-minded, positive people who wanted to better themselves, and had done so by becoming financially free through Property investment. I no longer felt isolated. For the whole of my life I'd tried to fit into a mould I wasn't comfortable in: permanent employment.

Divorce – an opportunity for personal growth

Sadly, that 3-day workshop crystallised many differences between me and my wife. It made me realise that we didn't want the same things from life and that realisation has been the most painful event in my life.

It wasn't about the money but about freedom (or at least the quest towards achieving it) and about growing as a person. Many people do not make a bid for freedom for fear of failing. I didn't want to spend the rest of my life not having tried. I owed it to myself and my children to show them that life can be very different. I'd rather fail trying than never try at all.

That weekend I saw people give up their weekends because they loved what they did. They didn't have to do it (they were financially free) but they chose to. They said "when you enjoy what you do you will never do another days work in your life again," and that's what I wanted! I wanted to jump out of bed and be excited about going to work. I don't mind working hard but it has to have passion and purpose now.

It was with a heavy heart then that I had to give up my dream of building a Property business with my wife and that I had to start again. However, I did so with a renewed passion as a result of the wealth education I'd had. That education enabled me to have as amicable a divorce as I could hope for because I no longer feared the loss of money and was able to provide the financial security that I wanted for my family. Against all legal advice I gave the Property business and Property to my wife rather than take the half I was entitled to. This would have forced a massive change to my wife's and kids' lifestyles, and that's not what I wanted for them. After all, one of my goals was to provide financial security for my family and now they have it. I'm free to now go and make my own mistakes safe in the knowledge they are taken care of.

> When you enjoy what you do you will never do another day of work in your life again

Birth of Investment Property Partners

So, Internet Property Centre has now risen like a phoenix from the ashes as Investment Property Partners. It is a one-stop shop for busy people who wish to achieve financial freedom through Property investment, and we manage that process, from finding a Property, to refurbishing it and then to managing it. By helping others achieve financial freedom, I also achieve financial freedom.

The journey continues

Although starting again in life, having ensured the mother of my children is secure and therefore they are too, the journey has become far more exciting because of all the opportunities I now see and the people that surround me. I'm a happier dad and love showing my boys how they too can make money other than through a J.O.B. (Just Over Broke). I took them to the Progressive Super Conference (they were the youngest Property investors there!) so they could hear Rob, Mark and Lord Alan Sugar tell them that we should stop giving them pocket money in order for them to develop the skills to make money themselves. Which brings me onto a deeper subject: Your Purpose in Life.

My life is unrecognisable compared to the one I had three years ago. I've undergone a radical transformation personally and professionally. Some say it's a mid-life crisis but I prefer to call it a mid-life review. You take stock of your life so far and look to the future to see if you want more of the same. I concluded I wanted change, and as Gandhi said, "Be the change you want to see in the world," so I changed my life. It was singularly the most terrifying and yet most liberating experience of my life. I didn't want to stay in the invisible cage for the rest of my life. I wanted to break free and follow a path to more freedom; to enjoy the work I did and to help others, particularly children, to develop their financial intelligence, to feel happier and fulfilled, to mix with like-minded people who supported you in your crazy adventures, to jump out of bed and feel giddy excitement at what the day would bring.

I have Property investing and the people I have met through it to thank for giving me the strength and courage to make the change to live a life with more purpose and passion. I hope it does for you too.

> Be the change you want to see in the world
>
> *Gandhi*

Humber Property Network

I started the Humber Property Network in Hull with my friend and fellow investor Simon Cartwright and through it we get to meet all the people active in Property north and south of the river Humber every month.

They come to us, which saves us having to go to them. They get to know, like and trust us over time and as a consequence we have been able to very quickly mix socially with experienced investors. Our profile, as a consequence, is raised within the city in which we invest, and also with the speakers who present at our event. It's taught us how to market a business; an invaluable skill for any business and it's taught us how to build our customer list.

We have learned how to run a high energy, "edu-taining" event every month to inspire, motivate, support and have fun at. That rubs off on people and they associate those feelings with me and Simon, which is no bad thing. After all, one of our goals in life, is to "Make a Difference."

Wild Catz Investment Club

I created a spin off club from the Humber Property Network called the Wild Catz Investment Club. Here, we use the principles familiar to the Property investor of buying, insuring and renting. However, instead of Property, the club buys shares. We buy assets (shares), insure them (put options), and then collect rent on them (sell call options). Whilst not Property, the principles are similar, and it's another long term wealth creation vehicle. Being a club, we meet at least once a month to discuss trades and investment proposals, and it keeps everyone motivated to continue to learn from each other and our club mentors. Pooling our money enables us to grow faster and the power of compounding our profits every month accelerates our wealth growth.

The Investment Property Exchange

Because of my internet marketing training and experience with the Internet Property Centre, I've always wanted to create a marketplace for buyers and sellers, so I created the Investment Property Exchange, a web site where Property investors can post their investment Property deals cost effectively to more Property buyers than they could reach by themselves. A Rightmove for investment deals if you like.

Whilst my divorce has been going through I've been sourcing investment Properties to investors to generate a fund for deposits so I can build my own Property portfolio. Now to the next exciting chapter in my life.

So, let's get started. The common thread of the interviewees is that they have all worked with Rob and Mark personally, either through attending their events, being mentored by them, being a member of the Joint Venture VIP Community, reading their best sellers, *getting educated...*

And taking action!

They are unedited versions of the actual interviews, so we disclaim ourselves from 'proper grammer' ;-) We wanted them to be in their raw, unedited and natural format, and you'll probably sit back, relax, and feel like you are talking to them all personally.

Other than their Progressive journey, each story is quite unique, and buried in each one are the keys to the treasure. It is up to you to find them.

Fortune favours the brave.

Robin's Contact Details

Email: robin.shaw@propertycentre.co.uk

Web Site: www.robin-shaw.com

Web Site: www.propertycentre.co.uk

Web Site: www.humberpropertynetwork.co.uk

Web Site: www.oboron.com

Web Site: www.grilltheproperty experts.com

Web Site: www.investmentpropertypartners.co.uk

Mobile: 07711 699 153

Acknowledgements

Writing a book is a team sport and I'd like to thank the many people who have inspired and supported me along the way to making this happen.

To Rob Moore, Mark Homer, Daniel Wagner, James Watson, my Mastermind group, the team at Progressive and of course every person I interviewed, you all helped me strengthen my resolve to succeed in Property and get a better life for myself and my boys.

And of course you. Without you there would be no book. Without you there would be no next generation of underground Property investing success stories. Without you I could not have achieved my dream.

And one day we hope to include you in these acknowledgements. This book is an evolution of success of ordinary, non silver-spoon-fed people looking for a better lifestyle.

Please let us know when you succeed. When you create all the things you desire. We would love to interview you too.

Rob.moore@progressiveproperty.co.uk

Thank you.

About Progressive Property

If you already know about Rob, Mark and the Progressive Property Group, you can either humour us with the updated version, or you can flick through to my story. ☺

Progressive Property has inspired most of the current UK Property investing scene to greater results and more cash flow through Property investing, and through developing the multi-millionaire mindset, myself included.

The ever-growing Progressive group is the UK's largest Property training company, with over 200,000 subscribers to their newsletter and community, the UK's largest annual Property event, the Property SuperConference, with guests such as James Caan & Lord Alan Sugar, and over 100,000 people trained at live paid Property training events since 2008.

So what, you may ask

Well what is most inspiring is that the founders, Rob Moore & Mark Homer, are little over 30 years old. The Progressive group has only been going just over 4 years yet the founders have written the two best selling Property books in the UK Property market: "Make Cash in a Property Market Crash" and "The 44 Most Closely Guarded Property Secrets," and they've bought and sold over 350 Properties in that time (at the time of writing), holding a current portfolio between themselves and their joint venture partners of over £20Million.

What inspired me, other than their reputation for stripy shirts, is the fact that they are both very down to earth, ordinary, accessible people (Rob won't like me for saying that), much like you and I and the interviewees in this book. OK, so they fly helicopters and drive Ferraris, but they are no different; they are very approachable
(one thing that set them apart for me is that you can still get a personal reply from Rob or Mark) and a lot of fun to be around.

Mark is the clever one (again, Rob won't like me for saying that), with a great brain for numbers and spread sheets. He scrutinises deals intensely and has been investing since he was 15 years old. He is more risk averse than Rob, but is the brain behind the trademarked Progressive Deal

Scrutiniser™ - the secret system which removes all human error from the Property buying process, and the mastermind of nearly all their joint Property purchases.

That being said, it wasn't always like this for Mark. I know he won't mind me sharing this personal information with you, but in his mid 20's his dad died of Cancer. He had one of the worst strains and endured a very painful death, and I can still tell that to this day it stays with him. I was very fortunate to hear him share the story with me, as he is not a public person, and you can still see that many of his decisions he makes in business and life are to prove things to his Dad, and it is truly sad that he is not with us to see Mark now.

Mark's uncle also died very closely to his father of Cancer, and so their close allegiance and fundraising for Cancer Research seems to have become as important as making money for their community and, of course, for themselves too. I am convinced these events keep the drive burning inside Mark, which, as you will read in this book, seems to be one of the common denominators of success.

Rob is the inspirational one (Rob will like me for saying that). When I interviewed him for this book he had the energy and drive of all the interviewees put together, and he had just days before had his first baby son, Bobby. He is engaging, confident, audacious, infectious and very inspiring. He is also very honest, to the point where you are able to get very close to him and really see how millionaires act and think without all the fluff and nonsense most marketers out there give you.

I believe it is this mix and polarity of personality that has made them such huge successes so fast. Inspirational to so many is the fact that when the recession and Property crash really kicked in 2007/8, almost all the UK's Property companies and many individuals went bust. Rob and Mark came out of nowhere, and within two years had placed themselves almost to the top of the UK Property market.

Yet in 2005, Rob was over £30,000 in debt and struggling as a self employed artist. I didn't think that the debt he had then was that large, but when I talked to him 'off the record,' he told me that this was all credit card debt from University and from struggling financially since, and that he needed over £1,800 a month just to pay his interest.

I have the feeling he was a good artist, but he says that a lack of confidence back then hindered his ability to actually sell it. He recounts a pivotal day in 2005, where he had opened his house as a gallery to sell his work locally. I don't get the impression making it as a modern artist is that easy in Peterborough, but he went for it anyway, and I admire that.

But I could see in his face the disappointment and even embarrassment when he told me that he never sold one painting in any of his open house exhibitions. In fact not even his family or friends bought one, and not even through sympathy. Many of his pieces still hang at his home. I wonder what such a public thing does to your confidence, and it certainly seemed one of the defining moments for Rob to make a decision to change things, and not be in that position again.

Fast-forward to now and they've built the largest active Property community in the UK. The best selling books, the cars and helicopters and the TV shows all seem to be a spin off from their Property systems and trainings they have developed. If you are lucky enough to meet them you will see that they are as normal and 'ordinary' as you can get. Rob had no money to start with and Mark had little confidence.

And naturally many people thought they were lucky, and their timing was 'perfect'. Actually, most people don't know that Rob and Mark bought their first 16 Properties as a partnership together, all at the same time in 2006 & 2007 – possibly the worst time in history to start a Property portfolio.

But with a mix of luck, as Mark admits, and an absolute refusal to give up, or sell, and a commitment to making their investments work, they turned a cash draining portfolio into a retirement funding one in just 12 months.

You won't see them retire though – absolutely not likely. When interviewing Rob he mentioned that he might consider retiring when he dies, and I think Rob bullies Mark into coming along for the ride. ☺

Another thing that drew me to Rob and Mark, and the entire Progressive team was their commitment to giving back. Last year they donated over £60,000 to charity, and raised over £30,000 at the 2011 Property SuperConference. Rob openly admits he was in it for himself in the early days, but now with the charity balls and events, they really are making a difference, as I have experienced with most wealthy people, contrary to belief down the local pub.

I'll save the rest for the book, as Rob and Mark become part of the story through the interviews.

On behalf of Rob and Mark, we would again like to thank you for reading this book.

A foreword from Rob

I feel very humbled by reading these stories.

I feel very grateful to have been a small or sometimes significant part in the success of the amazing people you are about to read about.

Let me make this clear: these are not multi-billionaire tycoons; those who you would probably never get to meet in your lifetime. These are 'ordinary', everyday next-door people with very little prior experience in Property, often no start up capital, and certainly no silver spoon.

Everyone in this book, ourselves included, are no different from you. Many of us started with less money than you, less knowledge than you, because you are reading this book for a reason and to be here you probably had to jump through some rings of fire.

Perhaps it is a sceptical partner, perhaps it is friends and family (the crabs who pull you back in the box), perhaps you have had to overcome fear, risk aversion, a (perceived) lack of time and money, a lack of confidence, experience and knowledge, and perhaps you are still working on that now.

Either way, where you are now is the perfect place to be, the perfect platform to spring from, whether it's a place of motivation or desperation, and believe me, you are on the verge of the most exciting, amazing, inspiring, financially and emotionally life changing journey.

So what is 'ordinary?'

Don't get me wrong, ordinary is not plain, vanilla boring and fade into the background. Ordinary is often one of the attributes of a multi-millionaire Property investor. Ordinary is you and me. Ordinary is approachable and friendly, ordinary is humble yet confident, ordinary is infinite possibility for all of us

And what's great about these 'ordinary' people is that they don't fit the mould. You can't define them; they define themselves. We have busy mums who work 70 hours a week, we have people who work 5-10 hours a week, we have 19 year olds and 61 year olds, we have men and women, we have different cultures, we have partners and lone rangers, and we have multiple strategies used to suit the individual. We have Marks and we have Robs.

And what blew me away, as I added in the Key Learnings section, was that there is so much to learn from every one of them. I don't care if you think you know it already; I'm supposed to know it all, yet learned so much from reading everyone's story, and I continue to commit to a lifelong journey of learning and improvement. I thank everyone in this book, and you, for allowing me to do that.

I learned that the more you learn, the more you know, and the more you know, the more you have to learn.

It's easy to skim through and read the 'surface words' that are on the page. But I urge you to go a little deeper. Look how creative every person in this book has been to common challenges – finance being an obvious example. Look how many jaw-dropping lessons are conveyed matter-of-factly, almost off the cuff and on a whim. Like they don't know just how profound what they said was.

Look how solution focused they all are when most people just focus on the problem.

This isn't 'Chicken Soup for the Soul' in that you won't find people who came back from the dead or defied gravity to move the Earth, but in my eyes these are everyday versions of just that, in their own world, in their own way, and in a way you and I can relate to so easily.

Thank you for reading this book. Thank you for being inspired enough to open these pages. When all is said and done, more is said than done, and as you know, this is just the beginning.

Paul McFadden

Young Scottish Joint 'Venturer'

Story At A Glance

Age: 25

J.O.B. Construction

Investment Areas: Glasgow

Strategies: Lease Options, Buy To Let, Joint Ventures, Package Deals

Vital Statistics:

Cash flow: 12 Months generated £10,000

Portfolio: £3.5Million

How did you get started in property, Paul?

When I was 19 I searched everywhere online trying to find any kind of get-rich-quick schemes. I think for me, the big motivation to make money came from not having my dad around, and seeing my mum struggle financially to bring up my two sisters and me.

During my childhood years, it was frustrating to miss out on all the material possessions that you see your friends enjoy – the Nike trainers, the Playstation's, etc., and like a typical child, I had blamed my mum for missing out on those things, without having the maturity to realise how hard it had been for her to cope with things.

So I kept searching online, wanting to see how to get rich, and Property just kept on popping up and that was at a time when there was no word of recession, so you could see the large returns that could be made.

Paul's Motto

"If you will do what nobody else will do, for the next twelve months – then you can have what nobody else can have, for the rest of your life" - *T Harv Eker!*

I came across Andy Shaw's book "Money for Nothing...and Your Property for Free", and while it left a lot of things unanswered, it did give me more curiosity into how it might actually work.

I kept searching and found free seminars in Glasgow; these were Russ Whitney and Brad Sugar's seminars. These seminars would then promote £7,000 courses, and being 19, just out of university, and starting my first job in IT, there was no way I could afford them.

How did you find out about Progressive?

I kept working in my job, but still researching and investigating, when I came across Progressive online. I read their books and got more interest and knowledge about how this Property business could actually be possible. Everyone I spoke to about Property – family, friends, and colleagues - said if you could buy a Property and hold it for five years, then it will have doubled in value. On that basis, it just seemed absurd not to get involved. The one thing I felt could possibly hold me back at that point: my young age.

How did you meet Progressive?

Around September 2008, I was about to book onto a Property Educators Mastermind Class, and the only reason I didn't was because I would have to take out a loan to pay for it. In the meantime, an email from Progressive appeared for a £50 training day in Manchester. I thought that before I committed to anything substantial in Property, I should probably try this low-cost training, rather than a more expensive course that might not lead to anything.

I drove from Glasgow to Manchester for the event and then straight home again, as I never had the money to stay overnight. I was blown away with what I learned that day and I made a commitment there that I'd find the money to go on a full training course.

After the one-day event what did you do next?

In March 2009 I went on the 3-day Masterclass; paying for it with a credit card. Knowing that there was already friction around money issues with my partner at the time, I felt that I really had to make the money work.

What did you do with the training and education?

I bought two investment Properties in the time between the 1-day event and the 3-day event, with a third purchase being my own home.

I had purchased these Properties using the creative financing strategies that were prevalent at the time, as well as getting another credit card to pay for the 5% deposit that was required.

After the training, however, the market completely changed. It was hard enough getting a 15% below market value deal, never mind 25%!

I spent the rest of the year completing further training; this time on T. Harv Eker courses, and I also bought another six Properties with my business partner.

I was working long hours in a construction job, but any spare moment I had was spent searching online for Property.

Completing the 3-day Masterclass expanded my mind to see more opportunities.

Have you made any mistakes along the way?

Loads! Although difficult and frustrating, mistakes are in fact one of the best ways to learn!

> It's not about avoiding mistakes. It's about learning from them.

From the one-day Progressive training I went out and did lots of viewings and spoke to many estate agents. I bought a Property that was worth £85,000 and I was getting it for £70,000. However, not being familiar with the creative finance strategies that were being used at that time, the surveyor involved valued the Property at the purchase price of £70,000. This left me with the major challenge of finding the 15% deposit, which I simply didn't have.

In the final days before that sale completed, I had to rush around trying to source the required funds. I increased my overdrafts, got another loan, and also borrowed money from a family member. I somehow pulled together just over £13,000 in five days.

It was a nightmare scenario trying to solve the problems and cover various fees for solicitors etc, and led to one of my main mottos for all future deals:

> When you have your back against the wall, you will find a solution.

Thankfully, I bought another Property that provided £5,000 cash back, which helped pay for the first mistake.

The entire market has shifted since that point, and I've witnessed a lot of changes. Very common strategies like creative financing completely changed; products such as 85% mortgages disappeared; and generally speaking it's been a very tough time for a lot of investors and home owners alike.

Did you do any other training?

Absolutely; my path for continual learning is the main reason behind what I've been able to achieve, and how I've been able to adapt.

I completed an intensive six-month period of very specialist courses with T. Harv Eker's training company. I took out a personal loan to pay for the Quantum Leap and Millionaire Mindset Intensive trainings in Singapore, Malaysia and London; an incredible set of experiences in my life.

What did you get from that additional training?

This training was instrumental in propelling me forward by changing my mind-set to THINK BIG.

If you're going to think, then

THINK BIG

It is so important to focus on developing yourself, your self-belief, and continual learning. It's also essential to learn to manage the money you already have, before you manage more, something that Harv deliberately focuses on.

Networking and connections are also very important, sometimes more so than actual knowledge or information. You just don't know who you are sitting next to. I met tax and finance experts at the Progressive training, who helped explain the processes, and it gave me more confidence to keep going and to buy more Properties.

What other property related things do you do?

I set up the Scottish Property Meet, as a major networking event to bring lots of Property people together on a regular basis.

I've launched Ashton Lloyd Ltd with some key business partners, where we provide one-stop Property services that specialise in the Scottish sector.

I also released my own training product – Property Jump Start – which was distributed online and teaches all of the essential information and strategies for getting started as a Property investor, with guides, reference sections, and videos.

Why did you set up the scottish property meet?

I've always believed that *your network is your net worth.* I therefore wanted to meet and bring all of the key players in Property, into one place, to generate new opportunities and build connections.

We're now broadening the aim of the meet to include different wealth creation vehicles, such as share trading and internet marketing, as well as also tackling personal development.

We've been able to provide a great service to the large number of members that attend every quarterly event, and we've been fortunate to be able to present some impressive main speakers, such as Shaf Rasul (online Dragon), Kevin Green (Secret Millionaire), Simon Zutshi (P.I.N.), Sarah Barrett (Lease Options), Glenn Armstrong (Ask Glenn), John Lee, Vincent Wong (Wealth Dragons) and Rob and Mark (Progressive).

When did you give up your J.O.B.?

It was towards the end of 2009 that I finally left my job.

At that time, my expenses were still greater than my income, but I just felt that I should go for it and that the release of available time would be able to provide me with new opportunities, and the ability to work on more deals.

And did those new opportunities appear?

My business partner and I had all these plans and about 90% of them never happened. Thankfully though, the first four months were really good, and we completed about five lease options.

My business partner and I then wanted to go in different directions, so there was a period spent separating our assets to go our own ways.

I was building up quite a large list of Investors, and my focus changed to servicing that list with opportunities that had been sourced, negotiated, and prepared for purchase.

I started surrounding myself with the right people, getting a couple of business partners that I had known for a long time and trusted; they could get mortgages and we were still able to buy even with all the lending restrictions that came about.

My best friend is an internet marketer, and using his lead generation skills and running the Scottish Property Meet, people would come to me with leads and deals to sell on. I started systemising that process, and by far it's been the most profitable thing of last year.

To date we've facilitated 52 deals, which represents about £6 million worth of Property. The average discount has been 31%, with yields of around 12%.

We've been adding to a portfolio at the rate of almost one a week with joint venture partners; I only have four Properties solely in my own name but I've got 20 with JV partners.

Why did you joint venture and not buy in your own name?

It all came down to the lending – my own situation, and the new restrictions from lenders.

My credit rating wasn't brilliant at the time. I had spent a small fortune on Property investment education and personal development - around £45k - all on credit cards, so the mortgage lenders probably weren't too impressed. ☺

Any deals you'd like to share?

I've got two Properties going through at the moment, with one that's just about to complete that we bought as "un-mortgageable". We purchased it for £50k with an end value of £150k. The refurbishment is costing £25k, and it will cover the bridging costs and release a large amount of profit.

My aim is to do four of those this year.

What challenges have you encountered?

Deals fall through at various stages, and it can be incredibly frustrating. It's a blow and I'd probably have ten more Properties by now, but it's just part of the business. Every business has a success ratio.

You just need to move on, and find more deals to raise that success ratio. Don't let it stop you. Find the wisdom in the situation and always learn from it, so that you reduce the risk of it repeating itself.

In such an ever-changing market of an ever-changing industry, you must learn to adapt. For example, it's a lot tougher to obtain financing in this current climate, so I always have to adapt and change the way things work and systemise them to grow into a business that can expand further.

When it comes to low-level detail like systemising, it's never been something I've enjoyed, so I've learned the importance of finding people in your business who love the stuff you hate and are good at it.

At first because of my age I struggled to believe I could do it. There were no other young guys doing it, but I realise now that I don't have to wait until I'm 30 or 40 before starting. Whatever your age, just get involved in Property NOW.

I read so many books where they had mentors or someone to turn to for help; I never had that.

I now meet up quite regularly with about 10-15 people and talk about things and hold each other to a higher level, and I see my mind-set changing and see what's possible.

If you want a better life, including financially and also the way you think about things and how you do things, then I think you need to surround yourself with the right people. And when it does come to the financial area, Property is by far the number one vehicle to become wealthy in the long term.

Any advice to anyone considering property investment?

If anyone said to me that I would end up spending £45k on my education and self-development before becoming successful, I wouldn't have bothered even starting.

But you ***have*** to invest in yourself. You must develop yourself as a person to allow success in, and to learn the technical skills of Investing.

Having read the book "The E-Myth", there are three types of people: technicians, managers and entrepreneurs. I'm an entrepreneur so the technician and, manager in me are weak; that means all the accounts, all the systems, all that stuff I don't like.

Thankfully I've got two business partners who are just awesome at that. I'm not always about making the most money in a particular deal. I prefer having a structured company with processes and systems that can make most deals work.

To this day I live by this motto:

> **"If you're prepared to do what no one else will do in the next 12 months, then you can have what everyone else dreams of"**

It's not for everyone, so for most people, they'll have to change their mind-set. Get some personal development to help with that change. Stick your toes in the water when it comes to Property investing. It's going to give you a better life; it's going to give you a second income; it's going to give you more time and freedom – which we all crave.

And what does the future hold for you?

One of my goals is to speak at schools, universities and colleges to tell my story to inspire others, and to show them they don't need to spend all of the huge money that I spent on training.

My product - Property Jump Start - shares most of the knowledge I've gained spending £24k on Property training courses, so I want to use that to 'jump start' others on their own journey. I also want to write a book to show people what can be achieved.

I want to own my own building contractors, and to have my own renovation team to manage refurbishments. With my background in construction, I've got access to a lot of good labour and I can source materials at good rates, so for a refurbishment most people would pay £20k, I'll be able to complete it for £12k, thereby providing a good service as well as making profit in that area too.

My goal in 10 years time is to have a construction company as big as the one I used to work for doing commercial Property.

I'm moving into my dream house in July; it's a townhouse over 3 floors with its own hot tub, cinema room; the works.

My friends are watching what's happened to me so far, and are starting to take an interest. A friend is now living his dream as a golf coach because of Property investing, which is great to see.

I love what I do now so it doesn't feel like work; I wouldn't want to change it for anything.

Key Learnings

- Invest in your education. Heavily. n
- When your back is against the wall, you can make amazing things happen.
- The market always changes, adapt and change with it and you will be successful.
- Do what others are not prepared to do.
- Find partners with different skills to you and align with them, always networking and meeting new people.
- Get mentors and push yourself. Love what you do and the rewards will come.
- Package deals for others as well as buying for yourself for greater income and larger chunks of cash.

Education

Progressive Property JV Buying Frenzy Networking Event [1-day]:

http://www.progressiveproperty.co.uk/jv-event

Progressive Property 3 Day Property Investing Masterclass Intensive:

http://www.progressiveproperty.co.uk/masterclass

Paul's Contact Details

Email: paul.mcfadden@ashtonlloyd.com

Web Site: www.ScottishPropertyMeet.com

Gill Alton

Building "Alton Towers"

Story At A Glance

Age: 42

J.O.B: Previously a Manager within Xerox but now focused on Property investment, around the family

Vital Statistics:

Properties: 15 Properties, nine of which have been purchased since attending Progressive Property training. The first of these nine were purchased at the end of Jan 2010.

Cash flow: £3,350 (this is calculated by taking the rent minus interest only mortgage payments and letting fees)

Equity: Our current equity across our Property portfolio is calculated at approx.. £566,000

Portfolio Value: Is currently calculated at approx.. £1.5M

How did you get started into property, Gill?

My husband bought a three-bedroom house in Bristol and rented out two rooms to raise some income. He then moved out completely because he realised he could get more money by letting out the whole house. So he was back living in student accommodation when I first met him. He then remortgaged his house in the rising market to buy more Properties. This was about 14 years ago.

When we moved to Maidenhead in 1999 he had a small portfolio and I had my residential home, we then sold several of these houses to afford our higher-priced home in Maidenhead, which left us with a portfolio of three in Bristol.

As a family we have our own mortgage business, Alton Mortgages Ltd, which my husband set up over six years ago and until about four years ago, I held a senior corporate role in Xerox, having worked for them for 12½ years.

Four years ago we decided that I would join him in the mortgage business because our daughter was just starting school and we wanted more flexibility around school runs and holidays. So I resigned from Xerox, having studied my mortgage exams in the evenings and weekends and I joined him on 1st September 2007.

We now know this turned out to be the start of the credit crunch, so not great timing on my behalf as the marketplace literally fell off the edge of a cliff within two or three months. It soon became apparent there wasn't enough mortgage activity to keep us both busy so Richard concentrated on the mortgages, while I focused on the life cover and critical illness work. I enjoyed this because essentially it was around helping people feel more secure.

We also joined Utility Warehouse as partners and initially I took the lead on this business, again this business is hugely enjoyable because it involves helping people to save money and build a better future for themselves. It has been a brilliant business to have alongside our mortgage and Property businesses as the skills of keeping going even when you are receiving rejection and negative comments are 'life skills' which are transferrable.

Then at the beginning of 2009 the mortgage network we were connected to for FSA Regulations went bankrupt. As one of the network's top mortgage brokers my husband was owed considerable money and unfortunately even after they went bankrupt, the bank still continued to pay our money to the network because that was the way the contracts were written.

In total we lost about £25,000 in a quiet market and with me having given up a big corporate salary, so it was a massive wake up call to think about things differently.

We had crazily thought our income streams were diversified, across mortgages, life cover, critical illness and insurance policies, we had never considered that the lynch pin would fail. So though we had multiple income streams the single point of failure was the weakness. This made us realise we needed to focus on income streams which were outside of the mortgage business.

By this time we had six Properties, made up of the original three in Bristol and then a further three which we had bought over the previous six years; however we had purchased these less wisely.

In fact, in purchasing these last three Properties we classically got swept along with all the 'hype' prior to this latest crash. For example, we did a two-day course with Inside Track and ended up buying an off-plan flat in Manchester city centre. The housing market stalled and the quoted growth in equity never materialised, and everybody was competing at the same time for tenants, so we never achieved the quoted rental figure either.

We also bought one through a company up in Newcastle, again after only minimal discussions with them, and really no due diligence. This has just about 'washed its face.'

Finally, we bought one in Maidenhead. It's embarrassing to say but we literally went out to buy a loaf of bread and came back with a flat. It was the show flat, and the last in a small complex for sale. We thought we did well, however in hindsight as it was new build we of course paid over the odds. We also took the developer's word on the value, not even looking at any comparables. Thankfully we have been saved by having a brilliant tenant in the Property from day one.

So having decided that we were going to start investing in Property again to increase this income stream into our family, we knew we had to go back to basics. From the mortgage business, we knew it was a buyer's market, but we needed to buy wisely. Thankfully, we had equity in our home, which we could release, so it was a case of getting the education to ensure I spent the money in a way which allowed us to achieve our objectives.

How did you meet Progressive?

Juswant Rai is now a friend of mine and knowing me and my personality he suggested Rob and Mark would be a good fit because of their different skills. As a family we decided I would take the lead on the education and attending the courses, so Richard could continue to focus on our mortgage business.

What attracted you to Progressive?

When I attended the first, £49 seminar in London with Progressive, I liked their style because I felt Rob and Mark represented the two extremes of the combined Gill Alton. For example I am very happy working on a spread sheet but I also thoroughly enjoy working with people, building teams and negotiating. Through my career at Xerox I spent time in sales, finance project management, service management and project management so I have been fortunate to develop a variety of different skills.

I recognised they had a great deal of knowledge, which attracted me and I felt with their guidance my experience and skills could be significantly improved. Being a passionate person myself, their extremely evident passion for the business also was a significant factor.

So you did some mortgage broker exams?

As per my story above I took my mortgage exams before I started with Progressive. These exams took me about four months to study and pass, as I was doing them in the evenings, around two very young children, and a career which engulfed me from 7:30am. However, I feel to make improvements in your life you often have to step out of your comfort zone and push myself and this was just one of those occasions. As we now know, I was only actually a mortgage broker for a few months, but the decision to leave Xerox was in fact the catalyst that got me where I am today.

Do you read property books?

I am embarrassed to say not until I started reading self-development books with Utility Warehouse and subsequently Property books via Progressive Property. Up till that point I read absolutely nothing, in fact I rarely picked up a book. Now I am proud to say we have a mini-library and am reading all the time.

When did you do your training?

September 2009 I did a one-day course for £49 and I followed this with a three-day Progressive Property Master-class course in November 2009. I also did the Lease Options course, and the Estate Agents course around the same times. After the trainings I followed what we had been taught and started to invest. The only thing I didn't follow was the advice to invest locally. Richard was brought up in Nottingham and through his mortgage business he had established a connection with an estate agent in Nottingham.

I had completed some analysis on our local area but having put my training into practice I worked out I could make our family money go further and achieve significantly higher rental yields in Nottingham. So at the end of January 2010 I went to Nottingham to look at an investment Property and to date I have now purchased 8.5 Properties for our family in Nottingham, the half Property being a joint venture purchase with our friends.

Any deals you'd like to share?

All my purchases have been below market value and have also delivered significant cash flow, however I was particularly pleased with the joint venture we did with our friends, mainly because they are both from senior financial backgrounds and were naturally cautious about the Property market. However they were curious enough to ask me to share my analysis with them and once I had, they surprised me by saying "We'd be interested in buying with you". It gave me a great boost of confidence. So we joint ventured on a house, their name is on the mortgage and everything is being split 50-50; from the deposit to the cash flow and the costs. It's all tied up in a contract.

How did you raise finances?

We raised the majority of our equity from our own home, and remortgaging our existing portfolio. We have also joint ventured with my parents, on two occasions. They had no desire to actually purchase Property, but they welcomed the idea of making their money work more effectively for them, while at the same time supporting us to grow our portfolio.

Have you made any mistakes?

Yes as mentioned we bought three Properties that barely cash flow when we got carried away and didn't do our homework. The Manchester flat has never achieved the rents quoted, the South Shields Property only just washes its face and the one in Maidenhead has money parked in it we are unable to extract. In all three cases we didn't do our due diligence correctly; basically we were lazy and relied on glossy sales literature.

However, I have learnt from these mistakes, I am now much more cautious and very detailed. For example an easy mistake to make with a repossession is to underestimate the cost of getting the Property back to a rentable standard. To avoid this I go through each room with my refurbishment manager and cost out everything that needs doing line by line, before we put the offer in. I find it's often the small things that can be overlooked which all add up.

So have you stopped buying for yourself?

No we are still investing, but in a controlled manner. However, as there are so many opportunities to invest I set up Alton Property Partners, so that I can work with others to help them take advantage of the current housing market. My service is very much around offering a complete solution for my investor. I am particularly aimed at the busy professional or business owner, who does not have the time, knowledge or connections required, but would like to benefit from holding a stock of Property. I use all the connections I have built up on our own portfolio, my experience, skills and education to deliver my service to them.

How many deals have you packaged?

I am currently in the process of hand-holding an investor through my 11th Alton Property Partners purchase. Most of these have been repossessions.

To date, my investors are based in the South, so they don't have the time and the ability to go to Nottingham regularly to review Property and manage the refurbishment. They want to simply hand the hassle over to me, knowing I will take the stress away and deliver the end result. One of my investors said "Gill, what you've achieved for me in four months would have taken me five years".

Put simply, I treat my investor's money as if it were my own money. To date, my Properties have achieved a gross rental yield of between 10-13% and voids have been minimal.

Once I have sourced the house, if the investor wishes to put an offer in, I work with them and liaise with the estate agent on their behalf. Once accepted, my husband and his mortgage business arrange the mortgage and we engage the solicitors on behalf of the investor. As soon as the sale is complete, my team then go in and refurbish to the agreed instructions.

Finally, I then coordinate with the letting agent so they market the Property ready for tenants. The Property belongs 100% to the investor so the cash flow is fully theirs and I don't have any equity stake in the house.

So, you've done this all in the past year?

Yes to date, since the end of January 2010. I've been involved in purchasing houses for our family, and also setting up Alton Property Partners to support investors. In total between both I have been instrumental in purchasing 20 houses.

How do you charge for your deal packaging?

I charge based on the equity that I deliver to my investor on completion of the refurbishment, which I feel is fair. So for example, if I source them a house for £55K and agree it's worth £70K in the current market when refurbished, but the refurbishment is going to cost £5k then the equity I have actually delivered is calculated at £10k. The financial commitment of the investor is to cover the deposit, the legals, the valuation, the refurbishment costs and my fees.

You don't pay cash for your repossessions?

We have only had to buy one house cash, and that wasn't because it was a repossession, but because it wasn't rentable in the current state and as such the mortgage company put 100% retention on it. Because my husband is a mortgage broker, I have the advantage of being able to work quickly and efficiently with him to arrange a mortgage for my investor, so purchasing a repossession with a mortgage has never been an issue. I have also primed my investor beforehand so they are ready; so it's a very smooth process.

So, to sum up your plans. You want to buy more properties for your family and deal package 20 for investors.

Yes I would like to continue to build our family Property portfolio, but I am also passionate about delivering my service to others through Alton

Property Partners, so I have set myself the personal target of helping secure 20 Properties for my investors this year.

I am fortunate that I feel that all my acquired skills have blended together in Alton Property Partners, and it was lovely to hear one of my Investors ask me (when the tenants moved in to their Property) "What do I have to do now because so far you've done everything for me?"

So your husband's mortgage business fits well

Yes it does. There has been so much doom and gloom in the press about the volume of mortgages dropping off due to the recession, but as many mortgage brokers have left the industry, the good ones have survived. Having my husband as part of my deal packaging process is brilliant, as I have direct access for my investors.

You mentioned getting out of your comfort zone. How are you going to do that?

I love building relationships and I am very comfortable with the financial side of the business. Actually there's not one side of the work I do in Alton Property Partners that I don't like. However, I would like to achieve more direct to vendor negotiation. That will push me out of my comfort zone simply because circumstances have meant I haven't done a lot of it yet. People buy from people they like and trust and so there would be an element of me having to prove myself to the vendor. I find doing anything new always pushes me outside of my comfort zone, but it's the way you grow.

So how did Progressive training help you?

The Progressive training has moved my knowledge up to current day, keeping me up to date with the movements in the Property marketplace. The combined knowledge of Rob and Mark is outstanding, covering everything from the economy and finances to inter-personal skills. As a specific one, of the most powerful things I have learnt from Progressive is how to analyse a deal effectively. Getting the financial fundamentals right is essential when investing in Property.

Has the VIP training made a difference to you?

Absolutely 'Yes'! Meeting once a month with other like-minded people has helped me to keep focused. Although I am very self-driven, the accountability has also made sure I have continued to prioritise my workload, which is great when you are first setting up a business. And this coupled with invaluable help and advice along the way has made it very worthwhile. Finally, I recognise being associated with Progressive has led to publicity I wouldn't have gained otherwise.

Any words of wisdom to share?

In any line of business you get knock-backs and Property investing is no different, so you should be prepared for them. Not everything will go right first time, so most importantly you just need to ensure you learn from your mistakes. The mantra within our house is to "do your best as you can't ask more of yourself than that, and if it doesn't work the first time, keep going. Don't give up."

Finally, if you're not passionate about something don't do it because you won't put your heart and soul into it.

What are your plans for the future?

As I have mentioned I am still very keen to build our family's portfolio and also to grow Alton Property Partners, as on a personal level I find helping others to achieve their investment goals, whether it is to buy one house or build a portfolio is extremely fulfilling. I am already helping to mentor at the Progressive Property VIP group and I am really enjoying that also.

One of my plans outside of the work I do with Progressive is to focus specifically on mentoring women and helping them get onto the Property investment ladder, as I feel it is a brilliant opportunity for women to take control of their finances and build an income to support their pensions.

From the many discussions I have, I know that sometimes the whole concept of getting started can be a bit daunting for women, so I would love to utilise my knowledge, skills and experience to work with them to support and encourage them, and help them lift off the ground. So watch this space for Venus Property Mentoring.

Key Learnings

- Regardless of what you have bought in the past, you can still make it right today.
- Invest in yourself. Network and read.
- Work hard, prioritise and get the important things done, so they fit around your personal lifestyle.
- Don't be afraid to approach friends and family for JV partners and finance.
- Spend time learning how to analyse a deal properly or work with someone who is good with numbers.
- Do the best you can and if it doesn't work the first time, just keep going.
- If you're not passionate about something you shouldn't do it.
- Be ready. Act fast. Don't give up.

Education

Progressive Property JV Buying Frenzy Networking Event [1 day]:

http://www.progressiveproperty.co.uk/jv-event

Progressive Property 3 Day Property Investing Masterclass Intensive:
http://www.progressiveproperty.co.uk/masterclass

Progressive Property Lease Options Training:

http://www.progressiveproperty.co.uk/lease-options-intensive

Progressive Property VIP JV Millionaires Club:
http://www.progressiveproperty.co.uk/vip-pmc

Progressive Property JV Portal Members Forum:
http://www.progressivepropertyforum.co.uk/

Gill's Contact Details

www.altonpropertypartners.co.uk

www.altonmortgages.co.uk

www.altonsavings4u.co.uk

www.altonmoney4u.co.uk

www.venuspropertymentoring.co.uk

Martin And Beckie Cooper

From Sticking Plasters To Plasterboards

Story At A Glance

Age: **Beckie:** 34 **Martin**: 43

J.O.B. Beckie: Nurse **Martin:** Plasterer

Investment Area: Hastings, East Sussex.

Vital Statistics:

Properties: 15 Properties.

Seven Properties in seven months since joining VIP with Progressive.

Cash flow: £5,499 net per month.

Portfolio: £1,460,000.

How did you get into property?

[Martin] The first investment Property was just a small flat back in '92 around the time of the recession. It was quite a bargain.

I then met Beckie, and at the same time, the flat downstairs came up for sale with the freehold, but I didn't have the deposit money, so Beckie very kindly lent me it.

In return, she asked for ten percent return on her money, which I gave her, and that was the start of our joint venturing and buying Property together.

Then Beckie and her brother, using money from an inheritance, bought a house along the seafront. I did it up while Beckie was studying in London. And then when she came back three years later, they sold it and with the funds from that, we bought our first home together.

Then in 1999 we bought a Property for £8,000. A poor chap, a friend of a friend, bought a flat and within a year the concrete floor had collapsed and cut off the water and electricity. Then he spent the next six years taking the Nationwide building surveyor to court. All the time he was paying the mortgage. He got a settlement but was thoroughly depressed and just wanted to get rid of it. So I offered him £8,000 and he accepted it. We spent £12,000 on it, and sold it three years later for £82,500 thanks to the rising market.

What did you do with that profit?

With that money we bought a plot of land on which to build our dream home which we are living in today. We then started investing in houses on a buy-to-let basis using self-certified mortgages, as I was a builder. Although my motivation can sometimes lack a little on my own Properties I now go out to work and get somebody else in to do it. We bought about eight Properties up to 2006.

What happened next?

[Beckie] We decided to move to Canada! We upped sticks and moved to

Canada with my job as a nurse. We did that for a year and a half. It was a great experience. We had a great time, did lots and saw a lot.

However, one of the major disadvantages was there was snow for six months of the year, which was cold. As a family, we love winter sports. We did lots of skiing, we did lots of boating, camping, all sorts; biking, all activities outside.

Although that was a major plus for us, there wasn't enough to keep us there at the time. So we came back at the beginning of March last year, 2010. I'd decided on setting up a letting agency by then because I didn't want to go back into nursing full-time, as I realised that what we did best was invest in Property.

So we decided that we'd start looking about for courses and seminars and things, and happened to come across the Property Super Conference, in April 2010. And that just set the ball rolling, really.

What impact did the property super conference have?

It opened up a whole new way of looking at Property because up until then, we were going at it alone and not realising all the other ways you can finance Property. We were just doing it the normal way, with a huge deposit, which we were lucky enough to have from taking equity out of our house.

But with the Progressive Property way, it just shows you that there are other people out there and different ways of buying Property, and there's a family, almost. I felt we were playing at it before. Now we're really serious and we really want to get quite a lot of Property.

You were there on stage at the 2011 property super conference as a result of the action you took.

Yes that was quite amazing. Getting up onstage is taking us to a whole different level of where we want to be, and what the future brings, so it's great and always opens doors.

We're very motivated in some aspects of our lives and we know what we want. We've got our goals set out for where we want to be. We're a great mix of different personalities and skills between the 2 of us. And really, really lucky because we know that other people are doing it on their own without husbands and wives.

We come home and we can discuss anything, at any time, and we've got support and accountability all rolled into one at any given moment. We love going to the meetings that we have. And we're very good friends now with several of the people on the VIP club, both from the first one and the second one, which is great accountability and lovely to meet up with like-minded people. We're just fortunate that we can carry it on when we're at home.

When did you join the VIP club?

We did the three-day Masterclass in July, and Rob did his Jedi mind tricks for which we are eternally grateful, and he convinced us all the answers lay in the VIP club which we signed up from September 2010. To date we have bought seven Properties in seven months.

Seven in seven months?

Actually, we're completing on two more now, so it will be nine in eight months. They're all in Hastings, which is our niche area as found for us on the Masterclass, which we obviously know very well because we've both been brought up in and around the Hastings areas and villages. So we've always lived here, always known peripherally what the market was doing.

And since we've been doing Property properly, we have learned a whole host of things; we can look at a Property and determine whether it's in the right ballpark for the figure they're offering. And also because I run a letting agency as well I have a very keen eye for what the rental income can be.

It is useful because I have to do that research and learn that market anyway for this business. I know what it will rent out at and therefore what's the right price to buy it for, to get the right yield, to get the right cash flow.

How are you financing the deals?

We've got two joint ventures that we've done with other people and some cash that we had from the sale of our house in Canada. Now we know the money is there we can keep going out to look at the Properties.

How did you find your joint venture partners?

We looked to family first. They've seen us doing it and how well it's going, so they wanted to invest as well.

What is the nature of the joint venture?

We borrow the money and use it to buy a Property below market value and then refinance and give them the money back with a return higher than the bank is paying them.

What is the VIP helping you achieve?

I think the accountability from meeting people. Setting, achieving and reviewing goals each month. This month has been probably the hardest one for us in a long time because the challenge for us is to promote ourselves, to brand ourselves and to get ourselves out there.

So Rob has set us a challenge this month of producing a short promotional video that we can upload to the Internet and our website. Rob's interviewing us this month, so to us, that's a different kettle of fish and slightly more of a challenge. Buying houses is not now the challenge for us.

It's very much accountability because we know that we don't want to obviously fall down, fall behind, disappoint anybody, all those things, so that's a great thing.

We've been very lucky with people that we've had our one-to-ones with on the VIP programme. They've been very supportive and set reasonable goals. I'm also quite competitive as well so that spurs me on to try and beat everybody in the same group. ;-)

Have you got an endpoint in mind at which you'll 'exit?'

I can't see an end. We'd like to build up a legacy to hand to the children. We're going to be doing this for a few years. The market will change, our strategies will change, but Property is it for now. That's going to be it for the rest of our 'working career.

Did you have challenges as a couple working together?

I think we've done that fairly well without actually locking horns. Most of these agents seem to be men and Beckie goes out and does the viewings with them.

Beckie is very good at negotiation and building relationships. We've been together a long time so I think we've done all our natural negotiating of what we're best at and who does what anyway in the relationship.

Beckie does the numbers and Martin manages the power team; his network of people. We're not competitive in our relationship. We're secure enough not to have to prove to each other that one is better than the other. We've been together so long that we know each other's strengths and weaknesses, and that's good as well because we're able to keep the other one accountable, and all those things that go along with it.

We still laugh. I dream about Property and I have often dreamt of the Progressive lot as well. Obviously, not in a strange way, ;-) but we've done so much with them and they've taught us so many different strategies.

Property to us now is just life. And there may be a Property situation that's going on that I'm immersed in and you can't switch your brain off. We're lucky we can state our case knowing that we're not going to be judged on what we're saying, which is often difficult for people. We can bring something no matter how mad it might seem to the table, and have an honest opinion about it.

What kind of properties are you investing in?

There's no real pattern. What we like to buy is ultimately ones that are going to rent out, that yield well, that cash flow well.

At the moment the Hastings market is crying out for three bedroom houses, but they're more difficult to get at the right price so that they yield and cash flow well. Having said that, having rapport with estate agents is really important, because they phoned me up and asked if we could help out on a deal.

The other Properties that we have been buying are flats. Ones that other people shy away from because there's an absent freeholder, or there's some problem with the lease. One of the flats we bought, the lease is short so you couldn't get a mortgage on it. We had to buy it for cash and extend the lease and then we will remortgage when the six months comes up, and make cash that way.

It's seeing an opportunity that someone else hasn't seen and hasn't understood. It's like "observe the masses and do the opposite," as Rob and James Caan have drummed into me!

How much cash flow are you making now?

We have 15 Properties and after the costs we're making £5,499 net after costs a month and yielding 11-12%. The one pre-Progressive left a lot to be desired; we now have rules in place which mean we won't buy anything that yields less than 8%.

Can you tell me more about the property with the short-term lease?

We've extended the lease and we're in the process of doing it up. The comparables in the area were anywhere between £60,000 and £70,000. So we plan to put it on the market in five months at £60,000 for a quick sale. It was originally priced at £46,000. We did offer £30,000, but they refused that, but they came back with £32,000 being okay, so I got a good discount.

How did you fix the short lease?

We just asked them if they'd extend it and they did for 10% of the purchase price, which was great. The freeholder arranged to have the lease extended for just the solicitor's costs and their fee.

You got that one fixed before you actually purchased?

We got the agreement that they would extend the lease before we completed on the purchase. We paid cash because it was below mortgage threshold and had a good conveyancer that had everything in place. After the six months comes up we will hopefully make 15-20K and take out all the cash to give us deposits for two or three Properties.

What are your plans for the future?

It's a very exciting year. We're now deal packaging and deal sourcing for people, and also setting up a hands-free portfolio service for people, as we've been taught by Progressive; we're following their model.

We are also planning on buying more Properties because that's where our cash flow is coming from. We're looking at opening up a system where we can mentor people as well that are interested in buying Properties in the surrounding area, or want to make Hastings a niche for them.

So, why are you creating all these new income streams?

We would never have thought about it had it not been for Progressive. We just thought buying Property was what you did and that was it.

We didn't realise that there were lots of different income streams: deal packaging, lease options, selling and flipping. We knew about flipping and selling but now we know these other strategies, we want to continue having our income coming from many sources when the market changes. This is so we can be financially free and not have to go to work so we can spend more time with our family, and do the things we want to.

It's highly leveraged active income isn't it?

Yes and do you know, I don't see it as a job at all. I'm not stressed and I don't have to manage people like I used to. We manage ourselves; we come and go when we please. I love doing it and it's just fantastic. I can't imagine doing anything else now.

They often say that when you do what you love, you'll never do a day's work ever again. I get to take my children to school and pick them up because I work my life around them and they didn't have that before. I didn't have that luxury.

And yes, I do work hard but it doesn't seem like hard work because I love doing what I'm doing. It's not luck either, because lots of people say, "Oh, you're so lucky". It's not luck at all. We've worked hard and we've had support. And we'll continue to have that support. I love going up to the

Progressive VIP meetings. It takes us four hours to get there and three hours to get back but it's well worth it to us, to meet like-minded people, to build an alliance and to have the support.

> When you do what you love, you'll never do a day's work ever again

What advice would you give to people coming along?

You need to do your homework. Find somebody who's done it. Find someone with experience. Someone with the knowledge and experience because lots of people out there will say, "Oh, yeah, look at this. Blah, blah, blah", and they're not actually doing it.

I think you need to align yourself with somebody who has actually got the knowledge and experience and that you can ask questions. Do your homework, look around, and then go for it.

There are lots of people we meet even now who are course junkies. You can go on so many courses. You need to do enough homework to dumb down some of the risk. It can never be a risk-free thing, Property investing. It's just not the way it works.

You have to weigh the risk, and you have to get the right risk profile. And lots of people obviously have different risk profiles, but also, there's no point just saying, "I'll do it tomorrow, I'll do it tomorrow", "Oh, I'm waiting until the time is right", because the time is never right. If you sit back and wait, you lose that opportunity. So that's why we're buying like crazy. My work ethos in my former job was see one, do one, teach one.

Beckie's Motto

See one, Do one, Teach One

You've got to feel the fear and do it. So just dive in once you've done a bit of homework. Mistakes are just opportunities you've got to flip on the head and change the way you look at it. You can't fail at this game as long as you learn to re-evaluate it and do something different next time, so you can't fail with the system we use.

Mistakes are just opportunities you've got to flip on their head

What's the plan for the letting agency?

The letting agency is just ticking along nicely. I am actively promoting that as well, but my ultimate aim is to hand that to an office manager so that I don't work in the business. It will then earn us a passive income. We source deals through the letting agency too.

Your thoughts for the future?

I would like to have 150 Properties, at least, with a decent cash flow so we can go off and do whatever we want. It sounds very simple but you just have to plug away at it. You have to do it every day to make those small gains. In the end, all those small gains add up and before you know it they add together to generate something special.

We also have a plan to live in the Mediterranean, and every day we get closer to that dream, which is now a goal and will soon be a reality.

Key Learnings

- Don't become a course junkie. Get out and make mistakes fast
- Mistakes are just opportunities you need to flip on their head
- When you love what you do you will never do a day's work ever again

Beckie and Martin's Contact Details

Website: www.epic-property.com

Email: Beckie@epic-property.com

Telephone: 0844 272 2618

Mobile: 07889 727381

Education

Property Super Conference:

http://www.propertysuperconference.co.uk

Progressive Property 3 Day Property Investing Masterclass Intensive:

http://www.progressiveproperty.co.uk/masterclass

Progressive Property Lease Options Training:

http://www.progressiveproperty.co.uk/lease-options-intensive

Progressive Property VIP JV Millionaires Club:
http://www.progressiveproperty.co.uk/vip-pmc

Trevor Cutmore

Faith, Purpose And A New "Lease" Of Life

Story At A Glance

Age: 49

J.O.B. Chef and Community Development.

Investment Area: Lincolnshire

Strategies: Lease options and buy-to-let.

Vital Statistics:

Properties: In the 12 months in the VIP Group I got seven deals and bought them in a variety of ways, plus almost £2Million of JV finance.

Cash flow: £3,500 per month.

Started a company to work with cash JV Investors.

How did you get into property, Trevor?

I was a chef for 25 years. I worked in London and Italy, but in 2003 I gave up chef-ing and moved into community development, which meant a drop in salary from £50,000 a year down to £19,000.

I did this because one of my goals in life is philanthropy. I love helping people, but after a good eight years of working in community development I realised that I wasn't going to get an income from this work that would enable me to help more people.

I've helped set up a school in Africa and lots of other things in the wider community. But these require money, so in 2004 with a friend of mine who is now my business partner, we decided to look at Property as a source of additional income.

We took over a large building on a lease that had some commercial units and it also has some flats on top as well, so that was the start. I started managing that myself, and that gave us some good experience. But, we said, "What we need to do is to start buying."

We had some money and so bought four holiday lets down in Cornwall. They were going to be buybacks after three years and guaranteed rent, so it looked quite a safe bet.

We put the money down. We did the traditional way of money-down, buy-to-let mortgages and on we went. We found another Property five miles away from us in Louth; a two up, two down – we said, "Yes, that's the sort of Property," because we'd been listening to some Property investment teaching.

We purchased a two up, two down – no problem. I managed to get about 17% discount on that just by being cheeky, but knowing what to spend, and that was it.

We bought five Properties in our portfolio and were forced to stop because we just had no more money to do anything else. That was 2007.

The crash came and the deposits we had were swallowed up with the dip; we had to leave 25% in, so that stopped us.

How did you meet Progressive?

Fast-forward to 2009 and I still to this day, do not know how I got to hear of Progressive Property. It must have been an e-mail but we went to a one-day event they did and it cost me £50 – an absolute bargain.

I went down, heard all these different strategies and different methods. It was all over my head, but I knew enough that this sounded really exciting; and education is something that is power or at least potential power. So, I came back. I brought my business partner up to speed and he said, "Right. This is what they're doing. Take the courses."

Did you do any other training?

I did the three-day Progressive Masterclass course and then the Lease Options training. That was at the end of 2009.

In January 2010, the Progressive VIP Millionaire's Club was launched. Again, I went back to my business partner, I discussed it. He's a chartered accountant. He understands accountability, responsibility and action, and we both knew that with a mentoring program, that would actually bring about results.

So, in I went. I loved the one-to-ones. I loved the speakers. The dynamics of the group and likeminded people was absolutely superb. It created friendly competition between us because each week: you'd find out and see what they did and it really encouraged you along.

Within months – bang – it was our first lease option and that was really good. We've not looked back. I did what the mentors told me to do and listened to what the speakers were saying.

We have done a lead generation site, but we haven't gone big in the IT or in the social media at present. But still, I'm looking at a cheap system to generate leads.

Are you planning to do a lead generation web site in the future?

Yes, we have got one up, but we're just not proactive in it because I am getting loads of leads anyway through leafleting and newspaper. I've got another two Properties to look at tomorrow, so that's never been a problem.

When did you discover that you wanted to help people?

There was a time when I was a very different person. I fought for Great Britain in judo. I was bullied as a kid and then I became a bit of a bully myself. I learned to fight and broke people's arms, noses and fingers. I was a nasty piece of work, but my life changed in 1994.

I used to swear constantly in six different languages and the day that I gave my life to the Lord, I haven't sworn since. I used drugs and almost divorced my wife. It was a really bad time in my life but I came into the Christian faith and that has been the most important part of my life since.

So, integrity is a huge part of what I want to achieve and reputation is very, very important even in the business world. I do like what Rob and Mark teach. I like the way that they're ethical and have integrity. That's very, very important to me. So somewhere along the line, my drive is my faith because I want to be in a position to help people.

I'm not perfect by any means. I know now how imperfect I am, but my faith is very, very good. It's what binds my life, my relationship. My wife, though we nearly divorced, is now my closest friend.

Has your wife been interested in property?

Well, at first she wasn't interested. We have three sons. Louis is 28, Jack is 24 and Clark is 21. When my wife was 45, she went to the doctor and found out she was pregnant, so we've got a four year old little girl, Joy and our lives have completely changed.

She's a teacher in a Christian school in Lincolnshire and has done that for many years.

Any tips you'd like to share?

I heard someone say, "knowledge is power". However, he clarified and said "knowledge is potential power," and he's absolutely right. "To know and to not do is to not know."

To know and to not do is to not know.

With all that you go through with the mentoring programs, you're given things to do. Make sure you do them, or it's absolutely pointless.

When mentors recommend things and they tell you to do something, you've got a choice and I chose to do what they said. So when they talked about books, I went and read the books. Now, what my wife and I would do is we read 10 pages a day of a book, usually a personal development book

Do you read books?

Oh, absolutely yes. I've read a book by Zig Ziglar. With that book, it's many stories of many people fighting adversity – all sorts of things. They make a stand.

For instance, there's one guy in America, he said, "We're not going to open Sunday". It was a burger stall. "We're not going to open on Sundays. We're going to give people the day off. Whether they want to go to Church or not, that's irrelevant. I just want to honour God."

It went into malls in America and they said, "No, our policy is open seven days a week". He said, "Okay, we won't come in". But, they changed their policy and let him in.

Now, I think his turnover is about £2.5 billion a year in over 5,000 places. Whether you agree with it or not, whether it's being religious or not, I like people of principle.

Third book – I've got something different. It's not personal development. I was illuminated by it so I could see things differently – Purple Cow by Seth Godin.

Have you made any mistakes along the way?

Well, yes. I'm still paying for them in Cornwall. The four holiday lets. Certainly, we buy closer to home now otherwise it's a 10-hour drive down to Cornwall for us.

Are you going with the strategy of finding somewhere within an hour's drive of your house?

Well, not wholly, but I don't think I'll buy down in Cornwall again either. I don't mind if it's the right Property in the right place and I can have it managed by a letting agent. I'd do it. However if it's on a leisure site I'm not going to.

Once bitten, twice shy. I'd much rather have two or three bedrooms, and the odd HMO would be nice. HMOs are higher to maintain and some agents don't want to touch them but the rewards are higher.

I'm actually looking at selling some commercial units that I've got to raise some cash, so I can do some cash buys. We want to be in a position to buy because we get some really good deals. I've got very good relationships with the estate agents who are offering me 20% below market value on deals.

I know that I could get over 25%, probably closer to 30% if I had the cash. So, I definitely am looking for cash rich Investors. I've got the knowledge and time to source Properties.

I don't want to deal-package. When I'm finding Property at 25%, 30%, 35% below market value, I want to do joint ventures and keep a share of it.

I've got mortgage hosts with Properties, so that's good. They put the money up. They've been supplying the deposits to put it in. Six months later, they remortgage to get their money back out because there's enough of a discount in there. Their name is on the mortgage. I oversee the whole deal. I install the letting agents and the tenants. We split the deal 50/50.

How do you find the joint venture partners?

Well, you've got friends and family to start with. As my profile has risen with the help of Progressive, I've attracted more Investors to me: they're motivated now because they can't get a return from the bank or stock market so attracting funds from them is easy.

I've got a lovely lease option which is just coming on now, which I've just sent to solicitors, so that's going to be a good one.

Do you want to tell us about lease options to show people what's being done in this market?

Yes, okay. It's a two-bedroom flat with a 96-year lease on it. It was on the market at £67,000. He works in another country, and she wants to go and join him. So, they wanted to sell, but couldn't sell at that price.

Their mortgage is £42,000 and they had reduced the Property down to £58,000 to try and sell. But, it's still not moving. Things just aren't shifting a lot unless it's Investors. But fortunately, she called me and I went to see it, liked everything, made a silly offer of – I generally work on 30% - about £40,000.

I said, "£40,000, £41,000 – the top would be £42,000." I knew that wasn't any good to her and then I talked about possibly a long-term lease. I would take control, it allowed her to move away and then we would buy it in a future time, again not giving them any jargon, any great details because otherwise you scare people with technical stuff. So, I was just gentle with her.

They didn't need the cash, just the mortgage taken care of?

That's right. He has a good job and she's going to join him. No problem at all, so they're fine. So, I put it out there. I had a look. I went back and saw her. We had another chat and she said, "Yes, I like the sound of it. My husband likes the sound of it." I said, "Okay, I'll put terms together and I'll e-mail it to you. Have a look. Give me a call and we'll have a chat."

I did say that there'd be seven years because lease options at the minute where it was normally 5 years, and you get a tenant buyer and cash out in three years – we can have that buffer – but since the market is not moving, it's harder to increase the value of the Property because Properties are going the wrong way at the minute up here.

So, tenant-buy is your best option. What I'm doing is I'm setting it for seven years. I'm going to rent it for four years, then I'm going to find myself a tenant-buyer for three years and monetise it that way, and it's really going to work. When I suggested, I said, "Right. I will service the mortgage, (which isn't much at £220 a month), for the period of time for the seven years."

They won't get anything from the deal which is obviously because I'm looking at buying it at £42,000, there's no equity in that – "But, I'm happy to pay you £52,000 in seven years' time."

I'm also going to give them 15% equity after seven years when we've sold it above the £52,000 of the net.

After all charges have been taken off, it's 15% of the net value so it's win-win.

Top Books

Rich Dad, Poor Dad – Robert Kiyosaki

God's Way is Still the Best Way – Zig Ziglar

Purple Cow – Seth Godin

It allows them to move on, doesn't it?

Yes. She wants to move at the end of March. I pay the legal fees. It's going to rent for £450 and will cash flow for about £260 a month. In seven years time it might not have doubled in value but it would be close to 100K.

You lay the seed, they come back and they say, "Look, can I talk to you a bit more about that?" because obviously what people don't know, people fear. So, it is a bit of an education and with some of the people that I've seen.

So you did the lease option training with progressive, but now you actually offer that training yourself?

Yes, so that's another thing. I didn't look at that when I started out two years ago or four years ago, but Rob & Mark think I have done so well on the VIP programme that they invited me to train as their Lease Options trainer, as they take a step back from the trainings themselves.

Plus it's another income stream for me: again one I would have never predicted two or four years ago.

Trevor Cutmore's Contact Details

Website: www.trevor.cutmore.co.uk

www.successinproperty.co.uk

Email: trevor.cutmore@gmail.com

Telephone: 07779018983

Key Learnings

- Invest in your education and training.
- Get accountability from someone or a group.
- Stay true to ethics and integrity.
- Find the best mentors and follow them.
- Read and never stop learning.
- Be creative and look at how you can offer solutions to people's problems that works for you and them, and always have their best interests at heart as well as your own.

Education

Progressive Property JV Buying Frenzy Networking Event [1-day]:

http://www.progressiveproperty.co.uk/jv-event

Progressive Property Lease Options Training:

http://www.progressiveproperty.co.uk/lease-options-intensive

Progressive Property VIP JV Millionaires Club:

http://www.progressiveproperty.co.uk/vip-pmc

Rob Moore

From Struggling Artist To Millionaire Entrepreneur

Story At A Glance

Age: 32

Investment Area: Peterborough

Vital Statistics

Cash flow [Business & Property]: £3Million

Equity: £2.1Million

Portfolio: Multiple JVs - £20Million+

How did you get into property Rob?

The reason I got into Property was because ultimately, I wasn't making enough money doing what I was doing. I was an artist, so I used to be very much a typical solopreneur artist. I used to paint the paintings myself. I used to go and try to hang them in galleries, and sell them myself, not very well. Actually, my art – the actual art was pretty good. I always had the feedback that I was a good artist. I got 100% at GCSE. I was the only person in the country to get 100% at GCSE art or 98% at A-level, and I think again one of the top five people in the country. So, I clearly had a talent, but I was crap at sales and marketing. Obviously, life is very different now. But back then, I just couldn't sell my work, not to the level that I wanted to be able to pay my £30,000 worth of debt off, to be able to pay the loans on the loans and the interest on the credit cards. £30,000 worth of debt doesn't sound like a lot now, but back then, it was braggable debt and the money I was earning selling paintings wasn't even paying off the interest, let alone the principal on all my loans.

That debt was acquired just by living above your means, was it?

Yes. I just wasn't financially savvy. I just wasn't aware of it. I hadn't been trained. I didn't know what I didn't know. So, I went to university and came back with all this debt. I didn't really know how to manage my money. I thought, yes, they're giving me a £1,500 overdraft. They're giving me a £5,000 credit card. Let's go and drink all that under the table, and have the best time of my life, which I did. Then, I came back with about £20,000 worth of debt, and then I decided to get a £10,000 loan and buy a car which was, I think, one or two years old. Within about 18 months, I had to sell the car to pay off some of the interest on my credit cards. I got about £3,500, £4,000 for a £10,000 car, but still had the £10,000 loan to pay. So, I just didn't know how to manage money. I just had no clue and I fell into Property by accident actually. Maybe it was just that I was looking for something else. But when you're not getting the results that you want even though you know you should be, and when you've been spending the first 25 years of your life not getting the things that you believe you deserve, sometimes you stumble upon things.

What did you do at university?

I did architecture – completely irrelevant. As most people, I went to university because I thought that's what clever people did. That's just what I thought.

I've just had a new son as you know. He's 7 months old. I don't want to force him to do anything like everyone thinks I will, but certainly if he's entrepreneurial and if he wants to set up a business, I'm not going to say to him, "You've got to go to university." I'm assuming he's going to be a smart kid if he's anything like his mum. But for me, unless you really know you want to be a doctor and that's the road you have to go down, I thought university was a waste of my time and a waste of the talents that I had.

So, I was hanging my pictures in a gallery and the guy who owned one of the galleries at the time said, "Look, Rob, you've got to get into Property." Of course, the first thing I said which is the first thing everyone says – I've heard probably 100,000 people say it to my face now because of the amount of people we've trained, "Well, I can't afford to get into Property because I can't afford to buy them", " I can't afford the deposit" or "I don't have the cash." It's the first thing I said. Mike at the time said, "You don't need money to get into Property." I said, "Yes, whatever, whatever." I batted it off for, actually, only a few weeks because for some reason, he wanted to help me and he worked on me. But you know, there are people who do this for years and years and years. Then finally, he said, "You've just got to come to this event. Read this book. Come to this event. That's all I can ask." I hadn't read a book since *Fantastic Mr. Fox* when I was eight or nine years old. I wasn't a reader. But, there was just something about Mike, and the way he seemed to be pushing and encouraging me in this. He bought a couple of units and said how much money he was making. So, I went back and I read this book in two days. Afterwards I said, "Oh my god!" All of a sudden I realized I've been spending my life buying liabilities rather than assets and it opened a door for me. About a week later, I went to an event – a really small, networking event in Peterborough with probably 10 people there. A presenter was standing in front of the slides. It was the driest and boring presentation I've ever seen. But at that networking event, I met Mark who obviously, as you know, is my business partner.

That was your very first networking event?

Yes, the very first one and I meet my future business partner. Shoot – score. It's all kind of gone from there really.

Tell me about your first property deal

I read this one book. I've met Mark. Mark and I had a chat at the bar after this networking event. We were both actually chasing a Property on the same street as luck happens. We were talking about it and I'd thought that I'd found this little goldmine street because instantly, that one book turned me into an avid reader. I read probably about 50 books a year now when you include the audio programs and I'll do that for the rest of my life. So, I was reading a few books, not just on Property, but on wealth creation like *Think and Grow Rich* and books like that. All of a sudden, I had this huge passion. So, I'd gone out, and I'd done a few viewings and bumped into Mark. Mark and I decided that we'd go on a couple of viewings together and just chat about Property – go down the pub, meet each other. Mark at the time was working for a chap in Peterborough for a Property sourcing company. He went back and he said, "Look, you've got to get Rob in. He's this bundle of energy and enthusiasm. I don't think he knows a lot yet, but that doesn't matter. You've got to somehow leverage him." So, they both got me into the office. They'd given me five book recommendations. I'd read them all in that week and I was just really hungry for it. Based on that, the guy hired me. I went in that room with the intention of working for free for them. I could paint through the night and I can work through the day. I don't need sleep. I had some funny working hours in my painting anyway. I did a lot of work through the night. So I thought, let's just get in there. Let's work for free. I think in a few months, I can really learn how to do this business. He started paying me £6 an hour which was pretty crap. But then, it was £8 an hour. Then, it was £10 an hour. Then, he started giving me commission. In that first year, I earned almost £100,000 and I've never earned £20,000 or £30,000 in a year before. So in that one year, I earned more than probably the four or five years previously as an artist, and in that same year, Mark and I, because we were both sitting next to each other in this office working, just started going out and buying Property together. I leveraged his skills, his knowledge, his money, his contacts because he'd been doing it quite awhile. I tagged along with him. I read a lot of personal development and wealth-creation books, so I was adding value on the mind-set side of things. I learned to become a life coach, so I was working on that with Mark. Yes, we bought, I think, just over 20 in our first year and my first nine months.

When you said you earned £100,000, how were you making that money?

Okay. That wasn't even included in the Properties. But, I earned that money through working for this guy, doing presentations for him because Mark and this guy, they didn't really have the personality or the courage to do public speaking. But, I said, "Right, I'll go and do all the talks." So, I started going around the country, doing the talks for him and stuff like that.

So, you travelled around the country networking?

Yes, absolutely. I got to every networking event I could. Also in that time, I was earning commissions on Properties we were selling. So, that was just my first ever Property salary, if you like. But also in one of the deals that Mark and I did, we made about £31,000 profit. Again, that was more than I'd earned in the previous probably two or three years as an artist. So, I was making money working for this guy, but for me, it wasn't about the money. I mean the money just came. It was about getting the knowledge and the education. I'm always telling people now, "Go and get an estate agent", "Go and find a Property sourcing company" or "Find someone like us. Find someone who's got a big brand, and go and offer to work for them for free." Not many people do it. I mean if they did it, they'd just do so well. We've had a lot of people who come and do work experience with us. But if someone came and worked for free for me, I'd certainly show them a bit more or give them a bit more than a normal member of staff because

That was the attitude I had at the time and as it turned out, I made nearly six figures. The real money was in the Property though. That was chump change compared to the money we were making both in the capital and the income from the Properties we were buying.

When was this?

This was December 15th, 2005. I remember because it was my dad's birthday. It was that day and around about that week where I met Mark, where I read this book and where a button just switched. It was like I'd known for so many years I wanted to be successful, wealthy and I wanted to be an entrepreneur. My dad had drummed it into me since I was three years old – "You can do anything you want, son. Just go out there and take what's yours." He gave me a good upbringing. GCSEs, A-levels, I got into girls and I got into booze. I turned around and I'm 25. I drifted along for years and had not really gotten anywhere. So that week in December, everything just happened. That was end of 2005. 2006, I worked in this company and at the end of 2006, Mark and I left. We set up Progressive, end of '06, start of '07 and we've turned that into a multi-million pound business now. We bought and sold around about 350 Properties since then.

Tell me about the first few deals that you did then. Were you confident? Were you nervous? Your first deal was a joint venture with Mark, wasn't it?

Yes, every single deal I've done bar two or three because whenever I buy a Property, I keep it. Now, we've sold a few that haven't gone very well, but I always buy with the intention to keep. Anything that I live in, I keep. Then when I move on, I keep the old one. So, I've got a handful of units that I bought for myself and kept. Mark's got a portfolio on his own as well that he had before me. But everything since we got together, we've bought together.

Well for me, I felt supremely confident. I don't really have a confidence issue problem as most people know. However, as a struggling artist I had zero confidence in selling my work. I was embarrassed and nervous about asking people for money. That translated through into most of my life like with girls. I became quite reclusive. But as a kid, I was good at sport. I played county sports and I was never worried about that. I was always worried about what people thought of me.

But when it came to Property, I don't know. I was going to say maybe it was because I had Mark there as a business partner. He had a lot of knowledge. We can just go out and do this. I've never known anything where you can leverage debt, where you can use other people's money, where you can make so much on the upside, where you can build multiple streams of income, and I said let's just get out there and take over the world. So, I didn't really think about what if. I didn't really think about what might happen if we don't do deals. What might happen? I was just like, we've got to go and do this. I think that helped drag Mark along with me because Mark is a lot more cautious than me. I often take the Mickey out of him for his spread sheets. He's quite risk-averse which works for us as a partnership. Mark had the knowledge, but I was, let's get out there. Let's go and do five viewings a night. Let's make loads of stupid offers. Who cares? Let's just do it.

The flip side to this is that Mark says you're much more of a reader. So, you'll go, prepare and research on the subject whereas he might just go in and learn by doing.

Yes, true. I suppose because I spend a lot of my time reading, I felt like I did have some knowledge even if it wasn't on-the-ground experience. I could always fall back on a few of the words that I'd known from the books that I'd read. I just think if you take fast action and you just keep doing it, there's a saying called, "Fail forward fast." I wasn't even thinking of failure. If you don't think of failure, you don't fail. But it was, yes, I'm going to make a few mistakes – so what? I don't really think about it now, to be honest.

But you know what it's like for people doing a deal for the first time. They're full of nerves and it sounds like you didn't have that because you equipped yourself with the knowledge and had the confidence.

I'd been sourcing Properties but that happened at the same time, so I hadn't been able to build up confidence sourcing before I bought Property myself because I was doing it at the same time.

If you've got any kind of problem, challenge or issue, just buy three books on it. So if you've not got much confidence, buy three books on confidence. If you're always scared, buy three books on overcoming fear. I think it's quite simple. Maybe I did have challenges or things I wanted to learn. I was reading loads of sales books because I wanted to learn how to sell. I didn't know how to sell obviously before art. I went from selling £10,000 worth of paintings a year to nearly £100,000 in my first proper year in the Property business. So, just grab a load of books and read the things that you don't think you're strong at. But also with the whole thing with fear and confidence, the only way – the only way to get over it is to go and do the thing. Whatever the beast is, whatever the demon is, you've just got to go and do that right in the face, head-on. I've now learned to enjoy that. If there's a problem, if there's an issue, if there's something I'm scared of or nervous about, I just make myself do it.

I have a friend who's scared of heights. He's jumped out of a plane eight times. He's done it more times than people who aren't scared of heights! Just do the things you fear most and get over it.

Exactly! Feel the fear and do it anyway. You'll find what you were afraid of wasn't real in the end.

You said you've bought and sold 350 properties. How much cash flow is there?

Our portfolio is quite complicated, so I'll tell you exactly what it's made up of. Since 2005, we've bought and sold 350. Of those, we've held just under 200 units. Of those, currently around about 50 are jointly owned by Mark and I, and the other 150 are joint and owned by myself, Mark and our JV partners. Then the other 150-odd, we've either bought and sold, or we have packaged up and sold to other people by sourcing them. I mean people who are new to Property probably don't yet understand the multitudes of different ways you can buy, package and create cash flow. It's not just about buying and holding. In fact, our aspirations of buying and holding have probably gone down a little. We wanted to buy 50 a year for ourselves when we started, but because there are other cash flow opportunities in building the brand and the businesses, writing the books, and all these other things which offer different vehicles for wealth – of that almost 200 units that are held in the portfolio, they'll generate, as an average, around about net £1,500 a year each, so just under £150,000 net of all costs, absolutely everything. So if you were to look at profit and loss, or management accounts, that's what would be left at the end of the year, roughly £1,500. Some of them pump out £2,500, £3,000 a year, some of them, more. But because some of them were bought in the early days they weren't so good. If you get £1,500 net out of a single let, we don't really do HMOs we couldn't make it work so well in our area, you're doing well. So if you times roughly £1,500 a month by roughly 200, you can kind of work out the cash flow from there.

And how much equity?

Goodness me! I haven't even thought about it. In terms of all the deals that Mark and I have done, and the joint venture partnerships, I think it's roughly about £25 million worth of actual Property value of which the loan to value is probably roughly at 60% at the moment but those that have been doing it 20 years, their loans to value are at 30%. We started about 4 or 5 years ago, so our loan to value has probably come down from 85% to about 60% through refinancing, or just holding them and not remortgaging them. So yes, they're the rough figures.

You say HMOs you've not got to work in your area.

Yes, because there's no university in Peterborough, there's no real high-end model. We're still trying. We've just converted one of our units into and HMO. We keep testing it all the time.

How about the professional market?

You're talking about Peterborough! I think there are three professionals in Peterborough.

No, but they commute into London now, don't they?

Yes, they do. When you've got models that are working, why keep flogging a dead horse that hasn't worked as well? HMO is one of a multitude of ways of making cash flow in Property. I make more money in a year from selling my books than I would if I had 10 HMOs or 20 HMOs. I'd just sell a few more thousand books a year.

So, it's where you put your energy?

Yes, exactly. When you do this, you don't know what you don't know and it's like there's a door that's closed. You don't know what's on the other side of the door. When you open the door, it's like a light shined through and you're like, wow, look at how amazing it is on the other side of this door. Then all of a sudden once you've opened that door for a while, then you have got another 500 doors that you can open. Then, you've got too many doors open.

You've got to choose which one.

You don't know which door to go down. If you're in one door, in the other and out, and in the other and out, you're just overwhelmed. Overwhelmed is frustrating.

I'm the sort of person that likes to do everything. I'm very proactive. I'm competitive. Sometimes, my problem is actually what do we say no to? The more successful you get, it's about what you say no to rather than what you say yes to, I've found.

Okay, at what point would you say you became financially free?

About 28 years old, so it was probably three months into the second year of us buying.

So, you'd have about 25 properties then?

Yes, something like that. Now, Mark and I chose a certain path, but ultimately, the asset value through a strategy of remortgaging or the income if we leverage them at the right loan to value rate gave us roughly the income that we needed passively per month to retire. At the time for me, that was £3,000 a month, then it was £5,000, then it's £10,000. It's funny. The figure always changes as you grow and I find that's very much the way it is in our world. You always want more money and the more successful you get…

I remember when I sold my first painting. £120 – that was a lot of money. £120 doesn't buy me a tie now. I remember when I thought that £100,000 was a ton of money. Now in our business, we need minimum £100,000 a month just to pay the bills.

So, the value of money and your perception of the value of money changes. So, this financial independence, financial freedom figure is an evolutionary thing. It moves. My goal was always to get £3,000 a month net when I was kind of 27 or 26 when I was starting this, and we achieved that between 10 and 15 months because it's difficult to say exactly at what day that was coming in. Your profit and loss accounts are a moving thing. But, it was around about the age of 28.

That was the target, but then you reset the target after you reached it.

Yes, £3,000 a month now doesn't pay for the girlfriend, so it's all different.

Imagine what it's going to cost once she's your wife.

Oh, man! Anyway moving on, what's the next question?

…and of course, kids

I've just had Bobby. He's seven months old. Yes, that's put the living expenses up but it's all worth it.

Okay, you achieved financial freedom at a relatively young age there. What was your motivation to continue working and then to create this business called progressive?

Okay. There's no doubt that retirement is overrated – 100%.

I was having a chat with Mark actually. We sat in the Ferrari. We were driving to the new office. We were looking at everything we got. We have roughly about 5,000, 6,000 square feet of office space which is a decent size. We do a few million pounds. I said to Mark, "When will it be enough, mate?" He looks at me and he went, " I don't know. Will it ever be enough?"

When I rewind to 2007 when we were sat in one of our little houses in a tiny, little room back-to-back working, just me and him – 20, 30 Properties, £3,000, £4,000 net would have been enough.

But of course, things always grow. For me, growth is one of my highest values – constant improvement, always challenging myself, competition. I can't fulfil those needs in retirement. Some people want to get to a certain amount of money and then they want to stop. Some people want to get to a certain amount of money and then they want to have the choice to stop. For me, I never want to stop. It's just not me. I'm too competitive. For me, stopping would be like death. I wouldn't feel like I'm giving value to the world. I wouldn't feel important. I wouldn't feel like I have a place. So, what we've got now is just the very start. The Progressive brand is growing and spreading. We've bought new companies. We're diversifying into other areas. I regard myself as much an entrepreneur now as I do a Property investor. For me, I won't retire. I just will never retire.

Would you slow down?

No. No way! No way! The more I leverage and the more I outsource, the more I give myself to do. When I'm 40, when I'm 50, when I'm 60, who knows? Switches might flip then.

Have there been any changes since having Bobby?

Well, all I really want now is more, so he can have more. My goal is for him to be world number 1 golfer and my goal is for him to be my biggest success in life. Again, that's just put more on my plate to do. Now, I've got to find time to play golf with Bobby twice a day.

I thought you wanted him to get to number 1? :)

Yes. Well, there you go. He needs to maybe play with me once a week then if he wants to become world number 1.

I don't know. I think it's just my personality. I'm sure people who are 20, 30 years older all say, "Rob is only 30. He's got a lot to learn about life." Maybe I have and me having a lot to learn about life is part of the passion of life, knowing that tomorrow is going to be different from today, knowing that I'm going to get new lessons, knowing that the failures are new opportunities. You know, in 20 years, we may be having a discussion and I might just be sitting on a boat. But at the moment, I hate boats, so who knows?

Yes, you don't know what you don't know. You don't know how you're going to feel in 20 years.

But if we keep growing at the same rate that we're growing even with a few down years, I think by the time we're 40 or 50, most of the world is going to know about us, and that's the way we want it at the moment.

You met Mark at this networking event and you've been partners ever since really? Is there anything that you don't do together?

Yes. We don't share girlfriends although they're both called Gemma! But other than that, no. Our Property portfolio is together. Our business is together. It's all completely 50-50. You know me. I do a fair few speaking gigs. I do a lot of the bigger ones now. If I go out and make £100,000 or £150,000 from my speaking gig, half of that goes to Mark. But day-to-day, I have zero to do with buying Property. I don't view. I don't make offers. I don't do any legals. All I do is sign pieces of paper that Mark puts under my nose. I wanted to be a Property investor in 2006. I wanted to go, and do viewings, make offers and buy. I got bored after about nine months of viewing shi**y houses that were smelly. It just wasn't really the thing that set me on fire. But, I knew that the results of that would set me on fire. Mark isn't really operational anymore, but he manages people in our office who buy for us and he's still very much involved in the buying of Property. But, Mark doesn't really do any of the speaking gigs. I'm not really up for putting all of our customers to sleep, so I keep him away from all of that. The good thing about us is we do everything together and there's 100% trust, but it's completely delineated. I see a lot of people who are doing joint ventures, partnerships, or there're three, four or ten10 of them, and they're all stepping on each other's toes doing things that each other is doing. I just don't think that's the right way to do it. I think you do what you do and you let your partners do their thing that you don't do, don't want to do, can't do. Then, you get the ultimate leverage.

From analysis of the roles that you both performed when you got together, was it quite clear that Mark was the numbers guy and you were the public face?

Yes, it was and it wasn't. It's kind of weird because actually five years down the line, now we have the biggest UK Property training business. I'm now teaching people how to joint venture. I didn't have this blueprint and model that I teach people five years ago. If I'd had it, I might have acted differently. So in a lot of ways – and I would just be honest – I think we were lucky. In a lot of ways, we set up in the worst time. We bought our first 20 units just before the crash. When people said to me, "It's alright for you, Rob. You've done this. You've got that," I think actually in a lot of ways, it was harder for us. But in other ways, the naivety that we had back then meant that we went and did what maybe we wouldn't do now which I'm very grateful for. One of those things was when Mark and I met, and we met at this Property networking event, we'd both just recently become single, wanted to get out on the town, and try and "interact", if you like. Also, we were both looking to buy similar Properties in similar areas. That was about where the similarities stopped, but that was the thing that attracted us to each other, which we didn't know at the time. This guy, he does what I'm doing. He's interested in what I'm doing. I want to get to know him. If I'd known everything about Mark, I can't imagine having a conversation with him without making me fall asleep – he probably would've thought, who's this guy, rah-rah, or look at him, who does he think he is mouthing off. So as it happens, we're completely different, but our passions are alike.

Yes and it brings me onto personalities and profiles in joint venture partners. Have you got any advice on the types you look for?

It's really simple. The first thing is truly understand who you are because most people live their life not understanding who they are, delusional about who they are.

How on earth do they get to do that?

Well, it's just be honest with yourself. To yourself, when you're marketing or you're selling, obviously you've got to portray an image and that's fine. But when it comes to yourself, just be honest about what you're good at and what you're cr*p at. Don't overestimate what you're good at. Don't underestimate what you're crap at. I'm genuinely good at this, this and this. I'm genuinely not good at this, this and this. Then, what you do is just find someone who is really good at the things you're not. But, the problem with people is they're naturally attracted to people with similarities. The attraction process is the wrong way around. If life meant that we were always attracted to opposites, certainly in business, it would be a lot easier. But, we're not. We're always attracted to the people who are similar. When I advise people on this, if there's a bit of frustration, if they don't really see the things the way you see the things, if working together is a bit frustrating, that's probably a good thing. It's like the best band in the world, in my opinion, like Radiohead, and they all have different musical tastes and styles. When they're writing songs, they can wind each other up and get frustrated because one person's going another way. They all have different backgrounds. But, the result is this amazingly creative, unique style of music. I think it's exactly the same in Property. It's like you've got to find people who are good at what you're not good at, who love what you hate. That's really important.

If you're really looking at joint venture partners and getting into this, all of the systems and processes really help. I didn't have that at the time and, like I said, I think in a lot of ways, I was fortunate. But, the great thing about this is it's quite liberating because I think a lot of people spend their life – I certainly did, maybe sometimes overestimating what I was good at, sometimes underestimating what I was good at and the same with the bad. But when you can just be honest with yourself and say, do you know what, I'm just not good at that, I'm just going to let it go – once you just let it go, how good is it to just be able to let go all the things that create you so much pain and tension.

I mean imagine if you could've dropped your three worst subjects at GCSE and just focused on the seven good ones, how much it would've helped the seven good ones, how much you'd have enjoyed it more. It's because we're not trained like that in this country, the government and the schooling system. Now, I don't want to go on about that. But, you're not allowed to drop the things you're not good at and find someone else to leverage. But, that's what I've been able to do. I hardly spend any of my time researching, or reading legal contracts and paperwork, which, to me, would ruin my day. Mark goes to a coffee shop with a contract the size of the Quran and he's excited about it!

I think there's an important lesson there. Just find those people who love the stuff you hate.

Yes, for sure. If you're writing the tips to wealth or the keys to success, it's got to be right up there.

How many joint venture partnerships have you got?

About 160 or 150. As I mentioned before, Mark and I have personal joint ventures where we own Properties together, and then we have joint ventures with other people. We've got lots of individual people who we have joint ventures with. Some people, we've got five or ten Properties with. Some people, we've got a handful with. I've also got joint ventures in business. So, I've created other businesses, bought businesses, created products. At the moment, I'm launching this product with you, which is a joint venture. So, my life is full of joint ventures and it's great because we're leveraging each other in this process of creating this book. We're also leveraging all of the amazing success stories in this book. If we were doing this on our own, it probably wouldn't happen. You know, there're plusses and minuses. For every successful joint venture, there's probably 0.2 that have failed. I won't go into it now, but I've got a few fairly big failures in joint ventures and that's just life.

You've created Progressive with Mark. What was the idea behind that?

It's quite simple. Mark and I got to the end of 2006, and for two young guys who had not really bought that many before. Mark had a few on his own, maybe 10 or 12 on his own, so he had experienced which helped. I had zero on my own before then. Yes, we just couldn't buy anymore. We were leveraged completely. We'd used a lot of Mark's funds. We'd done obviously a lot of fairly creative finance techniques. We just couldn't. We had no capacity to buy anymore. Mark also got the wobbles. He got the heebie-jeebies towards the end saying, "Blo*dy hell! I've got all this money all over the place, we've got all these deals and I can't keep up with them." We'd built some good relationships with eEstate agents. I've got one guy working at Progressive Property now who we were buying deals from five years ago, another guy who's still part of our community, the same people we were buying from five years ago that we've procured through the agents. So, we'd built all these relationships, and the last thing we wanted to do was go and tell them all, or stick a big advert or tattoo on our forehead, saying, "We're no longer buying," because we would have just lost a load of relationships. Estate agents are quite fickle and they've got a job to do, to sell Properties. But, they won't have any necessary allegiance to you. If you stop buying for three months, they would have found someone to replace you, fair enough. It's business. So, Mark and I said, right, we've got to monetize these deals. We've got to keep the agents warm. So, we started buying in family names. Obviously, we were still buying them, but we're buying in family names, so using family members. So, we were able to almost still give the illusion that we were still buying a lot. Then, we built a service to sell them unto other people because we were at capacity. That actually became quite a big machine because we never intended it. We went from buying one, one-and-a-half or two a month to now, we buy about 15 to 20 on a big month, six to eight on a quiet month and anywhere in-between. So, we're probably averaging 12 plus deals a month and you've got a little chap, a lad, an estate agent who's 25, looking at these guys who are a couple of years older, driving Ferraris and buying 10 deals a month. They just don't get it, but they're impressed. I always tell people all the time, "Right now when you start investing in Property, don't limit yourself to just buying yourself. Think about packaging, becoming a business because not only will you make multiple streams of income that way which is obviously sexy, but it's also you reduce your risk if you have multiple streams of income. But also, you'll create a better perception with the agents and you'll actually attract more deals that way." So, that's just how we started Progressive.

Then they moved into education.

Yes, because then we just started learning about business and all started realizing that there was a demand. A couple of things – number one when we started at Progressive and we started sourcing deals for other people, Mark and I didn't want to be the give-us-£2,500-£3,000-£4,000-and-we'll-source-you-a-Property-then-you-go-and-look-after-it. The thing with Property is you put the right Property in the wrong hands and it'll be a mess. By the same token, you can put not necessarily the best deal in the right hands and they'll sweat that asset the most. So, Mark and I didn't want to source for people who then would lose control. Then, they'd make a mess of it maybe and then they'd blame us. So, we decided to position ourselves quite highly and do the whole thing for them, the whole lot – investing, finding the tenants, managing and actually did a whole portfolio-building business. I didn't care if we had fewer customers. I just knew we'd have better customers, we'd give them a better service and they would ultimately benefit.

So, you'd manage their asset long-term?

Yes, exactly and we'd build them a portfolio of multiple Properties.

It makes sure it remains an asset rather than become a liability.

Yes. Now, the good thing about that is it was a good cash flow business because at the time when we started, I think £25,000 was the fee plus a profit share. So, you didn't need too many of those in year one to be able to fund your business. So, that was the first thing.

The next thing is I decided in 2007 that Mark and I knew enough to write a book. So, we built this business. Mark was sourcing the Properties. I was finding the customers. I, basically for three months, just stayed up pretty much most nights, all night, every night – I was still single at the time, so that was fine – and I just wrote this book. I grilled Mark for his knowledge. A lot of the book is Mark's knowledge. I went onto Amazon and I bought every single book I could find on Property. I read every single one, realized that a lot of them were full of fluff anyway, but if there were some nice nuggets in there, I'd transpose that into our book. So yes, I've written a book now. I'll go down to my local vanity publisher. I'll get them to print 20 for me. I'll give a couple to my mum and a couple to friends, I'll keep a few and I'm an author. Two years later, we've sold 20-odd-thousand. We've now sold 50-odd-thousand. We've sold more in the niche of Property than anybody else. Then, we're like, blo*dy hell, there are more ways to make money in Property than we'd thought and we were all of a sudden getting inundated. TV programmes were requesting us to do shows. People were asking, "I want you to teach me to do what you do." Of course in the business model world, we had a book for £15 and then a portfolio building for £25,000, but nothing in-between. So, those people who had £1,000, £2,000 or £3,000, or wanted to learn themselves; we had nothing for them, so we started adding in different services based on the demand.

In terms of revenue split, what brings in your income to your business now?

The books bring in pocket money for us. The books bring in maybe £100,000 to £150,000 a year.

The hands-free portfolio-building, it depends how many customers and clients we decide to service, but that's probably worth 20%, 25% of our income. The education business, so the seminars, the training events, the DVDs, the membership site and everything else, that brings in probably 40% or 50% of our income. Then, our portfolio is probably the rest.

Now you talked about becoming an entrepreneur and not just being a property investor, so you've bought other businesses.

Yes, I bought a business that was named Unlimited Success. I bought that from a failing seminar business at the end of last year. The recession and the crash hit so many businesses, and the seminar industry was one industry that was hit pretty hard. This business was being managed overseas and I think it was just difficult for them to make it work. Mark and I saw an opportunity because personal development and giving yourself the right mind-set is fairly closely linked to Property investing as you know, Robin. I just felt like there was a really good synergy between the community that we've built at Progressive Property, and wealth creation, personal development and that kind of thing. So yes, it was a new experience because I'd never bought a business. I'd always built a business. The difference between buying and building is significant. We had to go through quite a few months of legals, negotiations, and dealing with other cultures and other people who saw the world differently to us. But yes, that business is turning a profit now.

When did you buy that?

End of 2010, start of 2011.

Has it started to make profit yet?

Yes, for sure. I said let's get this rolling. Two months in, let's have our first event. Let's do this, this and this. Of course, we had too many partners in it and it just dragged out. It was six months before we did our first event. When we bought this business, we took on a big liability. There were about 800 customers who'd paid for trainings that if we hadn't put a rescue package together, they all would have lost either their money or their training. So, we invested heavily into resources and financially to deliver for these 800-odd people that took us about nine months to fulfil. We decided we didn't want to go out and do a load of new marketing for a business where we had 800 customers that needed our love and attention. So, we made them raving fans first. We spent, five months doing that. Now, we're just starting to launch new events, new products, build the brand back up. These opportunities come your way when you build a business around Property and anyone that's listening, whatever size they are, if they're a significant Property investor, then it's time to step up and build businesses around it. If they're just starting in Property, I would suggest seeing Property as a business and look for multiple streams of income, not just buying and holding.

So, do we see unlimited success coming out as the brand?

Our strategy is ultimately to build Progressive as a brand that is larger than any of its smaller parts and maybe they will merge together in the future. But ultimately, Unlimited Success is a different brand, so we're building it up as its own brand. It's not going to be branded around me and Mark like Progressive is. It's going to be branded around other people who are experts in that area. Mark and I know our limitations. We know what we're good at and what we're not good at, and we know how people see us. But, we're the masterminds behind that and we will drive that. For me, I always need something new, exciting and challenging. For Mark, he likes things to stay the same, and be regimented and systemised, but he still wants to make a load of money. So I guess in a lot of respects, this is my baby. This is the thing that I've driven. Mark just counts the money and he's quite happy with that. Yes, so it's good.

Just out of interest, where are you on the wealth dynamic profile?

Pretty much star all the way. I don't think that surprises you.

No, but there's an element of creator in you when you look forward to new challenges.

Yes.

Where does Mark sit on the wealth dynamics profile?

Deal maker, trader – pretty much the opposite. If anyone hasn't done wealth dynamics then check out Roger Hamilton's Entrepreneur Profiling System.

Are there any other businesses?

No, not yet. We had a venture that we started at the start of the year which we didn't pursue because we took on too much and the visions for the partners were different. But even myself who wants to take on the world and do everything, I realize that you can stretch yourself too much and you can put yourself beyond capacity. So this year and through to next year, we're focusing on continuing to build education. The market is changing all the time, and people need education and need continual education. So at the moment, we've got new products coming out that are helping people and teaching people how to do joint ventures, negotiation. I just continue to develop those and continue to develop the brand, and the same with Unlimited Success. We've just moved offices, so there's all that to deal with.

What about spreading Progressive around the country?

Yes, we've tested that. I know that some of the other companies, they do the little road shows all around the country. The challenge I have with that personally is that people will go to London, but not as many people from London will travel out. I mean I don't live in London. I live in Peterborough, so I have to go and travel there. But whenever we have an event in London, we get about a third of the people show up. The further north we've gone, the less people have understood us. I think that's the best way to put it. We've done events in Scotland, we've done events in Newcastle and stuff like that. At the end of the day, Mark and I are Southerners, and I'm just not sure if they really understand us. This is the rapport and the synergy. Also when you see these companies that are just pumping events all over the country, they're free, you know they're going to up-sell you a load of stuff and use all the sales tips and tricks, and you know that most of them don't even buy themselves and they're flown in from America – if we start using that same model, people are just going to put us in the same boat. We're not selling stuff. We're building a community. We have the largest Property community of any company and any business in the country. For us, that's a whole thing. It's about building a community. The community adds as much value to the community as it does from learning from Mark, Rob and Progressive Property. If we're holding an event all over the country everyday, there's no scarcity about that. It's not special. It's not unique. It's just a sales funnel machine.

I'm in business, so people there who need to be trained, I want to train them. People who want to invest in themselves; I want to be the person and the company that they invest with. Our trainings are better than anybody else's by a country mile and that's just not me bragging. That's the feedback we get. People spend tens of thousands of pounds with other companies, then come train with us. They spend a day with us that costs them £60 and they feel like they've learned more in that day. But, I don't want us to be a machine and an entity that isn't personal. If there's a demand and people want us to come out all over the country, maybe we'll do that.

But now, you want us to travel to Peterborough to your training firm instead of London.

Well, that's it. This is where we live. Yes, we've obviously got the new training facility that holds about 150 people, so we can do a lot. The great thing about that is people go to other training companies and they pay £10,000 to £12,000 for some of the trainings. Now, we're building bigger packages because I'd rather someone spend £10,000 to £12,000 with us than someone who's not going to give them the results. But, you can, cost-effectively for a couple of grand, get yourself pretty much fully educated with Progressive. You know, we keep the running cost of our business low, we have a training facility, which means we don't have to pay extortionate London hotel rates and we can keep the cost of the training accessible. We don't have to pay the fancy American trainers who want £10,000 a minute because Mark and I buy Properties every single day. I mean we won't be running the trainings forever. We'll train people through Progressive, but that's just where we're at now.

I guess you've talked about what you're doing at the moment. Plans for the coming year?

Consolidate. We've had some accelerated growth. We've got lots of new ventures on. A mentor of mine who's worth about £500 million said, "Don't spend the next year creating loads of new stuff. Just get better at what you are doing." Wise words.

Daniel Wagner says it's the creator's disease, isn't it? You want to create the next shiny object.

Yes. To a certain degree, I like the new and the exciting. But, new that doesn't work isn't exciting.

But, you don't know that until you do it.

No, exactly. The premises and the training facility, lots of these joint ventures, I want to see them through to fruition. You could write 20 books and sell one of each, or you can write one book and sell a million of them. I just want to focus on the projects that we've got going on and really bed them in. I'm just over 30 years old. So is Mark. It's not like I've got no time to go and do this.

Obviously, you know Mark and I buy probably anywhere between 20 and 35 units a year, so we'll just continue to buy. We bought our new office and we bought that for cash. You know also, we'll probably look at some commercial developments, but that's more Mark's bag.

So, he's moving into commercial rather than residential?

Yes, yes, yes.

In Peterborough?

Yes. You know, we'll keep it local because it's what we know. We know our limitations.

That's one of the things as well. If I go to Newcastle and start teaching people how to invest in Newcastle, I don't have any credibility. I've never bought anything in Newcastle. We have the Progressive system, the Progressive model which I believe is the best model for people being able to become successful in their own right in their own area. There're 65,000,

70,000 houses in Peterborough. We only need 1% of those. Not even that – 0.1%.

Have you set yourself a limit on the number of houses?

I don't set limits. Limits are restrictive.

Sorry, targets.

Mark deals with that. He'd be quite happy with 25 units a year for the rest of his life.

Just keep on buying 25 and then...

Yes, we're probably at the stage now where we can buy more, but Mark would rather buy 25 units at 35% to 40% discount than 50 units at 22% discount. He's quite selective. He's seen in the past that if you don't buy really well, then the money you're making is imaginary and it's all future-based. It's not real. So, he looks at sales value, not valuations and he's interested in the best deals. You know you can't get 100 of the very best deals a year. It just doesn't happen.

Have you got any mistakes that you'd like to share – top mistakes that you've made that you'd want others to avoid?

Wow, I could probably write a book on that!

Sometimes if you take too many things on, you can't do the things you're doing well, and that's one of my perennial challenges. I'm always having to evaluate am I doing too many things? A lot of people I know, once they open the door, then become very overwhelmed trying to do too many strategies. So, I would say, become a master of one thing rather than averagely good at a lot of things.

By the same token, an entrepreneur needs to be able to know management, sales, marketing – needs to have different facets. An entrepreneur is more of a generalist and needs a myriad of skills, but that's what's necessary. They're the different chapters of the book in being an entrepreneur and to become a great entrepreneur, you need to be good at those certain facets. To become a great Property investor, you need to have an understanding of the legal process, but you don't need to be a lawyer.

I would just say, focus on becoming great at one particular thing, or if you need two or three, fine. But, just don't spread yourself too thin. Don't try and chase all the things that shine at once. In wealth creation, you can make money out of Property, you can make money out of stocks, you can make money out of Internet, you can make money out of social media. You make money out of anything, but when you try and do more, you make money out of nothing. At the same time, Mark, on the flip side, is sometimes a bit limited and sometimes doesn't see opportunities that come because he's too focused on looking at one thing. So, that's where Mark and I have the balance. He keeps me focused and I keep him expanded.

So, I would say in terms of mistakes, most of the stuff we've done – if I've had any failed ventures, it's normally probably because I've just got too much on my plate, and I can't give it the love and attention that it needs.

Also, not leveraging quick enough – I always say to people, "If you're not ready to hire people, then hire people. If you're not ready to outsource some of your work, then outsource some of your work." I never sit here, thinking that was a good decision to delay leverage and a lot of people are always delaying leverage. I say, "I wish..." It doesn't make any difference. I don't regret. But, hiring an operations manager to take over all of the management of the Progressive companies, we did too late. Our first ever PA, we did too late. I don't care if you're on £30,000, £3,000 or £3 million. You should have a PA even if that PA does one hour a week for you. You should have a PA. Even PAs should have PAs. I wouldn't be able to survive in this world if I didn't have multiple assistants. So yes, leverage quicker because you'll grow bigger quicker.

This is about lifestyle as well. If you're running around doing everything, you can't sit back and enjoy it.

Well on that note, do you actually get time to enjoy it?

Yes. Sometimes Mark and I just push and push and push. We've spent a year and not really looked back. But, we do try and celebrate as much as we can. I think we're good to the Progressive team. I think we take them out on barbecues to try and do different things. Let's sit back and look at what you've achieved. Enjoy it. Be grateful. Wherever you are right now is just a fantastic place to be. I bet if we all think about it, we've got a multitude of things we're grateful for because if you don't think about those in life, it can be a bit unfulfilled.

Okay, so top tips would be: leverage before you're ready to leverage; invest in your education. I believe the investment in education is the best investment you'll ever make. I've invested six figures in my education, and I've still got so much to learn and so much money to pump in. The most wealthy and successful people spend money on themselves and I mean investing in their knowledge, their skills, their experience. Investing in your education is a lifelong thing. You don't buy one Property course and then that's it. Continue to invest in all different facets. It doesn't just have to be financially. It could be sweat equity. It could be time. It can be working for people for free. It could be meeting mentors for lunch. It could be going to business angel events and meeting millionaires. Constantly investing time, money and resource into your education for me is quite possibly the biggest. Everything that I've achieved now which is just such a drop in the ocean from where I want to be is all based on the people I've met and the books I've read. They're the two differences between where you are now and where you'll be in terms of being successful.

Top Books?

I've read a lot of how-to marketing books, how-to sell books. I find I learn as much if not more now from just reading autobiographies of successful people and just see how they did it. So, I thought Simon Cowell's autobiography was great. You just got real insight into how someone becomes a complete media mogul. I thought Christopher Reeve's was very emotional and very inspiring on how to overcome quite possibly the biggest challenges that people have. You have so many of those. I thought Gerald Ratner's one was how to bounce back from failures.

Top Books

Think and Grow Rich – *Napoleon Hill*

Make Cash in a Property Market Crash – *Rob Moore and Mark Homer*

Autobiographies – *Simon Cowell, Christopher Reeve, Gerald Ratner*

Francis And Jane Dolley

The Portfolio "Builders"

Story At A Glance

Ages: **Francis**: 52 **Jane:** 52

J.O.B.

Francis: (Previously) builder

Jane: local government accountant.

Investment Area: Taunton and Bridgwater in Somerset, and Bristol.

Strategies: Below market value, flips, HMO, lease option, JVs, corporate lets.

Vital Statistics:

Properties: 8 BTLs & 2 HMOs

Cash flow: £4,100pm - 9 corporate lets £5,000 pm cash flow

Equity: £440k

How did you get into property, Francis and Jane?

[Francis] I've always loved Property, the structure, the architecture and especially the history of the buildings. I had been running a small building firm for the past 20 years and employed three people in the firm with me, as well as many contractors as and when needed. It was quite stressful at the time, but I also enjoyed a lot of the aspects and the constant interaction with new people. I always knew I had the capacity to do more. At the same time I wanted to spend more time with my family and build a more secure future. In the building industry when there was no work due to the economy or bad weather, there was no income, and I felt often that it was out of my control.

Favourite Quote

"In the middle of every difficulty lies opportunity" – Einstein

Had you bought property before meeting Progressive?

[Jane] Yes we had. We bought our first house in 1980, a small end of terrace house, with a garage on the side. Those first few years were difficult. We had two young children, James and Emily, and neither of us earned very much.

It was hard to find enough money for the mortgage, so Francis turned the garage into a flat and we rented it out. We lived there for 15 years. When we decided to move on in 1995 we were able to rent out the house and the flat. The mortgage was gone then, and we were making £700 a month. We had no aspirations to become full-time Property investors at this point.

Did you buy any more property?

Yes. Three years ago our daughter Emily went to university in Bristol, and we decided it made sense to buy a house there. We didn't have a clue how to buy the correct way, and paid the asking price. We bought a three-bed end of terrace with garden to the side. Because of Francis' building skills it was easy to extend the house to a six-bed. The idea was that Emily lived there for free, and in return she ran the student house. This house makes over £1,000 a month at the moment. However we didn't think of this as a career until we met Rob and Mark.

How did you find out about Progressive?

[Francis] I had been searching for months on the Internet, looking at all sorts of experts out there offering the answers to all your dreams. I also knew there was a lot of bulls**t out there. I was very mistrusting, because everyone wanted your money, offering very little in return. However I found Progressive to be different.

They seemed to give you a lot. They imparted a lot of information. I was quite impressed with that. After researching and studying Property Investing for months, it became clear to me that we needed a mentor.

So next we carried out a process of elimination and narrowed it down to two potential mentors. Up to this point Jane was very apprehensive, but I knew that I had to get Jane on board to make this work.

We decided that we should meet them in person if we were going to take the next step. We went to a one-day event in London, and were so impressed with Rob and Mark that we completely forgot about the other mentor, and decided to train with Progressive.

When we met them they gave off tremendous energy, especially Rob, and they were both so knowledgeable and enthusiastic. I had a really good feeling about them that you just get from some people. I especially liked Rob's philosophy of 'abundance'.

The first person we met when we walked in the door was Rob, and I thought that was great. Here was this person I'd recently read about, warmly greeting people as they came in, just a normal guy, really friendly.

What happened after your one-day training?

I was really blown away by it. I thought this is definitely what we want to do, whereas up to that point I had been hesitant.

I came away with so much energy. I was really pleased, and relieved that Jane was no longer sceptical and was now very interested.

We simply had to go to the next step. We had to get educated. In the beginning we weren't very keen to spend money on our education as we didn't understand the real value. But now we realise it's the best thing you can do.

As well as the many different ways to buy and sell Property, the one-day training event also covered mind-set. It took us a while to understand the importance of adopting the correct mind-set. You need to constantly educate yourself, and you really need to keep up to date with what's going on.

After recognising you needed to get educated what did you do next?

We signed up for the three-day Progressive Masterclass in October 2009, and for me it was a doorway to a new world that I always knew was out there but didn't have access to.

We found ourselves surrounded by people who were likeminded, enthusiastic and positive. I was quite inspired by the group, by just being there. Jane was impressed by the information Rob and Mark were prepared to give you, and the learning process was such good fun.

It was actually our wedding anniversary during the course, so it was a bit strange for us, but the venue was beautiful and we really enjoyed our time there.

What did you do after the masterclass?

We had the knowledge now to start to put it all into action. Although we knew it wasn't going to be easy, we had paid for this education and understood we had to take action. So we immediately went out to view houses.

We drew a little equity out of our own house to start with, and bought three houses in the spring of 2010. All of the Properties were bought below market value and we added additional value using Francis' building skills. After refurbishment, each Property was remortgaged to get the deposits and majority of the refurbishment money back out. This enabled us to buy the next houses.

At the same time we started the VIP mentorship for the year.

How has the VIP mentorship helped you?

The best thing for us was the accountability. We knew we had to go out there and get results. We just had to. Otherwise we had to justify why we hadn't. There was constant momentum. In our one-to-ones we'd be asked "What where your goals for this month? Have you achieved them? If not. Why haven't you? What can we do to help you?"

As well as the one-to-ones we had group discussions to try to help and encourage each other. It just made you get on with it and keep going. As a result we replaced Jane's income last year and are well on our way to replacing mine.

We have over £50k in net annual cash flow from the 10 Properties in our portfolio. Our two multi-lets are our best earners at £13k and £14k. We flipped one three-bed house and made a net profit of £23k. This Property was bought at 36% below market value, and was sold on to a residential buyer.

Had you read any books on property investing?

The first book that I read about Property was "The 44 Most Closely

Guarded Property Secrets" and it opened my eyes to a whole new world. Since then my Property library has grown considerably – and I can't wait to read this book.

How did your wife Jane get involved?

Jane had been working as a local government accountant for many years. She'd often work late to meet deadlines. That meant evenings for us weren't quality time at all because we were both really tired, and we just couldn't see an end to it. It was the lack of quality time together, and with our family, that really pushed us both into the search for a different life.

You're doing property investing together as a couple. How do you find that?

Great! We still have our disagreements, but now we're finding our individual roles. We see plenty of couples embark on Property investing, but often one of the partners holds the other back. We've actually grown stronger, and over the course of the year we've seen each other develop new strengths.

Are you looking for seed capital to build your portfolio?

We have yet to package any deals to sell as we've had our hands full this year, and up until a few months ago we've had funds to be able to buy the houses ourselves.

Since we started to concentrate more on the larger Properties to convert to multi-lets or HMOs, the need for joint venture partners and investors looking for a good return on their money has become more necessary. This has been a whole new learning curve, and the relationship and trust between all parties is very important. The multi-lets are an area of the business that we are keen to expand so we are now actively looking for new Investors.

We are also joint venturing with Rob and Mark on a new lease option cash flow strategy!

Are you going to use any new strategies?

After completing Progressive's Lease Option course, we carried out a lot of advertising, leafleting and newspaper adverts including a half page article. We have built up a list of people who are potential tenant buyers. To date we have one deal making us £550 net per month.

We are also implementing a new strategy of corporate lets, which is greatly increasing our cash flow in a relatively short space of time. Watch this space.

Any inspirational moments along the way?

I never thought we would have got to this point so soon. So many people we have met during the year have been an inspiration to us. Rob has helped us push through our barriers and at times taken us right out of our comfort zone. We have made some amazing friends through the VIP group who I know will constantly inspire us with their achievements for years to come.

'I live the life I love, I love the life I live' -
Muddy Waters

Any deals you want to share with us?

This was a large three-storey four-bed Victorian house with an attached one-bed annexe. We agreed a price of £270k. The owners were divorcing.

The husband was getting the annexe, and the wife the main house. The deal didn't stack as it was. We obtained planning permission to split the house and annexe into two separate Properties. We have a lease option on the flat with an option to buy, sell or return to the owner in two years. We have refurbished and let the annexe, which now has a value of £100k. This enabled us to buy the main Property at the bargain price of £170k. We are converting this into a six-bed HMO, which has a RICS end valuation of £320k. When we remortgage, all funding will be returned to us. Rental income on the house is just over £1k net per month.

Do you attend any networking events?

We didn't at first. It wasn't easy to network, but now we're really in to it. We regularly attend the Berkshire Property Meet and the Bristol PIN, and Exeter PEN when we can. Also we go to the occasional breakfast or lunch meeting.

With some Property friends we are starting up a local networking event, Property Network West. We're starting to see the value of networking. It brings great benefits once you start building relationships with people. But you need to make the effort to attend, and take those first steps to talk. These events also help you to keep motivated.

Any challenges?

When we started out, and moved on from our very first house, the one that we split into a house and flat, we did have setbacks. Within the first 15 months at the two Properties we had a number of upsetting incidents and undesirable tenants.

Obviously we had all our friends saying "See! We told you it was going to be like this". We ignored them and persevered. The present family have lived there happily for the last 12 years.

Our current challenges are to continue systemising our business and raise jJoint vVenture finance.

You're building a family business?

Yes. Our daughter Emily studied architecture and planning at the University of the West of the England. She now works with us full time. Our son James studied computing and has also recently joined us. He deals with the IT side of the business, and builds our websites.

The corporate letting strategy is enabling our business cash flow to grow rapidly for very little monetary input. The idea is for Emily and James to control this between them after the initial start up.

We helped James to buy his first house. We put in the deposit and refurbishment costs and he worked on the house with us. The house was bought for £120k, and revalued at £160k after six months, returning the majority of our money. James rents this house to a young family giving him £200 a month net cash flow. Emily is more hands-on, managing our multi-lets.

And what are your plans for the future?

Our main objective this year is to attract more joint venture finance. This has worked well for us the past year. We already have a website to attract JV partners, and are currently setting up a commercial lending facility with a bank. Our intention is to continue down this JV route for the larger multi-lets.

We also have planned a steady expansion of our corporate let portfolio, which stands currently at nine Properties bringing in a net monthly cash flow of £5k. It is a difficult time for people who find themselves as accidental landlords and just can't rent or sell their Properties. This year we are planning to offer help as a landlord rescue service.

We are developing the corporate let strategy into a home study course as we feel it is a great way for people who are struggling financially to get into Property with very little cash.

The brand is next. We are keen to build our brand. We have continued with our Progressive Property training and are on the Grad Programme, which we are really enjoying and its helping us exponentially.

We are in the process of systemising the office and being more organised. We're getting there, but it's a work in progress.

Top Books

- Rich Dad, Poor Dad, *Robert Kiyosaki*
- The Slight Edge, *Jeff Olsen*
- 44 Most closely guarded Property secrets, *Rob Moore and Mark Homer*

Francis and Jane's Contact Details

www.yourlocalproperty.com

www.yourlocalinvestment.com

www.yourlocallets.com

Key Learnings

- Find the right mentors and work with them.
- Use the skills you already have and utilise them in Property investing.
- Have fun.
- Align with enthusiastic, positive and like-minded people. Network lots.
- Get over your personal scepticism.
- Use equity and other people's money to invest.
- Be accountable to someone or a group.
- Utilise other people's complementary strengths.
- Systemise your business so you can spend quality time with your family.
- Get your kids involved

Education

Progressive Property JV Buying Frenzy Networking Event [1-day]:

http://www.progressiveproperty.co.uk/jv-event

Progressive Property 3 Day Property Investing Masterclass Intensive:

http://www.progressiveproperty.co.uk/masterclass

Progressive Property Lease Options Training:

http://www.progressiveproperty.co.uk/lease-options-intensive

Progressive Property VIP JV Millionaires Club:

http://www.progressiveproperty.co.uk/vip-pmc

Progressive Property Graduate Millionaires Programme – Invitation Only

Andy Watkiss

"Keep On Trucking"

Story At A Glance

Age: 45

J.O.B. Haulage manager

Investment Area: Telford, Shropshire [but deals in UK]

Strategies: BTL, HMOs, joint ventures, deal packager

Vital Statistics

Properties: 48

Portfolio: £5.5 million. £3.4 million on mortgage.

Equity: £1.8 million.

How did you get into property?

I got into Property by watching Sarah Beeny's shows on TV and seeing what they did. Something came through the post from Inside Track. That was a day in Birmingham back in 2006 and then my wife Claire and I went on a two-day course. It did give us a lot of knowledge and it pushed us to go into Property,

We met up with a couple Jason and Karen while we were there, who lived in Stafford. He was a painter and decorator, had his own company, with a couple of crews out there. In the intervals, we were talking to each other as we were on the same table. He was saying, "I work for Investors all day long, week in week out, all year long, where I'm doing up houses for people, going into houses, doing a total or light refurbishment for them to sell them on. I'm seeing the money they're earning. But, I should be doing it myself. That's why I'm here".

So, it went from there we thought, "Shall we team up and see if we can buy houses either in Staffordshire or Telford? I'll find them and get the finance deposits one way or another, you do them up and we'll sell them on".

This was towards the end of 2006.

I started to look for Properties. Real, real rough places that needed doing up - a complete refurbishment. I went into estate agents in the Telford area. I went in there, saw a couple of Properties and went to view them. We did a deal. We looked at one for £85,000. We managed to get it at £70,000, which even in these days wouldn't be any good now. We managed to get the deal but further down the line, the deal fell through; the vendor decided they didn't want to sell for whatever reason and backed out.

From there then, we got a second Property we'd already looked at to buy with the actual estate agents.

So, we did a deal on the second one to buy, and the other couple decided that they could not go in on this one with us.

So I went to the estate agents and explained to them that the first one has fallen through and we can't proceed on the second one either now because we were going 50-50 on the deposit to buy, and the other couple could not proceed now.

So the owner of the estate agents said, "I buy Property. I'll join with you 50-50 if you like. Now James is my good friend and business partner with all of the portfolio of Properties, and with James having his Property sales and lettings agency it comes in very handy for us too.

Why are you doing property investing?

I'm doing this for our children. I've set up a trust that would be administered in the event of my death. I'm grateful to my wife who has been fully supportive whilst my partners and I were out viewing two or three Properties a night.

In the beginning my sister, Dad and Mum were all very sceptical, but now they're totally on board. They've lent money to help us.

When things were going crazy and we were locking cash in deals I'd ask my Dad if I could borrow some money. He'd say. "Son, get out of this transport business. I've been in it for donkey's years. Property is the way forward".

He retired last year at the age of 70.

I've been in transport all my life from before I left school. My father has been in transport all his life. He was a farmer before that. Granddad and Dad were farmers. Our farm was compulsory purchased and didn't get much for it back then.

We were robbed really, but that's one of the stories. Just before that, Dad had gotten into hauling, into moving aggregates - stones, tipper lorries, that sort of stuff.

Then, I was the age of five or six, I can't remember and I started to go with him in the lorry. Up over the years when I was in my teens 13, 14, 15 I was working in the fitting shop, helping him repair vehicles coming in. I was fully maintaining vehicles and we had a fleet of about 30 vehicles at that point.

So, rather than go to school I was naughty by skipping school and going to work on the lorries.

How many properties did you buy in 2007?

We bought nine Properties and towards the end of 2007 we refurbished and sold one, but we should have just kept it for the long term, but things were tightening up. We were buying with our own deposits with a mortgage, with no early penalty repayments with Northern Rock, then refurbishing them, remortgaging them, but always ending up one way or another having to leave £2-3k in the deals after all the deposit and refurbishment.

Money was running out.

What did you do next?

I had to look at a way of trying to do these Properties without using our own money. At this point, we still knew nothing about below market value. We were buying them at market price and then adding value by refurbishing.

Despite your training from Inside Track?

Yes. We didn't really pick up on buying below market value and not using your own money. The Inside Track way was all new build off plan with a market up lift, they hoped. We just bought at a good price and then would refinance out our deposit and refurbishment costs.

What did you do next?

I rang a few numbers in the local newspapers that said they buy houses quickly. I was curious how they did it so I rang a couple of them up and asked. I said we buy Properties. We're landlords. What are you doing with the ones you don't want? One of them said "Let's meet up and have a chat and I'll tell you how I do it".

He was buying for 18-20% below market value back in the days of 85% mortgages with Mortgage Express same day remortgages. So I asked what was he doing with all the 15% deals. He explained he sold them on for a finder's fee. I said I'd have some of them then.

However, we only bought two off him, he was a great help and we're thankful to him for his guidance in to the BMV world.

What stopped you buying more?

We picked up on the idea ourselves and started advertising and leafleting ourselves. "Do you need to sell your house quickly at no cost to you?" The phone didn't stop ringing!

When was this?

Late 2007, early 2008. We bought 28 Properties.

What's the story about a window cleaner?

A friend of ours is a window cleaner who cleaned our own house. His wife is a big friend of my wife. Their kids go to the same school and know each other. His engine blew up in his car. He said he didn't know what to do to get round my jobs. Well, with being in the transport business I said if "I supplied you with a van could we do a deal for you to deliver our leaflets using the van for both?"

We were having problems with the droppers shoving them through I letterbox and getting complaints from the council. He agreed to do his window cleaning in the mornings and leaflet drops in the afternoons. So I bought a van for £200 and got signs made for it with "Do you need to sell your house quickly?"

I would pay the running cost of it, as long as he put the fuel in. I insured and maintained it. He does around 600-800 leaflets a week.

When a lot of houses started coming through we also paid him a finder's fee too.

We bought a further nine Properties in 2009. We had about 38 Properties at that point. The deals were coming through and then the mortgage lenders were saying "No, you've got too many!"

Lending was getting very difficult by this point if you had more than 10 in your name and most with one lender group.

Is this when you started looking at deal packaging?

Yes it was, I was looking at other ways to make money from Property and had been to some Property group meetings. I spoke to some guys that were just Property trading for cash flow.

The PIN groups promoted a deal seller in the West Midlands so I got introduced to them, they were great guys.
I looked into buying leads from some of the Property BMV sale sites at 25% discount and set about ringing and converting them myself, which worked great.

I did about two-three Properties like this back at the end of 2009: just buying leads, ringing them up. The deal seller would sell them on for me as a full packaged deal.

At one of the pin meetings in Birmingham I met up with a guy who is now my second business partner in Property. He was also in Property with a portfolio in the West Midlands and also a mobile phone supplier, so I did a deal or two with phones and we started to meet up at a lot of the Property meeting groups to network.

Over the Christmas period my wife and two little girls and I visited him and his family.

When we were there I was chatting to him about the deals that I had done with the lead sellers, and was saying it's costly to buy all those leads to only get one or two out of them. I could do with my own lead web site out there.

He then mentioned that he has websites built and we agreed to pursue this a little more in the New Year.

He had a couple of websites made and started campaigns which started drawing plenty of people who want to sell quickly.

So he and I teamed up sharing all the costs, with both of us closing the deals, and going out to close the deal at vendors' Property all over the UK.

How did you meet Progressive?

I had been following Rob and Mark for some time with their website and emails, so when I found out that they were promoting a one-day workshop meeting in the West Midlands I just had to go and find out more about them.

On February 14th, Valentine's Day, my business partner and I went on the one-day workshop.

They approached both of us, because they were active both in marketing and buying their own Properties so we decided to go check them out. Rob went around the table asking "How many Properties do you have?"

Most people were saying one or two.

When they came to me and I said I have 38 Properties and explained about the van they asked to do an interview with me.

I must thank Rob at this point for that interview as after the interview came out, on Rob and Mark's Property forum site, the publicity we had after was phenomenal.

Wherever I was attending Property meetings up and down the UK people would come up and say, are you the guy with the van? It's amazing. Following Progressive Property; Rob and Mark, is a must.

They got us up on stage at the Property Super Conference 2010 and again we then we got flooded with requests from investors on the day and still to this day.

We've started following a lot of Rob's and Mark's strategies to flip

Property into auctions to make money.

Any Properties we bought outside our goldmine area we would put into auction. We bought one at £52K. We didn't refurbish it and sold for £85K in an auction in Derby. We made 20K profit.

Did you buy that one for cash?

Yes. We got the cash from deal packaging and being paid a finder's fee for selling deals on 25% below market value, but I could write a book on all of that alone!

Any tips you'd like to share?

I set up a Facebook page, which is Quick Cash Properties. There's a contact form on there. Through Facebook, through the recognition of the van and through advertising the logos, the silly cartoons, people have picked up on it (so brand yourself).

We've got 2,500 people on Facebook and about 1,000 of them are Telford people. It means when we have a room available, as soon as we have a house available, we've got flats, bungalows, houses, semis, detached and the HMO Property rooms, we put them onto Facebook and I just guide traffic to a letting agent and they take care of it from there.

I started using Facebook about 18 months ago. I started pushing it by joining every group I could find to do with Telford. Telford sales, Telford lettings, Telford football club, rugby club, even taxi people on there.

You make it sound very easy. Did you have any challenges?

The challenges lately have been around valuations. Trying to get mortgages ourselves personally. That's why we've gone into joint ventures now.

James and I have Properties with joint venture partners and friends who we have five or six Properties with, a couple that were on Sarah Benny's TV show a couple of years ago with a Property in Telford, and also from Telford too .

So you've been using joint venture partners as mortgage hosts?

Yes. For some time now with my wife, my sister. It's the only way forward for us to buy to hold at the moment.

As well as flipping Properties with joint venture partners with cash, I'm looking at ways to sell to first time buyers. We can only gift 5% legally but we're coming up with other ways around this, so we'll gift them 10% one way or another and leave just 5% in the Property in the deal.

So, you have a separate agreement?

Yes. We don't want the money now. We've got no interest in it. We will take it in five, six or seven years time. If you sell or remortgage, we'll know about it because we'll have a charge on it.

If you want to remortgage in five years time, we'll cut the 5% at the market value at that time. We'll collect it then, or if you want to sell it in three, four or five years time, we'll collect it then, which is a good way of building it up. It's a business with tangible assets, which if you wanted to you could sell on for a lot of money all the Properties you have with a 5% interest in.

That's a great way to view it. As a proper business with tangible assets.

Yes, the asset is in your name, with deeds and trusts which we get drawn up by solicitors.

I love the way you just pick up a new strategy, try it out and run with it.

Yes. It makes it interesting but I want to focus on helping others do the same now under the Progressive brand by teaching courses.

Is that something you saw yourself doing two years ago? Did you see yourself as a teacher, a mentor?

Absolutely not. At best I would have cringed. It would be the other way around. I'd be the one sat at the back of the room.

So, this journey has given you new confidence?

That's right. Any show we go to now, we've got t-shirts printed "Joint Venture Partners Required", we sit at the front whenever we can. 18 months ago I would have been at the back but now, I've got a passion for it. Anyone who asks, I just want to show them the ways of BMV buying Property.

I notice a change in your strategies since meeting Progressive

Before we were buying Properties doing it the standard formula way, but when we met Progressive they made us see new strategies. They also made us realise that the advertising on the window cleaners van was creative too and loved that and share it with their students now.

So, what are your plans for the future?

We aim to have 80 to 100 Properties in the next three-four years. More joint ventures with partners with cash to refurbish, sell and auction.

We get leads from all over the country so we'll find good Property deals at 30% off the market value and find an Investor who is buying in that area and joint venture with them.

We're looking to do training and one-to-one mentoring through Progressive.

Key Learnings

- Spot opportunities to joint venture with people to gain maximum leverage.
- Don't let changes in the market or economy affect you: embrace the change and see it as an opportunity.
- Be creative with investing and try out new strategies.
- Team up with other people with complementary skills.
- Package up and monetise deals you don't want to keep yourself.
- Get out there and network advertise yourself and have fun.

Education

Progressive Property JV Buying Frenzy Networking Event [1-day]:

http://www.progressiveproperty.co.uk/jv-event

Progressive Property JV Portal Members Forum:

http://www.progressivepropertyforum.co.uk

The Property SuperConference:

http://www.propertysuperconference.co.uk

Progressive Property Deal Packaging Cashflow Training

http://www.progressiveproperty.co.uk/deal-packaging-masterclass

Andy's Contact Details

Website: www.quick-cash-properties.co.uk
Email: andy.watkiss@blueyonder.co.uk
Mobile: 07971866697

Facebook: Andy Watkiss

Mark Homer

From School Boy Entrpreneur To Millionaire Business Man

Story At A Glance

Age: 31

Investment Area: Peterborough

Vital Statistics

Cash flow [Business & Property]: £3Million

Equity: £2.1Million

Portfolio: Multiple JVs - £20Million+

Mark, how did you get into property?

I started selling on eBay when I was at university so was developing the entrepreneurial side of myself. In the late 90s and early 2000s friends from school were investing in Property on the side from their day jobs; their parents had encouraged them. They would buy Properties and refurbish them or sell them.

They were buying them, they were going up and then they were selling them. They were making a killing and I didn't want to miss out! I also didn't think that they were necessarily and better than me, they just got in and did it, and I knew I needed to do that too.

What was your first property?

My first Property I signed up for in 2003. It was a ski flat in Bulgaria. I travelled to 4 different eastern European countries and did a lot of research. It was really the fact that Bulgaria was coming into the EU, the ski resort had only really just started, and most of the development was still to come. It had only been open three years. I also thought it could serve as a place for me to ski for myself.

How did that deal work out then?

I paid 64,000 Euros for it, and I've just accepted an offer to sell it for 25,000 Euros.

Right, so possibly not the best deal then?

Pretty bad.

Okay, so what impact did that have on your investing future?

Well, it just taught me that I really needed to stay local, have a deep understanding of the marketplace and what I was buying, and I'm sure Bulgarian Property makes people money but I would have thought it's probably the people who are based in Bulgaria that understand it best. I finished payments in 2007; I'd completed on it. It was delayed quite a lot, and then, by '07 I knew the rentals were really lacking.

So it was never going to achieve the cash flow that you expected?

No.

Did you buy that property with capital appreciation in mind or cash flow?

Both.

What did you do after that deal then?

My next one I bought a new build off plan in Peterborough.

How did that deal work out?

It was okay. It was ready by '05 and I sold it straight away. I made a small amount on it. I think I bought it for £131,000 and sold it for £155 000. I learned on that deal that when I came to sell mine, I could get significantly less for it than the developer was selling their units for.

So it showed me there was a dual market going on: that the resale value of new Properties is lower than a new Property that a developer would sell.

In 2005, when I sold it, I got 155,000 for it. The developer was pricing theirs at about £170,000. So immediately, I started to work out that, actually, I made that money, from a rising market, but if I just bought an existing one, I'd have made, probably, another ten or fifteen per cent.

I could have just bought an existing one from the developer, from another owner, or maybe just an existing one from another part of town.

So you haven't lost money on this deal, then.

No, I made money. But I was lucky. It was the rising market, and not the fact that I had the right strategy or secret knowledge.

Did that encourage you to do more?

Yes. I started buying existing units, small existing units, refurbishing them; small ex-council houses. Once I started to see the evidence of this working, because I had actually done it, and tried all the other strategies, I kept rolling it out and refined and perfected the model through 2005.

When you say 'perfected'...

Buying, refurbishing, then revaluing to get my money out to buy another, effectively making every deal no money left in.

And by perfecting the model, were you taking advice from other people?

Well, I'd seen a letting agent doing something similar. I read a few courses and packs and applied it to the local area with this local Property. And I was learning through making my own mistakes on the job, feeling the pain and then not making them again!

I now really see the value in education. I used to think I could scrimp by, not spend any money, learn as I go, or watch people from afar. That thinking actually cost me around £40,000 in my first deal. A couple of good courses and a community and support network would have cost me one tenth, and I'd have probably made more money faster.

So explain more about this model you perfected?

Well I learned that the low-value ones rented proportionally for much more than the more expensive ones. I also learned that the expenses were lower, and the risks were lower, because you could buy more for your (or other people's) money.

With the Bulgaria experience I knew it had to be local as the costs were crazy, I didn't understand the language or the legals, and nothing got done because I was in another country.

I didn't really understand how powerful it was investing locally until I started meeting other local investors. I could see that the more experienced ones seemed to get all the best, cheapest deals, fastest, before anyone else saw them. I started to think that they must be giving them backhanders, but soon realized that it was a question of trusting them to buy every time, and knowing them because they are doing it everyday.

Rob has this saying "visibility is credibility." We started to get the best deals because we were there, doing it, and everyone knew us, and you can't do that in remote or far away places.

So how many did you buy, and when was that?

I bought 15-20 with Rob between the end of 2005 and 2006?

How did you finance all those?

I used some cash that I'd saved from previous businesses. I also learned some creative ways to finance the deals, so I knew that I could continue to buy no matter what, because that's what I want to do – keep buying

Property.

I'm quite careful, I've always been an investor since I was 14.

Stocks, bonds? Safe ones?

Yeah, exactly, I still invest in equities and have a keen interest I the markets as they are a great indicator of what may come in other investment zones. Right from university I used my student loan money to invest and learnt a lot early on.

Is there a history of that in the family?

I really got that from my Dad. He was very much into saving and investing.

Well, they're very different things, aren't they? Was he into investing?

Probably more into saving. He wasn't into business. I learned a lot from him about how to keep money, but I also learned a lot about what not to do, as he would rarely invest or spend money. He never really got to enjoy any of his savings before he died, and he wasn't that old, and I don't want that to happen to me.

I'm a compulsive investor now and probably take a bit more risk than he did.

Where did this enterprising spirit come from?

I went to boarding school, and my father worked overseas; I was born in Asia. And when I was 12 I came back to boarding school. I was surrounded by wealthy people; all my friends' fathers – almost all of them – had their own businesses. And they were making serious money, most of them, because our school fees were very high; they had to. I used to go around to their houses and talk to their dads, and that really inspired me. I realised that business was a way to earn that money and I think it rubbed off on me being around those people. I am very grateful for that. Their level of wealth was on a completely different scale to other friends I had outside this arena. School surrounded me with the right people and gave me a great mindset.

Most people get their experiences from their parents, don't they?

Yes. Boarding school was really good for that, because my dad's been quite supportive, really. He was quite excited. He used to build roads and water systems for foreign governments and worked as a consultant in a big company but we still never seemed to have as much money for holidays as my friends. A few experiences then changed my life

In what way?

I had worked in a graduate training programme in a big company and I thought my plan was to work my way up through the company. However, I saw older people in the company who hadn't moved on much. I also saw my Dad work hard all his life and still not have much money to show for it and so when he died at 63, the same age as my uncle, it changed my perspective on what I wanted to do with my life.

I didn't want to be like that, and I wanted to take more risks to get higher rewards than my dad and uncle, but I didn't want to waste my money or time either. A combination of my dad's saving skills and my friends' dad's business and investing skills shaped what is important to me.

For me, investing is like a sport. I hated sport at school, but like all the other kids wanted the competition, the fun and the growth. And that is what our businesses and investing gives me.

I've tried, and continue to invest, in just about everything. Property, for me, ended being the best one for returns, leverage and security. Anything else I invest in will always be higher risk and therefore I'll use much less of my percentage of wealth.

What kind of prices were you buying your properties at?

I bought my first three on the same street. I paid £76,600 for the first, £77,000, and £77,000. They were all three-beds and they rented at £500. There was more cash flow in the lower end deals, even back in those days. There's even more now.

Did you buy them in the traditional way, or you were buying below market value?

I was buying them below market value through agents. It was probably 15-18%, once the refurbishment was done back in those days, which was actually quite good then.

Were there any networking events that you were going to at that time?

Rob and I met at one in early '06. I wasn't really going to them before that.

Was it love at first sight?

Well, I was impressed by his capacity for work, to be honest. When he actually said, "I'm going to go and do this", or, "I'm going to read this book" or whatever. When he came back, he'd done it. Laser speed; and I was like, "S**t, I've never managed to do that". I was blown away by all that, to be honest, and I just thought, "I've got to stay with this lad".

So that's a yes then!

[Laugh] That can be taken out of context.

Tell me what happened next then.

In mid '05 I went to work for a guy locally because I saw him buying new builds, and I thought it would be a good way for me to understand how the industry works a bit more. I thought if this guy can do it, surely I can too.

So I sold some new builds from there, learned a lot about how the market worked at that time, and plenty of people were making money accidentally. Then Rob joined. I said to the bloke who was running the company, "We've really got to get this Rob guy in, and get him selling", so he joined.

The bloke we were working for was a bit of a nightmare. It was a bit pressurized, so within a couple of months, we'd decided we were going to set up together at some point. We'd leave, and we needed to be together. That was in '07. Well, December '06, really. January '07. So we saw each other in the work environment during that period.

You worked together so you got to know each other pretty well?

Yeah, I saw him at work, and I saw how he could sell, and then of course, it was during that period he started presenting. And he'd present and sell stuff, he knew nothing about the month before ;-) Some people might look down on that, but he'd just go for it like some crazed fiend! He didn't know anything about any of this before, he'd lock himself away and immerse himself in it and learn at 10 times the speed of anyone else I'd ever met, and within a month he was standing on stage and telling the people all this stuff. It was unbelievable.

And of course, the bloke we were working for couldn't believe it either. And it was like, "Rob's presenting". Of course, Rob had been doing it in his pub, working for his Dad; he used to be the landlord at his dad's pub and was a training ground for his public speaking. I was petrified of the whole thing, so it was perfect.

He can crack on, he loved doing all the marketing and everything like that, so he can crack on and do that, and I can sort the Property stuff out.

So at this point, Rob's selling to make money to get a salary?

Correct. He was selling, but he was really focused on personal development because he'd come through his own journey. In '04, '05, he got into Anthony Robbins. And he really worked quite hard after that. So he introduced that, mixed it with Property when he was doing his presentations; almost fused the two things together, which, of course, people liked. They got quite excited by it.

I just wanted to invest in Property, but I now realize all the sales stuff Rob was learning at light speed was so important. It's not enough just to research and get clued up on Property investment, you've got to convince and persuade people (Vendors, Estate Agents) to deal with you and not your competitors.

I'm glad Rob took that stuff on, as I wasn't confident at it for a long long time. That being said, it's mostly down to me that we have the portfolio we do ☺

So when was Progressive Property formed?

January 2007.

Where did the name come from?

I wish we'd brainstormed it a little, but I'd kind of got it in my head. I went for a job interview, when I was looking to do my graduate scheme, and there was this company called Progressive Recruitment and I just loved the name; I thought it was a cool name. We've kind of taken that on now, what the actual word means and how we bring it to the market, but it wasn't intentional at first.

Why did you create Progressive Property?

We were trying to buy Properties for other people because we had so many deals coming in and we couldn't buy them all ourselves. We'd just started leapfrogging some of the old school investors and were getting the pick of many of the best deals.

We'd already built a reasonably sized portfolio, but we now had to buy for other people if we wanted to keep the deals flowing in. We thought we could sell them and have a small share in their portfolio.

This worked well for us and the people we bought for. Many people are too busy to do this, though love the idea of being a passive investor. Rob calls it 'the baby without the labour pains.'

Why not just carry on buying in your own names?

If you use other people's deposits, you can buy more Properties quicker. We had all these deals we wanted to buy, and we knew if we could get other people to in with us, almost as a Joint Venture, we have a share of their equity, and we find them deals that are of the quality we were buying for ourselves, we could all make a lot more money just by having a small share from a lot of people. We also wanted a business anyway. We wanted to be in business.

We were getting money to buy the Properties but then each deal we did for them we got a £10K of equity share. They buy the Property, below market value, then in the future, when they sell or remortgage, we'd get £10K of the equity. And we kept the deal flow coming through the agents that way.

How many properties did you buy in 2007 for yourselves and joint venture partners?

It took us six months to get our first client. It was really hard, we started in one of our houses and put £200 each into a bank account and set up shop. We were doing Property portfolios so it's a big lump of money to give to two young lads back then, which in hindsight was not really the right way to start, but we were very fixed in our ideas: we didn't just want to source average Properties like everyone else: we wanted to provide a fully hands free, upmarket and caring service. We were sourcing deals, refurbishing them and managing them too.

People often underestimate just what it takes to do this.

When did the education aspect of Progressive begin?

Progressive Education started in December '08. Since we wrote the first book so many people kept asking us to show them how to do it too, but we just didn't know how to teach it. We were just doing it and learning as we went along.

We thought it would be a good idea to introduce lower cost offers to the business too, so that there were lower barriers to entry for people with less money, to get involved in Property investing.

This was during the credit crunch?

Yes, the credit crunch came just as we moved into our proper offices! It's funny because Rob always said we should call our offices Progressive House. He thought it sounded official and grand. Ironically, it was a house when we started – a two bed one! Now we have 6,000 square feet, so we do actually have a real Progressive house!

All this growth while the market bottomed, people became very scared. Mortgages dried up and people stopped buying.

But you had become financially free through your portfolios.

Yes but then it depends how much money you want, right. It's funny, because every time we hit a goal, we wanted more money ☺ I don't think we are any different to anyone else like that. I remember when our running expenses were less than £500 per month. I also remember the first time our running expenses, or burn rate, went over £100,000 a month!

What training had you done during this time?

I'd done Chris Howard training and a variety of Property investment courses but I'm different from Rob. I'll go out and do stuff to learn making mistakes whereas he will read three books on it and perhaps take a quicker route.

So what made you think you should get into education?

We were already running our hands-free days for clients for our portfolio-builder service, so we were used to running events, and so the education developed from there. We were giving them a lot of value on that day and then we turned it into a paid course, which then went into a four-day Property Masterclass.

We're lucky because we've had a lot of professionals you would know train at our course, and so it helped put that course on the map. Rob would say it's the best in the UK!

How did it help your business?

It helped to smooth our cash flow. Sourcing is large sporadic sums of cash and is at the mercy of the Property buying lifecycle. We'd taken on greater overheads in offices and staff, so we had to meet our commitments. We needed to take smaller amounts, more times from more people to smooth the cash flow, and recession-proof the business.

It also builds your brand. In our first 18 months we had about 18 customers (albeit high paying ones), in the next 18 months we probably had 100,000 customers!

What did you do to expand the education arm of the business?

We provided more specialist courses on specific aspects of Property such as lease options, dealing with estate agents etc. I started doing mentorships with individual clients. There are so many strategies in Property that can make people money, and there's always a need for education, I think because people are so busy now, they don't want to make the mistakes like I did, and the want the fastest route to get the result.

How did you develop the mentorships?

People wanted more handholding in their area so I'd travel to their investment area and walk through what to do. However, with the travel, being away all day and out of the office, we felt we could provide a better service to more people. It was highly leveraged active income but it had its drawbacks.

I don't do them anymore because of time constraints. That was one to one, now Rob and I often do 1 to 800 on our webinars or at the Property SuperConference. It's better use of our time and we can reach and help more people.

You've become pretty synonymous with property investment education up and down the country. You've done regional events, one-day events, high-value, low-price events and then your three-day trainings. It's been successful wouldn't you say?

Yes. We did 80 last year. We'll probably do 120 next year. It's probably 60% of our business.

You launched the first property super conference in 2010. What was the thinking behind running an event like that?

Rob's desire to rule the world? [Laugh] No, seriously. It was very exciting. We'd seen these big name speakers and the draw that they create. The costs of running an event look horrendous. We'd been used to running events with 150-200 people but this was stepping up to 600+ people.

We had to work hard to get people there because it was three times as big an event as we'd ever run, but our community was getting bigger, and I think the ticket sales probably benefited from the speakers names. Because of the level and depth of content and the excitement it created on the weekend there was a ripple effect in registrations to all of our trainings, and the results people were getting.

Rob always said that running an event is about the experience and emotion that leads to the transformation. I thought it was just about learning the nuts and bolts of how to do something. I think we fused together both of these well in the end, after a few discussions/disagreements ☺

So what does the future hold, Mark?

We took on another company in February so we're busy integrating them. They are aimed at personal development, so we're branching out into different wealth creation vehicles. We're growing some of our VIP members to become part of the Progressive brand too.

No plans to open a Progressive letting agent in every major city then?

No. That's not something in our game plan. We have other plans.

So what advice would you give to people coming behind you about getting educated.

Get educated and leverage all our time and expense so you don't make all the mistakes I did. I signed up for three Properties on the east coast of Florida and managed to get out as the market crashed. That was a close shave.

I bought others off plan and lost money. I had to go through that journey, it was my "entrance fee" and you don't need to do that. You can just buy and invest in the assets that work using this knowledge.

Finally Mark, what has success brought you?

Freedom. I can choose what work I want to do, when I want to do it and where. I love cars and can buy my favourites. I have a nice house and don't have to worry about money when I go on holiday. I travel a lot now too and enjoy skiing. I also get to meet fantastic, inspiring people like James Caan, Lord Alan Sugar, Bob Geldof and Andreas Panayiotou.

I can also help so many more people now I have more time.

Simon Kennerley

"No Man Is An Island, But I'm Trying To Buy One"

Story At A Glance

Age: 39

J.O.B.: IT Consultant

Investment Area: Isle of Wight
Strategies: Buy to hold

Vital Statistics

Properties: Eight - all single lets varying from a one-bed flat to a three-bed house
Cash flow: £1500 per month after mortgage payments, lettings charges, and service charges
Portfolio: £1 million

Equity: £350,000

How did you get into property?

My parents own a mixed farm on the Isle of Wight and to help diversify from traditional farming they set up a farm cottage and a converted barn for holiday lets. I was given the opportunity to buy the farm cottage on the death of my grandma in 1996 and I continued to run this Property as a holiday let. The holiday let business is great for cash flow but has higher maintenance costs, so after a few years I changed the cottage to single lets and moved to a more standard re-mortgage and pull equity out strategy, which is possible in a rising house market.

How many properties did you buy using that method?

From 1996 I slowly built my Property portfolio starting with a probate Property which was a Victorian two-bed house which needed refurbishment, this gave an insight in the issues that come up in Properties. This was also the time I created a great relationship with a letting agent and learnt the value of a highly systemised company, who have trained and accredited staff – I can't stress enough how important lettings agents are. Not only do they find your tenants, but they also make sure you get your rents, and manage the maintenance and evictions.

Around this time I also started looking at some of the more exotic locations for Property development. I began to look at the up and coming European hot spots like Bulgaria, Spain, and Morocco and was tempted by the cheap inspection trips offered. Blinded by the hype and the slick marketing I jumped into the dream of owning a holiday Property that I could use and also rent out to cover the costs, and maybe make a small income.

It was off plan and during the trip there (a cold and wet November weekend – not showing the area at its best) I saw the plot of land where my apartment should be. Fast-forward 18 months and after struggling to get a mortgage and an administrative nightmare, I was out of pocket by thousands of Euros and lost my option to buy the apartment. It looked like a nightmare to try to get my money back, so I chalked this up to experience and moved on.

Returning to the UK market I picked up a great little one-bedroom flat which had just been finished and then I went on to a more ambitious recently built two-bed flat in Aldershot, which taught me the value of getting the right mortgage at the right time.

I was forced to take a tracker mortgage and at the time of purchase the rate looked good, but over time the interest rose and I got to the point of funding the mortgage out of my own pocket (not something I want to do again). But in a strange twist of fate this tracker is now the best value mortgage I have, and now this is my best cash flowing Property – long may the low interest rates last!

So, how did you meet Progressive?

I had slowed down my investing in Property during the credit crisis, as like the many others I was unsure of where the Property market was going, but as it levelled out I started looking for new opportunities and started to look at renewing my education in Property.

So looking round the 'Property scene' I began going to the free or low cost seminars, and it was at the Progressive Property one-day from there I decided to move on to do their Masterclass course. I have always maintained that if I can save the costs of the training in a deal I have done, then I feel the money has been well spent – this has happened with the Progressive Property!

What were your impressions?

I liked Rob and Mark. They certainly knew their stuff. They've certainly bought enough Properties to see most of the pitfalls. I was surprised on how they didn't just talk about how to buy Property, but more about the mind-set of how you should be buying Property, and what you need to succeed in that.

Did you do any more education?

Yes. I did the three-day Masterclass in May of 2010. This course gave me a refresher on buying Property, but also gave me the new strategies that Rob and Mark recommend. Also the other people on the course are like-minded and want to succeed in Property which means the course has high energy and lasting friendships are created.

I also went on the Lease Options course which I think is the most exciting strategy that has appeared recently.

I also try and get to all of the one-day Buying Frenzy Days as it makes a good location for networking and to help promote the Progressive brand.

What did you do after the three-day masterclass?

With the motivation of the Masterclass, I restarted my hunt for more Property. I applied and got accepted into the VIP club, which meant I had to up my game to make best use of the one-to-one mentoring, the extra speakers I was seeing and the networking it allows.

Back on the Property hunt I researched my 'goldmine' area and decided on the Isle of Wight, and then went about contacting estate agents and setting aside time to view Properties.

Overall I went and saw 50 Properties in the three months after the Masterclass. This gave me a good idea of the types of Property available and what kind of condition they were in. It gave me the opportunity also build relationships with the estate agents

Where do you invest and why?

I'm investing in the Isle of Wight. I was born there and grew up there and over the years built relationships with estate agents, letting agents, and builders. I have looked around at other areas in the south of England but the prices are too high for some of the strategies to work. I decided not to head north like other investors have. This does mean I have to travel a couple of hours to get to my 'goldmine' area but at least I get to see my family more.

What do you get out of the VIP club?

The monthly meetings forced me to do something every month. It is obviously a motivation to go there and say what's been done, what I need to do, and set a goal for the next month, which is, I think, the main reason why I enjoy the VIP club.

I'm quite lazy. I've tried to make sure that I can get to every meeting to make sure that I keep the motivation going. The information is very good and I've seen some of it before but I haven't seen everything before, I always try to learn something.

The one-to-one meeting obviously gives me suggestions to what I should be doing, I ask questions about whether I am doing something right or wrong or if there's anybody else I need to speak to about a particular idea or issue. It always forces me to do something that I should've done in the last month.

Since the VIP club membership have you bought any property?

Yes. I bought five Properties since the Masterclass with a couple more deals in the pipeline, which is more than I bought in the last three or four years. I have moved to looking at repossessions, auction Properties and lease option deals. I have got two repossessions, both of which have been good value purchases.

Are you using your own cash or someone else's?

I have been lucky that I have been able to release equity from my previous purchases and I have been using this to fund the Properties. I have also joint ventured with my mum to allow me to buy other Properties.

Do you attend networking events?

Yes, I try to go to the local Property networking events. This means I am a regular at the Berkshire Property Meet. I also try and go to the PIN meetings in Southampton and Bristol.

What type of properties do you buy?

Flats and houses. The cheaper ones tend to be flats and I don't have a problem finding tenants for them in the area I invest in.

What's the plan for the future?

I've set goals for the year and I am planning to buy six Properties this year. My challenge is finding finance but I have at least two Properties coming up that I should be able to pull the money back out again so I think that's two of them done.

What are your plans after your passive income exceeds your expenses?

I enjoy my job in IT but I'd prefer to work for myself and not work for somebody else. I've had a goal for a long time to retire at 40, which is next year. How close will I come to that? I don't know but that's always been my goal. Rob thinks I will achieve it!

So at the end of the year how many properties would you have?

13 Properties with 5-9% yield. I've never sold a Property. I'm a buy-to-hold person. I always thought it was going to be my pension fund.

Looks like you're on track for achieving that.

Yes, I'd like to think by the end of this year, I'm going to be at least half to two thirds of the way through getting enough income to not work and then the following year, get to a point when I think I'm in a position to not have to work anyway. I don't like the politics in my job but enjoy the technology.

Have you had any challenges?

I've made a lot of mistakes. I've bought off-plan at too high a price and I have struggled with foreign law systems. I have lost monies on foreign deals but all of my UK Properties are not in negative equity and I have positive cash flow from all of them too.

Did you buy abroad?

I was going to buy a Property in Bulgaria. I put the deposit down, and then had to wait the 18 months for it to be built. But due to a number of issues with mortgages, lawyers and the Property investments company, the deal fell though and I have had to write off the money.

I feel better because even Mark has lost money there in the early days! It's all part of the education, and the Progressive Education has saved me many more costly mistakes.

Key Learnings

- Get out there right away and action what you have learned. The more viewings you do, the more deals you will get.
- It doesn't matter if you did it wrong in the past, do it right today.
- Make mistakes and learn from them: keep going and don't give up.
- Buy for the long term.
- Set goals to replace your job income.
- Go to networking events and create contacts at these meetings

Education

Progressive Property JV Buying Frenzy Networking Event [1-day]:

http://www.progressiveproperty.co.uk/jv-event

Progressive Property 3 Day Property Investing Masterclass

http://www.progressiveproperty.co.uk/masterclass

The Property SuperConference

http://www.propertysuperconference.co.uk

Simons Contact Details

Email: property@simonkennerley.com

Willie Beveridge

From Iincapacity Benefit To

£1 Million Portfolio In 18 Months

Story At A Glance

Age: 47
J.O.B. Joiner
Investment Area: Dunfermline
Strategies: Distressed sellers

Vital Statistics:

Properties: 15 Properties
Value: 1.5 million
Cash Flow: 3k per month
Equity : Over 400k
Built in: Two years plus two months on my own

How did you get into property, Willie?

I'm a joiner builder. I used to do a Property up, sell it, buy another one and kept doing that.

When did you start buying property?

It was March 2009 I bought my first buy to let.

How did you meet Progressive?

At the time I was off work sick with back problems. It made me realise I had to do something different as the money stopped coming in when I wasn't working. I realised I had to get back into Property to rent them out rather than sell them. I just didn't know how to do it. I was 45 years old at the time and had never been out of work before. Due to injury I couldn't get work.

In February 2009 I went to a one-day progressive event in Manchester and Rob and Mark asked me what I wanted. I said "I'd like to have £1 million worth of Property in two years". I never thought at the time that I could do it but that was my goal which I set out on, and I actually did it quicker.

Did you do any other training?

I did a three-day Progressive Masterclass in May 2010 which galvanised me into action. Fortunately, Paul McFadden was there that day too and he signed up for the Masterclass as well, so I met up with him again then and stayed in touch. He's been a great help for me as well as somebody as young and motivated as he is. He's done really well.

Was it easy? What was the key to success?

No. I had the right team. I have a great broker Eddie Tweedie at First Choice Finance.

You seem to find the deals easily enough. How are you doing that?

I've sourced a few myself here and there. ☺

What kind of return are you getting on your properties?

I'm making at least £200 a month net cash flow after costs on each one. There's one I'm making £300 a month on. I've got three two-bedroom flats. I've got six three-bedroom houses and I've got a five-bedroom one. I had planned to convert that to an HMO but I've got a family in it so I'm making £300 a month on it.

Where are you investing?

I invest around Fife about 10 miles from Edinburgh. Most of my Properties are within five miles of where I live, as taught by Rob and Mark.

Do you manage the properties yourself?

Yes I do. I tried an agent but the first one just wasn't working. They were late every month with the rent.

Any mistakes?

Yes. Not getting them rented quick enough.

Have you done any joint ventures?

Yes. I met a boy at the Edinburgh Property Meet and he had found a house in Edinburgh. He asked me how I got my money in and out so we worked on it. That's making £230 per month net cash flow but there's a good deal of equity in it. We got a 30% discount on it. We eventually can get our money back out of the deal.

Do you do much networking?

I do yes. I attend events in Edinburgh, Glasgow and Fife to find out new ideas, new solutions.

Have you had challenges?

My wife was nervous about it but she's gone from not wanting to do it to having the Properties in her name so we can carry on buying. Finding finance is always a challenge.

How have you financed your deals?

I've provided the deposit for one of the deals but the others I have bridged the deposit but that's getting harder to do.

Do you recommend any books?

Obviously, the Progressive ones. Andy Shaw's book was one of the first ones to come out and I've just finished reading his "Bug Free Mind" book which tackles more the mind-set than the technical skills of Property investing.

Any advice to give to someone who is thinking of taking the next step?

You really need to want to change your life. Once you're ready to do that, go meet people at the Property networking events who have already done it, speak to them, read the books.

I had nothing a year and a half ago, but through determination I jumped the hurdles. Once you do one it gives you confidence to go and do it again.

I meet the same people over and over again at the Property meets but they don't do anything and it frustrates me. They just can't take the first step.

I reached a very low point whilst off sick with back trouble. I'd lost a lot of weight and I studied personal development books.
Find people who are supportive and have been there and done it. I've been very lucky and had people like John and Debra Rice and Clare Darwish to keep me going.

What are your plans for the future?

Continue to buy and build my portfolio and look at packaging deals for other Investors.

Your life has been transformed in the past year and a half hasn't it?

It certainly has. From incapacity benefit to having a £1 million worth of Property. I only borrowed £30K from my Dad's house and a £10K bank loan to get me going.

Any plans to do more joint ventures?

Yes I would like to.The first one has been good so hopefully I can do more from attending the networking events.

Top Tip

Get your Property let as soon as possible to help the cash flow.

Key Learnings

- Set your goals specifically and you will surprise yourself at how you achieve them.
- Break through your own personal challenges.
- Get your Properties rented out quickly and be proactive.
- Your friends and family may be nervous or sceptical but they will come around when you prove how well you are doing. Align with successful, motivated people.
- Have desire and determination: you can't not succeed.
- Keep on keeping on

Education

Progressive Property JV Buying Frenzy Networking Event [1-day]:

http://www.progressiveproperty.co.uk/jv-event

Progressive Property 3 Day Property Investing Masterclass

http://www.progressiveproperty.co.uk/3-day-masterclass

The Progressive Property Best Selling Books

http://www.progressiveproperty.co.uk/book-buy-now

Willies Contact Details

Website: www.rubyproperty.co.uk

Telephone: 07786436706

Email: willie@rubyproperty.co.uk

Peter Iwanizewski

27 And Sacked His Boss

Story At A Glance

Age: 27

J.O.B.: Recruitment

Investment Area: Coventry

Strategies: BMV

Vital Statistics:

Cash flow: £4.2K NET pcm

Portfolio: £1.45M

Equity: 450K

How did you get into property, Peter?

I used to work in recruitment after university, which was 2006. I left my first job in recruitment in 2007. I had that job for a year, but was made redundant and in the meantime ended up getting another job at E.ON in the sales department there.

I actually came across an advert for a course at that time and went on it. I'd had a couple of buy-to-lets at the time. I just bought my own home and then I decided that I wanted to get into it full-time.

One was a renovation I did before I went to uni, but was kept just as a buy-to-let. We meant to sell it, but ended up just keeping it as a buy-to-let. I bought my own home after that in 2007 and quickly bought a flat in Coventry just straight after that, not really planning on making a career out of it, and I went from there.

That's a bit unusual to get a couple of buy-to-lets before university. Is there a history of property investing in the family?

There was one before. Yes, my dad had a couple of buy-to-lets for his pension and that was something I'd seen, so I decided then. That was a renovation we did and then kept as a buy-to-let. I'd like to say when I bought my home in 2007, I actually bought that space below the market value of that, actually trying. Those were the days you could still remortgage, so I used the extra money to get another Property then.

You were aware you were buying it at a discount?

Yes but only from what the agent had it on a the time. However, as I've gotten more experience, I realised it's not just about what the estate agents have them on for, but what it was below what other Properties were selling for.

Okay, so 2007 you bought your home?

Yes and I went on a three-day training course and a mentorship that year. That was when I realised I wanted to try and make a career out of Property, but I worked up until 2009 just as a means of saving some extra money. So when I left, I obviously had a buffer to start with that I could use.

Did you buy any property after that mentorship and training?

Yes, I went out and I bought quite a few. At the same time I came across the Progressive trainings and after that, ended up buying more after their trainings as well.

How did you meet Progressive?

It was August 2009. I met them at a course they were doing in London. It was a one-day Progressive Mastermind course. I met Rob and Mark and then afterwards e-mailed Rob and it went from there, and that's what I liked about them. It's the fact that after the course, there was a core network, they were very personal and approachable and you could actually get to the CEOs; pretty unusual but very impressive.

Did you do other trainings with them?

I'd done some crewing for them (helping back of house at the Progressive Networking Events), and I was at the Super Conference last year. I certainly got good ideas from it, and to see the event run actually helping was a great experience that I learned a lot from.

How many properties have you bought since then?

I've bought nine Properties since then.

Is there a strategy you're using?

My main strategy is BMV buy-to-let. I always buy for cash flow rather than capital growth, although obviously the Properties are bought at a discount. It was nice to lock in real equity.

But, my main strategy was to build a buy-to-let portfolio that would allow me to leave my job, so I can be a full-time investor and then once I achieved that, then I started looking at more streams of cash flow.

But my goal was to get freedom, get enough Properties to leave my job, so I could live, to free up my time. Buy-to-let was the easiest way I could see of doing that or the most productive way.

Were you finding any problems getting mortgages?

I was quite lucky. The answer is yes and no. Yes when I did four or five deals quickly with a single mortgage company, but I have been able buy in joint names such as my dad's since then. There's strength in the credit score. I've kept the Properties tenanted and not missed payments. Something I always do is keep my credit score regularly monitored. I won't say that's a guarantee because sometimes I've done that, gone to get mortgages and it's still refused and there's nothing even on the file.

Have you read any books at all?

The usual, Rob & Mark's books and "Rich Dad, Poor Dad". Read some of the Property-related books. But no, I wouldn't say. Barring those, I hadn't read many to start with.

Any mistakes that you've made along the way?

Yes, I suppose when I first started. I won't say they are major mistakes, but you obviously learn things as you go along and learn how to deal with tenants. Learning on renovations, when you buy a Property and you're getting it ready to let – just make sure you're not waiting for materials.

It's about planning – being more organized, evolving, learning different ways of managing the Properties and getting the deals.

It's tough. Do your due diligence with all the Properties, stick to your plan and do not veer off.

Have you been buying distressed properties or is it just light refurbishments?

Yes, the earlier ones, there were more distressed Properties that needed work doing to them, not major refurbishments – nothing structural just complete overhauls on décor, kitchen, and bathroom. But recently, I've been buying Properties that are just light refurbishments or needs very little work doing at all.

How are you supplying deposits for these?

Different ways: private investment and JVs, remortgaging, working the job to start with a house I've been saving for a deposit as well, and then recently over the last year or so, using sourcing fees.

When I was buying Properties in Coventry, they were quite low, so I was able to get the deposits together. So at the start, I was still able to remortgage which was good.

So you actually source properties as well?

Yes, I do now. The last six months I did some, but now it's something I'm focusing on a lot heavier and upscaling.

Are you still working in your JOB?

No I left in July 2009 to go full-time into Property investing.

What are your plans for the year ahead?

Concentrate on sourcing more Properties, and looking to do work for first-time buyers now, getting them on the ladder through things like assisted sales and gifted deposits, for multiple streams of income, and buying when I can. A joint venture with someone on the Progressive VIP Millionaires Programme is something I'm looking into as well which hopefully will allow me to buy more Properties.

Some people have got lots of time and no money, and some people are the other way around, as they haven't got the experience. I meet some people that just say that the first ones they want to do are joint ventures, so that they can do them with someone who's a bit more experienced.

Do you do much networking at all?

Yes, I used to go to the Berkshire Property meet. I don't go there every month now, but I still go. I go to Parmdeep and Hanif's event in Birmingham. I sometimes go to the Leicester one and I actually run one in Coventry. It's just small at the moment. There are only about 20 to 25 people at the moment but we're looking to grow that as well.

How do you generate property leads?

In the early days it was with estate agents and I've still got relationships with three agents. I probably know ten Agents, but two or three that I know, call on the "bankers" as I've managed to complete on deals in the past. That's another tip I'd say.

What I've found is when you say you're going to do something, doing it is imperative, but if you can't do something or for any reason, be honest and just be upfront in what you're doing.

I started finding leads in newspapers, leaflets and the Internet. I've got a website, but I don't generate so many leads on the Internet at the moment as I do from my newspaper ads and leaflets.

Have you done any joint ventures?

I've done one joint venture with somebody and that was half the deposit each. It was with somebody I knew. I found the Property, we shared the monthly cash flow 50-50 and then I took "X" amount for the management of it monthly.

You manage properties as well?

Yes, I manage all mine and I have a couple of people, who I manage Properties for. It's not something I'm going to do a lot of now I've got contact with a local letting agent who would manage them anyway. But this particular one, I decided to manage because it put the person's mind at rest who was investing with me, as a service, and they wanted a hands-off experience.

Have you done any deals through estate agents?

I was going around agents because I didn't have any money at the time and I learned a lot on the estate agent's training. Once I bought three Properties through agents, once I started implementing some of what they were saying, it seemed to be getting to each of the agents I didn't know as well as the ones I did know!

What would you say to anyone coming behind you?

The more time you can devote to it, the better. Set out what it is you want specifically, and be realistic with your goals.

If you've only got an hour a week, the chances of you going to buying any Properties in a year almost can't happen. But, it's just being clear what you want and it can be achieved.

I worked two jobs at the start just so I can get enough money together to leave. It takes sacrifice, but again homework. Make the relationships. Property can feel like you're doing a lot of work at the start and not getting much back, but it's the conversations and relationships you build with agents is something that, over time, can come back and benefit you. And the work pays you back with passive income.

Key Learnings

- Use Property as a vehicle to create your own personal freedom and get out of a job.
- Start early, start now and learn things as you go along.
- Finance and investing conditions are always changing, you have to keep up with the market, and stay one step ahead.
- Plan, do your homework, do not veer from your plan, evolve and learn.
- When you say you're going to do something, do it, especially with estate agents.
- If something goes wrong, which will happen, be upfront about it.
- Do joint ventures to keep you buying through changing markets.
- The more time you can devote to investing, the better.
- Be realistic with your goals.
- Make sacrifices.
- Build the relationships and Property will pay you back big time.

Education

Progressive Property JV Buying Frenzy Networking Event [1-day]:

http://www.progressiveproperty.co.uk/jv-event

The Property SuperConference

http://www.propertysuperconference.co.uk

Progressive Property VIP JV Millionaires Club:

http://www.progressiveproperty.co.uk/vip-pmc

Peter's Contact Details

Email: peteriwaniszewski@hotmail.co.uk

Jackie Goodman And Colin Molloy

60 Hour Week Lawyers Help People Climb On The Property Ladder

Story At A Glance

Age: **Jackie:** 44 **Colin:** 52

J.O.B.

Colin: Barrister – head of Black Country Prosecution Service Area

Jackie: Solicitor – senior prosecutor, rape and serious sexual offences specialist

Investment Areas: Black Country and Shropshire

Strategies: BMV purchase & refinancing, lease options, deal packaging

Vital Statistics

Properties: Eight Properties

Cash flow: £2,000 (£24,000 p.a)

Portfolio Value: £782,000

How did you get into property Jackie?

I have always wanted my own business and more time freedom. My profession is a solicitor and Colin is a barrister. We both work as public prosecutors so we have extremely busy working lives. I now specialise in rape and very serious sexual offence cases. So as you can probably imagine, it's pretty pressurised, long hours, a lot of responsibility and at times quite harrowing.

During the daytime, it's very intense when I'm at work, which of course presents a challenge to building a business. With such a busy life it's important to be selective and have good time-management.

Colin is the head of the CPS area. His role is mostly management on a strategic level as well as overseeing and advising on top end serious cases. Being in the same work has enabled us to understand each other's pressures as much as anything else.

There are an awful lot of opportunities out there promising that you'll make £1 million overnight. I was looking for something that was a "solid business".

I think I came across a leaflet or a flyer, advertising a wealth seminar that was being run locally. It was a taster seminar for a couple of hours. I went along after work one evening and liked what I heard. From that, I went onto a one-day and then a three-day event with that company which was excellent. It was an introduction to wealth-creation – how to create independent wealth and become financially free.

It was interesting that, although it wasn't described as being a Property seminar, the majority of the content was Property-related, and the majority of the people who were teaching or mentoring on that particular seminar were financially free, principally from Property.

I came away thinking Property investment is the way to go. I've rented out before in the past, so I wasn't new to being a landlord but I'd never really thought about it as a viable business.

Shortly after that, we went on holiday and I spent the whole time there thinking through how to develop ideas into reality. Although I had the ideas and basic concepts, what I didn't have from that seminar was what I call "specific strategies" and that's when I came across Progressive.

How did you meet Progressive?

I really can't remember how I first heard about them but somehow I became aware of an event they were running. I asked Colin if he would come with me to a "Progressive" one-day event at Heathrow. He was initially sceptical but was really taken by it. At the end of the day, we had quite a long chat with Mark Homer. We actually looked at and discussed a Property deal we were interested in. Having spoken to him we realised we could benefit from his expert guidance.

We went on their three-day Progressive Masterclass and it was on that course that we learnt the variety of strategies that we now use in our Property business.

We went on and did various other training days with Progressive – Lease Options, Advanced Estate Agents etc, before becoming VIP students. We were in their first VIP group that began in January 2010, along with Trevor, Gill, Francis and Jane. We graduated from that at the end of last year in December and I have since done some mentoring for the next VIP group.

We have now built up a solid and good cash-flowing portfolio. We know we will continue to grow and build on this. Recognising the 'flat to down' trend of the market we have bought Properties that were in previously good performing areas to increase the likelihood of future capital growth when conditions improve.

We've used a variety of strategies including BMV, sourcing from estate agents and direct to vendor leads. We also use lease and purchase options where appropriate. These have been very lucrative. I personally like the tenant buyer scheme because I'm keen to help young couples get on the Property ladder.

We have put a lovely young couple into one of our Properties. They would never otherwise have been able to have such a nice house. They've got a little girl and they didn't have a large pot of money, so they weren't able to go out and buy outright in the usual way. They had enough capital to pay an option fee so using the rent-to-own scheme, we've been able to help this young couple and obviously there's good profit in it for us as well.

They're going to buy it off you eventually then?

Yes, that's it exactly. They live there as tenants but pay an additional amount each month, which we put aside in an interest bearing account as proof of deposit when they come to buy it.

We're doing a lot more of that work at the moment. We've got quite a lot of people now registered as tenant buyers, so we've started doing matching with other Investors who need qualified tenant buyers. There are an awful lot of people out there who are struggling and they just can't get onto the Property ladder, especially the young couples. We're both very keen to help them.

How did you put that deal together then?

We bought a Property below market value and our initial intention was to sell it on. We refurbished it to a high standard because we were looking to sell it. We didn't achieve the price that we wanted for it in the period of time that we'd given to market it. So, we went to plan B.

We always have at least one exit strategy in mind when we buy and this was one we preferred to move on than keep and rent out. So our second plan had been to do a purchase option with a tenant buyer if we failed to sell it outright in the time period we allotted.

We advertised locally. This young couple came forward and said they were really interested. They fell in love with the house. It was exactly where she wanted to live, but she never thought she'd be able to afford to live there.

By having knowledge and skills for various strategies, we are able to adapt accordingly. By using the tenant buyer option we have managed to move the Property on at the right price, which will be in three years' time.

In the meantime, it cash flows extremely well for us because we've got no management costs or void periods. Our tenant buyers look after it well because it will be their own home. With numerous people now registering on our rent to own scheme, we will be able to buy Properties with good future value for ourselves and other Investors ensuring high yields without void periods and little or no maintenance costs.

Where did you find your properties?

We've always managed to get our below market value deals through estate agents and more recently from direct to vendor leads in answer to our weekly adverts. We've built really good relationships with the agents because we've always been straight with them and we've never messed them around. They can have confidence in us and we with them.

One of our deals was particularly difficult. It was a nightmare because the couple were splitting up and couldn't stand the sight of each other, so much so that their own solicitors had had enough of them and effectively 'sacked' them in the middle of the transaction. The agent actually thanked us when it finally completed for sticking in there because other people might have pulled out. It has been because we have always completed on the ones that we said we would buy that we have built credibility and so we do get offered the good deals.

Another deal came to us because the vendor had sold his house three times and had been messed about, each time the buyer pulling out.

We were on the airport tarmac in Spain waiting to board a plane when we received a phone call from the agents who had recommended us as dependable investors. We made our offer which was actually less than it had sold for previously. His response:

"You know what? Just buy it. Take it away." So we did and we completed quickly which was just what the vendor wanted – a quick exit from this house that had become a real headache for him.

We've just recently refinanced one which was probably one of our best below market value deals. It's a three-bed we bought at £52,500 and we had it re-valued at £88,000. After refinancing it with a fixed mortgage at 4.99% for 4 years it still gives good positive cash flow.

We've been really lucky with the tenants on that house as well. Colin went to the first inspection and he was astonished because they're adding value to the Property!

They're making it their own and looking after it as though it is their house. They asked to landscape the garden and more recently they have put a new laminate floor in the kitchen and dining room. They have done such a good job that we will go halves on their next project which is to revamp the bathroom. Where can we find more of these tenants? ☺

Motto:

To always act in an ethical, trustworthy, skilled and professional way

Do you use a letting agent or do you manage them yourself?

A mix. The ones which are close to home, we manage ourselves, and the ones over in Shropshire, we've got fully managed. Even the ones that we let LHA, we've still refurbished to a good standard.

We take the view – if you offer people a really nice home, then they're more likely to look after it. So far, that's proved true for us. We've got good tenants who look after our Properties and have respected them because we've given them nice, fully-refurbished Property to move into, even the ones that are paying via LHA.

With greater experience and sourcing a good team we now do the refurbishment work more efficiently without compromising on standards.

That's good. That's nice to hear. So many times you hear about the hassle that tenants cause.

So far, we've not been saddled with any cannabis factories! As a prosecutor I've seen quite a few unlucky people who have discovered their house is now a cannabis farm with resident gardeners! It certainly does happen but our tenants are vetted well.

What effect did it have going on the one-day course and the three-day masterclass?

It has given us the strategies and knowledge to build up different aspects to the business. The three-day Masterclass is absolutely packed with information. Some of it, you'll go off and use straight away, and some of it, you'll "park" on the basis that you can't do everything at once.

It's important to choose a strategy or combination of strategies that work for you based on the amount of time you have available and your financial position.

We chose to begin by building rapport with estate agents before going direct-to-vendor. That worked for us because we wanted to start building the portfolio, gaining credibility and experience as well as getting confident with a strategy.

It's only been from the latter part of last year that I'm doing a lot more direct-to-vendor advertising, which I'm combining with my relationships with agents. It's a two-fold strategy now to get leads.

It also allows us to develop potential lease option deals. I have an arrangement with an agent who passes me dead or old listings that I may be able to work as a lease option.

We recently completed on a lease option that was a perfect solution for the vendor's situation and good back end profit for us. Again, it's about building relationships and knowing your personality.

There's an investor local to us who has no time for any of that and now passes us his potential lease option leads to work. Vendors have always commented on how professional and respectful we are when we deal with them. They also seem to feel comforted when we tell them what our professions are.

It's not always a race to get so many Properties in a short period of time. It's about careful, methodical research and sometimes the best decision you make is the deal you walk away from. If we feel uneasy, we don't do it. There's always another day. We now have a proven strategy and know how to buy our Properties well for maximum cash flow.

The training we've done has taught us many different ways to monetise

Property. We don't always buy; we can do lease options where we're controlling the Property for cash flow.

All of that is taught on the Masterclass course and the specific one-day courses. It's enabled me to get to where I am today which is not just having a portfolio, but building different strands of my business. We now have people coming to us and asking us to teach them what we've learned.

What was your main objective for this year?

Our main objective was to start building our own portfolio for residual income to enable me to start moving towards reducing my hours in the day job to then free up more time to take the business to the next level.

We set out a stage-managed approach. Our strategy was to build our portfolio by sourcing Properties below market value in good solid rental areas, to lock in equity and enable us to refinance and move our deposits on where appropriate.

I also wanted to set up something so I could stay close to other Property investors locally to me for motivation and support, because one of the things I found most valuable in the VIP is staying close to other investors.

I think one of the most difficult personal challenges for me has been the contrast between my day job environment and the energy of entrepreneurial people. I sometimes feel like Gwyneth Paltrow in Sliding Doors with two lives!

When I'm in the Property world I'm my own boss and I'm with a lot of entrepreneurial, like-minded people but when I go into my day job, I work with people with a different mind-set and I'm line-managed.

I do like all my colleagues, they're lovely people, but they just don't think the same as the people I work with in Property. You can be dragged into the employee mentality if you're not careful when you're there everyday.

It was because of this that I set up two local networking events : The Midlands Property Meet and the Shropshire Property Meet.

I set up the Midlands Property Meet with Pete Iwaniszewski who I met at one of Progressive's one-day events. We run it together in Coventry. We started that one earlier in August and that's growing month on month. About eight new people came last month and the feedback was excellent.

The format is informal. Deals are passed within the group and we keep each other motivated and up to date. It's a bit like a Mastermind group.

Similarly with the Shropshire Property Meet, we just felt that there was nothing in that part of the country which is one of our main investment areas. There's a big gap because everything seems to happen in London, Berkshire or Birmingham City centre.

I contacted Kerry, a leading letting agent. We agreed to use our contacts to set up the Shropshire Property Meet. For me, it's perfect because twice a month, I go to my own events and I'm mixing with many different Property investors who all use lots of different strategies.

One of the guys has over 200 Properties and several HMOs so he's a source of information and experience. I can sit next to somebody at one of the events and in 10 minutes of chatting, learn a solution to a problem I've got. Likewise, I can offer advice. It's really nice – social as well as educational.

When you come away from an event like that you're energized, aren't you?

Definitely, without a doubt. It refocuses your momentum on your goals as well because when you're sitting in a day job, and you've got this constant pressure and all the bureaucracy that goes with it, you can get a little bit dragged down if you're not careful.

Getting home late from work when my mind has been on rape cases all day and having to switch over to Property is hard. It's really, really hard. That's why a lot of people won't do it. The VIP Programme really helped with that aspect of it – it kept my mind focused.

Any other partnerships you've formed in property?

Yes, I'm working with Trevor Cutmore, a fellow Progressive VIP member.

We're putting together a newsletter called "Success in Property" which is about giving back some of what we've learnt.

Trevor and I have come together to give back because we both feel our lives have massively changed through Property and we hope that other people's can as well. He and his wife, Marie, are close friends of ours now.

I have to say that Progressive has made a difference in all of our lives in that respect because from going to the VIP club every month we've formed really close friendships, which includes Francis and Jane Dolley.

The six of us spend a lot of time together. We are all going off to Spain to a villa in September, which we bid for at the Progressive charity auction ball. We're all really looking forward to it, although we'll have to make sure we don't talk Property the whole of the time!

You've got a new set of friends then through property?

Yes. It's opened up our world to people who think the same as us, who are involved in Property and are entrepreneurial.

Without a doubt, Property has opened up a world of opportunities so we're very grateful to Progressive for that.

Had you read any property books before you went on the wealth seminar?

I've always had a strong interest in psychology, life coaching and mind-set and began reading books by authors like Fiona Harrold some years back. Around 13 years ago, I went on a course with someone to learn how to trade the stock market. That opened my mind to books that related to NLP for traders because like many things, trading is 90% about psychology and 10% methodology in my opinion. I also bought books like, "How to Think Like a Millionaire". I've always been interested in there being a better way than just going to work and getting a salary with all the pressure and lack of time freedom.

It's interesting how far back your wealth creation mind-set goes.

Yes but I never really found anything solid enough to take forward. Trading is great and I did it for a while (and still do the odd trade), but I was looking for something more solid and Property felt right for me.

At some point in the future when I've bought back some time I can start looking at some of these other wealth creation vehicles, but I wanted to just be very focused on Property for the time being.

You risk being scattered all over the place, don't you?

Yes, it's hard enough with a demanding job and doing Property, so add another thing into the mix, you risk doing nothing particularly well and just dabbling.

Did the VIP club give you a helping hand?

Yes. Through the VIP, it's meant that I've been close to other people who are moving forward. There was a core group of us that were quite naturally competitive anyway; I think that was quite healthy, in a very friendly way.

It was no surprise that it was Trevor, myself, Colin, Francis and Jane, and Gill who were the ones in the running for the VIP prize at the end of the year. There was only one vote in it between all of us.

We stayed close to each other, we stayed close to Progressive, we all went to every single meeting, we didn't miss one and we were, at the end of the year, the ones who'd done the most.

I don't think there was any coincidence in that. I think that's why it's so important if you want to become successful to keep close to people, to surround yourself with people who are on the same journey, some ahead of you and even some behind you because mentoring people who are behind you is a great way to keep yourself motivated.

That's a great point to make. When you teach someone else you get a kick out of it and it's a lesson for you as well.

It is and selflessly, I think. There's got to be some purpose to what you're doing. If you've learnt something and you don't use that to help other people, then it's quite selfish, just to say I've built a better life for myself and I'm not going to help anyone else to do it.

There's nothing more frustrating than knowing what you can achieve, what your potential is, but not being able to get there, whether it's because we don't believe in ourselves enough or because our situations are difficult. I think all a lot of people need is someone to give them confidence and offer a helping hand, especially women because I think we can be very hard on ourselves and we tend to underestimate what we can achieve.

Successful people should show others how to do it.

They're happy to share, aren't they?

Do you know that's an amazing thing about Property because if you're in a salaried position, chances are there's only one position going for promotion and everybody wants it and it can be very cut-throat, whereas in Property even if you're in the same town or looking for Properties on the same patch, people are still willing to help each other.

Talking of purpose then, once you're financially free, what are you going to do with your time?

I want to write. That's my passion and when I've got the time, that's what I will do. My dad was a writer and published author for over 40 years. I've always helped him proof read his work and I've always been interested in writing. So one day, I will give back through books as well as coaching.

Can you reduce your workload if you have income from property to the point where you can choose your work?

Yes that is part of our plan. When I've bought back some time I'll do much more mentoring to walk people into their first few deals. Also, one of the projects that Colin and I have talked about is providing secure housing for victims of extreme domestic violence.

There is a need for private landlords to provide that kind of housing which requires special equipment in undisclosed locations. That's something we've discussed as a project with our local authority housing team. The rents would be guaranteed for a period of time. We can provide a valuable service to the community and make a profit as well. Why not?

Do you plan to use joint venture partners for cash to buy properties?

Yes, that is the other thing that we've been looking at. We've got an informal arrangement at the moment with a family member who is going to be providing funds for an agreed return but we want to take that out to other people.

We know a lot of busy professionals. We're currently putting a brochure together to demonstrate the kind of work we've been doing and a contract to protect cash investments.

In terms of the future and property strategies, is there anything that you're going to be focusing on this year?

We're looking to do a lot more lease option work this year and are actively involved in three more deals. We're also sourcing for other investors. This will enable us to monetise the deals that are less than the expected 25-30% discounts. We are also about to move into HMOs for increased cash flow.

It has been frustrating at times because some of the people in Property that don't have full-time jobs are able to progress at a slightly different pace.

But irrespective of that, given the limitations on our time, we're very pleased with what we've achieved since we met Progressive at the end of 2009.

What advice would you give to someone who was thinking about taking that next step?

Ask yourself if you really want it. If you don't, it can be hard to keep going through. And I would say find a strategy that suits your budget and time available.

Surround yourself as much as possible with the people moving in the same direction as you. I think it increases your prospects of success.

I also think working in partnership can work well provided you have complementary skills. I know Colin and I take massive benefit in that respect from working together in the business – we keep each other motivated although we each have our own separate departments.

Colin does most of the research, he loves it, spends hours on it. He's a lot like Mark! He loves the refurbishing side as well. I do the marketing, networking, building business contacts and mostly dealing direct with vendors.

Also, Colin is rarely fazed by anything and is a very calming influence. I'm definitely the one who pushes us on more but I can also be the one to get stressed. We're a good team.

People must also be prepared to make short-term sacrifices for long-term gain. We speak to so many people, colleagues or otherwise, who are unwilling to do that. They prefer to watch TV than build their future.

The key is you've got to really want it and enjoy it because that's what keeps you going. I want to be retiring early to a villa in the sunshine and I will certainly sacrifice a few holidays and nights in front of the TV now.

Key Learnings

- You need to have a strong motivation and reason to succeed.
- Help others and you will get what you want.
- Stay close to mentors and build your own mastermind alliance.
- You can be a very busy person in a full time job and still make time to make Property investing a huge success.
- Property is the vehicle that will create the time and lifestyle that you want – and you get to choose it.
- Successful people have energy, drive and commitment.
- Have goals and tirelessly pursue them.
- Be persistent.
- Be fair in your negotiations with vendors. Leave a bit on the table for them. You don't have to make all your money out of one deal.
- Make sacrifices now to have the life you want later.

Education

Progressive Property JV Buying Frenzy Networking Event [1-day]:

http://www.progressiveproperty.co.uk/jv-event

Progressive Property 3 Day Property Investing Masterclass

http://www.progressiveproperty.co.uk/masterclass

Progressive Property VIP JV Millionaires Club:

http://www.progressiveproperty.co.uk/vip-pmc

Progressive Property Lease Options Training:

http://www.progressive-property.co.uk/lease-options

Progressive Property Deal Packaging Cashflow Training

http://www.progressiveproperty.co.uk/deal-packaging-masterclass

Top Books

Rich Dad, Poor Dad - *Robert Kiyosaki*

Feel the Fear and do it Anyway - *Susan Jeffers*

The Slight Edge - *Jeff Olsen*

Favourite Quote

"It's never too late to be who you might have been." By George Eliot

Jackie and Colin's Contacts

www.blackcountryhomebuyers.co.uk

www.wigandpenproperties.com

www.shropshirepropertymeet.co.uk

www.successinproperty.co.uk

www.moremoneymorechoice.co.uk

www.midlandspropertymeet.co.uk

Jackie Goodman:

Tel No: 07971 223675

Email: jackiegoodman@blueyonder.co.uk

Colin Molloy:

Tel No: 07792 410519

Email: cvm4908@yahoo.co.uk

Jim And Simone Whitfield

From Old Relics To Property Investing

Story At A Glance

Age: **Jim:** 40 **Simone:** 37

J.O.B.: **Jim**: Antiques dealer

Simone: Commercial analyst

Investment Area: Stafford

Strategies: BMV

Vital Statistics

Properties: Two NZ (trying to sell this year) two off-plan, six BMV local (one new one to complete next week)

Cash flow: £2K net per month

Equity: £215K in the UK £90K in NZ

How did you get into property, Jim?

I suppose looking back now, the only way my folks have made money is through Property. They had good jobs, but at the end of the day coming up to retirement and they haven't really saved anything – their pension isn't worth anything – so, Property is there for them.

I was doing antiques in about 2000 and it started to go downhill quite rapidly. I was sitting at our antique store, saying, "What are we going to do? I can't make a living like this anymore." It was a case of what can we do so we invested with a Property investment company.

They were doing it all for us with new-builds but they made the figures up. They got their own surveyors in. We bought two flats with them and then we put money into Florida, which never went through in the end.

We lost quite a bit of money there, letting somebody else do it. As soon as we bought them, you start to realise that they can't value up to the price they quoted. So, it was not quite the way to do it. We left it then and I just went back to antiques.

Then we received e-mails from Progressive so we went for the one-day seminar that was in Manchester and from that, we went out and found a third house. If they can do it – we can too. They're not making up the figures because they teach you how to do it and not to sell you new build Property. They tell you the basics and the strategies of how to work it, which looking back is brilliant.

When was that one-day event?

It must have been April 2009. They weren't saying, "Buy this off us and we'll do it." They were saying, "This is how we've done it and it works." And you can too.

We tried to do it. We'd already found a house that was only £60,000, which we thought was cheap, but you're not going to make the jump. It's still a scary situation. Are we doing the right thing? Is this going to work after losing so much with the previous company?

We still didn't want to take the step. It was still scary, but we thought we'll go ahead and do it. We put in the offer when we went on the three-day Progressive Masterclass which just put it all into perspective.

From then, we just carried on quite easily buying Properties at that time.

We bought the first one; did it up; rented it out; after six months, remortgaged; got the money out; and then bought the next one; and so on. We've got six now this way, and in all, we've got 11 Properties.

But, the two we bought with the previous company do make money now because of the market crash and interest rates so low. That was lucky.

We've got two in New Zealand because my wife is from there and we were going to move there, but one was actually just a house and we'd bought it online. That doesn't make us money. If only we had listened to Rob and Mark before that.

But, the one she had already before we met makes good money and we remortgaged that one to buy the other one.

So, you've still kept hold of your two properties that you bought from the previous company, pre progressive?

Yes. We couldn't sell them. A good lesson though.

What happened after you went on the three-day masterclass?

We bought the next five Properties within eight months because we had removed the fear. We knew what to do. It was just the first step that's the hardest, just thinking "is this the right thing?".

Looking back, it was the right thing, but at the time, you're just scared, thinking we've lost money with Property before. I'd lost quite a bit in stocks and shares as well. At least with Property, I'd still have something. Even if it was in negative equity, there'd still be something there.

My Mum had some money to spare. She wasn't getting any interest in the bank, so we asked her if we could borrow it. She said yes and we're using that money now.

It takes me two to three months to do a house. I do it. I get people to help me to do certain things like the electrics and plumbing. I can do the electrics, but you've still got to get it approved and signed off. It isn't long before you can get the money out anyway to buy more and repeat the process.

So your strategy is to buy a distressed property and refurbish it?

I just keep them and rent them out. There's no point in me going through all that trouble of refurbishing them to sell them. With each house, the most we would make is £30,000 if we sold it and then where would we be?

We'll make more just keeping it. We see no reason why we have to sell them unless we really need money, but you can just keep remortgaging. Mark and Rob told us about the council where we're renting out, some of the other house rents are going £100 cheaper than what we are getting! Council rents are a good strategy. They pay more and are better, longer tenants

What area do you invest in?

Stafford. The Properties are all in a three-mile radius of our house, so there's not much travelling involved. I'm really glad Rob and Mark taught us this, as it has been so much better than the overseas and distant Properties.

If I needed to, I could buy cheaper houses in Stoke but when you put the travelling into it, it's not worth it. I have bought them all here and I chase people here. I could get them to the other places, but it's going to cost more. It's just easier. The agency is managing them, and I can easily manage the agents.

Have you done any joint ventures with anyone?

Apart from with my Mum we haven't needed to at the moment. We're just doing it the easiest way without needing to get anyone else involved.

What are your plans for this year then?

I'm taking it easy now doing my garage conversion to turn it into an office, and then it will be back to getting more houses, because I won't have anything else to do!

I always look at Rightmove everyday just to see what's come up or check my e-mails because they send any new ones through from there. We looked over the Christmas period because that's when we bought them last year. We bought them all through that time.

They have gone up quite a bit, about £7,000 since last year.

Do you have a target of how many houses you want to buy this year?

No, I don't think it's worth getting worried about. When one comes along at the right price, I will buy it. If I'm going to say, "Yes, I'm going to do ten," and then I only do five. That'll annoy me.

So, it's just when they come up. Now, I know where we buy, how much we buy for, what I can get things done for, so I wouldn't go, "Yes, I've got to get this many." It's just whatever comes up because I feel satisfied with those six. They're all making money.

Have you given up the antiques business?

I still dabble. My dad still owns a shop, and I still go out and buy things. But, that's just a hobby now. It's just something I like to do whereas before it was something I had to do, but it was never going to make me the sort of money Property has.

Do you do the management of the lets or do you get a letting agent?

Like Mark and Rob said, it's not worth the hassle for the sort of percentage. We've been doing our tax return. Looking how much we pay them, we might start taking it on. On the next ones, we'll just pay them to find a tenant because they have to phone me if there are any problems.

Any new strategies you plan to use this year or are you just sticking with the tried-and-tested formula for the future?

We were thinking of putting flyers out, trying to find houses quicker. We are going to take it up a step and employ somebody to help me get the houses done quicker.

Property has enabled you to have a better lifestyle so you pick up the kids?

My dad had an antiques shop. He used to be in the shop seven days a week. I didn't see him, so I wanted a lifestyle where I could see my kids. It took the worry off.

Looking further into the future, the houses are going to pay for whatever we want to do. The security is the main thing for me that I've got with my kids, so I don't have to work like my dad. He's 75 and he's still got the antiques shop. The only way he's going to make any money is when he sells it.

Have you got any advice for someone who wanted to invest in property?

I'd tell that them what I've done and say, "Definitely go to Mark and Rob," because we've tried other ways. Progressive worked for us. The regret is we didn't do it sooner because we could've bought more, done more sooner and set ourselves up better than we are. But, that's probably it. Without them, we wouldn't be where we are now.

Any tips you'd like to share?

Go out and do it. Go out and learn. Find a house, make an offer; refurbish it. Just do it!

Have you read any property books?

Only Rich Dad, Poor Dad. Yes, it did change me. The other thing that has changed me is Christopher Howard. His course is really good and gives you a positive outlook on life. We still listen to that. After a while, you do go back into your old rut unless you have something to pick you up and go, "Hold on a minute." That's where I suppose Mark and Rob came in as well because you have a year with them. We can still talk to Mark if we want to.

So, it was a comfort to know that they were there for you to call them?

Yes, definitely. The biggest fear: is what you're doing the right thing? But if you've got somebody there who knows it inside out telling you that you can and have done it right it's reassuring.

My family, were dubious about it. They didn't think it was going to be the right thing to do even though Dad made money in it. They're worried. Are we going to lose our money? But, they've come around and now they're really happy with it. That's why my mum has lent me the money. She's done the figures of the other house and she was quite happy to do that.

Do you package deals for other people or lease options?

No. They're interesting but I haven't really got time to do it whilst I'm refurbishing the Properties. It's not something I like to do. I don't particularly like talking to people. I'm not that sort of person. That's why I like antiques and this. I'm my own boss who goes around and does what I want to do when I want to do it. I just like making money on my own the easy way buying Property for myself.

Yes, that's interesting because a lot of people don't like the negotiation and dealing with people, but it's good to see you can still make money out of it.

Yes, with the least amount of talking to people. ☺

Did you deal with the estate agents with all your properties then?

Yes. We bought the six Properties at five different agents. It's just whatever was cheapest on the market. There's one who keeps in touch, and tells us if there is anything cheap coming up and would we be interested. They're happy to phone us up, tell us this is coming up and share with us.

You make it sound so easy. What challenges did you have?

The only challenge was to do the first one. Once you've done that, you see that it will work.

Have you read any property books?

Only the Progressive books. I'm not a reader. I'm just lazy.

Key Learnings

- Like anything new, Property can be scary, but you've just got to dive in and do it **now**.
- Most people are getting no interest in the bank, you can help them earn, invest or be a JV partner and buy more deals yourself.
- Focus on the right area and the right Property type otherwise it can cost you big in mistakes.
- Build relationships with agents and surveyors, and it will help you invest without leaving any money in the deal.
- Leverage up and pay people to help you build your Property business.
- Property creates time that you can spend with your family.
- Go out and learn and then just DO IT.

Education

Progressive Property JV Buying Frenzy Networking Event [1-day]:

http://www.progressiveproperty.co.uk/jv-event

Progressive Property 3 Day Property Investing Masterclass

http://www.progressiveproperty.co.uk/masterclass

'Make Cash in a Property Market Crash"
http://www.progressiveproperty.co.uk/book-2-buy-now

"The 44 Most Closely Guarded Property Secrets"

http://www.progressiveproperty.co.uk/book-buy-now

Jim and Simone Contact Details

Email: staffordpropertybuyers@gmail.com

Andy Gelder
From Radio DJ To Managing 300 Properties

Story At A Glance

Age: 45

J.O.B.: Radio

Investment Area: Corby

Strategies: BMV, deal packaging

Vital Statistics

created a lettings agency with 390 units

How did you get into property Andy?

I have worked in radio for 20 years. I got into Property accidentally because I was living in Reading and had a job in Dunstable. I decided enough was enough after a two-hour journey home one Friday afternoon. I was about 25 so I said to my girlfriend at the time, who is now my wife, "I need a house in Bedfordshire!"

A wise old friend of mine said, "Whatever you do, don't sell your house. Rent it out." So, we did. We took out a let-to-buy mortgage on it, bought another place and four years later, it'd gone up fantastically in value. So, I sold it and used the money to buy a couple of flats and off we went.

I bought out the girlfriend that I bought the house with and as this friend said, "Whatever you do, don't sell it." The market was growing. It was a positive market and I rented it out. I pulled some money out to put a deposit down for the new house and sat on it for three years. It grew nicely. I sold it and then bought a couple of flats with the proceeds from that.

You make it sound easy. Was it?

Oh, it was then, yes. It was incredibly easy and for me, the odd thing that I just couldn't get my head around was I bought a flat in Luton which is near where I was working, because I met an estate agent who was an independent and I was looking for an investment. I don't know why, but I just knew I was.

Then, I sold that again, paid off the mortgage and I couldn't believe that I kept the profit. It was one of those real eye-opening moments.

For example, say I paid the mortgage back at £50,000, the Property had gone up to £100,000 and I kept the £50,000. I thought they want a share of that and I just couldn't believe it. Then thinking back three or four years down the line, I'm thinking why hadn't I done 5, 10, 15, 20 of those kinds of things, and realised that and spotted that little opportunity!

So how did you meet Progressive?

I was always freelancing on radio. I was always self-employed, so I'd always do a drive-time show or I was always doing a breakfast show. Basically like a breakfast show, I'd get in to work for 5:30, then by 10:00 or 11:00 in the morning, I'd be done for the day – tired, but done for the day and looking for other opportunities.

And I always loved cars, so I started renovating old MGs and selling them – buying them and selling them, doing that sort of thing. Then, we started doing it with Property. My now wife and I, we started in Property doing what my bank manager calls tarting-and-turning. We'd find a bit of a wreck. We'd do it up, flog it and make some money.

We were buying wrecks. I don't mean all real massive wrecks, but a full place where we'd go in and strip it back, tart it up, marry a new kitchen or bathroom in, make it pretty – nothing too structural – and sell it.

Our rule was very simple. If we thought we could make £5,000 out of it, we would do it and that was it. That was our parameters, so we'd go in and do it. The bank at the time would lend us the purchase price, so we're buying anywhere from £70,000 to £90,000 and they would also give us the refurbishment costs.

Yes, happy days. We'd sell it three or four months later, and because that was the stuff of the business, we weren't getting capital gains and we were just making a nice turn on it. That's what we did until the market turned and also what happened was my wife was looking around for other ideas in Property.

We'd been selling all these Properties and what we should've been doing is remortgaging them and keeping them because we'd moved through about 20 Properties over the years.

Later, I sat there at the desk in the hotel and I wrote on a piece of paper next to Kate. I said, "I feel sick. I wish we'd known this earlier." Honestly, it was just bonkers.

I went on a bit of a buying spree. I borrowed some money against the house that we live in now and started to build a portfolio, then using the strategies that we learned from making mistakes selling – remortgaged, pulled some money out from the existing Properties, started to move it forward.

I was talking to a really good friend of mine called Juswant Rai who runs the Berkshire Property Meet, turned to him and said, "I'm stuck! We can't move forward." He said, "Go and talk to Rob,"

I went up to meet him and said, "Look. I'm a friend who just wants to pick your brain kind of thing and I thought we'd have a cup of tea." So, I did that and I thought I better buy a couple of his books and loved them. I remember buying the books and putting them in the bag. I read one from cover-to-cover. I was flying out to France to go skiing and I read it cover-to-cover on the airplane. I was like "Wow! This is great."

Have you had any education with Progressive?

Yes, I did the estate agent course and we did a Masterclass course with them after that.

What impact did the courses have on you?

They were really good – very positive. I liked the style. Lots and lots of ideas, and that kind of then got me going into rethinking and rebuilding my portfolio. They came up with new strategies for the new economic climate.

We learned about packaging deals up, selling deals on – don't keep it to yourself, make money from the deals you don't keep for yourself – all of those kinds of strategies which were successful for us at the time.

Any mistakes you'd like to share?

1. Not starting sooner.
2. Being too gung-ho and having offers accepted but no finance to buy them.
3. Not having the education. I missed some big opportunities!

So what have you done since the education?

Sourced four Properties, did two lease options, and I set up a letting agency in Corby with a business partner I met and he's now a joint venture partner and has become a very good friend. I've got a joint venture Property deal going as well. We got it with a friend. I'm not mortgage-able at the moment. I'm up to the limit. I'm now struggling to get any finance.

So he's hosting the mortgage for you?

Yes and we go 50-50 on the cash flow.

What yields are you getting on your properties?

We look for anything over 10%.

Any advice for anyone coming behind you?

Think carefully, but take action. A lot of the professionals in the industry make it look easy and it isn't always. Stay focused on your goals and you will be in a better position than you were. Expect that you're going to have to lose some money. You've got to put some money into deals and you may not necessarily get it back.

Paying your entrance ticket whether that's in grafting or money!

I looked at my accounts recently and the amount of aborted survey fees where for example, the lender had pulled the plug or whatever. Make sure you factor this in.

Have you had any coaching?

Well, I have mentors from people who don't know that they're my mentors. Jim Rohn is my mentor. I've bought his books. Alan Sugar is a mentor. I don't have any regular coaching as such. But, I think it is important and it's something that we're going to look at this year. We were regrouping last year and paying a mortgage rather than paying a coach.

What are your plans for the future?

Make more money, grow our portfolio by six and grow the letting agency to be the number two in Corby. We would like it to be number one, but the number one guy has got a lot of units and just looking at what we have to achieve this year, we're not sure that'll be achievable. But, it'll be good to do it. It's a bit arrogant, but we think we'll be happy with number two.

Okay, which of you had the lettings agent experience before?

None of us! We made it up as we went along. What do they say? Get perfect later. We had no idea what we were doing, but we realised that we had a number of Properties between us. We were desperate. We knew we had to do something. The money wasn't coming in that we thought. So, let's do it. Let's set up a virtual letting agency.

We came up with a brand. We bought some software, set it up, put our Properties into it. It got us about another five or six, so we thought this isn't going to make us rich, but it's a start. Then, we saw a board on a Property in Corby. Nathan said, "Oh, they've got a few Properties. Let's go and give them a ring." We rang them up and said that we're a new agency – can we look after any of your Properties? The girl said, "Send us some information." We said, "Okay, we'll pop some in your post," put the phone down and went, "We haven't got any information. What do we do?!"

So, we made something up, went into Staples, bound it up on the ring binder, dropped it in the next day, got a phone call from the managing director who said, "Come in for a meeting." Then, we met the managing director and the owner of a portfolio. Three weeks later, he gave us the entire portfolio of 270 units and some commercial stuff to look after.

Get perfect later

What! You are joking?

No, I'm not joking. We do a fixed fee for him. Every month, we get a fixed fee. We work from his offices. He's given us his offices for free and his software. We look after his units and we've now grown it to a turnover of about £100,000 a year.

We just can't believe it and the opportunities it has created are phenomenal. The landlord owns a Property in Stoke that he wants to sell, so we've had it refurbished, and now, we're just contacting Investors to tell them about it.

It's incredible because we charge the tenants a setup fee. We've get room rentals and HMOs. We're taking up a few Properties here and there. We're just going through a rebranding process at the moment and getting a website.

But, it's phenomenal really and we're just looking at other opportunities within it.

Top Books

- Rob & Mark's Books
- Rich Dad, Poor Dad, *Robert Kiyosaki*
- Slight Edge, Jeff Olson
- 4 hour work week, *Tim Ferris*

Top tips

- Get as much education and networking as you can.
- Always look for yield.
- Put money aside for repairs.

Key Learnings

- Buy Properties and keep them: forever.
- Think carefully but take action.
- Get perfect later.
- Keep your investing strategies up to date.
- Create multiple streams of Property income to support your cash flow.
- Set goals and stick to them.
- Get educated and get a mentor.
- Don't be restricted by your own beliefs, you can do whatever you want to do, no matter how big.

Education

Progressive Property JV Buying Frenzy Networking Event [1-day]:

http://www.progressiveproperty.co.uk/jv-event

Progressive Property 3 Day Property investing Masterclass

http://www.progressiveproperty.co.uk/masterclass

"Make Cash in a Property Market Crash"
http://www.progressiveproperty.co.uk/book-2-buy-now

"The 44 Most Closely Guarded Property Secrets"

http://www.progressiveproperty.co.uk/book-buy-now

Progressive Property Deal Packaging Cash flow Training

http://www.progressiveproperty.co.uk/deal-packaging-masterclass

Andy Gelder's Contact Details

Web Site: www.lovelettings.co.uk

Tel No: 01536 540053

Paul Smith And Raj Limbachia

A Partnership On Fire

Story At A Glance

Age: **Paul**: 45

Raj: 19

J.O.B. Firefighter
Investment Area: Leeds and Bradford
Strategies: JVs, mortgage hosting, buy and hold

Vital Statistics

Cash flow: £2,500pm after all expenses.
Equity: £150,000
Portfolio Value: £450,000

How did you get into property, Paul?

It was the early 1990s. The first house I bought was just before the market started dropping; so very quickly, I found myself in negative equity. I had to ride it out. I bought a house with a friend and we rented the top part of it off as a flat. I had one floor and he had another floor as individual flats.

We had to ride that out because we quickly went into negative equity and I very quickly tired of living in a shared house environment, so I wanted out. I managed this through mortgage-hosting with my brother to get another flat which I moved into and then I rented my portion of that house out.

Eventually, the whole house got rented out. That's probably the very first step I took. I identified early on then that I could actually make a bit of money on this from cash flow on the rent. Also, I couldn't have sold the house at that time anyway because of the negative equity situation.

That was a time where I remember ringing every single bank in the Yellow Pages and asking them about getting a loan or mortgage to go buy a house to rent out. They all scoffed at me because at that time, there wasn't such a thing. They just said, "No, we don't do anything like that. You have to get a business loan."

So, it wasn't the easiest time to do things like that, but I did a bit of mortgage-hosting with other people, and also I bought a couple more in my own name with normal residential mortgages and built it like that originally.

It was a lot easier to do back then. Relatively quickly I built up a reasonably-sized portfolio which probably, as units renting, was about 13 houses and flats within it, all cash-flowing very well and also went up in value very fast once things started picking up again back then. That's over a period of 10 years.

Also at that time, I'd rented my own flat out and moved in with my then girlfriend. We moved out of her flat, and then got out and bought our house, which we're in now. So, it built on its own without aggressively buying Property to rent out.

We never sold anything. We just kept moving out, moving on and then renting them. As you can remember, the values just started going through the roof then.

I had a plan that was as long as I could make a couple of hundred quid a month on the rent after mortgage payments; I'll just keep buying. That worked for quite a while and obviously, I made quite a bit more than that as well.

Then what happened with the values going up – so far I was buying for like £25,000, £30,000 and getting £400 a month rent – the mortgage was £200, rent was £400. It was easy. But when the Property started going to £40,000, £50,000 to buy, suddenly the mortgage payment had gone up nearly towards what the rent was going to be.

So, that was the sort of time I was thinking it's not really worth it just because of the hassle that you got with the rent and everything else. It slowed off for me a bit then and that's why I stopped buying at that point.

So what happened to this portfolio?

I ended up, probably more by bad judgment, deciding to sell. I considered myself an amateur landlord back then. I didn't really know what I was doing. I didn't fully have a grip on it and it was quite time-consuming. I didn't have anything systemised. I didn't have any help.

I decided to sell, and also take the money, pay my own mortgage off which was really a nice position to be in and have some funds left to which I was going to invest in various things. That's basically what I did.

I sold everything I had. Everything that I basically sold, I did all right out of it. I paid a lot of tax, but then I was in a position where I had a nice house with no mortgage on it and quite a bit of money in the bank to do whatever I want to with going forward.

So, any mistakes you'd like others to learn from?

I foolishly invested quite a bit of that in stuff off plans abroad. If with hindsight you could have thought it through a bit more and maybe I'd had some help, or if I knew more then about Rob, Mark, Progressive and the networking opportunities that there are, if I'd have known a bit more and become more educated to how to run it better, then I wouldn't have sold.

Surely, I would've been advised against it and that would've been the right decision. But, that is the major thing. You basically sold it, paid a lot of the tax, got your money. At the time, people were making quite a bit of money off plans abroad. I did all right with the first one, which was an apartment in Spain. I didn't do badly at all with that, but I bought quite a few others that nothing ever came of, and one or two actually went into liquidation.

All sorts of things went wrong. Basically if I'd have kept the Property that I had, it probably would have gone up three or four times more again compared to what you were trying to achieve abroad, which just hasn't been anything like that.

My view was that I knew how to do it, but I really needed to be a lot more professional about it which sort of brought me around to looking into getting a bit more educated the second time around and trying to be more professional.

I went to a landlord networking event in Leeds and obviously spoke to a few people there before I bought any houses. I took a bit of advice off them, just listened to what different people were saying and the different speakers that were coming in, and obviously going on the Internet and doing research on that. I found quite a number of companies that were offering all sorts of different types of training to do with this and the other.

How did you meet Progressive?

I did a one-day Buying Frenzy training with Progressive. It was just two to three years ago thinking I'm going to do something like this and the actual taking-action part started probably about 18 months ago. I then decided to sign up for their three-day Property Masterclass course in September 2009.

What did you get out of the masterclass?

Quite a bit really. Obviously, you get an awful lot of motivation out of it. That's the big thing. You're inspired and you're motivated to go away and actually start making things happen. There were a lot of networking opportunities in it. I met the guy who I then decided to joint venture with and formed a partnership with. I met him there.

They taught me how to approach estate agents, how to speak to them, how to put a price in. Just a simple thing like making offers on a Property – you think you just go off and do what you want. They actually said, "There's actually a technique you can use which gets you to the figure where you're still getting a good discount, but it sounds like that's it, that's all you've got, there's nothing left, so there's more likelihood that they'll accept it." (Round no, Round no, Random no - strategy I learned at the Masterclass.)

Daft as it sounds, I didn't know how to use things like Rightmove very well, so they did a sit-down one-to-one with that, showing how to use Rightmove properly, effectively and also use it to find what they would call a gold-mine area, so you could establish what your best area is to buy in, and also compare other deals in and around that area.

You get shown what your average price is in that area and then shown how to find something that's considerably cheaper. There's a good chance that you're already buying it discount before you've even put a low offer in, just by knowing how to find it!

So you took all that information and put it into action?

Rob interviewed us for Progressive's YouTube channel because we had been one of the success stories from the Masterclass, and it is nice to have that follow up and also be able to look back on a good year or two.

What areas do you invest in?

I live in Leeds and my partner Raj, who I met at the Progressive Masterclass, lives in Leeds as well, in Pudsey.

One of the great things about the Progressive training is they get like minded people together, create the community for it, and teach you how to joint venture properly too.

Through meeting him, speaking to him, and looking at the Properties or deals that he'd already put together, we decided to buy in certain, select areas of Bradford initially.

We're not moving out anywhere else, so we're probably moving to Leeds as well. But, we're both close to Bradford and the Property prices over there were particularly cheap, the rent was quite high for what you're paying and it seemed to sort of add up.

How is it going?

It's going very well. Obviously, you're faced with the challenges, same as everyone else is, with the getting financing, mortgaging and things like that. That's the difficult part, but that aside, it's going very well. We've bought some really cheap houses, decent discounts and got some good tenants in. The yields are high. Purchase prices are low.

What are your yields?

In a perfect world where the tenant never missed a payment, it would probably be 12%. We've got one HMO and it wasn't an HMO when we bought it but we converted it. That would probably go nearer of 18 or 19%.

Any deals you'd like to share?

An example is one house went to auction and didn't sell, and we bought it for £38,500. We spent a small amount on it doing some improvements, not very much. When I say "small", I mean £2,000 or £3,000 – that was all.

We have a tenant in there that pays just under £500 a month. You work on a yield like that with that kind of outlay, it's fantastic.

We're now looking at remortgaging it because the value is £60,000. We should be pulling about £39,000 out of that when it completes. We know we can buy another one for a similar amount of money, so hopefully we'll have a path to move forward fairly briskly.

So how are you getting the finance?

Initially, we used Birmingham Midshires. I have four mortgages with them. Then unfortunately, they pulled the pin and it went down to three. That's three from nine. So, we went onto The Mortgage Works and a couple of others.

The only thing holding us back is the remortgage-within-six-months rule, so to get around that side of things, we approached commercial lenders for commercial mortgages and we found one that would do a remortgage on the value.

Assuming you paid £40,000 – the house increased its value by doing some refurbishments – and put a tenant in it that was paying a good market rent – I think they stress test it at 8.5% for the rent – if you can do that, they will then allow a mortgage against the new value.

Some months later, we go and say, "We think it's worth £60,000, £65,000." If they agree, see the tenancy agreement and see the improvements, they will lend 65% of that, so you can nearly get your money back, not quite get all your money back, but virtually get all your money back.

Wash, rinse, repeat. ☺

Great. Where are you sourcing your deals from?

Estate agents. We've had some good deals. Whether they're fully bottom drawer (as Rob & Mark would say) yet, I'm not sure.

But the deals that are out there regardless of whether you're in that scenario or not, there doesn't seem to be that many buyers for the sort that we're buying. I don't want to think we have to worry too much about what are the best bottom drawer deals, because we're doing okay just by seeing what's online.

We have got probably three estate agents who do selectively ring us up, say, "We've got this coming on. Do you want to have a look at it before it comes on?" and that's pretty good. My partner has got a good relationship with a letting agent in Bradford - he's actually working in his office a couple of days a week, helping him out. So anything at all that comes in, we've got first dibs at!

Yes, I think the estate agents at this present time haven't gotten an abundance of people knocking on their door, saying they want to buy houses. So, I think it's a little bit easier to get into a good position with them.

Probably the last six months, we've found that the deals are there and nobody is buying them anyway, so we don't have to worry too much. We do our very best to look after the estate agents. We don't mess them about. We do what we say we're going to do and we keep them informed. Once they've seen you do one quick, efficient deal, I think that's you onside with them.

Whether you get the absolute best deal that comes through, I'm not sure. But, we certainly get a good pick of the mix that comes through.

So you met your joint venture partner at the masterclass.

Yes. When I met Raj he was 18. He was on a different table from me, so somebody introduced us, we got talking and a few things impressed me about him. One was that he was 18. He was doing Property full-time already. He'd built up a portfolio of, I think, five or six houses already. He was doing it full-time, so he wasn't employed.

Also, he seemed pretty switched-on, quite eloquent, knew what he was talking about, and also very keen and motivated. I thought he's one to watch for the future. He'd achieved that already. When he doesn't work, he can't get a mortgage yet because of his lack of credit history.

He's only so young. But, he is mature. He's now 19, so he's a lot more mature than most people are at that age. Obviously if he carries on going like he is, I think he'll do very nicely out of it. When he's 25, 30, I think a lot of people will know his name because I think he'll make a good name for himself in Property and do very well out of it.

The best thing is he can do it full time. He has the time to deal with the day-to-day; little bits and pieces that crop up. I have quite a lot of time, but I cannot commit full time like he does at this time. So, it works very well because obviously I can get the mortgages, we can structure things how we think is fair and he has got full time availability.

How many properties have you bought together?

We started in December 2009. We got two in December, right off the back of the Masterclass (in fact I think we found them on the one-to-one day three Rightmove training, a great return on investment) and we got four last year, so that brings us up to six, one of which was an HMO. It wasn't licensed when we got it, but it is now. We can have six tenants in there. We have currently an offer on a seventh one which should go through pretty quickly. We also sorted out the finance with our new arrangement.

And what plans for the future?

Going forward if it works as it's supposed to work, we anticipate being able to buy one every two months. So, we're hoping that we can get maybe five or six this year as far as purchasing house s goes to rent out. Potentially, we may look at buying one or two to refurbish and sell as well.

We have a couple of other things that we'd like to do. We're thinking of doing the CeMAP training to become mortgage brokers.

Both of us are going to look at that because we're seeing the fees that we're paying out ourselves, and think we're involved and immersed in Property, and anyone in Property needs mortgages; so we can not only maybe help ourselves, but maybe help other people. So, there's a potential stream of income there.

We did look at a Property that was suitable to convert into a downstairs office/shop and a flat upstairs.

If we can find a deal like that, that stacks up before we do something like that and open the downstairs ourselves as a possible letting or estate agent that does mortgages as well, then the rent from the flat upstairs would cover the payment for the whole building. So, we virtually have an office and shop, rent-free.

So, the other thing above that is Raj currently working in his letting and estate agent's office. He's just secured a deal where he's getting an awful lot of repossessions coming through these books starting last month and into this month, and that the volume is increasing each month.

So, we're possibly looking at maybe packaging some of those deals up, cherry picking the best deals and then maybe through a network of people, try to pass them onto other Investors.

In return for Raj working for the agent, we can advertise our Properties on Rightmove for free and we're getting the first bite of the cherry of any deals that come in which will include the repossessions if we see them.

The other thing we're obviously aiming to do is get a web presence to generate some leads for Properties possibly. We were thinking we might organise our own Property network too.

Any tips you'd like to share?

Yes. Go to these events because they only cost a few quid but I always come away feeling quite motivated, thinking great ideas. You want to get started and it pushes you along again. It keeps you focused. It's a great thing and it's cheap. You meet loads of people all doing the same thing.

There are so many books out there. Read as many books as you can. Attend as many networking events as you can. Speak to those types of people as much as you can. Speak to them without selling anything and get as much as you can from them. They might then point you in the direction of who they consider to be good.

I wouldn't have any hesitation recommending the ones that I went on with Progressive Property. I think they were well worth the money. I would go on them again. They did exactly what they said they were going to do. They follow up with e-mails and phone calls. If you have any issues, you can ring up and speak to them.

Sometimes it can be quite comforting to have someone that had done it before Properly and say, "Look. I'm looking at this. What do you think?" and they say, "Well yes, it looks alright to me. We'd probably do it." So, it can just give you a bit of reassurance.

Last time I bought Property, I did it on my own. I think I'd much prefer working with somebody else because when there are things going wrong and you're on your own, it's quite a lonely place.

Education

Progressive Property JV Buying Frenzy Networking Event [1-day]:

http://www.progressiveproperty.co.uk/jv-event

Progressive Property 3 Day Property Investing Masterclass

http://www.progressiveproperty.co.uk/masterclass

Key Learnings:

- Buy Properties and keep them: forever.
- Turn residential Properties into buy-to -let.
- Don't buy new build or off plan Property.
- Invest like a professional, even if you are part time.
- Get motivated and get out there and do it now.
- You'll have challenges like everyone else; it's how you deal with them that counts.
- Don't let funds or a lack of finance be a barrier to your success.
- You don't have to get the absolute best deals to still make significant profit from Property.
- Do what you say you are going to do: be quick and efficient.
- Agents needs you at the moment get buying NOW!
- Work for an agent or Property company – you'll learn the insider secrets.
- Go the events and read lots.

Paul and Raj Contact details

Email: creativepropertyuk@googlemail.com

Geoff Whittaker

The Part Time, No BS Property Flipper

Story At A Glance

Age: 62

Investment Area: North Manchester

Strategies: Flip [buy and sell-on for profit]

Vital Statistics

Three Property flips generated £58.5K cash

How did you get into property, Geoff?

After leaving school, I went to Radio College and became a radio officer in the Merchant Navy. I sailed around the world for five years. Then, I got married, so that was the end of my seagoing career!

Because of my technical background, I got into corporate life working initially in the IT Industry for the next 25 years. Then as I'd been head-hunted several times before during the previous 25 years, I set up my own recruitment consultancy as a head hunter in the IT industry. I did this for about another 11 years.

Then approximately 18 months ago, I set up G and C Properties to work in the Property industry.

How did you meet Progressive?

I met Rob and Mark at one of their one-day seminars in London.

I had previously attended several Property seminars and I wasn't particularly enamoured by any of them. They were mainly American or Australian ones. My thoughts were that if it works in America and Australia and if their strategy is that clever, why aren't they still over there in their own countries making things happen as against them trying to sell their concepts over here?

The bottom line is that pension arrangements are not going to have enough money in the kitty to provide you, me and everybody else in the UK with a living standard anywhere near the one that you have been used to when you were working.

An e-mail came in from Progressive Property. I had a look on their website. It seemed interesting. I think the thing that really attracted me to Rob and Mark was that they were best-selling authors.

So at that first one-day Progressive Seminar that I attended, I purchased their two books. I read them and was very, very impressed with their very common sense, no-BS approach to making Property work for you. That's really what got me hooked on Progressive.

When was that?

That was about June 2009 when I did the one-day seminar in London. At that seminar I signed up for their three-day Master Class Course, which was around about October of the same year.

That's when I realised again that these guys were talking an awful lot of sense and based upon the fact that there were a lot of very experienced people at that seminar, it made me realise that a lot of the attendees already owned quite large portfolios of buy-to-let Properties but were still attending seminars to gain more knowledge.

This I found intriguing.

I could not understand what they hoped to learn when they appeared to me to be very experienced Property people. But of course when you're talking to these people, they just want one good idea that they can adopt which will more than pay for the seminar and get them ahead of the crowd.

After the Master Class Course, I did several other separate one day courses with Progressive such as the Estate Agents course and the Lease Options course. To date I have now done every course that Progressive offer and I 'crew' regularly at their seminars. Networking is what being successful in Property is all about as far as I am concerned.

Had you bought any property up until that point?

No, not investment Properties, but after March 2009 I set up a Property company, G and C Properties to buy, renovate and sell Property.

So what's your strategy?

What I do is I buy two-bedroom terraced houses in North Manchester. I renovate them and sell them on to first time buyers. I'm buying houses at less than £70,000 and I rely on the 'Bank of Mum and Dad' to fund the deposit for their son or daughter so that they can get on the Property ladder. This is generally the only way most young people can get on the housing ladder because they haven't got £15,000 to £20,000 deposits required.

So you're flipping on to first time buyers. Are mortgages a little easier to get than for investors?

Yes indeed, especially when Mum and Dad are the guarantors as well. Mum and Dad will either remortgage or use their own savings to give the kids a substantial deposit which also helps to keep the mortgage loan down for the kids and consequently they have lower monthly payments.

After completing the Master Class with Progressive, I started looking around at Properties, but as prices kept dropping it put me off buying. This was because if you buy something and you suddenly find out a month later you could have got it for £5,000 or £10,000 lower, it hits you hard in your pocket!

If you're thinking of renting out Properties, falling prices don't matter because the rents don't go down! Rents are in fact going up, so your yield will go up. But when you're buying to sell on, you don't want the prices to keep going down or you're going to end up with no profit.

> You make your profit when you buy, providing you buy way below market value (BMV)

You must be buying at prices that are as low as possible. I believe the only way you can do this is to buy Properties that are at the bottom end of the Property market: houses that people don't want to live in, particularly repossessions that have been smashed to pieces! When they come up for sale, there are very few viewers because of the condition of the Property.

Even if they are viewed, the condition of the Property knocks the youngsters for six because they just see a wreck. They walk through the front door. It smells! It's dreadful! It's awful! They won't even look at it, so in consequence it's difficult for the vendor to sell. This is where I come in.

The bottom line is that Rob and Mark constantly hammer into you the fact that you only buy properties BMV!

Their Estate Agents course was a real eye opener for me because I source my Properties through estate agents. That's my source of supply. I like estate agents simply because they're on every high street. You can visit five or even ten in a day at no cost. Their services are completely free!

It is essential to build up a 'rapport' with the employees in each of the estate agencies that you visit. You must be able to identify who are the 'wheeler dealers' in the agency and also who are the 'godfathers' or owners.You goal is to be offered the 'bottom drawer deals' that the estate agents only give to their pet investors and developers. You must become a 'banker' in the eyes of the agency.

How long did that take you to achieve?

It probably took me about eight weeks, but only after I'd done the Estate Agents course. Prior to doing anything with Progressive, I had trawled estate agents on many occasions and got absolutely nothing! It was at the original Master Class course that I attended, that I heard about the Estate Agents course. Mark and Rob employ several ex- estate agents and one of them spoke for an hour or so on the way they used to work within their estate agents office. The way they look after their pet Investors and developers, and especially the way they initially react to people walking into their offices for the first time.

I booked onto their next course and that was a real eye-opener! That course got me started on 1) sourcing through estate agents and 2) buying to renovate to sell on.

The repossessions they get are very reduced-commission for the agent. It's almost not worth their while in doing individual viewings as I now know. That's why they do block bookings because the commission is so low. It's just really not worth them putting the effort in.

But if then they can get somebody they know to come along and buy a Property quickly and renovate it to a good standard aimed at the first-time buyer, they're going to sell it quick. That's the area that I'm concentrating on at this moment in time.

Okay, so that's how they perceive you – as someone who can add the value and turn around a distressed property quickly to present them on to their customers, so that they can achieve a higher commission?

Yes absolutely, they'll get their full commission. Yes, absolutely very quickly!

How long does it take to turn a property around?

These days it is six months because I am limited to the six-months' rule instigated by most lenders in that they won't issue a mortgage to a buyer unless the owner, which is my case is me, has owned the Property for at least six months.

But the bottom line is by the time you've bought the Property, you've got three quotations at least from three different builders, plumber, plasterers, so on and so forth.

That's going to take a few weeks to sort out anyway. Then, they actually start work and good builders aren't available the next day. That's why they're good builders because they're very busy. Then, you're into six, eight, ten weeks depending on the amount of work you're doing. Then, it's presentable; it's ready, so on and so forth. You're four or five months down the road anyway. It could even be six months.

Are you buying these repossessions for cash?

Yes. The ones I've purchased so far have not been repossessions, but they've been effectively distressed Properties that needed work doing to them. You get better deals when you buy cash as I have come to learn, whether your cash or someone else's cash.

Do the estate agents work with you then once you've refurbished the property? Do you then give it back to them?

Yes absolutely. I always give it back to the agent that I purchased it from. I let them know straight upfront that they will get the Property to sell on when I have finished refurbing it and that I will pay their full fee. I don't try and cut anybody down on fees ever! That just doesn't pay. To try and shave off ½% when they are charging 1½% or 2 % will lose you total credibility from that agent – it's a non-starter because it's only a couple of hundred quid in reality. I want the agent to find me a buyer ASAP after I have finished the refurbishment.

So, you're pulling your cash out at the backend after six months when you have sold on?

Yes, I've done three so far. I'm taking it nice and easy. I want to be able to buy a Property for as low a price as possible. Then, if it didn't work out at the end of the day, I could always resell it and get all my money back including the costs.

The reality is on the first one I did, I made a 34% return-on-investment. Now at that particular time, the bank was giving me 0.1% interest for a whole year! They have since increased that to 2.2% pa which is still extremely low. This is with instant access of course. So yes, my first one – my return-on-investment was 32%. That for me is over £20,000 per deal.

Now, that really got me going because then it became obvious to me that if I can cut down the cost of purchasing even by £1,000 or £2,000 initially, that can add 4% or 5% when I sell on.

Until you've actually purchased, refurbished and sold on a Property, you do not know what the real costs involved are. It is only after your first one that you get an accurate idea of what the real costs involved are.

1. First House Purchase:

Bought for £55,000

Refurb. costs of £2,500

Cost of purchase and sales etc. £2,000

Sold for £79,995

Profit £20,495 = 34% ROI

2. Second House Purchase:

Bought for £67,000

Refurb. costs £16,000

Cost of purchase and sales £3,000

Sold for £109,000

Profit £23,000 = 26% ROI

3. Third House Purchase

Bought for £42,000

Refurb. costs £5,000

Cost of purchase and sales £3,500

Sold for £67,000

Profit £16,500 = 32% ROI

Are there any plans to convert that slush fund of capital into cash-flowing property?

At this moment in time, no. There are still a lot of Properties that are being repossessed which have not come on the market. I believe the government has asked the banks not to foreclose on people.

The reality is of the other 30,000 they didn't repossess, those people still are not paying the money, so their debts get bigger and bigger. The banks know full well they're never going to get that money back anyway. So, there comes a point where they've got to repossess the Property to try recover their costs if they can. That's the reality.

So, I firmly believe that this year, there will be a lot more repossessions coming onto the market.

I also believe that prices are going to go down more because once more repossessions come on the market and a lot of these are in such a bad state that they cannot be mortgaged, they can only be purchased by cash-buyers.

As I explained before, I buy at the low-end of the market where I don't want to pay more than £70,000 max. So, I firmly believe that prices are going to come down this year in the area that I'm in.

I've done three Properties so far. I'm taking it nice and easy. The first one, I made 34%, the next one, I made 26% and the one after that I made 32%. My total net cash profit after all costs is £59,995 cash in the bank.

My goal when I started was to make 20% return-on-investment for my money simply because the bank was giving me 0.1%. But then when I'd sold the first one and made 32% ROI, I thought that if I can make this type of return, why go into renting out at this moment in time?

I'm not thinking about building a pension portfolio or anything else, just making chunks of cash by turning over my money.

If you smooth that over the year, you're getting a higher return on what you would do with a buy-to-let?

Oh, absolutely! Yes, there's no question about it. I'm not knocking buy-to-let. It's a superb strategy and it's the best pension I believe you can get. Not only are you getting an income, but you own the Property and that Property will increase in value with time. As it increases in value, as we all know, two or three years down the road you can remortgage it and possibly pull £10,000 or £20,000 out of the increased equity without paying tax.

But at this moment in time unless you're buying right at the bottom end of the market, it's very difficult to make anything above 10% yield pa. I'm trying to make a minimum of 20% every six months return-on-investment.

Let say that a Property is worth a figure of £100,000 and can pay say £65,000 for it. Do a quick refurbishment which is a decorating job and say new carpets. Then put a tenant in. Straight away, you turn a redundant piece of real estate, which is what it was – that's why they got it so cheap because nobody else really wanted it, into an asset, a cash-producing asset and the value immediately jumps by at least 20% because it's now generating money.

A lot of people forget that, they keep saying, "House prices are going down." They are definitely going down in my opinion. There's no doubt about it, but as soon as you turn that piece of uninhabitable two or three-bedroom Property into a buy-to-let, it does become a cash-producing asset therefore the value goes up straightaway by at least 20% or even 25%.

Now if you go down the pub tonight and tell all of your friends that you've just bought a Property and that it has increased in value by 20%, they'll laugh at you. But the reality is that's what's happened when you turned it into an asset.

It's the media that's driving prices down, which is fine by me and everybody else who's in Property. All except for somebody who's trying to sell. But if you do a good job, you know the street price of the Property and you don't go above that street price with your refurbishment, then you should be able to sell it on for profit.

One of Geoff's top tips would be to know your market and stay in your market?

Yes, absolutely and that's exactly what the lads at Progressive taught me. Find your area and don't move out of that area which is why they're in Peterborough. 99% of their business is in Peterborough.

They know every street in the city and 85% of all of their business comes through estate agents. They'll happily tell you that. Well if these guys are making all this money and they're that successful, I just copy what they do and they tell me straight, "Copy what we do." In all the seminars they say to all of the attendees "Copy what we do."

Some people don't. They do their own thing. Well, I don't see the point. If there's a successful way of doing things, try it and then when the first one works do it again. Don't get clever, just follow what they do.

Again, another top tip – don't change the success formula.

Don't change the formula at all. Buy within your area. Don't move out of your area and don't buy any new-builds or off plan Properties. They are so difficult to value! This is what Rob and Mark hammer in to you at the various courses that they give.

Again, I'm putting bids in all the time for Properties. I'm now looking more and more at auctions because a lot of Properties are coming up at auction. Let's say there are a couple of hundred Properties for sale, I will view 20, I will bid on eight and I'll win one. That's the strategy I've got and that's the one I want out of 200 Properties. I'm not being greedy. I only want one.

Anybody can build up a portfolio of Properties, but it's making it cash flow positive that is the clever thing. You've got to buy the Property in as good a condition as you can when you're doing that because you've really got to keep your refurbishment costs down.

What's your plan then for this year and onward?

For this year, the plan at the moment is to buy five Properties. Now, it doesn't mean they're all going to be buy-to-sell. If they're the right deal and it's 10% + yield, one or two will certainly be in a portfolio.

But really, the name of the game, as far as I'm concerned is if I can buy a three-bed terraced house and turn it into a five-bed HMO. That's when you make the real money.

So, you have a terraced house with three bedrooms. You have downstairs. You go in your front door. You have the front room, the sitting room. You have the back room, which is the parlour. You might have the kitchen extension. The front room as you come in, you can turn into a bedroom and then go into the roof. So if you can turn a three-bedder into a five-bedder, that's when you make a substantial increase in money doing HMO and renting out at £300 to £320 per room per month.

But, you've still got to be buying around a maximum of £70,000 and you can't do that in Kensington, London.

It's difficult with the investor market as people can max out on the number of mortgages.

Yes. The thing about the investing side, the buy-to-let rents are going to keep increasing. There's no doubt about it. People cannot get deposits together therefore they can't get mortgages, so there's going to always be a rental demand. If you're operating in the right area you will make a good return on investment from a rental viewpoint.

Peterborough is the classic with I think 11,000 people on the waiting list because Rob and Mark rent exclusively to DHS-LHA (Local Housing Allowance) people. But, that's their market, so they've got 11,000 people banging on the door wanting to rent houses from them.

What challenges have you had?

I've made mistakes with tradesmen. You have to take a lot of people at face value initially. You try to get as many references as you can, but you want to start the refurbishment work moving fast.

I've fortunately not made too many mistakes, as I learned from Progressive first. The key is if you buy at the lowest possible price, then even if it all goes wrong at the end of the day, i.e. you spend too much on the refurbishment and you don't get the price that you really wanted when you sell, if you bought wisely at the outset then you will still make money when you sell on.

I learned fairly early on after the first debacle with a builder that the best place to find a power team of workmen as far as I'm concerned is to ring up the local council.

Let them know that you're an investor and that you're going to be buying Properties in their area to rent out to LHA people. Ask the council for a list of recommended tradesmen that they use to refurbish their own rental Properties, because you'd like to use those same people on your Properties to get them ready to house people.

They will send you a list of their recommended people that they'd been using for 5, 10, 15 or even 20 years.

It's not in the tradesman's interest to get a bad reputation with the council?

Correct, because when these guys have done a job for the council, the council inspector comes down, and if it's not 150%, they don't get paid and they'll be knocked off the council list.

Although the building trade at this moment is in dire straits, the refurbishment trade working for councils is not because council houses are always being trashed; they need maintenance and repair.

If you've got 10,000 council houses, almost 10% will always need some form of refurbishment to be done. That's where I get my tradesmen from.

For someone thinking of taking the next step into property investment education, what words of wisdom would you pass onto them?

First of all, you've got to latch onto a company like Progressive. You must have mentorship from people who have done it and have been doing it for years and most of all who are successful at doing it.

There're a lot of guys on the circuit who talk the talk, but don't walk the walk. They don't own any Properties. They might be American, they might be Australian, even Brits. You need to find and be mentored by somebody like the lads at Progressive. You can actually go to their offices in Peterborough and meet with them. I've been there many times.

They're real. They've got about 25 people working for them. They do portfolio-building as well, where they'll build a portfolio of investment Properties for people.

You've got to get mentored by people with a real track record and people you like to work with. Progressive are accessible. They do have a phone number. It's a British phone number. You ring it, somebody answers the phone and you can get through to these guys.

You don't have to be in a hurry to buy Property. You can put your bids in and wait for the right deal to materialise. Anybody can buy a Property, but not everybody can buy one at 30% or 40% below market value. I just prefer building a rapport with estate agents and they call me.

So, I would say to anybody, good mentorship is essential and decided as soon as you can what you strategy is going to be. Is it buy-to-let, is it buy, refurbish and hold or is it buy, refurbish and sell on or whatever? Stick with that strategy. Once you've decided what you're going to do, stick with it and give try it.

But to be on the safe side, buy at the bottom end of the market every time. Just don't pay more than £60,000 or £70,000 regardless of what your strategy is. If it's buy-to-let, just make sure you're going to get around about that 9% to 10% yield and you can only do that by buying at very low prices. Again if it's buy-to-sell you must be buying at lease 35% BMV.

Don't be afraid – everybody will learn this on mentorship of offering low prices. If a Property is say on Rightmove at an asking price of £70,000 offer them £45,000. You don't know people's circumstances. If the answer is No, Just move onto the next one and make another low offer. Just take the rebuff.

I think I read on Rob's Facebook page that if they're not insulted by your offer, you've not gone in low enough.

Provided that you did all of your calculations up front initially and that you are going to make at least 25% ROI go through with the purchase!

If you really wanted to make 30% + profit on the deal, as soon as you have got the agreement from the vendor to sell it to you, offer this same deal to other Property investors that you know for a finder's fee of say, £3,500 to £5,000, and sell it on. This helps the person who wants to sell; it helps the Investor who is looking for a good deal and it helps the estate agent who gets his full fee from the vendor for selling his Property. It's a win-win situation.

Again, that's what Rob and Mark keep hammering on. Everybody wants a win-win situation. The seller wants a win-win. The buyer and the investor want a win-win. The agent wants a win- win and you or me who initially recognised the deal want a win-win situation.

Key Learnings

- Pensions aren't going to pay out enough so you need to secure your own financial future.
- Focus and get great at one strategy and it will pay you dividend.
- You make your profit when you buy.
- Invest in building relationships with estate agents it will pay off in profits.
- If you are buying to flip, always pay and always pay the estate agents their full fee - never screw them down on price.
- Buy repossessions; don't buy new builds or off plan.
- Copy the successful strategies of successful people, such as the lads at Progressive. Don't re-invent the wheel.
- Buy Properties at the lowest prices that you can.

Top Books

- Read these two books written by Rob Moore and Mark Homer before you do anything else concerning Property!
- "Make Cash in a Property Market Crash", Rob Moore and Mark Homer
- "The 44 Most Closely Guarded Property Secrets", Rob Moore and Mark Homer

Education

Progressive Property JV Buying Frenzy Networking Event [1-day]:

http://www.progressiveproperty.co.uk/jv-event

Progressive Property 3 Day Property Investing Masterclass

http://www.progressiveproperty.co.uk/masterclass

What I've learned from writing the book

Well, all I can say is, "wow!": By interviewing these people and hearing their stories, they have certainly inspired me and so I really hope they inspire you too. I also hope I've done each story justice. My own personal journey in the past two years has seen me falter after taking the education whilst dealing with personal challenges but learning from these people and how they overcome challenges has renewed my belief and drive to continue my journey to success. It is our desire that this book does the same for you too.

Education

Many of the students I interviewed had already bought Property before they received their education. They'd made mistakes, parked money in Property, not achieved valuations, not got the rents that they were told were achievable, and had problem tenants to name a few.

However, since they have been trained they make fewer mistakes and have developed systems to overcome these eventualities, and rather than be 'hobbyist' Investors not making any money, they're making significant cash now.

Plenty of us mix with old school investors at networking events who have bought Property the "old" traditional way. They don't know to use other people's money and have learnt from their own mistakes. No one is saying that's wrong, it's just when you're educated you have learned from everyone else's mistakes too and it accelerates your success. Some of the "old boys" are amazed at the speed of success by the new educated Property Investor.

You have a serious advantage on them right now!

Health Warning!

Education is only of value when you implement it. Please do not become a seminar junkie where you attend seminar after workshop after webinar and not go out and implement what you have learned.

Get educated properly and **TAKE ACTION**.

Networking

Another common theme is that the people all network. At first they didn't really value it, weren't confident about what they were doing, not sure what they wanted. Now they see the value in meeting like-minded, solution oriented people and building relationships.

You will change your friends as you become more successful. It sounds clinical doesn't it, but it doesn't have to be. The reality is that you'll just see your old friends less often. You might find you can't discuss certain things with your old friends because they simply are not on your wavelength.

It's no one's fault; as much as we'd like to, we can't change them, and they can't change you. So, these new friends you meet through networking are more likely to be on a similar journey and will feature more in your lives in the future.

In running my own networking event, the feedback from people who attend tell me that it gives them a shot of positivity once a month, which gives them the energy, inspiration, motivation or whatever it is to help them jump over their hurdles until the next month. The energy from positive, like-minded people is addictive so you have to be careful.

Your net worth is linked to your network

Self or personal development

Often overlooked and certainly hard to 'sell' on a Property education workshop, but vitally important in determining your success is self or personal development.

I have been working on my own self-development for four years and so it was reassuring to hear others have been doing the same. When you step out into the relative unknown and sometimes frightening world of the investor or entrepreneur, from that of a paid employee, there aren't many other people on the same path.

It can be a lonely place and if you don't work on your self-esteem, self-belief, confidence, your fear of failure and happiness; it will be only too easy to slip back into the old mind-set and employment again.

To succeed as an entrepreneur, you must set aside your neediness for acceptance from others. Immunity to criticism is a "secret" shared by all the highly successful entrepreneurs that I know.

To succeed as an entrepreneur, you have to set aside your "Book of Excuses" once and for all. Making money as an entrepreneur and making excuses are mutually exclusive and wholly incompatible.

You can make money or

you can make excuses, but

you can't do both!

One of my coaches Daniel Wagner said that becoming an entrepreneur is a 365 day long personal development course. Every facet of your being is on display to the world. Any weaknesses are exposed and so it's a constant battle to first observe yourself, and then find a solution to improve yourself.

Just as we learn more from our mistakes more than our successes, we grow from the challenges we face. I cannot emphasise enough the importance of developing the right mind-set when undertaking investment of any sort so you can drive on to success after hitting the inevitable hurdles you come across.

In the new economy, the tests will come more frequently, more quickly and more furiously, but so will the opportunities.

Failure is part of the daily entrepreneurial experience – *Dan Kennedy*

F.O.C.U.S (Follow One Course Until Success)

A lot of the students have picked one strategy and implemented it until successful before going on to implement another one. Too often we can overwhelm ourselves by trying too many things at the same time and never doing each one justice. We then see failure and give up.

I cannot emphasise enough the power of concentration: to focus on one specific subject until you've made it successful before moving on to a new one. Nowhere is this more important than in wealth creation.

I trained in Property investing, share trading and internet marketing all at a similar time. I was excited by the endless possibilities for making money that these different lanes on the wealth motorway opened up for me.

However, I quickly came to realise that I was totally overwhelmed. I was spreading myself too thinly across each one. There was a steep, steep learning curve in each lane and I was struggling to work, spend time with the family and train.

Once I decided to drop share trading and internet marketing and focus on Property, things started to happen. And this book is a testament to that.

You must find ways to shield yourself from the many modern distractions we all encounter in daily life. Phone calls, emails, texts, colleagues, friends, clients, and suppliers all conspire to break your concentration on an hourly basis. It takes roughly 20 minutes to restore your concentration to its original state. This means that in an average day you're unlikely to have quality focused time for more than four hours each day.

The modern office just isn't conducive to sustained periods of uninterrupted quality thought time so be aware of this and develop deep immersive techniques to guard it.

Having a powerful 'why'

Trevor is a shining example of having a Powerful Why. His faith drives him to help others but in a sustainable way. Using his education he wants to teach people less well off how to fish and not to just give them fish.

This is something that's close to my heart too, and he and Jackie are exploring working together on a more socially enterprising project.

Jackie and Colin have loved helping young couples get a foot on the ladder through lease options. As Jackie says, investing isn't easy. She used all her annual leave, gives up her evenings twice a month to run Property meets, and after work does two or three viewings. Over the long term these challenges will test your resolve and that's why it's important to be absolutely clear to always know your Why.

Rob and Mark often open their hearts and share the pains they have faced with their immediate families' battles with cancer. There is absolutely no doubt that the pain of Mark losing his father and uncle, and Rob many of his family members, has driven them on so much more, because the reasons and necessities for success transcend their own personal interests.

Success habits

When you train in wealth creation you are taught to model successful people in your field. If you do what they do then success will follow. So often we don't seem to follow the systems that we have been taught.

Often you are just 2% away from success - if only you tweaked a specific aspect of your business system. It may be the marketing, the conversion, the product, the service or the delivery. Are you doing enough viewings to make enough offers, to find enough motivated sellers to accept your offers?

These people have common traits. They are prepared to do what most of us aren't on a regular basis. They have developed discipline. Can they be bothered to attend that 7am breakfast meeting or just spend an extra hour in bed? Should they watch that TV programme or make that phone call or analyse that deal?

> **It's easy to do and it's easy not to do -**
> ***Jeff Olsen***

Everyday, they chip away at the tasks that will bring them success over the years.

Support

Stepping out into the unknown new world of entrepreneurship is scary. Actually, it can be pretty damn terrifying. Whilst the reasons you have done that are exciting it is still nevertheless a nerve racking time.

People around you see you stepping away from them and their natural instinct is to pull you back into the crowd (remember Rob's crabs in the box). They will seize any opportunity to say "I told you so" as soon as you fail.

I know when I attended my three-day training that something inside me crystallised for the first time. I had finally found my tribe. I had found liked-minded, positive, spirited people who wished to be more than they were. Yes, they have failed from time to time but did it make them give up? No. They dusted themselves off, picked themselves back up and tried again.

I've come to meet some of the most generous spirited people I'd hoped to meet. They share and give on a daily basis. They do not fear competition. They believe you can achieve more by cooperation. That's why joint ventures are so prominent. Everyone looks for a win-win solution to help each other.

If your partner is not interested or actively preventing you from pursuing your education, there will be a clash sooner or later. Furthering yourself is an indication of your desire to grow as a person.

Suppressing that desire for growth is near enough impossible, and it will break through sooner rather than later, just like grass breaks through concrete. This can be threatening to your partner if they're not growing at the same rate. Your relationship is about to change shape as you embark on a journey of who you want to become.

Permanent employment is easy to understand. Entrepreneurship on the other hand is not easy to understand and can be quite complex. As humans we fear that which we don't understand. Your partner naturally will be fearful so it's up to you to show understanding. However, you cannot change a person. Only you can change yourself and this is where the friction can lie. I have direct experience here, including doing it wrong initially.

Goals, coaching and mastermind groups

Many of the investors interviewed say they were propelled forward by a mentor or coach as well as mixing with others in a similar group. Napoleon Hill in his book "Think and Grow Rich" speaks of the power of the mastermind group.

He defined mastermind as: "Coordination of knowledge and effort, in a spirit of harmony, between two or more people, for the attainment of a definite purpose."

It's no coincidence that many of the students interviewed have been in the Progressive JV VIP Property Millionaires Club and have subsequently gone on to become very good friends. They hold each other accountable and share openly ideas on what is working and help to solve each others' challenges.

They set clear goals to aim for, and are held accountable each month to their progress towards achieving them. Some of them have very ambitious goals and sometimes wonder how they are going to achieve them, but somehow they do.

If you want to propel your cash flow, make five times the money in one fifth of the time, want to spend more time doing the things you love with the people you love, want to play on a bigger stage and become known as a professional and profitable investor, and maybe one day teach others too, then watch this short video from Rob:

www.progressiveproperty.co.uk/vip-pmc

This is where many of the new professionals got started from this book, and you can too:

If you can see how you can achieve your goal your goal isn't big enough

Health

Whilst not mentioned explicitly in this book I'd like to make a personal observation of my own:

A healthy body is a healthy mind.

Speaking to and observing many successful people Rob and Mark included, they all have reduced the amount of convenience food and alcohol they consume and increased the amount of exercise they do. I have personally increased the amount of raw food and water in my diet and my energy levels have increased.

I've hired a personal trainer to teach me how to exercise effectively and to push me further than I would push myself ordinarily. This has resulted in me sleeping better but for less time, and having more waking hours in which to achieve. Gaining another two hours a day gives you back a whole working day each week. You could use this extra time to move forward faster as Mark and Rob do.

Win-win attitude – the heart and the head

Another common trait in all these people is the ethical way they conduct themselves. They seek out a win-win solution in making deals.

Too often Property investors are painted as preying on poor people who have fallen on hard times and paying rock bottom prices. The fact of the matter is that many Property investors stop repossession, prevent vendors from acquiring bad credit ratings, and enable them to move on in their lives.

Some investors have simply walked away from a deal because they didn't have a good "feeling" about the person or the deal. Something wasn't quite right. Rather than force themselves to do something every fibre in their being was telling them not to do they have quietly walked away.

I just want to talk about something that we rarely discuss in business. The heart! We often associate discussion about the heart with emotions, family and love and the head with cold, hard facts, logic and business decision making.

Well, having got to know a few of these people they make decisions with their heart too. Research is starting to show that there are neural pathways from the heart to the head, and that scientists have actually measured impulses firing from the heart first and triggering an action in the brain second.

The electromagnetic radiation emitted by the heart is 50 times stronger than that emitted by the brain and can be detected up to 10 feet outside the body.

We're only just getting a glimpse of the power of the heart in making decisions. Perhaps it controls those decisions we call "gut instincts". Those feelings we get in our stomach that tell us something isn't quite right about a person or a situation.

Numerous theories abound. Our education system is very left brain oriented and has suppressed our ability to "listen" to our creative instincts, but heart or emotional intelligence may well play a larger role than we suspect in decision making in the future to ensure win-win solutions. Those with good hearts in the long-term will succeed.

Just don't tell Mark this who can't live without all his spread sheets ☺

Now take ACTION – ready, fire, aim!

We come to the final and most important theme of the book. Every single one of the people interviewed had one defining characteristic. They took the knowledge they gained in the training and went out and put it into practice. Did they make mistakes? Yes. Did they look silly in front of people? Yes. Did it stop them? NO.

Many people spend a great deal of time in the analysis phase of a project, perfecting everything: getting things 'just so' before moving to the action phase. Paralysed by the "But what if?" syndrome.

I teach my children to make decisions quickly. I've told them they can always correct a wrong decision. You will only find out if it's a wrong decision though by taking some form of action. Then you can steer it back on track using the feedback from the action.

Grow your wings on the way down when you step off the cliff

Some people go out and throw a tremendous amount of effort at a particular task, but then don't achieve the results they think they deserve. This disheartens them and they eventually give up.

In reality, they are taking action but not necessarily the correct action. The key is to monitor your actions and measure your results. If you're not getting the desired results then you need to change the actions you take. After all, Einstein defined insanity as doing the same thing over and over again and expecting different results.

Insanity

Doing the same thing over and over and expecting different results

Sounds simple, doesn't it? Most people operate within their comfort zone and consequently don't take the successful actions needed which lie outside it. Fear is where the money is. I found it difficult to call vendors back. I realised it's because I couldn't always help them and felt like I was letting them down.

Recognising it was a block to my business, I resolved to make ten calls a day for a week. By picking up the phone and understanding the vendors' problems I was able to use my network to solve their problems.

The more I do it, the more I solve the problems, and now I don't feel so bad when I say "I'm afraid I can't help you". I'm at least helping some of the people, and it had to start with me picking up the phone and taking the action.

So, what's stopping you now...?

Rob's outro

'To know and not to do, is not to know'

Now is your time. You are suitably inspired, and that is the bridge between where you are now and where you desire to be. Be all that you can be, because you can.

'When all is said and done, more is said than done'

How are you going to be different? What is going to make you be a do-er? Don't spend all your time talking over your plans, go out and make mistakes, quickly. Go out and apply on the front line the strategies you've learned and put into action all your education.

'Get perfect later'

Learn. Do. Teach. Fast.

'Those who don't read have no advantage over those who can't read'

You are now a fully committed, life-long student of money, investing, Property, your mind-set, influence, people and your own personal development. It is never over, and the great thing about that is that there are no limits on what you can achieve.

'If you don't risk anything, you risk everything'

If you stay right where you are, in that uncomfortable comfortable place of 'something missing' and 'not enough', you will never be the person you want to be, have the things you want to have, and you will die unfulfilled without having made any impact on the universe.

That would be such a waste of your infinite potential. Everything you want in life, everything that you don't yet have, is just inches outside your comfort zone, and your current reality. Think just a tiny bit bigger, believe just a tiny bit more, do just a little bit more, and the compounded effect will be inconceivably different.

The bottom line is that you have come this far. Don't stop now. Never go back. A friend once told me that a brain, once expanded, can never go back to it's former shape. I don't know if he was being literal, or metaphorical, but now that you opened that door that leads to a million other doors, the world will never look the same again, and everything you've ever been missing starts at this door you've just opened.

'Is this the end, or is this just the beginning?'

The major common theme of progressive winners

One thing almost all Progressive success stories have in common is Joint Ventures. Specifically using other people's (non bank) leveraged finance to build portfolios and create income from scratch.

Their JV's extend to powerteams, communities, business partners and experts on hand to help them grow their property empire faster, no matter how difficult things were before.

If you'd like to achieve similar results to the Progressive winners in this book, and doing using other people' money, skills, time and resources, then the gift we are about to give you will be of the highest value to you:

The Progressive Joint Venture Be Your Own Bank Blueprint is a document that gives you the 7 steps, in full detail, needed to perform JV's successfully, getting the money in your bank and dealing JV deals.

This exclusive, trademarked report is waiting for you as a sincere thank you for reading this book:

https://progproperty.infusionsoft.com/go/JVB/

Most people don't get this far. You should be proud of yourself. And thank you from us, we really appreciate you. Here's your JV Blueprint, a gift from us:

https://progproperty.infusionsoft.com/go/JVB/

Glossary

BMV - Below market value.

HMO - House in multiple occupancy.

LTV - Loan to value.

LHA – Local Housing Allowance.

Flip – Buying and immediately selling a Property for profit.

Heads of Terms – Used to record what has been agreed in principle between parties prior to reaching the stage of entering into formal, contractual documentation.

Lease Option – An agreement to lease a Property and to buy it at a specific price within an agreed time in the future.

Mortgage Host - An investor or joint venture partner who is prepared to take out a mortgage on a Property you want in return for some financial benefit. A way to increase portfolio without being restricted by a traditional lender.

PIN – Property investors network.

Refurb – Refurbishment of a Property. Renovation.

Repos – Repossession Property that has been handed back to the mortgage lender usually due to mortgage arrears.

RICS – Royal Institution of Chartered Surveyors.

Essential Information

All of the interviewees in this book made reference to the Progressive trainings and educational materials that changed their lives. They are listed below, please choose which ones of these you want to take, invest in yourself, and take fast action to get your desired results.

There is absolutely nothing other than inaction stopping you from getting the results of everyone in this book, using the same strategies, working with the same people and following the same path.
And just 12 months or less from now, we hope to be adding your story to this book, which, year on year we will continually update. In fact commit right now; make it your goal to be one of the success stories. We need you, and you deserve it:

Please email us at rob.moore@progressiveproperty.co.uk

Put it down on (e)-paper, commit it to reality, allow us to make you accountable and take the first action step right now.

Progressive Property training

If you want to meet 150-300 likeminded Property investors of all experiences, be inspired, motivated, and learn the fundamentals of cash flow investing and giving up your job, go here:

Progressive Property JV Buying Frenzy Networking Event [1-day]:

http://www.progressiveproperty.co.uk/jv-event

If you would like to control assets with no deposit, no mortgage, regardless of your credit rating, quicker, faster, with lower risk, make job-leaving passive income, AND help more vendors and first time buyers, go here:

Progressive Property Lease Options Training:

http://www.progressive-property.co.uk/lease-options-intensive

If you would like to be part of the UK's largest underground community of professionally aspirational Property investors, be kept accountable to your cash flow goals, get personal attention and support to make them happen, grow your profile and brand, and get the best cash flow strategies before ANYONE else, go here:

Progressive Property VIP JV Millionaires Club:

http://www.progressiveproperty.co.uk/vip-pmc/

If you would like to go from where you are to complete professional in one closed door, four-day, life changing Property event, blowing away all negative and past energy and mistakes, and learn every single facet of total professional, low risk Property investment to replace any job or income within one year, go here:

Progressive Property Three-Day Property Investing Masterclass Intensive:

http://www.progressiveproperty.co.uk/masterclass/

If you would like to be part of a very low cost, online investor community with 1000s of people JV-ing to the tune of £300K per week, and get online fingertip access to 100s of hours of cash flow education, templates and resources, go here:

Progressive Property JV Portal Members Forum:

http://www.progressivepropertyeducation.co.uk/members/

If you would like to be a part, in the past or in the future, of the UK's largest Property event with the biggest name UK celebrity investors and entrepreneurs, teaching underground entrepreneurial cash flow tricks, go here:

The Property Super Conference:

http://www.propertysuperconference.co.uk/

If you would like to monetise every deal you find that you don't want to buy to the tune of £3K - £10K per deal, pre month, and become a known resource in the industry, servicing and helping other investors and building a business, go here:

Progressive Property Deal Packaging Cash flow Training:

http://www.progressiveproperty.co.uk/deal-packaging-masterclass

If you want to build one of the best libraries in the country and want Property knowledge most professionals don't know at your fingertips, go here:

The Progressive Property Best Selling Books

http://www.progressiveproperty.co.uk/book-buy-now

If you want to connect and stay in touch, go here:

Rob Moore's Facebook Page

http://www.facebook.com/robprogressive

If you want all the benefits of Property investing; you want the cash flow, the growth and the pension replacement, but with none of the hassle and completely handsfree: you want the baby without the labour pains, go here:

Progressive Property Handsfree Portfolio Building Service for Passive Investors:

email Rob on rob.moore@progressiveproperty.co.uk for details or go here:

http://www.progressiveproperty.co.uk/investment-opportunity

James Caan with Rob Moore and Mark Homer at Property Super Conference 2010

Lord Alan Sugar Keynote speaker at Property Super Conference 2011 with Rob Moore and Mark Homer

Sir Bob Geldoff at

Property Super Conference 2012

Rob Moore and Mark Homer with cheque raised for a charity close to their hearts

Get educated

Get motivated

Get out there

Change Your Life!

Rob Moore and Mark Homer with a few of the things that making money from Property can give them

(2) The considerations are—

(a) the general right of a defendant in criminal proceedings to know the identity of a witness in the proceedings;

(b) the extent to which the credibility of the witness concerned would be a relevant factor when the weight of his or her evidence comes to be assessed;

(c) whether evidence given by the witness might be the sole or decisive evidence implicating the defendant;

(d) whether the witness's evidence could be properly tested (whether on grounds of credibility or otherwise) without his or her identity being disclosed;

(e) whether there is any reason to believe that the witness—

(i) has a tendency to be dishonest, or

(ii) has any motive to be dishonest in the circumstances of the case,

having regard (in particular) to any previous convictions of the witness and to any relationship between the witness and the defendant or any associates of the defendant;

(f) whether it would be reasonably practicable to protect the witness by any means other than by making a witness anonymity order specifying the measures that are under consideration by the court.

90 Warning to jury

(1) Subsection (2) applies where, on a trial on indictment with a jury, any evidence has been given by a witness at a time when a witness anonymity order applied to the witness.

(2) The judge must give the jury such warning as the judge considers appropriate to ensure that the fact that the order was made in relation to the witness does not prejudice the defendant.

Discharge and variation

91 Discharge or variation of order

(1) A court that has made a witness anonymity order in relation to any criminal proceedings may in those proceedings subsequently discharge or vary (or further vary) the order if it appears to the court to be appropriate to do so in view of the provisions of sections 88 and 89 that apply to the making of an order.

(2) The court may do so—

(a) on an application made by a party to the proceedings if there has been a material change of circumstances since the relevant time, or

(b) on its own initiative.

(3) The court must give every party to the proceedings the opportunity to be heard—

(a) before determining an application made to it under subsection (2);

(b) before discharging or varying the order on its own initiative.

(4) But subsection (3) does not prevent the court hearing one or more of the parties to the proceedings in the absence of a defendant in the proceedings and his or her legal representatives, if it appears to the court to be appropriate to do so in the circumstances of the case.

(5) 'The relevant time' means—

(a) the time when the order was made, or

(b) if a previous application has been made under subsection (2), the time when the application (or the last application) was made.

92 Discharge or variation after proceedings

(1) This section applies if—

(a) a court has made a witness anonymity order in relation to a witness in criminal proceedings ('the old proceedings'), and

(b) the old proceedings have come to an end.

(2) The court that made the order may discharge or vary (or further vary) the order if it appears to the court to be appropriate to do so in view of—

(a) the provisions of sections 88 and 89 that apply to the making of a witness anonymity order, and
(b) such other matters as the court considers relevant.

(3) The court may do so—
(a) on an application made by a party to the old proceedings if there has been a material change of circumstances since the relevant time, or
(b) on an application made by the witness if there has been a material change of circumstances since the relevant time.

(4) The court may not determine an application made to it under subsection (3) unless in the case of each of the parties to the old proceedings and the witness—
(a) it has given the person the opportunity to be heard, or
(b) it is satisfied that it is not reasonably practicable to communicate with the person.

(5) Subsection (4) does not prevent the court hearing one or more of the persons mentioned in that subsection in the absence of a person who was a defendant in the old proceedings and that person's legal representatives, if it appears to the court to be appropriate to do so in the circumstances of the case.

(6) 'The relevant time' means—
(a) the time when the old proceedings came to an end, or
(b) if a previous application has been made under subsection (3), the time when the application (or the last application) was made.

93 Discharge or variation by appeal court

(1) This section applies if—
(a) a court has made a witness anonymity order in relation to a witness in criminal proceedings ('the trial proceedings'), and
(b) a defendant in the trial proceedings has in those proceedings—
(i) been convicted,
(ii) been found not guilty by reason of insanity, or
(iii) been found to be under a disability and to have done the act charged in respect of an offence.

(2) The appeal court may in proceedings on or in connection with an appeal by the defendant from the trial proceedings discharge or vary (or further vary) the order if it appears to the court to be appropriate to do so in view of—
(a) the provisions of sections 88 and 89 that apply to the making of a witness anonymity order, and
(b) such other matters as the court considers relevant.

(3) The appeal court may not discharge or vary the order unless in the case of each party to the trial proceedings—
(a) it has given the person the opportunity to be heard, or
(b) it is satisfied that it is not reasonably practicable to communicate with the person.

(4) But subsection (3) does not prevent the appeal court hearing one or more of the parties to the trial proceedings in the absence of a person who was a defendant in the trial proceedings and that person's legal representatives, if it appears to the court to be appropriate to do so in the circumstances of the case.

(5) In this section a reference to the doing of an act includes a reference to a failure to act.

(6) 'Appeal court' means—
(a) the Court of Appeal,
(b) the Court of Appeal in Northern Ireland, or
(c) the Court Martial Appeal Court.

Part II

Criminal Proceedings—Codes, Rules, and Guidelines

Code of Practice for the Detention, Treatment and Questioning of Persons by Police Officers (Code C)

(2017)

1 General

1.0 The powers and procedures in this Code must be used fairly, responsibly, with respect for the people to whom they apply and without unlawful discrimination. Under the Equality Act 2010, section 149 (Public sector Equality Duty), police forces must, in carrying out their functions, have due regard to the need to eliminate unlawful discrimination, harassment, victimisation and any other conduct which is prohibited by that Act, to advance equality of opportunity between people who share a relevant protected characteristic and people who do not share it, and to foster good relations between those persons. The Equality Act *also* makes it unlawful for police officers to discriminate against, harass or victimise any person on the grounds of the 'protected characteristics' of age, disability, gender reassignment, race, religion or belief, sex and sexual orientation, marriage and civil partnership, pregnancy and maternity, when using their powers. See *Notes 1A* and 1AA.

1.1 All persons in custody must be dealt with expeditiously, and released as soon as the need for detention no longer applies.

1.1A A custody officer must perform the functions in this Code as soon as practicable. A custody officer will not be in breach of this Code if delay is justifiable and reasonable steps are taken to prevent unnecessary delay. The custody record shall show when a delay has occurred and the reason. See *Note 1H*.

1.2 This Code of Practice must be readily available at all police stations for consultation by:

- police officers;
- police staff;
- detained persons;
- members of the public.

1.3 The provisions of this Code:

- include the *Annexes*
- do not include the *Notes for Guidance*.

1.4 If an officer has any suspicion, or is told in good faith, that a person of any age may be mentally disordered or otherwise mentally vulnerable, in the absence of clear evidence to dispel that suspicion, the person shall be treated as such for the purposes of this Code. See *Note 1G*.

1.5 Anyone who appears to be under 18, shall, in the absence of clear evidence that they are older and subject to *paragraph 1.5A*, be treated as a juvenile for the purposes of this Code and any other Code. See Note 1L

1.5A *Paragraph 1.5* does not change the statutory provisions in section 65(1) of PACE (appropriate consent) which require the consent of a juvenile's parent or guardian.

In this Code, section 65(1) is relevant to Annex A *paragraphs 2(b) and 2B* (Intimate searches) and *Annex K paragraphs 1(b) and 3* (X-Ray and ultrasound scan). In Code D (Identification), section 65(1)

is relevant to *paragraph 2.12* and *Note 2A,* which apply to identification procedures, to taking fingerprints, samples, footwear impressions, photographs and to evidential searches and examinations.

1.6 If a person appears to be blind, seriously visually impaired, deaf, unable to read or speak or has difficulty orally because of a speech impediment, they shall be treated as such for the purposes of this Code in the absence of clear evidence to the contrary.

1.7 'The appropriate adult' means, in the case of a:

(a) juvenile:

(i) the parent, guardian or, if the juvenile is in the care of a local authority or voluntary organisation, a person representing that authority or organisation (see *Note 1B*);

(ii) a social worker of a local authority (see *Note 1C*);

(iii) failing these, some other responsible adult aged 18 or over who is *not*:

~ a police officer;

~ employed by the police;

~ under the direction or control of the chief officer of a police force; or

~ a person who provides services under contractual arrangements (but without being employed by the chief officer of a police force), to assist that force in relation to the discharge of its chief officer's functions,

whether or not they are on duty at the time.

See *Note 1F.*

(b) person who is mentally disordered or mentally vulnerable: See *Note 1D.*

(i) a relative, guardian or other person responsible for their care or custody;

(ii) someone experienced in dealing with mentally disordered or mentally vulnerable people but who is not:

~ a police officer;

~ employed by the police;

~ under the direction or control of the chief officer of a police force; or

~ a person who provides services under contractual arrangements (but without being employed by the chief officer of a police force), to assist that force in relation to the discharge of its chief officer's functions,

whether or not they are on duty at the time;

(iii) failing these, some other responsible adult aged 18 or over other than a person described in the bullet points in *sub-paragraph (b)(ii)* above.

See *Note 1F.*

1.8 If this Code requires a person be given certain information, they do not have to be given it if at the time they are incapable of understanding what is said, are violent or may become violent or in urgent need of medical attention, but they must be given it as soon as practicable.

1.9 References to a custody officer include any police officer who, for the time being, is performing the functions of a custody officer.

1.9A When this Code requires the prior authority or agreement of an officer of at least inspector or superintendent rank, that authority may be given by a sergeant or chief inspector authorised to perform the functions of the higher rank under the Police and Criminal Evidence Act 1984 (PACE), section 107.

1.10 Subject to *paragraph 1.12,* this Code applies to people in custody at police stations in England and Wales, whether or not they have been arrested, and to those removed to a police station as a place of safety under the Mental Health Act 1983, sections 135 and 136, as a last resort (see paragraph 3.16). *Section 15* applies solely to people in police detention, e.g. those brought to a police station under arrest or arrested at a police station for an offence after going there voluntarily.

1.11 No part of this Code applies to a detained person:

(a) to whom PACE Code H applies because:

- they are detained following arrest under section 41 of the Terrorism Act 2000 (TACT) and not charged; or
- an authorisation has been given under section 22 of the Counter-Terrorism Act 2008 (CTACT) (post-charge questioning of terrorist suspects) to interview them.

(b) to whom the Code of Practice issued under paragraph 6 of Schedule 14 to TACT applies because they are detained for examination under Schedule 7 to TACT.

1.12 This Code does not apply to people in custody:

(i) arrested by officers under the Criminal Justice and Public Order Act 1994, section 136(2) on warrants issued in Scotland, or arrested or detained without warrant under section 137(2) by officers from a police force in Scotland. In these cases, police powers and duties and the person's rights and entitlements whilst at a police station in England or Wales are the same as those in Scotland;

(ii) arrested under the Immigration and Asylum Act 1999, section 142(3) in order to have their fingerprints taken;

(iii) whose detention has been authorised under Schedules 2 or 3 to the Immigration Act 1971 or section 62 of the Nationality, Immigration and Asylum Act 2002;

(iv) who are convicted or remanded prisoners held in police cells on behalf of the Prison Service under the Imprisonment (Temporary Provisions) Act 1980;

(v) Not used.

(vi) detained for searches under stop and search powers except as required by Code A.

The provisions on conditions of detention and treatment in *sections 8* and *9* must be considered as the minimum standards of treatment for such detainees.

1.13 In this Code:

(a) 'designated person' means a person other than a police officer, who has specified powers and duties conferred or imposed on them by designation under section 38 or 39 of the Police Reform Act 2002;

(b) reference to a police officer includes a designated person acting in the exercise or performance of the powers and duties conferred or imposed on them by their designation;

(c) where a search or other procedure to which this Code applies may only be carried out or observed by a person of the same sex as the detainee, the gender of the detainee and other parties present should be established and recorded in line with Annex L of this Code.

1.14 Designated persons are entitled to use reasonable force as follows:

(a) when exercising a power conferred on them which allows a police officer exercising that power to use reasonable force, a designated person has the same entitlement to use force; and

(b) at other times when carrying out duties conferred or imposed on them that also entitle them to use reasonable force, for example:

- when at a police station carrying out the duty to keep detainees for whom they are responsible under control and to assist any police officer or designated person to keep any detainee under control and to prevent their escape;
- when securing, or assisting any police officer or designated person in securing, the detention of a person at a police station;
- when escorting, or assisting any police officer or designated person in escorting, a detainee within a police station;
- for the purpose of saving life or limb;
- or preventing serious damage to property.

1.15 Nothing in this Code prevents the custody officer, or other police officer or designated person (see *paragraph 1.13*) given custody of the detainee by the custody officer, from allowing another person (see *(a)* and *(b)* below) to carry out individual procedures or tasks at the police station if the law allows. However, the officer or designated person given custody remains responsible for making sure the procedures and tasks are carried out correctly in accordance with the Codes of Practice (see *paragraph 3.5* and *Note 3F*). The other person who is allowed to carry out the procedures or tasks must be someone who *at that time*, is:

(a) under the direction and control of the chief officer of the force responsible for the police station in question; or

(b) providing services under contractual arrangements (but without being employed by the chief officer the police force), to assist a police force in relation to the discharge of its chief officer's functions.

1.16 Designated persons and others mentioned in *sub-paragraphs (a)* and *(b)* of *paragraph 1.15*, must have regard to any relevant provisions of the Codes of Practice.

1.17 In any provision of this or any other Code which allows or requires police officers or police staff to make a record in their report book, the reference to report book shall include any official report book or electronic recording device issued to them that enables the record in question to be made and dealt with in accordance with that provision. References in this and any other Code to written records, forms and signatures include electronic records and forms and electronic confirmation that identifies the person making the record or completing the form.

Chief officers must be satisfied as to the integrity and security of the devices, records and forms to which this *paragraph* applies and that use of those devices, records and forms satisfies relevant data protection legislation.

Notes for Guidance

1A Although certain sections of this Code apply specifically to people in custody at police stations, those there voluntarily to assist with an investigation should be treated with no less consideration, e.g. offered refreshments at appropriate times, and enjoy an absolute right to obtain legal advice or communicate with anyone outside the police station.

1AA In paragraph 1.0, under the Equality Act 2010, section 149, the 'relevant protected characteristics' are age, disability, gender reassignment, pregnancy and maternity, race, religion/belief and sex and sexual orientation. For further detailed guidance and advice on the Equality Act, see: https:// www.gov.uk/guidance/equality-act-2010-guidance.

1B A person, including a parent or guardian, should not be an appropriate adult if they:

- are:
  - ~ *suspected of involvement in the offence; the victim;*
  - ~ *a witness;*
  - ~ *involved in the investigation.*
- received admissions prior to attending to act as the appropriate adult.

Note: If a juvenile's parent is estranged from the juvenile, they should not be asked to act as the appropriate adult if the juvenile expressly and specifically objects to their presence.

1C If a juvenile admits an offence to, or in the presence of, a social worker or member of a youth offending team other than during the time that person is acting as the juvenile's appropriate adult, another appropriate adult should be appointed in the interest of fairness.

1D In the case of people who are mentally disordered or otherwise mentally vulnerable, it may be more satisfactory if the appropriate adult is someone experienced or trained in their care rather than a relative lacking such qualifications. But if the detainee prefers a relative to a better qualified stranger or objects to a particular person their wishes should, if practicable, be respected.

1E A detainee should always be given an opportunity, when an appropriate adult is called to the police station, to consult privately with a solicitor in the appropriate adult's absence if they want. An appropriate adult is not subject to legal privilege.

1F A solicitor or independent custody visitor who is present at the police station and acting in that capacity, may not be the appropriate adult.

1G 'Mentally vulnerable' applies to any detainee who, because of their mental state or capacity, may not understand the significance of what is said, of questions or of their replies. 'Mental disorder' is defined in the Mental Health Act 1983, section 1(2) as 'any disorder or disability of mind'. When the custody officer has any doubt about the mental state or capacity of a detainee, that detainee should be treated as mentally vulnerable and an appropriate adult called.

1H Paragraph 1.1A is intended to cover delays which may occur in processing detainees e.g. if:

- *a large number of suspects are brought into the station simultaneously to be placed in custody;*

- *interview rooms are all being used;*
- *there are difficulties contacting an appropriate adult, solicitor or interpreter.*

1I The custody officer must remind the appropriate adult and detainee about the right to legal advice and record any reasons for waiving it in accordance with section 6.

1J Not used.

1K This Code does not affect the principle that all citizens have a duty to help police officers to prevent crime and discover offenders. This is a civic rather than a legal duty; but when police officers are trying to discover whether, or by whom, offences have been committed they are entitled to question any person from whom they think useful information can be obtained, subject to the restrictions imposed by this Code. A person's declaration that they are unwilling to reply does not alter this entitlement.

1L Paragraph 1.5 reflects the statutory definition of 'arrested juvenile' in section 37(15) of PACE. This section was amended by section 42 of the Criminal Justice and Courts Act 2015 with effect from 26 October 2015, and includes anyone who appears to be under the age of 18. This definition applies for the purposes of the detention and bail provisions in sections 34 to 51 of PACE.

1M Not used.

2 Custody records

2.1A When a person:

- is brought to a police station under arrest
- is arrested at the police station having attended there voluntarily or attends a police station to answer bail

they must be brought before the custody officer as soon as practicable after their arrival at the station or if applicable, following their arrest after attending the police station voluntarily. This applies to both designated and non-designated police stations. A person is deemed to be 'at a police station' for these purposes if they are within the boundary of any building or enclosed yard which forms part of that police station.

2.1 A separate custody record must be opened as soon as practicable for each person brought to a police station under arrest or arrested at the station having gone there voluntarily or attending a police station in answer to street bail. All information recorded under this Code must be recorded as soon as practicable in the custody record unless otherwise specified. Any audio or video recording made in the custody area is not part of the custody record.

2.2 If any action requires the authority of an officer of a specified rank, subject to *paragraph 2.6A*, their name and rank must be noted in the custody record.

2.3 The custody officer is responsible for the custody record's accuracy and completeness and for making sure the record or copy of the record accompanies a detainee if they are transferred to another police station. The record shall show the:

- time and reason for transfer;
- time a person is released from detention.

2.3A If a person is arrested and taken to a police station as a result of a search in the exercise of any stop and search power to which PACE Code A (Stop and search) or the 'search powers code' issued under TACT applies, the officer carrying out the search is responsible for ensuring that the record of that stop and search is made as part of the person's custody record. The custody officer must then ensure that the person is asked if they want a copy of the search record and if they do, that they are given a copy as soon as practicable. The person's entitlement to a copy of the search record which is made as part of their custody record is in addition to, and does not affect, their entitlement to a copy of their custody record or any other provisions of section 2 (Custody records) of this Code. (See Code A *paragraph 4.2B* and the TACT search powers code *paragraph 5.3.5*).

2.4 The detainee's solicitor and appropriate adult must be permitted to inspect the whole of the detainee's custody record as soon as practicable after their arrival at the station and at any other time on request, whilst the person is detained. This includes the following *specific* records relating to the reasons for the detainee's arrest and detention and the offence concerned to which *paragraph 3.1(b)* refers:

(a) The information about the circumstances and reasons for the detainee's arrest as recorded in the custody record in accordance with *paragraph 4.3 of Code G*. This applies to any further offences for which the detainee is arrested whilst in custody;
(b) The record of the grounds for each authorisation to keep the person in custody. The authorisations to which this applies are the same as those described at items *(i)(a)* to *(d)* in the table in *paragraph 2* of *Annex M* of this Code.

Access to the records in *sub-paragraphs (a)* and *(b)* is *in addition* to the requirements in *paragraphs 3.4(b), 11.1A, 15.0, 15,7A(c) and 16.7A* to make certain documents and materials available and to provide information about the offence and the reasons for arrest and detention.

Access to the custody record for the purposes of this paragraph must be arranged and agreed with the custody officer and may not unreasonably interfere with the custody officer's duties. A record shall be made when access is allowed and whether it includes the records described in *sub-paragraphs (a)* and *(b)* above.

2.4A When a detainee leaves police detention or is taken before a court they, their legal representative or appropriate adult shall be given, on request, a copy of the custody record as soon as practicable. This entitlement lasts for 12 months after release.

2.5 The detainee, appropriate adult or legal representative shall be permitted to inspect the original custody record after the detainee has left police detention provided they give reasonable notice of their request. Any such inspection shall be noted in the custody record.

2.6 Subject to *paragraph 2.6A*, all entries in custody records must be timed and signed by the maker. Records entered on computer shall be timed and contain the operator's identification.

2.6A Nothing in this Code requires the identity of officers or other police staff to be recorded or disclosed:

(a) *Not used.*
(b) if the officer or police staff reasonably believe recording or disclosing their name might put them in danger.

In these cases, they shall use their warrant or other identification numbers and the name of their police station. See *Note 2A*.

2.7 The fact and time of any detainee's refusal to sign a custody record, when asked in accordance with this Code, must be recorded.

Note for Guidance

2A The purpose of paragraph 2.6A(b) is to protect those involved in serious organised crime investigations or arrests of particularly violent suspects when there is reliable information that those arrested or their associates may threaten or cause harm to those involved. In cases of doubt, an officer of inspector rank or above should be consulted.

3 Initial action

(a) Detained persons—normal procedure

3.1 When a person is brought to a police station under arrest or arrested at the station having gone there voluntarily, the custody officer must make sure the person is told clearly about:

(a) the following continuing rights, which may be exercised at any stage during the period in custody:
   (i) their right to consult privately with a solicitor and that free independent legal advice is available as in *section 6*;
   (ii) their right to have someone informed of their arrest as in *section 5*;
   (iii) their right to consult the Codes of Practice (see *Note 3D*); and
   (iv) if applicable, their right to interpretation and translation (see *paragraph 3.12*) and their right to communicate with their High Commission, Embassy or Consulate (see *paragraph 3.12A*).
(b) their right to be informed about the offence and (as the case may be) any further offences for which they are arrested whilst in custody and why they have been arrested

and detained in accordance with *paragraphs 2.4, 3.4(a)* and *11.1A* of this Code and *paragraph 3.3* of *Code G.*

3.2 The detainee must also be given a written notice, which contains information:

(a) to allow them to exercise their rights by setting out:

(i) their rights under paragraph 3.1, paragraph 3.12 and 3.12A;

(ii) the arrangements for obtaining legal advice, see section 6;

(iii) their right to a copy of the custody record as in paragraph 2.4A;

(iv) their right to remain silent as set out in the caution in the terms prescribed in section 10;

(v) their right to have access to materials and documents which are essential to effectively challenging the lawfulness of their arrest and detention for any offence and (as the case may be) any further offences for which they are arrested whilst in custody, in accordance with *paragraphs 3.4(b), 15.0, 15.7A(c)* and *16.7A* of this Code;

(vi) the maximum period for which they may be kept in police detention without being charged, when detention must be reviewed and when release is required;

(vii) their right to medical assistance in accordance with *section 9* of this Code;

(viii) their right, if they are prosecuted, to have access to the evidence in the case before their trial in accordance with the Criminal Procedure and Investigations Act 1996, the Attorney General's Guidelines on Disclosure, the common law and the Criminal Procedure Rules; and

(b) briefly setting out their other entitlements while in custody, by:

(i) mentioning:

~ the provisions relating to the conduct of interviews;

~ the circumstances in which an appropriate adult should be available to assist the detainee and their statutory rights to make representations whenever the need for their detention is reviewed;

(ii) listing the entitlements in this Code, concerning;

~ reasonable standards of physical comfort;

~ adequate food and drink;

~ access to toilets and washing facilities, clothing, medical attention, and exercise when practicable.

See Note 3A.

3.2A The detainee must be given an opportunity to read the notice and shall be asked to sign the custody record to acknowledge receipt of the notice. Any refusal to sign must be recorded on the custody record.

3.3 *Not used.*

3.3A An 'easy read' illustrated version should also be provided if available (see *Note 3A*).

3.4 (a) The custody officer shall:

- record the offence(s) that the detainee has been arrested for and the reason(s) for the arrest on the custody record. See *paragraph 10.3 and Code G paragraphs 2.2 and 4.3*;
- note on the custody record any comment the detainee makes in relation to the arresting officer's account but shall not invite comment. If the arresting officer is not physically present when the detainee is brought to a police station, the arresting officer's account must be made available to the custody officer remotely or by a third party on the arresting officer's behalf. If the custody officer authorises a person's detention, subject to *paragraph 1.8*, that officer must record the grounds for detention in the detainee's presence and at the same time, inform them of the grounds. The detainee must be informed of the grounds for their detention before they are questioned about any offence;

- note any comment the detainee makes in respect of the decision to detain them but shall not invite comment;
- not put specific questions to the detainee regarding their involvement in any offence, nor in respect of any comments they may make in response to the arresting officer's account or the decision to place them in detention. Such an exchange is likely to constitute an interview as in *paragraph 11.1A* and require the associated safeguards in *section 11*.

Note: This *sub-paragraph* also applies to any further offences and grounds for detention which come to light whilst the person is detained.

See *paragraph 11.13* in respect of unsolicited comments.

(b) Documents and materials which are essential to effectively challenging the lawfulness of the detainee's arrest and detention must be made available to the detainee or their solicitor. Documents and materials will be 'essential' for this purpose if they are capable of undermining the reasons and grounds which make the detainee's arrest and detention necessary. The decision about whether particular documents or materials must be made available for the purpose of this requirement therefore rests with the custody officer who determines whether detention is necessary, in consultation with the investigating officer who has the knowledge of the documents and materials in a particular case necessary to inform that decision. A note should be made in the detainee's custody record of the *fact* that documents or materials have been made available under this sub-paragraph and when. The investigating officer should make a separate note of what is made available and how it is made available in a particular case. This sub-paragraph also applies (with modifications) for the purposes of *sections 15 (Reviews and extensions of detention)* and *16 (Charging detained persons)*. See *Note 3ZA* and *paragraphs 15.0* and *16.7A*.

3.5 The custody officer or other custody staff as directed by the custody officer shall:

(a) ask the detainee whether at this time, they:

(i) would like legal advice, see *paragraph 6.5*;

(ii) want someone informed of their detention, see *section 5*;

(b) ask the detainee to sign the custody record to confirm their decisions in respect of *(a)*;

(c) determine whether the detainee:

(i) is, or might be, in need of medical treatment or attention, see *section 9*;

(ii) requires:

- an appropriate adult (see *paragraphs 1.4, 1.5, 1.5A* and *3.15)*; help to check documentation (see *paragraph 3.20*);
- an interpreter (see *paragraph 3.12 and Note 13B)*.

(d) record the decision in respect of (c).

Where any duties under this paragraph have been carried out by custody staff at the direction of the custody officer, the outcomes shall, as soon as practicable, be reported to the custody officer who retains overall responsibility for the detainee's care and treatment and ensuring that it complies with this Code. See *Note 3F*.

3.6 When the needs mentioned in *paragraph 3.5(c)* are being determined, the custody officer is responsible for initiating an assessment to consider whether the detainee is likely to present specific risks to custody staff, any individual who may have contact with detainee (e.g. legal advisers, medical staff) or themselves. This risk assessment must include the taking of reasonable steps to establish the detainee's identity and to obtain information about the detainee that is relevant to their safe custody, security and welfare and risks to others. Such assessments should therefore always include a check on the Police National Computer (PNC), to be carried out as soon as practicable, to identify any risks that have been highlighted in relation to the detainee. Although such assessments are primarily the custody officer's responsibility, it may be necessary for them to consult and involve others, e.g. the arresting officer or an appropriate healthcare professional, see *paragraph 9.13*. Other records held by or on behalf of the police and other UK law enforcement authorities that might provide information relevant to the detainee's safe custody, security and welfare and risk to others and to confirming their identity should also be checked. Reasons for delaying the initiation or completion of the assessment must be recorded.

3.7 Chief officers should ensure that arrangements for proper and effective risk assessments required by *paragraph 3.6* are implemented in respect of all detainees at police stations in their area.

3.8 Risk assessments must follow a structured process which clearly defines the categories of risk to be considered and the results must be incorporated in the detainee's custody record. The custody officer is responsible for making sure those responsible for the detainee's custody are appropriately briefed about the risks. If no specific risks are identified by the assessment, that should be noted in the custody record. See *Note 3E* and *paragraph 9.14*.

3.8A The content of any risk assessment and any analysis of the level of risk relating to the person's detention is not required to be shown or provided to the detainee or any person acting on behalf of the detainee. But information should not be withheld from any person acting on the detainee's behalf, for example, an appropriate adult, solicitor or interpreter, if to do so might put that person at risk.

3.9 The custody officer is responsible for implementing the response to any specific risk assessment, e.g.:

- reducing opportunities for self harm;
- calling an appropriate healthcare professional; increasing levels of monitoring or observation;
- reducing the risk to those who come into contact with the detainee. See *Note 3E*.

3.10 Risk assessment is an ongoing process and assessments must always be subject to review if circumstances change.

3.11 If video cameras are installed in the custody area, notices shall be prominently displayed showing cameras are in use. Any request to have video cameras switched off shall be refused.

(b) Detained persons—special groups

3.12 If the detainee appears to be someone who does not speak or understand English or who has a hearing or speech impediment, the custody officer must ensure:

(a) that without delay, arrangements (*see* paragraph 13.1ZA) are made for the detainee to have the assistance of an interpreter in the action under *paragraphs 3.1* to *3.5*. If the person appears to have a hearing or speech impediment, the reference to 'interpreter' includes appropriate assistance necessary to comply with *paragraphs 3.1* to 3.5. See paragraph 13.1C if the detainee is in Wales. See section 13 and Note 13B;

(b) that in addition to the continuing rights set out in *paragraph 3.1(a)(i)* to *(iv)*, the detainee is told clearly about their right to interpretation and translation;

(c) that the written notice given to the detainee in accordance with *paragraph 3.2* is in a language the detainee understands and includes the right to interpretation and translation together with information about the provisions in *section 13* and *Annex M*, which explain how the right applies (see *Note 3A*); and

(d) that if the translation of the notice is not available, the information in the notice is given through an interpreter and a written translation provided without undue delay.

3.12A If the detainee is a citizen of an independent Commonwealth country or a national of a foreign country, including the Republic of Ireland, the custody officer must ensure that in addition to the continuing rights set out in *paragraph 3.1(a)(i)* to *(iv)*, they are informed as soon as practicable about their rights of communication with their High Commission, Embassy or Consulate set out in *section 7*. This right must be included in the written notice given to the detainee in accordance with *paragraph 3.2*.

3.13 If the detainee is a juvenile, the custody officer must, if it is practicable, ascertain the identity of a person responsible for their welfare. That person:

- may be:
  - ~ the parent or guardian;

~ if the juvenile is in local authority or voluntary organisation care, or is otherwise being looked after under the Children Act 1989, a person appointed by that authority or organisation to have responsibility for the juvenile's welfare;
~ any other person who has, for the time being, assumed responsibility for the juvenile's welfare.

- must be informed as soon as practicable that the juvenile has been arrested, why they have been arrested and where they are detained. This right is in addition to the juvenile's right in *section 5* not to be held incommunicado. See *Note 3C*.

3.14 If a juvenile is known to be subject to a court order under which a person or organisation is given any degree of statutory responsibility to supervise or otherwise monitor them, reasonable steps must also be taken to notify that person or organisation (the 'responsible officer'). The responsible officer will normally be a member of a Youth Offending Team, except for a curfew order which involves electronic monitoring when the contractor providing the monitoring will normally be the responsible officer.

3.15 If the detainee is a juvenile, mentally disordered or otherwise mentally vulnerable, the custody officer must, as soon as practicable:

- inform the appropriate adult, who in the case of a juvenile may or may not be a person responsible for their welfare, as in *paragraph 3.13*, of:
  ~ the grounds for their detention;
  ~ their whereabouts.
- ask the adult to come to the police station to see the detainee.

3.16 It is imperative that a mentally disordered or otherwise mentally vulnerable person, detained under the Mental Health Act 1983, section 136, be assessed as soon as possible. A police station should only be used as a place of safety as a last resort but if that assessment is to take place at the police station, an approved mental health professional and a registered medical practitioner shall be called to the station as soon as possible to carry it out. See *Note 9D*. The appropriate adult has no role in the assessment process and their presence is not required. Once the detainee has been assessed and suitable arrangements made for their treatment or care, they can no longer be detained under section 136. A detainee must be immediately discharged from detention under section 136 if a registered medical practitioner, having examined them, concludes they are not mentally disordered within the meaning of the Act.

3.17 If the appropriate adult is:

- already at the police station, the provisions of *paragraphs 3.1* to *3.5* must be complied with in the appropriate adult's presence;
- not at the station when these provisions are complied with, they must be complied with again in the presence of the appropriate adult when they arrive,

and a copy of the notice given to the detainee in accordance with *paragraph 3.2*, shall also be given to the appropriate adult.

3.18 The detainee shall be advised that:

- the duties of the appropriate adult include giving advice and assistance;
- they can consult privately with the appropriate adult at any time.

3.19 If the detainee, or appropriate adult on the detainee's behalf, asks for a solicitor to be called to give legal advice, the provisions of *section 6* apply.

3.20 If the detainee is blind, seriously visually impaired or unable to read, the custody officer shall make sure their solicitor, relative, appropriate adult or some other person likely to take an interest in them and not involved in the investigation is available to help check any documentation. When this Code requires written consent or signing the person assisting may be asked to sign instead, if the detainee prefers. This paragraph does not require an appropriate adult to be called solely to assist in checking and signing documentation for a person who is not a juvenile, or mentally disordered or otherwise mentally vulnerable (see *paragraph 3.15* and *Note 13C*).

3.20A The Children and Young Persons Act 1933, section 31, requires that arrangements must be made for ensuring that a girl under the age of 18, while detained in a police station, is under the care of a woman. See *Note 3G*. It also requires that arrangements must be made for preventing any person under 18, while being detained in a police station, from associating with an adult charged with any offence, unless that adult is a relative or the adult is jointly charged with the same offence as the person under 18.

(c) Persons attending a police station or elsewhere voluntarily

3.21 Anybody attending a police station or other location (see *paragraph 3.22*) voluntarily to assist police with the investigation of an offence may leave at will unless arrested. See *Note 1K*. The person may only be prevented from leaving at will if their arrest on suspicion of committing the offence is necessary in accordance with Code G. See *Code G Note 2G*.

(a) If during an interview it is decided that their arrest is necessary, they must:
- be informed at once that they are under arrest and of the grounds and reasons as required by *Code G*, and
- be brought before the custody officer at the police station where they are arrested or, as the case may be, at the police station to which they are taken after being arrested elsewhere. The custody officer is then responsible for making sure that a custody record is opened and that they are notified of their rights in the same way as other detainees as required by this Code.

(b) If they are not arrested but are cautioned as in *section 10*, the person who gives the caution must, at the same time, inform them they are not under arrest and they are not obliged to remain at the station or other location, but if they agree to remain, they may obtain free and independent legal advice if they want. They shall also be given a copy of the notice explaining the arrangements for obtaining legal advice and told that the right to legal advice includes the right to speak with a solicitor on the telephone and be asked if they want advice. If advice is requested, the interviewer is responsible for securing its provision without delay by contacting the Defence Solicitor Call Centre. The interviewer is responsible for confirming that the suspect has given their agreement to be interviewed voluntarily. In the case of a juvenile or mentally vulnerable suspect, this must be given in the presence of the appropriate adult and for a juvenile, the agreement of a parent or guardian of the juvenile is also required. The interviewer must ensure that other provisions of this Code and Codes E and F concerning the conduct and recording of interviews of suspects and the rights and entitlements and safeguards for suspects who have been arrested and detained are followed insofar as they can be applied to suspects who are not under arrest. This includes:
- informing them of the offence and, as the case may be, any further offences, they are suspected of and the grounds and reasons for that suspicion and their right to be so informed (see *paragraph 3.1(b)*);
- the caution as required in *section 10*;
- determining whether they require an appropriate adult and help to check documentation (see *paragraph 3.5(c)(ii)*); and
- determining whether they require an interpreter and the provision of interpretation and translation services and informing them of that right. See *paragraphs 3.1(a)(iv), 3.5(c)(ii)* and *3.12, Note 6B* and *section 13*.

but does not include any requirement to provide a written notice in addition to that above which concerns the arrangements for obtaining legal advice.

3.22 If the other location mentioned in *paragraph 3.21* is any place or premises for which the interviewer requires the person's informed consent to remain, for example, the person's home, then the references that the person is 'not obliged to remain' and that they 'may leave at will' mean that the person may also withdraw their consent and require the interviewer to leave.

(d) Documentation

3.23 The grounds for a person's detention shall be recorded, in the person's presence if practicable. See *paragraph 1.8*.

3.24 Action taken under *paragraphs 3.12* to *3.20* shall be recorded.

(e) Persons answering street bail

3.25 When a person is answering street bail, the custody officer should link any documentation held in relation to arrest with the custody record. Any further action shall be recorded on the custody record in accordance with paragraphs 3.23 and 3.24 above.

(f) Requirements for suspects to be informed of certain rights

3.26 The provisions of this section identify the information which must be given to suspects who have been cautioned in accordance with *section 10 of this Code* according to whether or not they have been arrested and detained. It includes information required by EU Directive 2012/13 on the right to information in criminal proceedings. If a complaint is made by or on behalf of such a suspect that the information and (as the case may be) access to records and documents has not been provided as required, the matter shall be reported to an inspector to deal with as a complaint for the purposes of *paragraph 9.2*, or *paragraph 12.9* if the challenge is made during an interview. This would include, for example:

(a) in the case of a detained suspect:
- not informing them of their rights (see *paragraph 3.1*);
- not giving them a copy of the Notice (see *paragraph 3.2(a)*);
- not providing an opportunity to read the notice (see *paragraph 3.2A*);
- not providing the required information (see *paragraphs 3.2(a), 3.12(b)* and, *3.12A*;
- not allowing access to the custody record (see *paragraph 2.4*);
- not providing a translation of the Notice (see *paragraph 3.12(c)* and *(d)*); and

(b) in the case of a suspect who is not detained:
- not informing them of their rights or providing the required information (see *paragraph 3.21(b)*).

Notes for Guidance

3ZA For the purposes of paragraphs 3.4(b) and 15.0:

(a) Investigating officers are responsible for bringing to the attention of the officer who is responsible for authorising the suspect's detention or (as the case may be) continued detention (before or after charge), any documents and materials in their possession or control which appear to undermine the need to keep the suspect in custody. In accordance with Part IV of PACE, this officer will be either the custody officer, the officer reviewing the need for detention before or after charge (PACE, section 40), or the officer considering the need to extend detention without charge from 24 to 36 hours (PACE, section 42) who is then responsible for determining, which, if any, of those documents and materials are capable of undermining the need to detain the suspect and must therefore be made available to the suspect or their solicitor.

(b) the way in which documents and materials are 'made available', is a matter for the investigating officer to determine on a case by case basis and having regard to the nature and volume of the documents and materials involved. For example, they may be made available by supplying a copy or allowing supervised access to view. However, for view only access, it will be necessary to demonstrate that sufficient time is allowed for the suspect and solicitor to view and consider the documents and materials in question.

3A For access to currently available notices, including 'easy-read' versions, see https://www.gov.uk/guidance/notice-of-rights-and-entitlements-a-persons-rights-in-police-detention.

3B Not used.

3C If the juvenile is in local authority or voluntary organisation care but living with their parents or other adults responsible for their welfare, although there is no legal obligation to inform them, they should normally be contacted, as well as the authority or organisation unless they are suspected of involvement in the offence concerned. Even if the juvenile is not living with their parents, consideration should be given to informing them.

3D The right to consult the Codes of Practice does not entitle the person concerned to delay unreasonably any necessary investigative or administrative action whilst they do so. Examples of action which need not be delayed unreasonably include:

- *procedures requiring the provision of breath, blood or urine specimens under the Road Traffic Act 1988 or the Transport and Works Act 1992;*
- *searching detainees at the police station;*
- *taking fingerprints, footwear impressions or non-intimate samples without consent for evidential purposes.*

3E The Detention and Custody Authorised Professional Practice (APP) produced by the College of Policing (see http://www.app.college.police.uk) provides more detailed guidance on risk assessments and identifies key risk areas which should always be considered. See Home Office Circular 34/2007 (Safety of solicitors and probationary representatives at police stations).

3F A custody officer or other officer who, in accordance with this Code, allows or directs the carrying out of any task or action relating to a detainee's care, treatment, rights and entitlements to another officer or any other person, must be satisfied that the officer or person concerned is suitable, trained and competent to carry out the task or action in question.

3G Guidance for police officers and police staff on the operational application of section 31 of the Children and Young Persons Act 1933 has been published by the College of Policing and is available at: https://www.app.college.police.uk/app-content/detention-and-custody-2/detainee-care/children-and-young-persons/#girls.

4 Detainee's property

(a) Action

4.1 The custody officer is responsible for:

(a) ascertaining what property a detainee:

(i) has with them when they come to the police station, whether on: arrest or re-detention on answering to bail;

- commitment to prison custody on the order or sentence of a court;
- lodgement at the police station with a view to their production in court from prison custody;
- transfer from detention at another station or hospital;
- detention under the Mental Health Act 1983, section 135 or 136;
- remand into police custody on the authority of a court.

(ii) might have acquired for an unlawful or harmful purpose while in custody;

(b) the safekeeping of any property taken from a detainee which remains at the police station.

The custody officer may search the detainee or authorise their being searched to the extent they consider necessary, provided a search of intimate parts of the body or involving the removal of more than outer clothing is only made as in *Annex A*. A search may only be carried out by an officer of the same sex as the detainee. See *Note 4A* and *Annex L*.

4.2 Detainees may retain clothing and personal effects at their own risk unless the custody officer considers they may use them to cause harm to themselves or others, interfere with evidence, damage property, effect an escape or they are needed as evidence. In this event the custody officer may withhold such articles as they consider necessary and must tell the detainee why.

4.3 Personal effects are those items a detainee may lawfully need, use or refer to while in detention but do not include cash and other items of value.

(b) Documentation

4.4 It is a matter for the custody officer to determine whether a record should be made of the property a detained person has with him or had taken from him on arrest. Any record made is not required to be kept as part of the custody record but the custody record should be noted as to where such a record exists and that record shall be treated as being part of the custody record for the purpose of this and any other Code of Practice (see *paragraphs 2.4, 2.4A* and *2.5*). Whenever a record is made the detainee shall be allowed to check and sign the record of property as correct. Any refusal to sign shall be recorded.

4.5 If a detainee is not allowed to keep any article of clothing or personal effects, the reason must be recorded.

Notes for Guidance

4A PACE, Section 54(1) and paragraph 4.1 require a detainee to be searched when it is clear the custody officer will have continuing duties in relation to that detainee or when that detainee's behaviour or offence makes an inventory appropriate. They do not require every detainee to be searched, e.g. if it is clear a person will only be detained for a short period and is not to be placed in a cell, the custody officer may decide not to search them. In such a case the custody record will be endorsed 'not searched', paragraph 4.4 will not apply, and the detainee will be invited to sign the entry. If the detainee refuses, the custody officer will be obliged to ascertain what property they have in accordance with paragraph 4.1.

4B Paragraph 4.4 does not require the custody officer to record on the custody record property in the detainee's possession on arrest if, by virtue of its nature, quantity or size, it is not practicable to remove it to the police station.

4C Paragraph 4.4 does not require items of clothing worn by the person to be recorded unless withheld by the custody officer as in paragraph 4.2.

5 Right not to be held incommunicado

(a) Action

5.1 Subject to *paragraph 5.7B*, any person arrested and held in custody at a police station or other premises may, on request, have one person known to them or likely to take an interest in their welfare informed at public expense of their whereabouts as soon as practicable. If the person cannot be contacted the detainee may choose up to two alternatives. If they cannot be contacted, the person in charge of detention or the investigation has discretion to allow further attempts until the information has been conveyed. See *Notes 5C* and *5D*.

5.2 The exercise of the above right in respect of each person nominated may be delayed only in accordance with *Annex B*.

5.3 The above right may be exercised each time a detainee is taken to another police station.

5.4 If the detainee agrees, they may at the custody officer's discretion, receive visits from friends, family or others likely to take an interest in their welfare, or in whose welfare the detainee has an interest. See *Note 5B*.

5.5 If a friend, relative or person with an interest in the detainee's welfare enquires about their whereabouts, this information shall be given if the suspect agrees and *Annex B* does not apply. See *Note 5D*.

5.6 The detainee shall be given writing materials, on request, and allowed to telephone one person for a reasonable time, see *Notes 5A* and *5E*. Either or both of these privileges may be denied or delayed if an officer of inspector rank or above considers sending a letter or making a telephone call may result in any of the consequences in:

(a) *Annex B paragraphs 1* and *2* and the person is detained in connection with an indictable offence;

(b) *Not used*.

Nothing in this paragraph permits the restriction or denial of the rights in *paragraphs 5.1* and *6.1*.

5.7 Before any letter or message is sent, or telephone call made, the detainee shall be informed that what they say in any letter, call or message (other than in a communication to a solicitor) may be read or listened to and may be given in evidence. A telephone call may be terminated if it is being abused. The costs can be at public expense at the custody officer's discretion.

5.7A Any delay or denial of the rights in this section should be proportionate and should last no longer than necessary.

5.7B In the case of a person in police custody for specific purposes and periods in accordance with a direction under the Crime (Sentences) Act 1997, Schedule 1 (productions from prison etc.), the exercise of the rights in this section shall be subject to any additional conditions specified in the direction for the purpose of regulating the detainee's contact and communication with others whilst in police custody. See *Note 5F*.

(b) Documentation

5.8 A record must be kept of any:

(a) request made under this section and the action taken;

(b) letters, messages or telephone calls made or received or visit received;

(c) refusal by the detainee to have information about them given to an outside enquirer. The detainee must be asked to countersign the record accordingly and any refusal recorded.

Notes for Guidance

5A A person may request an interpreter to interpret a telephone call or translate a letter.

5B At the custody officer's discretion and subject to the detainee's consent, visits should be allowed when possible, subject to having sufficient personnel to supervise a visit and any possible hindrance to the investigation.

5C If the detainee does not know anyone to contact for advice or support or cannot contact a friend or relative, the custody officer should bear in mind any local voluntary bodies or other organisations who might be able to help. Paragraph 6.1 applies if legal advice is required.

5D In some circumstances it may not be appropriate to use the telephone to disclose information under paragraphs 5.1 and 5.5.

5E The telephone call at paragraph 5.6 is in addition to any communication under paragraphs 5.1 and 6.1.

5F Prison Service Instruction 26/2012 (Production of Prisoners at the Request of Warranted Law Enforcement Agencies) provides detailed guidance and instructions for police officers and Governors and Directors of Prisons regarding applications for prisoners to be transferred to police custody and their safe custody and treatment while in police custody.

6 Right to legal advice

(a) Action

6.1 Unless *Annex B* applies, all detainees must be informed that they may at any time consult and communicate privately with a solicitor, whether in person, in writing or by telephone, and that free independent legal advice is available. See *paragraph 3.1, Notes 1I, 6B and 6J*

6.2 *Not used.*

6.3 A poster advertising the right to legal advice must be prominently displayed in the charging area of every police station. See *Note 6H*.

6.4 No police officer should, at any time, do or say anything with the intention of dissuading any person who is entitled to legal advice in accordance with this Code, whether or not they have been arrested and are detained, from obtaining legal advice. See *Note 6ZA*.

6.5 The exercise of the right of access to legal advice may be delayed only as in *Annex B*. Whenever legal advice is requested, and unless *Annex B* applies, the custody officer must act without delay to secure the provision of such advice. If the detainee has the right to speak to a solicitor in person but declines to exercise the right the officer should point out that the right includes the right to speak with a solicitor on the telephone. If the detainee continues to waive this right, or a detainee whose right to free legal advice is limited to telephone advice from the Criminal Defence Service (CDS) Direct (*see Note 6B*) declines to exercise that right, the officer should ask them why and any reasons should be recorded on the custody record or the interview record as appropriate. Reminders of the right to legal advice must be given as in *paragraphs 3.5, 11.2, 15.4, 16.4, 16.5, 2B of Annex A, 3 of Annex K* and *5 of Annex M* of this Code and Code D, *paragraphs 3.17(ii)* and *6.3*. Once it is clear a detainee does not want to speak to a solicitor in person or by telephone they should cease to be asked their reasons. See *Note 6K*.

6.5A In the case of a person who is a juvenile or is mentally disordered or otherwise mentally vulnerable, an appropriate adult should consider whether legal advice from a solicitor is required. If such a detained person wants to exercise the right to legal advice, the appropriate action should be taken and should not be delayed until the appropriate adult arrives. If the person indicates that they do not want legal advice, the appropriate adult has the right to ask for a solicitor to attend if this would be in the best interests of the person. However, the person cannot be forced to see the solicitor if they are adamant that they do not wish to do so.

6.6 A detainee who wants legal advice may not be interviewed or continue to be interviewed until they have received such advice unless:

(a) *Annex B* applies, when the restriction on drawing adverse inferences from silence in *Annex C* will apply because the detainee is not allowed an opportunity to consult a solicitor; or

(b) an officer of superintendent rank or above has reasonable grounds for believing that:

(i) the consequent delay might:

- lead to interference with, or harm to, evidence connected with an offence; lead to interference with, or physical harm to, other people;
- lead to serious loss of, or damage to, property;
- lead to alerting other people suspected of having committed an offence but not yet arrested for it;
- hinder the recovery of property obtained in consequence of the commission of an offence.

See *Note 6A*

(ii) when a solicitor, including a duty solicitor, has been contacted and has agreed to attend, awaiting their arrival would cause unreasonable delay to the process of investigation.

Note: In these cases the restriction on drawing adverse inferences from silence in *Annex C* will apply because the detainee is not allowed an opportunity to consult a solicitor.

(c) the solicitor the detainee has nominated or selected from a list:

(i) cannot be contacted;

(ii) has previously indicated they do not wish to be contacted; or

(iii) having been contacted, has declined to attend; and

- the detainee has been advised of the Duty Solicitor Scheme but has declined to ask for the duty solicitor;
- in these circumstances the interview may be started or continued without further delay provided an officer of inspector rank or above has agreed to the interview proceeding.

Note: The restriction on drawing adverse inferences from silence in *Annex C* will not apply because the detainee is allowed an opportunity to consult the duty solicitor;

(d) the detainee changes their mind about wanting legal advice or (as the case may be) about wanting a solicitor present at the interview and states that they no longer wish to speak to a solicitor. In these circumstances, the interview may be started or continued without delay provided that:

(i) an officer of inspector rank or above:

- speaks to the detainee to enquire about the reasons for their change of mind (see *Note 6K*), and
- makes, or directs the making of, reasonable efforts to ascertain the solicitor's expected time of arrival and to inform the solicitor that the suspect has stated that they wish to change their mind and the reason (if given);

(ii) the detainee's reason for their change of mind (if given) and the outcome of the action in (i) are recorded in the custody record;

(iii) the detainee, after being informed of the outcome of the action in (i) above, confirms in writing that they want the interview to proceed without speaking or further speaking to a solicitor or (as the case may be) without a solicitor being present and do not wish to wait for a solicitor by signing an entry to this effect in the custody record;

(iv) an officer of inspector rank or above is satisfied that it is proper for the interview to proceed in these circumstances and:

- gives authority in writing for the interview to proceed and, if the authority is not recorded in the custody record, the officer must ensure that the custody record shows the date and time of the authority and where it is recorded, and
- takes, or directs the taking of, reasonable steps to inform the solicitor that the authority has been given and the time when the interview is expected to commence and records or causes to be recorded, the outcome of this action in the custody record.

(v) When the interview starts and the interviewer reminds the suspect of their right to legal advice (see *paragraph 11.2*, Code E *paragraph 4.5* and Code F *paragraph 4.5*), the interviewer shall then ensure that the following is recorded in the written interview record or the interview record made in accordance with Code E or F:

- confirmation that the detainee has changed their mind about wanting legal advice or (as the case may be) about wanting a solicitor present and the reasons for it if given;
- the fact that authority for the interview to proceed has been given and, subject to *paragraph 2.6A,* the name of the authorising officer;
- that if the solicitor arrives at the station before the interview is completed, the detainee will be so informed without delay and *a break will be taken* to allow them to speak to the solicitor if they wish, unless *paragraph 6.6(a)* applies, and
- that at any time during the interview, the detainee may again ask for legal advice and that if they do, a break will be taken to allow them to speak to the solicitor, unless *paragraph 6.6(a), (b), or (c)* applies.

Note: In these circumstances, the restriction on drawing adverse inferences from silence in *Annex C* will not apply because the detainee is allowed an opportunity to consult a solicitor if they wish.

6.7 If *paragraph 6.6(a)* applies, where the reason for authorising the delay ceases to apply, there may be no further delay in permitting the exercise of the right in the absence of a further authorisation unless *paragraph 6.6(b), (c)* or *(d)* applies. If *paragraph 6.6(b)(i)* applies, once sufficient information has been obtained to avert the risk, questioning must cease until the detainee has received legal advice unless *paragraph 6.6(a), (b)(ii), (c)* or *(d)* applies.

6.8 A detainee who has been permitted to consult a solicitor shall be entitled on request to have the solicitor present when they are interviewed unless one of the exceptions in *paragraph 6.6* applies.

6.9 The solicitor may only be required to leave the interview if their conduct is such that the interviewer is unable properly to put questions to the suspect. See *Notes 6D* and *6E.*

6.10 If the interviewer considers a solicitor is acting in such a way, they will stop the interview and consult an officer not below superintendent rank, if one is readily available, and otherwise an officer not below inspector rank not connected with the investigation. After speaking to the solicitor, the officer consulted will decide if the interview should continue in the presence of that solicitor. If they decide it should not, the suspect will be given the opportunity to consult another solicitor before the interview continues and that solicitor given an opportunity to be present at the interview. *See Note 6E.*

6.11 The removal of a solicitor from an interview is a serious step and, if it occurs, the officer of superintendent rank or above who took the decision will consider if the incident should be reported to the Solicitors Regulatory Authority. If the decision to remove the solicitor has been taken by an officer below superintendent rank, the facts must be reported to an officer of superintendent rank or above, who will similarly consider whether a report to the Solicitors Regulatory Authority would be appropriate. When the solicitor concerned is a duty solicitor, the report should be both to the Solicitors Regulatory Authority and to the Legal Aid Agency.

6.12 'Solicitor' in this Code means:

- a solicitor who holds a current practising certificate;
- an accredited or probationary representative included on the register of representatives maintained by the Legal Aid Agency.

6.12A An accredited or probationary representative sent to provide advice by, and on behalf of, a solicitor shall be admitted to the police station for this purpose unless an officer of inspector rank or above considers such a visit will hinder the investigation and directs otherwise. Hindering the investigation does not include giving proper legal advice to a detainee as in *Note 6D*. Once admitted to the police station, *paragraphs 6.6* to *6.10* apply.

6.13 In exercising their discretion under *paragraph 6.12A*, the officer should take into account in particular:

- whether:
  - ~ the identity and status of an accredited or probationary representative have been satisfactorily established;
  - ~ they are of suitable character to provide legal advice, e.g. a person with a criminal record is unlikely to be suitable unless the conviction was for a minor offence and not recent.
- any other matters in any written letter of authorisation provided by the solicitor on whose behalf the person is attending the police station. See *Note 6F*.

6.14 If the inspector refuses access to an accredited or probationary representative or a decision is taken that such a person should not be permitted to remain at an interview, the inspector must notify the solicitor on whose behalf the representative was acting and give them an opportunity to make alternative arrangements. The detainee must be informed and the custody record noted.

6.15 If a solicitor arrives at the station to see a particular person, that person must, unless *Annex B* applies, be so informed whether or not they are being interviewed and asked if they would like to see the solicitor. This applies even if the detainee has declined legal advice or, having requested it, subsequently agreed to be interviewed without receiving advice. The solicitor's attendance and the detainee's decision must be noted in the custody record.

(b) Documentation

6.16 Any request for legal advice and the action taken shall be recorded.

6.17 A record shall be made in the interview record if a detainee asks for legal advice and an interview is begun either in the absence of a solicitor or their representative, or they have been required to leave an interview.

Notes for Guidance

6ZA No police officer or police staff shall indicate to any suspect, except to answer a direct question, that the period for which they are liable to be detained, or if not detained, the time taken to complete the interview, might be reduced:

- *if they do not ask for legal advice or do not want a solicitor present when they are interviewed; or*
- *if they have asked for legal advice or (as the case may be) asked for a solicitor to be present when they are interviewed but change their mind and agree to be interviewed without waiting for a solicitor.*

6A In considering if paragraph 6.6(b) applies, the officer should, if practicable, ask the solicitor for an estimate of how long it will take to come to the station and relate this to the time detention is permitted, the time of day (i.e. whether the rest period under paragraph 12.2 is imminent) and the requirements of other investigations. If the solicitor is on their way or is to set off immediately, it will not normally be appropriate to begin an interview before they arrive. If it appears necessary to begin an interview before the solicitor's arrival, they should be given an indication of how long the police would be able to wait before 6.6(b) applies so there is an opportunity to make arrangements for someone else to provide legal advice.

6B A detainee has a right to free legal advice and to be represented by a solicitor. This Note for Guidance explains the arrangements which enable detainees to obtain legal advice. An outline of these arrangements is also included in the Notice of Rights and Entitlements given to detainees in accordance with paragraph 3.2. The arrangements also apply, with appropriate modifications, to persons attending a police station or other location voluntarily who are cautioned prior to being interviewed. See paragraph 3.21.

When a detainee asks for free legal advice, the Defence Solicitor Call Centre (DSCC) must be informed of the request.

Free legal advice will be limited to telephone advice provided by CDS Direct if a detainee is:

- *detained for a non-imprisonable offence;*
- *arrested on a bench warrant for failing to appear and being held for production at court (except where the solicitor has clear documentary evidence available that would result in the client being released from custody);*
- *arrested for drink driving (driving/in charge with excess alcohol, failing to provide a specimen, driving/in charge whilst unfit through drink), or*
- *detained in relation to breach of police or court bail conditions*

unless one or more exceptions apply, in which case the DSCC should arrange for advice to be given by a solicitor at the police station, for example:

- *the police want to interview the detainee or carry out an eye-witness identification procedure;*
- *the detainee needs an appropriate adult;*
- *the detainee is unable to communicate over the telephone;*
- *the detainee alleges serious misconduct by the police;*
- *the investigation includes another offence not included in the list,*
- *the solicitor to be assigned is already at the police station.*

When free advice is not limited to telephone advice, a detainee can ask for free advice from a solicitor they know or if they do not know a solicitor or the solicitor they know cannot be contacted, from the duty solicitor.

To arrange free legal advice, the police should telephone the DSCC. The call centre will decide whether legal advice should be limited to telephone advice from CDS Direct, or whether a solicitor known to the detainee or the duty solicitor should speak to the detainee.

When a detainee wants to pay for legal advice themselves:

- *the DSCC will contact a solicitor of their choice on their behalf;*
- *they may, when free advice is only available by telephone from CDS Direct, still speak to a solicitor of their choice on the telephone for advice, but the solicitor would not be paid by legal aid and may ask the person to pay for the advice;*
- *they should be given an opportunity to consult a specific solicitor or another solicitor from that solicitor's firm. If this solicitor is not available, they may choose up to two alternatives. If these alternatives are not available, the custody officer has discretion to allow further attempts until a solicitor has been contacted and agreed to provide advice;*
- *they are entitled to a private consultation with their chosen solicitor on the telephone or the solicitor may decide to come to the police station;*
- *If their chosen solicitor cannot be contacted, the DSCC may still be called to arrange free legal advice.*

Apart from carrying out duties necessary to implement these arrangements, an officer must not advise the suspect about any particular firm of solicitors.

6B1 Not used.

6B2 Not used.

6C Not used.

6D The solicitor's only role in the police station is to protect and advance the legal rights of their client. On occasions this may require the solicitor to give advice which has the effect of the client avoiding giving evidence which strengthens a prosecution case. The solicitor may intervene in order to seek clarification, challenge an improper question to their client or the manner in which it is put, advise their client not to reply to particular questions, or if they wish to give their client further legal advice. Paragraph 6.9 only applies if the solicitor's approach or conduct prevents or unreasonably obstructs proper questions being put to the suspect or the suspect's response being recorded. Examples of unacceptable conduct include answering questions on a suspect's behalf or providing written replies for the suspect to quote.

6E An officer who takes the decision to exclude a solicitor must be in a position to satisfy the court the decision was properly made. In order to do this they may need to witness what is happening.

6F If an officer of at least inspector rank considers a particular solicitor or firm of solicitors is persistently sending probationary representatives who are unsuited to provide legal advice, they should inform an officer of at least superintendent rank, who may wish to take the matter up with the Solicitors Regulation Authority.

6G Subject to the constraints of Annex B, a solicitor may advise more than one client in an investigation if they wish. Any question of a conflict of interest is for the solicitor under their professional code of conduct. If, however, waiting for a solicitor to give advice to one client may lead to unreasonable delay to the interview with another, the provisions of paragraph 6.6(b) may apply.

6H In addition to a poster in English, a poster or posters containing translations into Welsh, the main minority ethnic languages and the principal European languages should be displayed wherever they are likely to be helpful and it is practicable to do so.

6I Not used.

6J Whenever a detainee exercises their right to legal advice by consulting or communicating with a solicitor, they must be allowed to do so in private. This right to consult or communicate in private is fundamental. If the requirement for privacy is compromised because what is said or written by the detainee or solicitor for the purpose of giving and receiving legal advice is overheard, listened to, or read by others without the informed consent of the detainee, the right will effectively have been denied. When a detainee speaks to a solicitor on the telephone, they should be allowed to do so in private unless this is impractical because of the design and layout of the custody area or the location of telephones. However, the normal expectation should be that facilities will be available, unless they are being used, at all police stations to enable detainees to speak in private to a solicitor either face to face or over the telephone.

6K A detainee is not obliged to give reasons for declining legal advice and should not be pressed to do so.

7 Citizens of independent Commonwealth countries or foreign nationals

(a) Action

7.1 A detainee who is a citizen of an independent Commonwealth country or a national of a foreign country, including the Republic of Ireland, has the right, upon request, to communicate at any time with the appropriate High Commission, Embassy or Consulate. That detainee must be informed as soon as practicable of this right and asked if they want to have their High Commission, Embassy or Consulate told of their whereabouts and the grounds for their detention. Such a request should be acted upon as soon as practicable. See *Note 7A*.

7.2 A detainee who is a citizen of a country with which a bilateral consular convention or agreement is in force requiring notification of arrest must also be informed that subject to *paragraph 7.4*, notification of their arrest will be sent to the appropriate High Commission, Embassy or Consulate as soon as practicable, whether or not they request it. A list of the countries to which this requirement currently applies and contact details for the relevant High Commissions, Embassies and Consulates can be obtained from the Consular Directorate of the Foreign and Commonwealth Office (FCO) as follows:

- from the FCO web pages:
  - ~ *https://gov.uk/government/publications/table-of-consular-conventions-and-mandatory-notification-obligations, and*
  - ~ https://www.gov.uk/government/publications/foreign-embassies-in-the-uk
- by telephone to 020 7008 3100,

- by email to fcocorrespondence@fco.gov.uk.
- by letter to the Foreign and Commonwealth Office, King Charles Street, London, SW1A 2AH.

7.3 Consular officers may, if the detainee agrees, visit one of their nationals in police detention to talk to them and, if required, to arrange for legal advice. Such visits shall take place out of the hearing of a police officer.

7.4 Notwithstanding the provisions of consular conventions, if the detainee claims that they are a refugee or have applied or intend to apply for asylum, the custody officer must ensure that UK Visas and Immigration (UKVI) (formerly the UK Border Agency) is informed as soon as practicable of the claim. UKVI will then determine whether compliance with relevant international obligations requires notification of the arrest to be sent and will inform the custody officer as to what action police need to take.

(b) Documentation

7.5 A record shall be made:

- when a detainee is informed of their rights under this section and of any requirement in paragraph 7.2;
- of any communications with a High Commission, Embassy or Consulate, and
- of any communications with UKVI about a detainee's claim to be a refugee or to be seeking asylum and the resulting action taken by police.

Note for Guidance

7A The exercise of the rights in this section may not be interfered with even though Annex B applies.

8 Conditions of detention

(a) Action

8.1 So far as it is practicable, not more than one detainee should be detained in each cell. See *Note 8C*.

8.2 Cells in use must be adequately heated, cleaned and ventilated. They must be adequately lit, subject to such dimming as is compatible with safety and security to allow people detained overnight to sleep. No additional restraints shall be used within a locked cell unless absolutely necessary and then only restraint equipment, approved for use in that force by the chief officer, which is reasonable and necessary in the circumstances having regard to the detainee's demeanour and with a view to ensuring their safety and the safety of others. If a detainee is deaf, mentally disordered or otherwise mentally vulnerable, particular care must be taken when deciding whether to use any form of approved restraints.

8.3 Blankets, mattresses, pillows and other bedding supplied shall be of a reasonable standard and in a clean and sanitary condition. See *Note 8A*.

8.4 Access to toilet and washing facilities must be provided.

8.5 If it is necessary to remove a detainee's clothes for the purposes of investigation, for hygiene, health reasons or cleaning, replacement clothing of a reasonable standard of comfort and cleanliness shall be provided. A detainee may not be interviewed unless adequate clothing has been offered.

8.6 At least two light meals and one main meal should be offered in any 24-hour period. See *Note 8B*. Drinks should be provided at meal times and upon reasonable request between meals. Whenever necessary, advice shall be sought from the appropriate healthcare professional, see *Note 9A*, on medical and dietary matters. As far as practicable, meals provided shall offer a varied diet and meet any specific dietary needs or religious beliefs the detainee may have. The detainee may, at the custody officer's discretion, have meals supplied by their family or friends at their expense. See *Note 8A*.

8.7 Brief outdoor exercise shall be offered daily if practicable.

8.8 A juvenile shall not be placed in a police cell unless no other secure accommodation is available and the custody officer considers it is not practicable to supervise them if they are not placed in a cell or that a cell provides more comfortable accommodation than other secure accommodation in the station. A juvenile may not be placed in a cell with a detained adult.

(b) Documentation

8.9 A record must be kept of replacement clothing and meals offered.

8.10 If a juvenile is placed in a cell, the reason must be recorded.

8.11 The use of any restraints on a detainee whilst in a cell, the reasons for it and, if appropriate, the arrangements for enhanced supervision of the detainee whilst so restrained, shall be recorded. See paragraph 3.9.

Notes for Guidance

8A The provisions in paragraph 8.3 and 8.6 respectively are of particular importance in the case of a person likely to be detained for an extended period. In deciding whether to allow meals to be supplied by family or friends, the custody officer is entitled to take account of the risk of items being concealed in any food or package and the officer's duties and responsibilities under food handling legislation.

8B Meals should, so far as practicable, be offered at recognised meal times, or at other times that take account of when the detainee last had a meal.

8C The Detention and Custody Authorised Professional Practice (APP) produced by the College of Policing (see http://www.app.college.police.uk) provides more detailed guidance on matters concerning detainee healthcare and treatment and associated forensic issues which should be read in conjunction with sections 8 and 9 of this Code.

9 Care and treatment of detained persons

(a) General

9.1 Nothing in this section prevents the police from calling an appropriate healthcare professional to examine a detainee for the purposes of obtaining evidence relating to any offence in which the detainee is suspected of being involved. See *Notes 9A and 8C*.

9.2 If a complaint is made by, or on behalf of, a detainee about their treatment since their arrest, or it comes to notice that a detainee may have been treated improperly, a report must be made as soon as practicable to an officer of inspector rank or above not connected with the investigation. If the matter concerns a possible assault or the possibility of the unnecessary or unreasonable use of force, an appropriate healthcare professional must also be called as soon as practicable.

9.3 Detainees should be visited at least every hour. If no reasonably foreseeable risk was identified in a risk assessment, see *paragraphs 3.6 to 3.10,* there is no need to wake a sleeping detainee. Those suspected of being under the influence of drink or drugs or both or of having swallowed drugs, see *Note 9CA*, or whose level of consciousness causes concern must, subject to any clinical directions given by the appropriate healthcare professional, see *paragraph 9.13*:

- be visited and roused at least every half hour;
- have their condition assessed as in *Annex H;*
- and clinical treatment arranged if appropriate.

See *Notes 9B, 9C* and *9H*

9.4 When arrangements are made to secure clinical attention for a detainee, the custody officer must make sure all relevant information which might assist in the treatment of the detainee's condition is made available to the responsible healthcare professional. This applies whether or not the healthcare professional asks for such information. Any officer or police staff with relevant information must inform the custody officer as soon as practicable.

(b) Clinical treatment and attention

9.5 The custody officer must make sure a detainee receives appropriate clinical attention as soon as reasonably practicable if the person:

(a) appears to be suffering from physical illness; or
(b) is injured; or
(c) appears to be suffering from a mental disorder; or
(d) appears to need clinical attention.

9.5A This applies even if the detainee makes no request for clinical attention and whether or not they have already received clinical attention elsewhere. If the need for attention appears urgent, e.g. when indicated as in *Annex H*, the nearest available healthcare professional or an ambulance must be called immediately.

9.5B The custody officer must also consider the need for clinical attention as set out in *Note 9C* in relation to those suffering the effects of alcohol or drugs.

9.6 Paragraph 9.5 is not meant to prevent or delay the transfer to a hospital if necessary of a person detained under the Mental Health Act 1983, section 136. See Note 9D. When an assessment under that Act is to take place at a police station (see paragraph 3.16) the custody officer must consider whether an appropriate healthcare professional should be called to conduct an initial clinical check on the detainee. This applies particularly when there is likely to be any significant delay in the arrival of a suitably qualified medical practitioner.

9.7 If it appears to the custody officer, or they are told, that a person brought to a station under arrest may be suffering from an infectious disease or condition, the custody officer must take reasonable steps to safeguard the health of the detainee and others at the station. In deciding what action to take, advice must be sought from an appropriate healthcare professional. See *Note 9E*. The custody officer has discretion to isolate the person and their property until clinical directions have been obtained.

9.8 If a detainee requests a clinical examination, an appropriate healthcare professional must be called as soon as practicable to assess the detainee's clinical needs. If a safe and appropriate care plan cannot be provided, the appropriate healthcare professional's advice must be sought. The detainee may also be examined by a medical practitioner of their choice at their expense.

9.9 If a detainee is required to take or apply any medication in compliance with clinical directions prescribed before their detention, the custody officer must consult the appropriate healthcare professional before the use of the medication. Subject to the restrictions in *paragraph 9.10*, the custody officer is responsible for the safekeeping of any medication and for making sure the detainee is given the opportunity to take or apply prescribed or approved medication. Any such consultation and its outcome shall be noted in the custody record.

9.10 No police officer may administer or supervise the self-administration of medically prescribed controlled drugs of the types and forms listed in the Misuse of Drugs Regulations 2001, Schedule 2 or 3. A detainee may only self-administer such drugs under the personal supervision of the registered medical practitioner authorising their use or other appropriate healthcare professional. The custody officer may supervise the self-administration of, or authorise other custody staff to supervise the self-administration of, drugs listed in Schedule 4 or 5 if the officer has consulted the appropriate healthcare professional authorising their use and both are satisfied self-administration will not expose the detainee, police officers or anyone else to the risk of harm or injury.

9.11 When appropriate healthcare professionals administer drugs or authorise the use of other medications, supervise their self-administration or consult with the custody officer about allowing self-administration of drugs listed in Schedule 4 or 5, it must be within current medicines legislation and the scope of practice as determined by their relevant statutory regulatory body.

9.12 If a detainee has in their possession, or claims to need, medication relating to a heart condition, diabetes, epilepsy or a condition of comparable potential seriousness then, even though *paragraph 9.5* may not apply, the advice of the appropriate healthcare professional must be obtained.

9.13 Whenever the appropriate healthcare professional is called in accordance with this section to examine or treat a detainee, the custody officer shall ask for their opinion about:

- any risks or problems which police need to take into account when making decisions about the detainee's continued detention;
- when to carry out an interview if applicable;
- and the need for safeguards.

9.14 When clinical directions are given by the appropriate healthcare professional, whether orally or in writing, and the custody officer has any doubts or is in any way uncertain about any aspect of the directions, the custody officer shall ask for clarification. It is particularly important that directions concerning the frequency of visits are clear, precise and capable of being implemented. See *Note 9F*.

(c) Documentation

9.15 A record must be made in the custody record of:

(a) the arrangements made for an examination by an appropriate healthcare professional under *paragraph 9.2* and of any complaint reported under that paragraph together with any relevant remarks by the custody officer;

(b) any arrangements made in accordance with *paragraph 9.5*;

(c) any request for a clinical examination under *paragraph 9.8* and any arrangements made in response;

(d) the injury, ailment, condition or other reason which made it necessary to make the arrangements in *(a)* to (c); See *Note 9G*.

(e) any clinical directions and advice, including any further clarifications, given to police by a healthcare professional concerning the care and treatment of the detainee in connection with any of the arrangements made in *(a)* to (c); See *Notes 9E* and *9F*.

(f) if applicable, the responses received when attempting to rouse a person using the procedure in *Annex H*. See *Note 9H*.

9.16 If a healthcare professional does not record their clinical findings in the custody record, the record must show where they are recorded. See *Note 9G*. However, information which is necessary to custody staff to ensure the effective ongoing care and well being of the detainee must be recorded openly in the custody record, see *paragraph 3.8* and *Annex G, paragraph 7*.

9.17 Subject to the requirements of *Section 4*, the custody record shall include:

- a record of all medication a detainee has in their possession on arrival at the police station;
- a note of any such medication they claim to need but do not have with them.

Notes for Guidance

9A A 'healthcare professional' means a clinically qualified person working within the scope of practice *as determined by their relevant statutory regulatory body. Whether a healthcare professional is 'appropriate' depends on the circumstances of the duties they carry out at the time.*

9B Whenever possible juveniles and mentally vulnerable detainees should be visited more frequently.

9C A detainee who appears drunk or behaves abnormally may be suffering from illness, the effects of drugs or may have sustained injury, particularly a head injury which is not apparent. A detainee needing or dependent on certain drugs, including alcohol, may experience harmful effects within a short time of being deprived of their supply. In these circumstances, when there is any doubt, police should always act urgently to call an appropriate healthcare professional or an ambulance. Paragraph 9.5 does not apply to minor ailments or injuries which do not need attention. However, all such ailments or injuries must be recorded in the custody record and any doubt must be resolved in favour of calling the appropriate healthcare professional.

9CA Paragraph 9.3 would apply to a person in police custody by order of a magistrates' court under the Criminal Justice Act 1988, section 152 (as amended by the Drugs Act 2005, section 8) to facilitate the recovery of evidence after being charged with drug possession or drug trafficking and suspected of having swallowed drugs. In the case of the healthcare needs of a person who has swallowed drugs, the custody officer, subject to any clinical directions, should consider the necessity for rousing every half hour. This does not negate the need for regular visiting of the suspect in the cell.

9D Whenever practicable, arrangements should be made for persons detained for assessment under the Mental Health Act 1983, section 136 to be taken to a hospital. Chapter 10 of the Mental Health Act 1983 Code of Practice (as revised) provides more detailed guidance about arranging assessments under section 136 and transferring detainees from police stations to other places of safety.

9E It is important to respect a person's right to privacy and information about their health must be kept confidential and only disclosed with their consent or in accordance with clinical advice when it is necessary to protect the detainee's health or that of others who come into contact with them.

9F The custody officer should always seek to clarify directions that the detainee requires constant observation or supervision and should ask the appropriate healthcare professional to explain precisely what action needs to be taken to implement such directions.

9G Paragraphs 9.15 and 9.16 do not require any information about the cause of any injury, ailment or condition to be recorded on the custody record if it appears capable of providing evidence of an offence.

9H The purpose of recording a person's responses when attempting to rouse them using the procedure in Annex H is to enable any change in the individual's consciousness level to be noted and clinical treatment arranged if appropriate.

10 Cautions

(a) When a caution must be given

10.1 A person whom there are grounds to suspect of an offence, see *Note 10A*, must be cautioned before any questions about an offence, or further questions if the answers provide the grounds for suspicion, are put to them if either the suspect's answers or silence, (i.e. failure or refusal to answer or answer satisfactorily) may be given in evidence to a court in a prosecution. A person need not be cautioned if questions are for other necessary purposes, e.g.:

- (a) solely to establish their identity or ownership of any vehicle;
- (b) to obtain information in accordance with any relevant statutory requirement, see *paragraph 10.9*;
- (c) in furtherance of the proper and effective conduct of a search, e.g. to determine the need to search in the exercise of powers of stop and search or to seek co-operation while carrying out a search; or
- (d) to seek verification of a written record as in *paragraph 11.13*.
- (e) *Not used.*

10.2 Whenever a person not under arrest is initially cautioned, or reminded that they are under caution, that person must at the same time be told they are not under arrest and must be informed of the provisions of *paragraph 3.21* which explain that they need to agree to be interviewed, how they may obtain legal advice according to whether they are at a police station or elsewhere and the other rights and entitlements that apply to a voluntary interview. See *Note 10C*.

10.3 A person who is arrested, or further arrested, must be informed at the time if practicable or, if not, as soon as it becomes practicable thereafter, that they are under arrest and of the grounds and reasons for their arrest, see paragraph 3.4, *Note 10B* and *Code G, paragraphs 2.2 and 4.3*.

10.4 As required by *Code G, section 3*, a person who is arrested, or further arrested, must also be cautioned unless:

- (a) it is impracticable to do so by reason of their condition or behaviour at the time;
- (b) they have already been cautioned immediately prior to arrest as in *paragraph 10.1*.

(b) Terms of the cautions

10.5 The caution which must be given on:

- (a) arrest; or
- (b) all other occasions before a person is charged or informed they may be prosecuted; see *section 16*,

should, unless the restriction on drawing adverse inferences from silence applies, see *Annex C*, be in the following terms:

'You do not have to say anything. But it may harm your defence if you do not mention when questioned something which you later rely on in Court. Anything you do say may be given in evidence.'

Where the use of the Welsh Language is appropriate, a constable may provide the caution directly in Welsh in the following terms:

'Does dim rhaid i chi ddweud dim byd. Ond gall niweidio eich amddiffyniad os na fyddwch chi'n sôn, wrth gael eich holi, am rywbeth y byddwch chi'n dibynnu arno nes ymlaen yn y Llys. Gall unrhyw beth yr ydych yn ei ddweud gael ei roi fel tystiolaeth.'

See *Note 10G*

10.6 *Annex C, paragraph 2* sets out the alternative terms of the caution to be used when the restriction on drawing adverse inferences from silence applies.

10.7 Minor deviations from the words of any caution given in accordance with this Code do not constitute a breach of this Code, provided the sense of the relevant caution is preserved. See *Note 10D*.

10.8 After any break in questioning under caution, the person being questioned must be made aware they remain under caution. If there is any doubt the relevant caution should be given again in full when the interview resumes. See *Note 10E*.

10.9 When, despite being cautioned, a person fails to co-operate or to answer particular questions which may affect their immediate treatment, the person should be informed of any relevant consequences and that those consequences are not affected by the caution. Examples are when a person's refusal to provide:

- their name and address when charged may make them liable to detention;
- particulars and information in accordance with a statutory requirement, e.g. under the Road Traffic Act 1988, may amount to an offence or may make the person liable to a further arrest.

(c) Special warnings under the Criminal Justice and Public Order Act 1994, sections 36 and 37

10.10 When a suspect interviewed at a police station or authorised place of detention after arrest fails or refuses to answer certain questions, or to answer satisfactorily, after due warning, see *Note 10F*, a court or jury may draw such inferences as appear proper under the Criminal Justice and Public Order Act 1994, sections 36 and 37. Such inferences may only be drawn when:

(a) the restriction on drawing adverse inferences from silence, see *Annex C*, does not apply; and

(b) the suspect is arrested by a constable and fails or refuses to account for any objects, marks or substances, or marks on such objects found:
- on their person;
- in or on their clothing or footwear;
- otherwise in their possession;
- or in the place they were arrested;

(c) the arrested suspect was found by a constable at a place at or about the time the offence for which that officer has arrested them is alleged to have been committed, and the suspect fails or refuses to account for their presence there.

When the restriction on drawing adverse inferences from silence applies, the suspect may still be asked to account for any of the matters in *(b)* or *(c)* but the special warning described in *paragraph 10.11* will not apply and must not be given.

10.11 For an inference to be drawn when a suspect fails or refuses to answer a question about one of these matters or to answer it satisfactorily, the suspect must first be told in ordinary language:

(a) what offence is being investigated;
(b) what fact they are being asked to account for;
(c) this fact may be due to them taking part in the commission of the offence;
(d) a court may draw a proper inference if they fail or refuse to account for this fact; and
(e) a record is being made of the interview and it may be given in evidence if they are brought to trial.

(d) Juveniles and persons who are mentally disordered or otherwise mentally vulnerable

10.11A The information required in paragraph 10.11 must not be given to a suspect who is a juvenile or who is mentally disordered or otherwise mentally vulnerable unless the appropriate adult is present.

10.12 If a juvenile or a person who is mentally disordered or otherwise mentally vulnerable is cautioned in the absence of the appropriate adult, the caution must be repeated in the adult's presence.

10.12A *Not used.*

(e) Documentation

10.13 A record shall be made when a caution is given under this section, either in the interviewer's report book or in the interview record.

Notes for Guidance

10A There must be some reasonable, objective grounds for the suspicion, based on known facts or information which are relevant to the likelihood the offence has been committed and the person to be questioned committed it.

10B An arrested person must be given sufficient information to enable them to understand that they have been deprived of their liberty and the reason they have been arrested, e.g. when a person is arrested on suspicion of committing an offence they must be informed of the suspected offence's nature, when and where it was committed. The suspect must also be informed of the reason or reasons why the arrest is considered necessary. Vague or technical language should be avoided.

10C The restriction on drawing inferences from silence, see Annex C, paragraph 1, does not apply to a person who has not been detained and who therefore cannot be prevented from seeking legal advice if they want, see paragraph 3.21.

10D If it appears a person does not understand the caution, the person giving it should explain it in their own words.

10E It may be necessary to show to the court that nothing occurred during an interview break or between interviews which influenced the suspect's recorded evidence. After a break in an interview or at the beginning of a subsequent interview, the interviewer should summarise the reason for the break and confirm this with the suspect.

10F The Criminal Justice and Public Order Act 1994, sections 36 and 37 apply only to suspects who have been arrested by a constable or an officer of Revenue and Customs and are given the relevant warning by the police or Revenue and Customs officer who made the arrest or who is investigating the offence. They do not apply to any interviews with suspects who have not been arrested.

10G Nothing in this Code requires a caution to be given or repeated when informing a person not under arrest they may be prosecuted for an offence. However, a court will not be able to draw any inferences under the Criminal Justice and Public Order Act 1994, section 34, if the person was not cautioned.

11 Interviews—general

(a) Action

11.1A An interview is the questioning of a person regarding their involvement or suspected involvement in a criminal offence or offences which, under paragraph 10.1, must be carried out under caution. Before a person is interviewed, they and, if they are represented, their solicitor must be given sufficient information to enable them to understand the nature of any such offence, and why they are suspected of committing it (see *paragraphs 3.4(a)* and *10.3*), in order to allow for the effective exercise of the rights of the defence. However, whilst the information must always be sufficient for the person to understand the nature of any offence (see Note 11ZA), this does not require the disclosure of details at a time which might prejudice the criminal investigation. The decision about what needs to be disclosed for the purpose of this requirement therefore rests with the investigating officer who has sufficient knowledge of the case to make that decision. The officer who discloses the information shall make a record of the information disclosed and when it was disclosed. This record may be made in the interview record, in the officer's report book or other form provided for this purpose. Procedures under the Road Traffic Act 1988, section 7 or the Transport and Works Act 1992, section 31 do not constitute interviewing for the purpose of this Code.

11.1 Following a decision to arrest a suspect, they must not be interviewed about the relevant offence except at a police station or other authorised place of detention, unless the consequent delay would be likely to:

(a) lead to:

- interference with, or harm to, evidence connected with an offence;
- interference with, or physical harm to, other people; or
- serious loss of, or damage to, property;

(b) lead to alerting other people suspected of committing an offence but not yet arrested for it; or
(c) hinder the recovery of property obtained in consequence of the commission of an offence.

Interviewing in any of these circumstances shall cease once the relevant risk has been averted or the necessary questions have been put in order to attempt to avert that risk.

11.2 Immediately prior to the commencement or re-commencement of any interview at a police station or other authorised place of detention, the interviewer should remind the suspect of their entitlement to free legal advice and that the interview can be delayed for legal advice to be obtained, unless one of the exceptions in *paragraph 6.6* applies. It is the interviewer's responsibility to make sure all reminders are recorded in the interview record.

11.3 *Not used.*

11.4 At the beginning of an interview the interviewer, after cautioning the suspect, see *section 10*, shall put to them any significant statement or silence which occurred in the presence and hearing of a police officer or other police staff before the start of the interview and which have not been put to the suspect in the course of a previous interview. See *Note 11A*. The interviewer shall ask the suspect whether they confirm or deny that earlier statement or silence and if they want to add anything.

11.4A A significant statement is one which appears capable of being used in evidence against the suspect, in particular a direct admission of guilt. A significant silence is a failure or refusal to answer a question or answer satisfactorily when under caution, which might, allowing for the restriction on drawing adverse inferences from silence, see *Annex C*, give rise to an inference under the Criminal Justice and Public Order Act 1994, Part III.

11.5 No interviewer may try to obtain answers or elicit a statement by the use of oppression. Except as in *paragraph 10.9*, no interviewer shall indicate, except to answer a direct question, what action will be taken by the police if the person being questioned answers questions, makes a statement or refuses to do either. If the person asks directly what action will be taken if they answer questions, make a statement or refuse to do either, the interviewer may inform them what action the police propose to take provided that action is itself proper and warranted.

11.6 The interview or further interview of a person about an offence with which that person has not been charged or for which they have not been informed they may be prosecuted, must cease when:

(a) the officer in charge of the investigation is satisfied all the questions they consider relevant to obtaining accurate and reliable information about the offence have been put to the suspect, this includes allowing the suspect an opportunity to give an innocent explanation and asking questions to test if the explanation is accurate and reliable, e.g. to clear up ambiguities or clarify what the suspect said;
(b) the officer in charge of the investigation has taken account of any other available evidence; and
(c) the officer in charge of the investigation, or in the case of a detained suspect, the custody officer, see *paragraph 16.1*, reasonably believes there is sufficient evidence to provide a realistic prospect of conviction for that offence. See *Note 11B*.

This paragraph does not prevent officers in revenue cases or acting under the confiscation provisions of the Criminal Justice Act 1988 or the Drug Trafficking Act 1994 from inviting suspects to complete a formal question and answer record after the interview is concluded.

(b) Interview records

11.7 (a) An accurate record must be made of each interview, whether or not the interview takes place at a police station.

(b) The record must state the place of interview, the time it begins and ends, any interview breaks and, subject to *paragraph 2.6A*, the names of all those present; and must be made on the forms provided for this purpose or in the interviewer's report book or in accordance with Codes of Practice E or F.

(c) Any written record must be made and completed during the interview, unless this would not be practicable or would interfere with the conduct of the interview, and must constitute either a verbatim record of what has been said or, failing this, an account of the interview which adequately and accurately summarises it.

11.8 If a written record is not made during the interview it must be made as soon as practicable after its completion.

11.9 Written interview records must be timed and signed by the maker.

11.10 If a written record is not completed during the interview the reason must be recorded in the interview record.

11.11 Unless it is impracticable, the person interviewed shall be given the opportunity to read the interview record and to sign it as correct or to indicate how they consider it inaccurate. If the person interviewed cannot read or refuses to read the record or sign it, the senior interviewer present shall read it to them and ask whether they would like to sign it as correct or make their mark or to indicate how they consider it inaccurate. The interviewer shall certify on the interview record itself what has occurred. See *Note 11E.*

11.12 If the appropriate adult or the person's solicitor is present during the interview, they should also be given an opportunity to read and sign the interview record or any written statement taken down during the interview.

11.13 A record shall be made of any comments made by a suspect, including unsolicited comments, which are outside the context of an interview but which might be relevant to the offence. Any such record must be timed and signed by the maker. When practicable the suspect shall be given the opportunity to read that record and to sign it as correct or to indicate how they consider it inaccurate. See *Note 11E.*

11.14 Any refusal by a person to sign an interview record when asked in accordance with this Code must itself be recorded.

(c) Juveniles and mentally disordered or otherwise mentally vulnerable people

11.15 A juvenile or person who is mentally disordered or otherwise mentally vulnerable must not be interviewed regarding their involvement or suspected involvement in a criminal offence or offences, or asked to provide or sign a written statement under caution or record of interview, in the absence of the appropriate adult unless *paragraphs 11.1* or *11.18* to *11.20* apply. See *Note 11C.*

11.16 Juveniles may only be interviewed at their place of education in exceptional circumstances and only when the principal or their nominee agrees. Every effort should be made to notify the parent(s) or other person responsible for the juvenile's welfare and the appropriate adult, if this is a different person, that the police want to interview the juvenile and reasonable time should be allowed to enable the appropriate adult to be present at the interview. If awaiting the appropriate adult would cause unreasonable delay, and unless the juvenile is suspected of an offence against the educational establishment, the principal or their nominee can act as the appropriate adult for the purposes of the interview.

11.17 If an appropriate adult is present at an interview, they shall be informed:

- that they are not expected to act simply as an observer; and
- that the purpose of their presence is to:
  - ~ advise the person being interviewed;
  - ~ observe whether the interview is being conducted properly and fairly;
  - ~ and facilitate communication with the person being interviewed.

11.17A The appropriate adult may be required to leave the interview if their conduct is such that the interviewer is unable properly to put questions to the suspect. This will include situations where the appropriate adult's approach or conduct prevents or unreasonably obstructs proper questions being put to the suspect or the suspect's responses being recorded (see *Note 11F*). If the interviewer considers an appropriate adult is acting in such a way, they will stop the interview and consult an officer not below superintendent rank, if one is readily available, and otherwise an officer not below inspector rank not connected with the investigation. After speaking to the appropriate adult, the officer consulted must remind the adult that their role under *paragraph 11.17* does not allow them to obstruct proper questioning and give the adult an opportunity to respond. The officer consulted will then decide if the interview should continue without the attendance of that appropriate adult. If they decide it should, another appropriate adult must be obtained before the interview continues, unless the provisions of *paragraph 11.18* below apply.

(d) Vulnerable suspects—urgent interviews at police stations

11.18 The following interviews may take place only if an officer of superintendent rank or above considers delaying the interview will lead to the consequences in *paragraph 11.1(a)* to *(c)*, and is satisfied the interview would not significantly harm the person's physical or mental state (see *Annex G*):

(a) an interview of a detained juvenile or person who is mentally disordered or otherwise mentally vulnerable without the appropriate adult being present;

(b) an interview of anyone detained other than in *(a)* who appears unable to:
- appreciate the significance of questions and their answers; or
- understand what is happening because of the effects of drink, drugs or any illness, ailment or condition;

(c) an interview, without an interpreter having been arranged, of a detained person whom the custody officer has determined requires an interpreter (see *paragraphs 3.5(c)(ii)* and *3.12*) which is carried out by an interviewer speaking the suspect's own language or (as the case may be) otherwise establishing effective communication which is sufficient to enable the necessary questions to be asked and answered in order to avert the consequences. See *paragraphs 13.2* and *13.5*.

11.19 These interviews may not continue once sufficient information has been obtained to avert the consequences in *paragraph 11.1(a)* to *(c)*.

11.20 A record shall be made of the grounds for any decision to interview a person under *paragraph 11.18*.

Notes for Guidance

11ZA The requirement in paragraph 11.1A for a suspect to be given sufficient information about the offence applies prior to the interview and whether or not they are legally represented. What is sufficient will depend on the circumstances of the case, but it should normally include, as a minimum, a description of the facts relating to the suspected offence that are known to the officer, including the time and place in question. This aims to avoid suspects being confused or unclear about what they are supposed to have done and to help an innocent suspect to clear the matter up more quickly.

11A Paragraph 11.4 does not prevent the interviewer from putting significant statements and silences to a suspect again at a later stage or a further interview.

11B The Criminal Procedure and Investigations Act 1996 Code of Practice, paragraph 3.5 states 'In conducting an investigation, the investigator should pursue all reasonable lines of enquiry, whether these point towards or away from the suspect. What is reasonable will depend on the particular circumstances.' Interviewers should keep this in mind when deciding what questions to ask in an interview.

11C Although juveniles or people who are mentally disordered or otherwise mentally vulnerable are often capable of providing reliable evidence, they may, without knowing or wishing to do so, be particularly prone in certain circumstances to provide information that may be unreliable, misleading or self-incriminating. Special care should always be taken when questioning such a person, and the appropriate adult should be involved if there is any doubt about a person's age, mental state or capacity. Because of the risk of unreliable evidence it is also important to obtain corroboration of any facts admitted whenever possible.

11D Juveniles should not be arrested at their place of education unless this is unavoidable. When a juvenile is arrested at their place of education, the principal or their nominee must be informed.

11E Significant statements described in paragraph 11.4 will always be relevant to the offence and must be recorded. When a suspect agrees to read records of interviews and other comments and sign them as correct, they should be asked to endorse the record with, e.g. 'I agree that this is a correct record of what was said' and add their signature. If the suspect does not agree with the record, the interviewer should record the details of any disagreement and ask the suspect to read these details and sign them to the effect that they accurately reflect their disagreement. Any refusal to sign should be recorded.

11F The appropriate adult may intervene if they consider it is necessary to help the suspect understand any question asked and to help the suspect to answer any question. Paragraph 11.17A only applies if the appropriate adult's approach or conduct prevents or unreasonably obstructs proper questions being put to the suspect or the suspect's response being recorded. Examples of unacceptable conduct include answering questions on a suspect's behalf or providing written replies for the suspect to quote. An officer who takes the decision to exclude an appropriate adult must be in a position to satisfy the court the decision was properly made. In order to do this they may need to witness what is happening and give the suspect's solicitor (if they have one) who witnessed what happened, an opportunity to comment.

12 Interviews in police stations

(a) Action

12.1 If a police officer wants to interview or conduct enquiries which require the presence of a detainee, the custody officer is responsible for deciding whether to deliver the detainee into the officer's custody. An investigating officer who is given custody of a detainee takes over responsibility for the detainee's care and safe custody for the purposes of this Code until they return the detainee to the custody officer when they must report the manner in which they complied with the Code whilst having custody of the detainee.

12.2 Except as below, in any period of 24 hours a detainee must be allowed a continuous period of at least 8 hours for rest, free from questioning, travel or any interruption in connection with the investigation concerned. This period should normally be at night or other appropriate time which takes account of when the detainee last slept or rested. If a detainee is arrested at a police station after going there voluntarily, the period of 24 hours runs from the time of their arrest and not the time of arrival at the police station. The period may not be interrupted or delayed, except:

- (a) when there are reasonable grounds for believing not delaying or interrupting the period would:
  - (i) involve a risk of harm to people or serious loss of, or damage to, property;
  - (ii) delay unnecessarily the person's release from custody; or
  - (iii) otherwise prejudice the outcome of the investigation;
- (b) at the request of the detainee, their appropriate adult or legal representative;
- (c) when a delay or interruption is necessary in order to:
  - (i) comply with the legal obligations and duties arising under section 15; or
  - (ii) to take action required under *section 9* or in accordance with medical advice.

If the period is interrupted in accordance with *(a)*, a fresh period must be allowed. Interruptions under *(b)* and *(c)* do not require a fresh period to be allowed.

12.3 Before a detainee is interviewed, the custody officer, in consultation with the officer in charge of the investigation and appropriate healthcare professionals as necessary, shall assess whether the detainee is fit enough to be interviewed. This means determining and considering the risks to the detainee's physical and mental state if the interview took place and determining what safeguards are needed to allow the interview to take place. See *Annex G*. The custody officer shall not allow a detainee to be interviewed if the custody officer considers it would cause significant harm to the detainee's physical or mental state. Vulnerable suspects listed at *paragraph 11.18* shall be treated as always being at some risk during an interview and these persons may not be interviewed except in accordance with *paragraphs 11.18* to *11.20*.

12.4 As far as practicable interviews shall take place in interview rooms which are adequately heated, lit and ventilated.

12.5 A suspect whose detention without charge has been authorised under PACE because the detention is necessary for an interview to obtain evidence of the offence for which they have been arrested may choose not to answer questions but police do not require the suspect's consent or agreement to interview them for this purpose. If a suspect takes steps to prevent themselves being questioned or further questioned, e.g. by refusing to leave their cell to go to a suitable interview room or by trying to leave the interview room, they shall be advised their consent or agreement to interview is not required. The suspect shall be cautioned as in *section 10*, and informed if they fail or refuse to co-operate, the interview may take place in the cell and that their failure or refusal to co-operate may be given in evidence. The suspect shall then be invited to co-operate and go into the interview room.

12.6 People being questioned or making statements shall not be required to stand.

12.7 Before the interview commences each interviewer shall, subject to *paragraph 2.6A*, identify themselves and any other persons present to the interviewee.

12.8 Breaks from interviewing should be made at recognised meal times or at other times that take account of when an interviewee last had a meal. Short refreshment breaks shall be provided at approximately two hour intervals, subject to the interviewer's discretion to delay a break if there are reasonable grounds for believing it would:

(i) involve a:
- risk of harm to people;
- serious loss of, or damage to, property;

(ii) unnecessarily delay the detainee's release; or

(iii) otherwise prejudice the outcome of the investigation.

See *Note 12B*

12.9 If during the interview a complaint is made by or on behalf of the interviewee concerning the provisions of any of the Codes, or it comes to the interviewer's notice that the interviewee may have been treated improperly, the interviewer should:

(i) record the matter in the interview record; and

(ii) inform the custody officer, who is then responsible for dealing with it as in *section 9*.

(b) Documentation

12.10 A record must be made of the:
- time a detainee is not in the custody of the custody officer, and why
- reason for any refusal to deliver the detainee out of that custody.

12.11 A record shall be made of:

(a) the reasons it was not practicable to use an interview room; and

(b) any action taken as in *paragraph 12.5*.

The record shall be made on the custody record or in the interview record for action taken whilst an interview record is being kept, with a brief reference to this effect in the custody record.

12.12 Any decision to delay a break in an interview must be recorded, with reasons, in the interview record.

12.13 All written statements made at police stations under caution shall be written on forms provided for the purpose.

12.14 All written statements made under caution shall be taken in accordance with *Annex D*. Before a person makes a written statement under caution at a police station, they shall be reminded about the right to legal advice. See *Note 12A*.

Notes for Guidance

12A It is not normally necessary to ask for a written statement if the interview was recorded in writing and the record signed in accordance with paragraph 11.11 or audibly or visually recorded in accordance with Code E or F. Statements under caution should normally be taken in these circumstances only at the person's express wish. A person may however be asked if they want to make such a statement.

12B Meal breaks should normally last at least 45 minutes and shorter breaks after two hours should last at least 15 minutes. If the interviewer delays a break in accordance with paragraph 12.8 and prolongs the interview, a longer break should be provided. If there is a short interview and another short interview is contemplated, the length of the break may be reduced if there are reasonable grounds to believe this is necessary to avoid any of the consequences in paragraph 12.8(i) to (iii).

13 Interpreters

(a) General

13.1 Chief officers are responsible for making arrangements (see *paragraph 13.1ZA*) to provide appropriately qualified independent persons to act as interpreters and to provide translations of essential documents for:

(a) detained suspects who, in accordance with *paragraph 3.5(c)(ii)*, the custody officer has determined require an interpreter, and

(b) suspects who are not under arrest but are cautioned as in *section 10* who, in accordance with *paragraph 3.21(b)*, the interviewer has determined require an interpreter. In these cases, the responsibilities of the custody officer are, if appropriate, assigned to the interviewer. An interviewer who has any doubts about whether and what arrangements for an interpreter must be made or about how the provisions of this section should be applied to a suspect who is not under arrest should seek advice from an officer of the rank of sergeant or above.

If the suspect has a hearing or speech impediment, references to 'interpreter' and 'interpretation' in this Code include arrangements for appropriate assistance necessary to establish effective communication with that person. See *paragraph 13.1C* below if the person is in Wales.

13.1ZA References in *paragraph 13.1* above and elsewhere in this Code (see *paragraphs 3.12(a), 13.2, 13.2A, 13.5, 13.6, 13.9, 13.10, 13.10A, 13.10D and 13.11* below and in any other Code, to making arrangements for an interpreter to assist a suspect, mean making arrangements for the interpreter to be *physically* present in the same location as the suspect *unless* the provisions in *paragraph 13.12* below, and Part 1 of *Annex N*, allow live-link interpretation to be used.

13.1A The arrangements must comply with the minimum requirements set out in *Directive 2010/64/EU* of the European Parliament and of the Council of 20 October 2010 on the right to interpretation and translation in criminal proceedings (see *Note 13A*). The provisions *of this* Code implement the requirements for those to whom this Code applies. These requirements include the following:

- That the arrangements made and the quality of interpretation and translation provided shall be sufficient to 'safeguard the fairness of the proceedings, in particular by ensuring that suspected or accused persons have knowledge of the cases against them and are able to exercise their right of defence'. This term which is used by the Directive means that the suspect must be able to understand their position and be able to communicate effectively with police officers, interviewers, solicitors and appropriate adults as provided for by this and any other Code in the same way as a suspect who can speak and understand English and who does not have a hearing or speech impediment and who would therefore not require an interpreter. See *paragraphs 13.12 to 13.14* and *Annex N* for application to live-link interpretation.
- The provision of a written translation of all documents considered essential for the person to exercise their right of defence and to '*safeguard the fairness of the proceedings*' as described above. For the purposes of this Code, this includes any decision to authorise a person to be detained and details of any offence(s) with which the person has been charged or for which they have been told they may be prosecuted, see *Annex M*.
- Procedures to help determine:
  - ~ whether a suspect can speak and understand English and needs the assistance of an interpreter, see *paragraph 13.1* and *Notes 13B* and *13C*; and
  - ~ whether another interpreter should be arranged or another translation should be provided when a suspect complains about the quality of either or both, see *paragraphs 13.10A* and *13.10C*.

13.1B All reasonable attempts should be made to make the suspect understand that interpretation and translation will be provided at public expense.

13.1C With regard to persons in Wales, nothing in this or any other Code affects the application of the Welsh Language Schemes produced by police and crime commissioners in Wales in accordance with the Welsh Language Act 1993. See *paragraphs 3.12 and 13.1*.

(b) Interviewing suspects—foreign languages

13.2 Unless *paragraphs 11.1 or 11.18(c)* apply, a suspect who for the purposes of this Code requires an interpreter because they do not appear to speak or understand English (see *paragraphs 3.5(c)(ii)* and *3.12*) must not be interviewed unless arrangements are made for a person capable of interpreting to assist the suspect to understand and communicate.

13.2A If a person who is a juvenile or is mentally disordered or mentally vulnerable is interviewed and the person acting as the appropriate adult does not appear to speak or understand English, arrangements must be made for an interpreter to assist communication between the person, the appropriate adult and the interviewer, unless the interview is urgent and *paragraphs 11.1 or 11.18(c)* apply.

13.3 When a written record of the interview is made (see *paragraph 11.7*), the interviewer shall make sure the interpreter makes a note of the interview at the time in the person's language for use in the event of the interpreter being called to give evidence, and certifies its accuracy. The interviewer should allow sufficient time for the interpreter to note each question and answer after each is put, given and interpreted. The person should be allowed to read the record or have it read to them and sign it as correct or indicate the respects in which they consider it inaccurate. If an audio or visual record of the interview is made, the arrangements in Code E or F shall apply. See *paragraphs* 13.12 to *13.14* and Annex N for application to live-link interpretation.

13.4 In the case of a person making a statement under caution (see *Annex D)* to a police officer or other police staff in a language other than English:

(a) the interpreter shall record the statement in the language it is made;

(b) the person shall be invited to sign it;

(c) an official English translation shall be made in due course. See *paragraphs* 13.12 to *13.14* and Annex N for application to live-link interpretation.

(c) Interviewing suspects who have a hearing or speech impediment

13.5 Unless *paragraphs 11.1 or 11.18(c)* (urgent interviews) apply, a suspect who for the purposes of this Code requires an interpreter or other appropriate assistance to enable effective communication with them because they appear to have a hearing or speech impediment (see *paragraphs 3.5(c)(ii)* and *3.12)* must not be interviewed without arrangements having been made to provide an independent person capable of interpreting or of providing other appropriate assistance.

13.6 An interpreter should also be arranged if a person who is a juvenile or who is mentally disordered or mentally vulnerable is interviewed and the person who is present as the appropriate adult, appears to have a hearing or speech impediment, unless the interview is urgent and *paragraphs 11.1 or 11.18(c)* apply.

13.7 If a written record of the interview is made, the interviewer shall make sure the interpreter is allowed to read the record and certify its accuracy in the event of the interpreter being called to give evidence. If an audio or visual recording is made, the arrangements in Code E or F apply.

See *paragraphs* 13.12 to *13.14* and Annex N for application to live-link interpretation.

(d) Additional rules for detained persons

13.8 *Not used.*

13.9 If *paragraph 6.1* applies and the detainee cannot communicate with the solicitor because of language, hearing or speech difficulties, arrangements must be made for an interpreter to enable communication. A police officer or any other police staff may not be used for this purpose.

13.10 After the custody officer has determined that a detainee requires an interpreter (see *paragraph 3.5(c)(ii)*) and following the initial action in *paragraphs 3.1 to 3.5*, arrangements must also be made for an interpreter to:

- explain the grounds and reasons for any authorisation for their *continued* detention, before or after charge and any information about the authorisation given to them by the authorising officer and which is recorded in the custody record. See *paragraphs 15.3, 15.4* and *15.16(a)* and *(b)*;

- to provide interpretation at the magistrates' court for the hearing of an application for a warrant of further detention or any extension or further extension of such warrant to explain any grounds and reasons for the application and any information about the authorisation of their further detention given to them by the court (see PACE, sections 43 and 44 and *paragraphs 15.2* and *15.16(c)*); and
- explain any offence with which the detainee is charged or for which they are informed they may be prosecuted and any other information about the offence given to them by or on behalf of the custody officer, see *paragraphs 16.1* and *16.3*.

13.10A If a detainee complains that they are not satisfied with the quality of interpretation, the custody officer or (as the case may be) the interviewer, is responsible for deciding whether to make arrangements for a different interpreter in accordance with the procedures set out in the arrangements made by the chief officer, *see paragraph 13.1A*.

(e) Translations of essential documents

13.10B Written translations, oral translations and oral summaries of essential documents in a language the detainee understands shall be provided in accordance with Annex M (Translations of documents and records).

13.10C If a detainee complains that they are not satisfied with the quality of the translation, the custody officer or (as the case may be) the interviewer, is responsible for deciding whether a further translation should be provided in accordance with the procedures set out in the arrangements made by the chief officer, see *paragraph 13.1A*.

(f) Decisions not to provide interpretation and translation.

13.10D If a suspect challenges a decision:

- made by the custody officer or (as the case may be) by the interviewer, in accordance with this Code (see *paragraphs 3.5(c)(ii)* and *3.21(b))* that they do not require an interpreter, or
- made in accordance with *paragraphs 13.10A, 13.10B* or *13.10C* not to make arrangements to provide a different interpreter or another translation or not to translate a requested document,

the matter shall be reported to an inspector to deal with as a complaint for the purposes of *paragraph 9.2* or *paragraph 12.9* if the challenge is made during an interview.

(g) Documentation

13.11 The following must be recorded in the custody record or, as applicable, the interview record:

(a) Action taken to arrange for an interpreter, including the live-link requirements in Annex N as applicable;

(b) Action taken when a detainee is not satisfied about the standard of interpretation or translation provided, see *paragraphs 13.10A* and *13.10C*;

(c) When an urgent interview is carried out in accordance with *paragraph 13.2* or *13.5* in the absence of an interpreter;

(d) When a detainee has been assisted by an interpreter for the purpose of providing or being given information or being interviewed;

(e) Action taken in accordance with Annex M when:

- a written translation of an essential document is provided;
- an oral translation or oral summary of an essential document is provided instead of a written translation and the authorising officer's reason(s) why this would not prejudice the fairness of the proceedings (see *Annex M, paragraph 3*);
- a suspect waives their right to a translation of an essential document (see *Annex M, paragraph 4*);
- when representations that a document which is not included in the table is essential and that a translation should be provided are refused and the reason for the refusal (see *Annex M, paragraph 8*).

(h) Live-link interpretation

13.12 In this section and in Annex N, 'live-link interpretation' means an arrangement to enable communication between the suspect and an interpreter who is not *physically* present with the suspect. The arrangement must ensure that anything said by any person in the suspect's presence and hearing can be interpreted in the same way as if the interpreter was physically present at that time. The communication must be by audio *and* visual means for the purpose of an interview, and for all other purposes it may be *either*; by audio and visual means, or by audio means *only*, as follows:

(a) **Audio and visual communication**

This applies for the purposes of an interview conducted and recorded in accordance with Code E (Audio recording) or Code F (Visual recording) and during that interview, live link interpretation must *enable*:

(i) the suspect, the interviewer, solicitor, appropriate adult and any other person *physically* present with the suspect at any time during the interview and an interpreter who is not *physically* present, to *see* and *hear* each other; and

(ii) the interview to be conducted and recorded in accordance with the provisions of Codes C, E and F, subject to the modifications in Part 2 of Annex N.

(b) **Audio and visual or audio without visual communication.**

This applies to communication for the purposes of any provision of this or any other Code except as described in (a), which requires or permits information to be given to, sought from, or provided by a suspect, whether orally or in writing, which would include communication between the suspect and their solicitor and/or appropriate adult, and for these cases, live link interpretation must:

(i) *enable* the suspect, the person giving or seeking that information, any other person *physically* present with the suspect at that time and an interpreter who is not so present, to either *see* and *hear* each other, or to *hear without seeing* each other (for example by using a telephone); and

(ii) enable that information to be given to, sought from, or provided by, the suspect in accordance with the provisions of this or any other Code that apply to that information, as modified for the purposes of the live-link, by Part 2 of Annex N.

13.12A The requirement in *sub-paragraphs 13.12(a)(ii)* and *(b)(ii)*, that live-link interpretation must enable compliance with the relevant provisions of the Codes C, E and F, means that the arrangements must provide for any written or electronic record of what the suspect says in their own language which is made by the interpreter, to be securely transmitted without delay so that the suspect can be invited to read, check and if appropriate, sign or otherwise confirm that the record is correct or make corrections to the record.

13.13 Chief officers must be satisfied that live-link interpretation used in their force area for the purposes of paragraphs 3.12(a) and *(b)*, provides for accurate and secure communication with the suspect. This includes ensuring that at any time during which live link interpretation is being used: a person cannot see, hear or otherwise obtain access to any communications between the suspect and interpreter or communicate with the suspect or interpreter unless so authorised or allowed by the custody officer or, in the case of an interview, the interviewer and that as applicable, the confidentiality of any private consultation between a suspect and their solicitor and appropriate adult (see *paragraphs 13.2A, 13.6* and *13.9)* is maintained.. See Annex N *paragraph 4*.

Notes for Guidance

13A Chief officers have discretion when determining the individuals or organisations they use to provide interpretation and translation services for their forces provided that these are compatible with the requirements of the Directive. One example which chief officers may wish to consider is the Ministry of Justice commercial agreements for interpretation and translation services.

13B A procedure for determining whether a person needs an interpreter might involve a telephone interpreter service or using cue cards or similar visual aids which enable the detainee to indicate their ability to speak and understand English and their preferred language. This could be confirmed through an interpreter who could also assess the extent to which the person can speak and understand English.

13C There should also be a procedure for determining whether a suspect who requires an interpreter requires assistance in accordance with paragraph 3.20 to help them check and if applicable, sign any documentation.

14 Questioning—special restrictions

14.1 If a person is arrested by one police force on behalf of another and the lawful period of detention in respect of that offence has not yet commenced in accordance with PACE, section 41, no questions may be put to them about the offence while they are in transit between the forces except to clarify any voluntary statement they make.

14.2 If a person is in police detention at a hospital, they may not be questioned without the agreement of a responsible doctor. See *Note 14A*.

Note for Guidance

14A If questioning takes place at a hospital under paragraph 14.2, or on the way to or from a hospital, the period of questioning concerned counts towards the total period of detention permitted.

15 Reviews and extensions of detention

(a) Persons detained under PACE

15.0 The requirement in *paragraph 3.4(b)* that documents and materials essential to challenging the lawfulness of the detainee's arrest and detention must be made available to the detainee or their solicitor, applies for the purposes of this section as follows:

- (a) The officer reviewing the need for detention without charge (*PACE, section 40*), or (as the case may be) the officer considering the need to extend detention without charge from 24 to 36 hours (*PACE, section 42*), is responsible, in consultation with the investigating officer, for deciding which documents and materials are essential and must be made available.
- (b) When *paragraph 15.7A* applies (application for a warrant of further detention or extension of such a warrant), the officer making the application is responsible for deciding which documents and materials are essential and must be made available *before* the hearing. See *Note 3ZA*.

15.1 The review officer is responsible under PACE, section 40 for periodically determining if a person's detention, before or after charge, continues to be necessary. This requirement continues throughout the detention period and, except as in *paragraph 15.10*, the review officer must be present at the police station holding the detainee. See *Notes 15A* and *15B*.

15.2 Under PACE, section 42, an officer of superintendent rank or above who is responsible for the station holding the detainee may give authority any time after the second review to extend the maximum period the person may be detained without charge by up to 12 hours. Further detention without charge may be authorised only by a magistrates' court in accordance with PACE, sections 43 and 44. See *Notes 15C, 15D* and *15E*.

15.2A An authorisation under section 42(1) of PACE extends the maximum period of detention permitted before charge for indictable offences from 24 hours to 36 hours. Detaining a juvenile or mentally vulnerable person for longer than 24 hours will be dependent on the circumstances of the case and with regard to the person's:

- (a) special vulnerability;
- (b) the legal obligation to provide an opportunity for representations to be made prior to a decision about extending detention;
- (c) the need to consult and consider the views of any appropriate adult; and
- (d) any alternatives to police custody.

15.3 Before deciding whether to authorise continued detention the officer responsible under *paragraph 15.1* or *15.2* shall give an opportunity to make representations about the detention to:

- (a) the detainee, unless in the case of a review as in *paragraph 15.1*, the detainee is asleep;
- (b) the detainee's solicitor if available at the time; and
- (c) the appropriate adult if available at the time. See *Note 15CA*

15.3A Other people having an interest in the detainee's welfare may also make representations at the authorising officer's discretion.

15.3B Subject to *paragraph 15.10*, the representations may be made orally in person or by telephone or in writing. The authorising officer may, however, refuse to hear oral representations from the detainee if the officer considers them unfit to make representations because of their condition or behaviour. See *Note 15C*.

15.3C The decision on whether the review takes place in person or by telephone or by video conferencing (see Note 15G) is a matter for the review officer. In determining the form the review may take, the review officer must always take full account of the needs of the person in custody. The benefits of carrying out a review in person should always be considered, based on the individual circumstances of each case with specific additional consideration if the person is:

(a) a juvenile (and the age of the juvenile); or
(b) suspected of being mentally vulnerable; or
(c) in need of medical attention for other than routine minor ailments; or
(d) subject to presentational or community issues around their detention.

15.4 Before conducting a review or determining whether to extend the maximum period of detention without charge, the officer responsible must make sure the detainee is reminded of their entitlement to free legal advice, see *paragraph 6.5,* unless in the case of a review the person is asleep.

15.5 If, after considering any representations, the review officer under *paragraph 15.1* decides to keep the detainee in detention or the superintendent under *paragraph 15.2* extends the maximum period for which they may be detained without charge, then any comment made by the detainee shall be recorded. If applicable, the officer shall be informed of the comment as soon as practicable. See also *paragraphs 11.4* and *11.13*.

15.6 No officer shall put specific questions to the detainee:

- regarding their involvement in any offence; or
- in respect of any comments they may make:
  ~ when given the opportunity to make representations; or
  ~ in response to a decision to keep them in detention or extend the maximum period of detention.

Such an exchange could constitute an interview as in *paragraph 11.1A* and would be subject to the associated safeguards in *section 11* and, in respect of a person who has been charged, *paragraph 16.5*. See also *paragraph 11.13*.

15.7 A detainee who is asleep at a review, see *paragraph 15.1,* and whose continued detention is authorised must be informed about the decision and reason as soon as practicable after waking.

15.7A When an application is made to a magistrates' court under PACE, section 43 for a warrant of further detention to extend detention without charge of a person arrested for an *indictable offence*, or under section 44, to extend or further extend that warrant, the detainee:

(a) must be brought to court for the hearing of the application;
(b) is entitled to be legally represented if they wish, in which case, *Annex B* cannot apply; and
(c) must be given a copy of the information which supports the application and states:
  (i) the nature of the offence for which the person to whom the application relates has been arrested;
  (ii) the general nature of the evidence on which the person was arrested;
  (iii) what inquiries about the offence have been made and what further inquiries are proposed;
  (iv) the reasons for believing continued detention is necessary for the purposes of the further inquiries;

Note: A warrant of further detention can only be issued or extended if the court has reasonable grounds for believing that the person's further detention is necessary for the purpose of obtaining evidence of an indictable offence for which the person has been arrested and that the investigation is being conducted diligently and expeditiously.

See *paragraph 15.0(b)*.

15.8 *Not used.*

(b) Review of detention by telephone and video conferencing facilities

15.9 PACE, section 40A provides that the officer responsible under section 40 for reviewing the detention of a person who has not been charged, need not attend the police station holding the detainee and may carry out the review by telephone.

15.9A PACE, section 45A(2) provides that the officer responsible under section 40 for reviewing the detention of a person who has not been charged, need not attend the police station holding the detainee and may carry out the review by video conferencing facilities. See *Note 15G*.

15.9B A telephone review is not permitted where facilities for review by video conferencing exist and it is practicable to use them.

15.9C The review officer can decide at any stage that a telephone review or review by video conferencing should be terminated and that the review will be conducted in person. The reasons for doing so should be noted in the custody record.

See *Note 15F*.

15.10 When a review is carried out by telephone or by video conferencing facilities, an officer at the station holding the detainee shall be required by the review officer to fulfil that officer's obligations under PACE section 40 and this Code by:

(a) making any record connected with the review in the detainee's custody record;
(b) if applicable, making the record in *(a)* in the presence of the detainee; and
(c) for a review by telephone, giving the detainee information about the review.

15.11 When a review is carried out by telephone or by video conferencing facilities, the requirement in *paragraph 15.3* will be satisfied:

(a) if facilities exist for the immediate transmission of written representations to the review officer, e.g. fax or email message, by allowing those who are given the opportunity to make representations, to make their representations:
    (i) orally by telephone or (as the case may be) by means of the video conferencing facilities; or
    (ii) in writing using the facilities for the immediate transmission of written representations; and
(b) in all other cases, by allowing those who are given the opportunity to make representations, to make their representations orally by telephone or by means of the video conferencing facilities.

(c) Documentation

15.12 It is the officer's responsibility to make sure all reminders given under *paragraph 15.4* are noted in the custody record.

15.13 The grounds for, and extent of, any delay in conducting a review shall be recorded.

15.14 When a review is carried out by telephone or video conferencing facilities, a record shall be made of:

(a) the reason the review officer did not attend the station holding the detainee;
(b) the place the review officer was;
(c) the method representations, oral or written, were made to the review officer, see *paragraph 15.11*.

15.15 Any written representations shall be retained.

15.16 A record shall be made as soon as practicable of:

(a) the outcome of each review of detention before or after charge, and if *paragraph 15.7* applies, of when the person was informed and by whom;
(b) the outcome of any determination under PACE, section 42 by a superintendent whether to extend the maximum period of detention without charge beyond 24 hours from the relevant time. If an authorisation is given, the record shall state the number of hours and minutes by which the detention period is extended or further extended.

(c) the outcome of each application under PACE, section 43, for a warrant of further detention or under section 44, for an extension or further extension of that warrant. If a warrant for further detention is granted under section 43 or extended or further extended under 44, the record shall state the detention period authorised by the warrant and the date and time it was granted or (as the case may be) the period by which the warrant is extended or further extended.

Note: Any period during which a person is released on bail does not count towards the maximum period of detention without charge allowed under PACE, sections 41 to 44.

Notes for Guidance

15A Review officer for the purposes of:

- *PACE, sections 40, 40A and 45A means, in the case of a person arrested but not charged, an officer of at least inspector rank not directly involved in the investigation and, if a person has been arrested and charged, the custody officer.*

15B The detention of persons in police custody not subject to the statutory review requirement in paragraph 15.1 should still be reviewed periodically as a matter of good practice. Such reviews can be carried out by an officer of the rank of sergeant or above. The purpose of such reviews is to check the particular power under which a detainee is held continues to apply, any associated conditions are complied with and to make sure appropriate action is taken to deal with any changes. This includes the detainee's prompt release when the power no longer applies, or their transfer if the power requires the detainee be taken elsewhere as soon as the necessary arrangements are made. Examples include persons:

(a) arrested on warrant because they failed to answer bail to appear at court;

(b) arrested under the Bail Act 1976, section 7(3) for breaching a condition of bail granted after charge;

(c) in police custody for specific purposes and periods under the Crime (Sentences) Act 1997, Schedule 1;

(d) convicted, or remand prisoners, held in police stations on behalf of the Prison Service under the Imprisonment (Temporary Provisions) Act 1980, section 6;

(e) being detained to prevent them causing a breach of the peace;

(f) detained at police stations on behalf of Immigration Enforcement (formerly the UK Immigration Service);

(g) detained by order of a magistrates' court under the Criminal Justice Act 1988, section 152 (as amended by the Drugs Act 2005, section 8) to facilitate the recovery of evidence after being charged with drug possession or drug trafficking and suspected of having swallowed drugs.

The detention of persons remanded into police detention by order of a court under the Magistrates' Courts Act 1980, section 128 is subject to a statutory requirement to review that detention. This is to make sure the detainee is taken back to court no later than the end of the period authorised by the court or when the need for their detention by police ceases, whichever is the sooner.

15C In the case of a review of detention, but not an extension, the detainee need not be woken for the review. However, if the detainee is likely to be asleep, e.g. during a period of rest allowed as in paragraph 12.2, at the latest time a review or authorisation to extend detention may take place, the officer should, if the legal obligations and time constraints permit, bring forward the procedure to allow the detainee to make representations. A detainee not asleep during the review must be present when the grounds for their continued detention are recorded and must at the same time be informed of those grounds unless the review officer considers the person is incapable of understanding what is said, violent or likely to become violent or in urgent need of medical attention.

15CA In paragraph 15.3(b) and (c), 'available' includes being contactable in time to enable them to make representations remotely by telephone or other electronic means or in person by attending the station. Reasonable efforts should therefore be made to give the solicitor and appropriate adult sufficient notice of the time the decision is expected to be made so that they can make themselves available.

15D An application to a Magistrates' Court under PACE, sections 43 or 44 for a warrant of further detention or its extension should be made between 10am and 9pm, and if possible during normal court hours. It will not usually be practicable to arrange for a court to sit specially outside the hours of 10am to 9pm. If it appears a special sitting may be needed outside normal court hours but between 10am and 9pm, the clerk to the justices should be given notice and informed of this possibility, while the court is sitting if possible.

15E In paragraph 15.2, the officer responsible for the station holding the detainee includes a superintendent or above who, in accordance with their force operational policy or police regulations, is given that responsibility on a temporary basis whilst the appointed long-term holder is off duty or otherwise unavailable.

15F The provisions of PACE, section 40A allowing telephone reviews do not apply to reviews of detention after charge by the custody officer. When video conferencing is not required, they allow the use of a telephone to carry out a review of detention before charge. The procedure under PACE, section 42 must be done in person.

15G Video conferencing facilities means any facilities (whether a live television link or other facilities) by means of which the review can be carried out with the review officer, the detainee concerned and the detainee's solicitor all being able to both see and to hear each other. The use of video conferencing facilities for decisions about detention under section 45A of PACE is subject to regulations made by the Secretary of State being in force.

16 Charging detained persons

(a) Action

16.1 When the officer in charge of the investigation reasonably believes there is sufficient evidence to provide a realistic prospect of conviction for the offence (see *paragraph 11.6)*, they shall without delay, and subject to the following qualification, inform the custody officer who will be responsible for considering whether the detainee should be charged. See *Notes 11B* and *16A*. When a person is detained in respect of more than one offence it is permissible to delay informing the custody officer until the above conditions are satisfied in respect of all the offences, but see *paragraph 11.6*. If the detainee is a juvenile, mentally disordered or otherwise mentally vulnerable, any resulting action shall be taken in the presence of the appropriate adult if they are present at the time. See *Notes 16B* and *16C*.

16.1A Where guidance issued by the Director of Public Prosecutions under PACE, section 37A is in force the custody officer must comply with that Guidance in deciding how to act in dealing with the detainee. See *Notes 16AA* and *16AB*.

16.1B Where in compliance with the DPP's Guidance the custody officer decides that the case should be immediately referred to the CPS to make the charging decision, consultation should take place with a Crown Prosecutor as soon as is reasonably practicable. Where the Crown Prosecutor is unable to make the charging decision on the information available at that time, the detainee may be released without charge and on bail (with conditions if necessary) under section 37(7)(a). In such circumstances, the detainee should be informed that they are being released to enable the Director of Public Prosecutions to make a decision under section 37B.

16.2 When a detainee is charged with or informed they may be prosecuted for an offence, see *Note 16B*, they shall, unless the restriction on drawing adverse inferences from silence applies, see *Annex C*, be cautioned as follows:

> *'You do not have to say anything. But it may harm your defence if you do not mention now something which you later rely on in court. Anything you do say may be given in evidence.'*

Where the use of the Welsh Language is appropriate, a constable may provide the caution directly in Welsh in the following terms:

> *'Does dim rhaid i chi ddweud dim byd. Ond gall niweidio eich amddiffyniad os na fyddwch chi'n sôn, yn awr, am rywbeth y byddwch chi'n dibynnu arno nes ymlaen yn y llys. Gall unrhyw beth yr ydych yn ei ddweud gael ei roi fel tystiolaeth.'*

Annex C, paragraph 2 sets out the alternative terms of the caution to be used when the restriction on drawing adverse inferences from silence applies.

16.3 When a detainee is charged they shall be given a written notice showing particulars of the offence and, subject to *paragraph 2.6A*, the officer's name and the case reference number. As far as possible the particulars of the charge shall be stated in simple terms, but they shall also show the precise offence in law with which the detainee is charged. The notice shall begin:

'You are charged with the offence(s) shown below.' Followed by the caution.

If the detainee is a juvenile, mentally disordered or otherwise mentally vulnerable, a copy of the notice should also be given to the appropriate adult.

16.4 If, after a detainee has been charged with or informed they may be prosecuted for an offence, an officer wants to tell them about any written statement or interview with another person relating to such an offence, the detainee shall either be handed a true copy of the written statement or the content of the interview record brought to their attention. Nothing shall be done to invite any reply or comment except to:

(a) caution the detainee, *'You do not have to say anything, but anything you do say may be given in evidence.'*;

Where the use of the Welsh Language is appropriate, caution the detainee in the following terms:

'Does dim rhaid i chi ddweud dim byd, ond gall unrhyw beth yr ydych yn ei ddweud gael ei roi fel tystiolaeth.'

and

(b) remind the detainee about their right to legal advice.

16.4A If the detainee:

- cannot read, the document may be read to them;
- is a juvenile, mentally disordered or otherwise mentally vulnerable, the appropriate adult shall also be given a copy, or the interview record shall be brought to their attention.

16.5 A detainee may not be interviewed about an offence after they have been charged with, or informed they may be prosecuted for it, unless the interview is necessary:

- to prevent or minimise harm or loss to some other person, or the public
- to clear up an ambiguity in a previous answer or statement
- in the interests of justice for the detainee to have put to them, and have an opportunity to comment on, information concerning the offence which has come to light since they were charged or informed they might be prosecuted

Before any such interview, the interviewer shall:

(a) caution the detainee, *'You do not have to say anything, but anything you do say may be given in evidence.'*

Where the use of the Welsh Language is appropriate, the interviewer shall caution the detainee: *'Does dim rhaid i chi ddweud dim byd, ond gall unrhyw beth yr ydych yn ei ddweud gael ei roi fel tystiolaeth.'*

(b) remind the detainee about their right to legal advice.

See *Note 16B*

16.6 The provisions of *paragraphs 16.2* to *16.5* must be complied with in the appropriate adult's presence if they are already at the police station. If they are not at the police station then these provisions must be complied with again in their presence when they arrive unless the detainee has been released. See *Note 16C*.

16.7 When a juvenile is charged with an offence and the custody officer authorises their continued detention after charge, the custody officer must make arrangements for the juvenile to be taken into the care of a local authority to be detained pending appearance in court *unless* the custody officer certifies in accordance with PACE, section 38(6), that:

(a) for any juvenile; it is impracticable to do so and the reasons why it is impracticable must be set out in the certificate that must be produced to the court; or,

(b) in the case of a juvenile of at least 12 years old, no secure accommodation is available and other accommodation would not be adequate to protect the public from serious harm from that juvenile. See *Note 16D*.

Note: Chief officers should ensure that the operation of these provisions at police stations in their areas is subject to supervision and monitoring by an officer of the rank of inspector or above.

16.7A The requirement in *paragraph 3.4(b)* that documents and materials essential to effectively challenging the lawfulness of the detainee's arrest and detention must be made available to the detainee and, if they are represented, their solicitor, applies for the purposes of this section and a person's detention after charge. This means that the custody officer making the bail decision (PACE, section 38) or reviewing the need for detention after charge (*PACE, section 40*), is responsible for determining what, if any, documents or materials are essential and must be made available to the detainee or their solicitor. See *Note 3ZA*.

(b) Documentation

16.8 A record shall be made of anything a detainee says when charged.

16.9 Any questions put in an interview after charge and answers given relating to the offence shall be recorded in full during the interview on forms for that purpose and the record signed by the detainee or, if they refuse, by the interviewer and any third parties present. If the questions are audibly recorded or visually recorded the arrangements in Code E or F apply.

16.10 If arrangements for a juvenile's transfer into local authority care as in *paragraph 16.7* are not made, the custody officer must record the reasons in a certificate which must be produced before the court with the juvenile. See *Note 16D*.

Notes for Guidance

16A The custody officer must take into account alternatives to prosecution under the Crime and Disorder Act 1998 applicable to persons under 18, and in national guidance on the cautioning of offenders applicable to persons aged 18 and over.

16AA When a person is arrested under the provisions of the Criminal Justice Act 2003 which allow a person to be re-tried after being acquitted of a serious offence which is a qualifying offence specified in Schedule 5 to that Act and not precluded from further prosecution by virtue of section 75(3) of that Act the detention provisions of PACE are modified and make an officer of the rank of superintendent or above who has not been directly involved in the investigation responsible for determining whether the evidence is sufficient to charge.

16AB Where Guidance issued by the Director of Public Prosecutions under section 37B is in force, a custody officer who determines in accordance with that Guidance that there is sufficient evidence to charge the detainee, may detain that person for no longer than is reasonably necessary to decide how that person is to be dealt with under PACE, section 37(7)(a) to (d), including, where appropriate, consultation with the Duty Prosecutor. The period is subject to the maximum period of detention before charge determined by PACE, sections 41 to 44. Where in accordance with the Guidance the case is referred to the CPS for decision, the custody officer should ensure that an officer involved in the investigation sends to the CPS such information as is specified in the Guidance.

16B The giving of a warning or the service of the Notice of Intended Prosecution required by the Road Traffic Offenders Act 1988, section 1 does not amount to informing a detainee they may be prosecuted for an offence and so does not preclude further questioning in relation to that offence.

16C There is no power under PACE to detain a person and delay action under paragraphs 16.2 to 16.5 solely to await the arrival of the appropriate adult. Reasonable efforts should therefore be made to give the appropriate adult sufficient notice of the time the decision (charge etc.) is to be implemented so that they can be present. If the appropriate adult is not, or cannot be, present at that time, the detainee should be released on bail to return for the decision to be implemented when the adult is present, unless the custody officer determines that the absence of the appropriate adult makes the detainee unsuitable for bail for this purpose. After charge, bail cannot be refused, or release on bail delayed, simply because an appropriate adult is not available, unless the absence of that adult provides the custody officer with the necessary grounds to authorise detention after charge under PACE, section 38.

16D Except as in paragraph 16.7, neither a juvenile's behaviour nor the nature of the offence provides grounds for the custody officer to decide it is impracticable to arrange the juvenile's transfer to local authority care. Impracticability concerns the transport and travel requirements and the lack of secure accommodation which is provided for the purposes of restricting liberty does not make it impracticable to transfer the juvenile. The availability of secure accommodation is only a factor in relation to a juvenile aged 12 or over when other local authority accommodation would not be adequate to protect the public from serious harm from them. The obligation to transfer a juvenile to local authority accommodation applies as much to a juvenile charged during the daytime as to a juvenile to be held overnight, subject to a requirement to bring the juvenile before a court under PACE, section 46.

17 Testing persons for the presence of specified Class A drugs

(a) Action

17.1 This section of Code C applies only in selected police stations in police areas where the provisions for drug testing under section 63B of PACE (as amended by section 5 of the Criminal Justice Act 2003 and section 7 of the Drugs Act 2005) are in force and in respect of which the Secretary of State has given a notification to the relevant chief officer of police that arrangements for the taking of samples have been made. Such a notification will cover either a police area as a whole or particular stations within a police area. The notification indicates whether the testing applies to those arrested or charged or under the age of 18 as the case may be and testing can only take place in respect of the persons so indicated in the notification. Testing cannot be carried out unless the relevant notification has been given and has not been withdrawn. See *Note 17F.*

17.2 A sample of urine or a non-intimate sample may be taken from a person in police detention for the purpose of ascertaining whether they have any specified Class A drug in their body only where they have been brought before the custody officer and:

(a) either the arrest condition, see *paragraph 17.3,* or the charge condition, see *paragraph 17.4* is met;

(b) the age condition see *paragraph 17.5,* is met;

(c) the notification condition is met in relation to the arrest condition, the charge condition, or the age condition, as the case may be. (Testing on charge and/or arrest must be specifically provided for in the notification for the power to apply. In addition, the fact that testing of under 18s is authorised must be expressly provided for in the notification before the power to test such persons applies.). See *paragraph 17.1*; and

(d) a police officer has requested the person concerned to give the sample (the request condition).

17.3 The arrest condition is met where the detainee:

(a) has been arrested for a trigger offence, see *Note 17E,* but not charged with that offence; or

(b) has been arrested for any other offence but not charged with that offence and a police officer of inspector rank or above, who has reasonable grounds for suspecting that their misuse of any specified Class A drug caused or contributed to the offence, has authorised the sample to be taken.

17.4 The charge condition is met where the detainee:

(a) has been charged with a trigger offence, or

(b) has been charged with any other offence and a police officer of inspector rank or above, who has reasonable grounds for suspecting that the detainee's misuse of any specified Class A drug caused or contributed to the offence, has authorised the sample to be taken.

17.5 The age condition is met where:

(a) in the case of a detainee who has been arrested but not charged as in *paragraph 17.3,* they are aged 18 or over;

(b) in the case of a detainee who has been charged as in *paragraph 17.4,* they are aged 14 or over.

17.6 Before requesting a sample from the person concerned, an officer must:

(a) inform them that the purpose of taking the sample is for drug testing under PACE. This is to ascertain whether they have a specified Class A drug present in their body;

(b) warn them that if, when so requested, they fail without good cause to provide a sample they may be liable to prosecution;
(c) where the taking of the sample has been authorised by an inspector or above in accordance with *paragraph 17.3(b)* or *17.4(b)* above, inform them that the authorisation has been given and the grounds for giving it;
(d) remind them of the following rights, which may be exercised at any stage during the period in custody:
 (i) the right to have someone informed of their arrest [see section 5];
 (ii) the right to consult privately with a solicitor and that free independent legal advice is available [see section 6]; and
 (iii) the right to consult these Codes of Practice [see section 3].

17.7 In the case of a person who has not attained the age specified in section 63B(5A) of PACE—
(a) the making of the request for a sample under *paragraph 17.2(d)* above;
(b) the giving of the warning and the information under *paragraph 17.6* above; and
(c) the taking of the sample,

may not take place except in the presence of an appropriate adult. See *Note 17G*.

17.8 Authorisation by an officer of the rank of inspector or above within *paragraph 17.3(b)* or *17.4(b)* may be given orally or in writing but, if it is given orally, it must be confirmed in writing as soon as practicable.

17.9 If a sample is taken from a detainee who has been arrested for an offence but not charged with that offence as in *paragraph 17.3*, no further sample may be taken during the same continuous period of detention. If during that same period the charge condition is also met in respect of that detainee, the sample which has been taken shall be treated as being taken by virtue of the charge condition, see *paragraph 17.4*, being met.

17.10 A detainee from whom a sample may be taken may be detained for up to six hours from the time of charge if the custody officer reasonably believes the detention is necessary to enable a sample to be taken. Where the arrest condition is met, a detainee whom the custody officer has decided to release on bail without charge may continue to be detained, but not beyond 24 hours from the relevant time (as defined in section 41(2) of PACE), to enable a sample to be taken.

17.11 A detainee in respect of whom the arrest condition is met, but not the charge condition, see *paragraphs 17.3* and *17.4*, and whose release would be required before a sample can be taken had they not continued to be detained as a result of being arrested for a further offence which does not satisfy the arrest condition, may have a sample taken at any time within 24 hours after the arrest for the offence that satisfies the arrest condition.

(b) Documentation

17.12 The following must be recorded in the custody record:
(a) if a sample is taken following authorisation by an officer of the rank of inspector or above, the authorisation and the grounds for suspicion;
(b) the giving of a warning of the consequences of failure to provide a sample;
(c) the time at which the sample was given; and
(d) the time of charge or, where the arrest condition is being relied upon, the time of arrest and, where applicable, the fact that a sample taken after arrest but before charge is to be treated as being taken by virtue of the charge condition, where that is met in the same period of continuous detention. See *paragraph 17.9*.

(c) General

17.13 A sample may only be taken by a prescribed person. See *Note 17C*.

17.14 Force may not be used to take any sample for the purpose of drug testing.

17.15 The terms 'Class A drug' and 'misuse' have the same meanings as in the Misuse of Drugs Act 1971. 'Specified' (in relation to a Class A drug) and 'trigger offence' have the same meanings as in Part III of the Criminal Justice and Court Services Act 2000.

17.16 Any sample taken:

(a) may not be used for any purpose other than to ascertain whether the person concerned has a specified Class A drug present in his body; and

(b) can be disposed of as clinical waste unless it is to be sent for further analysis in cases where the test result is disputed at the point when the result is known, including on the basis that medication has been taken, or for quality assurance purposes.

(d) Assessment of misuse of drugs

17.17 Under the provisions of Part 3 of the Drugs Act 2005, where a detainee has tested positive for a specified Class A drug under section 63B of PACE a police officer may, at any time before the person's release from the police station, impose a requirement on the detainee to attend an initial assessment of their drug misuse by a suitably qualified person and to remain for its duration. Where such a requirement is imposed, the officer must, at the same time, impose a second requirement on the detainee to attend and remain for a follow-up assessment. The officer must inform the detainee that the second requirement will cease to have effect if, at the initial assessment they are informed that a follow-up assessment is not necessary These requirements may only be imposed on a person if:

(a) they have reached the age of 18

(b) notification has been given by the Secretary of State to the relevant chief officer of police that arrangements for conducting initial and follow-up assessments have been made for those from whom samples for testing have been taken at the police station where the detainee is in custody.

17.18 When imposing a requirement to attend an initial assessment and a follow-up assessment the police officer must:

(a) inform the person of the time and place at which the initial assessment is to take place;

(b) explain that this information will be confirmed in writing; and

(c) warn the person that they may be liable to prosecution if they fail without good cause to attend the initial assessment and remain for its duration and if they fail to attend the follow-up assessment and remain for its duration (if so required).

17.19 Where a police officer has imposed a requirement to attend an initial assessment and a follow-up assessment in accordance with *paragraph 17.17*, he must, before the person is released from detention, give the person notice in writing which:

(a) confirms their requirement to attend and remain for the duration of the assessments; and

(b) confirms the information and repeats the warning referred to in *paragraph 17.18*.

17.20 The following must be recorded in the custody record:

(a) that the requirement to attend an initial assessment and a follow-up assessment has been imposed; and

(b) the information, explanation, warning and notice given in accordance with *paragraphs 17.17* and *17.19*.

17.21 Where a notice is given in accordance with paragraph 17.19, a police officer can give the person a further notice in writing which informs the person of any change to the time or place at which the initial assessment is to take place and which repeats the warning referred to in *paragraph 17.18(c)*.

17.22 Part 3 of the Drugs Act 2005 also requires police officers to have regard to any guidance issued by the Secretary of State in respect of the assessment provisions.

Notes for Guidance

17A When warning a person who is asked to provide a urine or non-intimate sample in accordance with paragraph 17.6(b), the following form of words may be used:

'You do not have to provide a sample, but I must warn you that if you fail or refuse without good cause to do so, you will commit an offence for which you may be imprisoned, or fined, or both'.

Where the Welsh language is appropriate, the following form of words may be used:

'Does dim rhaid i chi roi sampl, ond mae'n rhaid i mi eich rhybuddio y byddwch chi'n cyflawni trosedd os byddwch chi'n methu neu yn gwrthod gwneud hynny heb reswm da, ac y gellir, oherwydd hynny, eich carcharu, eich dirwyo, neu'r ddau.'

17B A sample has to be sufficient and suitable. A sufficient sample is sufficient in quantity and quality to enable drug-testing analysis to take place. A suitable sample is one which by its nature, is suitable for a particular form of drug analysis.

17C A prescribed person in paragraph 17.13 is one who is prescribed in regulations made by the Secretary of State under section 63B(6) of the Police and Criminal Evidence Act 1984. [The regulations are currently contained in regulation SI 2001 No. 2645, the Police and Criminal Evidence Act 1984 (Drug Testing Persons in Police Detention) (Prescribed Persons) Regulations 2001.]

17D Samples, and the information derived from them, may not be subsequently used in the investigation of any offence or in evidence against the persons from whom they were taken.

17E Trigger offences are:

1. *Offences under the following provisions of the Theft Act 1968:*
   section 1 (theft)
   section 8 (robbery)
   section 9 (burglary)
   section 10 (aggravated burglary)
   section 12 (taking a motor vehicle or other conveyance without authority)
   section 12A (aggravated vehicle-taking)
   section 22 (handling stolen goods)
   section 25 (going equipped for stealing etc.)
2. *Offences under the following provisions of the Misuse of Drugs Act 1971, if committed in respect of a specified Class A drug:—*
   section 4 (restriction on production and supply of controlled drugs)
   section 5(2) (possession of a controlled drug)
   section 5(3) (possession of a controlled drug with intent to supply)
3. *Offences under the following provisions of the Fraud Act 2006:*
   section 1 (fraud)
   section 6 (possession etc. of articles for use in frauds)
   section 7 (making or supplying articles for use in frauds)

3A. An offence under section 1(1) of the Criminal Attempts Act 1981 if committed in respect of an offence under
   (a) any of the following provisions of the Theft Act 1968:
      section 1 (theft)
      section 8 (robbery)
      section 9 (burglary)
      section 22 (handling stolen goods)
   (b) section 1 of the Fraud Act 2006 (fraud)

4. *Offences under the following provisions of the Vagrancy Act 1824:*
   section 3 (begging)
   section 4 (persistent begging)

17F The power to take samples is subject to notification by the Secretary of State that appropriate arrangements for the taking of samples have been made for the police area as a whole or for the particular police station concerned for whichever of the following is specified in the notification:
   (a) persons in respect of whom the arrest condition is met;
   (b) persons in respect of whom the charge condition is met;
   (c) persons who have not attained the age of 18.

Note: Notification is treated as having been given for the purposes of the charge condition in relation to a police area, if testing (on charge) under section 63B(2) of PACE was in force immediately before section 7 of the Drugs Act 2005 was brought into force; and for the purposes of the age condition, in relation to a police area or police station, if immediately before that day, notification that arrangements had been made for the taking of samples from persons under the age of 18 (those aged 14-17) had been given and had not been withdrawn.

17G Appropriate adult in paragraph 17.7 means the person's–

- *(a) parent or guardian or, if they are in the care of a local authority or voluntary organisation, a person representing that authority or organisation; or*
- *(b) a social worker of a local authority; or*
- *(c) if no person falling within (a) or (b) above is available, any responsible person aged 18 or over who is not:*
  - *~ a police officer;*
  - *~ employed by the police;*
  - *~ under the direction or control of the chief officer of police force; or*
  - *~ a person who provides services under contractual arrangements (but without being employed by the chief officer of a police force), to assist that force in relation to the discharge of its chief officer's functions*

whether or not they are on duty at the time.

Note: Paragraph 1.5 *extends this Note to the person called to fulfil the role of the appropriate adult for a 17-year old detainee for the purposes of paragraph 17.7.*

Annex A Intimate and Strip Searches

A Intimate search

1. An intimate search consists of the physical examination of a person's body orifices other than the mouth. The intrusive nature of such searches means the actual and potential risks associated with intimate searches must never be underestimated.

(a) Action

2. Body orifices other than the mouth may be searched only:
   - (a) if authorised by an officer of inspector rank or above who has reasonable grounds for believing that the person may have concealed on themselves:
     - (i) anything which they could and might use to cause physical injury to themselves or others at the station; or
     - (ii) a Class A drug which they intended to supply to another or to export;

     and the officer has reasonable grounds for believing that an intimate search is the only means of removing those items; and
   - (b) if the search is under *paragraph 2(a)(ii)* (a drug offence search), the detainee's appropriate consent has been given in writing.

2A. Before the search begins, a police officer or designated detention officer, must tell the detainee:—

- (a) that the authority to carry out the search has been given;
- (b) the grounds for giving the authorisation and for believing that the article cannot be removed without an intimate search.

2B. Before a detainee is asked to give appropriate consent to a search under *paragraph 2(a)(ii)* (a drug offence search) they must be warned that if they refuse without good cause their refusal may harm their case if it comes to trial, see *Note A6*. This warning may be given by a police officer or member of police staff. In the case of juveniles, mentally vulnerable or mentally disordered suspects, the seeking and giving of consent must take place in the presence of the appropriate adult. A juvenile's consent is only valid if their parent's or guardian's consent is also obtained unless the juvenile is under 14, when their parent's or guardian's consent is sufficient in its own right. A detainee who is not legally represented must be reminded of their entitlement to have free legal advice, see Code C, *paragraph 6.5*, and the reminder noted in the custody record.

3. An intimate search may only be carried out by a registered medical practitioner or registered nurse, unless an officer of at least inspector rank considers this is not practicable and the search is to take place under *paragraph 2(a)(i)*, in which case a police officer may carry out the search. See *Notes A1* to *A5*.

3A. Any proposal for a search under *paragraph 2(a)(i)* to be carried out by someone other than a registered medical practitioner or registered nurse must only be considered as a last resort and when the authorising officer is satisfied the risks associated with allowing the item to remain with the detainee outweigh the risks associated with removing it. See *Notes A1* to *A5*.

4. An intimate search under:

- *paragraph 2(a)(i)* may take place only at a hospital, surgery, other medical premises or police station;
- *paragraph 2(a)(ii)* may take place only at a hospital, surgery or other medical premises and must be carried out by a registered medical practitioner or a registered nurse.

5. An intimate search at a police station of a juvenile or mentally disordered or otherwise mentally vulnerable person may take place only in the presence of an appropriate adult of the same sex (see Annex L), unless the detainee specifically requests a particular adult of the opposite sex who is readily available. In the case of a juvenile, the search may take place in the absence of the appropriate adult only if the juvenile signifies in the presence of the appropriate adult they do not want the adult present during the search and the adult agrees. A record shall be made of the juvenile's decision and signed by the appropriate adult.

6. When an intimate search under *paragraph 2(a)(i)* is carried out by a police officer, the officer must be of the same sex as the detainee (see *Annex L*). A minimum of two people, other than the detainee, must be present during the search. Subject to *paragraph 5*, no person of the opposite sex who is not a medical practitioner or nurse shall be present, nor shall anyone whose presence is unnecessary. The search shall be conducted with proper regard to the sensitivity and vulnerability of the detainee.

(b) Documentation

7. In the case of an intimate search, the following shall be recorded as soon as practicable in the detainee's custody record:

(a) for searches under paragraphs 2(a)(i) and (ii);
- the authorisation to carry out the search;
- the grounds for giving the authorisation;
- the grounds for believing the article could not be removed without an intimate search;
- which parts of the detainee's body were searched;
- who carried out the search;
- who was present;
- the result.

(b) for searches under paragraph 2(a)(ii):
- the giving of the warning required by *paragraph 2B*;
- the fact that the appropriate consent was given or (as the case may be) refused, and if refused, the reason given for the refusal (if any).

8. If an intimate search is carried out by a police officer, the reason why it was impracticable for a registered medical practitioner or registered nurse to conduct it must be recorded.

B Strip search

9. A strip search is a search involving the removal of more than outer clothing. In this Code, outer clothing includes shoes and socks.

(a) Action

10. A strip search may take place only if it is considered necessary to remove an article which a detainee would not be allowed to keep and the officer reasonably considers the detainee might have concealed such an article. Strip searches shall not be routinely carried out if there is no reason to consider that articles are concealed.

The conduct of strip searches

11. When strip searches are conducted:

(a) a police officer carrying out a strip search must be the same sex as the detainee (see *Annex L*);

(b) the search shall take place in an area where the detainee cannot be seen by anyone who does not need to be present, nor by a member of the opposite sex (see *Annex L*) except an appropriate adult who has been specifically requested by the detainee;

(c) except in cases of urgency, where there is risk of serious harm to the detainee or to others, whenever a strip search involves exposure of intimate body parts, there must be at least two people present other than the detainee, and if the search is of a juvenile or mentally disordered or otherwise mentally vulnerable person, one of the people must be the appropriate adult. Except in urgent cases as above, a search of a juvenile may take place in the absence of the appropriate adult only if the juvenile signifies in the presence of the appropriate adult that they do not want the adult to be present during the search and the adult agrees. A record shall be made of the juvenile's decision and signed by the appropriate adult. The presence of more than two people, other than an appropriate adult, shall be permitted only in the most exceptional circumstances;

(d) the search shall be conducted with proper regard to the sensitivity and vulnerability of the detainee in these circumstances and every reasonable effort shall be made to secure the detainee's co-operation and minimise embarrassment. Detainees who are searched shall not normally be required to remove all their clothes at the same time, e.g. a person should be allowed to remove clothing above the waist and redress before removing further clothing;

(e) if necessary to assist the search, the detainee may be required to hold their arms in the air or to stand with their legs apart and bend forward so a visual examination may be made of the genital and anal areas provided no physical contact is made with any body orifice;

(f) if articles are found, the detainee shall be asked to hand them over. If articles are found within any body orifice other than the mouth, and the detainee refuses to hand them over, their removal would constitute an intimate search, which must be carried out as in *Part A*;

(g) a strip search shall be conducted as quickly as possible, and the detainee allowed to dress as soon as the procedure is complete.

(b) Documentation

12. A record shall be made on the custody record of a strip search including the reason it was considered necessary, those present and any result.

Notes for Guidance

A1 Before authorising any intimate search, the authorising officer must make every reasonable effort to persuade the detainee to hand the article over without a search. If the detainee agrees, a registered medical practitioner or registered nurse should whenever possible be asked to assess the risks involved and, if necessary, attend to assist the detainee.

A2 If the detainee does not agree to hand the article over without a search, the authorising officer must carefully review all the relevant factors before authorising an intimate search. In particular, the officer must consider whether the grounds for believing an article may be concealed are reasonable.

A3 If authority is given for a search under paragraph 2(a)(i), a registered medical practitioner or registered nurse shall be consulted whenever possible. The presumption should be that the search will be conducted by the registered medical practitioner or registered nurse and the authorising officer must make every reasonable effort to persuade the detainee to allow the medical practitioner or nurse to conduct the search.

A4 A constable should only be authorised to carry out a search as a last resort and when all other approaches have failed. In these circumstances, the authorising officer must be satisfied the detainee might use the article for one or more of the purposes in paragraph 2(a)(i) and the physical injury likely to be caused is sufficiently severe to justify authorising a constable to carry out the search.

A5 If an officer has any doubts whether to authorise an intimate search by a constable, the officer should seek advice from an officer of superintendent rank or above.

A6 In warning a detainee who is asked to consent to an intimate drug offence search, as in paragraph 2B, the following form of words may be used:

'You do not have to allow yourself to be searched, but I must warn you that if you refuse without good cause, your refusal may harm your case if it comes to trial.'

Where the use of the Welsh Language is appropriate, the following form of words may be used:

'Nid oes rhaid i chi roi caniatâd i gael eich archwilio, ond mae'n rhaid i mi eich rhybuddio os gwrthodwch heb reswm da, y gallai eich penderfyniad i wrthod wneud niwed i'ch achos pe bai'n dod gerbron llys.'

Annex B Delay in Notifying Arrest or Allowing Access to Legal Advice

A Persons detained under PACE

1. The exercise of the rights in *Section 5* or *Section 6*, or both, may be delayed if the person is in police detention, as in PACE, section 118(2), in connection with an indictable offence, has not yet been charged with an offence and an officer of superintendent rank or above, or inspector rank or above only for the rights in *Section 5*, has reasonable grounds for believing their exercise will:
   - (i) lead to:
     - interference with, or harm to, evidence connected with an indictable offence; or
     - interference with, or physical harm to, other people; or
   - (ii) lead to alerting other people suspected of having committed an indictable offence but not yet arrested for it; or
   - (iii) hinder the recovery of property obtained in consequence of the commission of such an offence.
2. These rights may also be delayed if the officer has reasonable grounds to believe that:
   - (i) the person detained for an indictable offence has benefited from their criminal conduct (decided in accordance with Part 2 of the Proceeds of Crime Act 2002); and
   - (ii) the recovery of the value of the property constituting that benefit will be hindered by the exercise of either right.
3. Authority to delay a detainee's right to consult privately with a solicitor may be given only if the authorising officer has reasonable grounds to believe the solicitor the detainee wants to consult will, inadvertently or otherwise, pass on a message from the detainee or act in some other way which will have any of the consequences specified under *paragraphs 1 or 2*. In these circumstances, the detainee must be allowed to choose another solicitor. See *Note B3*.
4. If the detainee wishes to see a solicitor, access to that solicitor may not be delayed on the grounds they might advise the detainee not to answer questions or the solicitor was initially asked to attend the police station by someone else. In the latter case, the detainee must be told the solicitor has come to the police station at another person's request, and must be asked to sign the custody record to signify whether they want to see the solicitor.
5. The fact the grounds for delaying notification of arrest may be satisfied does not automatically mean the grounds for delaying access to legal advice will also be satisfied.
6. These rights may be delayed only for as long as grounds exist and in no case beyond 36 hours after the relevant time as in PACE, section 41. If the grounds cease to apply within this time, the detainee must, as soon as practicable, be asked if they want to exercise either right, the custody record must be noted accordingly, and action taken in accordance with the relevant section of the Code.
7. A detained person must be permitted to consult a solicitor for a reasonable time before any court hearing.

B Not used

C Documentation

13. The grounds for action under this Annex shall be recorded and the detainee informed of them as soon as practicable.

14. Any reply given by a detainee under *paragraphs 6* or *11* must be recorded and the detainee asked to endorse the record in relation to whether they want to receive legal advice at this point.

D Cautions and special warnings

15. When a suspect detained at a police station is interviewed during any period for which access to legal advice has been delayed under this Annex, the court or jury may not draw adverse inferences from their silence.

Notes for Guidance

B1 Even if Annex B applies in the case of a juvenile, or a person who is mentally disordered or otherwise mentally vulnerable, action to inform the appropriate adult and the person responsible for a juvenile's welfare, if that is a different person, must nevertheless be taken as in paragraph 3.13 and 3.15.

B2 In the case of Commonwealth citizens and foreign nationals, see Note 7A.

B3 A decision to delay access to a specific solicitor is likely to be a rare occurrence and only when it can be shown the suspect is capable of misleading that particular solicitor and there is more than a substantial risk that the suspect will succeed in causing information to be conveyed which will lead to one or more of the specified consequences.

Annex C Restriction on Drawing Adverse Inferences from Silence and Terms of the Caution when the Restriction Applies

(a) The restriction on drawing adverse inferences from silence

1. The Criminal Justice and Public Order Act 1994, sections 34, 36 and 37 as amended by the Youth Justice and Criminal Evidence Act 1999, section 58 describe the conditions under which adverse inferences may be drawn from a person's failure or refusal to say anything about their involvement in the offence when interviewed, after being charged or informed they may be prosecuted. These provisions are subject to an overriding restriction on the ability of a court or jury to draw adverse inferences from a person's silence. This restriction applies:

(a) to any detainee at a police station, see *Note 10C* who, before being interviewed, see *section 11* or being charged or informed they may be prosecuted, see *section 16,* has:
  - (i) asked for legal advice, see *section 6, paragraph 6.1*;
  - (ii) not been allowed an opportunity to consult a solicitor, including the duty solicitor, as in this Code; and
  - (iii) not changed their mind about wanting legal advice, see *section 6, paragraph 6.6(d).*

  Note the condition in (ii) will:
  - ~ apply when a detainee who has asked for legal advice is interviewed before speaking to a solicitor as in *section 6, paragraph 6.6(a)* or *(b)*;
  - ~ not apply if the detained person declines to ask for the duty solicitor, see *section 6, paragraphs 6.6(c)* and *(d).*

(b) to any person charged with, or informed they may be prosecuted for, an offence who:
  - (i) has had brought to their notice a written statement made by another person or the content of an interview with another person which relates to that offence, see *section 16, paragraph 16.4*;
  - (ii) is interviewed about that offence, see *section 16, paragraph 16.5*; or
  - (iii) makes a written statement about that offence, see *Annex D paragraphs 4* and *9.*

(b) Terms of the caution when the restriction applies

2. When a requirement to caution arises at a time when the restriction on drawing adverse inferences from silence applies, the caution shall be:

'You do not have to say anything, but anything you do say may be given in evidence.'

Where the use of the Welsh Language is appropriate, the caution may be used directly in Welsh in the following terms:

'Does dim rhaid i chi ddweud dim byd, ond gall unrhyw beth yr ydych chi'n ei ddweud gael ei roi fel tystiolaeth.'

3. Whenever the restriction either begins to apply or ceases to apply after a caution has already been given, the person shall be re-cautioned in the appropriate terms. The changed position on drawing inferences and that the previous caution no longer applies shall also be explained to the detainee in ordinary language. See *Note C2*.

Notes for Guidance

C1 The restriction on drawing inferences from silence does not apply to a person who has not been detained and who therefore cannot be prevented from seeking legal advice if they want to, see paragraphs 10.2 and 3.21.

C2 The following is suggested as a framework to help explain changes in the position on drawing adverse inferences if the restriction on drawing adverse inferences from silence:

(a) begins to apply:

'The caution you were previously given no longer applies. This is because after that caution:

(i) you asked to speak to a solicitor but have not yet been allowed an opportunity to speak to a solicitor. See paragraph 1(a); or

(ii) you have been charged with/informed you may be prosecuted. See paragraph 1(b).

'This means that from now on, adverse inferences cannot be drawn at court and your defence will not be harmed just because you choose to say nothing. Please listen carefully to the caution I am about to give you because it will apply from now on. You will see that it does not say anything about your defence being harmed.'

(b) ceases to apply before or at the time the person is charged or informed they may be prosecuted, see paragraph 1(a);

'The caution you were previously given no longer applies. This is because after that caution you have been allowed an opportunity to speak to a solicitor. Please listen carefully to the caution I am about to give you because it will apply from now on. It explains how your defence at court may be affected if you choose to say nothing.'

Annex D Written Statements Under Caution

(a) Written by a person under caution

1. A person shall always be invited to write down what they want to say.

2. A person who has not been charged with, or informed they may be prosecuted for, any offence to which the statement they want to write relates, shall:

(a) unless the statement is made at a time when the restriction on drawing adverse inferences from silence applies, see Annex C, be asked to write out and sign the following before writing what they want to say:

'I make this statement of my own free will. I understand that I do not have to say anything but that it may harm my defence if I do not mention when questioned something which I later rely on in court. This statement may be given in evidence.';

(b) if the statement is made at a time when the restriction on drawing adverse inferences from silence applies, be asked to write out and sign the following before writing what they want to say;

'I make this statement of my own free will. I understand that I do not have to say anything. This statement may be given in evidence.'

3. When a person, on the occasion of being charged with or informed they may be prosecuted for any offence, asks to make a statement which relates to any such offence and wants to write it they shall:

(a) unless the restriction on drawing adverse inferences from silence, see *Annex C*, applied when they were so charged or informed they may be prosecuted, be asked to write out and sign the following before writing what they want to say:
'I make this statement of my own free will. I understand that I do not have to say anything but that it may harm my defence if I do not mention when questioned something which I later rely on in court. This statement may be given in evidence.';

(b) if the restriction on drawing adverse inferences from silence applied when they were so charged or informed they may be prosecuted, be asked to write out and sign the following before writing what they want to say:
'I make this statement of my own free will. I understand that I do not have to say anything. This statement may be given in evidence.'

4. When a person who has already been charged with or informed they may be prosecuted for any offence asks to make a statement which relates to any such offence and wants to write it, they shall be asked to write out and sign the following before writing what they want to say:

'I make this statement of my own free will. I understand that I do not have to say anything. This statement may be given in evidence.';

5. Any person writing their own statement shall be allowed to do so without any prompting except a police officer or other police staff may indicate to them which matters are material or question any ambiguity in the statement.

(b) Written by a police officer or other police staff

6. If a person says they would like someone to write the statement for them, a police officer, or other police staff shall write the statement.

7. If the person has not been charged with, or informed they may be prosecuted for, any offence to which the statement they want to make relates they shall, before starting, be asked to sign, or make their mark, to the following:

(a) unless the statement is made at a time when the restriction on drawing adverse inferences from silence applies, see *Annex C*:
'I, ..., wish to make a statement. I want someone to write down what I say. I understand that I do not have to say anything but that it may harm my defence if I do not mention when questioned something which I later rely on in court. This statement may be given in evidence.';

(b) if the statement is made at a time when the restriction on drawing adverse inferences from silence applies:
'I, ..., wish to make a statement. I want someone to write down what I say. I understand that I do not have to say anything. This statement may be given in evidence.'

8. If, on the occasion of being charged with or informed they may be prosecuted for any offence, the person asks to make a statement which relates to any such offence they shall before starting be asked to sign, or make their mark to, the following:

(a) unless the restriction on drawing adverse inferences from silence applied, see *Annex C*, when they were so charged or informed they may be prosecuted:
'I, ..., wish to make a statement. I want someone to write down what I say. I understand that I do not have to say anything but that it may harm my defence if I do not mention when questioned something which I later rely on in court. This statement may be given in evidence.';

(b) if the restriction on drawing adverse inferences from silence applied when they were so charged or informed they may be prosecuted:
'I, ..., wish to make a statement. I want someone to write down what I say. I understand that I do not have to say anything. This statement may be given in evidence.'

9. If, having already been charged with or informed they may be prosecuted for any offence, a person asks to make a statement which relates to any such offence they shall before starting, be asked to sign, or make their mark to:

'I, ..., wish to make a statement. I want someone to write down what I say. I understand that I do not have to say anything. This statement may be given in evidence.'

10. The person writing the statement must take down the exact words spoken by the person making it and must not edit or paraphrase it. Any questions that are necessary, e.g. to make it more intelligible, and the answers given must be recorded at the same time on the statement form.

11. When the writing of a statement is finished the person making it shall be asked to read it and to make any corrections, alterations or additions they want. When they have finished reading they shall be asked to write and sign or make their mark on the following certificate at the end of the statement:

'I have read the above statement, and I have been able to correct, alter or add anything I wish. This statement is true. I have made it of my own free will.'

12. If the person making the statement cannot read, or refuses to read it, or to write the above mentioned certificate at the end of it or to sign it, the person taking the statement shall read it to them and ask them if they would like to correct, alter or add anything and to put their signature or make their mark at the end. The person taking the statement shall certify on the statement itself what has occurred.

Annex E Summary of Provisions Relating to Mentally Disordered and Otherwise Mentally Vulnerable People

1. If an officer has any suspicion, or is told in good faith, that a person of any age may be mentally disordered or otherwise mentally vulnerable, or mentally incapable of understanding the significance of questions or their replies that person shall be treated as mentally disordered or otherwise mentally vulnerable for the purposes of this Code. See *paragraph 1.4* and *Note E4*

2. In the case of a person who is mentally disordered or otherwise mentally vulnerable, 'the appropriate adult' means:

(a) a relative, guardian or other person responsible for their care or custody;

(b) someone experienced in dealing with mentally disordered or mentally vulnerable people but who is not a police officer or employed by the police;

(c) failing these, some other responsible adult aged 18 or over who is not a police officer or employed by the police.

See *paragraph 1.7(b) and Note 1D.*

3. If the custody officer authorises the detention of a person who is mentally vulnerable or appears to be suffering from a mental disorder, the custody officer must as soon as practicable inform the appropriate adult of the grounds for detention and the person's whereabouts, and ask the adult to come to the police station to see them. If the appropriate adult:

- is already at the station when information is given as in *paragraphs 3.1* to *3.5* the information must be given in their presence;
- is not at the station when the provisions of *paragraph 3.1* to *3.5* are complied with these provisions must be complied with again in their presence once they arrive.

See *paragraphs 3.15* to *3.17*

4. If the appropriate adult, having been informed of the right to legal advice, considers legal advice should be taken, the provisions of *section 6* apply as if the mentally disordered or otherwise mentally vulnerable person had requested access to legal advice. See *paragraphs 3.19, 6.5A* and *Note E1.*

5. The custody officer must make sure a person receives appropriate clinical attention as soon as reasonably practicable if the person appears to be suffering from a mental disorder or in urgent cases immediately call the nearest appropriate healthcare professional or an ambulance. It is not intended these provisions delay the transfer of a detainee to a place of safety under the

Mental Health Act 1983, section 136 if that is applicable. If an assessment under that Act is to take place at a police station, the custody officer must consider whether an appropriate healthcare professional should be called to conduct an initial clinical check on the detainee. See *paragraph 9.5* and *9.6*

6. It is imperative a mentally disordered or otherwise mentally vulnerable person detained under the Mental Health Act 1983, section 136 be assessed as soon as possible. A police station should only be used as a place of safety as a last resort but if that assessment is to take place at the police station, an approved social worker and registered medical practitioner shall be called to the station as soon as possible to carry it out. Once the detainee has been assessed and suitable arrangements been made for their treatment or care, they can no longer be detained under section 136. A detainee should be immediately discharged from detention if a registered medical practitioner having examined them, concludes they are not mentally disordered within the meaning of the Act. See *paragraph 3.16*.

7. If a mentally disordered or otherwise mentally vulnerable person is cautioned in the absence of the appropriate adult, the caution must be repeated in the appropriate adult's presence. See *paragraph 10.12*.

8. A mentally disordered or otherwise mentally vulnerable person must not be interviewed or asked to provide or sign a written statement in the absence of the appropriate adult unless the provisions of *paragraphs 11.1* or *11.18* to *11.20* apply. Questioning in these circumstances may not continue in the absence of the appropriate adult once sufficient information to avert the risk has been obtained. A record shall be made of the grounds for any decision to begin an interview in these circumstances. See *paragraphs 11.1, 11.15* and *11.18* to *11.20*.

9. If the appropriate adult is present at an interview, they shall be informed they are not expected to act simply as an observer and the purposes of their presence are to:

- advise the interviewee;
- observe whether or not the interview is being conducted properly and fairly;
- facilitate communication with the interviewee.

See *paragraph 11.17*

10. If the detention of a mentally disordered or otherwise mentally vulnerable person is reviewed by a review officer or a superintendent, the appropriate adult must, if available at the time, be given an opportunity to make representations to the officer about the need for continuing detention. See *paragraph 15.3*.

11. If the custody officer charges a mentally disordered or otherwise mentally vulnerable person with an offence or takes such other action as is appropriate when there is sufficient evidence for a prosecution this must be carried out in the presence of the appropriate adult if they are at the police station. A copy of the written notice embodying any charge must also be given to the appropriate adult. See *paragraphs 16.1* to *16.4A*

12. An intimate or strip search of a mentally disordered or otherwise mentally vulnerable person may take place only in the presence of the appropriate adult of the same sex, unless the detainee specifically requests the presence of a particular adult of the opposite sex. A strip search may take place in the absence of an appropriate adult only in cases of urgency when there is a risk of serious harm to the detainee or others. See *Annex A, paragraphs 5* and *11(c)*.

13. Particular care must be taken when deciding whether to use any form of approved restraints on a mentally disordered or otherwise mentally vulnerable person in a locked cell. See *paragraph 8.2*.

Notes for Guidance

E1 The purpose of the provisions at paragraphs 3.19 and 6.5A is to protect the rights of a mentally disordered or otherwise mentally vulnerable detained person who does not understand the significance of what is said to them. A mentally disordered or otherwise mentally vulnerable detained person should always be given an opportunity, when an appropriate adult is called to the police station, to consult privately with a solicitor in the absence of the appropriate adult if they want.

E2 Although people who are mentally disordered or otherwise mentally vulnerable are often capable of providing reliable evidence, they may, without knowing or wanting to do so, be particularly prone in certain circumstances to provide information that may be unreliable, misleading or self-incriminating. Special care should always be taken when questioning such a person, and the appropriate adult should be involved if there is any doubt about a person's mental state or capacity. Because of the risk of unreliable evidence, it is important to obtain corroboration of any facts admitted whenever possible.

E3 Because of the risks referred to in Note E2, which the presence of the appropriate adult is intended to minimise, officers of superintendent rank or above should exercise their discretion to authorise the commencement of an interview in the appropriate adult's absence only in exceptional cases, if it is necessary to avert an immediate risk of serious harm. See paragraphs 11.1 and 11.18 to 11.20.

E4 When a person is detained under section 136 of the Mental Health Act 1983 for assessment, the appropriate adult has no role in the assessment process and their presence is not required.

Annex F *Not used*

Annex G Fitness to be Interviewed

1. This Annex contains general guidance to help police officers and healthcare professionals assess whether a detainee might be at risk in an interview.

2. A detainee may be at risk in a interview if it is considered that:
   (a) conducting the interview could significantly harm the detainee's physical or mental state;
   (b) anything the detainee says in the interview about their involvement or suspected involvement in the offence about which they are being interviewed **might** be considered unreliable in subsequent court proceedings because of their physical or mental state.

3. In assessing whether the detainee should be interviewed, the following must be considered:
   (a) how the detainee's physical or mental state might affect their ability to understand the nature and purpose of the interview, to comprehend what is being asked and to appreciate the significance of any answers given and make rational decisions about whether they want to say anything;
   (b) the extent to which the detainee's replies may be affected by their physical or mental condition rather than representing a rational and accurate explanation of their involvement in the offence;
   (c) how the nature of the interview, which could include particularly probing questions, might affect the detainee.

4. It is essential healthcare professionals who are consulted consider the functional ability of the detainee rather than simply relying on a medical diagnosis, e.g. it is possible for a person with severe mental illness to be fit for interview.

5. Healthcare professionals should advise on the need for an appropriate adult to be present, whether reassessment of the person's fitness for interview may be necessary if the interview lasts beyond a specified time, and whether a further specialist opinion may be required.

6. When healthcare professionals identify risks they should be asked to quantify the risks. They should inform the custody officer:

- whether the person's condition:
  - ~ is likely to improve;
  - ~ will require or be amenable to treatment; and
- indicate how long it may take for such improvement to take effect.

7. The role of the healthcare professional is to consider the risks and advise the custody officer of the outcome of that consideration. The healthcare professional's determination and any advice or recommendations should be made in writing and form part of the custody record.

8. Once the healthcare professional has provided that information, it is a matter for the custody officer to decide whether or not to allow the interview to go ahead and if the interview is to proceed, to determine what safeguards are needed. Nothing prevents safeguards being provided in addition to those required under the Code. An example might be to have an appropriate healthcare professional present during the interview, in addition to an appropriate adult, in order constantly to monitor the person's condition and how it is being affected by the interview.

Annex H Detained Person: Observation List

1. If any detainee fails to meet any of the following criteria, an appropriate healthcare professional or an ambulance must be called.

2. When assessing the level of rousability, consider:

Rousability—can they be woken?

- go into the cell
- call their name
- shake gently

Response to questions—can they give appropriate answers to questions such as:

- What's your name?
- Where do you live?
- Where do you think you are?

Response to commands—can they respond appropriately to commands such as:

- Open your eyes!
- Lift one arm, now the other arm!

3. Remember to take into account the possibility or presence of other illnesses, injury, or mental condition; a person who is drowsy and smells of alcohol may also have the following:

- Diabetes
- Epilepsy
- Head injury
- Drug intoxication or overdose
- Stroke

Annex I *Not used*

Annex J *Not used*

Annex K X-Rays and Ultrasound Scans

(a) Action

1. PACE, section 55A allows a person who has been arrested and is in police detention to have an X-ray taken of them or an ultrasound scan to be carried out on them (or both) if:

(a) authorised by an officer of inspector rank or above who has reasonable grounds for believing that the detainee:

  (i) may have swallowed a Class A drug; and

  (ii) was in possession of that Class A drug with the intention of supplying it to another or to export; and

(b) the detainee's appropriate consent has been given in writing.

2. Before an x-ray is taken or an ultrasound scan carried out, a police officer or designated detention officer must tell the detainee:-

(a) that the authority has been given; and

(b) the grounds for giving the authorisation.

3. Before a detainee is asked to give appropriate consent to an x-ray or an ultrasound scan, they must be warned that if they refuse without good cause their refusal may harm their case if it comes

to trial, see *Notes K1* and *K2*. This warning may be given by a police officer or member of police staff. In the case of juveniles, mentally vulnerable or mentally disordered suspects the seeking and giving of consent must take place in the presence of the appropriate adult. A juvenile's consent is only valid if their parent's or guardian's consent is also obtained unless the juvenile is under 14, when their parent's or guardian's consent is sufficient in its own right. A detainee who is not legally represented must be reminded of their entitlement to have free legal advice, see Code C, *paragraph 6.5*, and the reminder noted in the custody record.

4. An x-ray may be taken, or an ultrasound scan may be carried out, only by a registered medical practitioner or registered nurse, and only at a hospital, surgery or other medical premises.

(b) Documentation

5. The following shall be recorded as soon as practicable in the detainee's custody record:
   - (a) the authorisation to take the x-ray or carry out the ultrasound scan (or both);
   - (b) the grounds for giving the authorisation;
   - (c) the giving of the warning required by *paragraph 3*; and
   - (d) the fact that the appropriate consent was given or (as the case may be) refused, and if refused, the reason given for the refusal (if any); and
   - (e) if an x-ray is taken or an ultrasound scan carried out:

   where it was taken or carried out;
     - who took it or carried it out;
     - who was present;
     - the result.

6. *Not used.*

Notes for Guidance

K1 If authority is given for an x-ray to be taken or an ultrasound scan to be carried out (or both), consideration should be given to asking a registered medical practitioner or registered nurse to explain to the detainee what is involved and to allay any concerns the detainee might have about the effect which taking an x-ray or carrying out an ultrasound scan might have on them. If appropriate consent is not given, evidence of the explanation *may, if the case comes to trial, be relevant to determining whether the detainee had a good cause for refusing.*

K2 In warning a detainee who is asked to consent to an X-ray being taken or an ultrasound scan being carried out (or both), as in paragraph 3, the following form of words may be used:

'You do not have to allow an x-ray of you to be taken or an ultrasound scan to be carried out on you, but I must warn you that if you refuse without good cause, your refusal may harm your case if it comes to trial.'

Where the use of the Welsh Language is appropriate, the following form of words may be provided in Welsh:

'Does dim rhaid i chi ganiatáu cymryd sgan uwchsain neu belydr-x (neu'r ddau) arnoch, ond mae'n rhaid i mi eich rhybuddio os byddwch chi'n gwrthod gwneud hynny heb reswm da, fe allai hynny niweidio eich achos pe bai'n dod gerbron llys.'

Annex L Establishing Gender of Persons for the Purpose of Searching

1. Certain provisions of this and other PACE Codes explicitly state that searches and other procedures may only be carried out by, or in the presence of, persons of the same sex as the person subject to the search or other procedure. See *Note L1*.

2. All searches and procedures must be carried out with courtesy, consideration and respect for the person concerned. Police officers should show particular sensitivity when dealing with transgender individuals (including transsexual persons) and transvestite persons (see *Notes L2, L3 and L4*).

(a) Consideration

3. In law, the gender (and accordingly the sex) of an individual is their gender as registered at birth unless they have been issued with a Gender Recognition Certificate (GRC) under the Gender Recognition Act 2004 (GRA), in which case the person's gender is their acquired gender. This means that if the acquired gender is the male gender, the person's sex becomes that of a man and, if it is the female gender, the person's sex becomes that of a woman and they must be treated as their acquired gender.

4. When establishing whether the person concerned should be treated as being male or female for the purposes of these searches and procedures, the following approach which is designed to minimise embarrassment and secure the person's co-operation should be followed:

(a) The person must not be asked whether they have a GRC (see paragraph 8);

(b) If there is no doubt as to as to whether the person concerned should be treated as being male or female, they should be dealt with as being of that sex.

(c) If at any time (including during the search or carrying out the procedure) there is doubt as to whether the person should be treated, or continue to be treated, as being male or female:

(i) the person should be asked what gender they consider themselves to be. If they express a preference to be dealt with as a particular gender, they should be asked to indicate and confirm their preference by signing the custody record or, if a custody record has not been opened, the search record or the officer's notebook. Subject to (ii) below, the person should be treated according to their preference;

(ii) if there are grounds to doubt that the preference in (i) accurately reflects the person's predominant lifestyle, for example, if they ask to be treated as a woman but documents and other information make it clear that they live predominantly as a man, or vice versa, they should be treated according to what appears to be their predominant lifestyle and not their stated preference;

(iii) If the person is unwilling to express a preference as in (i) above, efforts should be made to determine their predominant lifestyle and they should be treated as such. For example, if they appear to live predominantly as a woman, they should be treated as being female; or

(iv) if none of the above apply, the person should be dealt with according to what reasonably appears to have been their sex as registered at birth.

5. Once a decision has been made about which gender an individual is to be treated as, each officer responsible for the search or procedure should where possible be advised before the search or procedure starts of any doubts as to the person's gender and the person informed that the doubts have been disclosed. This is important so as to maintain the dignity of the person and any officers concerned.

(b) Documentation

6. The person's gender as established under *paragraph 4(c)(i)* to *(iv)* above must be recorded in the person's custody record or, if a custody record has not been opened, on the search record or in the officer's notebook.

7. Where the person elects which gender they consider themselves to be under *paragraph 4(b)(i)* but, following *4(b)(ii)* is not treated in accordance with their preference, the reason must be recorded in the search record, in the officer's notebook or, if applicable, in the person's custody record.

(c) *Disclosure of information*

8. Section 22 of the GRA defines any information relating to a person's application for a GRC or to a successful applicant's gender before it became their acquired gender as 'protected information'. Nothing in this Annex is to be read as authorising or permitting any police officer or any police staff who has acquired such information when acting in their official capacity to disclose that information to any other person in contravention of the GRA. Disclosure includes making a record of 'protected information' which is read by others.

Notes for Guidance

L1 Provisions to which paragraph 1 applies include:

- *In Code C; paragraph 4.1 and Annex A paragraphs 5, 6, and 11 (searches, strip and intimate searches of detainees under sections 54 and 55 of PACE);*
- *In Code A; paragraphs 2.8 and 3.6 and Note 4;*
- *In Code D; paragraph 5.5 and Note 5F (searches, examinations and photographing of detainees under section 54A of PACE) and paragraph 6.9 (taking samples);*
- *In Code H; paragraph 4.1 and Annex A paragraphs 6, 7 and 12 (searches, strip and intimate searches under sections 54 and 55 of PACE of persons arrested under section 41 of the Terrorism Act 2000).*

L2 While there is no agreed definition of transgender (or trans), it is generally used as an umbrella term to describe people whose gender identity (self-identification as being a woman, man, neither or both) differs from the sex they were registered as at birth. The term includes, but is not limited to, transsexual people.

L3 Transsexual means a person who is proposing to undergo, is undergoing or has undergone a process (or part of a process) for the purpose of gender reassignment, which is a protected characteristic under the Equality Act 2010 (see paragraph 1.0), by changing physiological or other attributes of their sex. This includes aspects of gender such as dress and title. It would apply to a woman making the transition to being a man and a man making the transition to being a woman, as well as to a person who has only just started out on the process of gender reassignment and to a person who has completed the process. Both would share the characteristic of gender reassignment with each having the characteristics of one sex, but with certain characteristics of the other sex.

L4 Transvestite means a person of one gender who dresses in the clothes of a person of the opposite gender. However, a transvestite does not live permanently in the gender opposite to their birth sex.

L5 Chief officers are responsible for providing corresponding operational guidance and instructions for the deployment of transgender officers and staff under their direction and control to duties which involve carrying out, or being present at, any of the searches and procedures described in paragraph 1. The guidance and instructions must comply with the Equality Act 2010 and should therefore complement the approach in this Annex.

Annex M Documents and Records to be Translated

1. For the purposes of Directive 2010/64/EU of the European Parliament and of the Council of 20 October 2010 and this Code, essential documents comprise records required to be made in accordance with this Code which are relevant to decisions to deprive a person of their liberty, to any charge and to any record considered necessary to enable a detainee to defend themselves in criminal proceedings and to safeguard the fairness of the proceedings. Passages of essential documents which are not relevant need not be translated. See *Note M1*

2. The table below lists the documents considered essential for the purposes of this Code and when (subject to paragraphs 3 to 7) written translations must be created and provided. See *paragraphs 13.12* to *13.14* and *Annex N* for application to live-link interpretation.

Table of essential documents:

	ESSENTIAL DOCUMENTS FOR THE PURPOSES OF THIS CODE	WHEN TRANSLATION TO BE CREATED	WHEN TRANSLATION TO BE PROVIDED.
(i)	The grounds for each of the following authorisations to keep the person in custody as they are described and referred to in the custody record: (a) Authorisation for detention before and after charge given by the custody officer and by the review officer, see Code C paragraphs 3.4 and 15.16(a). (b) Authorisation to extend detention without charge beyond 24 hours given by a superintendent, see Code C paragraph 15.16(b). (c) A warrant of further detention issued by a magistrates' court and any extension(s) of the warrant, see Code C paragraph 15.16(c). (d) An authority to detain in accordance with the directions in a warrant of arrest issued in connection with criminal proceedings including the court issuing the warrant.	As soon as practicable after each authorisation has been recorded in the custody record.	As soon as practicable after the translation has been created, whilst the person is detained or after they have been released (see Note M3).
(ii)	Written notice showing particulars of the offence charged required by Code C paragraph 16.3 or the offence for which the suspect has been told they may be prosecuted.	As soon as practicable after the person has been charged or reported.	
(iii)	Written interview records: Code C11.11, 13.3, 13.4 & Code E4.7 Written statement under caution: Code C Annex D.	To be created contemporaneously by the interpreter for the person to check and sign.	As soon as practicable after the person has been charged or told they may be prosecuted.

3. The custody officer may authorise an oral translation or oral summary of documents (i) to (ii) in the table (but not (iii)) to be provided (through an interpreter) instead of a written translation. Such an oral translation or summary may only be provided if it would not prejudice the fairness of the proceedings by in any way adversely affecting or otherwise undermining or limiting the ability of the suspect in question to understand their position and to communicate effectively with police officers, interviewers, solicitors and appropriate adults with regard to their detention and the investigation of the offence in question and to defend themselves in the event of criminal

proceedings. The quantity and complexity of the information in the document should always be considered and specific additional consideration given if the suspect is mentally disordered or otherwise mentally vulnerable or is a juvenile (see *Code C paragraph 1.5*). The reason for the decision must be recorded (see *paragraph 13.11(e)*)

4. Subject to paragraphs 5 to 7 below, a suspect may waive their right to a written translation of the essential documents described in the table but only if they do so voluntarily after receiving legal advice or having full knowledge of the consequences and give their unconditional and fully informed consent in writing (see *paragraph 9*).

5. The suspect may be asked if they wish to waive their right to a written translation and before giving their consent, they must be reminded of their right to legal advice and asked whether they wish to speak to a solicitor.

6. No police officer or police staff should do or say anything with the intention of persuading a suspect who is entitled to a written translation of an essential document to waive that right. See *Notes M2 and M3*.

7. For the purpose of the waiver:

   (a) the consent of a person who is mentally disordered or otherwise mentally vulnerable person is only valid if the information about the circumstances under which they can waive the right and the reminder about their right to legal advice mentioned in *paragraphs 3* to *5* and their consent is given in the presence of the appropriate adult.

   (b) the consent of a juvenile is only valid if their parent's or guardian's consent is also obtained unless the juvenile is under 14, when their parent's or guardian's consent is sufficient in its own right and the information and reminder mentioned in *sub-paragraph (a)* above and their consent is also given in the presence of the appropriate adult (who may or may not be a parent or guardian).

8. The detainee, their solicitor or appropriate adult may make representations to the custody officer that a document which is not included in the table is essential and that a translation should be provided. The request may be refused if the officer is satisfied that the translation requested is not essential for the purposes described in *paragraph 1* above.

9. If the custody officer has any doubts about

- providing an oral translation or summary of an essential document instead of a written translation (see paragraph 3);
- whether the suspect fully understands the consequences of waiving their right to a written translation of an essential document (see paragraph 4), or
- about refusing to provide a translation of a requested document (see *paragraph 7*), the officer should seek advice from an inspector or above.

Documentation

10. Action taken in accordance with this Annex shall be recorded in the detainee's custody record or interview record as appropriate (see *Code C paragraph 13.11(e)*).

Notes for Guidance

M1 It is not necessary to disclose information in any translation which is capable of undermining or otherwise adversely affecting any investigative processes, for example, by enabling the suspect to fabricate an innocent explanation or to conceal lies from the interviewer.

M2 No police officer or police staff shall indicate to any suspect, except to answer a direct question, whether the period for which they are liable to be detained or if not detained, the time taken to complete the interview, might be reduced:

- *if they do not ask for legal advice before deciding whether they wish to waive their right to a written translation of an essential document; or*
- *if they decide to waive their right to a written translation of an essential document.*

M3 There is no power under PACE to detain a person or to delay their release solely to create and provide a written translation of any essential document.

Annex N Live-Link Interpretation (para. 13.12)

Part 1: When the physical presence of the interpreter is not required.

1. EU Directive 2010/64 (see *paragraph 13.1*), Article 2(6) provides 'Where appropriate, communication technology such as videoconferencing, telephone or the Internet may be used, unless the physical presence of the interpreter is required in order to safeguard the fairness of the proceedings.' This Article permits, but does not require the use of a live-link, and the following provisions of this Annex determine whether the use of a live-link is appropriate in any particular case.

2. Decisions in accordance with this Annex that the physical presence of the interpreter is not required and to permit live-link interpretation, must be made on a case by case basis. Each decision must take account of the age, gender and vulnerability of the suspect, the nature and circumstances of the offence and the investigation and the impact on the suspect according to the particular purpose(s) for which the suspect requires the assistance of an interpreter and the time(s) when that assistance is required (see *Note N1*). For this reason, the custody officer in the case of a detained suspect, or in the case of a suspect who has not been arrested, the interviewer (subject to paragraph 13.1(b)), must consider whether the ability of the particular suspect, to communicate confidently and effectively for the purpose in question (see *paragraph 3*) is likely to be adversely affected or otherwise undermined or limited if the interpreter is not physically present and live-link interpretation is used. Although a suspect for whom an appropriate adult is required may be more likely to be adversely affected as described, it is important to note that a person who does not require an appropriate adult may also be adversely impacted by the use of live-link interpretation.

3. Examples of purposes referred to in *paragraph 2* include:
   - (a) understanding and appreciating their position having regard to any information given to them, or sought from them, in accordance with this or any other Code of Practice which, in particular, include:
     - the caution (see *paragraphs C10.1* and *10.12*).
     - the special warning (see *paragraphs 10.10* to *10.12*).
     - information about the offence (see *paragraphs 10.3, 11.1A* and *Note 11ZA*).
     - the grounds and reasons for detention (see *paragraphs 13.10* and *13.10A*).
     - the translation of essential documents (see *paragraph 13.10B* and *Annex M*).
     - their rights and entitlements (see *paragraph 3.12 and C3.21(b)*).
     - intimate and non-intimate searches of detained persons at police stations.
     - provisions and procedures to which Code D (Identification) applies concerning, for example, eye-witness identification, taking fingerprints, samples and photographs.
   - (b) understanding and seeking clarification from the interviewer of questions asked during an interview conducted and recorded in accordance with Code E or Code F and of anything else that is said by the interviewer and answering the questions.
   - (c) consulting privately with their solicitor and (if applicable) the appropriate adult (see *paragraphs 3.18, 13.2A, 13.6 and 13.9*):
     - (i) to help decide whether to answer questions put to them during interview; and
     - (ii) about any other matter concerning their detention and treatment whilst in custody.
   - (d) communicating with practitioners and others who have some formal responsibility for, or an interest in, the health and welfare of the suspect. Particular examples include appropriate healthcare professionals (see *section 9* of this Code), Independent Custody Visitors and drug arrest referral workers.

4. If the custody officer or the interviewer (subject to paragraph 13.1(b)) is satisfied that for a particular purpose as described in *paragraphs 2 and 3 above*, the live-link interpretation *would not* adversely affect or otherwise undermine or limit the suspect's ability to communicate confidently

and effectively for *that* purpose, they must so inform the suspect, their solicitor and (if applicable) the appropriate adult. At the same time, the operation of live-link interpretation must be explained and demonstrated to them, they must be advised of the chief officer's obligations concerning the security of live-link communications under *paragraph 13.13* (see *Note N2*) and they must be asked if they wish to make representations that live-link interpretation should not be used or if they require more information about the operation of the arrangements. They must also be told that at any time live-link interpretation is in use, they may make representations to the custody officer or the interviewer that its operation should cease and that the physical presence of an interpreter should be arranged.

When the authority of an inspector is required

5. If representations are made that live-link interpretation should not be used, or that at any time live-link interpretation is in use, its operation should cease and the physical presence of an interpreter arranged, and the custody officer or interviewer (subject to paragraph 13.1(b)) is unable to allay the concerns raised, live-link interpretation may not be used, or (as the case may be) continue to be used, *unless* authorised in writing by an officer of the rank of inspector or above, in accordance with *paragraph 6*.

6. Authority may be given if the officer is satisfied that for the purpose(s) in question at the time an interpreter is required, live-link interpretation is necessary and justified. In making this decision, the officer must have regard to:

(a) the circumstances of the suspect;
(b) the nature and seriousness of the offence;
(c) the requirements of the investigation, including its likely impact on both the suspect and any victim(s);
(d) the representations made by the suspect, their solicitor and (if applicable) the appropriate adult that live-link interpretation should not be used (see *paragraph 5*)
(e) the availability of a suitable interpreter to be *physically* present compared with the availability of a suitable interpreter for live-link interpretation (see *Note N3*); and
(f) the risk if the interpreter is not *physically* present, evidence obtained using link interpretation might be excluded in subsequent criminal proceedings; and
(g) the likely impact on the suspect and the investigation of any consequential delay to arrange for the interpreter to be *physically* present with the suspect.

7. For the purposes of Code E and live-link interpretation, there is no requirement to make a visual recording which shows the interpreter as viewed by the suspect and others present at the interview. The audio recording required by that Code is sufficient. However, the authorising officer, in consultation with the officer in charge of the investigation, may direct that the interview is conducted and recorded in accordance with Code F. This will require the visual record to show the live-link interpretation arrangements and the interpreter as seen and experienced by the suspect during the interview. This should be considered if it appears that the admissibility of interview evidence might be challenged because the interpreter was not *physically* present or if the suspect, solicitor or appropriate adult make representations that Code F should be applied.

Documentation

8. A record must be made of the actions, decisions, authorisations and outcomes arising from the requirements of this Annex. This includes representations made in accordance with *paragraphs 4* and *7*.

Part 2: Modifications for live-link interpretation

9. The following modification shall apply for the purposes of live-link interpretation:

(a) Code C paragraph 13.3:

For the third sentence, *substitute:* 'A clear legible copy of the complete record shall be sent without delay via the live-link to the interviewer. The interviewer, after confirming with the suspect that the copy is legible and complete, shall allow the suspect to read the record, or have the record read to them by the interpreter and to sign the copy as correct or indicate the respects in which they consider it inaccurate. The interviewer is responsible for ensuring that that the signed copy and the original record made by the interpreter are retained with the case papers for use in evidence if required and must advise the interpreter of their obligation to keep the original record securely for that purpose.';

(b) **Code C paragraph 13.4:**
For sub-paragraph (b), *substitute*: 'A clear legible copy of the complete statement shall be sent without delay via the live-link to the interviewer. The interviewer, after confirming with the suspect that the copy is legible and complete, shall invite the suspect to sign it. The interviewer is responsible for ensuring that that the signed copy and the original record made by the interpreter are retained with the case papers for use in evidence if required and must advise the interpreter of their obligation to keep the original record securely for that purpose.';

(c) **Code C paragraph 13.7:**
After the first sentence, *insert:* 'A clear legible copy of the certified record must be sent without delay via the live-link to the interviewer. The interviewer is responsible for ensuring that the original certified record and the copy are retained with the case papers for use as evidence if required and must advise the interpreter of their obligation to keep the original record securely for that purpose.'

(d) **Code C paragraph 11.2 and Codes E and F, paragraph 4.4—interviews**
At the beginning of each paragraph, *insert*: 'Before the interview commences, the operation of live-link interpretation shall be explained and demonstrated to the suspect, their solicitor and appropriate adult, unless it has been previously explained and demonstrated (see Code C Annex N *paragraph 4*).'

(e) **Codes E and F, paragraph 4.18 (signing master recording label)**
After the *third sentence,* insert, 'If live-link interpretation has been used, the interviewer should ask the interpreter to observe the removal and sealing of the master recording and to confirm in writing that they have seen it sealed and signed by the interviewer. A clear legible copy of the confirmation signed by the interpreter must be sent via the live-link to the interviewer. The interviewer is responsible for ensuring that the original confirmation and the copy are retained with the case papers for use in evidence if required and must advise the interpreter of their obligation to keep the original confirmation securely for that purpose.'

Notes for Guidance

N1 For purposes other than an interview, audio-only live-link interpretation, for example by telephone (see Code C paragraph 13.12(b)) may provide an appropriate option until an interpreter is physically present or audio-visual live-link interpretation becomes available. A particular example would be the initial action required when a detained suspect arrives at a police station to inform them of, and to explain, the reasons for their arrest and detention and their various rights and entitlements. Another example would be to inform the suspect by telephone, that an interpreter they will be able to see and hear is being arranged. In these circumstances, telephone live-link interpretation may help to allay the suspect's concerns and contribute to the completion of the risk assessment (see Code C paragraph 3.6).

N2 The explanation and demonstration of live-link interpretation is intended to help the suspect, solicitor and appropriate adult make an informed decision and to allay any concerns they may have.

N3 Factors affecting availability of a suitable interpreter will include the location of the police station and the language and type of interpretation (oral or sign language) required.

Code of Practice for the Identification of Persons by Police Officers (Code D)

(2017)

1 Introduction

1.1 This Code of Practice concerns the principal methods used by police to identify people in connection with the investigation of offences and the keeping of accurate and reliable criminal records. The powers and procedures in this code must be used fairly, responsibly, with respect for the people to whom they apply and without unlawful discrimination. Under the Equality Act 2010, section 149 (Public sector Equality Duty), police forces must, in carrying out their functions, have due regard to the need to eliminate unlawful discrimination, harassment, victimisation and any other conduct which is prohibited by that Act, to advance equality of opportunity between people who share a relevant protected characteristic and people who do not share it, and to foster good relations between those persons. The Equality Act also makes it unlawful for police officers to discriminate against, harass or victimise any person on the grounds of the 'protected characteristics' of age, disability, gender reassignment, race, religion or belief, sex and sexual orientation, marriage and civil partnership, pregnancy and maternity when using their powers. See *Note 1A*.

1.2 In this Code, identification by an eye-witness arises when a witness who has seen the offender committing the crime and is given an opportunity to identify a person suspected of involvement in the offence in a video identification, identification parade or similar procedure. These eye-witness identification procedures which are in Part A of section 3 below, are designed to:

- test the eye-witness' ability to identify the suspect as the person they saw on a previous occasion
- provide safeguards against mistaken identification.

While this Code concentrates on visual identification procedures, it does not prevent the police making use of aural identification procedures such as a 'voice identification parade', where they judge that appropriate. See *Note 1B*.

1.2A In this Code, separate provisions in Part B of section 3 below, apply when any person, including a police officer, is asked if they recognise anyone they see in an image as being someone who is known to them and to test their claim that they recognise that person. These separate provisions are not subject to the eye-witnesses identification procedures described in *paragraph 1.2*.

1.2B Part C applies when a film, photograph or image relating to the offence or any description of the suspect is broadcast or published in any national or local media or on any social networking site or on any local or national police communication systems.

1.3 Identification by fingerprints applies when a person's fingerprints are taken to: compare with fingerprints found at the scene of a crime

- check and prove convictions
- help to ascertain a person's identity.

1.3A Identification using footwear impressions applies when a person's footwear impressions are taken to compare with impressions found at the scene of a crime.

1.4 Identification by body samples and impressions includes taking samples such as a cheek swab, hair or blood to generate a DNA profile for comparison with material obtained from the scene of a crime, or a victim.

1.5 Taking photographs of arrested people applies to recording and checking identity and locating and tracing persons who:

- are wanted for offences
- fail to answer their bail.

1.6 Another method of identification involves searching and examining detained suspects to find, e.g., marks such as tattoos or scars which may help establish their identity or whether they have been involved in committing an offence.

1.7 The provisions of the Police and Criminal Evidence Act 1984 (PACE) and this Code are designed to make sure fingerprints, samples, impressions and photographs are taken, used and retained, and identification procedures carried out, only when justified and necessary for preventing, detecting or investigating crime. If these provisions are not observed, the application of the relevant procedures in particular cases may be open to question.

1.8 The provisions of this Code do not authorise, or otherwise permit, fingerprints or samples to be taken from a person detained solely for the purposes of assessment under section 136 of the Mental Health Act 1983.

Note for Guidance

1A In paragraph 1.1, under the Equality Act 1949, section 149, the 'relevant protected characteristics' are: age, disability, gender reassignment, pregnancy and maternity, race, religion/belief, sex and sexual orientation. For further detailed guidance and advice on the Equality Act, see: https://www. gov.uk/guidance/equality-act-2010-guidance.

1B See Home Office Circular 57/2003 *'Advice on the use of voice identification parades'.*

2 General

2.1 This Code must be readily available at all police stations for consultation by:

- police officers and police staff
- detained persons
- members of the public

2.2 The provisions of this Code:

- include the Annexes
- do not include the Notes for guidance.

2.3 Code C, paragraph 1.4 and the *Notes for guidance* applicable to those provisions apply to this Code with regard to a suspected person who may be mentally disordered or otherwise mentally vulnerable.

2.4 Code C, paragraphs 1.5 and 1.5A and the *Notes for guidance* applicable to those provisions apply to this Code with regard to a suspected person who appears to be under the age of 18.

2.5 Code C, paragraph 1.6 applies to this Code with regard to a suspected person who appears to be blind, seriously visually impaired, deaf, unable to read or speak or has difficulty communicating orally because of a speech impediment.

2.6 In this Code:

- 'appropriate adult' means the same as in Code C, *paragraph 1.7*
- 'solicitor' means the same as in Code C, *paragraph 6.12*

and the *Notes for guidance* applicable to those provisions apply to this Code.

- where a search or other procedure under this Code may only be carried out or observed by a person of the same sex as the person to whom the search or procedure applies, the gender of the detainee and other persons present should be established and recorded in line with Annex L of Code C.

2.7 References to a custody officer include any police officer who, for the time being, is performing the functions of a custody officer, see *paragraph 1.9* of Code C.

2.8 When a record of any action requiring the authority of an officer of a specified rank is made under this Code, subject to *paragraph 2.18,* the officer's name and rank must be recorded.

2.9 When this Code requires the prior authority or agreement of an officer of at least inspector or superintendent rank, that authority may be given by a sergeant or chief inspector who has been authorised to perform the functions of the higher rank under PACE, section 107.

2.10 Subject to *paragraph 2.18,* all records must be timed and signed by the maker.

2.11 Records must be made in the custody record, unless otherwise specified. In any provision of this Code which allows or requires police officers or police staff to make a record in their report book, the reference to 'report book' shall include any official report book or electronic recording device issued to them that enables the record in question to be made and dealt with in accordance with that provision. References in this Code to written records, forms and signatures include electronic records and forms and electronic confirmation that identifies the person completing the record or form.

Chief officers must be satisfied as to the integrity and security of the devices, records and forms to which this *paragraph* applies and that use of those devices, records and forms satisfies relevant data protection legislation.

(taken from *Code C paragraph 1.17).*

2.12 If any procedure in this Code requires a person's consent, the consent of a:

- mentally disordered or otherwise mentally vulnerable person is only valid if given in the presence of the appropriate adult
- juvenile is only valid if their parent's or guardian's consent is also obtained unless the juvenile is under 14, when their parent's or guardian's consent is sufficient in its own right. If the only obstacle to an identification procedure in *section 3* is that a juvenile's parent or guardian refuses consent or reasonable efforts to obtain it have failed, the identification officer may apply the provisions of paragraph 3.21 (suspect known but not available). See *Note 2A*.

2.13 If a person is blind, seriously visually impaired or unable to read, the custody officer or identification officer shall make sure their solicitor, relative, appropriate adult or some other person likely to take an interest in them and not involved in the investigation is available to help check any documentation. When this Code requires written consent or signing, the person assisting may be asked to sign instead, if the detainee prefers. This paragraph does not require an appropriate adult to be called solely to assist in checking and signing documentation for a person who is not a juvenile, or mentally disordered or otherwise mentally vulnerable (see *Note 2B* and Code C *paragraph 3.15*).

2.14 If any procedure in this Code requires information to be given to or sought from a suspect, it must be given or sought in the appropriate adult's presence if the suspect is mentally disordered, otherwise mentally vulnerable or a juvenile. If the appropriate adult is not present when the information is first given or sought, the procedure must be repeated in the presence of the appropriate adult when they arrive. If the suspect appears deaf or there is doubt about their hearing or speaking ability or ability to understand English, the custody officer or identification officer must ensure that the necessary arrangements in accordance with Code C are made for an interpreter to assist the suspect.

2.15 Any procedure in this Code involving the participation of a suspect who is mentally disordered, otherwise mentally vulnerable or a juvenile must take place in the presence of the appropriate adult. See Code C *paragraph 1.4*.

2.15A Any procedure in this Code involving the participation of a witness who is or appears to be mentally disordered, otherwise mentally vulnerable or a juvenile should take place in the presence of a pre-trial support person unless the witness states that they do not want a support person to be present. A support person must not be allowed to prompt any identification of a suspect by a witness. See *Note 2AB*.

2.16 References to:

- 'taking a photograph', include the use of any process to produce a single, still or moving, visual image
- 'photographing a person', should be construed accordingly
- 'photographs', 'films', 'negatives' and 'copies' include relevant visual images recorded, stored, or reproduced through any medium
- 'destruction' includes the deletion of computer data relating to such images or making access to that data impossible

2.17 This Code does not affect or apply to, the powers and procedures:

(i) for requiring and taking samples of breath, blood and urine in relation to driving offences, etc., when under the influence of drink, drugs or excess alcohol under the:
   - Road Traffic Act 1988, sections 4 to 11
   - Road Traffic Offenders Act 1988, sections 15 and 16
   - Transport and Works Act 1992, sections 26 to 38;

(ii) under the Immigration Act 1971, Schedule 2, paragraph 18, for taking photographs, measuring and identifying and taking biometric information (not including DNA) from persons detained or liable to be detained under that Act, Schedule 2, paragraph 16 (Administrative Provisions as to Control on Entry etc.); or for taking fingerprints in accordance with the Immigration and Asylum Act 1999, sections 141 and 142(4), or other methods for collecting information about a person's external physical characteristics provided for by regulations made under that Act, section 144;

(iii) under the Terrorism Act 2000, Schedule 8, for taking photographs, fingerprints, skin impressions, body samples or impressions from people:
- arrested under that Act, section 41,
- detained for the purposes of examination under that Act, Schedule 7, and to whom the Code of Practice issued under that Act, Schedule 14, paragraph 6, applies ('the terrorism provisions')

(iv) for taking photographs, fingerprints, skin impressions, body samples or impressions from people who have been:
- arrested on warrants issued in Scotland, by officers exercising powers mentioned in Part X of the Criminal Justice and Public Order Act 1994;
- arrested or detained without warrant by officers from a police force in Scotland exercising their powers of arrest or detention mentioned in Part X of the Criminal Justice and Public Order Act 1994.

Note: In these cases, police powers and duties and the person's rights and entitlements whilst at a police station in England and Wales are the same as if the person had been arrested in Scotland by a Scottish police officer.

2.18 Nothing in this Code requires the identity of officers or police staff to be recorded or disclosed:

(a) in the case of enquiries linked to the investigation of terrorism;

(b) if the officers or police staff reasonably believe recording or disclosing their names might put them in danger.

In these cases, they shall use their warrant or other identification numbers and the name of their police station. *See Note 2D.*

2.19 In this Code:

(a) 'designated person' means a person other than a police officer, who has specified powers and duties conferred or imposed on them by designation under section 38 or 39 of the Police Reform Act 2002;

(b) any reference to a police officer includes a designated person acting in the exercise or performance of the powers and duties conferred or imposed on them by their designation.

2.20 If a power conferred on a designated person:

(a) allows reasonable force to be used when exercised by a police officer, a designated person exercising that power has the same entitlement to use force;

(b) includes power to use force to enter any premises, that power is not exercisable by that designated person except:

(i) in the company, and under the supervision, of a police officer; or

(ii) for the purpose of:
- saving life or limb; or
- preventing serious damage to property.

2.21 In the case of a detained person, nothing in this Code prevents the custody officer, or other police officer or designated person given custody of the detainee by the custody officer for the purposes of the investigation of an offence for which the person is detained, from allowing another person (see *(a)* and *(b)* below) to carry out individual procedures or tasks at the police station if the law allows. However, the officer or designated person given custody remains responsible for making sure the procedures and tasks are carried out correctly in accordance with the Codes of Practice. The other person who is allowed to carry out the procedures or tasks must be *someone who at that time* is:

(a) under the direction and control of the chief officer of the force responsible for the police station in question; or;

(b) providing services under contractual arrangements (but without being employed by the chief officer the police force), to assist a police force in relation to the discharge of its chief officer's functions.

2.22 Designated persons and others mentioned in *sub-paragraphs (a)* and *(b)* of *paragraph 2.21* must have regard to any relevant provisions of the Codes of Practice.

Notes for guidance

2A For the purposes of paragraph 2.12, the consent required from a parent or guardian may, for a juvenile in the care of a local authority or voluntary organisation, be given by that authority or organisation. In the case of a juvenile, nothing in paragraph 2.12 requires the parent, guardian or representative of a local authority or voluntary organisation to be present to give their consent, unless they are acting as the appropriate adult under paragraphs 2.14 or 2.15. However, it is important that a parent or guardian not present is fully informed before being asked to consent. They must be given the same information about the procedure and the juvenile's suspected involvement in the offence as the juvenile and appropriate adult. The parent or guardian must also be allowed to speak to the juvenile and the appropriate adult if they wish. Provided the consent is fully informed and is not withdrawn, it may be obtained at any time before the procedure takes place.

2AB The Youth Justice and Criminal Evidence Act 1999 guidance 'Achieving Best Evidence in Criminal Proceedings' indicates that a pre-trial support person should accompany a vulnerable witness during any identification procedure unless the witness states that they do not want a support person to be present. It states that this support person should not be (or not be likely to be) a witness in the investigation.

2B People who are seriously visually impaired or unable to read may be unwilling to sign police documents. The alternative, i.e. their representative signing on their behalf, seeks to protect the interests of both police and suspects.

2C Not used

2D The purpose of paragraph 2.18(b) is to protect those involved in serious organised crime investigations or arrests of particularly violent suspects when there is reliable information that those arrested or their associates may threaten or cause harm to the officers. In cases of doubt, an officer of inspector rank or above should be consulted.

3 Identification and recognition of suspects

Part (A) Identification of a suspect by an eye-witness

3.0 This part applies when an eye-witness has seen a person committing a crime or in any other circumstances which tend to prove or disprove the involvement of the person they saw in a crime, for example, close to the scene of the crime, immediately before or immediately after it was committed. It sets out the procedures to be used to test the ability of that eye-witness to identify a person suspected of involvement in the offence ('the suspect') as the person they saw on the previous occasion. This part does not apply to the procedure described in Part B (see Note 3AA) which is used to test the ability of someone who is not an eye-witness, to recognise anyone whose image they see.

3.1 A record shall be made of the description of the suspect as first given by the eye-witness. This record must:

(a) be made and kept in a form which enables details of that description to be accurately produced from it, in a visible and legible form, which can be given to the suspect or the suspect's solicitor in accordance with this Code; and

(b) unless otherwise specified, be made before the eye-witness takes part in any identification procedures under *paragraphs 3.5 to 3.10, 3.21, 3.23* or Annex E (Showing Photographs to Eye-Witnesses).

A copy of the record shall where practicable, be given to the suspect or their solicitor before any procedures under *paragraphs 3.5* to *3.10, 3.21 or 3.23* are carried out. See *Note 3E.*

3.1A References in this Part:

(a) to the identity of the suspect being 'known' mean that there is sufficient information known to the police to establish, in accordance with Code G (Arrest), that there are reasonable grounds to suspect a particular person of involvement in the offence;

(b) to the suspect being 'available' mean that the suspect is immediately available, or will be available within a reasonably short time, in order that they can be invited to take part in at least one of the eye-witness identification procedures under *paragraphs 3.5* to *3.10* and it is practicable to arrange an effective procedure under *paragraphs 3.5 to 3.10*; and

(c) to the eye-witness identification procedures under *paragraphs 3.5* to *3.10* mean:

- Video identification (*paragraphs 3.5* and *3.6*);
- Identification parade (*paragraphs 3.7* and *3.8*); and
- Group identification (*paragraphs 3.9* and *3.10*).

(a) Cases when the suspect's identity is not known

3.2 In cases when the suspect's identity is not known, an eye-witness may be taken to a particular neighbourhood or place to see whether they can identify the person they saw on a previous occasion. Although the number, age, sex, race, general description and style of clothing of other people present at the location and the way in which any identification is made cannot be controlled, the principles applicable to the formal procedures under *paragraphs 3.5* to *3.10* shall be followed as far as practicable. For example:

(a) where it is practicable to do so, a record should be made of the eye-witness' description of the person they saw on the previous occasion, as in *paragraph 3.1(a)*, before asking the eye-witness to make an identification;

(b) Care must be taken not provide the eye-witness with any information concerning the description of the suspect (if such information is available) and not to direct the eye-witness' attention to any individual unless, taking into account all the circumstances, this cannot be avoided. However, this does not prevent an eye-witness being asked to look carefully at the people around at the time or to look towards a group or in a particular direction, if this appears necessary to make sure that the witness does not overlook a possible suspect simply because the eye-witness is looking in the opposite direction and also to enable the eye-witness to make comparisons between any suspect and others who are in the area;

(c) where there is more than one eye-witness, every effort should be made to keep them separate and eye-witnesses should be taken to see whether they can identify a person independently;

(d) once there is sufficient information to establish, in accordance with *paragraph 3.1A(a)*, that the suspect is 'known', e.g. after the eye-witness makes an identification, the provisions set out from *paragraph 3.4* onwards shall apply for that and any other eye-witnesses in relation to that individual;

(e) the officer or police staff accompanying the eye-witness must record, in their report book, the action taken as soon as practicable and in as much detail, as possible. The record should include:

(i) the date, time and place of the relevant occasion when the eye-witness claims to have previously seen the person committing the offence in question or in any other circumstances which tend to prove or disprove the involvement of the person they saw in a crime (see *paragraph 3.0*); and

(ii) where any identification was made:

- how it was made and the conditions at the time (e.g., the distance the eye-witness was from the suspect, the weather and light);
- if the eye-witness's attention was drawn to the suspect; the reason for this; and
- anything said by the eye-witness or the suspect about the identification or the conduct of the procedure.

See Note 3F

3.3 An eye-witness must not be shown photographs, computerised or artist's composite likenesses or similar likenesses or pictures (including 'E-fit' images) if in accordance with *paragraph 3.1A*, the identity of the suspect is known and they are available to take part in one of the procedures under *paragraphs 3.5* to *3.10*. If the suspect's identity is not known, the showing of any such images to an eye-witness to see if they can identify a person whose image they are shown as the person they saw on a previous occasion must be done in accordance with *Annex E*.

(b) Cases when the suspect is known and available

3.4 If the suspect's identity is known to the police (see *paragraph 3.1A(a)*) and they are available (see *paragraph 3.1A(b)*), the identification procedures that may be used are set out in *paragraphs 3.5* to *3.10* below as follows:

(i) video identification;
(ii) identification parade; or
(iii) group identification.

(i) Video identification

3.5 A 'video identification' is when the eye-witness is shown images of a known suspect, together with similar images of others who resemble the suspect. *Moving* images must be used unless the conditions in sub-paragraph (a) or (b) below apply:

(a) this sub-paragraph applies if:

(i) the identification officer, in consultation with the officer in charge of the investigation, is satisfied that because of aging, or other physical changes or differences, the appearance of the suspect has significantly changed since the previous occasion when the eye-witness claims to have seen the suspect (see *paragraph 3.0* and *Note 3ZA*);

(ii) an image (moving or still) is available which the identification officer and the officer in charge of the investigation reasonably believe shows the appearance of the suspect as it was at the time the suspect was seen by the eye-witness; and

(iii) having regard to the extent of change and the purpose of eye-witness identification procedures (see *paragraph 3.0*), the identification officer believes that that such an image should be shown to the eye-witness.

In such a case, the identification officer may arrange a video identification procedure using the image described in (ii). In accordance with the 'Notice to suspect' (see paragraph 3.17(vi)), the suspect must first be given an opportunity to provide their own image(s) for use in the procedure but it is for the identification officer and officer in charge of the investigation to decide whether, following (ii) and (iii), any image(s) provided by the suspect should be used.

A video identification using an image described above may, at the discretion of the identification officer be arranged in addition to, or as an alternative to, a video identification using *moving* images taken after the suspect has been given the information and notice described in *paragraphs 3.17* and *3.18*.

See paragraph 3.21 and Note 3D in any case where the suspect deliberately takes steps to frustrate the eye-witness identification arrangements and procedures.

(b) this sub-paragraph applies if, in accordance with *paragraph 2A* of *Annex A* of this Code, the identification officer does not consider that replication of a physical feature or concealment of the location of the feature can be achieved using a moving image. In these cases, still images may be used.

3.6 Video identifications must be carried out in accordance with *Annex A*.

(ii) Identification parade

3.7 An 'identification parade' is when the eye-witness sees the suspect in a line of others who resemble the suspect.

3.8 Identification parades must be carried out in accordance with *Annex B*.

(iii) Group identification

3.9 A 'group identification' is when the eye-witness sees the suspect in an informal group of people.

3.10 Group identifications must be carried out in accordance with *Annex C*.

Arranging eye-witness identification procedures—duties of identification officer

3.11 Except as provided for in *paragraph 3.19*, the arrangements for, and conduct of, the eye-witness identification procedures in *paragraphs 3.5 to 3.10* and circumstances in which any such identification procedure must be held shall be the responsibility of an officer not below inspector rank who is not involved with the investigation ('the identification officer'). The identification officer may direct another officer or police staff, see *paragraph 2.21*, to make arrangements for, and to conduct, any of these identification procedures and except as provided for in *paragraph 7* of *Annex A*, any reference in this section to the identification officer includes the officer or police staff to whom the arrangements for, and/or conduct of, any of these procedure has been delegated. In delegating these arrangements and procedures, the identification officer must be able to supervise effectively and either intervene or be contacted for advice. Where any action referred to in this paragraph is taken by another officer or police staff at the direction of the identification officer, the outcome shall, as soon as practicable, be reported to the identification officer. For the purpose of these procedures, the identification officer retains overall responsibility for ensuring that the procedure complies with this Code and in addition, in the case of detained suspect, their care and treatment until returned to the custody officer. Except as permitted by this Code, no officer or any other person involved with the investigation of the case against the suspect may take any part in these procedures or act as the identification officer.

This paragraph does not prevent the identification officer from consulting the officer in charge of the investigation to determine which procedure to use. When an identification procedure is required, in the interest of fairness to suspects and eye-witnesses, it must be held as soon as practicable.

Circumstances in which an eye-witness identification procedure must be held

3.12 If, before any identification procedure set out in *paragraphs 3.5* to *3.10* has been held

(a) an eye-witness has identified a suspect or purported to have identified them; or

(b) there is an eye-witness available who expresses an ability to identify the suspect; or

(c) there is a reasonable chance of an eye-witness being able to identify the suspect,

and the eye-witness in (a) to (c) has not been given an opportunity to identify the suspect in any of the procedures set out in *paragraphs 3.5* to *3.10*, then an identification procedure shall be held if the suspect disputes being the person the eye-witness claims to have seen on a previous occasion (see *paragraph 3.0*), unless:

(i) it is not practicable to hold any such procedure; or

(ii) any such procedure would serve no useful purpose in proving or disproving whether the suspect was involved in committing the offence, for example

- where the suspect admits being at the scene of the crime and gives an account of what took place and the eye-witness does not see anything which contradicts that; or
- when it is not disputed that the suspect is already known to the eye-witness who claims to have recognised them when seeing them commit the crime.

3.13 An eye-witness identification procedure may also be held if the officer in charge of the investigation, after consultation with the identification officer, considers it would be useful.

Selecting an eye-witness identification procedure

3.14 If, because of paragraph 3.12, an identification procedure is to be held, the suspect shall initially be invited to take part in a video identification unless:

(a) a video identification is not practicable; or
(b) an identification parade is both practicable and more suitable than a video identification; or
(c) *paragraph 3.16* applies.

The identification officer and the officer in charge of the investigation shall consult each other to determine which option is to be offered. An identification parade may not be practicable because of factors relating to the witnesses, such as their number, state of health, availability and travelling requirements. A video identification would normally be more suitable if it could be arranged and completed sooner than an identification parade. Before an option is offered the suspect must also be reminded of their entitlement to have free legal advice, see Code C, *paragraph 6.5.*

3.15 A suspect who refuses the identification procedure in which the suspect is first invited to take part shall be asked to state their reason for refusing and may get advice from their solicitor and/or if present, their appropriate adult. The suspect, solicitor and/or appropriate adult shall be allowed to make representations about why another procedure should be used. A record should be made of the reasons for refusal and any representations made. After considering any reasons given, and representations made, the identification officer shall, if appropriate, arrange for the suspect to be invited to take part in an alternative which the officer considers suitable and practicable. If the officer decides it is not suitable and practicable to invite the suspect to take part in an alternative identification procedure, the reasons for that decision shall be recorded.

3.16 A suspect may initially be invited to take part in a group identification if the officer in charge of the investigation considers it is more suitable than a video identification or an identification parade and the identification officer considers it practicable to arrange.

Notice to suspect

3.17 Unless *paragraph 3.20* applies, before any eye-witness identification procedure set out in *paragraphs 3.5* to *3.10* is arranged, the following shall be explained to the suspect:

(i) the purpose of the procedure (see *paragraph 3.0*);
(ii) their entitlement to free legal advice; see Code C, *paragraph 6.5*;
(iii) the procedures for holding it, including their right, subject to *Annex A, paragraph 9*, to have a solicitor or friend present;
(iv) that they do not have to consent to or co-operate in the procedure;
(v) that if they do not consent to, and co-operate in, a procedure, their refusal may be given in evidence in any subsequent trial and police may proceed covertly without their consent or make other arrangements to test whether an eye-witness can identify them, see *paragraph 3.21*;
(vi) whether, for the purposes of a video identification procedure, images of them have previously been obtained either:
  - in accordance with *paragraph 3.20*, and if so, that they may co-operate in providing further, suitable images to be used instead; or
  - in accordance with paragraph 3.5(a), and if so, that they may provide their own images for the identification officer to consider using.

(vii) if appropriate, the special arrangements for juveniles;
(viii) if appropriate, the special arrangements for mentally disordered or otherwise mentally vulnerable people;
(ix) that if they significantly alter their appearance between being offered an identification procedure and any attempt to hold an identification procedure, this may be given in evidence if the case comes to trial, and the identification officer may then consider other forms of identification, see *paragraph 3.21* and *Note 3C*;

(x) that a moving image or photograph may be taken of them when they attend for any identification procedure;

(xi) whether, before their identity became known, the eye-witness was shown photographs, a computerised or artist's composite likeness or similar likeness or image by the police, see *Note 3B;*

(xii) that if they change their appearance before an identification parade, it may not be practicable to arrange one on the day or subsequently and, because of the appearance change, the identification officer may consider alternative methods of identification, see *Note 3C;*

(xiii) that they or their solicitor will be provided with details of the description of the suspect as first given by any eye-witnesses who are to attend the procedure or confrontation, see *paragraph 3.1.*

3.18 This information must also be recorded in a written notice handed to the suspect. The suspect must be given a reasonable opportunity to read the notice, after which, they should be asked to sign a copy of the notice to indicate if they are willing to co-operate with the making of a video or take part in the identification parade or group identification. The signed copy shall be retained by the identification officer.

3.19 In the case of a detained suspect, the duties under *paragraphs 3.17* and *3.18* may be performed by the custody officer or by another officer or police staff not involved in the investigation as directed by the custody officer, if:

(a) it is proposed to release the suspect in order that an identification procedure can be arranged and carried out and an inspector is not available to act as the identification officer, see *paragraph 3.11,* before the suspect leaves the station; or

(b) it is proposed to keep the suspect in police detention whilst the procedure is arranged and carried out and waiting for an inspector to act as the identification officer, see *paragraph 3.11,* would cause unreasonable delay to the investigation.

The officer concerned shall inform the identification officer of the action taken and give them the signed copy of the notice. See *Note 3C.*

3.20 If the identification officer and officer in charge of the investigation suspect, on reasonable grounds that if the suspect was given the information and notice as in *paragraphs 3.17* and *3.18,* they would then take steps to avoid being seen by a witness in any identification procedure, the identification officer may arrange for images of the suspect suitable for use in a video identification procedure to be obtained before giving the information and notice. If suspect's images are obtained in these circumstances, the suspect may, for the purposes of a video identification procedure, co-operate in providing new images which if suitable, would be used instead, see *paragraph 3.17(vi).*

(c) Cases when the suspect is known but not available

3.21 When a known suspect is not available or has ceased to be available, see *paragraph 3.1A,* the identification officer may make arrangements for a video identification (see *paragraph 3.5* and *Annex A*). If necessary, the identification officer may follow the video identification procedures using any suitable moving or still images and these may be obtained covertly if necessary. Alternatively, the identification officer may make arrangements for a group identification without the suspect's consent (see Annex C *paragraph 34*). See *Note 3D.* These provisions may also be applied to juveniles where the consent of their parent or guardian is either refused or reasonable efforts to obtain that consent have failed (see *paragraph 2.12*).

3.22 Any covert activity should be strictly limited to that necessary to test the ability of the eye-witness to identify the suspect as the person they saw on the relevant previous occasion.

3.23 The identification officer may arrange for the suspect to be confronted by the eye-witness if none of the options referred to in *paragraphs 3.5* to *3.10* or *3.21* are practicable. A 'confrontation' is when the suspect is directly confronted by the eye-witness. A confrontation does not require the suspect's consent. Confrontations must be carried out in accordance with Annex D.

3.24 Requirements for information to be given to, or sought from, a suspect or for the suspect to be given an opportunity to view images before they are shown to an eye-witness, do not apply if the suspect's lack of co-operation prevents the necessary action.

(d) Documentation

3.25 A record shall be made of the video identification, identification parade, group identification or confrontation on forms provided for the purpose.

3.26 If the identification officer considers it is not practicable to hold a video identification or identification parade requested by the suspect, the reasons shall be recorded and explained to the suspect.

3.27 A record shall be made of a person's failure or refusal to co-operate in a video identification, identification parade or group identification and, if applicable, of the grounds for obtaining images in accordance with *paragraph 3.20*.

(e) Not used

3.28 *Not used.*

3.29 *Not used.*

(f) Destruction and retention of photographs taken or used in eye-witness identification procedures

3.30 PACE, section 64A, see *paragraph 5.12*, provides powers to take photographs of suspects and allows these photographs to be used or disclosed only for purposes related to the prevention or detection of crime, the investigation of offences or the conduct of prosecutions by, or on behalf of, police or other law enforcement and prosecuting authorities inside and outside the United Kingdom or the enforcement of a sentence. After being so used or disclosed, they may be retained but can only be used or disclosed for the same purposes.

3.31 Subject to *paragraph 3.33,* the photographs (and all negatives and copies), of suspects *not* taken in accordance with the provisions in *paragraph 5.12* which are taken for the purposes of, or in connection with, the identification procedures in *paragraphs 3.5* to *3.10, 3.21 or 3.23* must be destroyed unless the suspect:

- (a) is charged with, or informed they may be prosecuted for, a recordable offence;
- (b) is prosecuted for a recordable offence;
- (c) is cautioned for a recordable offence or given a warning or reprimand in accordance with the Crime and Disorder Act 1998 for a recordable offence; or
- (d) gives informed consent, in writing, for the photograph or images to be retained for purposes described in *paragraph 3.30*.

3.32 When *paragraph 3.31* requires the destruction of any photograph, the person must be given an opportunity to witness the destruction or to have a certificate confirming the destruction if they request one within five days of being informed that the destruction is required.

3.33 Nothing in *paragraph 3.31* affects any separate requirement under the Criminal Procedure and Investigations Act 1996 to retain material in connection with criminal investigations.

Part (B) Recognition by <u>controlled</u> showing of films, photographs and images

3.34 This Part of this section applies when, for the purposes of obtaining evidence of recognition, arrangements are made for a person, including a police officer, who is <u>not</u> an eye-witness (see *Note 3AA)*:

- (a) to view a film, photograph or any other visual medium; and
- (b) on the occasion of the viewing, to be asked whether they recognise anyone whose image is shown in the material as someone who is known to them.

The arrangements for such viewings may be made by the officer in charge of the relevant investigation. Although there is no requirement for the identification officer to make the arrangements or to be consulted about the arrangements, nothing prevents this. See *Notes 3AA* and *3G*.

3.35 To provide safeguards against mistaken recognition and to avoid any possibility of collusion, on the occasion of the viewing, the arrangements should ensure:

(a) that the films, photographs and other images are shown on an individual basis;
(b) that any person who views the material;
(i) is unable to communicate with any other individual to whom the material has been, or is to be, shown;
(ii) is not reminded of any photograph or description of any individual whose image is shown or given any other indication as to the identity of any such individual;
(iii) is not be told whether a previous witness has recognised any one;
(c) that immediately before a person views the material, they are told that:
(i) an individual who is known to them may, or may not, appear in the material they are shown and that if they do not recognise anyone, they should say so;
(ii) at any point, they may ask to see a particular part of the material frozen for them to study and there is no limit on how many times they can view the whole or any part or parts of the material; and
(d) that the person who views the material is not asked to make any decision as to whether they recognise anyone whose image they have seen as someone known to them until they have seen the whole of the material at least twice, unless the officer in charge of the viewing decides that because of the number of images the person has been invited to view, it would not be reasonable to ask them to view the whole of the material for a second time. A record of this decision must be included in the record that is made in accordance with *paragraph 3.36*.

(see *Note 3G*).

3.36 A record of the circumstances and conditions under which the person is given an opportunity to recognise an individual must be made and the record must include:
(a) whether the person knew or was given information concerning the name or identity of any suspect;
(b) what the person has been told *before* the viewing about the offence, the person(s) depicted in the images or the offender and by whom;
(c) how and by whom the witness was asked to view the image or look at the individual;
(d) whether the viewing was alone or with others and if with others, the reason for it;
(e) the arrangements under which the person viewed the film or saw the individual and by whom those arrangements were made;
(f) subject to *paragraph 2.18*, the name and rank of the officer responsible for deciding that the viewing arrangements should be made in accordance with this Part;
(g) the date time and place images were viewed or further viewed or the individual was seen;
(h) the times between which the images were viewed or the individual was seen;
(i) how the viewing of images or sighting of the individual was controlled and by whom;
(j) whether the person was familiar with the location shown in any images or the place where they saw the individual and if so, why;
(k) whether or not, on this occasion, the person claims to recognise any image shown, or any individual seen, as being someone known to them, and if they do:
(i) the reason;
(ii) the words of recognition;
(iii) any expressions of doubt; and
(iv) what features of the image or the individual triggered the recognition.

3.37 The record required under *paragraph 3.36* may be made by the person who views the image or sees the individual and makes the recognition; and if applicable, by the officer or police staff in charge of showing the images to that person or in charge of the conditions under which that person sees the individual. The person must be asked to read and check the completed record and as applicable, confirm that it is correctly and accurately reflects the part they played in the viewing (see *Note 3H*).

Part (C) Recognition by uncontrolled viewing of films, photographs and images

3.38 This Part applies when, for the purpose of identifying and tracing suspects, films and photographs of incidents or other images are:

(a) shown to the public (which may include police officers and police staff as well as members of the public) through the national or local media or any social media networking site; or

(b) circulated through local or national police communication systems for viewing by police officers and police staff; and

the viewing is not formally controlled and supervised as set out in Part B.

3.39 A copy of the relevant material released to the national or local media for showing as described in sub-paragraph 3.38(a), shall be kept. The suspect or their solicitor shall be allowed to view such material before any eye-witness identification procedure under *paragraphs 3.5* to *3.10*, *3.21* or *3.23* of Part A are carried out, provided it is practicable and would not unreasonably delay the investigation. This paragraph does not affect any separate requirement under the Criminal Procedure and Investigations Act 1996 to retain material in connection with criminal investigations that might apply to *sub-paragraphs 3.38(a)* and *(b)*.

3.40 Each eye-witness involved in any eye-witness identification procedure under *paragraphs 3.5* to *3.10*, *3.21* or *3.23* shall be asked, *after they have taken part*, whether they have seen any film, photograph or image relating to the offence or any description of the suspect which has been broadcast or published as described in *paragraph 3.38(a)* and their reply recorded. If they have, they should be asked to give details of the circumstances and subject to the eye-witness's recollection, the record described in *paragraph 3.41* should be completed.

3.41 As soon as practicable after an individual (member of the public, police officer or police staff) indicates in response to a viewing that they may have information relating to the identity and whereabouts of anyone they have seen in that viewing, arrangements should be made to ensure that they are asked to give details of the circumstances and, subject to the individual's recollection, a record of the circumstances and conditions under which the viewing took place is made. This record shall be made in accordance with the provisions of *paragraph 3.36* insofar as they can be applied to the viewing in question (see *Note 3H*).

Notes for guidance

3AA The eye-witness identification procedures in Part A should not be used to test whether a witness can recognise a person as someone they know and would be able to give evidence of recognition along the lines that 'On (describe date, time, location and circumstances) I saw an image of an individual who I recognised as AB.' In these cases, the procedures in Part B shall apply if the viewing is controlled and the procedure in Part C shall apply if the viewing is not controlled.

3ZA In paragraph 3.5(a)(i), examples of physical changes or differences that the identification officer may wish to consider include hair style and colour, weight, facial hair, wearing or removal of spectacles and tinted contact lenses, facial injuries, tattoos and makeup.

3A Except for the provisions of Annex E, paragraph 1, a police officer who is a witness for the purposes of this part of the Code is subject to the same principles and procedures as a civilian witness.

3B When an eye-witness attending an identification procedure has previously been shown photographs, or been shown or provided with computerised or artist's composite likenesses, or similar likenesses or pictures, it is the officer in charge of the investigation's responsibility to make the identification officer aware of this.

3C The purpose of paragraph 3.19 is to avoid or reduce delay in arranging identification procedures by enabling the required information and warnings, see sub-paragraphs 3.17(ix) and 3.17(xii), to be given at the earliest opportunity.

3D Paragraph 3.21 would apply when a known suspect becomes 'unavailable' and thereby delays or frustrates arrangements for obtaining identification evidence. It also applies when a suspect refuses or fails to take part in a video identification, an identification parade or a group identification, or refuses or fails to take part in the only practicable options from that list. It enables any suitable images of the suspect, moving or still, which are available or can be obtained, to be used in an identification procedure. Examples include images from custody and other CCTV systems and from visually recorded interview records, see Code F Note for Guidance 2D.

3E When it is proposed to show photographs to a witness in accordance with Annex E, it is the responsibility of the officer in charge of the investigation to confirm to the officer responsible for supervising and directing the showing, that the first description of the suspect given by that eye-witness has been recorded. If this description has not been recorded, the procedure under Annex E must be postponed, see Annex E paragraph 2.

3F The admissibility and value of identification evidence obtained when carrying out the procedure under paragraph 3.2 may be compromised if:

- *(a) before a person is identified, the eye-witness' attention is specifically drawn to that person;* or
- *(b) the suspect's identity becomes known before the procedure.*

3G The admissibility and value of evidence of recognition obtained when carrying out the procedures in Part B may be compromised if, before the person is recognised, the witness who has claimed to know them is given or is made, or becomes aware of, information about the person which was not previously known to them personally but which they have purported to rely on to support their claim that the person is in fact known to them.

3H It is important that the record referred to in paragraphs 3.36 and 3.41 is made as soon as practicable after the viewing and whilst it is fresh in the mind of the individual who makes the recognition.

4 Identification by fingerprints and footwear impressions

(A) Taking fingerprints in connection with a criminal investigation

(a) General

4.1 References to 'fingerprints' means any record, produced by any method, of the skin pattern and other physical characteristics or features of a person's:

- (i) fingers; or
- (ii) palms.

(b) Action

4.2 A person's fingerprints may be taken in connection with the investigation of an offence only with their consent or if *paragraph 4.3* applies. If the person is at a police station, consent must be in writing.

4.3 PACE, section 61, provides powers to take fingerprints without consent from any person aged ten or over as follows:

- (a) under *section 61(3)*, from a person detained at a police station in consequence of being arrested for a recordable offence, see *Note 4A*, if they have not had their fingerprints taken in the course of the investigation of the offence unless those previously taken fingerprints are not a complete set or some or all of those fingerprints are not of sufficient quality to allow satisfactory analysis, comparison or matching.
- (b) under *section 61(4)*, from a person detained at a police station who has been charged with a recordable offence, see *Note 4A*, or informed they will be reported for such an offence if they have not had their fingerprints taken in the course of the investigation of the offence unless those previously taken fingerprints are not a complete set or some or all of those fingerprints are not of sufficient quality to allow satisfactory analysis, comparison or matching.
- (c) under *section 61(4A)*, from a person who has been bailed to appear at a court or police station if the person:
  - (i) has answered to bail for a person whose fingerprints were taken previously and there are reasonable grounds for believing they are not the same person; or
  - (ii) who has answered to bail claims to be a different person from a person whose fingerprints were previously taken;

and in either case, the court or an officer of inspector rank or above, authorises the fingerprints to be taken at the court or police station (an inspector's authority may be given in writing or orally and confirmed in writing, as soon as practicable);

(ca) under *section 61(5A)* from a person who has been arrested for a recordable offence and released if the person:
   (i) is on bail and has not had their fingerprints taken in the course of the investigation of the offence, or;
   (ii) has had their fingerprints taken in the course of the investigation of the offence, but they do not constitute a complete set or some, or all, of the fingerprints are not of sufficient quality to allow satisfactory analysis, comparison or matching.

(cb) under *section 61(5B)* from a person not detained at a police station who has been charged with a recordable offence or informed they will be reported for such an offence if:
   (i) they have not had their fingerprints taken in the course of the investigation; or
   (ii) their fingerprints have been taken in the course of the investigation of the offence but either:
   - they do not constitute a complete set or some, or all, of the fingerprints are not of sufficient quality to allow satisfactory analysis, comparison or matching; or
   - the investigation was discontinued but subsequently resumed and, before the resumption, their fingerprints were destroyed pursuant to section 63D(3).

(d) under *section 61(6)*, from a person who has been:
   (i) convicted of a recordable offence; or
   (ii) given a caution in respect of a recordable offence (see Note 4A) which, at the time of the caution, the person admitted;

   if, since being convicted or cautioned:
   - their fingerprints have not been taken; or
   - their fingerprints which have been taken do not constitute a complete set or some, or all, of the fingerprints are not of sufficient quality to allow satisfactory analysis, comparison or matching;

   and in either case, an officer of inspector rank or above is satisfied that taking the fingerprints is necessary to assist in the prevention or detection of crime and authorises the taking;

(e) under *section 61(6A)* from a person a constable reasonably suspects is committing or attempting to commit, or has committed or attempted to commit, any offence if either:
   (i) the person's name is unknown to, and cannot be readily ascertained by, the constable; or
   (ii) the constable has reasonable grounds for doubting whether a name given by the person as their name is their real name.

   Note: fingerprints taken under this power are not regarded as having been taken in the course of the investigation of an offence.
   [See *Note 4C*]

(f) under *section 61(6D)* from a person who has been convicted outside England and Wales of an offence which if committed in England and Wales would be a qualifying offence as defined by PACE, section 65A (see Note 4AB) if:
   (i) the person's fingerprints have not been taken previously under this power or their fingerprints have been so taken on a previous occasion but they do not constitute a complete set or some, or all, of the fingerprints are not of sufficient quality to allow satisfactory analysis, comparison or matching; and
   (ii) a police officer of inspector rank or above is satisfied that taking fingerprints is necessary to assist in the prevention or detection of crime and authorises them to be taken.

4.4 PACE, section 63A(4) and Schedule 2A provide powers to:

(a) make a requirement (in accordance with Annex G) for a person to attend a police station to have their fingerprints taken in the exercise of one of the following powers (described in *paragraph 4.3* above) within certain periods as follows:

(i) *section 61(5A)*—Persons arrested for a recordable offence and released, see *paragraph 4.3(ca)*: In the case of a person whose fingerprints were taken in the course of the investigation but those fingerprints do not constitute a complete set or some, or all, of the fingerprints are not of sufficient quality, the requirement may not be made more than six months from the day the investigating officer was informed that the fingerprints previously taken were incomplete or below standard. In the case of a person whose fingerprints were destroyed prior to the resumption of the investigation, the requirement may not be made more than six months from the day on which the investigation resumed.

(ii) *section 61(5B)*—Persons not detained at a police station charged etc. with a recordable offence, see *paragraph 4.3(cb)*: The requirement may not be made more than six months from:

- the day the person was charged or informed that they would be reported, if fingerprints have not been taken in the course of the investigation of the offence; or
- the day the investigating officer was informed that the fingerprints previously taken were incomplete or below standard, if fingerprints have been taken in the course of the investigation but those fingerprints do not constitute a complete set or some, or all, of the fingerprints are not of sufficient quality; or
- the day on which the investigation was resumed, in the case of a person whose fingerprints were destroyed prior to the resumption of the investigation.

(iii) *section 61(6)*—Persons convicted or cautioned for a recordable offence in England and Wales, see *paragraph 4.3(d)*: Where the offence for which the person was convicted or cautioned is a qualifying offence (see Note 4AB), there is no time limit for the exercise of this power. Where the conviction or caution is for a recordable offence which is not a qualifying offence, the requirement may not be made more than two years from:

- in the case of a person who has not had their fingerprints taken since the conviction or caution, the day on which the person was convicted or cautioned, or, if later, the day on which Schedule 2A came into force (March 7, 2011), ; or
- in the case of a person whose fingerprints have been taken in the course of the investigation but those fingerprints do not constitute a complete set or some, or all, of the fingerprints are not of sufficient quality, the day on which an officer from the force investigating the offence was informed that the fingerprints previously taken were incomplete or below standard, or, if later, the day on which Schedule 2A came into force (March 7, 2011).

(iv) *section 61(6D)*—A person who has been convicted of a qualifying offence (see *Note 4AB*) outside England and Wales, see paragraph 4.3(g): There is no time limit for making the requirement.

Note: A person who has had their fingerprints taken under any of the powers in section 61 mentioned in *paragraph 4.3* on two occasions in relation to any offence may not be required under Schedule 2A to attend a police station for their fingerprints to be taken again under section 61 in relation to that offence, unless authorised by an officer of inspector rank or above. The fact of the authorisation and the reasons for giving it must be recorded as soon as practicable.

(b) arrest, without warrant, a person who fails to comply with the requirement.

4.5 A person's fingerprints may be taken, as above, electronically.

4.6 Reasonable force may be used, if necessary, to take a person's fingerprints without their consent under the powers as in *paragraphs 4.3* and *4.4*.

4.7 Before any fingerprints are taken:

(a) without consent under any power mentioned in *paragraphs 4.3* and *4.4* above, the person must be informed of:

(i) the reason their fingerprints are to be taken;

(ii) the power under which they are to be taken; and

(iii) the fact that the relevant authority has been given if any power mentioned in *paragraph 4.3(c), (d)* or *(f)* applies

(b) with or without consent at a police station or elsewhere, the person must be informed:

(i) that their fingerprints may be subject of a speculative search against other fingerprints, see *Note 4B*; and

(ii) that their fingerprints may be retained in accordance with *Annex F, Part (a)* unless they were taken under the power mentioned in paragraph 4.3(e) when they must be destroyed after they have being checked (See *Note 4C*).

(c) Documentation

4.8A A record must be made as soon as practicable after the fingerprints are taken, of:

- the matters in paragraph 4.7(a)(i) to (iii) and the fact that the person has been informed of those matters; and
- the fact that the person has been informed of the matters in paragraph 4.7(b)(i) and (ii).

The record must be made in the person's custody record if they are detained at a police station when the fingerprints are taken.

4.8 If force is used, a record shall be made of the circumstances and those present.

4.9 Not used

(B) Not used

4.10 *Not used*

4.11 *Not used*

4.12 *Not used*

4.13 *Not used*

4.14 *Not used*

4.15 *Not used*

(C) Taking footwear impressions in connection with a criminal investigation

(a) Action

4.16 Impressions of a person's footwear may be taken in connection with the investigation of an offence only with their consent or if *paragraph 4.17* applies. If the person is at a police station consent must be in writing.

4.17 PACE, section 61A, provides power for a police officer to take footwear impressions without consent from any person over the age of ten years who is detained at a police station:

(a) in consequence of being arrested for a recordable offence, see *Note 4A*; or if the detainee has been charged with a recordable offence, or informed they will be reported for such an offence; and

(b) the detainee has not had an impression of their footwear taken in the course of the investigation of the offence unless the previously taken impression is not complete or is not of sufficient quality to allow satisfactory analysis, comparison or matching (whether in the case in question or generally).

4.18 Reasonable force may be used, if necessary, to take a footwear impression from a detainee without consent under the power in *paragraph 4.17*.

4.19 Before any footwear impression is taken with, or without, consent as above, the person must be informed:

(a) of the reason the impression is to be taken;

(b) that the impression may be retained and may be subject of a speculative search against other impressions, see *Note 4B*, unless destruction of the impression is required in accordance with *Annex F, Part B*.

(b) Documentation

4.20 A record must be made, as soon as possible, of the reason for taking a person's footwear impressions without consent. If force is used, a record shall be made of the circumstances and those present.

4.21 A record shall be made when a person has been informed under the terms of *paragraph 4.19(b)*, of the possibility that their footwear impressions may be subject of a speculative search.

Notes for guidance

4A References to 'recordable offences' in this Code relate to those offences for which convictions or cautions may be recorded in national police records. See PACE, section 27(4). The recordable offences current at the time when this Code was prepared, are any offences which carry a sentence of imprisonment on conviction (irrespective of the period, or the age of the offender or actual sentence passed) as well as the non-imprisonable offences under the Vagrancy Act 1824 sections 3 and 4 (begging and persistent begging), the Street Offences Act 1959, section 1 (loitering or soliciting for purposes of prostitution), the Road Traffic Act 1988, section 25 (tampering with motor vehicles), the Criminal Justice and Public Order Act 1994, section 167 (touting for hire car services) and others listed in the National Police Records (Recordable Offences) Regulations 2000 as amended.

4AB A qualifying offence is one of the offences specified in PACE, section 65A. These include offences which involve the use or threat of violence or unlawful force against persons, sexual offences, offences against children and other offences, for example:

- murder, false imprisonment, kidnapping contrary to Common law
- manslaughter, conspiracy to murder, threats to kill, wounding with intent to cause grievous bodily harm (GBH), causing GBH and assault occasioning actual bodily harm contrary to the Offences Against the Person Act 1861;
- criminal possession or use of firearms contrary to sections 16 to 18 of the Firearms Act 1968;
- robbery, burglary and aggravated burglary contrary to sections 8, 9 or 10 of the Theft Act 1968 or an offence under section 12A of that Act involving an accident which caused a person's death;
- criminal damage required to be charged as arson contrary to section 1 of the Criminal Damage Act 1971;
- taking, possessing and showing indecent photographs of children contrary to section 1 of the Protection of Children Act 1978;
- rape, sexual assault, child sex offences, exposure and other offences contrary to the Sexual Offences Act 2003.

4B Fingerprints, footwear impressions or a DNA sample (and the information derived from it) taken from a person arrested on suspicion of being involved in a recordable offence, or charged with such an offence, or informed they will be reported for such an offence, may be subject of a speculative search. This means the fingerprints, footwear impressions or DNA sample may be checked against other fingerprints, footwear impressions and DNA records held by, or on behalf of, the police and other law enforcement authorities in, or outside, the UK, or held in connection with, or as a result of, an investigation of an offence inside or outside the UK.

4C The power under section 61(6A) of PACE described in paragraph 4.3(e) allows fingerprints of a suspect who has not been arrested, and whose name is not known or cannot be ascertained, or who gave a doubtful name, to be taken in connection with any offence (whether recordable or not) using a mobile device and then checked on the street against the database containing the national fingerprint collection. Fingerprints taken under this power cannot be retained after they have been checked. The results may make an arrest for the suspected offence based on the name condition unnecessary (See Code G paragraph 2.9(a)) and enable the offence to be disposed of without arrest, for example, by summons/

charging by post, penalty notice or words of advice. If arrest for a non-recordable offence is necessary for any other reasons, this power may also be exercised at the station. Before the power is exercised, the officer should:

- inform the person of the nature of the suspected offence and why they are suspected of committing it.
- give them a reasonable opportunity to establish their real name before deciding that their name is unknown and cannot be readily ascertained or that there are reasonable grounds to doubt that a name they have given is their real name.
- as applicable, inform the person of the reason why their name is not known and cannot be readily ascertained or of the grounds for doubting that a name they have given is their real name, including, for example, the reason why a particular document the person has produced to verify their real name, is not sufficient.

4D Not used.

5 Examinations to establish identity and the taking of photographs

(A) Detainees at police stations

(a) Searching or examination of detainees at police stations

5.1 PACE, section 54A(1), allows a detainee at a police station to be searched or examined or both, to establish:

(a) whether they have any marks, features or injuries that would tend to identify them as a person involved in the commission of an offence and to photograph any identifying marks, see *paragraph 5.5*; or

(b) their identity, see *Note 5A*.

A person detained at a police station to be searched under a stop and search power, see Code A, is not a detainee for the purposes of these powers.

5.2 A search and/or examination to find marks under section 54A (1) (a) may be carried out without the detainee's consent, see *paragraph 2.12*, only if authorised by an officer of at least inspector rank when consent has been withheld or it is not practicable to obtain consent, see *Note 5D.*

5.3 A search or examination to establish a suspect's identity under section 54A (1) (b) may be carried out without the detainee's consent, see *paragraph 2.12*, only if authorised by an officer of at least inspector rank when the detainee has refused to identify themselves or the authorising officer has reasonable grounds for suspecting the person is not who they claim to be.

5.4 Any marks that assist in establishing the detainee's identity, or their identification as a person involved in the commission of an offence, are identifying marks. Such marks may be photographed with the detainee's consent, see *paragraph 2.12*; or without their consent if it is withheld or it is not practicable to obtain it, see *Note 5D.*

5.5 A detainee may only be searched, examined and photographed under section 54A, by a police officer of the same sex.

5.6 Any photographs of identifying marks, taken under section 54A, may be used or disclosed only for purposes related to the prevention or detection of crime, the investigation of offences or the conduct of prosecutions by, or on behalf of, police or other law enforcement and prosecuting authorities inside, and outside, the UK. After being so used or disclosed, the photograph may be retained but must not be used or disclosed except for these purposes, see *Note 5B.*

5.7 The powers, as in *paragraph 5.1*, do not affect any separate requirement under the Criminal Procedure and Investigations Act 1996 to retain material in connection with criminal investigations.

5.8 Authority for the search and/or examination for the purposes of *paragraphs 5.2* and *5.3* may be given orally or in writing. If given orally, the authorising officer must confirm it in writing as soon as practicable. A separate authority is required for each purpose which applies.

5.9 If it is established a person is unwilling to co-operate sufficiently to enable a search and/or examination to take place or a suitable photograph to be taken, an officer may use reasonable force to:

(a) search and/or examine a detainee without their consent; and
(b) photograph any identifying marks without their consent.

5.10 The thoroughness and extent of any search or examination carried out in accordance with the powers in section 54A must be no more than the officer considers necessary to achieve the required purpose. Any search or examination which involves the removal of more than the person's outer clothing shall be conducted in accordance with Code C, Annex A, paragraph 11.

5.11 An intimate search may not be carried out under the powers in section 54A.

(b) Photographing detainees at police stations and other persons elsewhere than at a police station

5.12 Under PACE, section 64A, an officer may photograph:

(a) any person whilst they are detained at a police station; and
(b) any person who is elsewhere than at a police station and who has been:
  (i) arrested by a constable for an offence;
  (ii) taken into custody by a constable after being arrested for an offence by a person other than a constable;
  (iii) made subject to a requirement to wait with a community support officer under paragraph 2(3) or (3B) of Schedule 4 to the Police Reform Act 2002;
  (iiia) given a direction by a constable under section 27 of the Violent Crime Reduction Act 2006.
  (iv) given a penalty notice by a constable in uniform under Chapter 1 of Part 1 of the Criminal Justice and Police Act 2001, a penalty notice by a constable under section 444A of the Education Act 1996, or a fixed penalty notice by a constable in uniform under section 54 of the Road Traffic Offenders Act 1988;
  (v) given a notice in relation to a relevant fixed penalty offence (within the meaning of paragraph 1 of Schedule 4 to the Police Reform Act 2002) by a community support officer by virtue of a designation applying that paragraph to him;
  (vi) given a notice in relation to a relevant fixed penalty offence (within the meaning of paragraph 1 of Schedule 5 to the Police Reform Act 2002) by an accredited person by virtue of accreditation specifying that that paragraph applies to him; or
  (viii) given a direction to leave and not return to a specified location for up to 48 hours by a police constable (under section 27 of the Violent Crime Reduction Act 2006).

5.12A Photographs taken under PACE, section 64A:

(a) may be taken with the person's consent, or without their consent if consent is withheld or it is not practicable to obtain their consent, see *Note 5E*; and
(b) may be used or disclosed only for purposes related to the prevention or detection of crime, the investigation of offences or the conduct of prosecutions by, or on behalf of, police or other law enforcement and prosecuting authorities inside and outside the United Kingdom or the enforcement of any sentence or order made by a court when dealing with an offence. After being so used or disclosed, they may be retained but can only be used or disclosed for the same purposes. See *Note 5B*.

5.13 The officer proposing to take a detainee's photograph may, for this purpose, require the person to remove any item or substance worn on, or over, all, or any part of, their head or face. If they do not comply with such a requirement, the officer may remove the item or substance.

5.14 If it is established the detainee is unwilling to co-operate sufficiently to enable a suitable photograph to be taken and it is not reasonably practicable to take the photograph covertly, an officer may use reasonable force, see *Note 5F*.

(a) to take their photograph without their consent; and
(b) for the purpose of taking the photograph, remove any item or substance worn on, or over, all, or any part of, the person's head or face which they have failed to remove when asked.

5.15 For the purposes of this Code, a photograph may be obtained without the person's consent by making a copy of an image of them taken at any time on a camera system installed anywhere in the police station.

(c) Information to be given

5.18 When a person is searched, examined or photographed under the provisions as in *paragraph 5.1* and *5.12*, or their photograph obtained as in *paragraph 5.15*, they must be informed of the:

(a) purpose of the search, examination or photograph;
(b) grounds on which the relevant authority, if applicable, has been given; and
(c) purposes for which the photograph may be used, disclosed or retained.

This information must be given before the search or examination commences or the photograph is taken, except if the photograph is:

(i) to be taken covertly;
(ii) obtained as in *paragraph 5.15*, in which case the person must be informed as soon as practicable after the photograph is taken or obtained.

(d) Documentation

5.17 A record must be made when a detainee is searched, examined, or a photograph of the person, or any identifying marks found on them, are taken. The record must include the:

(a) identity, subject to paragraph 2.18, of the officer carrying out the search, examination or taking the photograph;
(b) purpose of the search, examination or photograph and the outcome;
(c) detainee's consent to the search, examination or photograph, or the reason the person was searched, examined or photographed without consent;
(d) giving of any authority as in *paragraphs 5.2* and *5.3*, the grounds for giving it and the authorising officer.

5.18 If force is used when searching, examining or taking a photograph in accordance with this section, a record shall be made of the circumstances and those present.

(B) Persons at police stations not detained

5.19 When there are reasonable grounds for suspecting the involvement of a person in a criminal offence, but that person is at a police station **voluntarily** and not detained, the provisions of *paragraphs 5.1* to *5.18* should apply, subject to the modifications in the following paragraphs.

5.20 References to the 'person being detained' and to the powers mentioned in *paragraph 5.1* which apply only to detainees at police stations shall be omitted.

5.21 Force may not be used to:

(a) search and/or examine the person to:
  (i) discover whether they have any marks that would tend to identify them as a person involved in the commission of an offence; or
  (ii) establish their identity, see *Note 5A*;
(b) take photographs of any identifying marks, see *paragraph 5.4*; or
(c) take a photograph of the person.

5.22 Subject to *paragraph 5.24*, the photographs of persons or of their identifying marks which are not taken in accordance with the provisions mentioned in *paragraphs 5.1* or *5.12*, must be destroyed (together with any negatives and copies) unless the person:

(a) is charged with, or informed they may be prosecuted for, a recordable offence;
(b) is prosecuted for a recordable offence;
(c) is cautioned for a recordable offence or given a warning or reprimand in accordance with the Crime and Disorder Act 1998 for a recordable offence; or
(d) gives informed consent, in writing, for the photograph or image to be retained as in *paragraph 5.6*.

5.23 When *paragraph 5.22* requires the destruction of any photograph, the person must be given an opportunity to witness the destruction or to have a certificate confirming the destruction provided they so request the certificate within five days of being informed the destruction is required.

5.24 Nothing in *paragraph 5.22* affects any separate requirement under the Criminal Procedure and Investigations Act 1996 to retain material in connection with criminal investigations.

Notes for guidance

5A The conditions under which fingerprints may be taken to assist in establishing a person's identity, are described in Section 4.

5B Examples of purposes related to the prevention or detection of crime, the investigation of offences or the conduct of prosecutions include:

(a) checking the photograph against other photographs held in records or in connection with, or as a result of, an investigation of an offence to establish whether the person is liable to arrest for other offences;

(b) when the person is arrested at the same time as other people, or at a time when it is likely that other people will be arrested, using the photograph to help establish who was arrested, at what time and where;

(c) when the real identity of the person is not known and cannot be readily ascertained or there are reasonable grounds for doubting a name and other personal details given by the person, are their real name and personal details. In these circumstances, using or disclosing the photograph to help to establish or verify their real identity or determine whether they are liable to arrest for some other offence, e.g. by checking it against other photographs held in records or in connection with, or as a result of, an investigation of an offence;

(d) when it appears any identification procedure in section 3 may need to be arranged for which the person's photograph would assist;

(e) when the person's release without charge may be required, and if the release is:

(i) on bail to appear at a police station, using the photograph to help verify the person's identity when they answer their bail and if the person does not answer their bail, to assist in arresting them; or

(ii) without bail, using the photograph to help verify their identity or assist in locating them for the purposes of serving them with a summons to appear at court in criminal proceedings;

(f) when the person has answered to bail at a police station and there are reasonable grounds for doubting they are the person who was previously granted bail, using the photograph to help establish or verify their identity;

(g) when the person arrested on a warrant claims to be a different person from the person named on the warrant and a photograph would help to confirm or disprove their claim;

(h) when the person has been charged with, reported for, or convicted of, a recordable offence and their photograph is not already on record as a result of (a) to (f) or their photograph is on record but their appearance has changed since it was taken and the person has not yet been released or brought before a court.

5C There is no power to arrest a person convicted of a recordable offence solely to take their photograph. The power to take photographs in this section applies only where the person is in custody as a result of the exercise of another power, e.g. arrest for fingerprinting under PACE, Schedule 2A, paragraph 17.

5D Examples of when it would not be practicable to obtain a detainee's consent, see paragraph 2.12, to a search, examination or the taking of a photograph of an identifying mark include:

(a) when the person is drunk or otherwise unfit to give consent;

(b) when there are reasonable grounds to suspect that if the person became aware a search or examination was to take place or an identifying mark was to be photographed, they would take steps to prevent this happening, e.g. by violently resisting, covering or concealing the

mark etc. and it would not otherwise be possible to carry out the search or examination or to photograph any identifying mark;

(c) in the case of a juvenile, if the parent or guardian cannot be contacted in sufficient time to allow the search or examination to be carried out or the photograph to be taken.

5E Examples of when it would not be practicable to obtain the person's consent, see paragraph 2.12, to a photograph being taken include:

(a) when the person is drunk or otherwise unfit to give consent;

(b) when there are reasonable grounds to suspect that if the person became aware a photograph, suitable to be used or disclosed for the use and disclosure described in paragraph 5.6, was to be taken, they would take steps to prevent it being taken, e.g. by violently resisting, covering or distorting their face etc., and it would not otherwise be possible to take a suitable photograph;

(c) when, in order to obtain a suitable photograph, it is necessary to take it covertly; and

(d) in the case of a juvenile, if the parent or guardian cannot be contacted in sufficient time to allow the photograph to be taken.

5F The use of reasonable force to take the photograph of a suspect elsewhere than at a police station must be carefully considered. In order to obtain a suspect's consent and co-operation to remove an item of religious headwear to take their photograph, a constable should consider whether in the circumstances of the situation the removal of the headwear and the taking of the photograph should be by an officer of the same sex as the person. It would be appropriate for these actions to be conducted out of public view (see paragraph 1.1 *and* Note 1A*).*

6 Identification by body samples and impressions

(A) General

6.1 References to:

(a) an 'intimate sample' mean a dental impression or sample of blood, semen or any other tissue fluid, urine, or pubic hair, or a swab taken from any part of a person's genitals or from a person's body orifice other than the mouth;

(b) a 'non-intimate sample' means:

  (i) a sample of hair, other than pubic hair, which includes hair plucked with the root, see *Note 6A*;

  (ii) a sample taken from a nail or from under a nail;

  (iii) a swab taken from any part of a person's body other than a part from which a swab taken would be an intimate sample;

  (iv) saliva;

  (v) a skin impression which means any record, other than a fingerprint, which is a record, in any form and produced by any method, of the skin pattern and other physical characteristics or features of the whole, or any part of, a person's foot or of any other part of their body.

(B) Action

(a) Intimate samples

6.2 PACE, section 62, provides that intimate samples may be taken under:

(a) section 62(1), from a person in police detention only:

  (i) if a police officer of inspector rank or above has reasonable grounds to believe such an impression or sample will tend to confirm or disprove the suspect's involvement in a recordable offence, see *Note 4A*, and gives authorisation for a sample to be taken; and

  (ii) with the suspect's written consent;

(b) section 62(1A), from a person not in police detention but from whom two or more non-intimate samples have been taken in the course of an investigation of an offence and the samples, though suitable, have proved insufficient if:

(i) a police officer of inspector rank or above authorises it to be taken; and
(ii) the person concerned gives their written consent. See *Notes 6B* and *6C*

(c) section 62(2A), from a person convicted outside England and Wales of an offence which if committed in England and Wales would be qualifying offence as defined by PACE, section 65A (see *Note 4AB*) from whom two or more non-intimate samples taken under section 63(3E) (see *paragraph 6.6(h)* have proved insufficient if:
(i) a police officer of inspector rank or above is satisfied that taking the sample is necessary to assist in the prevention or detection of crime and authorises it to be taken; and
(ii) the person concerned gives their written consent.

6.2A PACE, section 63A(4) and Schedule 2A provide powers to:

(a) make a requirement (in accordance with Annex G) for a person to attend a police station to have an intimate sample taken in the exercise of one of the following powers (see *paragraph 6.2*):
(i) *section 62(1A)*—Persons from whom two or more non-intimate samples have been taken and proved to be insufficient, see paragraph 6.2(b): There is no time limit for making the requirement.
(ii) *section 62(2A)*—Persons convicted outside England and Wales from whom two or more non-intimate samples taken under section 63(3E) (see paragraph 6.6(g) have proved insufficient, see *paragraph 6.2(c)*: There is no time limit for making the requirement.

(b) arrest without warrant a person who fails to comply with the requirement

6.3 Before a suspect is asked to provide an intimate sample, they must be:

(a) informed:
(i) of the reason, including the nature of the suspected offence (except if taken under paragraph 6.2(c) from a person convicted outside England and Wales.
(ii) that authorisation has been given and the provisions under which given;
(iii) that a sample taken at a police station may be subject of a speculative search;

(b) warned that if they refuse without good cause their refusal may harm their case if it comes to trial, see *Note 6D*. If the suspect is in police detention and not legally represented, they must also be reminded of their entitlement to have free legal advice, see Code C, *paragraph 6.5*, and the reminder noted in the custody record. If *paragraph 6.2(b)* applies and the person is attending a station voluntarily, their entitlement to free legal advice as in Code C, *paragraph 3.21* shall be explained to them.

6.4 Dental impressions may only be taken by a registered dentist. Other intimate samples, except for samples of urine, may only be taken by a registered medical practitioner or registered nurse or registered paramedic.

(b) Non-intimate samples

6.5 A non-intimate sample may be taken from a detainee only with their written consent or if *paragraph 6.6* applies.

6.6 A non-intimate sample may be taken from a person without the appropriate consent in the following circumstances:

(a) under *section 63(2A)* from a person who is in police detention as a consequence of being arrested for a recordable offence and who has not had a non-intimate sample of the same type and from the same part of the body taken in the course of the investigation of the offence by the police or they have had such a sample taken but it proved insufficient.

(b) Under *section 63(3)* from a person who is being held in custody by the police on the authority of a court if an officer of at least the rank of inspector authorises it to be taken. An authorisation may be given:

(i) if the authorising officer has reasonable grounds for suspecting the person of involvement in a recordable offence and for believing that the sample will tend to confirm or disprove that involvement, and

(ii) in writing or orally and confirmed in writing, as soon as practicable;

but an authorisation may not be given to take from the same part of the body a further non-intimate sample consisting of a skin impression unless the previously taken impression proved insufficient

(c) under *section 63(3ZA)* from a person who has been arrested for a recordable offence and released if:

(i) in the case of a person who is on bail, they have not had a sample of the same type and from the same part of the body taken in the course of the investigation of the offence, or;

(ii) in any case, the person has had such a sample taken in the course of the investigation of the offence, but either:

- it was not suitable or proved insufficient; or
- the investigation was discontinued but subsequently resumed and before the resumption, any DNA profile derived from the sample was destroyed and the sample itself was destroyed pursuant to section 63R(4), (5) or (12).

(d) under *section 63(3A)*, from a person (whether or not in police detention or held in custody by the police on the authority of a court) who has been charged with a recordable offence or informed they will be reported for such an offence if the person:

(i) has not had a non-intimate sample taken from them in the course of the investigation of the offence; or

(ii) has had a sample so taken, but it was not suitable or proved insufficient, see *Note 6B*; or

(iii) has had a sample taken in the course of the investigation of the offence and the sample has been destroyed and in proceedings relating to that offence there is a dispute as to whether a DNA profile relevant to the proceedings was derived from the destroyed sample.

(e) under *section 63(3B)*, from a person who has been:

(i) convicted of a recordable offence; or

(ii) given a caution in respect of a recordable offence which, at the time of the caution, the person admitted;

if, since their conviction or caution a non-intimate sample has not been taken from them or a sample which has been taken since then was not suitable or proved insufficient and in either case, an officer of inspector rank or above, is satisfied that taking the fingerprints is necessary to assist in the prevention or detection of crime and authorises the taking;

(f) under *section 63(3C)* from a person to whom section 2 of the Criminal Evidence (Amendment) Act 1997 applies (persons detained following acquittal on grounds of insanity or finding of unfitness to plead).

(g) under *section 63(3E)* from a person who has been convicted outside England and Wales of an offence which if committed in England and Wales would be a qualifying offence as defined by PACE, section 65A (see *Note 4AB*) if:

(i) a non-intimate sample has not been taken previously under this power or unless a sample was so taken but was not suitable or proved insufficient; and

(ii) a police officer of inspector rank or above is satisfied that taking a sample is necessary to assist in the prevention or detection of crime and authorises it to be taken.

6.6A PACE, *section 63A(4)* and *Schedule 2A* provide powers to:

(a) make a requirement (in accordance with Annex G) for a person to attend a police station to have a non-intimate sample taken in the exercise of one of the following powers (see *paragraph 6.6* above) within certain time limits as follows:
   (i) *section 63(3ZA)*—Persons arrested for a recordable offence and released, see paragraph 6.6(c): In the case of a person from whom a non-intimate sample was taken in the course of the investigation but that sample was not suitable or proved insufficient, the requirement may not be made more than six months from the day the investigating officer was informed that the sample previously taken was not suitable or proved insufficient. In the case of a person whose DNA profile and sample was destroyed prior to the resumption of the investigation, the requirement may not be made more than six months from the day on which the investigation resumed.
   (ii) *section 63(3A)*—Persons charged etc. with a recordable offence, see paragraph 6.6(d): The requirement may not be made more than six months from:
   - the day the person was charged or informed that they would be reported, if a sample has not been taken in the course of the investigation;
   - the day the investigating officer was informed that the sample previously taken was not suitable or proved insufficient, if a sample has been taken in the course of the investigation but the sample was not suitable or proved insufficient; or
   - the day on which the investigation was resumed, in the case of a person whose DNA profile and sample were destroyed prior to the resumption of the investigation.

   (iii) *section 63(3B)*—Person convicted or cautioned for a recordable offence in England and Wales, see paragraph 6.6(e): Where the offence for which the person was convicted etc. is also a qualifying offence (see *Note 4AB*), there is no time limit for the exercise of this power. Where the conviction etc. was for a recordable offence that is <u>not</u> a qualifying offence, the requirement may not be made more than two years from:
   - in the case of a person whose sample has not been taken since they were convicted or cautioned, the day the person was convicted or cautioned, , or, if later. the day Schedule 2A came into force (March 7 2011); or
   - in the case of a person whose sample has been taken but was not suitable or proved insufficient, the day an officer from the force investigating the offence was informed that the sample previously taken was not suitable or proved insufficient or, if later, the day Schedule 2A came into force (March 7 2011).

   (iv) *section 63(3E)*—A person who has been convicted of qualifying offence (see *Note 4AB*) outside England and Wales, see *paragraph 6.6(h)*: There is no time limit for making the requirement.

   Note: A person who has had a non-intimate sample taken under any of the powers in section 63 mentioned in paragraph 6.6 on two occasions in relation to any offence may not be required under Schedule 2A to attend a police station for a sample to be taken again under section 63 in relation to that offence, unless authorised by an officer of inspector rank or above. The fact of the authorisation and the reasons for giving it must be recorded as soon as practicable.

(b) arrest, without warrant, a person who fails to comply with the requirement.

6.7 Reasonable force may be used, if necessary, to take a non-intimate sample from a person without their consent under the powers mentioned in *paragraph 6.6*.

6.8 Before any non-intimate sample is taken:

(a) without consent under any power mentioned in paragraphs 6.6 and 6.6A, the person must be informed of:
   (i) the reason for taking the sample;
   (ii) the power under which the sample is to be taken;

(iii) the fact that the relevant authority has been given if any power mentioned in *paragraph 6.6(b), (e)* or *(g)* applies, including the nature of the suspected offence (except if taken under *paragraph 6.6(e)* from a person convicted or cautioned, or under *paragraph 6.6(g)* if taken from a person convicted outside England and Wales;

(b) with or without consent at a police station or elsewhere, the person must be informed:

(i) that their sample or information derived from it may be subject of a speculative search against other samples and information derived from them, see *Note 6E* and

(ii) that their sample and the information derived from it may be retained in accordance with Annex F, Part (a).

(c) Removal of clothing

6.9 When clothing needs to be removed in circumstances likely to cause embarrassment to the person, no person of the opposite sex who is not a registered medical practitioner or registered health care professional shall be present, (unless in the case of a juvenile, mentally disordered or mentally vulnerable person, that person specifically requests the presence of an appropriate adult of the opposite sex who is readily available) nor shall anyone whose presence is unnecessary. However, in the case of a juvenile, this is subject to the overriding proviso that such a removal of clothing may take place in the absence of the appropriate adult only if the juvenile signifies in their presence, that they prefer the adult's absence and they agree.

(d) Documentation

6.10 A record must be made as soon as practicable after the sample is taken of:

- The matters in *paragraph 6.8(a)(i)* to *(iii)* and the fact that the person has been informed of those matters; and
- The fact that the person has been informed of the matters in paragraph 6.8(b)(i) and (ii).

6.10A If force is used, a record shall be made of the circumstances and those present.

6.11 A record must be made of a warning given as required by *paragraph 6.3*.

6.12 *Not used*

Notes for guidance

6A When hair samples are taken for the purpose of DNA analysis (rather than for other purposes such as making a visual match), the suspect should be permitted a reasonable choice as to what part of the body the hairs are taken from. When hairs are plucked, they should be plucked individually, unless the suspect prefers otherwise and no more should be plucked than the person taking them reasonably considers necessary for a sufficient sample.

6B (a) An insufficient sample is one which is not sufficient either in quantity or quality to provide information for a particular form of analysis, such as DNA analysis. A sample may also be insufficient if enough information cannot be obtained from it by analysis because of loss, destruction, damage or contamination of the sample or as a result of an earlier, unsuccessful attempt at analysis.

(b) An unsuitable sample is one which, by its nature, is not suitable for a particular form of analysis.

6C Nothing in paragraph 6.2 prevents intimate samples being taken for elimination purposes with the consent of the person concerned but the provisions of paragraph 2.12 relating to the role of the appropriate adult, should be applied. Paragraph 6.2(b) does not, however, apply where the non-intimate samples were previously taken under the Terrorism Act 2000, Schedule 8, paragraph 10.

6D In warning a person who is asked to provide an intimate sample as in paragraph 6.3, the following form of words may be used:

'You do not have to provide this sample/allow this swab or impression to be taken, but I must warn you that if you refuse without good cause, your refusal may harm your case if it comes to trial.'

6E Fingerprints or a DNA sample and the information derived from it taken from a person arrested on suspicion of being involved in a recordable offence, or charged with such an offence, or informed they will be reported for such an offence, may be subject of a speculative search. This means they may be checked against other fingerprints and DNA records held by, or on behalf of, the police and other law enforcement authorities in or outside the UK or held in connection with, or as a result of, an investigation of an offence inside or outside the UK.

See Annex F regarding the retention and use of fingerprints and samples taken with consent for elimination purposes.

6F Samples of urine and non-intimate samples taken in accordance with sections 63B and 63C of PACE may not be used for identification purposes in accordance with this Code. See Code C Note for guidance 17D.

Annex A Video Identification

(a) General

1. The arrangements for obtaining and ensuring the availability of a suitable set of images to be used in a video identification must be the responsibility of an identification officer (see *paragraph 3.11* of this Code) who has no direct involvement with the case.

2. The set of images must include the suspect and at least eight other people who, so far as possible, and subject to *paragraph 7*, resemble the suspect in age, general appearance and position in life. Only one suspect shall appear in any set unless there are two suspects of roughly similar appearance, in which case they may be shown together with at least twelve other people.

2A If the suspect has an unusual physical feature, e.g., a facial scar, tattoo or distinctive hairstyle or hair colour which does not appear on the images of the other people that are available to be used, steps may be taken to:

(a) conceal the location of the feature on the images of the suspect and the other people; or
(b) replicate that feature on the images of the other people.

For these purposes, the feature may be concealed or replicated electronically or by any other method which it is practicable to use to ensure that the images of the suspect and other people resemble each other. The identification officer has discretion to choose whether to conceal or replicate the feature and the method to be used.

2B If the identification officer decides that a feature should be concealed or replicated, the reason for the decision and whether the feature was concealed or replicated in the images shown to any eye-witness shall be recorded.

2C If the eye-witness requests to view any image where an unusual physical feature has been concealed or replicated without the feature being concealed or replicated, the identification officer has discretion to allow the eye-witness to view such image(s) if they are available.

3. The images used to conduct a video identification shall, as far as possible, show the suspect and other people in the same positions or carrying out the same sequence of movements. They shall also show the suspect and other people under identical conditions unless the identification officer reasonably believes:

(a) because of the suspect's failure or refusal to co-operate or other reasons, it is not practicable for the conditions to be identical; and
(b) any difference in the conditions would not direct an eye-witness' attention to any individual image.

4. The reasons identical conditions are not practicable shall be recorded on forms provided for the purpose.

5. Provision must be made for each person shown to be identified by number.

6. If police officers are shown, any numerals or other identifying badges must be concealed. If a prison inmate is shown, either as a suspect or not, then either all, or none of, the people shown should be in prison clothing.

7. The suspect or their solicitor, friend, or appropriate adult must be given a reasonable opportunity to see the complete set of images before it is shown to any eye-witness. If the suspect has a reasonable objection to the set of images or any of the participants, the suspect shall be asked to

state the reasons for the objection. Steps shall, if practicable, be taken to remove the grounds for objection. If this is not practicable, the suspect and/or their representative shall be told why their objections cannot be met and the objection, the reason given for it and why it cannot be met shall be recorded on forms provided for the purpose. The requirement in *paragraph 2* that the images of the other people 'resemble' the suspect does not require the images to be identical or extremely similar (see *Note A1).*

8. Before the images are shown in accordance with *paragraph 7,* the suspect or their solicitor shall be provided with details of the first description of the suspect by any eye-witnesses who are to attend the video identification. When a broadcast or publication is made, as in *paragraph 3.38(a),* the suspect or their solicitor must also be allowed to view any material released to the media by the police for the purpose of recognising or tracing the suspect, provided it is practicable and would not unreasonably delay the investigation.

9. No unauthorised people may be present when the video identification is conducted. The suspect's solicitor, if practicable, shall be given reasonable notification of the time and place the video identification is to be conducted. The suspect's solicitor may only be present at the video identification on request and with the prior agreement of the identification officer, if the officer is satisfied that the solicitor's presence will not deter or distract any eye-witness from viewing the images and making an identification. If the identification officer is not satisfied and does not agree to the request, the reason must be recorded. The solicitor must be informed of the decision and the reason for it. and that they may then make representations about why they should be allowed to be present. The representations may be made orally or in writing, in person or remotely by electronic communication and must be recorded. These representations must be considered by an officer of at least the rank of inspector who is not involved with the investigation and responsibility for this may not be delegated under *paragraph 3.11.* If, after considering the representations, the officer is satisfied that the solicitor's presence will deter or distract the eye-witness, the officer shall inform the solicitor of the decision and reason for it and ensure that any response by the solicitor is also recorded. If allowed to be present, the solicitor is not entitled to communicate in any way with an eye-witness during the procedure but this does not prevent the solicitor from communicating with the identification officer. The suspect may not be present when the images are shown to any eye-witness and is not entitled to be informed of the time and place the video identification procedure is to be conducted. The video identification procedure itself shall be recorded on video with sound. The recording must show all persons present within the sight or hearing of the eye-witness whilst the images are being viewed and must include what the eye-witness says and what is said to them by the identification officer and by any other person present at the video identification procedure. A supervised viewing of the recording of the video identification procedure by the suspect and/or their solicitor may be arranged on request, at the discretion of the investigating officer. Where the recording of the video identification procedure is to be shown to the suspect and/or their solicitor, the investigating officer may arrange for anything in the recording that might allow the eye-witness to be identified to be concealed if the investigating officer considers that this is justified (see *Note A2).* In accordance with *paragraph 2.18,* the investigating officer may also arrange for anything in that recording that might allow any police officers or police staff to be identified to be concealed.

(b) Conducting the video identification

10. The identification officer is responsible for making the appropriate arrangements to make sure, before they see the set of images, eye-witnesses are not able to communicate with each other about the case, see any of the images which are to be shown, see, or be reminded of, any photograph or description of the suspect or be given any other indication as to the suspect's identity, or overhear an eye-witness who has already seen the material. There must be no discussion with the eye-witness about the composition of the set of images and they must not be told whether a previous eye-witness has made any identification.

11. Only one eye-witness may see the set of images at a time. Immediately before the images are shown, the eye-witness shall be told that the person they saw on a specified earlier occasion may, or

may not, appear in the images they are shown and that if they cannot make an identification, they should say so. The eye-witness shall be advised that at any point, they may ask to see a particular part of the set of images or to have a particular image frozen for them to study. Furthermore, it should be pointed out to the eye-witness that there is no limit on how many times they can view the whole set of images or any part of them. However, they should be asked not to make any decision as to whether the person they saw is on the set of images until they have seen the whole set at least twice.

12. Once the eye-witness has seen the whole set of images at least twice and has indicated that they do not want to view the images, or any part of them, again, the eye-witness shall be asked to say whether the individual they saw in person on a specified earlier occasion has been shown and, if so, to identify them by number of the image. The eye-witness will then be shown that image to confirm the identification, see *paragraph 17*.

13. Care must be taken not to direct the eye-witness' attention to any one individual image or give any indication of the suspect's identity. Where an eye-witness has previously made an identification by photographs, or a computerised or artist's composite or similar likeness, they must not be reminded of such a photograph or composite likeness once a suspect is available for identification by other means in accordance with this Code. Nor must the eye-witness be reminded of any description of the suspect.

13A. If after the video identification procedure has ended, the eye-witness informs any police officer or police staff involved in the post-viewing arrangements that they wish to change their decision about their identification, or they have not made an identification when in fact they could have made one, an accurate record of the words used by the eye-witness and of the circumstances immediately after the procedure ended, shall be made. If the eye-witness has not had an opportunity to communicate with other people about the procedure, the identification officer has the discretion to allow the eye-witness a second opportunity to make an identification by repeating the video identification procedure using the same images but in different positions.

14. After the procedure, action required in accordance with *paragraph 3.40* applies.

(c) Image security and destruction

15. Arrangements shall be made for all relevant material containing sets of images used for specific identification procedures to be kept securely and their movements accounted for. In particular, no-one involved in the investigation shall be permitted to view the material prior to it being shown to any witness.

16. As appropriate, *paragraph 3.30* or *3.31* applies to the destruction or retention of relevant sets of images.

(d) Documentation

17. A record must be made of all those participating in, or seeing, the set of images whose names are known to the police.

18. A record of the conduct of the video identification must be made on forms provided for the purpose. This shall include anything said by the witness about any identifications or the conduct of the procedure and any reasons it was not practicable to comply with any of the provisions of this Code governing the conduct of video identifications. This record is in addition to any statement that is taken from any eye-witness after the procedure.

Note for guidance

A1 The purpose of the video identification is to test the eye-witness' ability to distinguish the suspect from others and it would not be a fair test if all the images shown were identical or extremely similar to each other. The identification officer is responsible for ensuring that the images shown are suitable for the purpose of this test.

A2 The purpose of allowing the identity of the eye-witness to be concealed is to protect them in cases when there is information that suspects or their associates, may threaten the witness or cause them harm or when the investigating officer considers that special measures may be required to protect their identity during the criminal process.

Annex B Identification Parades

(a) General

1. A suspect must be given a reasonable opportunity to have a solicitor or friend present, and the suspect shall be asked to indicate on a second copy of the notice whether or not they wish to do so.

2. An identification parade may take place either in a normal room or one equipped with a screen permitting witnesses to see members of the identification parade without being seen. The procedures for the composition and conduct of the identification parade are the same in both cases, subject to *paragraph 8* (except that an identification parade involving a screen may take place only when the suspect's solicitor, friend or appropriate adult is present or the identification parade is recorded on video).

3. Before the identification parade takes place, the suspect or their solicitor shall be provided with details of the first description of the suspect by any witnesses who are attending the identification parade. When a broadcast or publication is made as in *paragraph 3.38(a)*, the suspect or their solicitor should also be allowed to view any material released to the media by the police for the purpose of identifying and tracing the suspect, provided it is practicable to do so and would not unreasonably delay the investigation.

(b) Identification parades involving prison inmates

4. If a prison inmate is required for identification, and there are no security problems about the person leaving the establishment, they may be asked to participate in an identification parade or video identification.

5. An identification parade may be held in a Prison Department establishment but shall be conducted, as far as practicable under normal identification parade rules. Members of the public shall make up the identification parade unless there are serious security, or control, objections to their admission to the establishment. In such cases, or if a group or video identification is arranged within the establishment, other inmates may participate. If an inmate is the suspect, they are not required to wear prison clothing for the identification parade unless the other people taking part are other inmates in similar clothing, or are members of the public who are prepared to wear prison clothing for the occasion.

(c) Conduct of the identification parade

6. Immediately before the identification parade, the suspect must be reminded of the procedures governing its conduct and cautioned in the terms of Code C, paragraphs 10.5 or 10.6, as appropriate.

7. All unauthorised people must be excluded from the place where the identification parade is held.

8. Once the identification parade has been formed, everything afterwards, in respect of it, shall take place in the presence and hearing of the suspect and any interpreter, solicitor, friend or appropriate adult who is present (unless the identification parade involves a screen, in which case everything said to, or by, any witness at the place where the identification parade is held, must be said in the hearing and presence of the suspect's solicitor, friend or appropriate adult or be recorded on video).

9. The identification parade shall consist of at least eight people (in addition to the suspect) who, so far as possible, resemble the suspect in age, height, general appearance and position in life. Only one suspect shall be included in an identification parade unless there are two suspects of roughly similar appearance, in which case they may be paraded together with at least twelve other people. In no circumstances shall more than two suspects be included in one identification parade and where there are separate identification parades, they shall be made up of different people.

10. If the suspect has an unusual physical feature, e.g., a facial scar, tattoo or distinctive hairstyle or hair colour which cannot be replicated on other members of the identification parade, steps may be taken to conceal the location of that feature on the suspect and the other members of the identification parade if the suspect and their solicitor, or appropriate adult, agree. For example,

by use of a plaster or a hat, so that all members of the identification parade resemble each other in general appearance.

11. When all members of a similar group are possible suspects, separate identification parades shall be held for each unless there are two suspects of similar appearance when they may appear on the same identification parade with at least twelve other members of the group who are not suspects. When police officers in uniform form an identification parade any numerals or other identifying badges shall be concealed.

12. When the suspect is brought to the place where the identification parade is to be held, they shall be asked if they have any objection to the arrangements for the identification parade or to any of the other participants in it and to state the reasons for the objection. The suspect may obtain advice from their solicitor or friend, if present, before the identification parade proceeds. If the suspect has a reasonable objection to the arrangements or any of the participants, steps shall, if practicable, be taken to remove the grounds for objection. When it is not practicable to do so, the suspect shall be told why their objections cannot be met and the objection, the reason given for it and why it cannot be met, shall be recorded on forms provided for the purpose.

13. The suspect may select their own position in the line, but may not otherwise interfere with the order of the people forming the line. When there is more than one witness, the suspect must be told, after each witness has left the room, that they can, if they wish, change position in the line. Each position in the line must be clearly numbered, whether by means of a number laid on the floor in front of each identification parade member or by other means.

14. Appropriate arrangements must be made to make sure, before witnesses attend the identification parade, they are not able to:

(i) communicate with each other about the case or overhear a witness who has already seen the identification parade;
(ii) see any member of the identification parade;
(iii) see, or be reminded of, any photograph or description of the suspect or be given any other indication as to the suspect's identity; or
(iv) see the suspect before or after the identification parade.

15. The person conducting a witness to an identification parade must not discuss with them the composition of the identification parade and, in particular, must not disclose whether a previous witness has made any identification.

16. Witnesses shall be brought in one at a time. Immediately before the witness inspects the identification parade, they shall be told the person they saw on a specified earlier occasion may, or may not, be present and if they cannot make an identification, they should say so. The witness must also be told they should not make any decision about whether the person they saw is on the identification parade until they have looked at each member at least twice.

17. When the officer or police staff (see *paragraph 3.11*) conducting the identification procedure is satisfied the witness has properly looked at each member of the identification parade, they shall ask the witness whether the person they saw on a specified earlier occasion is on the identification parade and, if so, to indicate the number of the person concerned, see *paragraph 28*.

18. If the witness wishes to hear any identification parade member speak, adopt any specified posture or move, they shall first be asked whether they can identify any person(s) on the identification parade on the basis of appearance only. When the request is to hear members of the identification parade speak, the witness shall be reminded that the participants in the identification parade have been chosen on the basis of physical appearance only. Members of the identification parade may then be asked to comply with the witness' request to hear them speak, see them move or adopt any specified posture.

19. If the witness requests that the person they have indicated remove anything used for the purposes of *paragraph 10* to conceal the location of an unusual physical feature, that person may be asked to remove it.

20. If the witness makes an identification after the identification parade has ended, the suspect and, if present, their solicitor, interpreter or friend shall be informed. When this occurs, consideration should be given to allowing the witness a second opportunity to identify the suspect.

21. After the procedure, action required in accordance with *paragraph 3.40* applies.

22. When the last witness has left, the suspect shall be asked whether they wish to make any comments on the conduct of the identification parade.

(d) Documentation

23. A video recording must normally be taken of the identification parade. If that is impracticable, a colour photograph must be taken. A copy of the video recording or photograph shall be supplied, on request, to the suspect or their solicitor within a reasonable time.

24. As appropriate, *paragraph 3.30* or *3.31*, should apply to any photograph or video taken as in *paragraph 23*.

25. If any person is asked to leave an identification parade because they are interfering with its conduct, the circumstances shall be recorded.

26. A record must be made of all those present at an identification parade whose names are known to the police.

27. If prison inmates make up an identification parade, the circumstances must be recorded.

28. A record of the conduct of any identification parade must be made on forms provided for the purpose. This shall include anything said by the witness or the suspect about any identifications or the conduct of the procedure, and any reasons it was not practicable to comply with any of this Code's provisions.

Annex C Group Identification

(a) General

1. The purpose of this Annex is to make sure, as far as possible, group identifications follow the principles and procedures for identification parades so the conditions are fair to the suspect in the way they test the witness' ability to make an identification.

2. Group identifications may take place either with the suspect's consent and co-operation or covertly without their consent.

3. The location of the group identification is a matter for the identification officer, although the officer may take into account any representations made by the suspect, appropriate adult, their solicitor or friend.

4. The place where the group identification is held should be one where other people are either passing by or waiting around informally, in groups such that the suspect is able to join them and be capable of being seen by the witness at the same time as others in the group. For example people leaving an escalator, pedestrians walking through a shopping centre, passengers on railway and bus stations, waiting in queues or groups or where people are standing or sitting in groups in other public places.

5. If the group identification is to be held covertly, the choice of locations will be limited by the places where the suspect can be found and the number of other people present at that time. In these cases, suitable locations might be along regular routes travelled by the suspect, including buses or trains or public places frequented by the suspect.

6. Although the number, age, sex, race and general description and style of clothing of other people present at the location cannot be controlled by the identification officer, in selecting the location the officer must consider the general appearance and numbers of people likely to be present. In particular, the officer must reasonably expect that over the period the witness observes the group, they will be able to see, from time to time, a number of others whose appearance is broadly similar to that of the suspect.

7. A group identification need not be held if the identification officer believes, because of the unusual appearance of the suspect, none of the locations it would be practicable to use, satisfy the requirements of *paragraph 6* necessary to make the identification fair.

8. Immediately after a group identification procedure has taken place (with or without the suspect's consent), a colour photograph or video should be taken of the general scene, if practicable, to give a general impression of the scene and the number of people present. Alternatively, if it is practicable, the group identification may be video recorded.

9. If it is not practicable to take the photograph or video in accordance with *paragraph 8*, a photograph or film of the scene should be taken later at a time determined by the identification officer if the officer considers it practicable to do so.

10. An identification carried out in accordance with this Code remains a group identification even though, at the time of being seen by the witness, the suspect was on their own rather than in a group.

11. Before the group identification takes place, the suspect or their solicitor shall be provided with details of the first description of the suspect by any witnesses who are to attend the identification. When a broadcast or publication is made, as in *paragraph 3.38(a)*, the suspect or their solicitor should also be allowed to view any material released by the police to the media for the purposes of identifying and tracing the suspect, provided that it is practicable and would not unreasonably delay the investigation.

12. After the procedure, action required in accordance with *paragraph 3.40* applies.

(b) Identification with the consent of the suspect

13. A suspect must be given a reasonable opportunity to have a solicitor or friend present. They shall be asked to indicate on a second copy of the notice whether or not they wish to do so.

14. The witness, the person carrying out the procedure and the suspect's solicitor, appropriate adult, friend or any interpreter for the witness, may be concealed from the sight of the individuals in the group they are observing, if the person carrying out the procedure considers this assists the conduct of the identification.

15. The person conducting a witness to a group identification must not discuss with them the forthcoming group identification and, in particular, must not disclose whether a previous witness has made any identification.

16. Anything said to, or by, the witness during the procedure about the identification should be said in the presence and hearing of those present at the procedure.

17. Appropriate arrangements must be made to make sure, before witnesses attend the group identification, they are not able to:

(i) communicate with each other about the case or overhear a witness who has already been given an opportunity to see the suspect in the group;

(ii) see the suspect; or

(iii) see, or be reminded of, any photographs or description of the suspect or be given any other indication of the suspect's identity.

18. Witnesses shall be brought one at a time to the place where they are to observe the group. Immediately before the witness is asked to look at the group, the person conducting the procedure shall tell them that the person they saw on a specified earlier occasion may, or may not, be in the group and that if they cannot make an identification, they should say so. The witness shall be asked to observe the group in which the suspect is to appear. The way in which the witness should do this will depend on whether the group is moving or stationary.

Moving group

19. When the group in which the suspect is to appear is moving, e.g. leaving an escalator, the provisions of *paragraphs 20* to *24* should be followed.

20. If two or more suspects consent to a group identification, each should be the subject of separate identification procedures. These may be conducted consecutively on the same occasion.

21. The person conducting the procedure shall tell the witness to observe the group and ask them to point out any person they think they saw on the specified earlier occasion.

22. Once the witness has been informed as in *paragraph 21* the suspect should be allowed to take whatever position in the group they wish.

23. When the witness points out a person as in *paragraph 21* they shall, if practicable, be asked to take a closer look at the person to confirm the identification. If this is not practicable, or they cannot confirm the identification, they shall be asked how sure they are that the person they have indicated is the relevant person.

24. The witness should continue to observe the group for the period which the person conducting the procedure reasonably believes is necessary in the circumstances for them to be able to make comparisons between the suspect and other individuals of broadly similar appearance to the suspect as in *paragraph 6*.

Stationary groups

25. When the group in which the suspect is to appear is stationary, e.g. people waiting in a queue, the provisions of *paragraphs 26* to *29* should be followed.

26. If two or more suspects consent to a group identification, each should be subject to separate identification procedures unless they are of broadly similar appearance when they may appear in the same group. When separate group identifications are held, the groups must be made up of different people.

27. The suspect may take whatever position in the group they wish. If there is more than one witness, the suspect must be told, out of the sight and hearing of any witness, that they can, if they wish, change their position in the group.

28. The witness shall be asked to pass along, or amongst, the group and to look at each person in the group at least twice, taking as much care and time as possible according to the circumstances, before making an identification. Once the witness has done this, they shall be asked whether the person they saw on the specified earlier occasion is in the group and to indicate any such person by whatever means the person conducting the procedure considers appropriate in the circumstances. If this is not practicable, the witness shall be asked to point out any person they think they saw on the earlier occasion.

29. When the witness makes an indication as in *paragraph 28,* arrangements shall be made, if practicable, for the witness to take a closer look at the person to confirm the identification. If this is not practicable, or the witness is unable to confirm the identification, they shall be asked how sure they are that the person they have indicated is the relevant person.

All cases

30. If the suspect unreasonably delays joining the group, or having joined the group, deliberately conceals themselves from the sight of the witness, this may be treated as a refusal to co-operate in a group identification.

31. If the witness identifies a person other than the suspect, that person should be informed what has happened and asked if they are prepared to give their name and address. There is no obligation upon any member of the public to give these details. There shall be no duty to record any details of any other member of the public present in the group or at the place where the procedure is conducted.

32. When the group identification has been completed, the suspect shall be asked whether they wish to make any comments on the conduct of the procedure.

33. If the suspect has not been previously informed, they shall be told of any identifications made by the witnesses.

(c) Group Identification without the suspect's consent

34. Group identifications held covertly without the suspect's consent should, as far as practicable, follow the rules for conduct of group identification by consent.

35. A suspect has no right to have a solicitor, appropriate adult or friend present as the identification will take place without the knowledge of the suspect.

36. Any number of suspects may be identified at the same time.

(d) Identifications in police stations

37. Group identifications should only take place in police stations for reasons of safety, security or because it is not practicable to hold them elsewhere.

38. The group identification may take place either in a room equipped with a screen permitting witnesses to see members of the group without being seen, or anywhere else in the police station that the identification officer considers appropriate.

39. Any of the additional safeguards applicable to identification parades should be followed if the identification officer considers it is practicable to do so in the circumstances.

(e) Identifications involving prison inmates

40. A group identification involving a prison inmate may only be arranged in the prison or at a police station.

41. When a group identification takes place involving a prison inmate, whether in a prison or in a police station, the arrangements should follow those in *paragraphs 37* to *39*. If a group identification takes place within a prison, other inmates may participate. If an inmate is the suspect, they do not have to wear prison clothing for the group identification unless the other participants are wearing the same clothing.

(f) Documentation

42. When a photograph or video is taken as in *paragraph 8* or *9*, a copy of the photograph or video shall be supplied on request to the suspect or their solicitor within a reasonable time.

43. *Paragraph 3.30* or *3.31*, as appropriate, shall apply when the photograph or film taken in accordance with *paragraph 8* or *9* includes the suspect.

44. A record of the conduct of any group identification must be made on forms provided for the purpose. This shall include anything said by the witness or suspect about any identifications or the conduct of the procedure and any reasons why it was not practicable to comply with any of the provisions of this Code governing the conduct of group identifications.

Annex D Confrontation by an Eye-Witness

1. Before the confrontation takes place, the eye-witness must be told that the person they saw on a specified earlier occasion may, or may not, be the person they are to confront and that if they are not that person, then the witness should say so.

2. Before the confrontation takes place the suspect or their solicitor shall be provided with details of the first description of the suspect given by any eye-witness who is to attend. When a broadcast or publication is made, as in *paragraph 3.38(a)*, the suspect or their solicitor should also be allowed to view any material released to the media for the purposes of recognising or tracing the suspect, provided it is practicable to do so and would not unreasonably delay the investigation.

3. Force may not be used to make the suspect's face visible to the eye-witness.

4. Confrontation must take place in the presence of the suspect's solicitor, interpreter or friend unless this would cause unreasonable delay.

5. The suspect shall be confronted independently by each eye-witness, who shall be asked 'Is this the person?'. If the eye-witness identifies the person but is unable to confirm the identification, they shall be asked how sure they are that the person is the one they saw on the earlier occasion.

6. The confrontation should normally take place in the police station, either in a normal room or one equipped with a screen permitting the eye-witness to see the suspect without being seen. In both cases, the procedures are the same except that a room equipped with a screen may be used only when the suspect's solicitor, friend or appropriate adult is present or the confrontation is recorded on video.

7. After the procedure, action required in accordance with paragraph 3.40 applies.

Annex E Showing Photographs to Eye-Witnesses

(a) Action

1. An officer of sergeant rank or above shall be responsible for supervising and directing the showing of photographs. The actual showing may be done by another officer or police staff, see *paragraph 3.11*.

2. The supervising officer must confirm the first description of the suspect given by the eye-witness has been recorded before they are shown the photographs. If the supervising officer is unable to confirm the description has been recorded they shall postpone showing the photographs.

3. Only one eye-witness shall be shown photographs at any one time. Each witness shall be given as much privacy as practicable and shall not be allowed to communicate with any other eye-witness in the case.

4. The eye-witness shall be shown not less than twelve photographs at a time, which shall, as far as possible, all be of a similar type.

5. When the eye-witness is shown the photographs, they shall be told the photograph of the person they saw on a specified earlier occasion may, or may not, be amongst them and if they cannot make an identification, they should say so. The eye-witness shall also be told they should not make a decision until they have viewed at least twelve photographs. The eye-witness shall not be prompted or guided in any way but shall be left to make any selection without help.

6. If an eye-witness makes an identification from photographs, unless the person identified is otherwise eliminated from enquiries or is not available, other eye-witnesses shall not be shown photographs. But both they, and the eye-witness who has made the identification, shall be asked to attend a video identification, an identification parade or group identification unless there is no dispute about the suspect's identification.

7. If the eye-witness makes a selection but is unable to confirm the identification, the person showing the photographs shall ask them how sure they are that the photograph they have indicated is the person they saw on the specified earlier occasion.

8. When the use of a computerised or artist's composite or similar likeness has led to there being a known suspect who can be asked to participate in a video identification, appear on an identification parade or participate in a group identification, that likeness shall not be shown to other potential eye-witnesses.

9. When an eye-witness attending a video identification, an identification parade or group identification has previously been shown photographs or computerised or artist's composite or similar likeness (and it is the responsibility of the officer in charge of the investigation to make the identification officer aware that this is the case), the suspect and their solicitor must be informed of this fact before the identification procedure takes place.

10. None of the photographs shown shall be destroyed, whether or not an identification is made, since they may be required for production in court. The photographs shall be numbered and a separate photograph taken of the frame or part of the album from which the eye-witness made an identification as an aid to reconstituting it.

(b) Documentation

11. Whether or not an identification is made, a record shall be kept of the showing of photographs on forms provided for the purpose. This shall include anything said by the eye-witness about any identification or the conduct of the procedure, any reasons it was not practicable to comply with any of the provisions of this Code governing the showing of photographs and the name and rank of the supervising officer.

12. The supervising officer shall inspect and sign the record as soon as practicable.

Annex F Fingerprints, Samples and Footwear Impressions—Destruction And Speculative Searches

Part A: Fingerprints and samples

Paragraphs 1 to 12 summarise and update information which is available at: https://www.gov.uk/government/publications/protection-of-freedoms-act-2012-dna-and-fingerprint-provisions/protection-of-freedoms-act-2012-how-dna-and-fingerprint-evidence-is-protected-in-law

DNA samples

1. A DNA sample is an individual's biological material, containing all of their genetic information. The Act requires all DNA samples to be destroyed within 6 months of being taken. This allows sufficient time for the sample to be analysed and a DNA profile to be produced for use on the database.

2. The only exception to this is if the sample is or may be required for disclosure as evidence, in which case it may be retained for as long as this need exists under the Criminal Procedure and Investigations Act 1996.

DNA profiles and fingerprints

3. A DNA profile consists of a string of 16 pairs of numbers and 2 letters (XX for women, XY for men) to indicate gender. This number string is stored on the National DNA Database (NDNAD). It allows the person to be identified if they leave their DNA at a crime scene.

4. Fingerprints are usually scanned electronically from the individual in custody and the images stored on IDENT1, the national fingerprint database.

Retention Periods: Fingerprints and DNA profiles

5. The retention period depends on the outcome of the investigation of the recordable offence in connection with which the fingerprints and DNA samples was taken, the age of the person at the time the offence was committed and whether the *recordable* offence is a qualifying offence and whether it is an excluded offence (See Table *Notes (a)* to *(c)*), as follows:

Table—Retention periods

(a) Convictions

Age when offence committed	Outcome	Retention Period
Any age	Convicted or given a caution or youth caution for a recordable offence which is also a qualifying offence	INDEFINITE
18 or over	Convicted or given a caution for a recordable offence which is NOT a qualifying offence	INDEFINITE
Under 18	Convicted or given a youth caution for a recordable offence which is NOT a qualifying offence.	1st conviction or youth caution—5 years plus length of any prison sentence. Indefinite if prison sentence 5 years or more 2nd conviction or youth caution: Indefinite

(b) Non-Convictions

Age when offence committed	Outcome	Retention Period
Any age	Charged but not convicted of a recordable qualifying offence.	3 years plus a 2 year extension if granted by a District Judge (or indefinite if the individual has a previous conviction for a recordable offence which is not excluded)
Any age	Arrested for, but not charged with, a recordable qualifying offence	3 years if granted by the Biometrics Commissioner plus a 2 year extension if granted by a District Judge (or indefinite if the individual has a previous conviction for a recordable offence which is not excluded)
Any age	Arrested for or charged with a recordable offence which is not a qualifying offence.	Indefinite if the person has a previous conviction for a recordable offence which is not excluded otherwise NO RETENTION)
18 or over	Given Penalty Notice for Disorder for recordable offence	2 years

Table Notes:

(a) A 'recordable' offence is one for which the police are required to keep a record. Generally speaking, these are imprisonable offences; however, it also includes a number of non-imprisonable offences such as begging and taxi touting. The police are not able to take or retain the DNA or fingerprints of an individual who is arrested for an offence which is not recordable.

(b) A 'qualifying' offence is one listed under section 65A of the Police and Criminal Evidence Act 1984 (the list comprises sexual, violent, terrorism and burglary offences).

(c) An 'excluded' offence is a recordable offence which is not a qualifying offence, was committed when the individual was under 18, for which they received a sentence of fewer than 5 years imprisonment and is the only recordable offence for which the person has been convicted

Speculative searches

6. Where the retention framework above requires the deletion of a person's DNA profile and fingerprints, the Act first allows a *speculative search* of their DNA and fingerprints against DNA and fingerprints obtained from crime scenes which are stored on NDNAD and IDENT1. Once the speculative search has been completed, the profile and fingerprints are deleted unless there is a match, in which case they will be retained for the duration of any investigation and thereafter in accordance with the retention framework (e.g. if that investigation led to a conviction for a qualifying offence, they would be retained indefinitely).

Extensions of retention period

7. For qualifying offences, PACE allows chief constables to apply for extensions to the given retention periods for DNA profiles and fingerprints if considered necessary for prevention or detection of crime.

8. Section 20 of the Protection of Freedoms Act 2012 established the independent office of Commissioner for the Retention and Use of Biometric Material ('the 'Biometrics Commissioner'). For details, see https://www.gov.uk/government/organisations/biometrics-commissioner.

9. Where an individual is arrested for, but not charged with, a qualifying offence, their DNA profile and fingerprint record will normally be deleted. However, the police can apply to the Biometrics Commissioner for permission to retain their DNA profile and fingerprint record for a

period of 3 years. The application must be made within 28 days of the decision not to proceed with a prosecution.

10. If the police make such an application, the Biometrics Commissioner would first give both them and the arrested individual an opportunity to make written representations and then, taking into account factors including the age and vulnerability of the victim(s) of the alleged offences, and their relationship to the suspect, make a decision on whether or not retention is appropriate.

11. If after considering the application, the Biometrics Commissioner decides that retention is not appropriate, the DNA profile and fingerprint record in question must be destroyed.

12. If the Biometrics Commissioner agrees to allow retention, the police will be able to retain that individual's DNA profile and fingerprint record for a period of 3 years from the date the samples were taken. At the end of that period, the police will be able to apply to a District Judge (Magistrates' Courts) for a single 2 year extension to the retention period. If the application is rejected, the force must then destroy the DNA profile and fingerprint record.

Part B: Footwear impressions

13. Footwear impressions taken in accordance with section 61A of PACE (see *paragraphs 4.16* to *4.21*) may be retained for as long as is necessary for purposes related to the prevention or detection of crime, the investigation of an offence or the conduct of a prosecution.

Part C: Fingerprints, samples and footwear impressions taken in connection with a criminal investigation from a person *not suspected of committing* the offence under investigation for elimination purposes.

14. When fingerprints, footwear impressions or DNA samples are taken from a person in connection with an investigation and the person is *not suspected of having committed the offence*, see *Note F1*, they must be destroyed as soon as they have fulfilled the purpose for which they were taken unless:

(a) they were taken for the purposes of an investigation of an offence for which a person has been convicted; and

(b) fingerprints, footwear impressions or samples were also taken from the convicted person for the purposes of that investigation.

However, subject to *paragraph 14,* the fingerprints, footwear impressions and samples, and the information derived from samples, may not be used in the investigation of any offence or in evidence against the person who is, or would be, entitled to the destruction of the fingerprints, footwear impressions and samples, see *Note F2*.

15. The requirement to destroy fingerprints, footwear impressions and DNA samples, and information derived from samples and restrictions on their retention and use in *paragraph 14* do not apply if the person gives their written consent for their fingerprints, footwear impressions or sample to be retained and used after they have fulfilled the purpose for which they were taken, see *Note F1*. This consent can be withdrawn at any time.

16. When a person's fingerprints, footwear impressions or sample are to be destroyed:

(a) any copies of the fingerprints and footwear impressions must also be destroyed; and

(b) neither the fingerprints, footwear impressions, the sample, or any information derived from the sample, may be used in the investigation of any offence or in evidence against the person who is, or would be, entitled to its destruction.

Notes for guidance

F1 Fingerprints, footwear impressions and samples given voluntarily for the purposes of elimination play an important part in many police investigations. It is, therefore, important to make sure innocent volunteers are not deterred from participating and their consent to their fingerprints, footwear impressions and DNA being used for the purposes of a specific investigation is fully informed and voluntary. If the police or volunteer seek to have the fingerprints, footwear impressions or samples retained for use after the specific investigation ends, it is important the volunteer's consent to this is also fully informed and voluntary. The volunteer must be told that they may withdraw their consent at any time.

The consent must be obtained in writing using current nationally agreed forms provided for police use according to the purpose for which the consent is given. This purpose may be either:

- *DNA/fingerprints/footwear impressions—to be used only for the purposes of a specific investigation; or*
- *DNA/fingerprints/footwear impressions—to be used in the specific investigation and retained by the police for future use.*

To minimise the risk of confusion:

- *if a police officer or member of police staff has any doubt about:*
  - ~ *how the consent forms should be completed and signed, or*
  - ~ *whether a consent form they propose to use and refer to is fully compliant with the current nationally agreed form,*

  the relevant national police helpdesk (for DNA or fingerprints) should be contacted.
- *in each case, the meaning of consent should be explained orally and care taken to ensure the oral explanation accurately reflects the contents of the written form the person is to be asked to sign.*

F2 The provisions for the retention of fingerprints, footwear impressions and samples in paragraph 15 allow for all fingerprints, footwear impressions and samples in a case to be available for any subsequent miscarriage of justice investigation.

Annex G Requirement for a Person to Attend a Police Station for Fingerprints and Samples (paragraphs 4.4, 6.2A and 6.6A).

1. A requirement under Schedule 2A for a person to attend a police station to have fingerprints or samples taken:
   (a) must give the person a period of at least seven days within which to attend the police station; and
   (b) may direct them to attend at a specified time of day or between specified times of day.

2. When specifying the period and times of attendance, the officer making the requirements must consider whether the fingerprints or samples could reasonably be taken at a time when the person is required to attend the police station for any other reason. See *Note G1*.

3. An officer of the rank of inspector or above may authorise a period shorter than 7 days if there is an urgent need for person's fingerprints or sample for the purposes of the investigation of an offence. The fact of the authorisation and the reasons for giving it must be recorded as soon as practicable.

4. The constable making a requirement and the person to whom it applies may agree to vary it so as to specify any period within which, or date or time at which, the person is to attend. However, variation shall not have effect for the purposes of enforcement, unless it is confirmed by the constable in writing.

Notes for guidance

G1 The specified period within which the person is to attend need not fall within the period allowed (if applicable) for making the requirement.

G2 To justify the arrest without warrant of a person who fails to comply with a requirement, (see paragraphs 4.4(b) and 6.7(b) above), the officer making the requirement, or confirming a variation, should be prepared to explain how, when and where the requirement was made or the variation was confirmed and what steps were taken to ensure the person understood what to do and the consequences of not complying with the requirement.

Code of Practice on Audio Recording Interviews with Suspects (Code E)

(2015)

1 General

1.0 The procedures in this Code must be used fairly, responsibly, with respect for the people to whom they apply and without unlawful discrimination. Under the Equality Act 2010, section 149, when police officers are carrying out their functions, they also have a duty to have due regard to the need to eliminate unlawful discrimination, harassment and victimisation, to advance equality of opportunity between people who share a relevant protected characteristic and people who do not share it, and to take steps to foster good relations between those persons. See *Note 1B*.

1.1 This Code of Practice must be readily available for consultation by:

- police officers
- police staff
- detained persons
- members of the public.

1.2 The *Notes for Guidance* included are not provisions of this Code.

1.3 Nothing in this Code shall detract from the requirements of Code C, the Code of Practice for the detention, treatment and questioning of persons by police officers.

1.4 The interviews to which this Code applies are described in *section 3*.

1.5 The term:

- 'appropriate adult' has the same meaning as in Code C, *paragraph 1.7* and in the case of a 17 year old suspect, includes the person called to fulfil that role in accordance with *paragraph 1.5A* of Code C.
- 'solicitor' has the same meaning as in Code C, *paragraph 6.12*.
- 'interview' has the same meaning as in Code C, *paragraph 11.1A*.

1.5A Recording of interviews shall be carried out openly to instil confidence in its reliability as an impartial and accurate record of the interview.

1.6 In this Code:

(aa) 'recording media' means any removable, physical audio recording medium (such as magnetic tape, optical disc or solid state memory) which can be played and copied.

(a) 'designated person' means a person other than a police officer, designated under the Police Reform Act 2002, Part 4 who has specified powers and duties of police officers conferred or imposed on them;

(b) any reference to a police officer includes a designated person acting in the exercise or performance of the powers and duties conferred or imposed on them by their designation.

(c) 'secure digital network' is a computer network system which enables an original interview recording to be stored as a digital multi media file or a series of such files, on a secure file server which is accredited by the National Accreditor for Police Information Systems in accordance with the UK Government Protective Marking Scheme. (See *section 7* of this Code.)

1.7 *Sections 2* to *6* of this Code set out the procedures and requirements which apply to all audio recorded interviews together with the provisions which apply only to interviews which are audio recorded using *removable* media. *Section 7* sets out the provisions which apply to interviews which are audio recorded using a *secure digital network* and specifies the provisions in *sections 2* to *6* which do not apply to secure digital network recording. The Annex to this Code sets out the terms and conditions of the exemption from the requirement to audio record interviews about indictable offences referred to in *paragraph 3.1(a)(iii)*.

1.8 Nothing in this Code prevents the custody officer, or other officer given custody of the detainee, from allowing police staff who are not designated persons to carry out individual procedures or tasks at the police station if the law allows. However, the officer remains responsible for making sure the procedures and tasks are carried out correctly in accordance with this Code. Any such police staff must be:

(a) a person employed by a police force and under the control and direction of the Chief Officer of that force; or

(b) employed by a person with whom a police force has a contract for the provision of services relating to persons arrested or otherwise in custody.

1.9 Designated persons and other police staff must have regard to any relevant provisions of the Codes of Practice.

1.10 References to pocket book include any official report book issued to police officers or police staff.

1.11 References to a custody officer include those performing the functions of a custody officer as in *paragraph 1.9* of Code C.

1.12 In the application of this Code to the conduct and recording of an interview of a suspect who has not been arrested:

(a) references to the 'custody officer' include references to an officer of the rank of sergeant or above who is not directly involved in the investigation of the offence(s);

(b) if the interview takes place elsewhere than at a police station, references to 'interview room' include any place or location which the interviewer is satisfied will enable the interview to be conducted and recorded in accordance with this Code and where the suspect is present voluntarily (see *Note 1A*), and

(c) provisions in addition to those which expressly apply to these interviews shall be followed insofar as they are relevant and can be applied in practice.

Notes for Guidance

1A An interviewer who is not sure, or has any doubt, about the suitability of a place or location of an interview to be carried out elsewhere than at a police station, should consult an officer of the rank of sergeant or above for advice.

1B In paragraph 1.0, the 'relevant protected characteristics' are: age, disability, gender reassignment, pregnancy and maternity, race, religion/belief, sex and sexual orientation.

2 Recording and sealing master recordings

2.1 *Not used.*

2.2 One recording, the master recording, will be sealed in the suspect's presence. A second recording will be used as a working copy. The master recording is any of the recordings made by a multi-deck/drive machine or the only recording made by a single deck/drive machine. The working copy is one of the other recordings made by a multi-deck/drive machine or a copy of the master recording made by a single deck/drive machine. (See *Note 2A*.)

[This paragraph does not apply to interviews recorded using a secure digital network, see paragraphs 7.4 to 7.6.]

2.3 Nothing in this Code requires the identity of officers or police staff conducting interviews to be recorded or disclosed:

(a) *Not used.*

(b) if the interviewer reasonably believes recording or disclosing their name might put them in danger.

In these cases interviewers should use warrant or other identification numbers and the name of their police station. Such instances and the reasons for them shall be recorded in the custody record or the interviewer's pocket book. (See *Note 2C*.)

Notes for guidance

2A The purpose of sealing the master recording before it leaves the suspect's presence is to establish their confidence that the integrity of the recording is preserved. If a single deck/drive machine is used the working copy of the master recording must be made in the suspect's presence and without the master recording leaving their sight. The working copy shall be used for making further copies if needed.

2B Not used.

2C The purpose of paragraph 2.3(b) is to protect those involved in serious organised crime investigations or arrests of particularly violent suspects when there is reliable information that those arrested or their associates may threaten or cause harm to those involved. In cases of doubt, an officer of inspector rank or above should be consulted.

3 Interviews to be audio recorded

3.1 Subject to *paragraph 3.4*, audio recording shall be used for any interview:

(a) with a person cautioned under Code C, *section 10* in respect of any *indictable* offence, which includes any offence triable either way, except when :

(i) that person has been arrested and the interview takes place elsewhere than at a police station in accordance with Code C *paragraph 11.1* for which a written record would be required;

(ii) the conditions in *paragraph 3.3A* are satisfied and authority not to audio record the interview is given by:

- the custody officer in the case of a detained suspect, or
- an officer of the rank of sergeant or above in the case of a suspect who has not been arrested and to whom *paragraphs 3.21* and *3.22* of Code C (Persons attending a police station or elsewhere voluntarily) apply; or

(iii) the conditions in Part 1 of the Annex to this Code are satisfied, in which case the interview must be conducted and recorded in writing, in accordance with *section 11 of Code C.*

(See *Note 3A.*)

(b) which takes place as a result of an interviewer exceptionally putting further questions to a suspect about an *indictable* offence after they have been charged with, or told they may be prosecuted for, that offence, see Code C, *paragraph 16.5 and Note 3E.*

(c) when an interviewer wants to tell a person, after they have been charged with, or informed they may be prosecuted for, an *indictable* offence, about any written statement or interview with another person, see Code C, *paragraph 16.4 and Note 3F.*

See *Note 3D*

3.2 The Terrorism Act 2000 and the Counter-Terrorism Act 2008 make separate provisions for a Code of Practice for the video recording with sound of:

- interviews of persons detained under section 41 of, or Schedule 7 to, the 2000 Act, and
- post-charge questioning of persons authorised under section 22 or 23 of the 2008 Act. The provisions of this Code do not apply to such interviews or questioning. (See *Note 3C.*)

3.3 *Not used*

3.3A The conditions referred to in *paragraph 3.1(a)(ii)* are:

(a) it is not reasonably practicable to audio record, or as the case may be, continue to audio record, the interview because of equipment failure or the unavailability of a suitable interview room or recording equipment; and

(b) the authorising officer considers, on reasonable grounds, that the interview or continuation of the interview should not be delayed until the failure has been rectified or until a suitable room or recording equipment becomes available.

In these cases:

- the interview must be recorded or continue to be recorded in writing in accordance with Code C, *section 11*; and
- the authorising officer shall record the specific reasons for not audio recording and the interviewer is responsible for ensuring that the written interview record shows the date and time of the authority, the authorising officer and where the authority is recorded. (See *Note 3B.*)

3.4 If a detainee refuses to go into or remain in a suitable interview room, see Code C *paragraph 12.5*, and the custody officer considers, on reasonable grounds, that the interview should not be delayed the interview may, at the custody officer's discretion, be conducted in a cell using portable recording equipment or, if none is available, recorded in writing as in Code C, *section 11*. The reasons for this shall be recorded in accordance with Code C *paragraph 12.11*.

3.5 The whole of each interview shall be audio recorded, including the taking and reading back of any statement.

3.6 A sign or indicator which is visible to the suspect must show when the recording equipment is recording.

Notes for guidance

3A Nothing in this Code is intended to preclude audio recording at police discretion of interviews at police stations or elsewhere with people cautioned in respect of offences not covered by paragraph 3.1, or responses made by persons after they have been charged with, or told they may be prosecuted for, an offence, provided this Code is complied with.

3B A decision made in accordance with paragraphs 3.1(a)(ii) and 3.3A not to audio record an interview for any reason may be the subject of comment in court. The authorising officer should be prepared to justify that decision.

3C If, during the course of an interview under this Code, it becomes apparent that the interview should be conducted under the terrorism code for the video recording with sound of interviews the interview should only continue in accordance with that code.

3D Attention is drawn to the provisions set out in Code C about the matters to be considered when deciding whether a detained person is fit to be interviewed.

3E Code C sets out the circumstances in which a suspect may be questioned about an offence after being charged with it.

3F Code C sets out the procedures to be followed when a person's attention is drawn after charge, to a statement made by another person. One method of bringing the content of an interview with another person to the notice of a suspect may be to play them a recording of that interview.

4 The interview

(a) General

4.1 The provisions of Code C:

- *sections 10 and 11*, and the applicable *Notes for Guidance* apply to the conduct of interviews to which this Code applies.
- *paragraphs 11.7 to 11.14* apply only when a written record is needed.

4.2 Code C, *paragraphs 10.10, 10.11* and *Annex C* describe the restriction on drawing adverse inferences from an arrested suspect's failure or refusal to say anything about their involvement in the offence when interviewed or after being charged or informed they may be prosecuted, and how it affects the terms of the caution and determines if and by whom a special warning under sections 36 and 37 of the Criminal Justice and Public Order Act 1994 can be given.

(b) Commencement of interviews

4.3 When the suspect is brought into the interview room the interviewer shall, without delay but in the suspect's sight, load the recorder with new recording media and set it to record. The recording media must be unwrapped or opened in the suspect's presence.

[This paragraph does not apply to interviews recorded using a secure digital network, see paragraphs 7.4 and 7.5.]

4.4 The interviewer should tell the suspect about the recording process and point out the sign or indicator which shows that the recording equipment is activated and recording. (See *paragraph 3.6*.) The interviewer shall:

(a) explain that the interview is being audibly recorded;
(b) subject to *paragraph 2.3*, give their name and rank and that of any other interviewer present;
(c) ask the suspect and any other party present, e.g. the appropriate adult, a solicitor or interpreter, to identify themselves;

(d) state the date, time of commencement and place of the interview; and

(e) state the suspect will be given a notice about what will happen to the recording. *[This sub-paragraph does not apply to interviews recorded using a secure digital network, see paragraphs 7.4 and 7.6 to 7.7.]*

See *Note 4A*

4.4A Any person entering the interview room after the interview has commenced shall be invited by the interviewer to identify themselves for the purpose of the audio recording and state the reason why they have entered the interview room.

4.5 The interviewer shall:

- caution the suspect, see Code C *section 10*; and
- if they are detained, remind them of their entitlement to free legal advice, see Code C, *paragraph 11.2*; or
- if they are not detained under arrest, explain this and their entitlement to free legal advice, see Code C, *paragraph 3.21*.

4.6 The interviewer shall put to the suspect any significant statement or silence, see Code C, *paragraph 11.4*.

(c) Interviews with suspects who appear to have a hearing impediment

4.7 If the suspect appears to have a hearing impediment, the interviewer shall make a written note of the interview in accordance with Code C, at the same time as audio recording it in accordance with this Code. (See *Notes 4B* and *4C*.)

(d) Objections and complaints by the suspect

4.8 If the suspect or an appropriate adult on their behalf, objects to the interview being audibly recorded either at the outset, during the interview or during a break, the interviewer shall explain that the interview is being audibly recorded and that this Code requires the objections to be recorded on the audio recording. When any objections have been audibly recorded or the suspect or appropriate adult have refused to have their objections recorded, the interviewer shall say they are turning off the recorder, give their reasons and turn it off. The interviewer shall then make a written record of the interview as in Code C, *section 11*. If, however, the interviewer reasonably considers they may proceed to question the suspect with the audio recording still on, the interviewer may do so. This procedure also applies in cases where the suspect has previously objected to the interview being visually recorded, see Code F *paragraph 4.8*, and the investigating officer has decided to audibly record the interview. (See *Note 4D*.)

4.9 If in the course of an interview a complaint is made by or on behalf of the person being questioned concerning the provisions of this or any other Codes, or it comes to the interviewer's notice that the person may have been treated improperly, the interviewer shall act as in Code C, *paragraph 12.9*. (See *Notes 4E* and *4F*.)

4.10 If the suspect indicates they want to tell the interviewer about matters not directly connected with the offence of which they are suspected and they are unwilling for these matters to be audio recorded, the suspect should be given the opportunity to tell the interviewer about these matter after the conclusion of the formal interview.

(e) Changing recording media

4.11 When the recorder shows the recording media only has a short time left to run, the interviewer shall so inform the person being interviewed and round off that part of the interview. If the interviewer leaves the room for a second set of recording media, the suspect shall not be left unattended. The interviewer will remove the recording media from the recorder and insert the new recording media which shall be unwrapped or opened in the suspect's presence. The recorder should be set to record on the new media. To avoid confusion between the recording media, the interviewer shall mark the media with an identification number immediately after it is removed from the recorder.

[This paragraph does not apply to interviews recorded using a secure digital network as this does not use removable media, see paragraphs 1.6(c), 7.4 and 7.14 to 7.15.]

(f) Taking a break during interview

4.12 When a break is taken, the fact that a break is to be taken, the reason for it and the time shall be recorded on the audio recording.

4.12A When the break is taken and the interview room vacated by the suspect, the recording media shall be removed from the recorder and the procedures for the conclusion of an interview followed, see *paragraph 4.18*.

4.13 When a break is a short one and both the suspect and an interviewer remain in the interview room, the recording may be stopped. There is no need to remove the recording media and when the interview recommences the recording should continue on the same recording media. The time the interview recommences shall be recorded on the audio recording.

4.14 After any break in the interview the interviewer must, before resuming the interview, remind the person being questioned of their right to legal advice if they have not exercised it and that they remain under caution or, if there is any doubt, give the caution in full again. (See *Note 4G*.)

[Paragraphs 4.12 to 4.14 do not apply to interviews recorded using a secure digital network, see paragraphs 7.4 and 7.8 to 7.10.]

(g) Failure of recording equipment

4.15 If there is an equipment failure which can be rectified quickly, e.g. by inserting new recording media, the interviewer shall follow the appropriate procedures as in *paragraph 4.11*. When the recording is resumed the interviewer shall explain what happened and record the time the interview recommences. If, however, it will not be possible to continue recording on that recorder and no replacement recorder is readily available, the interview may continue without being audibly recorded. If this happens, the interviewer shall seek the authority as in *paragraph 3.1(a)(ii)* of the custody officer, or as applicable, a sergeant or above. (See *Note 4H*.)

[This paragraph does not apply to interviews recorded using a secure digital network, see paragraphs 7.4 and 7.11.]

(h) Removing recording media from the recorder

4.16 Recording media which is removed from the recorder during the interview shall be retained and the procedures in *paragraph 4.18* followed.

[This paragraph does not apply to interviews recorded using a secure digital network as this does not use removable media, see 1.6(c), 7.4 and 7.14 to 7.15.]

(i) Conclusion of interview

4.17 At the conclusion of the interview, the suspect shall be offered the opportunity to clarify anything they have said and asked if there is anything they want to add.

4.18 At the conclusion of the interview, including the taking and reading back of any written statement, the time shall be recorded and the recording shall be stopped. The interviewer shall seal the master recording with a master recording label and treat it as an exhibit in accordance with force standing orders. The interviewer shall sign the label and ask the suspect and any third party present during the interview to sign it. If the suspect or third party refuse to sign the label an officer of at least the rank of inspector, or if not available the custody officer, or if the suspect has not been arrested, a sergeant, shall be called into the interview room and asked, subject to *paragraph 2.3*, to sign it.

4.19 The suspect shall be handed a notice which explains:

- how the audio recording will be used;
- the arrangements for access to it;
- that if they are charged or informed they will be prosecuted, a copy of the audio recording will be supplied as soon as practicable or as otherwise agreed between the suspect and the police or on the order of a court.

[Paragraphs 4.17 to 4.19 do not apply to interviews recorded using a secure digital network, see paragraphs 7.4 and 7.12 to 7.13.]

Notes for guidance

4A For the purpose of voice identification the interviewer should ask the suspect and any other people present to identify themselves.

4B This provision is to give a person who is deaf or has impaired hearing equivalent rights of access to the full interview record as far as this is possible using audio recording.

4C The provisions of Code C on interpreters for suspects who do not appear to speak or understand English or who appear to have a hearing or speech impediment, continue to apply.

4D The interviewer should remember that a decision to continue recording against the wishes of the suspect may be the subject of comment in court.

4E If the custody officer, or in the case of a person who has not been arrested, a sergeant, is called to deal with the complaint, the recorder should, if possible, be left on until the officer has entered the room and spoken to the person being interviewed. Continuation or termination of the interview should be at the interviewer's discretion pending action by an inspector under Code C, paragraph 9.2.

4F If the complaint is about a matter not connected with this Code or Code C, the decision to continue is at the interviewer's discretion. When the interviewer decides to continue the interview, they shall tell the suspect that at the conclusion of the interview, the complaint will be brought to the attention of the custody officer, or in the case of a person who has not been arrested, a sergeant. When the interview is concluded the interviewer must, as soon as practicable, inform the custody officer or, as the case may be, the sergeant, about the existence and nature of the complaint made.

4G In considering whether to caution again after a break, the interviewer should bear in mind that they may have to satisfy a court that the person understood that they were still under caution when the interview resumed. The interviewer should also remember that it may be necessary to show to the court that nothing occurred during a break or between interviews which influenced the suspect's recorded evidence. After a break or at the beginning of a subsequent interview, the interviewer should consider summarising on the record the reason for the break and confirming this with the suspect.

4H Where the interview is being recorded and the media or the recording equipment fails the interviewer should stop the interview immediately. Where part of the interview is unaffected by the error and is still accessible on the media, that part shall be copied and sealed in the suspect's presence as a master copy and the interview recommenced using new equipment/media as required. Where the content of the interview has been lost in its entirety, the media should be sealed in the suspect's presence and the interview begun again. If the recording equipment cannot be fixed or no replacement is immediately available, the interview should be recorded in accordance with Code C, section 11.

5 After the interview

5.1 The interviewer shall make a note in their pocket book that the interview has taken place and that it was audibly recorded, the time it commenced, its duration and date and identification number of the master recording.

5.2 If no proceedings follow in respect of the person whose interview was recorded, the recording media must be kept securely as in *paragraph 6.1* and *Note 6A*.

[This section (paragraphs 5.1, 5.2 and Note 5A) does not apply to interviews recorded using a secure digital network, see paragraphs 7.4 and 7.14 to 7.15.]

Note for guidance

5A Any written record of an audio recorded interview should be made in accordance with current national guidelines for police officers, police staff and CPS prosecutors concerned with the preparation, processing and submission of prosecution files.

6 Master Recording security

(a) General

6.1 The officer in charge of each police station at which interviews with suspects are recorded or as the case may be, where recordings of interviews carried out elsewhere than at a police station are held, shall make arrangements for master recordings to be kept securely and their movements accounted for on the same basis as material which may be used for evidential purposes, in accordance with force standing orders. (See *Note 6A*.)

(b) Breaking master recording seal for criminal proceedings

6.2 A police officer has no authority to break the seal on a master recording which is required for criminal trial or appeal proceedings. If it is necessary to gain access to the master recording, the police officer shall arrange for its seal to be broken in the presence of a representative of the Crown Prosecution Service. The defendant or their legal adviser should be informed and given a reasonable opportunity to be present. If the defendant or their legal representative is present they shall be invited to re-seal and sign the master recording. If either refuses or neither is present this should be done by the representative of the Crown Prosecution Service. (See *Notes 6B and 6C*.)

(c) Breaking master recording seal: other cases

6.3 The chief officer of police is responsible for establishing arrangements for breaking the seal of the master copy where no criminal proceedings result, or the criminal proceedings to which the interview relates, have been concluded and it becomes necessary to break the seal. These arrangements should be those which the chief officer considers are reasonably necessary to demonstrate to the person interviewed and any other party who may wish to use or refer to the interview record that the master copy has not been tampered with and that the interview record remains accurate. (See *Note 6D*.)

6.3A Subject to *paragraph 6.3C*, a representative of each party must be given a reasonable opportunity to be present when the seal is broken and the master recording copied and re-sealed.

6.3B If one or more of the parties is not present when the master copy seal is broken because they cannot be contacted or refuse to attend or paragraph 6.3C applies, arrangements should be made for an independent person such as a custody visitor, to be present. Alternatively, or as an additional safeguard, arrangements should be made for a film or photographs to be taken of the procedure.

6.3C *Paragraph 6.3A* does not require a person to be given an opportunity to be present when;

(a) it is necessary to break the master copy seal for the proper and effective further investigation of the original offence or the investigation of some other offence; and

(b) the officer in charge of the investigation has reasonable grounds to suspect that allowing an opportunity might prejudice any such an investigation or criminal proceedings which may be brought as a result or endanger any person. (See *Note 6E*.)

(d) Documentation

6.4 When the master recording seal is broken, a record must be made of the procedure followed, including the date, time, place and persons present.

[This section (paragraphs 6.1 to 6.4 and Notes 6A to 6E) does not apply to interviews recorded using a secure digital network, see paragraphs 7.4 and 7.14 to 7.15.]

Notes for guidance

6A This section is concerned with the security of the master recording sealed at the conclusion of the interview. Care must be taken of working recordings because their loss or destruction may lead unnecessarily to the need to access master recordings.

6B If the master recording has been delivered to the crown court for their keeping after committal for trial the crown prosecutor will apply to the chief clerk of the crown court centre for the release of the recording for unsealing by the crown prosecutor.

6C Reference to the Crown Prosecution Service or to the crown prosecutor in this part of the Code should be taken to include any other body or person with a statutory responsibility for the proceedings for which the police recorded interview is required.

6D The most common reasons for needing access to master copies that are not required for criminal proceedings arise from civil actions and complaints against police and civil actions between individuals arising out of allegations of crime investigated by police.

6E Paragraph 6.3C could apply, for example, when one or more of the outcomes or likely outcomes of the investigation might be; (i) the prosecution of one or more of the original suspects; (ii) the prosecution of someone previously not suspected, including someone who was originally a witness, and (iii) any original suspect being treated as a prosecution witness and when premature disclosure of any police action, particularly through contact with any parties involved, could lead to a real risk of compromising the investigation and endangering witnesses.

7 Recording of Interviews by Secure Digital Network

7.1 A secure digital network does not use removable media and this section specifies the provisions which will apply when a secure digital network is used.

7.2 *Not used.*

7.3 The following requirements are solely applicable to the use of a secure digital network for the recording of interviews.

(a) Application of sections 1 to 6 of Code E

7.4 *Sections 1* to 6 of Code E above apply except for the following paragraphs:

- *Paragraph 2.2* under 'Recording and sealing of master recordings'
- *Paragraph 4.3* under '(b) Commencement of interviews'
- *Paragraph 4.4(e)* under '(b) Commencement of interviews'
- *Paragraphs 4.11* to *4.19* under '(e) Changing recording media', '(f) Taking a break during interview', '(g) Failure of recording equipment', '(h) Removing recording media from the recorder' and '(i) Conclusion of interview'
- *Paragraphs 6.1* to *6.4* and *Notes 6A* to *6E* under 'Media security'

(b) Commencement of Interviews

7.5 When the suspect is brought into the interview room, the interviewer shall without delay and in the sight of the suspect, switch on the recording equipment and enter the information necessary to log on to the secure network and start recording.

7.6 The interviewer must then inform the suspect that the interview is being recorded using a secure digital network and that recording has commenced.

7.7 In addition to the requirements of *paragraph 4.4(a)* to *(d)* above, the interviewer must inform the person that:

- they will be given access to the recording of the interview in the event that they are charged or informed that they will be prosecuted but if they are not charged or informed that they will be prosecuted they will only be given access as agreed with the police or on the order of a court; and
- they will be given a written notice at the end of the interview setting out their rights to access the recording and what will happen to the recording.

(c) Taking a break during interview

7.8 When a break is taken, the fact that a break is to be taken, the reason for it and the time shall be recorded on the audio recording. The recording shall be stopped and the procedures in *paragraphs 7.12* and *7.13* for the conclusion of an interview followed.

7.9 When the interview recommences the procedures in *paragraphs 7.5* to *7.7* for commencing an interview shall be followed to create a new file to record the continuation of the interview. The time the interview recommences shall be recorded on the audio recording.

7.10 After any break in the interview the interviewer must, before resuming the interview, remind the person being questioned that they remain under caution or, if there is any doubt, give the caution in full again. (See *Note 4G*.)

(d) Failure of recording equipment

7.11 If there is an equipment failure which can be rectified quickly, e.g. by commencing a new secure digital network recording, the interviewer shall follow the appropriate procedures as in *paragraphs 7.8* to *7.10*. When the recording is resumed the interviewer shall explain what happened and record the time the interview recommences. If, however, it is not possible to continue recording on the secure digital network the interview should be recorded on removable media as in *paragraph 4.3* unless the necessary equipment is not available. If this happens the interview may continue without being audibly recorded and the interviewer shall seek the authority of the custody officer authority or a sergeant as in *paragraph 3.3(a) or (b)*. (See *Note 4H*.)

(e) Conclusion of interview

7.12 At the conclusion of the interview, the suspect shall be offered the opportunity to clarify anything he or she has said and asked if there is anything they want to add.

7.13 At the conclusion of the interview, including the taking and reading back of any written statement:

(a) the time shall be orally recorded.

(b) the suspect shall be handed a notice (see *Note 7A)* which explains:
- how the audio recording will be used
- the arrangements for access to it
- that if they are charged or informed that they will be prosecuted, they will be given access to the recording of the interview either electronically or by being given a copy on removable recording media, but if they are not charged or informed that they will prosecuted, they will only be given access as agreed with the police or on the order of a court.

(c) the suspect must be asked to confirm that he or she has received a copy of the notice at *sub-paragraph (b)* above. If the suspect fails to accept or to acknowledge receipt of the notice, the interviewer will state for the recording that a copy of the notice has been provided to the suspect and that he or she has refused to take a copy of the notice or has refused to acknowledge receipt.

(d) the time shall be recorded and the interviewer shall notify the suspect that the recording is being saved to the secure network. The interviewer must save the recording in the presence of the suspect. The suspect should then be informed that the interview is terminated.

(f) After the interview

7.14 The interviewer shall make a note in their pocket book that the interview has taken place and that it was audibly recorded, time it commenced, its duration and date and the identification number of the original recording.

7.15 If no proceedings follow in respect of the person whose interview was recorded, the recordings must be kept securely as in *paragraphs 7.16 and 7.17*.

(See *Note 5A*.)

(g) Security of secure digital network interview records

7.16 Interview record files are stored in read only format on non-removable storage devices, for example, hard disk drives, to ensure their integrity. The recordings are first saved locally to a secure non-removable device before being transferred to the remote network device. If for any reason the network connection fails, the recording remains on the local device and will be transferred when the network connections are restored.

7.17 Access to interview recordings, including copying to removable media, must be strictly controlled and monitored to ensure that access is restricted to those who have been given specific permission to access for specified purposes when this is necessary. For example, police officers and CPS lawyers involved in the preparation of any prosecution case, persons interviewed if they have been charged or informed they may be prosecuted and their legal representatives.

Note for Guidance

7A The notice at paragraph 7.13 above should provide a brief explanation of the secure digital network and how access to the recording is strictly limited. The notice should also explain the access rights of the suspect, his or her legal representative, the police and the prosecutor to the recording of the interview. Space should be provided on the form to insert the date and the file reference number for the interview.

ANNEX: PARAGRAPH 3.1(A)(III)—EXEMPTION FROM THE REQUIREMENT TO AUDIO RECORD INTERVIEWS FOR INDICTABLE OFFENCES—CONDITIONS.

[See *Notes A1, A2 and A3*]

Part 1: Four specified indictable offence types—four conditions

1. The **first** condition is that the person has not been arrested.

2. The **second** condition is that the interview takes place elsewhere than at a police station (see *Note A4*).

3. The **third** condition is that the *indictable* offence in respect of which the person has been cautioned is *one* of the following:

(a) Possession of a controlled drug contrary to section 5(2) of the Misuse of Drugs Act 1971 if the drug is cannabis as defined by that Act but it is not cannabis oil (see *Note A5*);

(b) Possession of a controlled drug contrary to section 5(2) of the Misuse of Drugs Act 1971 if the drug is khat as defined by that Act (see *Note A5*);

(c) Retail theft (shoplifting) contrary to section 1 of the Theft Act 1968 (see *Note A6)*; and

(d) Criminal damage to property contrary to section 1(1) of the Criminal Damage Act 1971 (see *Note A6),*

and in this paragraph, the reference to each of the above offences applies to an attempt to commit that offence as defined by section 1 of the Criminal Attempts Act 1981.

4. The **fourth** condition is that:

(a) where the person has been cautioned in respect of an offence described in *paragraph 3(a)* (Possession of cannabis) or *paragraph 3(b)* (Possession of khat), the requirements of *paragraphs 5* and *6* are satisfied; or

(b) where the person has been cautioned in respect of an offence described in *paragraph 3(c)* (Retail theft), the requirements of *paragraphs 5* and *7* are satisfied; or

(c) where the person has been cautioned in respect of an offence described in *paragraph 3(d)* (criminal damage), the requirements of *paragraphs 5* and *8* are satisfied.

5. The requirements of this paragraph that apply to all four offences described in *paragraph 3* are that:

(i) the person suspected of committing the offence:
- appears to be aged 18 or over;
- does *not* require an appropriate adult (see *paragraph 1.5* of this Code);
- appears to be able to appreciate the significance of questions and their answers;
- does *not* appear to be unable to understand what is happening because of the effects of drink, drugs or illness, ailment or condition; and
- does *not* require an interpreter in accordance with Code C *section 13*.

(ii) it appears that the commission of the offence:
- has *not* resulted in any injury to any person;
- has *not* involved any realistic threat or risk of injury to any person; and
- has *not* caused any *substantial* financial or material loss to the private property of any individual.

(iii) in accordance with Code G (Arrest), the person's arrest is *not* necessary in order to investigate the offence; and

(iv) the person is not being interviewed about any other offence.

See *Notes A3* and *A8*.

6. The requirements of this paragraph that apply to the offences described in *paragraph 3(a)* (possession of cannabis) and *paragraph 3(b)* (possession of khat) are that a police officer who is experienced in the recognition of the physical appearance, texture and smell of cannabis or (as the case may be) khat, is able to say that the substance which has been found in the suspect's possession by that officer or, as the case may be, by any other officer not so experienced and trained:

(i) is a controlled drug being either cannabis which is not cannabis oil or khat; and
(ii) the quantity of the substance found is consistent with personal use by the suspect and does not provide any grounds to suspect an intention to supply others.

See *Note A5*.

7. The requirements of this paragraph that apply to the offence described in *paragraph 3(c)* (retail theft), are that it appears to the officer:

(i) that the value of the property stolen does not exceed £100 inclusive of VAT;
(ii) that the stolen property has been recovered and remains fit for sale unless the items stolen comprised drink or food and have been consumed; and
(iii) that the person suspected of stealing the property is not employed (whether paid or not) by the person, company or organisation to which the property belongs.

See *Note A3*.

8. The requirements of this paragraph that apply to the offence described in *paragraph 3(d)* (Criminal damage), are that it appears to the officer:

(i) that the value of the criminal damage does *not exceed* £300; and
(ii) that the person suspected of damaging the property is not employed (whether paid or not) by the person, company or organisation to which the property belongs.

See *Note A3*

Part 2: Other provisions applicable to all interviews to which this Annex applies

9. Subject to *paragraph 10*, the provisions of *paragraphs 3.21* and *3.22* of Code C (Persons attending a police station or elsewhere voluntarily) regarding the suspect's right to free legal advice and the other rights and entitlements that apply to all voluntary interviews, irrespective of where they take place, will apply to any interview to which this Annex applies. See *Note A7*.

10. If it appears to the interviewing officer that before the conclusion of an interview, any of the requirements in *paragraphs 5 to 8* of *Part 1* that apply to the offence in question described in *paragraph 3* of Part 1 have ceased to apply; this Annex shall cease to apply. The person being interviewed must be so informed and a break in the interview must be taken. The reason must be recorded in the interview record and the continuation of the interview shall be audio recorded in accordance with *sections 1* to *7* of this Code. For the purpose of the continuation, the provisions of paragraphs 4.3 and 7.5 (Commencement of interviews) shall apply. See *Note A8*.

Notes for Guidance

A1 This Annex sets out conditions and requirements of the limited exemption referred to in paragraph 3.1(a)(iii), from the requirement to make an audio recording of an interview about an indictable offence, including offences triable either way.

A2 The purpose of the exemption is to support the policy which gives police in England and Wales, options for dealing with low-level offences quickly and non-bureaucratically in a proportionate manner. Guidance for police about these options is available at: https://www.app.college.police.uk/app-content/prosecution-and-case-management/justice-outcomes/.

A3 A decision in relation to a particular offence that the conditions and requirements in this Annex for an audio-recording exemption are satisfied is an operational matter for the interviewing officer according to all the particular circumstances of the case. These circumstances include the outcome of the officer's investigation at that time and any other matters that are relevant to the officer's consideration as to how to deal with the matter.

A4 An interviewer who is not sure, or has any doubt, about the suitability of a place or location for carrying out an interview elsewhere than at a police station, should consult an officer of the rank of sergeant or above for advice. (Repeated from Note 1A).

A5 Under the Misuse of Drugs Act 1971 as at the date this Code comes into force:

(a) cannabis includes any part of the cannabis plant but not mature stalks and seeds separated from the plant, cannabis resin and cannabis oil, but paragraph 3(a) does not apply to the possession of cannabis oil; and

(b) khat includes the leaves, stems and shoots of the plant.

A6 The power to issue a Penalty Notice for Disorder (PND) for an offence contrary to section 1 of the Theft Act 1968 applies when the value of the goods stolen does not exceed £100 inclusive of VAT. The power to issue a PND for an offence contrary to section 1(1) of the Criminal Damage Act 1971 applies when the value of the damage does not exceed £300.

A7 The interviewing officer is responsible for ensuring compliance with the provisions of Code C applicable to the conduct and recording of voluntary interviews to which this Annex applies. These include the right to free legal advice and the provision of a notice explaining the arrangements (see Code C paragraph 3.21 and section 6), the provision of information about the offence before the interview (see Code C paragraph 11.1A) and the right to interpretation and translation (see Code C section 13).

A8 The requirements in paragraph 5 of Part 1 will cease to apply if, for example during the course of an interview, as a result of what the suspect says or other information which comes to the interviewing officer's notice:

- *it appears that the suspect:*
  - ~ *is aged under 18;*
  - ~ *does require an appropriate adult;*
  - ~ *is unable to appreciate the significance of questions and their answers;*
  - ~ *is unable to understand what is happening because of the effects of drink, drugs or illness, ailment or condition; or*
  - ~ *requires an interpreter; or*
- *the police officer decides that the suspect's arrest is now necessary (see Code G).*

Code of Practice on Visual Recording with Sound of Interviews with Suspects (Code F)

(2015)

1 General

1.0 The procedures in this Code must be used fairly, responsibly, with respect for the people to whom they apply and without unlawful discrimination. Under the Equality Act 2010, section 149, when police officers are carrying out their functions, they also have a duty to have due regard to the need to eliminate unlawful discrimination, harassment and victimisation, to advance equality of opportunity between people who share a relevant protected characteristic and people who do not share it, and to take steps to foster good relations between those persons. See *Note 1C*.

1.1 This code of practice must be readily available for consultation by police officers and other police staff, detained persons and members of the public.

1.2 The *Notes for Guidance* included are not provisions of this code. They form guidance to police officers and others about its application and interpretation.

1.3 Nothing in this code shall be taken as detracting in any way from the requirements of the Code of Practice for the Detention, Treatment and Questioning of Persons by Police Officers (Code C). (See *Note 1A*.)

1.4 The interviews to which this Code applies are described in section 3.

1.5 In this code, the term 'appropriate adult', 'solicitor' and 'interview' have the same meaning as those set out in Code C and in the case of a 17 year old suspect, 'appropriate adult' includes the person called to fulfil that role in accordance with C *paragraph 1.5A* of Code C. The corresponding provisions and Notes for Guidance in Code C applicable to those terms shall also apply where appropriate.

1.5A The visual recording of interviews shall be carried out openly to instil confidence in its reliability as an impartial and accurate record of the interview.

1.6 Any reference in this code to visual recording shall be taken to mean visual recording with sound and in this code:

(aa) 'recording media' means any removable, physical audio recording medium (such as magnetic tape, optical disc or solid state memory) which can be played and copied.

(a) 'designated person' means a person other than a police officer, designated under the Police Reform Act 2002, Part 4 who has specified powers and duties of police officers conferred or imposed on them;

(b) any reference to a police officer includes a designated person acting in the exercise or performance of the powers and duties conferred or imposed on them by their designation.

(c) 'secure digital network' is a computer network system which enables an original interview recording to be stored as a digital multi media file or a series of such files, on a secure file server which is accredited by the National Accreditor for Police Information Systems in accordance with the UK Government Protective Marking Scheme. See *paragraph 1.6A* and section 7 of this Code.

1.6A Section 7 below sets out the provisions which apply to interviews visually recorded using a secure digital network by reference to Code E and by excluding provisions of sections 1 to 6 of this Code which relate or apply only to removable media.

1.7 References to 'pocket book' in this Code include any official report book issued to police officers.

1.8 In the application of this Code to the conduct and visual recording of an interview of a suspect who has not been arrested:

(a) references to the 'custody officer' include references to an officer of the rank of sergeant or above who is not directly involved in the investigation of the offence(s);

(b) if the interview takes place elsewhere than at a police station, references to 'interview room' include any place or location which the interviewer is satisfied will enable the interview to be conducted and recorded in accordance with this Code and where the suspect is present voluntarily (see *Note 1B*); and

(c) provisions in addition to those which expressly apply to these interviews shall be followed insofar as they are relevant and can be applied in practice.

Notes for Guidance

1A As in paragraph 1.9 of Code C, references to custody officers include those carrying out the functions of a custody officer.

1B An interviewer who is not sure, or has any doubt, about the suitability of a place or location of an interview to be carried out elsewhere than at a police station, should consult an officer of the rank of sergeant or above for advice.

1C In paragraph 1.0, 'relevant protected characteristic' includes: age, disability, gender reassignment, pregnancy and maternity, race, religion/belief, sex and sexual orientation.

2 Recording and sealing of master recordings

2.1 *Not used.*

2.2 The camera(s) shall be placed in the interview room so as to ensure coverage of as much of the room as is practicably possible whilst the interviews are taking place. (See *Note 2A*.)

2.3 When the recording medium is placed in the recorder and it is switched on to record, the correct date and time, in hours, minutes and seconds, will be superimposed automatically, second by second, during the whole recording, see *Note 2B*. See section 7 regarding the use of a secure digital network to record the interview.

2.4 One recording, referred to in this code as the master recording copy, will be sealed before it leaves the presence of the suspect. A second recording will be used as a working copy. (See *Notes 2C* and *2D*.)

2.5 Nothing in this code requires the identity of an officer or police staff to be recorded or disclosed:

(a) *Not used.*

(b) if the interviewer reasonably believes that recording or disclosing their name might put them in danger.

In these cases, the interviewer will have their back to the camera and shall use their warrant or other identification number and the name of the police station to which they are attached. Such instances and the reasons for them shall be recorded in the custody record or the interviewer's pocket book. (See *Note 2E*.)

Notes for Guidance

2A Interviewers will wish to arrange that, as far as possible, visual recording arrangements are unobtrusive. It must be clear to the suspect, however, that there is no opportunity to interfere with the recording equipment or the recording media.

2B In this context, the recording medium should be capable of having an image of the date and time superimposed as the interview is recorded.

2C The purpose of sealing the master recording before it leaves the presence of the suspect is to establish their confidence that the integrity of the recording is preserved.

2D The visual recording of the interview may be used for identification procedures in accordance with paragraph 3.21 or Annex E of Code D.

2E The purpose of the paragraph 2.5(b) is to protect police officers and others involved in the investigation of serious organised crime or the arrest of particularly violent suspects when there is reliable information that those arrested or their associates may threaten or cause harm to the officers, their families or their personal property. In cases of doubt, an officer of inspector rank should be consulted.

3 Interviews to be visually recorded

3.1 Subject to paragraph 3.2 below, when an interviewer is deciding whether to make a visual recording, these are the areas where it might be appropriate:

(a) with a suspect in respect of an indictable offence (including an offence triable either way) (see *Notes 3A* and *3B*);

(b) which takes place as a result of an interviewer exceptionally putting further questions to a suspect about an offence described in sub-paragraph (a) above after they have been charged with, or informed they may be prosecuted for, that offence (see *Note 3C*);

(c) in which an interviewer wishes to bring to the notice of a person, after that person has been charged with, or informed they may be prosecuted for an offence described in sub-paragraph (a) above, any written statement made by another person, or the content of an interview with another person (see *Note 3D*);

(d) with, or in the presence of, a deaf or deaf/blind or speech impaired person who uses sign language to communicate;

(e) with, or in the presence of anyone who requires an appropriate adult, or

(f) in any case where the suspect or their representative requests that the interview be recorded visually.

3.2 The Terrorism Act 2000 and the Counter-Terrorism Act 2008 make separate provisions for a Code of Practice for the video recording with sound of:

- interviews of persons detained under section 41 of, or Schedule 7 to, the 2000 Act; and
- post-charge questioning of persons authorised under section 22 or 23 of the 2008 Act.

The provisions of this code do not therefore apply to such interviews. (See *Note 3E*.)

3.3 Following a decision by an interviewer to *visually record* any interview mentioned in paragraph 3.1 above, the custody officer in the case of a detained person, or a sergeant in the case of a suspect who has not been arrested, may authorise the interviewer not to make a *visual record* and for the purpose of this Code (F), the provisions of Code E *paragraphs 3.1, 3.2, 3.3, 3.3A* and *3.4* shall apply as appropriate. However, authority not to make a *visual recording* does not detract in any way from the requirement for *audio recording*. This would require a further authorisation not to make in accordance with Code E. (See *Note 3F*.)

3.5 The whole of each interview shall be recorded visually, including the taking and reading back of any statement.

3.6 A sign or indicator which is visible to the suspect must show when the visual recording equipment is recording.

Notes for Guidance

3A Nothing in the code is intended to preclude visual recording at police discretion of interviews at police stations or elsewhere with people cautioned in respect of offences not covered by paragraph 3.1, or responses made by persons after they have been charged with, or informed they may be prosecuted for, an offence, provided that this code is complied with.

3B Attention is drawn to the provisions set out in Code C about the matters to be considered when deciding whether a detained person is fit to be interviewed.

3C Code C sets out the circumstances in which a suspect may be questioned about an offence after being charged with it.

3D Code C sets out the procedures to be followed when a person's attention is drawn after charge, to a statement made by another person. One method of bringing the content of an interview with another person to the notice of a suspect may be to play them a recording of that interview.

3E If, during the course of an interview under this Code, it becomes apparent that the interview should be conducted under the terrorism code for the video recording with sound of interviews, the interview should only continue in accordance with that code.

3F A decision not to record an interview visually for any reason may be the subject of comment in court. The authorising officer should therefore be prepared to justify their decision in each case.

4 The Interview

(a) General

4.1 The provisions of Code C in relation to cautions and interviews and the *Notes for Guidance* applicable to those provisions shall apply to the conduct of interviews to which this Code applies.

4.2 Particular attention is drawn to those parts of Code C that describe the restrictions on drawing adverse inferences from an arrested suspect's failure or refusal to say anything about their involvement in the offence when interviewed, or after being charged or informed they may be prosecuted and how those restrictions affect the terms of the caution and determine whether a special warning under Sections 36 and 37 of the Criminal Justice and Public Order Act 1994 can be given.

(b) Commencement of interviews

4.3 When the suspect is brought into the interview room the interviewer shall without delay, but in sight of the suspect, load the recording equipment and set it to record. The recording media must be unwrapped or otherwise opened in the presence of the suspect. (See *Note 4A*.)

4.4 The interviewer shall then tell the suspect formally about the visual recording and point out the sign or indicator which shows that the recording equipment is activated and recording (see *paragraph 3.6*). The interviewer shall:

(a) explain that the interview is being visually recorded;

(b) subject to paragraph 2.5, give their name and rank, and that of any other interviewer present;

(c) ask the suspect and any other party present (e.g. the appropriate adult, a solicitor or interpreter) to identify themselves;

(d) state the date, time of commencement and place of the interview, and

(e) state that the suspect will be given a notice about what will happen to the recording.

See Note 4AA

4.4A Any person entering the interview room after the interview has commenced shall be invited by the interviewer to identify themselves for the purpose of the recording and state the reason why they have entered the interview room.

4.5 The interviewer shall then caution the suspect, see Code C, section 10 and:

- if they are detained, remind them of their entitlement to free legal advice, see Code C *paragraph 11.2*, or
- if they are not detained under arrest, explain this and their entitlement to free legal advice, see Code C *paragraph 3.21*.

4.6 The interviewer shall then put to the suspect any significant statement or silence, see Code C, *paragraph 11.4*.

(c) Interviews suspects who appear to require an interpreter

4.7 The provisions of Code C on interpreters for suspects who do not appear to speak or understand English, or who appear to have a hearing or speech impediment, continue to apply.

(d) Objections and complaints by the suspect

4.8 If the suspect or an appropriate adult on their behalf, objects to the interview being visually recorded either at the outset or during the interview or during a break in the interview, the interviewer shall explain that the interview is being visually recorded and that this Code requires that the objections to be recorded on the visual recording. When any objections have been recorded or the suspect or the appropriate adult have refused to have their objections recorded, the interviewer shall say that they are turning off the visual recording, give their reasons and turn it off. If a separate audio recording is being maintained, the interviewer shall ask the person to record the reasons for refusing to agree to the interview being visually recorded. *Paragraph 4.8* of Code E will apply if the person also objects to the interview being audio recorded. If the interviewer reasonably considers they may proceed to question the suspect with the visual recording still on, the interviewer may do so. (See *Note 4G*.)

4.9 If in the course of an interview a complaint is made by the person being questioned, or on their behalf, concerning the provisions of this or any other Code, or it comes to the interviewer's notice that the person may have been treated improperly, then the interviewer shall act as in Code C, paragraph 12.9. (See *Notes 4B* and *4C*.)

4.10 If the suspect indicates that they wish to tell the interviewer about matters not directly connected with the offence of which they are suspected and that they are unwilling for these matters to be visually recorded, the suspect should be given the opportunity to tell the interviewer about these matters after the conclusion of the formal interview.

(e) Changing the recording media

4.11 In instances where the recording medium is not of sufficient length to record all of the interview with the suspect, further certified recording medium will be used. When the recording equipment indicates that the recording medium has only a short time left to run, the interviewer shall advise the suspect and round off that part of the interview. If the interviewer wishes to continue the interview but does not already have further certified recording media with him, they shall obtain a set. The suspect should not be left unattended in the interview room. The interviewer will remove the recording media from the recording equipment and insert the new ones which have been unwrapped or otherwise opened in the suspect's presence. The recording equipment shall then be set to record. Care must be taken, particularly when a number of sets of recording media have been used, to ensure that there is no confusion between them. This could be achieved by marking the sets of recording media with consecutive identification numbers.

(f) Taking a break during the interview

4.12 When a break is taken, the fact that a break is to be taken, the reason for it and the time shall be recorded on the visual record.

4.12A When the break is taken and the interview room vacated by the suspect, the recording media shall be removed from the recorder and the procedures for the conclusion of an interview followed. (See *paragraph 4.18*.)

4.13 When a break is a short one and both the suspect and an interviewer remain in the interview room, the recording may be stopped. There is no need to remove the recording media and when the interview recommences the recording should continue on the same recording media. The time at which the interview recommences shall be recorded.

4.14 After any break in the interview the interviewer must, before resuming the interview, remind the person being questioned of their right to legal advice if they have not exercised it and that they remain under caution or, if there is any doubt, give the caution in full again. (See *Notes 4D* and *4E*.)

(g) Failure of recording equipment

4.15 If there is a failure of equipment which can be rectified quickly, the appropriate procedures set out in paragraph 4.12 shall be followed. When the recording is resumed the interviewer shall explain what has happened and record the time the interview recommences. If, however, it is not possible to continue recording on that particular recorder and no alternative equipment is readily available, the interview may continue without being recorded visually. In such circumstances, the procedures set out in paragraph 3.3 of this code for seeking the authority of the custody officer or a sergeant will be followed. (See *Note 4F*.)

(h) Removing used recording media from recording equipment

4.16 Where used recording media are removed from the recording equipment during the course of an interview, they shall be retained and the procedures set out in paragraph 4.18 below followed.

(i) Conclusion of interview

4.17 Before the conclusion of the interview, the suspect shall be offered the opportunity to clarify anything he or she has said and asked if there is anything that they wish to add.

4.18 At the conclusion of the interview, including the taking and reading back of any written statement, the time shall be recorded and the recording equipment switched off. The master recording shall be removed from the recording equipment, sealed with a master recording label and treated as an exhibit in accordance with the force standing orders. The interviewer shall sign the label and also ask the suspect and any third party present during the interview to sign it. If the suspect or third party refuses to sign the label, an officer of at least the rank of inspector, or if one is not available, the custody officer or, if the suspect has not been arrested, a sergeant, shall be called into the interview room and asked, subject to *paragraph 2.5*, to sign it.

4.19 The suspect shall be handed a notice which explains the use which will be made of the recording and the arrangements for access to it. The notice will also advise the suspect that a copy of the tape shall be supplied as soon as practicable if the person is charged or informed that he will be prosecuted.

Notes for Guidance

4AA For the purpose of voice identification the interviewer should ask the suspect and any other people present to identify themselves.

4A The interviewer should attempt to estimate the likely length of the interview and ensure that an appropriate quantity of certified recording media and labels with which to seal the master copies are available in the interview room.

4B Where the custody officer, or in the case of a person who has not been arrested, a sergeant, is called to deal with the complaint, wherever possible the recorder should be left to run until the officer has entered the interview room and spoken to the person being interviewed. Continuation or termination of the interview should be at the discretion of the interviewer pending action by an inspector under Code C paragraph 9.2.

4C Where the complaint is about a matter not connected with this Code or Code C, the decision to continue with the interview is at the interviewer's discretion. Where the interviewer decides to continue with the interview, the person being interviewed shall be told that at the conclusion of the interview, the complaint will be brought to the attention of the custody officer, or in the case of a person who has not been arrested, a sergeant. When the interview is concluded, the interviewer must, as soon as practicable, inform the custody officer or the sergeant of the existence and nature of the complaint made.

4D In considering whether to caution again after a break, the interviewer should bear in mind that they may have to satisfy a court that the person understood that they were still under caution when the interview resumed.

4E The officer should bear in mind that it may be necessary to satisfy the court that nothing occurred during a break in an interview or between interviews which influenced the suspect's recorded evidence. On the re-commencement of an interview, the interviewer should consider summarising on the record the reason for the break and confirming this with the suspect.

4F Where the interview is being recorded and the media or the recording equipment fails, the interviewer should stop the interview immediately. Where part of the interview is unaffected by the error and is still accessible on the media, that part shall be copied and sealed in the suspect's presence as a master copy and the interview recommenced using new equipment/media as required. Where the content of the interview has been lost in its entirety, the media should be sealed in the suspect's presence and the interview begun again. If the recording equipment cannot be fixed or no replacement is immediately available, the interview should be audio recorded in accordance with Code E.

4G The interviewer should be aware that a decision to continue recording against the wishes of the suspect may be the subject of comment in court.

5 After the Interview

5.1 The interviewer shall make a note in his or her pocket book of the fact that the interview has taken place and has been recorded, its time, duration and date and the identification number of the master copy of the recording media.

5.2 Where no proceedings follow in respect of the person whose interview was recorded, the recording media must nevertheless be kept securely in accordance with paragraph 6.1 and *Note 6A*.

Note for Guidance

5A Any written record of a recorded interview shall be made in accordance with current national guidelines for police officers, police staff and CPS prosecutors concerned with the preparation, processing and submission of files.

6 Master Recording Security

(a) General

6.1 The officer in charge of the police station at which interviews with suspects are recorded or as the case may be, where recordings of interviews carried out elsewhere than at a police station are held, shall make arrangements for the master copies to be kept securely and their movements accounted for on the same basis as other material which may be used for evidential purposes, in accordance with force standing orders. (See *Note 6A*.)

(b) Breaking master recording seal for criminal proceedings

6.2 A police officer has no authority to break the seal on a master copy which is required for criminal trial or appeal proceedings. If it is necessary to gain access to the master copy, the police officer shall arrange for its seal to be broken in the presence of a representative of the Crown Prosecution Service. The defendant or their legal adviser shall be informed and given a reasonable opportunity to be present. If the defendant or their legal representative is present they shall be invited to reseal and sign the master copy. If either refuses or neither is present, this shall be done by the representative of the Crown Prosecution Service. (See *Notes 6B* and *6C*.)

(c) Breaking master recording seal: other cases

6.3 The chief officer of police is responsible for establishing arrangements for breaking the seal of the master copy where no criminal proceedings result, or the criminal proceedings to which the interview relates, have been concluded and it becomes necessary to break the seal. These arrangements should be those which the chief officer considers are reasonably necessary to demonstrate to the person interviewed and any other party who may wish to use or refer to the interview record that the master copy has not been tampered with and that the interview record remains accurate. (See *Note 6D*.)

6.4 Subject to paragraph 6.6, a representative of each party must be given a reasonable opportunity to be present when the seal is broken and the master recording copied and re-sealed.

6.5 If one or more of the parties is not present when the master copy seal is broken because they cannot be contacted or refuse to attend or paragraph 6.6 applies, arrangements should be made for an independent person such as a custody visitor, to be present. Alternatively, or as an additional safeguard, arrangement should be made for a film or photographs to be taken of the procedure.

6.6 Paragraph 6.4 does not require a person to be given an opportunity to be present when:

(a) it is necessary to break the master copy seal for the proper and effective further investigation of the original offence or the investigation of some other offence; and

(b) the officer in charge of the investigation has reasonable grounds to suspect that allowing an opportunity might prejudice any such an investigation or criminal proceedings which may be brought as a result or endanger any person. (See *Note 6E*.)

(d) Documentation

6.7 When the master copy seal is broken, copied and re-sealed, a record must be made of the procedure followed, including the date time and place and persons present.

Notes for Guidance

6A This section is concerned with the security of the master recordings which will have been sealed at the conclusion of the interview. Care should, however, be taken of working recordings since their loss or destruction may lead unnecessarily to the need to have access to master copies.

6B If the master recording has been delivered to the Crown Court for their keeping after committal for trial, the Crown Prosecutor will apply to the Chief Clerk of the Crown Court Centre for its release for unsealing by the Crown Prosecutor.

6C Reference to the Crown Prosecution Service or to the Crown Prosecutor in this part of the code shall be taken to include any other body or person with a statutory responsibility for prosecution for whom the police conduct any recorded interviews.

6D The most common reasons for needing access to master recordings that are not required for criminal proceedings arise from civil actions and complaints against police and civil actions between individuals arising out of allegations of crime investigated by police.

6E Paragraph 6.6 could apply, for example, when one or more of the outcomes or likely outcomes of the investigation might be: (i) the prosecution of one or more of the original suspects; (ii) the prosecution of someone previously not suspected, including someone who was originally a witness; and (iii) any original suspect being treated as a prosecution witness and when premature disclosure of any police action, particularly through contact with any parties involved, could lead to a real risk of compromising the investigation and endangering witnesses.

7 Visual Recording of Interviews by Secure Digital Network

7.1 This section applies if an officer wishes to make a visual recording with sound of an interview mentioned in section 3 of this Code using a secure digital network which does not use removable media (see *paragraph 1.6(c)* above.

7.3 The provisions of sections 1 to 6 of this Code which relate or apply only to removable media will not apply to a secure digital network recording.

7.4 The statutory requirement and provisions for the audio recording of interviews using a secure digital network set out in section 7 of Code E should be applied to the visual recording with sound of interviews mentioned in section 3 of this code as if references to audio recordings of interviews include visual recordings with sound.

Code of Practice for the Statutory Power of Arrest by Police Officers (Code G)

(2012)

This Code applies to any arrest made by a police officer after midnight on 12 November 2012

1 Introduction

1.1 This Code of Practice deals with the statutory power of police to arrest a person who is involved, or suspected of being involved, in a criminal offence. The power of arrest must be used fairly, responsibly, with respect for people suspected of committing offences and without unlawful discrimination. The Equality Act 2010 makes it unlawful for police officers to discriminate against, harass or victimise any person on the grounds of the 'protected characteristics' of age, disability, gender reassignment, race, religion or belief, sex and sexual orientation, marriage and civil partnership, pregnancy and maternity when using their powers. When police forces are carrying out their functions they also have a duty to have regard to the need to eliminate unlawful discrimination, harassment and victimisation and to take steps to foster good relations.

1.2 The exercise of the power of arrest represents an obvious and significant interference with the Right to liberty and security under Article 5 of the European Convention on Human Rights set out in Part I of Schedule 1 to the Human Rights Act 1998.

1.3 The use of the power must be fully justified and officers exercising the power should consider if the necessary objectives can be met by other, less intrusive means. Absence of justification for exercising the power of arrest may lead to challenges should the case proceed to court. It could also lead to civil claims against police for unlawful arrest and false imprisonment. When the power of arrest is exercised it is essential that it is exercised in a non-discriminatory and proportionate manner which is compatible with the Right to liberty under Article 5. See *Note 1B*.

1.4 Section 24 of the Police and Criminal Evidence Act 1984 (as substituted by section 110 of the Serious Organised Crime and Police Act 2005) provides the statutory power for a constable to arrest without warrant for all offences. If the provisions of the Act and this Code are not observed, both the arrest and the conduct of any subsequent investigation may be open to question.

1.5 This Code of Practice must be readily available at all police stations for consultation by police officers and police staff, detained persons and members of the public.

1.6 The notes for guidance are not provisions of this code.

2 Elements of Arrest under section 24 PACE

2.1 A lawful arrest requires two elements:

A person's involvement or suspected involvement or attempted involvement in the commission of a criminal offence;

AND

Reasonable grounds for *believing* that the person's arrest is necessary.

- both elements must be satisfied, and
- it can never be necessary to arrest a person unless there are reasonable grounds to suspect them of committing an offence.

2.2 The arrested person must be informed that they have been arrested, even if this fact is obvious, and of the relevant circumstances of the arrest in relation to both the above elements. The custody officer must be informed of these matters on arrival at the police station. See *paragraphs 2.9, 3.3* and *Note 3* and *Code C paragraph 3.4*.

(a) 'Involvement in the commission of an offence'

2.3 A constable may arrest without warrant in relation to any offence (see *Notes 1* and *1A*) anyone:

- who is about to commit an offence or is in the act of committing an offence;
- whom the officer has reasonable grounds for suspecting is about to commit an offence or to be committing an offence;
- whom the officer has reasonable grounds to suspect of being guilty of an offence which he or she has reasonable grounds for suspecting has been committed;
- anyone who is guilty of an offence which has been committed or anyone whom the officer has reasonable grounds for suspecting to be guilty of that offence.

2.3A There must be some reasonable, objective grounds for the suspicion, based on known facts and information which are relevant to the likelihood the offence has been committed and the person liable to arrest committed it. See *Notes 2* and *2A*.

(b) Necessity criteria

2.4 The power of arrest is **only** exercisable if the constable has reasonable grounds for *believing* that it is necessary to arrest the person. The statutory criteria for what may constitute necessity are set out in paragraph 2.9 and it remains an operational decision at the discretion of the constable to decide:

- which one or more of the necessity criteria (if any) applies to the individual; and
- if any of the criteria do apply, whether to arrest, grant street bail after arrest, report for summons or for charging by post, issue a penalty notice or take any other action that is open to the officer.

2.5 In applying the criteria, the arresting officer has to be satisfied that at least one of the reasons supporting the need for arrest is satisfied.

2.6 Extending the power of arrest to all offences provides a constable with the ability to use that power to deal with any situation. However applying the necessity criteria requires the constable to examine and justify the reason or reasons why a person needs to be arrested or (as the case may be) further arrested, for an offence for the custody officer to decide whether to authorise their detention for that offence. See *Note 2C*

2.7 The criteria in paragraph 2.9 below which are set out in section 24 of PACE as substituted by section 110 of the Serious Organised Crime and Police Act 2005 are exhaustive. However, the circumstances that may satisfy those criteria remain a matter for the operational discretion of individual officers. Some examples are given to illustrate what those circumstances might be and what officers might consider when deciding whether arrest is necessary.

2.8 In considering the individual circumstances, the constable must take into account the situation of the victim, the nature of the offence, the circumstances of the suspect and the needs of the investigative process.

2.9 When it is practicable to tell a person why their arrest is necessary (as required by paragraphs 2.2, 3.3 and *Note 3*), the constable should outline the facts, information and other circumstances which provide the grounds for believing that their arrest is necessary and which the officer considers satisfy one or more of the statutory criteria in sub-paragraphs (a) to (f), namely:

(a) to enable the name of the person in question to be ascertained (in the case where the constable does not know, and cannot readily ascertain, the person's name, or has reasonable grounds for doubting whether a name given by the person as his name is his real name):

An officer might decide that a person's name cannot be readily ascertained if they fail or refuse to give it when asked, particularly after being warned that failure or refusal is likely to make their arrest necessary (see *Note 2D*). Grounds to doubt a name given may arise if the person appears reluctant or hesitant when asked to give their name or to verify the name they have given.

Where mobile fingerprinting is available and the suspect's name cannot be ascertained or is doubted, the officer should consider using the power under section 61(6A) of PACE (see *Code D paragraph 4.3(e)*) to take and check the fingerprints of a suspect as this may avoid the need to arrest solely to enable their name to be ascertained.

(b) correspondingly as regards the person's address:

An officer might decide that a person's address cannot be readily ascertained if they fail or refuse to give it when asked, particularly after being warned that such a failure or refusal is likely to make their arrest necessary. See *Note 2D*. Grounds to doubt an address given may arise if the person appears reluctant or hesitant when asked to give their address or is unable to provide verifiable details of the locality they claim to live in.

When considering reporting to consider summons or charging by post as alternatives to arrest, an address would be satisfactory if the person will be at it for a sufficiently long period for it to be possible to serve them with the summons or requisition and charge; or, that some other person at that address specified by the person will accept service on their behalf. When considering issuing a penalty notice, the address should be one where the person will be in the event of enforcement action if the person does not pay the penalty or is convicted and fined after a court hearing.

(c) to prevent the person in question:

(i) causing physical injury to himself or any other person;

This might apply where the suspect has already used or threatened violence against others and it is thought likely that they may assault others if they are not arrested. See *Note 2D*

(ii) suffering physical injury;

This might apply where the suspect's behaviour and actions are believed likely to provoke, or have provoked, others to want to assault the suspect unless the suspect is arrested for their own protection. See *Note 2D*

(iii) causing loss or damage to property;

This might apply where the suspect is a known persistent offender with a history of serial offending against property (theft and criminal damage) and it is thought likely that they may continue offending if they are not arrested.

(iv) committing an offence against public decency (only applies where members of the public going about their normal business cannot reasonably be expected to avoid the person in question);

This might apply when an offence against public decency is being committed in a place to which the public have access and is likely to be repeated in that or some other public place at a time when the public are likely to encounter the suspect. See *Note 2D*

(v) causing an unlawful obstruction of the highway;

This might apply to any offence where its commission causes an unlawful obstruction which it is believed may continue or be repeated if the person is not arrested, particularly if the person has been warned that they are causing an obstruction. See *Note 2D*

(d) to protect a child or other vulnerable person from the person in question.

This might apply when the health (physical or mental) or welfare of a child or vulnerable person is likely to be harmed or is at risk of being harmed, if the person is not arrested in cases where it is not practicable and appropriate to make alternative arrangements to prevent the suspect from having any harmful or potentially harmful contact with the child or vulnerable person.

(e) to allow the prompt and effective investigation of the offence or of the conduct of the person in question. See *Note 2E*

This may arise when it is thought likely that unless the person is arrested and then either taken in custody to the police station or granted 'street bail' to attend the station later, see *Note 2J*, further action considered necessary to properly investigate their involvement in the offence would be frustrated, unreasonably delayed or otherwise hindered and therefore be impracticable. Examples of such actions include:

(i) *interviewing the suspect* on occasions when the person's voluntary attendance is not considered to be a practicable alternative to arrest, because for example:

- it is thought unlikely that the person would attend the police station voluntarily to be interviewed.
- it is necessary to interview the suspect about the outcome of other investigative action for which their arrest is necessary, see (ii) to (v) below.
- arrest would enable the special warning to be given in accordance with Code C paragraphs 10.10 and 10.11 when the suspect is found:
  - in possession of incriminating objects, or at a place where such objects are found;
  - at or near the scene of the crime at or about the time it was committed.
- the person has made false statements and/or presented false evidence;
- it is thought likely that the person:
  - may steal or destroy evidence;
  - may collude or make contact with, co-suspects or conspirators;
  - may intimidate or threaten or make contact with, witnesses. See *Notes 2F and 2G*

(ii) when considering arrest in connection with the investigation of an *indictable offence* (see *Note 6*), there is a need:
- to enter and search without a search warrant any premises occupied or controlled by the arrested person or where the person was when arrested or immediately before arrest;
- to prevent the arrested person from having contact with others;
- to detain the arrested person for more than 24 hours before charge.

(iii) when considering arrest in connection with any *recordable offence* and it is necessary to secure or preserve evidence of that offence by taking fingerprints, footwear impressions or samples from the suspect for evidential comparison or matching with other material relating to that offence, for example, from the crime scene. See *Note 2H*

(iv) when considering arrest in connection with any offence and it is necessary to search, examine or photograph the person to obtain evidence. See *Note 2H*

(v) when considering arrest in connection with an offence to which the statutory Class A drug testing requirements in Code C section 17 apply, to enable testing when it is thought that drug misuse might have caused or contributed to the offence. See *Note 2I.*

(f) to prevent any prosecution for the offence from being hindered by the disappearance of the person in question.

This may arise when it is thought that:
- if the person is not arrested they are unlikely to attend court if they are prosecuted;
- the address given is not a satisfactory address for service of a summons or a written charge and requisition to appear at court because the person will not be at it for a sufficiently long period for the summons or charge and requisition to be served and no other person at that specified address will accept service on their behalf.

3 Information to be given on Arrest

(a) Cautions—when a caution must be given

3.1 Code C paragraphs 10.1 and 10.2 set out the requirement for a person whom there are grounds to suspect of an offence (see *Note 2*) to be cautioned before being questioned or further questioned about an offence.

3.2 *Not used.*

3.3 A person who is arrested, or further arrested, must be informed at the time if practicable, or if not, as soon as it becomes practicable thereafter, that they are under arrest and of the grounds and reasons for their arrest, see paragraphs 2.2 and *Note 3.*

3.4 A person who is arrested, or further arrested, must be cautioned unless:

(a) it is impracticable to do so by reason of their condition or behaviour at the time;

(b) they have already been cautioned immediately prior to arrest as in *paragraph 3.1.*

(b) Terms of the caution (Taken from Code C section 10)

3.5 The caution, which must be given on arrest, should be in the following terms:

'You do not have to say anything. But it may harm your defence if you do not mention when questioned something which you later rely on in Court. Anything you do say may be given in evidence.'

Where the use of the Welsh Language is appropriate, a constable may provide the caution directly in Welsh in the following terms:

'Does dim rhaid i chi ddweud dim byd. Ond gall niweidio eich amddiffyniad os na fyddwch chi'n sôn, wrth gael eich holi, am rywbeth y byddwch chi'n dibynnu arno nes ymlaen yn y Llys. Gall unrhyw beth yr ydych yn ei ddweud gael ei roi fel tystiolaeth.'

See *Note 5*

3.6 Minor deviations from the words of any caution given in accordance with this Code do not constitute a breach of this Code, provided the sense of the relevant caution is preserved. See *Note 6*

3.7 *Not used.*

4 Records of Arrest

(a) General

4.1 The arresting officer is required to record in his pocket book or by other methods used for recording information:

- the nature and circumstances of the offence leading to the arrest;
- the reason or reasons why arrest was necessary;
- the giving of the caution; and
- anything said by the person at the time of arrest.

4.2 Such a record should be made at the time of the arrest unless impracticable to do. If not made at that time, the record should then be completed as soon as possible thereafter.

4.3 On arrival at the police station or after being first arrested at the police station, the arrested person must be brought before the custody officer as soon as practicable and a custody record must be opened in accordance with section 2 of Code C. The information given by the arresting officer on the circumstances and reason or reasons for arrest shall be recorded as part of the custody record. Alternatively, a copy of the record made by the officer in accordance with paragraph 4.1 above shall be attached as part of the custody record. See *paragraph 2.2* and *Code C paragraphs 3.4* and *10.3*.

4.4 The custody record will serve as a record of the arrest. Copies of the custody record will be provided in accordance with paragraphs 2.4 and 2.4A of Code C and access for inspection of the original record in accordance with paragraph 2.5 of Code C.

(b) Interviews and arrests

4.5 Records of interview, significant statements or silences will be treated in the same way as set out in sections 10 and 11 of Code C and in Codes E and F (audio and visual recording of interviews).

Notes for guidance

1 For the purposes of this Code, 'offence' means any statutory or common law offence for which a person may be tried by a magistrates' court or the Crown court and punished if convicted. Statutory offences include assault, rape, criminal damage, theft, robbery, burglary, fraud, possession of controlled drugs and offences under road traffic, liquor licensing, gambling and immigration legislation and local government byelaws. Common law offences include murder, manslaughter, kidnapping, false imprisonment, perverting the course of justice and escape from lawful custody.

1A This code does not apply to powers of arrest conferred on constables under any arrest warrant, for example, a warrant issued under the Magistrates' Courts Act 1980, sections 1 or 13, or the Bail Act 1976, section 7(1), or to the powers of constables to arrest without warrant other than under section 24 of PACE for an offence. These other powers to arrest without warrant do not depend on the arrested person committing any specific offence and include:

- *PACE, section 46A, arrest of person who fails to answer police bail to attend police station or is suspected of breaching any condition of that bail for the custody officer to decide whether they should be kept in police detention which applies whether or not the person commits an offence under section 6 of the Bail Act 1976 (e.g. failing without reasonable cause to surrender to custody);*
- *Bail Act 1976, section 7(3), arrest of person bailed to attend court who is suspected of breaching, or is believed likely to breach, any condition of bail to take them to court for bail to be re-considered;*
- *Children & Young Persons Act 1969, section 32(1A) (absconding)—arrest to return the person to the place where they are required to reside;*
- *Immigration Act 1971, Schedule 2 to arrest a person liable to examination to determine their right to remain in the UK;*
- *Mental Health Act 1983, section 136 to remove person suffering from mental disorder to place of safety for assessment;*
- *Prison Act 1952, section 49, arrest to return person unlawfully at large to the prison etc. where they are liable to be detained;*

- *Road Traffic Act 1988, section 6D arrest of driver following the outcome of a preliminary roadside test requirement to enable the driver to be required to provide an evidential sample;*
- *Common law power to stop or prevent a Breach of the Peace—after arrest a person aged 18 or over may be brought before a justice of the peace court to show cause why they should not be bound over to keep the peace—not criminal proceedings.*

1B Juveniles should not be arrested at their place of education unless this is unavoidable. When a juvenile is arrested at their place of education, the principal or their nominee must be informed. (From Code C Note 11D)

2 Facts and information relevant to a person's suspected involvement in an offence should not be confined to those which tend to indicate the person has committed or attempted to commit the offence. Before making a decision to arrest, a constable should take account of any facts and information that are available, including claims of innocence made by the person, that might dispel the suspicion.

2A Particular examples of facts and information which might point to a person's innocence and may tend to dispel suspicion include those which relate to the statutory defence provided by the Criminal Law Act 1967, section 3(1) which allows the use of reasonable force in the prevention of crime or making an arrest and the common law of self-defence. This may be relevant when a person appears, or claims, to have been acting reasonably in defence of themselves or others or to prevent their property or the property of others from being stolen, destroyed or damaged, particularly if the offence alleged is based on the use of unlawful force, e.g. a criminal assault. When investigating allegations involving the use of force by school staff, the power given to all school staff under the Education and Inspections Act 2006, section 93, to use reasonable force to prevent their pupils from committing any offence, injuring persons, damaging property or prejudicing the maintenance of good order and discipline may be similarly relevant. The Association of Chief Police Officers and the Crown Prosecution Service have published joint guidance to help the public understand the meaning of reasonable force and what to expect from the police and CPS in cases which involve claims of self defence. Separate advice for school staff on their powers to use reasonable force is available from the Department for Education

2B If a constable who is dealing with an allegation of crime and considering the need to arrest becomes an investigator for the purposes of the Code of Practice under the Criminal Procedure and Investigations Act 1996, the officer should, in accordance with paragraph 3.5 of that Code, 'pursue all reasonable lines of inquiry, whether these point towards or away from the suspect. What is reasonable in each case will depend on the particular circumstances.'

2C For a constable to have reasonable grounds for believing it necessary to arrest, he or she is not required to be satisfied that there is no viable alternative to arrest. However, it does mean that in all cases, the officer should consider that arrest is the practical, sensible and proportionate option in all the circumstances at the time the decision is made. This applies equally to a person in police detention after being arrested for an offence who is suspected of involvement in a further offence and the necessity to arrest them for that further offence is being considered.

2D Although a warning is not expressly required, officers should if practicable, consider whether a warning which points out their offending behaviour, and explains why, if they do not stop, the resulting consequences may make their arrest necessary. Such a warning might:

- *if heeded, avoid the need to arrest, or*
- *if it is ignored, support the need to arrest and also help prove the mental element of certain offences, for example, the person's intent or awareness, or help to rebut a defence that they were acting reasonably.*

A person who is warned that they may be liable to arrest if their real name and address cannot be ascertained, should be given a reasonable opportunity to establish their real name and address before deciding that either or both are unknown and cannot be readily ascertained or that there are reasonable grounds to doubt that a name and address they have given is their real name and address. They should be told why their name is not known and cannot be readily ascertained and (as the case may be) of the grounds for doubting that a name and address they have given is their real name and address, including, for example, the reason why a particular document the person has produced to verify their real name and/or address, is not sufficient.

2E The meaning of 'prompt' should be considered on a case by case basis taking account of all the circumstances. It indicates that the progress of the investigation should not be delayed to the extent that it would adversely affect the effectiveness of the investigation. The arresting officer also has discretion to release the arrested person on 'street bail' as an alternative to taking the person directly to the station. See Note 2J.

2F An officer who believes that it is necessary to interview the person suspected of committing the offence must then consider whether their arrest is necessary in order to carry out the interview. The officer is not required to interrogate the suspect to determine whether they will attend a police station voluntarily to be interviewed but they must consider whether the suspect's voluntary attendance is a practicable alternative for carrying out the interview. If it is, then arrest would not be necessary. Conversely, an officer who considers this option but is not satisfied that it is a practicable alternative, may have reasonable grounds for deciding that the arrest is necessary at the outset 'on the street'. Without such considerations, the officer would not be able to establish that arrest was necessary in order to interview.

Circumstances which suggest that a person's arrest 'on the street' would not be necessary to interview them might be where the officer:

- *is satisfied as to their identity and address and that they will attend the police station voluntarily to be interviewed, either immediately or by arrangement at a future date and time; and*
- *is not aware of any other circumstances which indicate that voluntary attendance would not be a practicable alternative. See paragraph 2.9(e)(i) to (v).*

When making arrangements for the person's voluntary attendance, the officer should tell the person:

- *that to properly investigate their suspected involvement in the offence they must be interviewed under caution at the police station, but in the circumstances their arrest for this purpose will not be necessary if they attend the police station voluntarily to be interviewed;*
- *that if they attend voluntarily, they will be entitled to free legal advice before, and to have a solicitor present at, the interview;*
- *that the date and time of the interview will take account of their circumstances and the needs of the investigation; and*
- *that if they do not agree to attend voluntarily at a time which meets the needs of the investigation, or having so agreed, fail to attend, or having attended, fail to remain for the interview to be completed, their arrest will be necessary to enable them to be interviewed.*

2G When the person attends the police station voluntarily for interview by arrangement as in Note 2F above, their arrest on arrival at the station prior to interview would only be justified if:

- *new information coming to light after the arrangements were made indicates that from that time, voluntary attendance ceased to be a practicable alternative and the person's arrest became necessary; and*
- *it was not reasonably practicable for the person to be arrested before they attended the station.*

If a person who attends the police station voluntarily to be interviewed decides to leave before the interview is complete, the police would at that point be entitled to consider whether their arrest was necessary to carry out the interview. The possibility that the person might decide to leave during the interview is therefore not a valid reason for arresting them before the interview has commenced. See Code C paragraph 3.21.

2H The necessity criteria do not permit arrest solely to enable the routine taking, checking (speculative searching) and retention of fingerprints, samples, footwear impressions and photographs when there are no prior grounds to believe that checking and comparing the fingerprints etc. or taking a photograph would provide relevant evidence of the person's involvement in the offence concerned or would help to ascertain or verify their real identity.

2I The necessity criteria do not permit arrest for an offence solely because it happens to be one of the statutory drug testing 'trigger offences' (see Code C Note 17E) when there is no suspicion that Class A drug misuse might have caused or contributed to the offence.

2J Having determined that the necessity criteria have been met and having made the arrest, the officer can then consider the use of street bail on the basis of the effective and efficient progress of the investigation of the offence in question. It gives the officer discretion to compel the person to attend a police station at a date/time that best suits the overall needs of the particular investigation. Its use is not confined to dealing with child care issues or allowing officers to attend to more urgent operational duties and granting street bail does not retrospectively negate the need to arrest.

3 An arrested person must be given sufficient information to enable them to understand they have been deprived of their liberty and the reason they have been arrested, as soon as practicable after the arrest, e.g. when a person is arrested on suspicion of committing an offence they must be informed of the nature of the suspected offence and when and where it was committed. The suspect must also be informed of the reason or reasons why arrest is considered necessary. Vague or technical language should be avoided. When explaining why one or more of the arrest criteria apply, it is not necessary to disclose any specific details that might undermine or otherwise adversely affect any investigative processes. An example might be the conduct of a formal interview when prior disclosure of such details might give the suspect an opportunity to fabricate an innocent explanation or to otherwise conceal lies from the interviewer.

4 Nothing in this Code requires a caution to be given or repeated when informing a person not under arrest they may be prosecuted for an offence. However, a court will not be able to draw any inferences under the Criminal Justice and Public Order Act 1994, section 34, if the person was not cautioned.

5 If it appears a person does not understand the caution, the person giving it should explain it in their own words.

6 Certain powers available as the result of an arrest—for example, entry and search of premises, detention without charge beyond 24 hours, holding a person incommunicado and delaying access to legal advice—only apply in respect of indictable offences and are subject to the specific requirements on authorisation as set out in PACE and the relevant Code of Practice.

Criminal Procedure and Investigations Act 1996: Code of Practice under Part II

Preamble

This code of practice is issued under Part II of the Criminal Procedure and Investigations Act 1996 ('the Act'). It sets out the manner in which police officers are to record, retain and reveal to the prosecutor material obtained in a criminal investigation and which may be relevant to the investigation, and related matters.

1. Introduction

1.1 This code of practice applies in respect of criminal investigations conducted by police officers which begin on or after the day on which this code comes into effect. Persons other than police officers who are charged with the duty of conducting an investigation as defined in the Act are to have regard to the relevant provisions of the code, and should take these into account in applying their own operating procedures.

1.2 This code does not apply to persons who are not charged with the duty of conducting an investigation as defined in the Act.

1.3 Nothing in this code applies to material intercepted in obedience to a warrant issued under section 2 of the Interception of Communications Act 1985 or section 5 of the Regulation of Investigatory Powers Act 2000, or to any copy of that material as defined in section 10 of the 1985 Act or section 15 of the 2000 Act.

1.4 This code extends only to England and Wales.

2. Definitions

2.1 In this code:

- *a criminal investigation* is an investigation conducted by police officers with a view to it being ascertained whether a person should be charged with an offence, or whether a person charged with an offence is guilty of it. This will include:

  - investigations into crimes that have been committed;
  - investigations whose purpose is to ascertain whether a crime has been committed, with a view to the possible institution of criminal proceedings; and
  - investigations which begin in the belief that a crime may be committed, for example when the police keep premises or individuals under observation for a period of time, with a view to the possible institution of criminal proceedings;
- charging a person with an offence includes prosecution by way of summons or postal requisition;
- *an investigator* is any police officer involved in the conduct of a criminal investigation. All investigators have a responsibility for carrying out the duties imposed on them under this code, including in particular recording information, and retaining records of information and other material;
- the *officer in charge of an investigation* is the police officer responsible for directing a criminal investigation. He is also responsible for ensuring that proper procedures are in place for recording information, and retaining records of information and other material, in the investigation;
- the *disclosure officer* is the person responsible for examining material retained by the police during the investigation; revealing material to the prosecutor during the investigation and any criminal proceedings resulting from it, and certifying that he has done this; and disclosing material to the accused at the request of the prosecutor;
- the *prosecutor* is the authority responsible for the conduct, on behalf of the Crown, of criminal proceedings resulting from a specific criminal investigation;
- *material* is material of any kind, including information and objects, which is obtained or inspected in the course of a criminal investigation and which may be relevant to the investigation. This includes not only material coming into the possession of the investigator (such as documents seized in the course of searching premises) but also material generated by him (such as interview records);
- material may be *relevant to an investigation* if it appears to an investigator, or to the officer in charge of an investigation, or to the disclosure officer, that it has some bearing on any offence under investigation or any person being investigated, or on the surrounding circumstances of the case, unless it is incapable of having any impact on the case;
- *sensitive material* is material, the disclosure of which, the disclosure officer believes, would give rise to a real risk of serious prejudice to an important public interest;
- references to *prosecution disclosure* are to the duty of the prosecutor under sections 3 and 7A of the Act to disclose material which is in his possession or which he has inspected in pursuance of this code, and which might reasonably be considered capable of undermining the case against the accused, or of assisting the case for the accused;
- references to the disclosure of material to a person accused of an offence include references to the disclosure of material to his legal representative;
- references to police officers and to the chief officer of police include those employed in a police force as defined in section 3(3) of the Prosecution of Offences Act 1985.

3. General responsibilities

3.1 The functions of the investigator, the officer in charge of an investigation and the disclosure officer are separate. Whether they are undertaken by one, two or more persons will depend on the complexity of the case and the administrative arrangements within each police force. Where they are undertaken by more than one person, close consultation between them is essential to the effective performance of the duties imposed by this code.

3.2 In any criminal investigation, one or more deputy disclosure officers may be appointed to assist the disclosure officer, and a deputy disclosure officer may perform any function of a disclosure officer as defined in paragraph 2.1.

3.3 The chief officer of police for each police force is responsible for putting in place arrangements to ensure that in every investigation the identity of the officer in charge of an investigation and the disclosure officer is recorded. The chief officer of police for each police force shall ensure that disclosure officers and deputy disclosure officers have sufficient skills and authority, commensurate with the complexity of the investigation, to discharge their functions effectively. An individual must not be appointed as disclosure officer, or continue in that role, if that is likely to result in a conflict of interest, for instance, if the disclosure officer is the victim of the alleged crime which is the subject of the investigation. The advice of a more senior officer must always be sought if there is doubt as to whether a conflict of interest precludes an individual acting as disclosure officer. If thereafter the doubt remains, the advice of a prosecutor should be sought.

3.4 The officer in charge of an investigation may delegate tasks to another investigator, to civilians employed by the police force, or to other persons participating in the investigation under arrangements for joint investigations, but he remains responsible for ensuring that these have been carried out and for accounting for any general policies followed in the investigation. In particular, it is an essential part of his duties to ensure that all material which may be relevant to an investigation is retained, and either made available to the disclosure officer or (in exceptional circumstances) revealed directly to the prosecutor.

3.5 In conducting an investigation, the investigator should pursue all reasonable lines of inquiry, whether these point towards or away from the suspect. What is reasonable in each case will depend on the particular circumstances. For example, where material is held on computer, it is a matter for the investigator to decide which material on the computer it is reasonable to inquire into, and in what manner.

3.6 If the officer in charge of an investigation believes that other persons may be in possession of material that may be relevant to the investigation, and if this has not been obtained under paragraph 3.5 above, he should ask the disclosure officer to inform them of the existence of the investigation and to invite them to retain the material in case they receive a request for its disclosure. The disclosure officer should inform the prosecutor that they may have such material. However, the officer in charge of an investigation is not required to make speculative enquiries of other persons; there must be some reason to believe that they may have relevant material. That reason may come from information provided to the police by the accused or from other inquiries made or from some other source.

3.7 If, during a criminal investigation, the officer in charge of an investigation or disclosure officer for any reason no longer has responsibility for the functions falling to him, either his supervisor or the police officer in charge of criminal investigations for the police force concerned must assign someone else to assume that responsibility. That person's identity must be recorded, as with those initially responsible for these functions in each investigation.

4. Recording of information

4.1 If material which may be relevant to the investigation consists of information which is not recorded in any form, the officer in charge of an investigation must ensure that it is recorded in a durable or retrievable form (whether in writing, on video or audio tape, or on computer disk).

4.2 Where it is not practicable to retain the initial record of information because it forms part of a larger record which is to be destroyed, its contents should be transferred as a true record to a durable and more easily-stored form before that happens.

4.3 Negative information is often relevant to an investigation. If it may be relevant it must be recorded. An example might be a number of people present in a particular place at a particular time who state that they saw nothing unusual.

4.4 Where information which may be relevant is obtained, it must be recorded at the time it is obtained or as soon as practicable after that time. This includes, for example, information obtained in house-to-house enquiries, although the requirement to record information promptly does not require an investigator to take a statement from a potential witness where it would not otherwise be taken.

5. Retention of material

(a) Duty to retain material

5.1 The investigator must retain material obtained in a criminal investigation which may be relevant to the investigation. Material may be photographed, video-recorded, captured digitally or otherwise retained in the form of a copy rather than the original at any time, if the original is perishable; the original was supplied to the investigator rather than generated by him and is to be returned to its owner; or the retention of a copy rather than the original is reasonable in all the circumstances.

5.2 Where material has been seized in the exercise of the powers of seizure conferred by the Police and Criminal Evidence Act 1984, the duty to retain it under this code is subject to the provisions on the retention of seized material in section 22 of that Act.

5.3 If the officer in charge of an investigation becomes aware as a result of developments in the case that material previously examined but not retained (because it was not thought to be relevant) may now be relevant to the investigation, he should, wherever practicable, take steps to obtain it or ensure that it is retained for further inspection or for production in court if required.

5.4 The duty to retain material includes in particular the duty to retain material falling into the following categories, where it may be relevant to the investigation:

- crime reports (including crime report forms, relevant parts of incident report books or police officers' notebooks);
- custody records;
- records which are derived from tapes of telephone messages (for example, 999 calls) containing descriptions of an alleged offence or offender;
- final versions of witness statements (and draft versions where their content differs from the final version), including any exhibits mentioned (unless these have been returned to their owner on the understanding that they will be produced in court if required);
- interview records (written records, or audio or video tapes, of interviews with actual or potential witnesses or suspects);
- communications between the police and experts such as forensic scientists, reports of work carried out by experts, and schedules of scientific material prepared by the expert for the investigator, for the purposes of criminal proceedings;
- records of the first description of a suspect by each potential witness who purports to identify or describe the suspect, whether or not the description differs from that of subsequent descriptions by that or other witnesses;
- any material casting doubt on the reliability of a witness.

5.5 The duty to retain material, where it may be relevant to the investigation, also includes in particular the duty to retain material which may satisfy the test for prosecution disclosure in the Act, such as:

- information provided by an accused person which indicates an explanation for the offence with which he has been charged;
- any material casting doubt on the reliability of a confession;
- any material casting doubt on the reliability of a prosecution witness.

5.6 The duty to retain material falling into these categories does not extend to items which are purely ancillary to such material and possess no independent significance (for example, duplicate copies of records or reports).

(b) Length of time for which material is to be retained

5.7 All material which may be relevant to the investigation must be retained until a decision is taken whether to institute proceedings against a person for an offence.

5.8 If a criminal investigation results in proceedings being instituted, all material which may be relevant must be retained at least until the accused is acquitted or convicted or the prosecutor decides not to proceed with the case.

5.9 Where the accused is convicted, all material which may be relevant must be retained at least until:

- the convicted person is released from custody, or discharged from hospital, in cases where the court imposes a custodial sentence or a hospital order;
- six months from the date of conviction, in all other cases.

If the court imposes a custodial sentence or hospital order and the convicted person is released from custody or discharged from hospital earlier than six months from the date of conviction, all material which may be relevant must be retained at least until six months from the date of conviction.

5.10 If an appeal against conviction is in progress when the release or discharge occurs, or at the end of the period of six months specified in paragraph 5.9, all material which may be relevant must be retained until the appeal is determined. Similarly, if the Criminal Cases Review Commission is considering an application at that point in time, all material which may be relevant must be retained at least until the Commission decides not to refer the case to the Court.

6. Preparation of material for prosecutor

(a) Introduction

6.1 The officer in charge of the investigation, the disclosure officer or an investigator may seek advice from the prosecutor about whether any particular item of material may be relevant to the investigation.

6.2 Material which may be relevant to an investigation, which has been retained in accordance with this code, and which the disclosure officer believes will not form part of the prosecution case, must be listed on a schedule. This process will differ depending on whether the case is likely to be heard in the magistrates' court or the Crown Court.

(b) Magistrates' Court

Anticipated Guilty pleas

6.3 If the accused is charged with a summary offence or an either-way offence that is likely to remain in the magistrates' court, and it is considered that he is likely to plead guilty (e.g. because he has admitted the offence), a schedule or streamlined disclosure certificate is not required. However, the Common Law duty to disclose material which may assist the defence at bail hearings or in the early preparation of their case remains, and where there is such material the certification on the Police Report (MG5/SDF) must be completed. Where there is no such material, a certificate to that effect must be completed in like form to that attached at the Annex.

6.4 If, contrary to the expectation of a guilty plea being entered, the accused pleads not guilty at the first hearing, the disclosure officer must ensure that the streamlined disclosure certificate is prepared and submitted as soon as is reasonably practicable after that happens.

Anticipated Not Guilty pleas

6.5 If the accused is charged with a summary offence or an either-way offence that is likely to remain in the magistrates' court, and it is considered that he is likely to plead not guilty, a streamlined disclosure certificate must be completed in like form to that attached at the Annex.

Material which may assist the defence

6.6 In every case, irrespective of the anticipated plea, if there is material known to the disclosure officer that might assist the defence with the early preparation of their case or at a bail hearing (for example, a key prosecution witness has relevant previous convictions or a witness has withdrawn his or her statement), a note must be made on the MG5 (or other format agreed under the National File Standards). The material must be disclosed to the prosecutor who will disclose it to the defence if he thinks it meets this Common Law test.

No undermining or assisting material and sensitive material—magistrates' court cases

6.7 If there is no material which might fall to be disclosed as undermining the prosecution case or assisting the defence, the officer should complete the appropriate entry on the streamlined disclosure certificate. If there is any sensitive unused material the officer should complete a sensitive material schedule (MG6D or similar) and attach it to the prosecution file. In exceptional circumstances, when its existence is so sensitive that it cannot be listed, it should be revealed to the prosecutor separately.

(c) Crown Court

6.8 For cases to be held in the Crown Court, the unused material schedules (MG6 series) are used.

6.9 The disclosure officer must ensure that a schedule is prepared in the following circumstances:

- the accused is charged with an offence which is triable only on indictment;
- the accused is charged with an offence which is triable either way, and it is considered that the case is likely to be tried on indictment.

6.10 Material which the disclosure officer does not believe is sensitive must be listed on a schedule of non-sensitive material. The schedule must include a statement that the disclosure officer does not believe the material is sensitive.

Way in which material is to be listed on schedule

6.11 For indictable only cases or either-way cases sent to the Crown Court, schedules MG6 C, D and E should be completed to facilitate service of the MG6C with the prosecution case, wherever possible. The disclosure officer should ensure that each item of material is listed separately on the schedule, and is numbered consecutively. The description of each item should make clear the nature of the item and should contain sufficient detail to enable the prosecutor to decide whether he needs to inspect the material before deciding whether or not it should be disclosed.

6.12 In some enquiries it may not be practicable to list each item of material separately. For example, there may be many items of a similar or repetitive nature. These may be listed in a block and described by quantity and generic title.

6.13 Even if some material is listed in a block, the disclosure officer must ensure that any items among that material which might satisfy the test for prosecution disclosure are listed and described individually.

(d) Sensitive material—Crown Court

6.14 Any material which is believed to be sensitive either must be listed on a schedule of sensitive material or, in exceptional circumstances where its existence is so sensitive that it cannot be listed, it should be revealed to the prosecutor separately. If there is no sensitive material, the disclosure officer must record this fact on a schedule of sensitive material, or otherwise so indicate.

6.15 Subject to paragraph 6.16 below, the disclosure officer must list on a sensitive schedule any material the disclosure of which he believes would give rise to a real risk of serious prejudice to an important public interest, and the reason for that belief. The schedule must include a statement that the disclosure officer believes the material is sensitive. Depending on the circumstances, examples of such material may include the following among others:

- material relating to national security;
- material received from the intelligence and security agencies;
- material relating to intelligence from foreign sources which reveals sensitive intelligence gathering methods;
- material given in confidence;
- material relating to the identity or activities of informants, or undercover police officers, or witnesses, or other persons supplying information to the police who may be in danger if their identities are revealed;
- material revealing the location of any premises or other place used for police surveillance, or the identity of any person allowing a police officer to use them for surveillance;
- material revealing, either directly or indirectly, techniques and methods relied upon by a police officer in the course of a criminal investigation, for example covert surveillance techniques, or other methods of detecting crime;
- material whose disclosure might facilitate the commission of other offences or hinder the prevention and detection of crime;
- material upon the strength of which search warrants were obtained;
- material containing details of persons taking part in identification parades;
- material supplied to an investigator during a criminal investigation which has been generated by an official of a body concerned with the regulation or supervision of bodies corporate or of persons engaged in financial activities, or which has been generated by a person retained by such a body;
- material supplied to an investigator during a criminal investigation which relates to a child or young person and which has been generated by a local authority social services department, an Area Child Protection Committee or other party contacted by an investigator during the investigation;
- material relating to the private life of a witness.

6.16 In exceptional circumstances, where an investigator considers that material is so sensitive that its revelation to the prosecutor by means of an entry on the sensitive schedule is inappropriate, the existence of the material must be revealed to the prosecutor separately. This will apply only where compromising the material would be likely to lead directly to the loss of life, or directly threaten national security.

6.17 In such circumstances, the responsibility for informing the prosecutor lies with the investigator who knows the detail of the sensitive material. The investigator should act as soon as is reasonably practicable after the file containing the prosecution case is sent to the prosecutor. The investigator must also ensure that the prosecutor is able to inspect the material so that he can assess whether it is disclosable and, if so, whether it needs to be brought before a court for a ruling on disclosure.

7. Revelation of material to prosecutor

7.1 Certain unused material must be disclosed to the accused at Common Law if it would assist the defence with the early preparation of their case or at a bail hearing. This material may consist of items such as a previous relevant conviction of a key prosecution witness or the withdrawal of support for the prosecution by a witness. This material must be revealed to the prosecutor for service on the defence with the initial details of the prosecution case.

7.1A In anticipated not guilty plea cases for hearing in the magistrates' court the disclosure officer must give the streamlined disclosure certificate to the prosecutor at the same time as he gives the prosecutor the file containing the material for the prosecution case.

7.1B In cases sent to the Crown Court, wherever possible, the disclosure officer should give the schedules concerning unused material to the prosecutor at the same time as the prosecution file in preparation for the first hearing and any case management that the judge may wish to conduct at that stage.

7.2 The disclosure officer should draw the attention of the prosecutor to any material an investigator has retained (including material to which paragraph 6.16 applies) which may satisfy the test for prosecution disclosure in the Act, and should explain why he has come to that view.

7.3 At the same time as complying with the duties in paragraphs 7.1 and 7.2, the disclosure officer must give the prosecutor a copy of any material which falls into the following categories (unless such material has already been given to the prosecutor as part of the file containing the material for the prosecution case):

- information provided by an accused person which indicates an explanation for the offence with which he has been charged;
- any material casting doubt on the reliability of a confession;
- any material casting doubt on the reliability of a prosecution witness;
- any other material which the investigator believes may satisfy the test for prosecution disclosure in the Act.

7.4 If the prosecutor asks to inspect material which has not already been copied to him, the disclosure officer must allow him to inspect it. If the prosecutor asks for a copy of material which has not already been copied to him, the disclosure officer must give him a copy. However, this does not apply where the disclosure officer believes, having consulted the officer in charge of the investigation, that the material is too sensitive to be copied and can only be inspected.

7.5 If material consists of information which is recorded other than in writing, whether it should be given to the prosecutor in its original form as a whole, or by way of relevant extracts recorded in the same form, or in the form of a transcript, is a matter for agreement between the disclosure officer and the prosecutor.

8. Subsequent action by disclosure officer

8.1 At the time when a streamlined disclosure certificate is prepared for magistrates' court cases, or a schedule of non-sensitive material is prepared for Crown Court cases, the disclosure officer may not know exactly what material will form the case against the accused. In addition, the prosecutor may not have given advice about the likely relevance of particular items of material. Once these matters have been determined, the disclosure officer must give the prosecutor, where necessary, an amended certificate or schedule listing any additional material:

- which may be relevant to the investigation,

- which does not form part of the case against the accused,
- which is not already listed on the schedule, and
- which he believes is not sensitive,

unless he is informed in writing by the prosecutor that the prosecutor intends to disclose the material to the defence.

8.2 Section 7A of the Act imposes a continuing duty on the prosecutor, for the duration of criminal proceedings against the accused, to disclose material which satisfies the test for disclosure (subject to public interest considerations). To enable him to do this, any new material coming to light should be treated in the same way as the earlier material.

8.3 In particular, after a defence statement has been given, or details of the issues in dispute have been recorded on the effective trial preparation form, the disclosure officer must look again at the material which has been retained and must draw the attention of the prosecutor to any material which might reasonably be considered capable of undermining the case for the prosecution against the accused or of assisting the case for the accused; and he must reveal it to him in accordance with paragraphs 7.4 and 7.5 above.

9. Certification by disclosure officer

9.1 The disclosure officer must certify to the prosecutor that, to the best of his knowledge and belief, all relevant material which has been retained and made available to him has been revealed to the prosecutor in accordance with this code. He must sign and date the certificate. It will be necessary to certify not only at the time when the schedule and accompanying material is submitted to the prosecutor, and when relevant material which has been retained is reconsidered after the accused has given a defence statement, but also whenever a schedule is otherwise given or material is otherwise revealed to the prosecutor.

10. Disclosure of material to accused

10.1 Other than early disclosure under Common Law, in the magistrates' court the streamlined certificate at the Annex (and any relevant unused material to be disclosed under it) must be disclosed to the accused either:

- at the hearing where a not guilty plea is entered, or
- as soon as possible following a formal indication from the accused or representative that a not guilty plea will be entered at the hearing.

10.1A If material has not already been copied to the prosecutor, and he requests its disclosure to the accused on the ground that:

- it satisfies the test for prosecution disclosure, **or**
- the court has ordered its disclosure after considering an application from the accused,

the disclosure officer must disclose it to the accused.

10.2 If material has been copied to the prosecutor, and it is to be disclosed, whether it is disclosed by the prosecutor or the disclosure officer is a matter of agreement between the two of them.

10.3 The disclosure officer must disclose material to the accused either by giving him a copy or by allowing him to inspect it. If the accused person asks for a copy of any material which he has been allowed to inspect, the disclosure officer must give it to him, unless in the opinion of the disclosure officer that is either not practicable (for example because the material consists of an object which cannot be copied, or because the volume of material is so great), or not desirable (for example because the material is a statement by a child witness in relation to a sexual offence).

10.4 If material which the accused has been allowed to inspect consists of information which is recorded other than in writing, whether it should be given to the accused in its original form or in the form of a transcript is a matter for the discretion of the disclosure officer. If the material is transcribed, the disclosure officer must ensure that the transcript is certified to the accused as a true record of the material which has been transcribed.

10.5 If a court concludes that an item of sensitive material satisfies the prosecution disclosure test and that the interests of the defence outweigh the public interest in withholding disclosure, it will be necessary to disclose the material if the case is to proceed. This does not mean that sensitive documents must always be disclosed in their original form: for example, the court may agree that sensitive details still requiring protection should be blocked out, or that documents may be summarised, or that the prosecutor may make an admission about the substance of the material under section 10 of the Criminal Justice Act 1967.

ANNEX

1. FOR USE IN GAP CASES AT 1ST HEARING WHERE THERE IS NOTHING TO DISCLOSE PURSUANT TO R v DPP *ex parte* LEE

URN: **Defendant:** First Name Last Name

Reporting Officer's Certification
In accordance with Common Law I certify that to the best of my knowledge and belief there is no relevant unused material that might reasonably assist the defence with the early preparation of their case or at a bail hearing.
Reporting Officer Name
SIGNATURE
Date

2. FOR USE IN ALL NGAP CASES AT 1ST HEARING WHERE THERE IS NOTHING TO DISCLOSE

URN: **Defendant:** First Name Last Name

	SCHEDULE OF NON-SENSITIVE UNUSED MATERIAL—NOT FOR DISCLOSURE	
No.	Police use (Brief description of materials)	CPS use
1		Having applied the disclosure tests set out in the CPIA 1996, I am satisfied from the descriptions listed in this schedule that the items in question are clearly not disclosable.
2		
3		
4		
5		
6		
7		
8		
9		
10		

Disclosure Officer's Certification I certify— • that any relevant unused material has been recorded and retained in accordance with the CPIA 1996 Code of Practice (as amended), • that such material as is non-sensitive is shown on the schedule above, • and that to the best of my knowledge and belief there are no items shown in the schedule that might reasonably undermine the prosecution case, or, so far as it is apparent, assist the defence with the early preparation of their case or at a bail hearing. Disclosure Officer Name SIGNATURE:	 CPS Prosecutor Name SIGNATURE:
Date	Date

3. FOR USE IN ALL NGAP CASES AT 1ST HEARING WHERE THERE ARE SOME ITEMS TO DISCLOSE

URN: **Defendant:** First Name Last Name

SCHEDULE OF NON-SENSITIVE UNUSED MATERIAL		
No.	Police use	CPS use
	(Brief description of materials including those falling under para.7.3 of the Code)	(Against each item insert **D** for disclose; **I** for inspect; **CND** for clearly not disclosable)
1		
2		
3		
4		
5		
6		
7		
8		
9		
10		

Disclosure Officer's Certification I certify— • that any relevant unused material has been recorded and retained in accordance with the CPIA 1996 Code of Practice (as amended) • that such material as is non-sensitive is shown on the schedule above, • and that to the best of my knowledge and belief items …

in the schedule might reasonably undermine the prosecution case, or assist the defence with the early preparation of their case or at a bail hearing, because ...

Disclosure Officer Name	CPS Prosecutor Name
SIGNATURE:	SIGNATURE:
Date	Date

Criminal Procedure Rules 2015

(SI 2015, No. 1490)

PART 16 WITNESS STATEMENTS

16.1. When this Part applies

This Part applies where a party wants to introduce a written witness statement in evidence under section 9 of the Criminal Justice Act 1967.

16.2. Content of written witness statement

The statement must contain—

(a) at the beginning—

(i) the witness' name, and

(ii) the witness' age, if under 18;

(b) a declaration by the witness that—

(i) it is true to the best of the witness' knowledge and belief, and

(ii) the witness knows that if it is introduced in evidence, then it would be an offence wilfully to have stated in it anything that the witness knew to be false or did not believe to be true;

(c) if the witness cannot read the statement, a signed declaration by someone else that that person read it to the witness; and

(d) the witness' signature.

16.3. Reference to exhibit

Where the statement refers to a document or object as an exhibit—

(a) the statement must contain such a description of that exhibit as to identify it clearly; and

(b) the exhibit must be labelled or marked correspondingly, and the label or mark signed by the maker of the statement.

16.4. Written witness statement in evidence

(1) A party who wants to introduce in evidence a written witness statement must—

(a) before the hearing at which that party wants to introduce it, serve a copy of the statement on—

(i) the court officer, and

(ii) each other party; and

(b) at or before that hearing, serve on the court officer the statement or an authenticated copy.

(2) If that party relies on only part of the statement, that party must mark the copy in such a way as to make that clear.

(3) A prosecutor must serve on a defendant, with the copy of the statement, a notice—

(a) of the right to object to the introduction of the statement in evidence instead of the witness giving evidence in person;

(b) of the time limit for objecting under this rule; and

(c) that if the defendant does not object in time, the court—
 (i) can nonetheless require the witness to give evidence in person, but
 (ii) may decide not to do so.

(4) A party served with a written witness statement who objects to its introduction in evidence must—
(a) serve notice of the objection on—
 (i) the party who served it, and
 (ii) the court officer; and
(b) serve the notice of objection not more than 7 days after service of the statement unless—
 (i) the court extends that time limit, before or after the statement was served,
 (ii) rule 24.8 (Written guilty plea: special rules) applies, in which case the time limit is the later of 7 days after service of the statement or 7 days before the hearing date, or
 (iii) rule 24.9 (Single justice procedure: special rules) applies, in which case the time limit is 21 days after service of the statement.

(5) The court may exercise its power to require the witness to give evidence in person—
(a) on application by any party; or
(b) on its own initiative.

(6) A party entitled to receive a copy of a statement may waive that entitlement by so informing—
(a) the party who would have served it; and
(b) the court.

PART 17 WITNESS SUMMONSES, WARRANTS AND ORDERS

17.1. When this Part applies

(1) This Part applies in magistrates' courts and in the Crown Court where—
(a) a party wants the court to issue a witness summons, warrant or order under—
 (i) section 97 of the Magistrates' Courts Act 1980,
 (ii) paragraph 4 of Schedule 3 to the Crime and Disorder Act 1998,
 (iii) section 2 of the Criminal Procedure (Attendance of Witnesses) Act 1965, or
 (iv) section 7 of the Bankers' Books Evidence Act 1879;
(b) the court considers the issue of such a summons, warrant or order on its own initiative as if a party had applied; or
(c) one of those listed in rule 17.7 wants the court to withdraw such a summons, warrant or order.

(2) A reference to a 'witness' in this Part is a reference to a person to whom such a summons, warrant or order is directed.

17.2. Issue etc. of summons, warrant or order with or without a hearing

(1) The court may issue or withdraw a witness summons, warrant or order with or without a hearing.

(2) A hearing under this Part must be in private unless the court otherwise directs.

17.3. Application for summons, warrant or order: general rules

(1) A party who wants the court to issue a witness summons, warrant or order must apply as soon as practicable after becoming aware of the grounds for doing so.

(2) A party applying for a witness summons or order must—

(a) identify the proposed witness;
(b) explain—
(i) what evidence the proposed witness can give or produce,
(ii) why it is likely to be material evidence, and
(iii) why it would be in the interests of justice to issue a summons, order or warrant as appropriate.

(3) A party applying for an order to be allowed to inspect and copy an entry in bank records must—
(a) identify the entry;
(b) explain the purpose for which the entry is required; and
(c) propose—
(i) the terms of the order, and
(ii) the period within which the order should take effect, if 3 days from the date of service of the order would not be appropriate.

(4) The application may be made orally unless—
(a) rule 17.5 applies; or
(b) the court otherwise directs.

(5) The applicant must serve any order made on the witness to whom, or the bank to which, it is directed.

17.4. Written application: form and service

(1) An application in writing under rule 17.3 must be in the form set out in the Practice Direction, containing the same declaration of truth as a witness statement.

(2) The party applying must serve the application—
(a) in every case, on the court officer and as directed by the court; and
(b) as required by rule 17.5, if that rule applies.

17.5. Application for summons to produce a document, etc.: special rules

(1) This rule applies to an application under rule 17.3 for a witness summons requiring the proposed witness—
(a) to produce in evidence a document or thing; or
(b) to give evidence about information apparently held in confidence, that relates to another person.

(2) The application must be in writing in the form required by rule 17.4.

(3) The party applying must serve the application—
(a) on the proposed witness, unless the court otherwise directs; and
(b) on one or more of the following, if the court so directs—
(i) a person to whom the proposed evidence relates,
(ii) another party.

(4) The court must not issue a witness summons where this rule applies unless—
(a) everyone served with the application has had at least 14 days in which to make representations, including representations about whether there should be a hearing of the application before the summons is issued; and
(b) the court is satisfied that it has been able to take adequate account of the duties and rights, including rights of confidentiality, of the proposed witness and of any person to whom the proposed evidence relates.

(5) This rule does not apply to an application for an order to produce in evidence a copy of an entry in bank records.

17.6. Application for summons to produce a document, etc.: court's assessment of relevance and confidentiality

(1) This rule applies where a person served with an application for a witness summons requiring the proposed witness to produce in evidence a document or thing objects to its production on the ground that—

(a) it is not likely to be material evidence; or

(b) even if it is likely to be material evidence, the duties or rights, including rights of confidentiality, of the proposed witness or of any person to whom the document or thing relates, outweigh the reasons for issuing a summons.

(2) The court may require the proposed witness to make the document or thing available for the objection to be assessed.

(3) The court may invite—

(a) the proposed witness or any representative of the proposed witness; or

(b) a person to whom the document or thing relates or any representative of such a person,

to help the court assess the objection.

17.7. Application to withdraw a summons, warrant or order

(1) The court may withdraw a witness summons, warrant or order if one of the following applies for it to be withdrawn—

(a) the party who applied for it, on the ground that it no longer is needed;

(b) the witness, on the grounds that—

(i) he was not aware of any application for it, and

(ii) he cannot give or produce evidence likely to be material evidence, or

(iii) even if he can, his duties or rights, including rights of confidentiality, or those of any person to whom the evidence relates, outweigh the reasons for the issue of the summons, warrant or order; or

(c) any person to whom the proposed evidence relates, on the grounds that—

(i) he was not aware of any application for it, and

(ii) that evidence is not likely to be material evidence, or

(iii) even if it is, his duties or rights, including rights of confidentiality, or those of the witness, outweigh the reasons for the issue of the summons, warrant or order.

(2) A person applying under the rule must—

(a) apply in writing as soon as practicable after becoming aware of the grounds for doing so, explaining why he wants the summons, warrant or order to be withdrawn; and

(b) serve the application on the court officer and as appropriate on—

(i) the witness,

(ii) the party who applied for the summons, warrant or order, and

(iii) any other person who he knows was served with the application for the summons, warrant or order.

(3) Rule 17.6 applies to an application under this rule that concerns a document or thing to be produced in evidence.

17.8. Court's power to vary requirements under this Part

(1) The court may—

(a) shorten or extend (even after it has expired) a time limit under this Part; and

(b) where a rule or direction requires an application under this Part to be in writing, allow that application to be made orally instead.

(2) Someone who wants the court to allow an application to be made orally under paragraph (1)(b) of this rule must—

(a) give as much notice as the urgency of his application permits to those on whom he would otherwise have served an application in writing; and

(b) in doing so explain the reasons for the application and for wanting the court to consider it orally.

PART 18 MEASURES TO ASSIST A WITNESS OR DEFENDANT TO GIVE EVIDENCE

GENERAL RULES

18.1. When this Part applies

This Part applies—

(a) where the court can give a direction (a 'special measures direction'), under section 19 of the Youth Justice and Criminal Evidence Act 1999, on an application or on its own initiative, for any of the following measures—
  (i) preventing a witness from seeing the defendant (section 23 of the 1999 Act),
  (ii) allowing a witness to give evidence by live link (section 24 of the 1999 Act),
  (iii) hearing a witness' evidence in private (section 25 of the 1999 Act),
  (iv) dispensing with the wearing of wigs and gowns (section 26 of the 1999 Act),
  (v) admitting video recorded evidence (sections 27 and 28 of the 1999 Act),
  (vi) questioning a witness through an intermediary (section 29 of the 1999 Act),
  (vii) using a device to help a witness communicate (section 30 of the 1999 Act);

(b) where the court can vary or discharge such a direction, under section 20 of the 1999 Act;

18.2. Meaning of 'witness'

In this Part, 'witness' means anyone (other than a defendant) for whose benefit an application, direction or order is made.

18.3. Making an application for a direction or order

A party who wants the court to exercise its power to give or make a direction or order must—

(a) apply in writing as soon as reasonably practicable, and in any event not more than—
  (i) 28 days after the defendant pleads not guilty, in a magistrates' court, or
  (ii) 14 days after the defendant pleads not guilty, in the Crown Court; and

(b) serve the application on—
  (i) the court officer, and
  (ii) each other party.

18.4. Decisions and reasons

(1) A party who wants to introduce the evidence of a witness who is the subject of an application, direction or order must—

(a) inform the witness of the court's decision as soon as reasonably practicable; and

(b) explain to the witness the arrangements that as a result will be made for him or her to give evidence.

(2) The court must announce, at a hearing in public before the witness gives evidence, the reasons for a decision—

(a) to give, make, vary or discharge a direction or order; or

(b) to refuse to do so.

18.5. Court's power to vary requirements under this Part

(1) The court may—

(a) shorten or extend (even after it has expired) a time limit under this Part; and

(b) allow an application or representations to be made in a different form to one set out in the Practice Direction, or to be made orally.

(2) A person who wants an extension of time must—

(a) apply when serving the application or representations for which it is needed; and

(b) explain the delay.

18.6. Custody of documents

Unless the court otherwise directs, the court officer may—

(a) keep a written application or representations; or

(b) arrange for the whole or any part to be kept by some other appropriate person, subject to any conditions that the court may impose.

18.7. Declaration by intermediary

(1) This rule applies where—

(a) a video recorded interview with a witness is conducted through an intermediary;

(b) the court directs the examination of a witness or defendant through an intermediary.

(2) An intermediary must make a declaration—

(a) before such an interview begins;

(b) before the examination begins (even if such an interview with the witness was conducted through the same intermediary).

(3) The declaration must be in these terms—

'I solemnly, sincerely and truly declare [*or* I swear by Almighty God] that I will well and faithfully communicate questions and answers and make true explanation of all matters and things as shall be required of me according to the best of my skill and understanding.'

SPECIAL MEASURES DIRECTIONS

18.8. Exercise of court's powers

The court may decide whether to give, vary or discharge a special measures direction—

(a) at a hearing, in public or in private, or without a hearing;

(b) in a party's absence, if that party—

(i) applied for the direction, variation or discharge, or

(ii) has had at least 14 days in which to make representations.

18.9. Special measures direction for a young witness

(1) This rule applies where, under section 21 or section 22 of the Youth Justice and Criminal Evidence Act 1999, the primary rule requires the court to give a direction for a special measure to assist a child witness or a qualifying witness—

(a) on an application, if one is made; or

(b) on the court's own initiative, in any other case.

(2) A party who wants to introduce the evidence of such a witness must as soon as reasonably practicable—

(a) notify the court that the witness is eligible for assistance;

(b) provide the court with any information that the court may need to assess the witness' views, if the witness does not want the primary rule to apply; and

(c) serve any video recorded evidence on—

(i) the court officer, and

(ii) each other party.

18.10. Content of application for a special measures direction

An applicant for a special measures direction must—

(a) explain how the witness is eligible for assistance;

(b) explain why special measures would be likely to improve the quality of the witness' evidence;

(c) propose the measure or measures that in the applicant's opinion would be likely to maximise, so far as practicable, the quality of that evidence;

(d) report any views that the witness has expressed about—

(i) his or her eligibility for assistance,

(ii) the likelihood that special measures would improve the quality of his or her evidence, and

(iii) the measure or measures proposed by the applicant;

(e) in a case in which a child witness or a qualifying witness does not want the primary rule to apply, provide any information that the court may need to assess the witness' views;

(f) in a case in which the applicant proposes that the witness should give evidence by live link—

(i) identify someone to accompany the witness while the witness gives evidence,

(ii) name that person, if possible, and

(iii) explain why that person would be an appropriate companion for the witness, including the witness' own views;

(g) in a case in which the applicant proposes the admission of video recorded evidence, identify—

(i) the date and duration of the recording,

(ii) which part the applicant wants the court to admit as evidence, if the applicant does not want the court to admit all of it;

(h) attach any other material on which the applicant relies; and

(i) if the applicant wants a hearing, ask for one, and explain why it is needed.

18.11. Application to vary or discharge a special measures direction

(1) A party who wants the court to vary or discharge a special measures direction must—

(a) apply in writing, as soon as reasonably practicable after becoming aware of the grounds for doing so; and

(b) serve the application on—

(i) the court officer, and

(ii) each other party.

(2) The applicant must—

(a) explain what material circumstances have changed since the direction was given (or last varied, if applicable);

(b) explain why the direction should be varied or discharged; and

(c) ask for a hearing, if the applicant wants one, and explain why it is needed.

18.12. Application containing information withheld from another party

(1) This rule applies where—

(a) an applicant serves an application for a special measures direction, or for its variation or discharge; and

(b) the application includes information that the applicant thinks ought not be revealed to another party.

(2) The applicant must—

(a) omit that information from the part of the application that is served on that other party;

(b) mark the other part to show that, unless the court otherwise directs, it is only for the court; and

(c) in that other part, explain why the applicant has withheld that information from that other party.

(3) Any hearing of an application to which this rule applies—

(a) must be in private, unless the court otherwise directs; and

(b) if the court so directs, may be, wholly or in part, in the absence of a party from whom information has been withheld.

(4) At any hearing of an application to which this rule applies—

(a) the general rule is that the court must consider, in the following sequence—

(i) representations first by the applicant and then by each other party, in all the parties' presence, and then

(ii) further representations by the applicant, in the absence of a party from whom information has been withheld; but

(b) the court may direct other arrangements for the hearing.

18.13. Representations in response

(1) This rule applies where a party wants to make representations about—

(a) an application for a special measures direction;

(b) an application for the variation or discharge of such a direction; or

(c) a direction, variation or discharge that the court proposes on its own initiative.

(2) Such a party must—

(a) serve the representations on—

(i) the court officer, and

(ii) each other party;

(b) do so not more than 14 days after, as applicable—

(i) service of the application, or

(ii) notice of the direction, variation or discharge that the court proposes; and

(c) ask for a hearing, if that party wants one, and explain why it is needed.

(3) Where representations include information that the person making them thinks ought not be revealed to another party, that person must—

(a) omit that information from the representations served on that other party;

(b) mark the information to show that, unless the court otherwise directs, it is only for the court; and

(c) with that information include an explanation of why it has been withheld from that other party.

(4) Representations against a special measures direction must explain, as appropriate—

(a) why the witness is not eligible for assistance;

(b) if the witness is eligible for assistance, why—

(i) no special measure would be likely to improve the quality of the witness' evidence,

(ii) the proposed measure or measures would not be likely to maximise, so far as practicable, the quality of the witness' evidence, or

(iii) the proposed measure or measures might tend to inhibit the effective testing of that evidence;

(c) in a case in which the admission of video recorded evidence is proposed, why it would not be in the interests of justice for the recording, or part of it, to be admitted as evidence.

(5) Representations against the variation or discharge of a special measures direction must explain why it should not be varied or discharged.

DEFENDANT'S EVIDENCE DIRECTIONS

18.14. Exercise of court's powers

The court may decide whether to give, vary or discharge a defendant's evidence direction—

(a) at a hearing, in public or in private, or without a hearing;

(b) in a party's absence, if that party—

(i) applied for the direction, variation or discharge, or

(ii) has had at least 14 days in which to make representations.

18.15. Content of application for a defendant's evidence direction

An applicant for a defendant's evidence direction must—

(a) explain how the proposed direction meets the conditions prescribed by the Youth Justice and Criminal Evidence Act 1999;

(b) in a case in which the applicant proposes that the defendant give evidence by live link—

(i) identify a person to accompany the defendant while the defendant gives evidence, and
(ii) explain why that person is appropriate;
(c) ask for a hearing, if the applicant wants one, and explain why it is needed.

18.16. Application to vary or discharge a defendant's evidence direction

(1) A party who wants the court to vary or discharge a defendant's evidence direction must—
(a) apply in writing, as soon as reasonably practicable after becoming aware of the grounds for doing so; and
(b) serve the application on—
(i) the court officer, and
(ii) each other party.
(2) The applicant must—
(a) on an application to discharge a live link direction, explain why it is in the interests of justice to do so;
(b) on an application to discharge a direction for an intermediary, explain why it is no longer necessary in order to ensure that the defendant receives a fair trial;
(c) on an application to vary a direction for an intermediary, explain why it is necessary for the direction to be varied in order to ensure that the defendant receives a fair trial; and
(d) ask for a hearing, if the applicant wants one, and explain why it is needed.

18.17. Representations in response

(1) This rule applies where a party wants to make representations about—
(a) an application for a defendant's evidence direction;
(b) an application for the variation or discharge of such a direction; or
(c) a direction, variation or discharge that the court proposes on its own initiative.
(2) Such a party must—
(a) serve the representations on—
(i) the court officer, and
(ii) each other party;
(b) do so not more than 14 days after, as applicable—
(i) service of the application, or
(ii) notice of the direction, variation or discharge that the court proposes; and
(c) ask for a hearing, if that party wants one, and explain why it is needed.

(3) Representations against a direction, variation or discharge must explain why the conditions prescribed by the Youth Justice and Criminal Evidence Act 1999 are not met.

WITNESS ANONYMITY ORDERS

18.18. Exercise of court's powers

(1) The court may decide whether to make, vary or discharge a witness anonymity order—
(a) at a hearing (which must be in private, unless the court otherwise directs), or without a hearing (unless any party asks for one);
(b) in the absence of a defendant.

(2) The court must not exercise its power to make, vary or discharge a witness anonymity order, or to refuse to do so—
(a) before or during the trial, unless each party has had an opportunity to make representations;
(b) on an appeal by the defendant to which applies Part 34 (Appeal to the Crown Court) or Part 39 (Appeal to the Court of Appeal about conviction or sentence), unless in each party's case—
(i) that party has had an opportunity to make representations, or

(ii) the appeal court is satisfied that it is not reasonably practicable to communicate with that party;

(c) after the trial and any such appeal are over, unless in the case of each party and the witness—

(i) each has had an opportunity to make representations, or

(ii) the court is satisfied that it is not reasonably practicable to communicate with that party or witness.

18.19. Content and conduct of application for a witness anonymity order

(1) An applicant for a witness anonymity order must—

(a) include in the application nothing that might reveal the witness' identity;

(b) describe the measures proposed by the applicant;

(c) explain how the proposed order meets the conditions prescribed by section 88 of the Coroners and Justice Act 2009;

(d) explain why no measures other than those proposed will suffice, such as—

(i) an admission of the facts that would be proved by the witness,

(ii) an order restricting public access to the trial,

(iii) reporting restrictions, in particular under sections 45, 45A or 46 of the Youth Justice and Criminal Evidence Act 1999,

(iv) a direction for a special measure under section 19 of the Youth Justice and Criminal Evidence Act 1999,

(v) introduction of the witness' written statement as hearsay evidence, under section 116 of the Criminal Justice Act 2003, or

(vi) arrangements for the protection of the witness;

(e) attach to the application—

(i) a witness statement setting out the proposed evidence, edited in such a way as not to reveal the witness' identity,

(ii) where the prosecutor is the applicant, any further prosecution evidence to be served, and any further prosecution material to be disclosed under the Criminal Procedure and Investigations Act 1996, similarly edited, and

(iii) any defence statement that has been served, or as much information as may be available to the applicant that gives particulars of the defence; and

(f) ask for a hearing, if the applicant wants one.

(2) At any hearing of the application, the applicant must—

(a) identify the witness to the court, unless at the prosecutor's request the court otherwise directs; and

(b) present to the court, unless it otherwise directs—

(i) the unedited witness statement from which the edited version has been prepared,

(ii) where the prosecutor is the applicant, the unedited version of any further prosecution evidence or material from which an edited version has been prepared, and

(iii) such further material as the applicant relies on to establish that the proposed order meets the conditions prescribed by section 88 of the 2009 Act.

(3) At any such hearing—

(a) the general rule is that the court must consider, in the following sequence—

(i) representations first by the applicant and then by each other party, in all the parties' presence, and then

(ii) information withheld from a defendant, and further representations by the applicant, in the absence of any (or any other) defendant; but

(b) the court may direct other arrangements for the hearing.

(4) Before the witness gives evidence, the applicant must identify the witness to the court—

(a) if not already done;

(b) without revealing the witness' identity to any other party or person; and
(c) unless at the prosecutor's request the court otherwise directs.

18.20. Duty of court officer to notify the Director of Public Prosecutions

The court officer must notify the Director of Public Prosecutions of an application, unless the prosecutor is, or acts on behalf of, a public authority.

18.21. Application to vary or discharge a witness anonymity order

(1) A party who wants the court to vary or discharge a witness anonymity order, or a witness who wants the court to do so when the case is over, must—
(a) apply in writing, as soon as reasonably practicable after becoming aware of the grounds for doing so; and
(b) serve the application on—
(i) the court officer, and
(ii) each other party.

(2) The applicant must—
(a) explain what material circumstances have changed since the order was made (or last varied, if applicable);
(b) explain why the order should be varied or discharged, taking account of the conditions for making an order; and
(c) ask for a hearing, if the applicant wants one.

(3) Where an application includes information that the applicant thinks might reveal the witness' identity, the applicant must—
(a) omit that information from the application that is served on a defendant;
(b) mark the information to show that it is only for the court and the prosecutor (if the prosecutor is not the applicant); and
(c) with that information include an explanation of why it has been withheld.

(4) Where a party applies to vary or discharge a witness anonymity order after the trial and any appeal are over, the party who introduced the witness' evidence must serve the application on the witness.

18.22. Representations in response

(1) This rule applies where a party or, where the case is over, a witness, wants to make representations about—
(a) an application for a witness anonymity order;
(b) an application for the variation or discharge of such an order; or
(c) a variation or discharge that the court proposes on its own initiative.

(2) Such a party or witness must—
(a) serve the representations on—
(i) the court officer, and
(ii) each other party;
(b) do so not more than 14 days after, as applicable—
(i) service of the application, or
(ii) notice of the variation or discharge that the court proposes; and
(c) ask for a hearing, if that party or witness wants one.

(3) Where representations include information that the person making them thinks might reveal the witness' identity, that person must—
(a) omit that information from the representations served on a defendant;
(b) mark the information to show that it is only for the court (and for the prosecutor, if relevant); and
(c) with that information include an explanation of why it has been withheld.

(4) Representations against a witness anonymity order must explain why the conditions for making the order are not met.

(5) Representations against the variation or discharge of such an order must explain why it would not be appropriate to vary or discharge it, taking account of the conditions for making an order.

(6) A prosecutor's representations in response to an application by a defendant must include all information available to the prosecutor that is relevant to the conditions and considerations specified by sections 88 and 89 of the Coroners and Justice Act 2009.

LIVE LINK DIRECTIONS

18.23. Exercise of court's powers

The court may decide whether to give or discharge a live link direction—

(a) at a hearing, in public or in private, or without a hearing;
(b) in a party's absence, if that party—
  (i) applied for the direction or discharge, or
  (ii) has had at least 14 days in which to make representations in response to an application by another party.

18.24. Content of application for a live link direction

An applicant for a live link direction must—

(a) unless the court otherwise directs, identify the place from which the witness will give evidence;
(b) if that place is in the United Kingdom, explain why it would be in the interests of the efficient or effective administration of justice for the witness to give evidence by live link;
(c) if the applicant wants the witness to be accompanied by another person while giving evidence—
  (i) name that person, if possible, and
  (ii) explain why it is appropriate for the witness to be accompanied;
(d) ask for a hearing, if the applicant wants one, and explain why it is needed.

18.25. Application to discharge a live link direction

(1) A party who wants the court to discharge a live link direction must—
  (a) apply in writing, as soon as reasonably practicable after becoming aware of the grounds for doing so; and
  (b) serve the application on—
    (i) the court officer, and
    (ii) each other party.

(2) The applicant must—
  (a) explain what material circumstances have changed since the direction was given;
  (b) explain why it is in the interests of justice to discharge the direction; and
  (c) ask for a hearing, if the applicant wants one, and explain why it is needed.

18.26. Representations in response

(1) This rule applies where a party wants to make representations about an application for a live link direction or for the discharge of such a direction.

(2) Such a party must—
  (a) serve the representations on—
    (i) the court officer, and
    (ii) each other party;
  (b) do so not more than 14 days after service of the application; and—
  (c) ask for a hearing, if that party wants one, and explain why it is needed.

(3) Representations against a direction or discharge must explain, as applicable, why the conditions prescribed by the Criminal Justice Act 1988 or the Criminal Justice Act 2003 are not met.

PART 19 EXPERT EVIDENCE

19.1. When this Part applies

(1) This Part applies where a party wants to introduce expert opinion evidence.

(2) A reference to an 'expert' in this Part is a reference to a person who is required to give or prepare expert evidence for the purpose of criminal proceedings, including evidence required to determine fitness to plead or for the purpose of sentencing.

19.2. Expert's duty to the court

(1) An expert must help the court to achieve the overriding objective—

(a) by giving opinion which is—

(i) objective and unbiased, and

(ii) within the expert's area or areas of expertise; and

(b) by actively assisting the court in fulfilling its duty of case management under rule 3.2, in particular by—

(i) complying with directions made by the court, and

(ii) at once informing the court of any significant failure (by the expert or another) to take any step required by such a direction.

(2) This duty overrides any obligation to the person from whom the expert receives instructions or by whom the expert is paid.

(3) This duty includes obligations—

(a) to define the expert's area or areas of expertise—

(i) in the expert's report, and

(ii) when giving evidence in person;

(b) when giving evidence in person, to draw the court's attention to any question to which the answer would be outside the expert's area or areas of expertise; and

(c) to inform all parties and the court if the expert's opinion changes from that contained in a report served as evidence or given in a statement.

19.3. Introduction of expert evidence

(1) A party who wants another party to admit as fact a summary of an expert's conclusions must serve that summary—

(a) on the court officer and on each party from whom that admission is sought;

(b) as soon as practicable after the defendant whom it affects pleads not guilty.

(2) A party on whom such a summary is served must—

(a) serve a response stating—

(i) which, if any, of the expert's conclusions are admitted as fact, and

(ii) where a conclusion is not admitted, what are the disputed issues concerning that conclusion; and

(b) serve the response—

(i) on the court officer and on the party who served the summary,

(ii) as soon as practicable, and in any event not more than 14 days after service of the summary.

(3) A party who wants to introduce expert evidence otherwise than as admitted fact must—

(a) serve a report by the expert which complies with rule 19.4 (Content of expert's report) on—

(i) the court officer, and

(ii) each other party;

(b) serve the report as soon as practicable, and in any event with any application in support of which that party relies on that evidence;

(c) serve with the report notice of anything of which the party serving it is aware which might reasonably be thought capable of detracting substantially from the credibility of that expert;

(d) if another party so requires, give that party a copy of, or a reasonable opportunity to inspect—
   (i) a record of any examination, measurement, test or experiment on which the expert's findings and opinion are based, or that were carried out in the course of reaching those findings and opinion, and
   (ii) anything on which any such examination, measurement, test or experiment was carried out.

(4) Unless the parties otherwise agree or the court directs, a party may not—
(a) introduce expert evidence if that party has not complied with paragraph (3);
(b) introduce in evidence an expert report if the expert does not give evidence in person.

19.4. Content of expert's report

Where rule 19.3(3) applies, an expert's report must—
(a) give details of the expert's qualifications, relevant experience and accreditation;
(b) give details of any literature or other information which the expert has relied on in making the report;
(c) contain a statement setting out the substance of all facts given to the expert which are material to the opinions expressed in the report, or upon which those opinions are based;
(d) make clear which of the facts stated in the report are within the expert's own knowledge;
(e) where the expert has based an opinion or inference on a representation of fact or opinion made by another person for the purposes of criminal proceedings (for example, as to the outcome of an examination, measurement, test or experiment)—
   (i) identify the person who made that representation to the expert,
   (ii) give the qualifications, relevant experience and any accreditation of that person, and
   (iii) certify that that person had personal knowledge of the matters stated in that representation;
(f) where there is a range of opinion on the matters dealt with in the report—
   (i) summarise the range of opinion, and
   (ii) give reasons for the expert's own opinion;
(g) if the expert is not able to give an opinion without qualification, state the qualification;
(h) include such information as the court may need to decide whether the expert's opinion is sufficiently reliable to be admissible as evidence;
(i) contain a summary of the conclusions reached;
(j) contain a statement that the expert understands an expert's duty to the court, and has complied and will continue to comply with that duty; and
(k) contain the same declaration of truth as a witness statement.

19.5. Expert to be informed of service of report

A party who serves on another party or on the court a report by an expert must, at once, inform that expert of that fact.

19.6. Pre-hearing discussion of expert evidence

(1) This rule applies where more than one party wants to introduce expert evidence.
(2) The court may direct the experts to—
(a) discuss the expert issues in the proceedings; and
(b) prepare a statement for the court of the matters on which they agree and disagree, giving their reasons.

(3) Except for that statement, the content of that discussion must not be referred to without the court's permission.

(4) A party may not introduce expert evidence without the court's permission if the expert has not complied with a direction under this rule.

19.7. Court's power to direct that evidence is to be given by a single joint expert

(1) Where more than one defendant wants to introduce expert evidence on an issue at trial, the court may direct that the evidence on that issue is to be given by one expert only.

(2) Where the co-defendants cannot agree who should be the expert, the court may—

(a) select the expert from a list prepared or identified by them; or

(b) direct that the expert be selected in another way.

19.8. Instructions to a single joint expert

(1) Where the court gives a direction under rule 19.7 for a single joint expert to be used, each of the co-defendants may give instructions to the expert.

(2) A co-defendant who gives instructions to the expert must, at the same time, send a copy of the instructions to each other co-defendant.

(3) The court may give directions about—

(a) the payment of the expert's fees and expenses; and

(b) any examination, measurement, test or experiment which the expert wishes to carry out.

(4) The court may, before an expert is instructed, limit the amount that can be paid by way of fees and expenses to the expert.

(5) Unless the court otherwise directs, the instructing co-defendants are jointly and severally liable for the payment of the expert's fees and expenses.

19.9. Court's power to vary requirements under this Part

(1) The court may extend (even after it has expired) a time limit under this Part.

(2) A party who wants an extension of time must—

(a) apply when serving the report, summary or notice for which it is required; and

(b) explain the delay.

PART 20 HEARSAY EVIDENCE

20.1. When this Part applies

This Part applies—

(a) in a magistrates' court and in the Crown Court;

(b) where a party wants to introduce hearsay evidence, within the meaning of section 114 of the Criminal Justice Act 2003.

20.2. Notice to introduce hearsay evidence

(1) This rule applies where a party wants to introduce hearsay evidence for admission under any of the following sections of the Criminal Justice Act 2003—

(a) section 114(1)(d) (evidence admissible in the interests of justice);

(b) section 116 (evidence where a witness is unavailable);

(c) section 117(1)(c) (evidence in a statement prepared for the purposes of criminal proceedings);

(d) section 121 (multiple hearsay).

(2) That party must—

(a) serve notice on—

(i) the court officer, and

(ii) each other party;

(b) in the notice—

(i) identify the evidence that is hearsay,

(ii) set out any facts on which that party relies to make the evidence admissible,

(iii) explain how that party will prove those facts if another party disputes them, and

(iv) explain why the evidence is admissible; and

(c) attach to the notice any statement or other document containing the evidence that has not already been served.

(3) A prosecutor who wants to introduce such evidence must serve the notice not more than—

(a) 28 days after the defendant pleads not guilty, in a magistrates' court; or

(b) 14 days after the defendant pleads not guilty, in the Crown Court.

(4) A defendant who wants to introduce such evidence must serve the notice as soon as reasonably practicable.

(5) A party entitled to receive a notice under this rule may waive that entitlement by so informing—

(a) the party who would have served it; and

(b) the court.

20.3. Opposing the introduction of hearsay evidence

(1) This rule applies where a party objects to the introduction of hearsay evidence.

(2) That party must—

(a) apply to the court to determine the objection;

(b) serve the application on—

(i) the court officer, and

(ii) each other party;

(c) serve the application as soon as reasonably practicable, and in any event not more than 14 days after—

(i) service of notice to introduce the evidence under rule 20.2,

(ii) service of the evidence to which that party objects, if no notice is required by that rule, or

(iii) the defendant pleads not guilty

whichever of those events happens last; and

(d) in the application, explain—

(i) which, if any, facts set out in a notice under rule 20.2 that party disputes,

(ii) why the evidence is not admissible, and

(iii) any other objection to the evidence.

(3) The court—

(a) may determine an application—

(i) at a hearing, in public or in private, or

(ii) without a hearing;

(b) must not determine the application unless the party who served the notice—

(i) is present, or

(ii) has had a reasonable opportunity to respond;

(c) may adjourn the application; and

(d) may discharge or vary a determination where it can do so under—

(i) section 8B of the Magistrates' Courts Act 1980 (ruling at pre-trial hearing in a magistrates' court), or

(ii) section 9 of the Criminal Justice Act 1987, or section 31 or 40 of the Criminal Procedure and Investigations Act 1996 (ruling at preparatory or other pre-trial hearing in the Crown Court).

20.4. Unopposed hearsay evidence

(1) This rule applies where—

(a) a party has served notice to introduce hearsay evidence under rule 20.2; and

(b) no other party has applied to the court to determine an objection to the introduction of the evidence.

(2) The court must treat the evidence as if it were admissible by agreement.

20.5. Court's power to vary requirements under this Part

(1) The court may—

(a) shorten or extend (even after it has expired) a time limit under this Part;

(b) allow an application or notice to be in a different form to one set out in the Practice Direction, or to be made or given orally;

(c) dispense with the requirement for notice to introduce hearsay evidence.

(2) A party who wants an extension of time must—

(a) apply when serving the application or notice for which it is needed; and

(b) explain the delay.

PART 21 EVIDENCE OF BAD CHARACTER

21.1. When this Part applies

This Part applies—

(a) in a magistrates' court and in the Crown Court;

(b) where a party wants to introduce evidence of bad character, within the meaning of section 98 of the Criminal Justice Act 2003.

21.2. Content of application or notice

(1) A party who wants to introduce evidence of bad character must—

(a) make an application under rule 21.3, where it is evidence of a non-defendant's bad character;

(b) give notice under rule 21.4, where it is evidence of a defendant's bad character.

(2) An application or notice must—

(a) set out the facts of the misconduct on which that party relies,

(b) explain how that party will prove those facts (whether by certificate of conviction, other official record, or other evidence), if another party disputes them, and

(c) explain why the evidence is admissible.

21.3. Application to introduce evidence of a non-defendant's bad character

(1) This rule applies where a party wants to introduce evidence of the bad character of a person other than the defendant.

(2) That party must serve an application to do so on—

(a) the court officer; and

(b) each other party.

(3) The applicant must serve the application—

(a) as soon as reasonably practicable; and in any event

(b) not more than 14 days after the prosecutor discloses material on which the application is based (if the prosecutor is not the applicant).

(4) A party who objects to the introduction of the evidence must—

(a) serve notice on—

(i) the court officer, and

(ii) each other party not more than 14 days after service of the application; and

(b) in the notice explain, as applicable—

(i) which, if any, facts of the misconduct set out in the application that party disputes,

(ii) what, if any, facts of the misconduct that party admits instead,

(iii) why the evidence is not admissible, and

(iv) any other objection to the application.

(5) The court—

(a) may determine an application—

(i) at a hearing, in public or in private, or

(ii) without a hearing;

(b) must not determine the application unless each party other than the applicant—
 (i) is present, or
 (ii) has had at least 14 days in which to serve a notice of objection;
(c) may adjourn the application; and
(d) may discharge or vary a determination where it can do so under—
 (i) section 8B of the Magistrates' Courts Act 1980 (ruling at pre-trial hearing in a magistrates' court), or
 (ii) section 9 of the Criminal Justice Act 1987, or section 31 or 40 of the Criminal Procedure and Investigations Act 1996 (ruling at preparatory or other pre-trial hearing in the Crown Court).

21.4. Notice to introduce evidence of a defendant's bad character

(1) This rule applies where a party wants to introduce evidence of a defendant's bad character.
(2) A prosecutor or co-defendant who wants to introduce such evidence must serve notice on—
 (a) the court officer; and
 (b) each other party.
(3) A prosecutor must serve any such notice not more than—
 (a) 28 days after the defendant pleads not guilty, in a magistrates' court; or
 (b) 14 days after the defendant pleads not guilty, in the Crown Court.
(4) A co-defendant must serve any such notice—
 (a) as soon as reasonably practicable; and in any event
 (b) not more than 14 days after the prosecutor discloses material on which the notice is based.
(5) A party who objects to the introduction of the evidence identified by such a notice must—
 (a) apply to the court to determine the objection;
 (b) serve the application on—
  (i) the court officer, and
  (ii) each other party not more than 14 days after service of the notice; and
 (c) in the application explain, as applicable—
  (i) which, if any, facts of the misconduct set out in the notice that party disputes,
  (ii) what, if any, facts of the misconduct that party admits instead,
  (iii) why the evidence is not admissible,
  (iv) why it would be unfair to admit the evidence, and
  (v) any other objection to the notice.
(6) The court—
 (a) may determine such an application—
  (i) at a hearing, in public or in private, or
  (ii) without a hearing;
 (b) must not determine the application unless the party who served the notice—
  (i) is present, or
  (ii) has had a reasonable opportunity to respond;
 (c) may adjourn the application; and
 (d) may discharge or vary a determination where it can do so under—
  (i) section 8B of the Magistrates' Courts Act 1980 (ruling at pre-trial hearing in a magistrates' court), or
  (ii) section 9 of the Criminal Justice Act 1987, or section 31 or 40 of the Criminal Procedure and Investigations Act 1996 (ruling at preparatory or other pre-trial hearing in the Crown Court).
(7) A party entitled to receive such a notice may waive that entitlement by so informing—
 (a) the party who would have served it; and
 (b) the court.

(8) A defendant who wants to introduce evidence of his or her own bad character must—
   (a) give notice, in writing or orally—
      (i) as soon as reasonably practicable, and in any event
      (ii) before the evidence is introduced, either by the defendant or in reply to a question asked by the defendant of another party's witness in order to obtain that evidence; and
   (b) in the Crown Court, at the same time give notice (in writing, or orally) of any direction about the defendant's character that the defendant wants the court to give the jury under rule 25.14 (Directions to the jury and taking the verdict)

21.5. Reasons for decisions

The court must announce at a hearing in public (but in the absence of the jury, if there is one) the reasons for a decision—
   (a) to admit evidence as evidence of bad character, or to refuse to do so; or
   (b) to direct an acquittal or a retrial under section 107 of the Criminal Justice Act 2003.

21.6. Court's power to vary requirements under this Part

(1) The court may—
   (a) shorten or extend (even after it has expired) a time limit under this Part;
   (b) allow an application or notice to be in a different form to one set out in the Practice Direction, or to be made or given orally;
   (c) dispense with a requirement for notice to introduce evidence of a defendant's bad character.
(2) A party who wants an extension of time must—
   (a) apply when serving the application or notice for which it is needed; and
   (b) explain the delay.

PART 22 EVIDENCE OF A COMPLAINANT'S PREVIOUS SEXUAL BEHAVIOUR

22.1. When this Part applies

This Part applies—
   (a) in a magistrates' court and in the Crown Court;
   (b) where—
      (i) section 41 of the Youth Justice and Criminal Evidence Act 1999 prohibits the introduction of evidence or cross-examination about any sexual behaviour of the complainant of a sexual offence, and
      (ii) despite that prohibition, a defendant wants to introduce such evidence or to cross-examine a witness about such behaviour.

22.2. Exercise of court's powers

The court—
   (a) must determine an application under rule 22.4 (Application for permission to introduce evidence or cross-examine)—
      (i) at a hearing in private, and
      (ii) in the absence of the complainant;
   (b) must not determine the application unless—
      (i) each party other than the applicant is present, or has had at least 14 days in which to make representations, and
      (ii) the court is satisfied that it has been able to take adequate account of the complainant's rights;
   (c) may adjourn the application; and

(d) may discharge or vary a determination where it can do so under—
(i) section 8B of the Magistrates' Courts Act 1980 (ruling at pre-trial hearing in a magistrates' court), or
(ii) section 9 of the Criminal Justice Act 1987, or section 31 or 40 of the Criminal Procedure and Investigations Act 1996 (ruling at preparatory or other pre-trial hearing in the Crown Court).

22.3. Decisions and reasons

(1) A prosecutor who wants to introduce the evidence of a complainant in respect of whom the court allows the introduction of evidence or cross-examination about any sexual behaviour must—
(a) inform the complainant of the court's decision as soon as reasonably practicable; and
(b) explain to the complainant any arrangements that as a result will be made for him or her to give evidence.
(2) The court must—
(a) promptly determine an application; and
(b) allow the prosecutor sufficient time to comply with the requirements of—
(i) paragraph (1), and
(ii) the code of practice issued under section 32 of the Domestic Violence, Crime and Victims Act 2004.
(3) The court must announce at a hearing in public—
(a) the reasons for a decision to allow or refuse an application under rule 22.4; and
(b) if it allows such an application, the extent to which evidence may be introduced or questions asked.

22.4. Application for permission to introduce evidence or cross-examine

(1) A defendant who wants to introduce evidence or cross-examine a witness about any sexual behaviour of the complainant must—
(a) serve an application for permission to do so on—
(i) the court officer, and
(ii) each other party;
(b) serve the application—
(i) as soon as reasonably practicable after becoming aware of the grounds for doing so, and in any event
(ii) not more than 14 days after the prosecutor discloses material on which the application is based.
(2) The application must—
(a) identify the issue to which the defendant says the complainant's sexual behaviour is relevant;
(b) give particulars of—
(i) any evidence that the defendant wants to introduce, and
(ii) any questions that the defendant wants to ask;
(c) identify the exception to the prohibition in section 41 of the Youth Justice and Criminal Evidence Act 1999 on which the defendant relies; and
(d) give the name and date of birth of any witness whose evidence about the complainant's sexual behaviour the defendant wants to introduce.

22.5. Application containing information withheld from another party

(1) This rule applies where—
(a) an applicant serves an application under rule 22.4 (Application for permission to introduce evidence or cross-examine); and
(b) the application includes information that the applicant thinks ought not be revealed to another party.

(2) The applicant must—
(a) omit that information from the part of the application that is served on that other party;
(b) mark the other part to show that, unless the court otherwise directs, it is only for the court; and
(c) in that other part, explain why the applicant has withheld that information from that other party.

(3) If the court so directs, the hearing of an application to which this rule applies may be, wholly or in part, in the absence of a party from whom information has been withheld.

(4) At the hearing of an application to which this rule applies—
(a) the general rule is that the court must consider, in the following sequence—
(i) representations first by the applicant and then by each other party, in all the parties' presence, and then
(ii) further representations by the applicant, in the absence of a party from whom information has been withheld; but
(b) the court may direct other arrangements for the hearing.

22.6. Representations in response

(1) This rule applies where a party wants to make representations about—
(a) an application under rule 22.4 (Application for permission to introduce evidence or cross-examine); or
(b) a proposed variation or discharge of a decision allowing such an application.

(2) Such a party must—
(a) serve the representations on—
(i) the court officer, and
(ii) each other party; and
(b) do so not more than 14 days after, as applicable—
(i) service of the application, or
(ii) notice of the proposal to vary or discharge.

(3) Where representations include information that the person making them thinks ought not be revealed to another party, that person must—
(a) omit that information from the representations served on that other party;
(b) mark the information to show that, unless the court otherwise directs, it is only for the court; and
(c) with that information include an explanation of why it has been withheld from that other party.

(4) Representations against an application under rule 22.4 must explain the grounds of objection.

(5) Representations against the variation or discharge of a decision must explain why it should not be varied or discharged.

22.7. Special measures, etc. for a witness

(1) This rule applies where the court allows an application under rule 22.4 (Application for permission to introduce evidence or cross-examine).

(2) Despite the time limits in rule 18.3 (Making an application for a direction or order)—
(a) a party may apply not more than 14 days after the court's decision for a special measures direction or for the variation of an existing special measures direction; and
(b) the court may shorten the time for opposing that application.

(3) Where the court allows the cross-examination of a witness, the court must give directions for the appropriate treatment and questioning of that witness in accordance with rule 3.9(6) and (7) (setting ground rules for the conduct of questioning).

22.8. Court's power to vary requirements under this Part

The Court may shorten or extend (even after it has expired) a time limit under this Part.

PART 23 RESTRICTION ON CROSS-EXAMINATION BY A DEFENDANT

GENERAL RULES

23.1. When this Part applies

This Part applies where—

(a) a defendant may not cross-examine in person a witness because of section 34 or section 35 of the Youth Justice and Criminal Evidence Act 1999 (Complainants in proceedings for sexual offences; Child complainants and other child witnesses);

(b) the court can prohibit a defendant from cross-examining in person a witness under section 36 of that Act (Direction prohibiting accused from cross-examining particular witness).

23.2. Appointment of advocate to cross-examine witness

(1) This rule applies where a defendant may not cross-examine in person a witness in consequence of—

(a) the prohibition imposed by section 34 or section 35 of the Youth Justice and Criminal Evidence Act 1999; or

(b) a prohibition imposed by the court under section 36 of the 1999 Act.

(2) The court must, as soon as practicable, explain in terms the defendant can understand (with help, if necessary)—

(a) the prohibition and its effect;

(b) that if the defendant will not be represented by a lawyer with a right of audience in the court for the purposes of the case then the defendant is entitled to arrange for such a lawyer to cross-examine the witness on his or her behalf;

(c) that the defendant must notify the court officer of the identity of any such lawyer, with details of how to contact that person, by no later than a date set by the court;

(d) that if the defendant does not want to make such arrangements, or if the defendant gives no such notice by that date, then—

(i) the court must decide whether it is necessary in the interests of justice to appoint such a lawyer to cross-examine the witness in the defendant's interests, and

(ii) if the court decides that that is necessary, the court will appoint a lawyer chosen by the court who will not be responsible to the defendant.

(3) Having given those explanations, the court must—

(a) ask whether the defendant wants to arrange for a lawyer to cross-examine the witness, and set a date by when the defendant must notify the court officer of the identity of that lawyer if the answer to that question is 'yes';

(b) if the answer to that question is 'no', or if by the date set the defendant has given no such notice—

(i) decide whether it is necessary in the interests of justice for the witness to be cross-examined by an advocate appointed to represent the defendant's interests, and

(ii) if the court decides that that is necessary, give directions for the appointment of such an advocate.

(4) The court may give the explanations and ask the questions required by this rule—

(a) at a hearing, in public or in private; or

(b) without a hearing, by written notice to the defendant.

(5) The court may extend (even after it has expired) the time limit that it sets under paragraph (3)(a)—

(a) on application by the defendant; or

(b) on its own initiative.

(6) Paragraphs (7), (8), (9) and (10) apply where the court appoints an advocate.

(7) The directions that the court gives under paragraph (3)(b)(ii) must provide for the supply to the advocate of a copy of—

(a) all material served by one party on the other, whether before or after the advocate's appointment, to which applies—

(i) Part 8 (Initial details of the prosecution case),

(ii) in the Crown Court, rule 9.15 (service of prosecution evidence in a case sent for trial),

(iii) Part 16 (Written witness statements),

(iv) Part 19 (Expert evidence),

(v) Part 20 (Hearsay evidence),

(vi) Part 21 (Evidence of bad character),

(vii) Part 22 (Evidence of a complainant's previous sexual behaviour);

(b) any material disclosed, given or served, whether before or after the advocate's appointment, which is—

(i) prosecution material disclosed to the defendant under section 3 (Initial duty of prosecutor to disclose) or section 7A (Continuing duty of prosecutor to disclose) of the Criminal Procedure and Investigations Act 1996,

(ii) a defence statement given by the defendant under section 5 (Compulsory disclosure by accused) or section 6 (Voluntary disclosure by accused) of the 1996 Act,

(iii) a defence witness notice given by the defendant under section 6C of that Act (Notification of intention to call defence witnesses), or

(iv) an application by the defendant under section 8 of that Act (Application by accused for disclosure);

(c) any case management questionnaire prepared for the purposes of the trial or, as the case may be, the appeal; and

(d) all case management directions given by the court for the purposes of the trial or the appeal.

(8) Where the defendant has given a defence statement—

(a) section 8(2) of the Criminal Procedure and Investigations Act 1996 is modified to allow the advocate, as well as the defendant, to apply for an order for prosecution disclosure under that subsection if the advocate has reasonable cause to believe that there is prosecution material concerning the witness which is required by section 7A of the Act to be disclosed to the defendant and has not been; and

(b) rule 15.5 (Defendant's application for prosecution disclosure) applies to an application by the advocate as it does to an application by the defendant.

(9) Before receiving evidence the court must establish, with the active assistance of the parties and of the advocate, and in the absence of any jury in the Crown Court—

(a) what issues will be the subject of the advocate's cross-examination; and

(b) whether the court's permission is required for any proposed question, for example where Part 21 or Part 22 applies.

(10) The appointment terminates at the conclusion of the cross-examination of the witness.

APPLICATION TO PROHIBIT CROSS-EXAMINATION

23.3. Exercise of court's powers

(1) The court may decide whether to impose or discharge a prohibition against cross-examination under section 36 of the Youth Justice and Criminal Evidence Act 1999—

(a) at a hearing, in public or in private, or without a hearing;

(b) in a party's absence, if that party—

(i) applied for the prohibition or discharge, or

(ii) has had at least 14 days in which to make representations.

(2) The court must announce, at a hearing in public before the witness gives evidence, the reasons for a decision—

(a) to impose or discharge such a prohibition; or

(b) to refuse to do so.

23.4. Application to prohibit cross-examination

(1) This rule applies where under section 36 of the Youth Justice and Criminal Evidence Act 1999 the prosecutor wants the court to prohibit the cross-examination of a witness by a defendant in person.

(2) The prosecutor must—

(a) apply in writing, as soon as reasonably practicable after becoming aware of the grounds for doing so; and

(b) serve the application on—

(i) the court officer,

(ii) the defendant who is the subject of the application, and

(iii) any other defendant, unless the court otherwise directs.

(3) The application must—

(a) report any views that the witness has expressed about whether he or she is content to be cross-examined by the defendant in person;

(b) identify—

(i) the nature of the questions likely to be asked, having regard to the issues in the case,

(ii) any relevant behaviour of the defendant at any stage of the case, generally and in relation to the witness,

(iii) any relationship, of any nature, between the witness and the defendant,

(iv) any other defendant in the case who is subject to such a prohibition in respect of the witness, and

(v) any special measures direction made in respect of the witness, or for which an application has been made;

(c) explain why the quality of evidence given by the witness on cross-examination—

(i) is likely to be diminished if no such prohibition is imposed, and

(ii) would be likely to be improved if it were imposed; and

(d) explain why it would not be contrary to the interests of justice to impose the prohibition.

23.5. Application to discharge prohibition imposed by the court

(1) A party who wants the court to discharge a prohibition against cross-examination which the court imposed under section 36 of the Youth Justice and Criminal Evidence Act 1999 must—

(a) apply in writing, as soon as reasonably practicable after becoming aware of the grounds for doing so; and

(b) serve the application on—

(i) the court officer, and

(ii) each other party.

(2) The applicant must—

(a) explain what material circumstances have changed since the prohibition was imposed; and

(b) ask for a hearing, if the applicant wants one, and explain why it is needed.

23.6. Application containing information withheld from another party

(1) This rule applies where—

(a) an applicant serves an application for the court to impose a prohibition against cross-examination, or for the discharge of such a prohibition; and

(b) the application includes information that the applicant thinks ought not be revealed to another party.

(2) The applicant must—
(a) omit that information from the part of the application that is served on that other party;
(b) mark the other part to show that, unless the court otherwise directs, it is only for the court; and
(c) in that other part, explain why the applicant has withheld that information from that other party.
(3) Any hearing of an application to which this rule applies—
(a) must be in private, unless the court otherwise directs; and
(b) if the court so directs, may be, wholly or in part, in the absence of a party from whom information has been withheld.
(4) At any hearing of an application to which this rule applies—
(a) the general rule is that the court must consider, in the following sequence—
(i) representations first by the applicant and then by each other party, in all the parties' presence, and then
(ii) further representations by the applicant, in the absence of a party from whom information has been withheld; but
(b) the court may direct other arrangements for the hearing.

23.7. Representations in response

(1) This rule applies where a party wants to make representations about—
(a) an application under rule 23.4 for a prohibition against cross-examination;
(b) an application under rule 23.5 for the discharge of such a prohibition; or
(c) a prohibition or discharge that the court proposes on its own initiative.
(2) Such a party must—
(a) serve the representations on—
(i) the court officer, and
(ii) each other party;
(b) do so not more than 14 days after, as applicable—
(i) service of the application, or
(ii) notice of the prohibition or discharge that the court proposes; and
(c) ask for a hearing, if that party wants one, and explain why it is needed.

(3) Representations against a prohibition must explain in what respect the conditions for imposing it are not met.

(4) Representations against the discharge of a prohibition must explain why it should not be discharged.

(5) Where representations include information that the person making them thinks ought not be revealed to another party, that person must—
(a) omit that information from the representations served on that other party;
(b) mark the information to show that, unless the court otherwise directs, it is only for the court; and
(c) with that information include an explanation of why it has been withheld from that other party.

23.8. Court's power to vary requirements

(1) The court may—
(a) shorten or extend (even after it has expired) a time limit under rule 23.4 (Application to prohibit cross-examination), rule 23.5 (Application to discharge prohibition imposed by the court) or rule 23.7 (Representations in response); and
(b) allow an application or representations required by any of those rules to be made in a different form to one set out in the Practice Direction, or to be made orally.
(2) A person who wants an extension of time must—
(a) apply when serving the application or representations for which it is needed; and
(b) explain the delay.

Attorney General's Guidelines on Disclosure for investigators, prosecutors and defence practitioners

(Issued December 2013)

Introduction

These Guidelines are issued by the Attorney General for investigators, prosecutors and defence practitioners on the application of the disclosure regime contained in the Criminal Procedure and Investigations Act 1996 ('CPIA'). The Guidelines emphasise the importance of prosecution-led disclosure and the importance of applying the CPIA regime in a 'thinking manner', tailored, where appropriate, to the type of investigation or prosecution in question.

The Guidelines do not contain the detail of the disclosure regime; they outline the high level principles which should be followed when the disclosure regime is applied.

These Guidelines replace the existing Attorney General's Guidelines on Disclosure issued in 2005 and the Supplementary Guidelines on Digital Material issued in 2011, which is an annex to the general guidelines.

The Guidelines are intended to operate alongside the Judicial Protocol on the Disclosure of Unused Material in Criminal Cases. They are not designed to be an unequivocal statement of the law at any one time, nor are they a substitute for a thorough understanding of the relevant legislation, codes of practice, case law and procedure.

Readers should note that a review of disclosure in the magistrates' courts is currently being undertaken by HHJ Kinch QC and the Chief Magistrate, on behalf of Lord Justice Gross, the Senior Presiding Judge. Amendments may therefore be made to these documents following the recommendations of that review, and in accordance with other forthcoming changes to the criminal justice system.

The Importance of Disclosure

1. The statutory framework for criminal investigations and disclosure is contained in the Criminal Procedure and Investigations Act 1996 (the CPIA) and the CPIA Code of Practice. The CPIA aims to ensure that criminal investigations are conducted in a fair, objective and thorough manner, and requires prosecutors to disclose to the defence material which has not previously been disclosed to the accused and which might reasonably be considered capable of undermining the case for the prosecution against the accused or of assisting the case for the accused. The CPIA requires a timely dialogue between the prosecution, defence and the court to enable the prosecution properly to identify such material.

2. Every accused person has a right to a fair trial, a right long embodied in our law and guaranteed by Article 6 of the European Convention on Human Rights (ECHR). A fair trial is the proper object and expectation of all participants in the trial process. Fair disclosure to the accused is an inseparable part of a fair trial. A fair trial should not require consideration of irrelevant material and should not involve spurious applications or arguments which serve to divert the trial process from examining the real issues before the court.

3. Properly applied, the CPIA should ensure that material is not disclosed which overburdens the participants in the trial process, diverts attention from the relevant issues, leads to unjustifiable delay, and is wasteful of resources. Consideration of disclosure issues should be an integral part of a good investigation and not something that exists separately.

Disclosure: general principles

4. Disclosure refers to providing the defence with copies of, or access to, any prosecution material which might reasonably be considered capable of undermining the case for the prosecution against the accused, or of assisting the case for the accused, and which has not previously been disclosed (section 3 CPIA).

5. Prosecutors will only be expected to anticipate what material might undermine their case or strengthen the defence in the light of information available at the time of the disclosure decision, and they may take into account information revealed during questioning.

6. In deciding whether material satisfies the disclosure test, consideration should be given amongst other things to:

a. the use that might be made of it in cross-examination;

b. its capacity to support submissions that could lead to:

(i) the exclusion of evidence;

(ii) a stay of proceedings, where the material is required to allow a proper application to be made;

(iii) a court or tribunal finding that any public authority had acted incompatibly with the accused's rights under the ECHR;

c. its capacity to suggest an explanation or partial explanation of the accused's actions;

d. the capacity of the material to have a bearing on scientific or medical evidence in the case.

7. It should also be borne in mind that while items of material viewed in isolation may not be reasonably considered to be capable of undermining the prosecution case or assisting the accused, several items together can have that effect.

8. Material relating to the accused's mental or physical health, intellectual capacity, or to any ill treatment which the accused may have suffered when in the investigator's custody is likely to fall within the test for disclosure set out in paragraph 4 above.

9. Disclosure must not be an open-ended trawl of unused material. A critical element to fair and proper disclosure is that the defence play their role to ensure that the prosecution are directed to material which might reasonably be considered capable of undermining the prosecution case or assisting the case for the accused. This process is key to ensuring prosecutors make informed determinations about disclosure of unused material. The defence statement is important in identifying the issues in the case and why it is suggested that the material meets the test for disclosure.

10. Disclosure should be conducted in a thinking manner and never be reduced to a box-ticking exercise; at all stages of the process, there should be consideration of **why** the CPIA disclosure regime requires a particular course of action and what should be done to achieve that aim.

11. There will always be a number of participants in prosecutions and investigations: senior investigation officers, disclosure officers, investigation officers, reviewing prosecutors, leading counsel, junior counsel, and sometimes disclosure counsel. Communication within the 'prosecution team' is vital to ensure that all matters which could have a bearing on disclosure issues are given sufficient attention by the right person. This is especially so given many reviewing lawyers will be unable to sit behind the trial advocate throughout the trial. In practice, this is likely to mean that a full log of disclosure decisions (with reasons) must be kept on the file and made available as appropriate to the prosecution team.

12. The role of the reviewing lawyer will be central to ensuring all members of the prosecution team are aware of, and carry out, their duties and role(s). Where this involves counsel or more than one reviewing lawyer, this should be done by giving clear written instructions and record keeping.

13. The centrality of the reviewing lawyer does not mean that he or she has to do all the work personally; on the contrary, it will often mean effective delegation. Where the conduct of a prosecution is assigned to more than one prosecutor, steps must be taken to ensure that all involved in the case properly record their decisions. Subsequent prosecutors must be able to see and understand previous disclosure decisions before carrying out their continuous review function.

14. Investigators must always be alive to the potential need to reveal and prosecutors to the potential need to disclose material, in the interests of justice and fairness in the particular circumstances of any case, after the commencement of proceedings but before their duty arises under the Act. For instance, disclosure ought to be made of significant information that might affect a bail decision. This is likely to depend on what the defence chooses to reveal at that stage.

Investigators and Disclosure Officers

15. Investigators and disclosure officers must be fair and objective and must work together with prosecutors to ensure that disclosure obligations are met. Investigators and disclosure officers should be familiar with the CPIA Code of Practice, in particular their obligations to **retain** and **record** relevant material, to **review** it and to **reveal** it to the prosecutor.

16. Whether a case is a summary only matter or a long and complex trial on indictment, it is important that investigators and disclosure officers should approach their duties in a 'thinking manner' and not as a box ticking exercise. Where necessary, the reviewing lawyer should be consulted. It is important that investigators and disclosure officers are deployed on cases which are commensurate with their training, skills and experience. The conduct of an investigation provides the foundation for the entire case, and may even impact the conduct of linked cases. It is vital that there is always consideration of disclosure matters at the outset of an investigation, regardless of its size.

17. A fair investigation involves the pursuit of material following all reasonable lines of enquiry, whether they point towards or away from the suspect. What is 'reasonable' will depend on the context of the case. A fair investigation does not mean an endless investigation: investigators and disclosure officers must give thought to defining, and thereby limiting, the scope of their investigations, seeking the guidance of the prosecutor where appropriate

18. Where there are a number of disclosure officers assigned to a case, there should be a lead disclosure officer who is the focus for enquiries and whose responsibility it is to ensure that the investigator's disclosure obligations are complied with. Where appropriate, regular case conferences and other meetings should be held to ensure prosecutors are apprised of all relevant developments in investigations. Full records should be kept of such meetings.

19. The CPIA Code of Practice encourages investigators and disclosure officers to seek advice from prosecutors about whether any particular item of material may be relevant to the investigation, and if so, how. Investigators and disclosure officers should record key decisions taken on these matters and be prepared to account for their actions later. An identical approach is not called for in each and every case.

20. Investigators are to approach their task seeking to establish what actually happened. They are to be fair and objective.

21. Disclosure officers (or their deputies) must inspect, view, listen to or search all relevant material that has been retained by the investigator and the disclosure officer must provide a personal declaration to the effect that this task has been undertaken. In some cases, a detailed examination of all material seized may be required. In others, however, a detailed examination of every item of material seized would be virtually impossible: see the **Annex**.

22. Prosecutors only have knowledge of matters which are revealed to them by investigators and disclosure officers, and the schedules are the written means by which that revelation takes place. Whatever the approach taken by investigators or disclosure officers to examining the material gathered or generated in the course of an investigation, it is crucial that disclosure officers record their reasons for a particular approach in writing.

23. In meeting the obligations in paragraph 6.9 and 8.1 of the Code, schedules must be completed in a form which not only reveals sufficient information to the prosecutor, but which demonstrates a transparent and thinking approach to the disclosure exercise, to command the confidence of the defence and the court. Descriptions on non-sensitive schedules must be clear and accurate, and must contain sufficient detail to enable the prosecutor to make an informed decision on disclosure. The use of abbreviations and acronyms can be problematic and lead to difficulties in appreciating the significance of the material.

24. Sensitive schedules must contain sufficiently clear descriptions to enable the prosecutor to make an informed decision as to whether or not the material itself should be viewed, to the extent possible without compromising the confidentiality of the information.

25. It may become apparent to an investigator that some material obtained in the course of an investigation, either because it was considered to be potentially relevant, or because it was inextricably

linked to material that was relevant, is, in fact, incapable of impact. It is not necessary to retain such material, although the investigator should err on the side of caution in reaching that conclusion and should be particularly mindful of the fact that some investigations continue over some time and that what is incapable of impact may change over time. The advice of the prosecutor should be sought where appropriate.

26. Disclosure officers must specifically draw material to the attention of the prosecutor for consideration where they have any doubt as to whether it might reasonably be considered capable of undermining the prosecution case or of assisting the case for the accused.

27. Disclosure officers must seek the advice and assistance of prosecutors when in doubt as to their responsibility as early as possible. They must deal expeditiously with requests by the prosecutor for further information on material, which may lead to disclosure.

Prosecutors

28. Prosecutors are responsible for making proper disclosure in consultation with the disclosure officer. The duty of disclosure is a continuing one and disclosure should be kept under review. In addition, prosecutors should ensure that advocates in court are properly instructed as to disclosure issues. Prosecutors must also be alert to the need to provide advice to, and where necessary probe actions taken by, disclosure officers to ensure that disclosure obligations are met. There should be no aspects of an investigation about which prosecutors are unable to ask probing questions.

29. Prosecutors must review schedules prepared by disclosure officers thoroughly and must be alert to the possibility that relevant material may exist which has not been revealed to them or material included which should not have been. If no schedules have been provided, or there are apparent omissions from the schedules, or documents or other items are inadequately described or are unclear, the prosecutor must at once take action to obtain properly completed schedules. Likewise schedules should be returned for amendment if irrelevant items are included. If prosecutors remain dissatisfied with the quality or content of the schedules they must raise the matter with a senior investigator to resolve the matter satisfactorily.

30. Where prosecutors have reason to believe that the disclosure officer has not discharged the obligation in paragraph 21 to inspect, view, listen to or search relevant material, they must at once raise the matter with the disclosure officer and request that it be done. Where appropriate the matter should be raised with the officer in the case or a senior officer.

31. Prosecutors should copy the defence statement to the disclosure officer and investigator as soon as reasonably practicable and prosecutors should advise the investigator if, in their view, reasonable and relevant lines of further enquiry should be pursued. If the defence statement does point to other reasonable lines of enquiry, further investigation is required and evidence obtained as a result of these enquiries may be used as part of the prosecution case or to rebut the defence.

32. It is vital that prosecutors consider defence statements thoroughly. Prosecutors cannot comment upon, or invite inferences to be drawn from, failures in defence disclosure otherwise than in accordance with section 11 of the CPIA. Prosecutors may cross-examine the accused on differences between the defence case put at trial and that set out in his or her defence statement. In doing so, it may be appropriate to apply to the judge under section 6E of the CPIA for copies of the statement to be given to a jury, edited if necessary to remove inadmissible material. Prosecutors should examine the defence statement to see whether it points to other lines of enquiry.

33. Prosecutors should challenge the lack of, or inadequate, defence statements in writing, copying the document to the court and the defence and seeking directions from the court to require the provision of an adequate statement from the defence.

34. If the material does not fulfil the disclosure test there is no requirement to disclose it. For this purpose, the parties' respective cases should not be restrictively analysed but must be carefully analysed to ascertain the specific facts the prosecution seek to establish and the specific grounds on which the charges are resisted.

Prosecution advocates

35. Prosecution advocates should ensure that all material which ought to be disclosed under the Act is disclosed to the defence. However, prosecution advocates cannot be expected to disclose material if they are not aware of its existence. As far as is possible, prosecution advocates must place themselves in a fully informed position to enable them to make decisions on disclosure.

36. Upon receipt of instructions, prosecution advocates should consider as a priority all the information provided regarding disclosure of material. Prosecution advocates should consider, in every case, whether they can be satisfied that they are in possession of all relevant documentation and that they have been fully instructed regarding disclosure matters. If as a result the advocate considers that further information or action is required, written advice should promptly be provided setting out the aspects that need clarification or action.

37. The prosecution advocate must keep decisions regarding disclosure under review until the conclusion of the trial, whenever possible in consultation with the reviewing prosecutor. The prosecution advocate must in every case specifically consider whether he or she can satisfactorily discharge the duty of continuing review on the basis of the material supplied already, or whether it is necessary to inspect further material or to reconsider material already inspected. Prosecution advocates must not abrogate their responsibility under the CPIA by disclosing material which does not pass the test for disclosure, set out in paragraph 4, above.

38. There remains no basis in practice or law for counsel to counsel disclosure.

Defence

39. Defence engagement must be early and meaningful for the CPIA regime to function as intended. Defence statements are an integral part of this and are intended to help focus the attention of the prosecutor, court and co-defendants on the relevant issues in order to identify exculpatory unused material. Defence statements should be drafted in accordance with the relevant provisions of the CPIA.

40. Defence requests for further disclosure should ordinarily only be answered by the prosecution if the request is relevant to and directed to an issue identified in the defence statement. If it is not, then a further or amended defence statement should be sought by the prosecutor and obtained before considering the request for further disclosure.

41. In some cases that involve extensive unused material that is within the knowledge of a defendant, the defence will be expected to provide the prosecution and the court with assistance in identifying material which is suggested to pass the test for disclosure.

42. The prosecution's continuing duty to keep disclosure under review is crucial, and particular attention must be paid to understanding the significance of developments in the case on the unused material and earlier disclosure decisions. Meaningful defence engagement will help the prosecution to keep disclosure under review. The continuing duty of review for prosecutors is less likely to require the disclosure of further material to the defence if the defence have clarified and articulated their case, as required by the CPIA.

43. In the magistrates' courts, where the provision of a defence statement is not mandatory, early identification of the material issues by the defence, whether through a defence statement, case management form or otherwise, will help the prosecution to focus its preparation of the case and allow any defence disclosure queries to be dealt with promptly and accurately.

Magistrates' Courts (including the Youth Court)

44. The majority of criminal cases are heard in the magistrates' court. The requirement for the prosecution to provide initial disclosure only arises after a not guilty plea has been entered but prosecutors should be alert to the possibility that material may exist which should be disclosed to the defendant prior to the CPIA requirements applying to the case.

45. Where a not guilty plea is entered in the magistrates' court, prosecutors should ensure that any issues of dispute which are raised are noted on the file. They should also seek to obtain a copy of any Magistrates' Court Trial Preparation Form. Consideration of the issues raised in court and on

the Trial Preparation Form will assist in deciding what material undermines the prosecution case or assists the defendant.

46. Where a matter is set down for trial in the magistrates' court, prosecutors should ensure that the investigator is requested to supply any outstanding disclosure schedules as a matter of urgency. Prosecutors should serve initial disclosure in sufficient time to ensure that the trial date is effective.

47. There is no requirement for a defence statement to be served in the magistrates' court but it should be noted that if none is given the court has no power to hear an application for further prosecution disclosure under section 8 of the CPIA and the Criminal Procedure Rules.

Cases in the Crown Court

48. The exponential increase in the use of technology in society means that many routine Crown Court cases are increasingly likely to have to engage with digital material of some form. It is not only in large and complex cases that there may be large quantities of such material. Where such investigations involve digital material, it will be virtually impossible for investigators (or prosecutors) to examine every item of such material individually and there should be no expectation that such material will be so examined. Having consulted with the prosecution as appropriate, disclosure officers should determine what their approach should be to the examination of the material. Investigators or disclosure officers should decide how best to pursue a reasonable line of enquiry in relation to the relevant digital material, and ensure that the extent and manner of the examination are commensurate with the issues in the case.

49. Consideration should be given to any local or national agreements in relation to disclosure in 'Early Guilty Plea Scheme' cases.

Large and complex cases in the Crown Court

50. The particular challenges presented by large and complex criminal prosecutions require an approach to disclosure which is specifically tailored to the needs of such cases. In these cases more than any other is the need for careful thought to be given to prosecution-led disclosure matters from the very earliest stage. It is essential that the prosecution takes a grip on the case and its disclosure requirements from the very outset of the investigation, which must continue throughout all aspects of the case preparation.

Disclosure Management Documents

51. Accordingly, investigations and prosecutions of large and complex cases should be carefully defined and accompanied by a clear investigation and prosecution strategy. The approach to disclosure in such cases should be outlined in a document which should be served on the defence and the court at an early stage. Such documents, sometimes known as Disclosure Management Documents, will require careful preparation and presentation, tailored to the individual case. They may include:

a. Where prosecutors and investigators operate in an integrated office, an explanation as to how the disclosure responsibilities have been managed;
b. A brief summary of the prosecution case and a statement outlining how the prosecutor's general approach will comply with the CPIA regime, these Guidelines and the Judicial Protocol on the Disclosure of Unused Material in Criminal Cases;
c. The prosecutor's understanding of the defence case, including information revealed during interview;
d. An outline of the prosecution's general approach to disclosure, which may include detail relating to:
    (i) Digital material: explaining the method and extent of examination, in accordance with the **Annex** to these Guidelines;
    (ii) Video footage;
    (iii) Linked investigations: explaining the nexus between investigations, any memoranda of understanding or disclosure agreements between investigators;

(iv) Third party and foreign material, including steps taken to obtain the material;
(v) Reasonable lines of enquiry: a summary of the lines pursued, particularly those that point away from the suspect, or which may assist the defence;
(vi) Credibility of a witness: confirmation that witness checks, including those of professional witnesses have, or will be, carried out.

52. Thereafter the prosecution should follow the Disclosure Management Document. They are living documents and should be amended in light of developments in the case; they should be kept up to date as the case progresses. Their use will assist the court in its own case management and will enable the defence to engage from an early stage with the prosecution's proposed approach to disclosure.

Material not held by the prosecution

Involvement of other agencies: material held by other Government departments and third parties

53. Where it appears to an investigator, disclosure officer or prosecutor that a Government department or other Crown body has material that may be relevant to an issue in the case, reasonable steps should be taken to identify and consider such material. Although what is reasonable will vary from case to case, the prosecution should inform the department or other body of the nature of its case and of relevant issues in the case in respect of which the department or body might possess material, and ask whether it has any such material.

54. It should be remembered that investigators, disclosure officers and prosecutors cannot be regarded to be in constructive possession of material held by Government departments or Crown bodies simply by virtue of their status as Government departments or Crown bodies.

55. Where, after reasonable steps have been taken to secure access to such material, access is denied, the investigator, disclosure officer or prosecutor should consider what if any further steps might be taken to obtain the material or inform the defence. The final decision on any further steps will be for the prosecutor.

Third party material: other domestic bodies

56. There may be cases where the investigator, disclosure officer or prosecutor believes that a third party (for example, a local authority, a social services department, a hospital, a doctor, a school, a provider of forensic services) has material or information which might be relevant to the prosecution case. In such cases, investigators, disclosure officers and prosecutors should take reasonable steps to identify, secure and consider material held by any third party where it appears to the investigator, disclosure officer or prosecutor that (a) such material exists and (b) that it may be relevant to an issue in the case.

57. If the investigator, disclosure officer or prosecutor seeks access to the material or information but the third party declines or refuses to allow access to it, the matter should not be left. If despite any reasons offered by the third party it is still believed that it is reasonable to seek production of the material or information, and the requirements of section 2 of the Criminal Procedure (Attendance of Witnesses) Act 1965 or as appropriate section 97 of the Magistrates Courts Act 1980 are satisfied (or any other relevant power), then the prosecutor or investigator should apply for a witness summons causing a representative of the third party to produce the material to the court.

58. Sometimes, for example through multi-agency working arrangements, investigators, disclosure officers or prosecutors may become aware of the content or nature of material held by a third party. Consultation with the relevant third party must always take place before disclosure is made; there may be public interest reasons to apply to the Court for an order for non-disclosure in the public interest, in accordance with the procedure outlined in paragraph 65 and following.

International matters

59. The obligations under the CPIA Code to pursue all reasonable lines of enquiry apply to material held overseas.

60. Where it appears that there is relevant material, the prosecutor must take reasonable steps to obtain it, either informally or making use of the powers contained in the Crime (International Co-operation) Act 2003 and any EU and international conventions. See CPS Guidance 'Obtaining Evidence and Information from Abroad'.

61. There may be cases where a foreign state or a foreign court refuses to make the material available to the investigator or prosecutor. There may be other cases where the foreign state, though willing to show the material to investigators, will not allow the material to be copied or otherwise made available and the courts of the foreign state will not order its provision.

62. It is for these reasons that there is no absolute duty on the prosecutor to disclose relevant material held overseas by entities not subject to the jurisdiction of the courts in England and Wales. However consideration should be given to whether the type of material believed to be held can be provided to the defence.

63. The obligation on the investigator and prosecutor under the CPIA is to take reasonable steps. Where investigators are allowed to examine files of a foreign state but are not allowed to take copies or notes or list the documents held, there is no breach by the prosecution in its duty of disclosure by reason of its failure to obtain such material, provided reasonable steps have been taken to try and obtain the material. Prosecutors have a margin of consideration as to what steps are appropriate in the particular case but prosecutors must be alive to their duties and there may be some circumstances where these duties cannot be met. Whether the prosecutor has taken reasonable steps is for the court to determine in each case if the matter is raised.

64. In these circumstances it is important that the position is clearly set out in writing so that the court and the defence know what the position is. Investigators and prosecutors must record and explain the situation and set out, insofar as they are permitted by the foreign state, such information as they can and the steps they have taken.

Applications for non-disclosure in the public interest

65. The CPIA allows prosecutors to apply to the court for an order to withhold material which would otherwise fall to be disclosed if disclosure would give rise to a real risk of serious prejudice to an important public interest. Before making such an application, prosecutors should aim to disclose as much of the material as they properly can (for example, by giving the defence redacted or edited copies or summaries). Neutral material or material damaging to the defendant need not be disclosed and there is no need to bring it to the attention of the court. Only in truly borderline cases should the prosecution seek a judicial ruling on whether material in its possession should be disclosed.

66. Prior to the hearing, the prosecutor and the prosecution advocate must examine all material which is the subject matter of the application and make any necessary enquiries of the investigator. The investigator must be frank with the prosecutor about the full extent of the sensitive material. Prior to or at the hearing, the court must be provided with full and accurate information about the material

67. The prosecutor (or representative) and/or investigator should attend such applications. Section 16 of the CPIA allows a person claiming to have an interest in the sensitive material to apply to the court for the opportunity to be heard at the application.

68. The principles set out at paragraph 36 of *R v H & C* [2004] 2 Cr. App. R. 10 [2004] UKHL 3 should be applied rigorously, firstly by the prosecutor and then by the court considering the material. It is essential that these principles are scrupulously adhered to, to ensure that the procedure for examination of material in the absence of the accused is compliant with Article 6.

69. If prosecutors conclude that a fair trial cannot take place because material which satisfies the test for disclosure cannot be disclosed, and that this cannot be remedied by the above procedure; how the case is presented; or by any other means, they should not continue with the case.

Other disclosure

70. Disclosure of any material that is made outside the ambit of CPIA will attract confidentiality by virtue of *Taylor v SFO* [1999] 2 AC 177.

Material relevant to sentence

71. In all cases the prosecutor must consider disclosing in the interests of justice any material which is relevant to sentence (e.g. information which might mitigate the seriousness of the offence or assist the accused to lay blame in part upon a co-accused or another person).

Post-conviction

72. Where, after the conclusion of the proceedings, material comes to light, that might cast doubt upon the safety of the conviction, the prosecutor must consider disclosure of such material.

Applicability of these Guidelines

73. These Guidelines shall have immediate effect.

...*

* **Editor's Note:** The guidelines reproduced above are followed by an 'Annex: Attorney General's Guidelines on Disclosure: Supplementary Guidelines on Digitally Stored Material (2011)' to which further reference may be made.

Human Rights—Act and Convention

Human Rights Act 1998

(1998, c. 42)

Introduction

1 The Convention Rights

(1) In this Act 'the Convention rights' means the rights and fundamental freedoms set out in—

(a) Articles 2 to 12 and 14 of the Convention,

(b) Articles 1 to 3 of the First Protocol, and

(c) Article 1 of the Thirteenth Protocol,

as read with Articles 16 to 18 of the Convention.

(2) Those Articles are to have effect for the purposes of this Act subject to any designated derogation or reservation (as to which see sections 14 and 15).

(3) The Articles are set out in Schedule 1.

(4) The Secretary of State may by order make such amendments to this Act as he considers appropriate to reflect the effect, in relation to the United Kingdom, of a protocol.

(5) In subsection (4) 'protocol' means a protocol to the Convention—

(a) which the United Kingdom has ratified; or

(b) which the United Kingdom has signed with a view to ratification.

(6) No amendment may be made by an order under subsection (4) so as to come into force before the protocol concerned is in force in relation to the United Kingdom.

2 Interpretation of Convention rights

(1) A court or tribunal determining a question which has arisen in connection with a Convention right must take into account any—

(a) judgment, decision, declaration or advisory opinion of the European Court of Human Rights,

(b) opinion of the Commission given in a report adopted under Article 31 of the Convention,

(c) decision of the Commission in connection with Article 26 or 27(2) of the Convention, or

(d) decision of the Committee of Ministers taken under Article 46 of the Convention,

whenever made or given, so far as, in the opinion of the court or tribunal, it is relevant to the proceedings in which that question has arisen.

(2) Evidence of any judgment, decision, declaration or opinion of which account may have to be taken under this section is to be given in proceedings before any court or tribunal in such manner as may be provided by rules.

(3) In this section 'rules' means rules of court or, in the case of proceedings before a tribunal, rules made for the purposes of this section—

(a) by the Lord Chancellor or the Secretary of State, in relation to any proceedings outside Scotland;

(b) by the Secretary of State, in relation to proceedings in Scotland; or
(c) by a Northern Ireland department, in relation to proceedings before a tribunal in Northern Ireland—
(i) which deals with transferred matters; and
(ii) for which no rules made under paragraph (a) are in force.

Legislation

3 Interpretation of legislation

(1) So far as it is possible to do so, primary legislation and subordinate legislation must be read and given effect in a way which is compatible with the Convention rights.

(2) This section—
(a) applies to primary legislation and subordinate legislation whenever enacted;
(b) does not affect the validity, continuing operation or enforcement of any incompatible primary legislation; and
(c) does not affect the validity, continuing operation or enforcement of any incompatible subordinate legislation if (disregarding any possibility of revocation) primary legislation prevents removal of the incompatibility.

4 Declaration of incompatibility

(1) Subsection (2) applies in any proceedings in which a court determines whether a provision of primary legislation is compatible with a Convention right.

(2) If the court is satisfied that the provision is incompatible with a Convention right, it may make a declaration of that incompatibility.

(3) Subsection (4) applies in any proceedings in which a court determines whether a provision of subordinate legislation, made in the exercise of a power conferred by primary legislation, is compatible with a Convention right.

(4) If the court is satisfied—
(a) that the provision is incompatible with a Convention right, and
(b) that (disregarding any possibility of revocation) the primary legislation concerned prevents removal of the incompatibility,

it may make a declaration of that incompatibility.

(5) In this section 'court' means—
(a) the Supreme Court;
(b) the Judicial Committee of the Privy Council;
(c) the Court Martial Appeal Court;
(d) in Scotland, the High Court of Justiciary sitting otherwise than as a trial court or the Court of Session;
(e) in England and Wales or Northern Ireland, the High Court or the Court of Appeal.
(f) the Court of Protection, in any matter being dealt with by the President of the Family Division, the Vice-Chancellor or a puisne judge of the High Court.

(6) A declaration under this section ('a declaration of incompatibility')—
(a) does not affect the validity, continuing operation or enforcement of the provision in respect of which it is given; and
(b) is not binding on the parties to the proceedings in which it is made.

5 Right of Crown to intervene

(1) Where a court is considering whether to make a declaration of incompatibility, the Crown is entitled to notice in accordance with rules of court.

(2) In any case to which subsection (1) applies—
(a) a Minister of the Crown (or a person nominated by him),
(b) a member of the Scottish Executive,
(c) a Northern Ireland Minister,
(d) a Northern Ireland department,

is entitled, on giving notice in accordance with rules of court, to be joined as a party to the proceedings.

(3) Notice under subsection (2) may be given at any time during the proceedings.

(4) A person who has been made a party to criminal proceedings (other than in Scotland) as the result of a notice under subsection (2) may, with leave, appeal to the Supreme Court against any declaration of incompatibility made in the proceedings.

(5) In subsection (4)—

'criminal proceedings' includes all proceedings before the Court Martial Appeal Court; and

'leave' means leave granted by the court making the declaration of incompatibility or by the Supreme Court.

Public authorities

6 Acts of public authorities

(1) It is unlawful for a public authority to act in a way which is incompatible with a Convention right.

(2) Subsection (1) does not apply to an act if—

(a) as the result of one or more provisions of primary legislation, the authority could not have acted differently; or

(b) in the case of one or more provisions of, or made under, primary legislation which cannot be read or given effect in a way which is compatible with the Convention rights, the authority was acting so as to give effect to or enforce those provisions.

(3) In this section 'public authority' includes—

(a) a court or tribunal, and

(b) any person certain of whose functions are functions of a public nature,

but does not include either House of Parliament or a person exercising functions in connection with proceedings in Parliament.

(4) ...

(5) In relation to a particular act, a person is not a public authority by virtue only of subsection (3)(b) if the nature of the act is private.

(6) 'An act' includes a failure to act but does not include a failure to—

(a) introduce in, or lay before, Parliament a proposal for legislation; or

(b) make any primary legislation or remedial order.

7 Proceedings

(1) A person who claims that a public authority has acted (or proposes to act) in a way which is made unlawful by section 6(1) may—

(a) bring proceedings against the authority under this Act in the appropriate court or tribunal, or

(b) rely on the Convention right or rights concerned in any legal proceedings, but only if he is (or would be) a victim of the unlawful act.

(2) In subsection (1)(a) 'appropriate court or tribunal' means such court or tribunal as may be determined in accordance with rules; and proceedings against an authority include a counterclaim or similar proceeding.

(3) If the proceedings are brought on an application for judicial review, the applicant is to be taken to have a sufficient interest in relation to the unlawful act only if he is, or would be, a victim of that act.

(4) ...*

(5) Proceedings under subsection (1)(a) must be brought before the end of—

(a) the period of one year beginning with the date on which the act complained of took place; or

(b) such longer period as the court or tribunal considers equitable having regard to all the circumstances,

but that is subject to any rule imposing a stricter time limit in relation to the procedure in question.

* **Editor's Note:** Applies to Scotland only.

(6) In subsection (1)(b) 'legal proceedings' includes—
(a) proceedings brought by or at the instigation of a public authority; and
(b) an appeal against the decision of a court or tribunal.

(7) For the purposes of this section, a person is a victim of an unlawful act only if he would be a victim for the purposes of Article 34 of the Convention if proceedings were brought in the European Court of Human Rights in respect of that act.

(8) Nothing in this Act creates a criminal offence.

(9) In this section 'rules' means—
(a) in relation to proceedings before a court or tribunal outside Scotland, rules made by the Lord Chancellor or the Secretary of State for the purposes of this section or rules of court,
(b) . . .*
(c) . . .**
and includes provision made by order under section 1 of the Courts and Legal Services Act 1990.

(10) In making rules, regard must be had to section 9.

(11) The Minister who has power to make rules in relation to a particular tribunal may, to the extent he considers it necessary to ensure that the tribunal can provide an appropriate remedy in relation to an act (or proposed act) of a public authority which is (or would be) unlawful as a result of section 6(1), by order add to—
(a) the relief or remedies which the tribunal may grant; or
(b) the grounds on which it may grant any of them.

(12) An order made under subsection (11) may contain such incidental, supplemental, consequential or transitional provision as the Minister making it considers appropriate.

(13) 'The Minister' includes the Northern Ireland department concerned.

8 Judicial remedies

(1) In relation to any act (or proposed act) of a public authority which the court finds is (or would be) unlawful, it may grant such relief or remedy, or make such order, within its powers as it considers just and appropriate.

(2) But damages may be awarded only by a court which has power to award damages, or to order the payment of compensation, in civil proceedings.

(3) No award of damages is to be made unless, taking account of all the circumstances of the case, including—
(a) any other relief or remedy granted, or order made, in relation to the act in question (by that or any other court), and
(b) the consequences of any decision (of that or any other court) in respect of that act,
the court is satisfied that the award is necessary to afford just satisfaction to the person in whose favour it is made.

(4) In determining—
(a) whether to award damages, or
(b) the amount of an award,
the court must take into account the principles applied by the European Court of Human Rights in relation to the award of compensation under Article 41 of the Convention.

(5) A public authority against which damages are awarded is to be treated—
(a) . . .***
(b) for the purposes of the Civil Liability (Contribution) Act 1978 as liable in respect of damage suffered by the person to whom the award is made.

(6) In this section—
'court' includes a tribunal;
'damages' means damages for an unlawful act of a public authority; and
'unlawful' means unlawful under section 6(1).

* **Editor's Note:** Applies to Scotland only.
** **Editor's Note:** Applies to Northern Ireland only.
*** **Editor's Note:** Applies to Scotland only.

9 Judicial acts

(1) Proceedings under section 7(1)(a) in respect of a judicial act may be brought only—

(a) by exercising a right of appeal;

(b) on an application . . . for judicial review; or

(c) in such other forum as may be prescribed by rules.

(2) That does not affect any rule of law which prevents a court from being the subject of judicial review.

(3) In proceedings under this Act in respect of a judicial act done in good faith, damages may not be awarded otherwise than to compensate a person to the extent required by Article 5(5) of the Convention.

(4) An award of damages permitted by subsection (3) is to be made against the Crown; but no award may be made unless the appropriate person, if not a party to the proceedings, is joined.

(5) In this section—

'appropriate person' means the Minister responsible for the court concerned, or a person or government department nominated by him;

'court' includes a tribunal;

'judge' includes a member of a tribunal, a justice of the peace and a clerk or other officer entitled to exercise the jurisdiction of a court;

'judicial act' means a judicial act of a court and includes an act done on the instructions, or on behalf, of a judge; and

'rules' has the same meaning as in section 7(9).

Remedial action

10 Power to take remedial action

(1) This section applies if—

(a) a provision of legislation has been declared under section 4 to be incompatible with a Convention right and, if an appeal lies—

(i) all persons who may appeal have stated in writing that they do not intend to do so;

(ii) the time for bringing an appeal has expired and no appeal has been brought within that time; or

(iii) an appeal brought within that time has been determined or abandoned;

or

(b) it appears to a Minister of the Crown or Her Majesty in Council that, having regard to a finding of the European Court of Human Rights made after the coming into force of this section in proceedings against the United Kingdom, a provision of legislation is incompatible with an obligation of the United Kingdom arising from the Convention.

(2) If a Minister of the Crown considers that there are compelling reasons for proceeding under this section, he may by order make such amendments to the legislation as he considers necessary to remove the incompatibility.

(3) If, in the case of subordinate legislation, a Minister of the Crown considers—

(a) that it is necessary to amend the primary legislation under which the subordinate legislation in question was made, in order to enable the incompatibility to be removed, and

(b) that there are compelling reasons for proceeding under this section,

he may by order make such amendments to the primary legislation as he considers necessary.

(4) This section also applies where the provision in question is in subordinate legislation and has been quashed, or declared invalid, by reason of incompatibility with a Convention right and the Minister proposes to proceed under paragraph 2(b) of Schedule 2.

(5) If the legislation is an Order in Council, the power conferred by subsection (2) or (3) is exercisable by Her Majesty in Council.

(6) In this section 'legislation' does not include a Measure of the Church Assembly or of the General Synod of the Church of England.

(7) Schedule 2 makes further provision about remedial orders.

21 Interpretation etc.

(1) In this Act—

'amend' includes repeal and apply (with or without modifications);

'the appropriate Minister' means the Minister of the Crown having charge of the appropriate authorised government department (within the meaning of the Crown Proceedings Act 1947);

'the Commission' means the European Commission of Human Rights;

'the Convention' means the Convention for the Protection of Human Rights and Fundamental Freedoms, agreed by the Council of Europe at Rome on 4th November 1950 as it has effect for the time being in relation to the United Kingdom;

'declaration of incompatibility' means a declaration under section 4;

'Minister of the Crown' has the same meaning as in the Ministers of the Crown Act 1975;

'primary legislation' means any—

(a) public general Act;
(b) local and personal Act;
(c) private Act;
(d) Measure of the Church Assembly;
(e) Measure of the General Synod of the Church of England;
(f) Order in Council—
  (i) made in exercise of Her Majesty's Royal Prerogative;
  (ii) . . .*
  (iii) amending an Act of a kind mentioned in paragraph (a), (b) or (c);

and includes an order or other instrument made under primary legislation . . . to the extent to which it operates to bring one or more provisions of that legislation into force or amends any primary legislation;

'the First Protocol' means the protocol to the Convention agreed at Paris on 20th March 1952;

'the Eleventh Protocol' means the protocol to the Convention (restructuring the control machinery established by the Convention) agreed at Strasbourg on 11th May 1994;

'the Thirteenth Protocol' means the protocol to the Convention (concerning the abolition of the death penalty in all circumstances) agreed at Vilnius on 3rd May 2002;

'remedial order' means an order under section 10;

'subordinate legislation' means any—

(a) Order in Council other than one—
  (i) made in exercise of Her Majesty's Royal Prerogative;
  (ii) . . .**
  (iii) amending an Act of a kind mentioned in the definition of primary legislation;
(b) . . .
(c) . . .
(d) . . .
(e) . . .
(f) order, rules, regulations, scheme, warrant, byelaw or other instrument made under primary legislation (except to the extent to which it operates to bring one or more provisions of that legislation into force or amends any primary legislation);
(g) . . .
(h) . . .

'tribunal' means any tribunal in which legal proceedings may be brought.

(2) The references in paragraphs (b) and (c) of section 2(1) to Articles are to Articles of the Convention as they had effect immediately before the coming into force of the Eleventh Protocol.

(3) The reference in paragraph (d) of section 2(1) to Article 46 includes a reference to Articles 32 and 54 of the Convention as they had effect immediately before the coming into force of the Eleventh Protocol.

* **Editor's Note:** Applies to Northern Ireland only.
** **Editor's Note:** Applies to Northern Ireland only.

(4) The references in section 2(1) to a report or decision of the Commission or a decision of the Committee of Ministers include references to a report or decision made as provided by paragraphs 3, 4 and 6 of Article 5 of the Eleventh Protocol (transitional provisions).

(5) Any liability under the Army Act 1955, the Air Force Act 1955 or the Naval Discipline Act 1957 to suffer death for an offence is replaced by a liability to imprisonment for life or any less punishment authorised by those Acts; and those Acts shall accordingly have effect with the necessary modifications.

22 Short title, commencement, application and extent

(1) This Act may be cited as the Human Rights Act 1998.

(2) Section 18, 20 and 21(5) and this section come into force on the passing of this Act.

(3) The other provisions of this Act come into force on such day as the Secretary of State may by order appoint; and different days may be appointed for different purposes.

(4) Paragraph (b) of subsection (1) of section 7 applies to proceedings brought by or at the instigation of a public authority whenever the act in question took place; but otherwise that subsection does not apply to an act taking place before the coming into force of that section.

(5) This Act binds the Crown.

(6) ...

(7) Section 21(5), so far as it relates to any provision contained in the Army Act 1955, the Air Force Act 1955 or the Naval Discipline Act 1957, extends to any place to which that provision extends.

Convention for the Protection of Human Rights and Fundamental Freedoms*

(Rome, 4.11.1950)[1]

The governments signatory hereto, being members of the Council of Europe,

Considering the Universal Declaration of Human Rights proclaimed by the General Assembly of the United Nations on 10th December 1948;

Considering that this declaration aims at securing the universal and effective recognition and observance of the rights therein declared;

Considering that the aim of the Council of Europe is the achievement of greater unity between its members and that one of the methods by which that aim is to be pursued is the maintenance and further realisation of human rights and fundamental freedoms;

Reaffirming their profound belief in those fundamental freedoms which are the foundation of justice and peace in the world and are best maintained on the one hand by an effective political democracy and on the other by a common understanding and observance of the human rights upon which they depend;

Being resolved, as the governments of European countries which are like-minded and have a common heritage of political traditions, ideals, freedom and the rule of law, to take the first steps for the collective enforcement of certain of the rights stated in the Universal Declaration,

Have agreed as follows:

Article 1

The High Contracting Parties shall secure to everyone within their jurisdiction the rights and freedoms defined in Section 1 of this Convention.

* Reproduced with permission from the Council of Europe.

[1] European Treaty Series, No. 5. Text amended according to the provisions of Protocol No. 3 (ETS No. 45), which entered into force on 21 September 1970, of Protocol No. 5 (ETS No. 55), which entered into force on 20 December 1971, and of Protocol No. 8 (ETS No. 118), which entered into force on 1 January 1990, and comprising also the text of Protocol No. 2 (ETS No. 44) which, in accordance with Article 5, paragraph 3, therefore, has been an integral part of the Convention since its entry into force on 21 September 1970.

Section I

Article 2

1. Everyone's right to life shall be protected by law. No one shall be deprived of his life intentionally save in the execution of a sentence of a court following his conviction of a crime for which this penalty is provided by law.

2. Deprivation of life shall not be regarded as inflicted in contravention of this article when it results from the use of force which is no more than absolutely necessary:

(a) in defence of any person from unlawful violence;

(b) in order to effect a lawful arrest or to prevent the escape of a person lawfully detained;

(c) in action lawfully taken for the purpose of quelling a riot or insurrection.

Article 3

No one shall be subjected to torture or to inhuman or degrading treatment or punishment.

Article 4

1. No one shall be held in slavery or servitude.

2. No one shall be required to perform forced or compulsory labour.

3. For the purpose of this article the term 'forced or compulsory labour' shall not include:

(a) any work required to be done in the ordinary course of detention imposed according to the provisions of Article 5 of this Convention or during conditional release from such detention;

(b) any service of a military character or, in case of conscientious objectors in countries where they are recognised, service exacted instead of compulsory military service;

(c) any service exacted in case of an emergency or calamity threatening the life or well-being of the community;

(d) any work or service which forms part of normal civic obligations.

Article 5

1. Everyone has the right to liberty and security of person. No one shall be deprived of his liberty save in the following cases and in accordance with a procedure prescribed by law:

(a) the lawful detention of a person after conviction by a competent court;

(b) the lawful arrest or detention of a person for non-compliance with the lawful order of a court or in order to secure the fulfilment of any obligation prescribed by law;

(c) the lawful arrest or detention of a person effected for the purpose of bringing him before the competent legal authority on reasonable suspicion of having committed an offence or when it is reasonably considered necessary to prevent his committing an offence or fleeing after having done so;

(d) the detention of a minor by lawful order for the purpose of educational supervision or his lawful detention for the purpose of bringing him before the competent legal authority;

(e) the lawful detention of persons for the prevention of the spreading of infectious diseases, of persons of unsound mind, alcoholics or drug addicts or vagrants;

(f) the lawful arrest or detention of a person to prevent his effecting an unauthorised entry into the country or of a person against whom action is being taken with a view to deportation or extradition.

2. Everyone who is arrested shall be informed promptly, in a language which he understands, of the reasons for his arrest and of any charge against him.

3. Everyone arrested or detained in accordance with the provisions of paragraph 1(c) of this article shall be brought promptly before a judge or other officer authorised by law to exercise judicial power and shall be entitled to trial within a reasonable time or to release pending trial. Release may be conditioned by guarantees to appear for trial.

4. Everyone who is deprived of his liberty by arrest or detention shall be entitled to take proceedings by which the lawfulness of his detention shall be decided speedily by a court and his release ordered if the detention is not lawful.

5. Everyone who has been the victim of arrest or detention in contravention of the provisions of this article shall have an enforceable right to compensation.

Article 6

1. In the determination of his civil rights and obligations or of any criminal charge against him, everyone is entitled to a fair and public hearing within a reasonable time by an independent and impartial tribunal established by law. Judgment shall be pronounced publicly but the press and public may be excluded from all or part of the trial in the interests of morals, public order or national security in a democratic society, where the interests of juveniles or the protection of the private life of the parties so require, or to the extent strictly necessary in the opinion of the court in special circumstances where publicity would prejudice the interests of justice.

2. Everyone charged with a criminal offence shall be presumed innocent until proved guilty according to law.

3. Everyone charged with a criminal offence has the following minimum rights;

(a) to be informed promptly, in a language which he understands and in detail, of the nature and cause of the accusation against him;
(b) to have adequate time and facilities for the preparation of his defence;
(c) to defend himself in person or through legal assistance of his own choosing or, if he has not sufficient means to pay for legal assistance, to be given it free when the interests of justice so require;
(d) to examine or have examined witnesses against him and to obtain the attendance and examination of witnesses on his behalf under the same conditions as witnesses against him;
(e) to have the free assistance of an interpreter if he cannot understand or speak the language used in court.

Article 7

1. No one shall be held guilty of any criminal offence on account of any act or omission which did not constitute a criminal offence under national or international law at the time when it was committed. Nor shall a heavier penalty be imposed than the one that was applicable at the time the criminal offence was committed.

2. This article shall not prejudice the trial and punishment of any person for any act or omission which, at the time when it was committed, was criminal according to the general principles of law recognised by civilised nations.

Article 8

1. Everyone has the right to respect for his private and family life, his home and his correspondence.

2. There shall be no interference by a public authority with the exercise of this right except such as is in accordance with the law and is necessary in a democratic society in the interests of national security, public safety or the economic well-being of the country, for the prevention of disorder or crime, for the protection of health or morals, or for the protection of the rights and freedoms of others.

Article 9

1. Everyone has the right to freedom of thought, conscience and religion; this right includes freedom to change his religion or belief and freedom, either alone or in community with others and in public or private, to manifest his religion or belief, in worship, teaching, practice and observance.

2. Freedom to manifest one's religion or beliefs shall be subject only to such limitations as are prescribed by law and are necessary in a democratic society in the interests of public safety, for the protection of public order, health or morals, or for the protection of the rights and freedoms of others.

Article 10

1. Everyone has the right to freedom of expression. This right shall include freedom to hold opinions and to receive and impart information and ideas without interference by public authority and

regardless of frontiers. This article shall not prevent States from requiring the licensing of broadcasting, television or cinema enterprises.

2. The exercise of these freedoms, since it carries with it duties and responsibilities, may be subject to such formalities, conditions, restrictions or penalties as are prescribed by law and are necessary in a democratic society, in the interests of national security, territorial integrity or public safety, for the prevention of disorder or crime, for the protection of health or morals, for the protection of the reputation of rights of others, for preventing the disclosure of information received in confidence, or for maintaining the authority and impartiality of the judiciary.

Article 11

1. Everyone has the right to freedom of peaceful assembly and to freedom of association with others, including the right to form and to join trade unions for the protection of his interests.

2. No restrictions shall be placed on the exercise of these rights other than such as are prescribed by law and are necessary in a democratic society in the interests of national security or public safety, for the prevention of disorder or crime, for the protection of health or morals or for the protection of the rights and freedoms of others. This article shall not prevent the imposition of lawful restrictions on the exercise of these rights by members of the armed forces, of the police or of the administration of the state.

Article 12

Men and women of marriageable age have the right to marry and to found a family, according to the national laws governing the exercise of this right.

Article 13

Everyone whose rights and freedoms as set forth in this Convention are violated shall have an effective remedy before a national authority notwithstanding that the violation has been committed by persons acting in an official capacity.

Article 14

The employment of the rights and freedoms set forth in this Convention shall be secured without discrimination on any ground such as sex, race, colour, language, religion, political or other opinion, national or social origin, association with a national minority, property, birth or other status.

Article 15

1. In time of war or other public emergency threatening the life of the nation any High Contracting Party may take measures derogating from its obligations under this Convention to the extent strictly required by the exigencies of the situation, provided that such measures are not inconsistent with its other obligations under international law.

2. No derogation from Article 2, except in respect of deaths resulting from lawful acts of war, or from Articles 3, 4 (paragraph 1) and 7 shall be made under this provision.

3. Any High Contracting Party availing itself of this right of derogation shall keep the Secretary General of the Council of Europe fully informed of the measures which it has taken and the reasons therefor. It shall also inform the Secretary General of the Council of Europe when such measures have ceased to operate and the provisions of the Convention are again being fully executed.

Article 16

Nothing in Articles 10, 11 and 14 shall be regarded as preventing the High Contracting Parties from imposing restrictions on the political activity of aliens.

Article 17

Nothing in this Convention may be interpreted as implying for any State, group or person any right to engage in any activity or perform any act aimed at the destruction of any of the rights and freedoms set forth herein or at their limitation to a greater extent than is provided for in the Convention.

Article 18

The restrictions permitted under this Convention to the said rights and freedoms shall not be applied for any purpose other than those for which they have been prescribed.

Part IV

Civil Proceedings—Statutes and Rules

Civil Evidence Act 1968

(1968, c. 64)

11 Convictions as evidence in civil proceedings

(1) In any civil proceedings the fact that a person has been convicted of an offence by or before any court in the United Kingdom or of a service offence anywhere shall (subject to subsection (3) below) be admissible in evidence for the purpose of proving, where to do so is relevant to any issue in those proceedings, that he committed that offence, whether he was so convicted upon a plea of guilty or otherwise and whether or not he is a party to the civil proceedings; but no conviction other than a subsisting one shall be admissible in evidence by virtue of this section.

(2) In any civil proceedings in which by virtue of this section a person is proved to have been convicted of an offence by or before any court in the United Kingdom or of a service offence—

- (a) he shall be taken to have committed that offence unless the contrary is proved; and
- (b) without prejudice to the reception of any other admissible evidence for the purpose of identifying the facts on which the conviction was based, the contents of any document which is admissible as evidence of the conviction, and the contents of the information, complaint, indictment or charge-sheet on which the person in question was convicted, shall be admissible in evidence for that purpose.

(3) Nothing in this section shall prejudice the operation of section 13 of this Act or any other enactment whereby a conviction or a finding of fact in any criminal proceedings is for the purposes of any other proceedings made conclusive evidence of any fact.

(4) Where in any civil proceedings the contents of any document are admissible in evidence by virtue of subsection (2) above, a copy of that document, or of the material part thereof, purporting to be certified or otherwise authenticated by or on behalf of the court or authority having custody of that document shall be admissible in evidence and shall be taken to be a true copy of that document or part unless the contrary is shown.

(5) Nothing in any of the following enactments, that is to say—

- (a) section 14 of the Powers of Criminal Courts (Sentencing) Act 2000 (under which a conviction leading to discharge is to be disregarded except as therein mentioned);
- (aa) section 187 of the Armed Forces Act 2006 (which makes similar provision in respect of service convictions);
- (b) section 191 of the Criminal Procedure (Scotland) Act 1975 (which makes similar provision in respect of convictions on indictment in Scotland); and
- (c) section 8 of the Probation Act (Northern Ireland) 1950 (which corresponds to the said section 12) or any corresponding enactment of the Parliament of Northern Ireland for the time being in force,

shall affect the operation of this section; and for the purposes of this section any order made by a court of summary jurisdiction in Scotland under section 383 or section 384 of the said Act of 1975 shall be treated as a conviction.

(7) In this section—

'service offence' has the same meaning as in the Armed Forces Act 2006;

'conviction' includes anything that under section 376(1) and (2) of that Act is to be treated as a conviction, and 'convicted' is to be read accordingly.

12 Findings of adultery and paternity as evidence in civil proceedings

(1) In any civil proceedings—

(a) the fact that a person has been found guilty of adultery in any matrimonial proceedings; and

(b) the fact that a person has been found to be the father of a child in relevant proceedings before any court in England and Wales or Northern Ireland or has been adjudged to be the father of a child in affiliation proceedings before any court in the United Kingdom;

shall (subject to subsection (3) below) be admissible in evidence for the purpose of proving, where to do so is relevant to any issue in those civil proceedings, that he committed the adultery to which the finding relates or, as the case may be, is (or was) the father of that child, whether or not he offered any defence to the allegation of adultery or paternity and whether or not he is a party to the civil proceedings; but no finding or adjudication other than a subsisting one shall be admissible in evidence by virtue of this section.

(2) In any civil proceedings in which by virtue of this section a person is proved to have been found guilty of adultery as mentioned in subsection (1)(a) above or to have been found or adjudged to be the father of a child as mentioned in subsection (1)(b) above—

(a) he shall be taken to have committed the adultery to which the finding relates or, as the case may be, to be (or have been) the father of that child, unless the contrary is proved; and

(b) without prejudice to the reception of any other admissible evidence for the purpose of identifying the facts on which the finding or adjudication was based, the contents of any document which was before the court, or which contains any pronouncement of the court, in the other proceedings in question shall be admissible in evidence for that purpose.

(3) Nothing in this section shall prejudice the operation of any enactment whereby a finding of fact in any matrimonial or affiliation proceedings is for the purposes of any other proceedings made conclusive evidence of any fact.

(4) Subsection (4) of section 11 of this Act shall apply for the purposes of this section as if the reference to subsection (2) were a reference to subsection (2) of this section.

(5) In this section—

'matrimonial proceedings' means any matrimonial cause in the High Court or a county court in England and Wales or in the High Court in Northern Ireland, any consistorial action in Scotland, or any appeal arising out of any such cause or action;

'relevant proceedings' means—

(a) . . .;

(b) proceedings under the Children Act 1989;

(c) proceedings which would have been relevant proceedings for the purposes of this section in the form in which it was in force before the passing of the Children Act 1989.

13 Conclusiveness of convictions for purposes of defamation actions

(1) In an action for libel or slander in which the question whether the plaintiff did or did not commit a criminal offence is relevant to an issue arising in the action, proof that, at the time when that issue falls to be determined, he stands convicted of that offence shall be conclusive evidence that he committed that offence; and his conviction thereof shall be admissible in evidence accordingly.

(2) In any such action as aforesaid in which by virtue of this section the plaintiff is proved to have been convicted of an offence, the contents of any document which is admissible as evidence of the conviction, and the contents of the information, complaint, indictment or charge-sheet on which he was convicted, shall, without prejudice to the reception of any other admissible evidence for the purpose of identifying the facts on which the conviction was based, be admissible in evidence for the purpose of identifying those facts.

(2A) In the case of an action for libel or slander in which there is more than one plaintiff—

(a) the references in subsections (1) and (2) above to the plaintiff shall be construed as references to any of the plaintiffs, and

(b) proof that any of the plaintiffs stands convicted of an offence shall be conclusive evidence that he committed that offence so far as that fact is relevant to any issue arising in relation to his cause of action or that of any other plaintiff.

(3) For the purposes of this section a person shall be taken to stand convicted of an offence if but only if there subsists against him a conviction of that offence by or before a court in the United Kingdom or by a court-martial there or elsewhere.

(4) Subsections (4) to (7) of section 11 of this Act shall apply for the purposes of this section as they apply for the purposes of that section, but as if in the said subsection (4) the reference to subsection (2) were a reference to subsection (2) of this section.

(5) The foregoing provisions of this section shall apply for the purposes of any action begun after the passing of this Act, whenever the cause of action arose, but shall not apply for the purposes of any action begun before the passing of this Act or any appeal or other proceedings arising out of any such action.

Civil Evidence Act 1972

(1972, c. 30)

3 Admissibility of expert opinion and certain expressions of non-expert opinion

(1) Subject to any rules of court made in pursuance of . . . this Act, where a person is called as a witness in any civil proceedings, his opinion on any relevant matter on which he is qualified to give expert evidence shall be admissible in evidence.

(2) It is hereby declared that where a person is called as a witness in any civil proceedings, a statement of opinion by him on any relevant matter on which he is not qualified to give expert evidence, if made as a way of conveying relevant facts personally perceived by him, is admissible as evidence of what he perceived.

(3) In this section 'relevant matter' includes an issue in the proceedings in question.

Children Act 1989

(1989, c. 41)

96 Evidence given by, or with respect to, children

(1) Subsection (2) applies where a child who is called as a witness in any civil proceedings does not, in the opinion of the court, understand the nature of an oath.

(2) The child's evidence may be heard by the court if, in its opinion—

(a) he understands that it is his duty to speak the truth; and

(b) he has sufficient understanding to justify his evidence being heard.

(3) The Lord Chancellor may with the concurrence of the Lord Chief Justice by order make provision for the admissibility of evidence which would otherwise be inadmissible under any rule of law relating to hearsay.

(4) An order under subsection (3) may only be made with respect to—
(a) civil proceedings in general or such civil proceedings, or class of civil proceedings, as may be prescribed; and
(b) evidence in connection with the upbringing, maintenance or welfare of a child.
(5) An order under subsection (3)—
(a) may, in particular, provide for the admissibility of statements which are made orally or in a prescribed form or which are recorded by any prescribed method of recording;
(b) may make different provision for different purposes and in relation to different descriptions of court; and
(c) may make such amendments and repeals in any enactment relating to evidence (other than in this Act) as the Lord Chancellor considers necessary or expedient in consequence of the provision made by the order.
(6) Subsection (5)(b) is without prejudice to section 104(4).
(7) In this section—
'civil proceedings' means civil proceedings, before any tribunal, in relation to which the strict rules of evidence apply, whether as a matter of law or agreement between the parties, and reference to 'the court' shall be construed accordingly; and
'prescribed' means prescribed by an order under subsection (3).

98 Self-incrimination

(1) In any proceedings in which a court is hearing an application for an order under Part IV or V, no person shall be excused from—
(a) giving evidence on any matter; or
(b) answering any question put to him in the course of his giving evidence,
on the ground that doing so might incriminate him or his spouse or civil partner of an offence.
(2) A statement or admission made in such proceedings shall not be admissible in evidence against the person making it or his spouse or civil partner in proceedings for an offence other than perjury.

Civil Evidence Act 1995

(1995, c. 38)

Admissibility of hearsay evidence

1 Admissibility of hearsay evidence

(1) In civil proceedings evidence shall not be excluded on the ground that it is hearsay.
(2) In this Act—
(a) 'hearsay' means a statement made otherwise than by a person while giving oral evidence in the proceedings which is tendered as evidence of the matters stated; and
(b) references to hearsay include hearsay of whatever degree.
(3) Nothing in this Act affects the admissibility of evidence admissible apart from this section.
(4) The provisions of sections 2 to 6 (safeguards and supplementary provisions relating to hearsay evidence) do not apply in relation to hearsay evidence admissible apart from this section, notwithstanding that it may also be admissible by virtue of this section.

Safeguards in relation to hearsay evidence

2 Notice of proposal to adduce hearsay evidence

(1) A party proposing to adduce hearsay evidence in civil proceedings shall, subject to the following provisions of this section, give to the other party or parties to the proceedings—
(a) such notice (if any) of that fact, and
(b) on request, such particulars of or relating to the evidence,
as is reasonable and practicable in the circumstances for the purpose of enabling him or them to deal with any matters arising from its being hearsay.

(2) Provision may be made by rules of court—

(a) specifying classes of proceedings or evidence in relation to which subsection (1) does not apply, and

(b) as to the manner in which (including the time within which) the duties imposed by that subsection are to be complied with in the cases where it does apply.

(3) Subsection (1) may also be excluded by agreement of the parties; and compliance with the duty to give notice may in any case be waived by the person to whom notice is required to be given.

(4) A failure to comply with subsection (1), or with rules under subsection (2)(b), does not affect the admissibility of the evidence but may be taken into account by the court—

(a) in considering the exercise of its powers with respect to the course of proceedings and costs, and

(b) as a matter adversely affecting the weight to be given to the evidence in accordance with section 4.

3 Power to call witness for cross-examination on hearsay statement

Rules of court may provide that where a party to civil proceedings adduces hearsay evidence of a statement made by a person and does not call that person as a witness, any other party to the proceedings may, with the leave of the court, call that person as a witness and cross-examine him on the statement as if he had been called by the first-mentioned party and as if the hearsay statement were his evidence in chief.

4 Considerations relevant to weighing of hearsay evidence

(1) In estimating the weight (if any) to be given to hearsay evidence in civil proceedings the court shall have regard to any circumstances from which any inference can reasonably be drawn as to the reliability or otherwise of the evidence.

(2) Regard may be had, in particular, to the following—

(a) whether it would have been reasonable and practicable for the party by whom the evidence was adduced to have produced the maker of the original statement as a witness;

(b) whether the original statement was made contemporaneously with the occurrence or existence of the matters stated;

(c) whether the evidence involves multiple hearsay;

(d) whether any person involved had any motive to conceal or misrepresent matters;

(e) whether the original statement was an edited account, or was made in collaboration with another or for a particular purpose;

(f) whether the circumstances in which the evidence is adduced as hearsay are such as to suggest an attempt to prevent proper evaluation of its weight.

Supplementary provisions as to hearsay evidence

5 Competence and credibility

(1) Hearsay evidence shall not be admitted in civil proceedings if or to the extent that it is shown to consist of, or to be proved by means of, a statement made by a person who at the time he made the statement was not competent as a witness.

For this purpose 'not competent as a witness' means suffering from such mental or physical infirmity, or lack of understanding, as would render a person incompetent as a witness in civil proceedings; but a child shall be treated as competent as a witness if he satisfies the requirements of section 96(2)(a) and (b) of the Children Act 1989 (conditions for reception of unsworn evidence of child).

(2) Where in civil proceedings hearsay evidence is adduced and the maker of the original statement, or of any statement relied upon to prove another statement, is not called as a witness—

(a) evidence which if he had been so called would be admissible for the purpose of attacking or supporting his credibility as a witness is admissible for that purpose in the proceedings; and

(b) evidence tending to prove that, whether before or after he made the statement, he made any other statement inconsistent with it is admissible for the purpose of showing that he had contradicted himself.

Provided that evidence may not be given of any matter of which, if he had been called as a witness and had denied that matter in cross-examination, evidence could not have been adduced by the cross-examining party.

6 Previous statements of witnesses

(1) Subject as follows, the provisions of this Act as to hearsay evidence in civil proceedings apply equally (but with any necessary modifications) in relation to a previous statement made by a person called as a witness in the proceedings.

(2) A party who has called or intends to call a person as a witness in civil proceedings may not in those proceedings adduce evidence of a previous statement made by that person, except—

(a) with the leave of the court, or

(b) for the purpose of rebutting a suggestion that his evidence has been fabricated.

This shall not be construed as preventing a witness statement (that is, a written statement of oral evidence which a party to the proceedings intends to lead) from being adopted by a witness in giving evidence or treated as his evidence.

(3) Where in the case of civil proceedings section 3, 4 or 5 of the Criminal Procedure Act 1865 applies, which make provision as to—

(a) how far a witness may be discredited by the party producing him,

(b) the proof of contradictory statements made by a witness, and

(c) cross-examination as to previous statements in writing,

this Act does not authorise the adducing of evidence of a previous inconsistent or contradictory statement otherwise than in accordance with those sections.

This is without prejudice to any provision made by rules of court under section 3 above (power to call witness for cross-examination on hearsay statement).

(4) Nothing in this Act affects any of the rules of law as to the circumstances in which, where a person called as a witness in civil proceedings is cross-examined on a document used by him to refresh his memory, that document may be made evidence in the proceedings.

(5) Nothing in this section shall be construed as preventing a statement of any description referred to above from being admissible by virtue of section 1 as evidence of the matters stated.

7 Evidence formerly admissible at common law

(1) The common law rule effectively preserved by section 9(1) and (2)(a) of the Civil Evidence Act 1968 (admissibility of admissions adverse to a party) is superseded by the provisions of this Act.

(2) The common law rules effectively preserved by section 9(1) and (2)(b) to (d) of the Civil Evidence Act 1968, that is, any rule of law whereby in civil proceedings—

(a) published works dealing with matters of a public nature (for example, histories, scientific works, dictionaries and maps) are admissible as evidence of facts of a public nature stated in them,

(b) public documents (for example, public registers, and returns made under public authority with respect to matters of public interest) are admissible as evidence of facts stated in them, or

(c) records (for example, the records of certain courts, treaties, Crown grants, pardons and commissions) are admissible as evidence of facts stated in them, shall continue to have effect.

(3) The common law rules effectively preserved by section 9(3) and (4) of the Civil Evidence Act 1968, that is, any rule of law whereby in civil proceedings—

(a) evidence of a person's reputation is admissible for the purpose of proving his good or bad character, or

(b) evidence of reputation or family tradition is admissible—
   (i) for the purpose of proving or disproving pedigree or the existence of a marriage, or
   (ii) for the purpose of proving or disproving the existence of any public or general right or of identifying any person or thing,

shall continue to have effect in so far as they authorise the court to treat such evidence as proving or disproving that matter.

Where any such rule applies, reputation or family tradition shall be treated for the purposes of this Act as a fact and not as a statement or multiplicity of statements about the matter in question.

(4) The words in which a rule of law mentioned in this section is described are intended only to identify the rule and shall not be construed as altering it in any way.

Other matters

8 Proof of statements contained in documents

(1) Where a statement contained in a document is admissible as evidence in civil proceedings, it may be proved—

(a) by the production of that document, or
(b) whether or not that document is still in existence, by the production of a copy of that document or of the material part of it,

authenticated in such manner as the court may approve.

(2) It is immaterial for this purpose how many removes there are between a copy and the original.

9 Proof of records of business or public authority

(1) A document which is shown to form part of the records of a business or public authority may be received in evidence in civil proceedings without further proof.

(2) A document shall be taken to form part of the records of a business or public authority if there is produced to the court a certificate to that effect signed by an officer of the business or authority to which the records belong.

For this purpose—

(a) a document purporting to be a certificate signed by an officer of a business or public authority shall be deemed to have been duly given by such an officer and signed by him; and
(b) a certificate shall be treated as signed by a person if it purports to bear a facsimile of his signature.

(3) The absence of an entry in the records of a business or public authority may be proved in civil proceedings by affidavit of an officer of the business or authority to which the records belong.

(4) In this section—

'records' means records in whatever form;

'business' includes any activity regularly carried on over a period of time, whether for profit or not, by any body (whether corporate or not) or by an individual;

'officer' includes any person occupying a responsible position in relation to the relevant activities of the business or public authority or in relation to its records; and

'public authority' includes any public or statutory undertaking, any government department and any person holding office under Her Majesty.

(5) The court may, having regard to the circumstances of the case, direct that all or any of the above provisions of this section do not apply in relation to a particular document or record, or description of documents or records.

10 Admissibility and proof of Ogden Tables

(1) The actuarial tables (together with explanatory notes) for use in personal injury and fatal accident cases issued from time to time by the Government Actuary's Department are admissible in evidence for the purpose of assessing, in an action for personal injury, the sum to be awarded as general damages for future pecuniary loss.

(2) They may be proved by the production of a copy published by Her Majesty's Stationery Office.

(3) For the purposes of this section—

(a) 'personal injury' includes any disease and any impairment of a person's physical or mental condition; and

(b) 'action for personal injury' includes an action brought by virtue of the Law Reform (Miscellaneous Provisions) Act 1934 or the Fatal Accidents Act 1976.

General

11 Meaning of 'civil proceedings'

In this Act 'civil proceedings' means civil proceedings, before any tribunal, in relation to which the strict rules of evidence apply, whether as a matter of law or by agreement of the parties.

References to 'the court' and 'rules of court' shall be construed accordingly.

12 Provisions as to rules of court

(1) Any power to make rules of court regulating the practice or procedure of the court in relation to civil proceedings includes power to make such provision as may be necessary or expedient for carrying into effect the provisions of this Act.

(2) Any rules of court made for the purposes of this Act as it applies in relation to proceedings in the High Court apply, except in so far as their operation is excluded by agreement, to arbitration proceedings to which this Act applies, subject to such modifications as may be appropriate.

Any question arising as to what modifications are appropriate shall be determined, in default of agreement, by the arbitrator or umpire, as the case may be.

13 Interpretation

In this Act—

'civil proceedings' has the meaning given by section 11 and 'court' and 'rules of court' shall be construed in accordance with that section;

'document' means anything in which information of any description is recorded, and 'copy', in relation to a document, means anything onto which information recorded in the document has been copied, by whatever means and whether directly or indirectly;

'hearsay' shall be construed in accordance with section 1(2);

'oral evidence' includes evidence which, by reason of a defect of speech or hearing, a person called as a witness gives in writing or by signs;

'the original statement', in relation to hearsay evidence, means the underlying statement (if any) by—

(a) in the case of evidence of fact, a person having personal knowledge of the fact, or

(b) in the case of evidence of opinion, the person whose opinion it is; and

'statement' means any representation of fact or opinion, however made.

14 Savings

(1) Nothing in this Act affects the exclusion of evidence on grounds other than that it is hearsay.

This applies whether the evidence falls to be excluded in pursuance of any enactment or rule of law, for failure to comply with rules of court or an order of the court, or otherwise.

(2) Nothing in this Act affects the proof of documents by means other than those specified in section 8 or 9.

(3) Nothing in this Act affects the operation of the following enactments—

(a) section 2 of the Documentary Evidence Act 1868 (mode of proving certain official documents);

(b) section 2 of the Documentary Evidence Act 1882 (documents printed under the superintendence of Stationery Office);

(c) section 1 of the Evidence (Colonial Statutes) Act 1907 (proof of statutes of certain legislatures);

(d) section 1 of the Evidence (Foreign, Dominion and Colonial Documents) Act 1933 (proof and effect of registers and official certificates of certain countries);

(e) section 5 of the Oaths and Evidence (Overseas Authorities and Countries) Act 1963 (provision in respect of public registers of other countries).

16 Short title commencement and extent

(1) This Act may be cited as the Civil Evidence Act 1995.

(4) This Act extends to England and Wales.

Civil Partnership Act 2004

(2004, c. 33)

84 Evidence

(1) Any enactment or rule of law relating to the giving of evidence by a spouse applies in relation to a civil partner as it applies in relation to the spouse.

(2) Subsection (1) is subject to any specific amendment made by or under this Act which relates to the giving of evidence by a civil partner.

(3) For the avoidance of doubt, in any such amendment, references to a person's civil partner do not include a former civil partner.

(4) References in subsections (1) and (2) to giving evidence are to giving evidence in any way (whether by supplying information, making discovery, producing documents or otherwise).

(5) Any rule of law—

(a) which is preserved by section 7(3) of the Civil Evidence Act 1995 or section 118(1) of the Criminal Justice Act 2003, and

(b) under which in any proceedings evidence of reputation or family tradition is admissible for the purpose of proving or disproving the existence of a marriage,

is to be treated as applying in an equivalent way for the purpose of proving or disproving the existence of a civil partnership.

Civil Procedure Rules 1998

(SI 1998, No. 3132 (L. 17))

32.1 Power of court to control evidence

(1) The court may control the evidence by giving directions as to—

(a) the issues on which it requires evidence;

(b) the nature of the evidence which it requires to decide those issues; and

(c) the way in which the evidence is to be placed before the court.

(2) The court may use its power under this rule to exclude evidence that would otherwise be admissible.

(3) The court may limit cross-examination.

32.2 Evidence of witnesses—general rule

(1) The general rule is that any fact which needs to be proved by the evidence of witnesses is to be proved—

(a) at trial, by their oral evidence given in public; and

(b) at any other hearing, by their evidence in writing.

(2) This is subject—

(a) to any provision to the contrary contained in these Rules or elsewhere; or

(b) to any order of the court.

(3) The court may give directions—

(a) identifying or limiting the issues to which factual evidence may be directed;

(b) identifying the witnesses who may be called or whose evidence may be read; or

(c) limiting the length or format of witness statements.

32.3 Evidence by video link or other means

The court may allow a witness to give evidence through a video link or by other means.

32.4 Requirement to serve witness statements for use at trial

(1) A witness statement is a written statement signed by a person which contains the evidence which that person would be allowed to give orally.

(2) The court will order a party to serve on the other parties any witness statement of the oral evidence which the party serving the statement intends to rely on in relation to any issues of fact to be decided at the trial.

(3) The court may give directions as to—

(a) the order in which witness statements are to be served; and

(b) whether or not the witness statements are to be filed.

32.5 Use at trial of witness statements which have been served

(1) If—

(a) a party has served a witness statement; and

(b) he wishes to rely at trial on the evidence of the witness who made the statement,

he must call the witness to give oral evidence unless the court orders otherwise or he puts the statement in as hearsay evidence.

(Part 33 contains provisions about hearsay evidence)

(2) Where a witness is called to give oral evidence under paragraph (1), his witness statement shall stand as his evidence in chief unless the court orders otherwise.

(3) A witness giving oral evidence at trial may with the permission of the court—

(a) amplify his witness statement; and

(b) give evidence in relation to new matters which have arisen since the witness statement was served on the other parties.

(4) The court will give permission under paragraph (3) only if it considers that there is good reason not to confine the evidence of the witness to the contents of his witness statement.

(5) If a party who has served a witness statement does not—

(a) call the witness to give evidence at trial; or

(b) put the witness statement in as hearsay evidence, any other party may put the witness statement in as hearsay evidence.

32.6 Evidence in proceedings other than at trial

(1) Subject to paragraph (2), the general rule is that evidence at hearings other than the trial is to be by witness statement unless the court, a practice direction or any other enactment requires otherwise.

(2) At hearings other than the trial, a party may, rely on the matters set out in—

(a) his statement of case; or

(b) his application notice, if the statement of case or application notice is verified by a statement of truth.

32.7 Order for cross-examination

(1) Where, at a hearing other than the trial, evidence is given in writing, any party may apply to the court for permission to cross-examine the person giving the evidence.

(2) If the court gives permission under paragraph (1) but the person in question does not attend as required by the order, his evidence may not be used unless the court gives permission.

32.8 Form of witness statement

A witness statement must comply with the requirements set out in Practice Direction 32.

(Part 22 requires a witness statement to be verified by a statement of truth)

32.9 Witness summaries

(1) A party who—

(a) is required to serve a witness statement for use at trial; but
(b) is unable to obtain one, may apply, without notice, for permission to serve a witness summary instead.

(2) A witness summary is a summary of—
(a) the evidence, if known, which would otherwise be included in a witness statement; or
(b) if the evidence is not known, the matters about which the party serving the witness summary proposes to question the witness.

(3) Unless the court orders otherwise, a witness summary must include the name and address of the intended witness.

(4) Unless the court orders otherwise, a witness summary must be served within the period in which a witness statement would have had to be served.

(5) Where a party serves a witness summary, so far as practicable rules 32.4 (requirement to serve witness statements for use at trial), 32.5(3) (amplifying witness statements), and 32.8 (form of witness statement) shall apply to the summary.

32.10 Consequence of failure to serve witness statement or summary

If a witness statement or a witness summary for use at trial is not served in respect of an intended witness within the time specified by the court, then the witness may not be called to give oral evidence unless the court gives permission.

32.11 Cross-examination on a witness statement

Where a witness is called to give evidence at trial, he may be cross-examined on his witness statement whether or not the statement or any part of it was referred to during the witness's evidence in chief.

32.12 Use of witness statements for other purposes

(1) Except as provided by this rule, a witness statement may be used only for the purpose of the proceedings in which it is served.

(2) Paragraph (1) does not apply if and to the extent that—
(a) the witness gives consent in writing to some other use of it;
(b) the court gives permission for some other use; or
(c) the witness statement has been put in evidence at a hearing held in public.

32.13 Availability of witness statements for inspection

(1) A witness statement which stands as evidence in chief is open to inspection during the course of the trial unless the court otherwise directs.

(2) Any person may ask for a direction that a witness statement is not open to inspection.

(3) The court will not make a direction under paragraph (2) unless it is satisfied that a witness statement should not be open to inspection because of—
(a) the interests of justice;
(b) the public interest;
(c) the nature of any expert medical evidence in the statement;
(d) the nature of any confidential information (including information relating to personal financial matters) in the statement; or
(e) the need to protect the interests of any child or protected party.

(4) The court may exclude from inspection words or passages in the statement.

32.14 False statements

(1) Proceedings for contempt of court may be brought against a person if he makes, or causes to be made, a false statement in a document verified by a statement of truth without an honest belief in its truth.

(Part 22 makes provision for a statement of truth)

32.15 Affidavit evidence

(1) Evidence must be given by affidavit instead of or in addition to a witness statement if this is required by the court, a provision contained in any other rule, a practice direction or any other enactment.

(2) Nothing in these Rules prevents a witness giving evidence by affidavit at a hearing other than the trial if he chooses to do so in a case where paragraph (1) does not apply, but the party putting forward the affidavit may not recover the additional cost of making it from any other party unless the court orders otherwise.

32.16 Form of affidavit

An affidavit must comply with the requirements set out in Practice Direction 32.

32.17 Affidavit made outside the jurisdiction

A person may make an affidavit outside the jurisdiction in accordance with—

(a) this Part; or

(b) the law of the place where he makes the affidavit.

32.18 Notice to admit facts

(1) A party may serve notice on another party requiring him to admit the facts, or the part of the case of the serving party, specified in the notice.

(2) A notice to admit facts must be served no later than 21 days before the trial.

(3) Where the other party makes any admission in response to the notice, the admission may be used against him only—

(a) in the proceedings in which the notice to admit is served; and

(b) by the party who served the notice.

(4) The court may allow a party to amend or withdraw any admission made by him on such terms as it thinks just.

32.19 Notice to admit or produce documents

(1) A party shall be deemed to admit the authenticity of a document disclosed to him under Part 31 (disclosure and inspection of documents) unless he serves notice that he wishes the document to be proved at trial.

(2) A notice to prove a document must be served—

(a) by the latest date for serving witness statements; or

(b) within 7 days of disclosure of the document,

whichever is later.

32.20 Notarial acts and instruments

A notarial act or instrument may be received in evidence without further proof as duly authenticated in accordance with the requirements of law unless the contrary is proved.

PD 32 PRACTICE DIRECTION WRITTEN EVIDENCE

EVIDENCE IN GENERAL

1.1

Rule 32.2 sets out how evidence is to be given and facts are to be proved.

1.2

Evidence at a hearing other than the trial should normally be given by witness statement (see paragraph 17 onwards). However a witness may give evidence by affidavit if he wishes to do so (and see paragraph 1.4 below).

1.3

Statements of case (see paragraph 26 onwards) and application notices may also be used as evidence provided that their contents have been verified by a statement of truth.

(For information regarding evidence by deposition see Part 34 and Practice Direction 34A.)

1.4

Affidavits must be used as evidence in the following instances:

(1) where sworn evidence is required by an enactment, rule, order or practice direction, and

(2) in any application for a search order, a freezing injunction, or an order requiring an occupier to permit another to enter his land. (Part 81—Applications and proceedings in relation to contempt of court, and the Practice Direction accompanying that Part, contain provisions about evidence in relation to contempt of court. Particular attention is drawn to rules 81.10, 81.11, 81.14, 81.15, 81.26 and Practice Direction 81 paragraphs 4.5 and 14.1.)

1.5

If a party believes that sworn evidence is required by a court in another jurisdiction for any purpose connected with the proceedings, he may apply to the court for a direction that evidence shall be given only by affidavit on any pre-trial applications.

1.6

The court may give a direction under rule 32.15 that evidence shall be given by affidavit instead of or in addition to a witness statement or statement of case:

(1) on its own initiative, or

(2) after any party has applied to the court for such a direction.

1.7

An affidavit, where referred to in the Civil Procedure Rules or a practice direction, also means an affirmation unless the context requires otherwise.

AFFIDAVITS

Deponent

2

A deponent is a person who gives evidence by affidavit or affirmation.

Heading

3.1

The affidavit should be headed with the title of the proceedings (see paragraph 4 of Practice Direction 7A and paragraph 7 of Practice Direction 20); where the proceedings are between several parties with the same status it is sufficient to identify the parties as follows:

	Number:
A.B. (and others)	Claimants/Applicants
C.D. (and others)	Defendants/Respondents
	(as appropriate)

3.2

At the top right hand corner of the first page (and on the backsheet) there should be clearly written:

(1) the party on whose behalf it is made,

(2) the initials and surname of the deponent,

(3) the number of the affidavit in relation to that deponent,

(4) the identifying initials and number of each exhibit referred to, and

(5) the date sworn.

Body of affidavit

4.1
The affidavit must, if practicable, be in the deponent's own words, the affidavit should be expressed in the first person and the deponent should:

(1) commence 'I (*full name*) of (*address*) state on oath......',

(2) if giving evidence in his professional, business or other occupational capacity, give the address at which he works in (1) above, the position he holds and the name of his firm or employer,

(3) give his occupation or, if he has none, his description, and

(4) state if he is a party to the proceedings or employed by a party to the proceedings, if it be the case.

4.2
An affidavit must indicate:

(1) which of the statements in it are made from the deponent's own knowledge and which are matters of information or belief, and

(2) the source for any matters of information or belief.

4.3
Where a deponent:

(1) refers to an exhibit or exhibits, he should state 'there is now shown to me marked '...' the (*description of exhibit*)', and

(2) makes more than one affidavit (to which there are exhibits) in the same proceedings, the numbering of the exhibits should run consecutively throughout and not start again with each affidavit.

Jurat

5.1
The jurat of an affidavit is a statement set out at the end of the document which authenticates the affidavit.

5.2
It must:

(1) be signed by all deponents,

(2) be completed and signed by the person before whom the affidavit was sworn whose name and qualification must be printed beneath his signature,

(3) contain the full address of the person before whom the affidavit was sworn, and

(4) follow immediately on from the text and not be put on a separate page.

Format of affidavits

6.1
An affidavit should:

(1) be produced on durable quality A4 paper with a 3.5cm margin,

(2) be fully legible and should normally be typed on one side of the paper only,

(3) where possible, be bound securely in a manner which would not hamper filing, or otherwise each page should be endorsed with the case number and should bear the initials of the deponent and of the person before whom it was sworn,

(4) have the pages numbered consecutively as a separate document (or as one of several documents contained in a file),

(5) be divided into numbered paragraphs,

(6) have all numbers, including dates, expressed in figures, and

(7) give the reference to any document or documents mentioned either in the margin or in bold text in the body of the affidavit.

6.2
It is usually convenient for an affidavit to follow the chronological sequence of events or matters dealt with; each paragraph of an affidavit should as far as possible be confined to a distinct portion of the subject.

Inability of Deponent to read or sign affidavit

7.1
Where an affidavit is sworn by a person who is unable to read or sign it, the person before whom the affidavit is sworn must certify in the jurat that:

(1) he read the affidavit to the deponent,
(2) the deponent appeared to understand it, and
(3) the deponent signed or made his mark, in his presence.

7.2
If that certificate is not included in the jurat, the affidavit may not be used in evidence unless the court is satisfied that it was read to the deponent and that he appeared to understand it. Two versions of the form of jurat with the certificate are set out at Annex 1 to this practice direction.

Alterations to affidavits

8.1
Any alteration to an affidavit must be initialled by both the deponent and the person before whom the affidavit was sworn.

8.2
An affidavit which contains an alteration that has not been initialled may be filed or used in evidence only with the permission of the court.

Who may administer oaths and take affidavits

9.1
Only the following may administer oaths and take affidavits:

(1) A commissioner for oaths;
(2) omitted
(3) other persons specified by statute;
(4) certain officials of the Senior Courts;
(5) a circuit judge or district judge;
(6) any justice of the peace; and
(7) certain officials of any county court appointed by the judge of that court for the purpose.

9.2
An affidavit must be sworn before a person independent of the parties or their representatives.

Filing of affidavits

10.1
If the court directs that an affidavit is to be filed, it must be filed in the court or Division, or Office or Registry of the court or Division where the action in which it was or is to be used, is proceeding or will proceed.

10.2
Where an affidavit is in a foreign language:

(1) the party wishing to rely on it—
    (a) must have it translated, and
    (b) must file the foreign language affidavit with the court, and

(2) the translator must make and file with the court an affidavit verifying the translation and exhibiting both the translation and a copy of the foreign language affidavit.

EXHIBITS

Manner of exhibiting documents

11.1

A document used in conjunction with an affidavit should be:

(1) produced to and verified by the deponent, and remain separate from the affidavit, and
(2) identified by a declaration of the person before whom the affidavit was sworn.

11.2

The declaration should be headed with the name of the proceedings in the same way as the affidavit.

11.3

The first page of each exhibit should be marked:

(1) as in paragraph 3.2 above, and
(2) with the exhibit mark referred to in the affidavit.

Letters

12.1

Copies of individual letters should be collected together and exhibited in a bundle or bundles. They should be arranged in chronological order with the earliest at the top, and firmly secured.

12.2

When a bundle of correspondence is exhibited, the exhibit should have a front page attached stating that the bundle consists of original letters and copies. They should be arranged and secured as above and numbered consecutively.

Other documents

13.1

Photocopies instead of original documents may be exhibited provided the originals are made available for inspection by the other parties before the hearing and by the judge at the hearing.

13.2

Court documents must not be exhibited (official copies of such documents prove themselves).

13.3

Where an exhibit contains more than one document, a front page should be attached setting out a list of the documents contained in the exhibit; the list should contain the dates of the documents.

Exhibits other than documents

14.1

Items other than documents should be clearly marked with an exhibit number or letter in such a manner that the mark cannot become detached from the exhibit.

14.2

Small items may be placed in a container and the container appropriately marked.

General provisions

15.1

Where an exhibit contains more than one document:

(1) the bundle should not be stapled but should be securely fastened in a way that does not hinder the reading of the documents, and

(2) the pages should be numbered consecutively at bottom centre.

15.2
Every page of an exhibit should be clearly legible; typed copies of illegible documents should be included, paginated with 'a' numbers.

15.3
Where affidavits and exhibits have become numerous, they should be put into separate bundles and the pages numbered consecutively throughout.

15.4
Where on account of their bulk the service of exhibits or copies of exhibits on the other parties would be difficult or impracticable, the directions of the court should be sought as to arrangements for bringing the exhibits to the attention of the other parties and as to their custody pending trial.

Affirmations

16
All provisions in this or any other practice direction relating to affidavits apply to affirmations with the following exceptions:

(1) the deponent should commence 'I (*name*) of (*address*) do solemnly and sincerely affirm ......', and

(2) in the jurat the word 'sworn' is replaced by the word 'affirmed'.

WITNESS STATEMENTS

Heading

17.1
The witness statement should be headed with the title of the proceedings (see paragraph 4 of Practice Direction 7A and paragraph 7 of Practice Direction 20); where the proceedings are between several parties with the same status it is sufficient to identify the parties as follows:

	Number:
A.B. (and others)	Claimants/Applicants
C.D. (and others)	Defendants/Respondents
	(as appropriate)

17.2
At the top right hand corner of the first page there should be clearly written:

(1) the party on whose behalf it is made,
(2) the initials and surname of the witness,
(3) the number of the statement in relation to that witness,
(4) the identifying initials and number of each exhibit referred to, and
(5) the date the statement was made.

Body of witness statement

18.1
The witness statement must, if practicable, be in the intended witness's own words, the statement should be expressed in the first person and should also state:

(1) the full name of the witness,

(2) his place of residence or, if he is making the statement in his professional, business or other occupational capacity, the address at which he works, the position he holds and the name of his firm or employer,

(3) his occupation, or if he has none, his description, and

(4) the fact that he is a party to the proceedings or is the employee of such a party if it be the case.

18.2

A witness statement must indicate:

(1) which of the statements in it are made from the witness's own knowledge and which are matters of information or belief, and

(2) the source for any matters of information or belief.

18.3

An exhibit used in conjunction with a witness statement should be verified and identified by the witness and remain separate from the witness statement.

18.4

Where a witness refers to an exhibit or exhibits, he should state 'I refer to the (*description of exhibit*) marked '...''.

18.5

The provisions of paragraphs 11.3 to 15.4 (exhibits) apply similarly to witness statements as they do to affidavits.

18.6

Where a witness makes more than one witness statement to which there are exhibits, in the same proceedings, the numbering of the exhibits should run consecutively throughout and not start again with each witness statement.

Format of witness statement

19.1

A witness statement should:

(1) be produced on durable quality A4 paper with a 3.5cm margin,

(2) be fully legible and should normally be typed on one side of the paper only,

(3) where possible, be bound securely in a manner which would not hamper filing, or otherwise each page should be endorsed with the case number and should bear the initials of the witness,

(4) have the pages numbered consecutively as a separate statement (or as one of several statements contained in a file),

(5) be divided into numbered paragraphs,

(6) have all numbers, including dates, expressed in figures, and

(7) give the reference to any document or documents mentioned either in the margin or in bold text in the body of the statement.

19.2

It is usually convenient for a witness statement to follow the chronological sequence of the events or matters dealt with, each paragraph of a witness statement should as far as possible be confined to a distinct portion of the subject.

Statement of Truth

20.1

A witness statement is the equivalent of the oral evidence which that witness would, if called, give in evidence; it must include a statement by the intended witness that he believes the facts in it are true.

20.2

To verify a witness statement the statement of truth is as follows:

'I believe that the facts stated in this witness statement are true'.

20.3

Attention is drawn to rule 32.14 which sets out the consequences of verifying a witness statement containing a false statement without an honest belief in its truth.

(Paragraph 3A of Practice Direction 22 sets out the procedure to be followed where the person who should sign a document which is verified by a statement of truth is unable to read or sign the document.)

21
Omitted

Alterations to witness statements

22.1
Any alteration to a witness statement must be initialled by the person making the statement or by the authorised person where appropriate (see paragraph 21).

22.2
A witness statement which contains an alteration that has not been initialled may be used in evidence only with the permission of the court.

Filing of witness statements

23.1
If the court directs that a witness statement is to be filed, it must be filed in the court or Division, or Office or Registry of the court or Division where the action in which it was or is to be used, is proceeding or will proceed.

23.2
Where the court has directed that a witness statement in a foreign language is to be filed:

(1) the party wishing to rely on it must—

(a) have it translated, and

(b) file the foreign language witness statement with the court, and

(2) the translator must make and file with the court an affidavit verifying the translation and exhibiting both the translation and a copy of the foreign language witness statement.

Certificate of court officer

24.1
Where the court has ordered that a witness statement is not to be open to inspection by the public or that words or passages in the statement are not to be open to inspection the court officer will so certify on the statement and make any deletions directed by the court under rule 32.13(4).

Defects in affidavits, witness statements and exhibits

25.1
Where:

(1) an affidavit,

(2) a witness statement, or

(3) an exhibit to either an affidavit or a witness statement,

does not comply with Part 32 or this practice direction in relation to its form, the court may refuse to admit it as evidence and may refuse to allow the costs arising from its preparation.

25.2
Permission to file a defective affidavit or witness statement or to use a defective exhibit may be obtained from a judge in the court where the case is proceeding.

STATEMENTS OF CASE

26.1
A statement of case may be used as evidence in an interim application provided it is verified by a statement of truth.

26.2

To verify a statement of case the statement of truth should be set out as follows:

'[I believe] [the *(party on whose behalf the statement of case is being signed)* believes] that the facts stated in the statement of case are true'.

26.3

Attention is drawn to rule 32.14 which sets out the consequences of verifying a witness statement containing a false statement without an honest belief in its truth.

(For information regarding statements of truth see Part 22 and Practice Direction 22.)

(Practice Directions 7A and 17 provide further information concerning statements of case.)

AGREED BUNDLES FOR HEARINGS

27.1

The court may give directions requiring the parties to use their best endeavours to agree a bundle or bundles of documents for use at any hearing.

27.2

All documents contained in bundles which have been agreed for use at a hearing shall be admissible at that hearing as evidence of their contents, unless—

(1) the court orders otherwise; or

(2) a party gives written notice of objection to the admissibility of particular documents.

VIDEO CONFERENCING

29.1

Guidance on the use of video conferencing in the civil courts is set out at Annex 3 to this practice direction.

A list of the sites which are available for video conferencing can be found on Her Majesty's Courts Service website at www.hmcourts-service.gov.uk.

ANNEX 1

Certificate to be used where a deponent to an affidavit is unable to read or sign it

Sworn at .... this ...... day of .... Before me, I having first read over the contents of this affidavit to the deponent [*if there are exhibits, add* 'and explained the nature and effect of the exhibits referred to in it'] who appeared to understand it and approved its content as accurate, and made his mark on the affidavit in my presence.

Or; (after, *Before me*) the witness to the mark of the deponent having been first sworn that he had read over etc. (*as above*) and that he saw him make his mark on the affidavit. (*Witness must sign*).

Certificate to be used where a deponent to an affirmation is unable to read or sign it

Affirmed at .... this ...... day of .... Before me, I having first read over the contents of this affirmation to the deponent [*if there are exhibits, add* 'and explained the nature and effect of the exhibits referred to in it'] who appeared to understand it and approved its content as accurate, and made his mark on the affirmation in my presence.

Or, (after, *Before me*) the witness to the mark of the deponent having been first sworn that he had read over etc. (*as above*) and that he saw him make his mark on the affirmation. (*Witness must sign*).

ANNEX 2

Omitted

ANNEX 3

VIDEO CONFERENCING GUIDANCE

This guidance is for the use of video conferencing (VCF) in civil proceedings. It is in part based, with permission, upon the protocol of the Federal Court of Australia. It is intended to provide a guide to all persons involved in the use of VCF, although it does not attempt to cover all the practical questions which might arise.

Video conferencing generally

1.
The guidance covers the use of VCF equipment both (a) in a courtroom, whether via equipment which is permanently placed there or via a mobile unit, and (b) in a separate studio or conference room. In either case, the location at which the judge sits is referred to as the 'local site'. The other site or sites to and from which transmission is made are referred to as 'the remote site' and in any particular case any such site may be another courtroom. The guidance applies to cases where VCF is used for the taking of evidence and also to its use for other parts of any legal proceedings (for example, interim applications, case management conferences, pre-trial reviews).

2.
VCF may be a convenient way of dealing with any part of proceedings: it can involve considerable savings in time and cost. Its use for the taking of evidence from overseas witnesses will, in particular, be likely to achieve a material saving of costs, and such savings may also be achieved by its use for taking domestic evidence. It is, however, inevitably not as ideal as having the witness physically present in court. Its convenience should not therefore be allowed to dictate its use. A judgment must be made in every case in which the use of VCF is being considered not only as to whether it will achieve an overall cost saving but as to whether its use will be likely to be beneficial to the efficient, fair and economic disposal of the litigation. In particular, it needs to be recognised that the degree of control a court can exercise over a witness at the remote site is or may be more limited than it can exercise over a witness physically before it.

3.
When used for the taking of evidence, the objective should be to make the VCF session as close as possible to the usual practice in a trial court where evidence is taken in open court. To gain the maximum benefit, several differences have to be taken into account. Some matters, which are taken for granted when evidence is taken in the conventional way, take on a different dimension when it is taken by VCF: for example, the administration of the oath, ensuring that the witness understands who is at the local site and what their various roles are, the raising of any objections to the evidence and the use of documents.

4.
It should not be presumed that all foreign governments are willing to allow their nationals or others within their jurisdiction to be examined before a court in England or Wales by means of VCF. If there is any doubt about this, enquiries should be directed to the Foreign and Commonwealth Office (International Legal Matters Unit, Consular Division) with a view to ensuring that the country from which the evidence is to be taken raises no objection to it at diplomatic level. The party who is directed to be responsible for arranging the VCF (see paragraph 8 below) will be required to make all necessary inquiries about this well in advance of the VCF and must be able to inform the court what those inquiries were and of their outcome.

5.
Time zone differences need to be considered when a witness abroad is to be examined in England or Wales by VCF. The convenience of the witness, the parties, their representatives and the court must all be taken into account. The cost of the use of a commercial studio is usually greater outside normal business hours.

6.
Those involved with VCF need to be aware that, even with the most advanced systems currently available, there are the briefest of delays between the receipt of the picture and that of the accompanying sound. If due allowance is not made for this, there will be a tendency to 'speak over' the witness,

whose voice will continue to be heard for a millisecond or so after he or she appears on the screen to have finished speaking.

7.

With current technology, picture quality is good, but not as good as a television picture. The quality of the picture is enhanced if those appearing on VCF monitors keep their movements to a minimum.

Preliminary arrangements

8.

The court's permission is required for any part of any proceedings to be dealt with by means of VCF. Before seeking a direction, the applicant should notify the listing officer, diary manager or other appropriate court officer of the intention to seek it, and should enquire as to the availability of court VCF equipment for the day or days of the proposed VCF. The application for a direction should be made to the Master, District Judge or Judge, as may be appropriate. If all parties consent to a direction, permission can be sought by letter, fax or e-mail, although the court may still require an oral hearing. All parties are entitled to be heard on whether or not such a direction should be given and as to its terms. If a witness at a remote site is to give evidence by an interpreter, consideration should be given at this stage as to whether the interpreter should be at the local site or the remote site. If a VCF direction is given, arrangements for the transmission will then need to be made. The court will ordinarily direct that the party seeking permission to use VCF is to be responsible for this. That party is hereafter referred to as 'the VCF arranging party'.

9.

Subject to any order to the contrary, all costs of the transmission, including the costs of hiring equipment and technical personnel to operate it, will initially be the responsibility of, and must be met by, the VCF arranging party. All reasonable efforts should be made to keep the transmission to a minimum and so keep the costs down. All such costs will be considered to be part of the costs of the proceedings and the court will determine at such subsequent time as is convenient or appropriate who, as between the parties, should be responsible for them and (if appropriate) in what proportions.

10.

The local site will, if practicable, be a courtroom but it may instead be an appropriate studio or conference room. The VCF arranging party must contact the listing officer, diary manager or other appropriate officer of the court which made the VCF direction and make arrangements for the VCF transmission. Details of the remote site, and of the equipment to be used both at the local site (if not being supplied by the court) and the remote site (including the number of ISDN lines and connection speed), together with all necessary contact names and telephone numbers, will have to be provided to the listing officer, diary manager or other court officer. The court will need to be satisfied that any equipment provided by the parties for use at the local site and also that at the remote site is of sufficient quality for a satisfactory transmission. The VCF arranging party must ensure that an appropriate person will be present at the local site to supervise the operation of the VCF throughout the transmission in order to deal with any technical problems. That party must also arrange for a technical assistant to be similarly present at the remote site for like purposes.

11.

It is recommended that the judge, practitioners and witness should arrive at their respective VCF sites about 20 minutes prior to the scheduled commencement of the transmission.

12.

If the local site is not a courtroom, but a conference room or studio, the judge will need to determine who is to sit where. The VCF arranging party must take care to ensure that the number of microphones is adequate for the speakers and that the panning of the camera for the practitioners' table encompasses all legal representatives so that the viewer can see everyone seated there.

13.
The proceedings, wherever they may take place, form part of a trial to which the public is entitled to have access (unless the court has determined that they should be heard in private). If the local site is to be a studio or conference room, the VCF arranging party must ensure that it provides sufficient accommodation to enable a reasonable number of members of the public to attend.

14.
In cases where the local site is a studio or conference room, the VCF arranging party should make arrangements, if practicable, for the royal coat of arms to be placed above the judge's seat.

15.
In cases in which the VCF is to be used for the taking of evidence, the VCF arranging party must arrange for recording equipment to be provided by the court which made the VCF direction so that the evidence can be recorded. An associate will normally be present to operate the recording equipment when the local site is a courtroom. The VCF arranging party should take steps to ensure that an associate is present to do likewise when it is a studio or conference room. The equipment should be set up and tested before the VCF transmission. It will often be a valuable safeguard for the VCF arranging party also to arrange for the provision of recording equipment at the remote site. This will provide a useful back-up if there is any reduction in sound quality during the transmission. A direction from the court for the making of such a back-up recording must, however, be obtained first. This is because the proceedings are court proceedings and, save as directed by the court, no other recording of them must be made. The court will direct what is to happen to the back-up recording.

16.
Some countries may require that any oath or affirmation to be taken by a witness accord with local custom rather than the usual form of oath or affirmation used in England and Wales. The VCF arranging party must make all appropriate prior inquiries and put in place all arrangements necessary to enable the oath or affirmation to be taken in accordance with any local custom. That party must be in a position to inform the court what those inquiries were, what their outcome was and what arrangements have been made. If the oath or affirmation can be administered in the manner normal in England and Wales, the VCF arranging party must arrange in advance to have the appropriate holy book at the remote site. The associate will normally administer the oath.

17.
Consideration will need to be given in advance to the documents to which the witness is likely to be referred. The parties should endeavour to agree on this. It will usually be most convenient for a bundle of the copy documents to be prepared in advance, which the VCF arranging party should then send to the remote site.

18.
Additional documents are sometimes quite properly introduced during the course of a witness's evidence. To cater for this, the VCF arranging party should ensure that equipment is available to enable documents to be transmitted between sites during the course of the VCF transmission. Consideration should be given to whether to use a document camera. If it is decided to use one, arrangements for its use will need to be established in advance. The panel operator will need to know the number and size of documents or objects if their images are to be sent by document camera. In many cases, a simpler and sufficient alternative will be to ensure that there are fax transmission and reception facilities at the participating sites.

The hearing

19.
The procedure for conducting the transmission will be determined by the judge. He will determine who is to control the cameras. In cases where the VCF is being used for an application in the course of the proceedings, the judge will ordinarily not enter the local site until both sites are on line. Similarly,

at the conclusion of the hearing, he will ordinarily leave the local site while both sites are still on line. The following paragraphs apply primarily to cases where the VCF is being used for the taking of the evidence of a witness at a remote site. In all cases, the judge will need to decide whether court dress is appropriate when using VCF facilities. It might be appropriate when transmitting from courtroom to courtroom. It might not be when a commercial facility is being used.

20.

At the beginning of the transmission, the judge will probably wish to introduce himself and the advocates to the witness. He will probably want to know who is at the remote site and will invite the witness to introduce himself and anyone else who is with him. He may wish to give directions as to the seating arrangements at the remote site so that those present are visible at the local site during the taking of the evidence. He will probably wish to explain to the witness the method of taking the oath or of affirming, the manner in which the evidence will be taken, and who will be conducting the examination and cross-examination. He will probably also wish to inform the witness of the matters referred to in paragraphs 6 and 7 above (co-ordination of picture with sound, and picture quality).

21.

The examination of the witness at the remote site should follow as closely as possible the practice adopted when a witness is in the courtroom. During examination, cross-examination and re-examination, the witness must be able to see the legal representative asking the question and also any other person (whether another legal representative or the judge) making any statements in regard to the witness's evidence. It will in practice be most convenient if everyone remains seated throughout the transmission.

PART 33 MISCELLANEOUS RULES ABOUT EVIDENCE

33.1 Introductory

In this Part—

(a) 'hearsay' means a statement made, otherwise than by a person while giving oral evidence in proceedings, which is tendered as evidence of the matters stated; and

(b) references to hearsay include hearsay of whatever degree.

33.2 Notice of intention to rely on hearsay evidence

(1) Where a party intends to rely on hearsay evidence at trial and either—

(a) that evidence is to be given by a witness giving oral evidence; or

(b) that evidence is contained in a witness statement of a person who is not being called to give oral evidence;

that party complies with section 2(1)(a) of the Civil Evidence Act 1995 serving a witness statement on the other parties in accordance with the court's order.

(2) Where paragraph (1)(b) applies, the party intending to rely on the hearsay evidence must, when he serves the witness statement—

(a) inform the other parties that the witness is not being called to give oral evidence; and

(b) give the reason why the witness will not be called.

(3) In all other cases where a party intends to rely on hearsay evidence at trial, that party complies with section 2(1)(a) of the Civil Evidence Act 1995 by serving a notice on the other parties which—

(a) identifies the hearsay evidence;

(b) states that the party serving the notice proposes to rely on the hearsay evidence at trial; and

(c) gives the reason why the witness will not be called.

(4) The party proposing to rely on the hearsay evidence must—
- (a) serve the notice no later than the latest date for serving witness statements; and
- (b) if the hearsay evidence is to be in a document, supply a copy to any party who requests him to do so.

33.3 Circumstances in which notice of intention to rely on hearsay evidence is not required

Section 2(1) of the Civil Evidence Act 1995 (duty to give notice of intention to rely on hearsay evidence) does not apply—
- (a) to evidence at hearings other than trials;
- (aa) to an affidavit or witness statement which is to be used at trial but which does not contain hearsay evidence;
- (b) to a statement which a party to a probate action wishes to put in evidence and which is alleged to have been made by the person whose estate is the subject of the proceedings; or
- (c) where the requirement is excluded by a practice direction.

33.4 Power to call witness for cross-examination on hearsay evidence

(1) Where a party—
- (a) proposes to rely on hearsay evidence; and
- (b) does not propose to call the person who made the original statement to give oral evidence,

the court may, on the application of any other party, permit that party to call the maker of the statement to be cross-examined on the contents of the statement.

(2) An application for permission to cross-examine under this rule must be made not more than 14 days after the day on which a notice of intention to rely on the hearsay evidence was served on the applicant.

33.5 Credibility

(1) Where a party—
- (a) proposes to rely on hearsay evidence; but
- (b) does not propose to call the person who made the original statement to give oral evidence; and
- (c) another party wishes to call evidence to attack the credibility of the person who made the statement,

the party who so wishes must give notice of his intention to the party who proposes to give the hearsay statement in evidence.

(2) A party must give notice under paragraph (1) not more than 14 days after the day on which a hearsay notice relating to the hearsay evidence was served on him.

33.6 Use of plans, photographs and models as evidence

(1) This rule applies to evidence (such as a plan, photograph or model) which is not—
- (a) contained in a witness statement, affidavit or expert's report;
- (b) to be given orally at trial; or
- (c) evidence of which prior notice must be given under rule 33.2.

(2) This rule includes documents which may be received in evidence without further proof under section 9 of the Civil Evidence Act 1995.

(3) Unless the court orders otherwise the evidence shall not be receivable at a trial unless the party intending to put it in evidence has given notice to the other parties in accordance with this rule.

(4) Where the party intends to use the evidence as evidence of any fact then, except where paragraph (6) applies, he must give notice not later than the latest date for serving witness statements.

(5) He must give notice at least 21 days before the hearing at which he proposes to put in the evidence, if—

(a) there are not to be witness statements; or

(b) he intends to put in the evidence solely in order to disprove an allegation made in a witness statement.

(6) Where the evidence forms part of expert evidence, he must give notice when the expert's report is served on the other party.

(7) Where the evidence is being produced to the court for any reason other than as part of factual or expert evidence, he must give notice at least 21 days before the hearing at which he proposes to put in the evidence.

(8) Where a party has given notice that he intends to put in the evidence, he must give every other party an opportunity to inspect it and to agree to its admission without further proof.

33.7 Evidence of finding on question of foreign law

(1) This rule sets out the procedure which must be followed by a party who intends to put in evidence a finding on a question of foreign law by virtue of section 4(2) of the Civil Evidence Act 1972.

(2) He must give any other party notice of his intention.

(3) He must give the notice—

(a) if there are to be witness statements, not later than the latest date for serving them; or

(b) otherwise, not less than 21 days before the hearing at which he proposes to put the finding in evidence.

(4) The notice must—

(a) specify the question on which the finding was made; and

(b) enclose a copy of a document where it is reported or recorded.

33.8 Evidence of consent of trustee to act

A document purporting to contain the written consent of a person to act as trustee and to bear his signature verified by some other person is evidence of such consent.

33.9 Human Rights

(1) This rule applies where a claim is—

(a) for a remedy under section 7 of the Human Rights Act 1998 in respect of a judicial act which is alleged to have infringed the claimant's Article 5 Convention rights; and

(b) based on a finding by a court or tribunal that the claimant's Convention rights have been infringed.

(2) The court hearing the claim—

(a) may proceed on the basis of the finding of that other court or tribunal that there has been an infringement but it is not required to do so, and

(b) may reach its own conclusion in the light of that finding and of the evidence heard by that other court or tribunal.

PART 34 WITNESSES, DEPOSITIONS AND EVIDENCE FOR FOREIGN COURTS

I WITNESSES AND DEPOSITIONS

34.1 Scope of this Section

(1) This Section of this Part provides—

(a) for the circumstances in which a person may be required to attend court to give evidence or to produce a document; and

(b) for a party to obtain evidence before a hearing to be used at the hearing.

(2) In this Section, reference to a hearing includes a reference to the trial.

34.2 Witness summonses

(1) A witness summons is a document issued by the court requiring a witness to—

(a) attend court to give evidence; or

(b) produce documents to the court.

(2) A witness summons must be in the relevant practice form.

(3) There must be a separate witness summons for each witness.

(4) A witness summons may require a witness to produce documents to the court either—

(a) on the date fixed for a hearing; or

(b) on such date as the court may direct.

(5) The only documents that a summons under this rule can require a person to produce before a hearing are documents which that person could be required to produce at the hearing.

34.3 Issue of a witness summons

(1) A witness summons is issued on the date entered on the summons by the court.

(2) A party must obtain permission from the court where he wishes to—

(a) have a summons issued less than 7 days before the date of the trial;

(b) have a summons issued for a witness to attend court to give evidence or to produce documents on any date except the date fixed for the trial; or

(c) have a summons issued for a witness to attend court to give evidence or to produce documents at any hearing except the trial.

(3) A witness summons must be issued by—

(a) the court where the case is proceeding; or

(b) the court where the hearing in question will be held.

(4) The court may set aside or vary a witness summons issued under this rule.

34.4 Witness summons in aid of inferior court or of tribunal

(1) The court may issue a witness summons in aid of an inferior court or of a tribunal.

(2) The court which issued the witness summons under this rule may set it aside.

(3) In this rule, 'inferior court or tribunal' means any court or tribunal that does not have power to issue a witness summons in relation to proceedings before it.

34.5 Time for serving a witness summons

(1) The general rule is that a witness summons is binding if it is served at least 7 days before the date on which the witness is required to attend before the court or tribunal.

(2) The court may direct that a witness summons shall be binding although it will be served less than 7 days before the date on which the witness is required to attend before the court or tribunal.

(3) A witness summons which is—

(a) served in accordance with this rule; and

(b) requires the witness to attend court to give evidence,

is binding until the conclusion of the hearing at which the attendance of the witness is required.

34.6 Who is to serve a witness summons

(1) A witness summons is to be served by the court unless the party on whose behalf it is issued indicates in writing, when he asks the court to issue the summons, that he wishes to serve it himself.

(2) Where the court is to serve the witness summons, the party on whose behalf it is issued must deposit, in the court office, the money to be paid or offered to the witness under rule 34.7.

34.7 Right of witness to travelling expenses and compensation for loss of time

At the time of service of a witness summons the witness must be offered or paid—

(a) a sum reasonably sufficient to cover his expenses in travelling to and from the court; and

(b) such sum by way of compensation for loss of time as may be specified in Practice Direction 34A.

34.8 Evidence by deposition

(1) A party may apply for an order for a person to be examined before the hearing takes place.

(2) A person from whom evidence is to be obtained following an order under this rule is referred to as a 'deponent' and the evidence is referred to as a 'deposition'.

(3) An order under this rule shall be for a deponent to be examined on oath before—

(a) a judge;

(b) an examiner of the court; or

(c) such other person as the court appoints.

(Rule 34.15 makes provision for the appointment of examiners of the court)

(4) The order may require the production of any document which the court considers is necessary for the purposes of the examination.

(5) The order must state the date, time and place of the examination.

(6) At the time of service of the order the deponent must be offered or paid—

(a) a sum reasonably sufficient to cover his expenses in travelling to and from the place of examination; and

(b) such sum by way of compensation for loss of time as may be specified in Practice Direction 34A.

(7) Where the court makes an order for a deposition to be taken, it may also order the party who obtained the order to serve a witness statement or witness summary in relation to the evidence to be given by the person to be examined.

(Part 32 contains the general rules about witness statements and witness summaries)

34.9 Conduct of examination

(1) Subject to any directions contained in the order for examination, the examination must be conducted in the same way as if the witness were giving evidence at a trial.

(2) If all the parties are present, the examiner may conduct the examination of a person not named in the order for examination if all the parties and the person to be examined consent.

(3) The examiner may conduct the examination in private if he considers it appropriate to do so.

(4) The examiner must ensure that the evidence given by the witness is recorded in full.

(5) The examiner must send a copy of the deposition—

(a) to the person who obtained the order for the examination of the witness; and

(b) to the court where the case is proceeding.

(6) The party who obtained the order must send each of the other parties a copy of the deposition which he receives from the examiner.

34.10 Enforcing attendance of witness

(1) If a person served with an order to attend before an examiner—

(a) fails to attend; or

(b) refuses to be sworn for the purpose of the examination or to answer any lawful question or produce any document at the examination,

a certificate of his failure or refusal, signed by the examiner, must be filed by the party requiring the deposition.

(2) On the certificate being filed, the party requiring the deposition may apply to the court for an order requiring that person to attend or to be sworn or to answer any question or produce any document, as the case may be.

(3) An application for an order under this rule may be made without notice.

(4) The court may order the person against whom an order is made under this rule to pay any costs resulting from his failure or refusal.

34.11 Use of deposition at a hearing

(1) A deposition ordered under rule 34.8 may be given in evidence at a hearing unless the court orders otherwise.

(2) A party intending to put in evidence a deposition at a hearing must serve notice of his intention to do so on every other party.

(3) He must serve the notice at least 21 days before the day fixed for the hearing.

(4) The court may require a deponent to attend the hearing and give evidence orally.

(5) Where a deposition is given in evidence at trial, it shall be treated as if it were a witness statement for the purposes of rule 32.13 (availability of witness statements for inspection).

34.12 Restrictions on subsequent use of deposition taken for the purpose of any hearing except the trial

(1) Where the court orders a party to be examined about his or any other assets for the purpose of any hearing except the trial, the deposition may be used only for the purpose of the proceedings in which the order was made.

(2) However, it may be used for some other purpose—

(a) by the party who was examined;

(b) if the party who was examined agrees; or

(c) if the court gives permission.

34.13 Where a person to be examined is out of the jurisdiction—letter of request

(1) This rule applies where a party wishes to take a deposition from a person who is—

(a) out of the jurisdiction; and

(b) not in a Regulation State within the meaning of Section III of this Part.

(1A) The High Court may order the issue of a letter of request to the judicial authorities of the country in which the proposed deponent is.

(2) A letter of request is a request to a judicial authority to take the evidence of that person, or arrange for it to be taken.

(3) The High Court may make an order under this rule in relation to county court proceedings.

(4) If the government of a country allows a person appointed by the High Court to examine a person in that country, the High Court may make an order appointing a special examiner for that purpose.

(5) A person may be examined under this rule on oath or affirmation or in accordance with any procedure permitted in the country in which the examination is to take place.

(6) If the High Court makes an order for the issue of a letter of request, the party who sought the order must file—

(a) the following documents and, except where paragraph (7) applies, a translation of them—

(i) a draft letter of request;

(ii) a statement of the issues relevant to the proceedings;

(iii) a list of questions or the subject matter of questions to be put to the person to be examined; and

(b) an undertaking to be responsible for the Secretary of State's expenses.

(7) There is no need to file a translation if—

(a) English is one of the official languages of the country where the examination is to take place; or

(b) a practice direction has specified that country as a country where no translation is necessary.

34.13A Letter of request—Proceeds of Crime Act 2002

(1) This rule applies where a party to existing or contemplated proceedings in—

(a) the High Court; or

(b) a magistrates' court,

under Part 5 of the Proceeds of Crime Act 2002 (civil recovery of the proceeds etc. of unlawful conduct) wishes to take a deposition from a person who is out of the jurisdiction.

(2) The High Court may, on the application of such a party, order the issue of a letter of request to the judicial authorities of the country in which the proposed deponent is.

(3) Paragraphs (4) to (7) of rule 34.13 shall apply irrespective of where the proposed deponent is, and rule 34.23 shall not apply in cases where the proposed deponent is in a Regulation State within the meaning of Section III of this Part.

34.14 Fees and expenses of examiner of the court

(1) An examiner of the court may charge a fee for the examination.

(2) He need not send the deposition to the court unless the fee is paid.

(3) The examiner's fees and expenses must be paid by the party who obtained the order for examination.

(4) If the fees and expenses due to an examiner are not paid within a reasonable time, he may report that fact to the court.

(5) The court may order the party who obtained the order for examination to deposit in the court office a specified sum in respect of the examiner's fees and, where it does so, the examiner will not be asked to act until the sum has been deposited.

(6) An order under this rule does not affect any decision as to the party who is ultimately to bear the costs of the examination.

34.15 Examiners of the court

(1) The Lord Chancellor shall appoint persons to be examiners of the court.

(2) The persons appointed shall be barristers or solicitor-advocates who have been practising for a period of not less than three years.

(3) The Lord Chancellor may revoke an appointment at any time.

II EVIDENCE FOR FOREIGN COURTS

34.16 Scope and interpretation

(1) This Section applies to an application for an order under the 1975 Act for evidence to be obtained, other than an application made as a result of a request by a court in another Regulation State.

(2) In this Section—

(a) 'the 1975 Act' means the Evidence (Proceedings in Other Jurisdictions) Act 1975; and

(b) 'Regulation State' has the same meaning as in Section III of this Part.

34.17 Application for order

An application for an order under the 1975 Act for evidence to be obtained—

(a) must be—

(i) made to the High Court;

(ii) supported by written evidence; and

(iii) accompanied by the request as a result of which the application is made, and where appropriate, a translation of the request into English; and

(b) may be made without notice.

34.18 Examination

(1) The court may order an examination to be taken before—

(a) any fit and proper person nominated by the person applying for the order;

(b) an examiner of the court; or

(c) any other person whom the court considers suitable.

(2) Unless the court orders otherwise—

(a) the examination will be taken as provided by rule 34.9; and

(b) rule 34.10 applies.

(3) The court may make an order under rule 34.14 for payment of the fees and expenses of the examination.

34.19 Dealing with deposition

(1) The examiner must send the deposition of the witness to the Senior Master unless the court orders otherwise.

(2) The Senior Master will—

- (a) give a certificate sealed with the seal of the Senior Courts for use out of the jurisdiction identifying the following documents—
  - (i) the request;
  - (ii) the order of the court for examination; and
  - (iii) the deposition of the witness; and
- (b) send the certificate and the documents referred to in paragraph (a) to—
  - (i) the Secretary of State; or
  - (ii) where the request was sent to the Senior Master by another person in accordance with a Civil Procedure Convention, to that other person,

  for transmission to the court or tribunal requesting the examination.

34.20 Claim to privilege

(1) This rule applies where—

- (a) a witness claims to be exempt from giving evidence on the ground specified in section 3(1)(b) of the 1975 Act; and
- (b) That claim is not supported or conceded as referred to in section 3(2) of that Act.

(2) The examiner may require the witness to give the evidence which he claims to be exempt from giving.

(3) Where the examiner does not require the witness to give that evidence, the court may order the witness to do so.

(4) An application for an order under paragraph (3) may be made by the person who obtained the order under section 2 of the 1975 Act.

(5) Where such evidence is taken—

- (a) it must be contained in a document separate from the remainder of the deposition;
- (b) the examiner will send to the Senior Master—
  - (i) the deposition; and
  - (ii) a signed statement setting out the claim to be exempt and the ground on which it was made;

(6) On receipt of the statement referred to in paragraph (5)(b)(ii), the Senior Master will—

- (a) retain the document containing the part of the witness's evidence to which the claim to be exempt relates; and
- (b) send the statement and a request to determine that claim to the foreign court or tribunal together with the documents referred to in rule 34.17.

(7) The Senior Master will—

- (a) if the claim to be exempt is rejected by the foreign court or tribunal, send the document referred to in paragraph (5)(a) to that court or tribunal;
- (b) if the claim is upheld, send the document to the witness; and
- (c) in either case, notify the witness and person who obtained the order under section 2 of the foreign court or tribunal's decision.

34.21 Order under 1975 Act as applied by Patents Act 1977

Where an order is made for the examination of witnesses under section 1 of the 1975 Act as applied by section 92 of the Patents Act 1977 the court may permit an officer of the European Patent Office to—

- (a) attend the examination and examine the witnesses; or
- (b) request the court or the examiner before whom the examination takes place to put specified questions to them.

III TAKING OF EVIDENCE—MEMBER STATES OF THE EUROPEAN UNION

34.22 Interpretation

In this Section—

(a) 'designated court' has the meaning given in Practice Direction 34A;

(b) 'Regulation State' has the same meaning as 'Member State' in the Taking of Evidence Regulation, that is all Member States except Denmark;

(c) 'the Taking of Evidence Regulation' means Council Regulation (EC) No. 1206/2001 of 28 May 2001 on co-operation between the courts of the Member States in the taking of evidence in civil and commercial matters.

34.23 Where a person to be examined is in another Regulation State

(1) Subject to rule 34.13A, this rule applies where a party wishes to take a deposition from a person who is in another Regulation State—

(a) outside the jurisdiction; and

(b) in a Regulation State.

(2) The court may order the issue of a request to a designated court ('the requested court') in the Regulation State in which the proposed deponent is.

(3) If the court makes an order for the issue of a request, the party who sought the order must file—

(a) a draft Form A as set out in the annex to the Taking of Evidence Regulation (request for the taking of evidence);

(b) except where paragraph (4) applies, a translation of the form;

(c) an undertaking to be responsible for costs sought by the requested court in relation to—

(i) fees paid to experts and interpreters; and

(ii) where requested by that party, the use of special procedures or communications technology; and

(d) an undertaking to be responsible for the court's expenses.

(4) There is no need to file a translation if—

(a) English is one of the official languages of the Regulation State where the examination is to take place; or

(b) the Regulation State has indicated, in accordance with the Taking of Evidence Regulation, that English is a language which it will accept.

(5) Where article 17 of the Taking of Evidence Regulation (direct taking of evidence by the requested court) allows evidence to be taken directly in another Regulation State, the court may make an order for the submission of a request in accordance with that article.

(6) If the court makes an order for the submission of a request under paragraph (5), the party who sought the order must file—

(a) a draft Form I as set out in the annex to the Taking of Evidence Regulation (request for direct taking of evidence);

(b) except where paragraph (4) applies, a translation of the form; and

(c) an undertaking to be responsible for the court's expenses.

34.24 Evidence for courts of other Regulation States

(1) This rule applies where a court in another Regulation State ('the requesting court') issues a request for evidence to be taken from a person who is in the jurisdiction.

(2) An application for an order for evidence to be taken—

(a) must be made to a designated court;

(b) must be accompanied by—

(i) the form of request for the taking of evidence as a result of which the application is made; and

(ii) where appropriate, a translation of the form of request; and

(c) may be made without notice.

(3) Rule 34.18(1) and (2) apply.

(4) The examiner must send—

(a) the deposition to the court for transmission to the requesting court; and

(b) a copy of the deposition to the person who obtained the order for evidence to be taken.

PRACTICE DIRECTION

DEPOSITIONS AND COURT ATTENDANCE BY WITNESSES

This Practice Direction supplements CPR Part 34

WITNESS SUMMONSES

Issue of witness summons

1.1

A witness summons may require a witness to:

(1) attend court to give evidence,

(2) produce documents to the court, or

(3) both,

on either a date fixed for the hearing or such date as the court may direct.

1.2

Two copies of the witness summons should be filed with the court for sealing, one of which will be retained on the court file.

1.3

A mistake in the name or address of a person named in a witness summons may be corrected if the summons has not been served.

1.4

The corrected summons must be re-sealed by the court and marked 'Amended and Re-Sealed'.

Witness summons issued in aid of an inferior court or tribunal

2.1

A witness summons may be issued in the High Court or a county court in aid of a court or tribunal which does not have the power to issue a witness summons in relation to the proceedings before it.

2.2

A witness summons referred to in paragraph 2.1 may be set aside by the court which issued it.

2.3

An application to set aside a witness summons referred to in paragraph 2.1 will be heard:

(1) in the High Court by a Master at the Royal Courts of Justice or by a district judge in a District Registry, and

(2) in a county court by a district judge.

2.4

Unless the court otherwise directs, the applicant must give at least 2 days' notice to the party who issued the witness summons of the application, which will normally be dealt with at a hearing.

Travelling expenses and compensation for loss of time

3.1

When a witness is served with a witness summons he must be offered a sum to cover his travelling expenses to and from the court and compensation for his loss of time.

3.2

If the witness summons is to be served by the court, the party issuing the summons must deposit with the court:

(1) a sum sufficient to pay for the witness's expenses in travelling to the court and in returning to his home or place of work, and

(2) a sum in respect of the period during which earnings or benefit are lost, or such lesser sum as it may be proved that the witness will lose as a result of his attendance at court in answer to the witness summons.

3.3

The sum referred to in 3.2(2) is to be based on the sums payable to witnesses attending the Crown Court.

3.4

Where the party issuing the witness summons wishes to serve it himself, he must:

(1) notify the court in writing that he wishes to do so, and

(2) at the time of service offer the witness the sums mentioned in paragraph 3.2 above.

DEPOSITIONS

To be taken in England and Wales for use as evidence in proceedings in courts in England and Wales

4.1

A party may apply for an order for a person to be examined on oath before:

(1) a judge,

(2) an examiner of the court, or

(3) such other person as the court may appoint.

4.2

The party who obtains an order for the examination of a deponent before an examiner of the court must:

(1) apply to the Foreign Process Section of the Masters' Secretary's Department at the Royal Courts of Justice for the allocation of an examiner,

(2) when allocated, provide the examiner with copies of all documents in the proceedings necessary to inform the examiner of the issues, and

(3) pay the deponent a sum to cover his travelling expenses to and from the examination and compensation for his loss of time.

4.3

In ensuring that the deponent's evidence is recorded in full, the court or the examiner may permit it to be recorded on audiotape or videotape, but the deposition must always be recorded in writing by him or by a competent shorthand writer or stenographer.

4.4

If the deposition is not recorded word for word, it must contain, as nearly as may be, the statement of the deponent; the examiner may record word for word any particular questions and answers which appear to him to have special importance.

4.5

If a deponent objects to answering any question or where any objection is taken to any question, the examiner must:

(1) record in the deposition or a document attached to it—

(a) the question,

(b) the nature of and grounds for the objection, and

(c) any answer given, and

(2) give his opinion as to the validity of the objection and must record it in the deposition or a document attached to it.

The court will decide as to the validity of the objection and any question of costs arising from it.

4.6

Documents and exhibits must:

(1) have an identifying number or letter marked on them by the examiner, and

(2) be preserved by the party or his legal representative who obtained the order for the examination, or as the court or the examiner may direct.

4.7

The examiner may put any question to the deponent as to:

(1) the meaning of any of his answers, or

(2) any matter arising in the course of the examination.

4.8

Where a deponent:

(1) fails to attend the examination, or

(2) refuses to:

(a) be sworn, or

(b) answer any lawful question, or

(c) produce any document,

the examiner will sign a certificate of such failure or refusal and may include in his certificate any comment as to the conduct of the deponent or of any person attending the examination.

4.9

The party who obtained the order for the examination must file the certificate with the court and may apply for an order that the deponent attend for examination or as may be. The application may be made without notice.

4.10

The court will make such order on the application as it thinks fit including an order for the deponent to pay any costs resulting from his failure or refusal.

4.11

A deponent who wilfully refuses to obey an order made against him under Part 34 may be proceeded against for contempt of court.

4.12

A deposition must:

(1) be signed by the examiner,

(2) have any amendments to it initialled by the examiner and the deponent,

(3) be endorsed by the examiner with—

(a) a statement of the time occupied by the examination, and

(b) a record of any refusal by the deponent to sign the deposition and of his reasons for not doing so, and

(4) be sent by the examiner to the court where the proceedings are taking place for filing on the court file.

4.13

Rule 34.14 deals with the fees and expenses of an examiner.

Depositions to be taken abroad for use as evidence in proceedings before courts in England and Wales (where the Taking of Evidence Regulation does not apply)

5.1

Where a party wishes to take a deposition from a person outside the jurisdiction, the High Court may order the issue of a letter of request to the judicial authorities of the country in which the proposed deponent is.

5.2

An application for an order referred to in paragraph 5.1 should be made by application notice in accordance with Part 23.

5.3

The documents which a party applying for an order for the issue of a letter of request must file with his application notice are set out in rule 34.13(6). They are as follows:

(1) a draft letter of request in the form set out in Annex A to this practice direction,

(2) a statement of the issues relevant to the proceedings,

(3) a list of questions or the subject matter of questions to be put to the proposed deponent,

(4) a translation of the documents in (1), (2) and (3) above, unless the proposed deponent is in a country of which English is an official language, and

(5) an undertaking to be responsible for the expenses of the Secretary of State

In addition to the documents listed above the party applying for the order must file a draft order.

5.4

The above documents should be filed with the Masters' Secretary in Room E214, Royal Courts of Justice, Strand, London WC2A 2LL.

5.5

The application will be dealt with by the Senior Master of the Queen's Bench Division of the High Court who will, if appropriate, sign the letter of request.

5.6

Attention is drawn to the provisions of rule 23.10 (application to vary or discharge an order made without notice).

5.7

If parties are in doubt as to whether a translation under paragraph 5.3(4) above is required, they should seek guidance from the Foreign Process Section of the Masters' Secretary's Department.

5.8

A special examiner appointed under rule 34.13(4) may be the British Consul or the Consul-General or his deputy in the country where the evidence is to be taken if:

(1) there is in respect of that country a Civil Procedure Convention providing for the taking of evidence in that country for the assistance of proceedings in the High Court or other court in this country, or

(2) with the consent of the Secretary of State.

5.9

The provisions of paragraphs 4.1 to 4.12 above apply to the depositions referred to in this paragraph.

Depositions to be taken in England and Wales for use as evidence in proceedings before courts abroad pursuant to letters of request (where the Taking of Evidence Regulation does not apply)

6.1
Section II of Part 34 relating to obtaining evidence for foreign courts applies to letters of request and should be read in conjunction with this part of the practice direction.

6.2
The Evidence (Proceedings in Other Jurisdictions) Act 1975 applies to these depositions.

6.3
The written evidence supporting an application under rule 34.17 (which should be made by application notice—see Part 23) must include or exhibit—

(1) a statement of the issues relevant to the proceedings;
(2) a list of questions or the subject matter of questions to be put to the proposed deponent;
(3) a draft order; and
(4) a translation of the documents in (1) and (2) into English, if necessary.

6.4

(1) The Senior Master will send to the Treasury Solicitor any request—
  (a) forwarded by the Secretary of State with a recommendation that effect should be given to the request without requiring an application to be made; or
  (b) received by him in pursuance of a Civil Procedure Convention providing for the taking of evidence of any person in England and Wales to assist a court or tribunal in a foreign country where no person is named in the document as the applicant.
(2) In relation to such a request, the Treasury Solicitor may, with the consent of the Treasury—
  (a) apply for an order under the 1975 Act; and
  (b) take such other steps as are necessary to give effect to the request.

6.5
The order for the deponent to attend and be examined together with the evidence upon which the order was made must be served on the deponent.

6.6
Attention is drawn to the provisions of rule 23.10 (application to vary or discharge an order made without notice).

6.7
Arrangements for the examination to take place at a specified time and place before an examiner of the court or such other person as the court may appoint shall be made by the applicant for the order and approved by the Senior Master.

6.8
The provisions of paragraph 4.2 to 4.12 apply to the depositions referred to in this paragraph, except that the examiner must send the deposition to the Senior Master.

(For further information about evidence see Part 32 and Practice Direction 32.)

TAKING OF EVIDENCE BETWEEN EU MEMBER STATES

Taking of Evidence Regulation

7.1
Where evidence is to be taken—

(a) from a person in another Member State of the European Union for use as evidence in proceedings before courts in England and Wales; or

(b) from a person in England and Wales for use as evidence in proceedings before a court in another Member State,

Council Regulation (EC) No 1206/2001 of 28 May 2001 on co-operation between the courts of the Member States in the taking of evidence in civil or commercial matters ('the Taking of Evidence Regulation') applies.

7.2

The Taking of Evidence Regulation is annexed to this practice direction as Annex B.

7.3

The Taking of Evidence Regulation does not apply to Denmark. In relation to Denmark, therefore, rule 34.13 and Section II of Part 34 will continue to apply.

(Article 21(1) of the Taking of Evidence Regulation provides that the Regulation prevails over other provisions contained in bilateral or multilateral agreements or arrangements concluded by the Member States and in particular the Hague Convention of 1 March 1954 on Civil Procedure and the Hague Convention of 18 March 1970 on the Taking of Evidence Abroad in Civil or Commercial Matters)

Originally published in the official languages of the European Community in the *Official Journal of the European Communities* by the Office for Official Publications of the European Communities.

Meaning of 'designated court'

8.1

In accordance with the Taking of Evidence Regulation, each Regulation State has prepared a list of courts competent to take evidence in accordance with the Regulation indicating the territorial and, where appropriate, special jurisdiction of those courts.

8.2

Where Part 34, Section III refers to a 'designated court' in relation to another Regulation State, the reference is to the court, referred to in the list of competent courts of that State, which is appropriate to the application in hand.

8.3

Where the reference is to the 'designated court' in England and Wales, the reference is to the appropriate competent court in the jurisdiction. The designated courts for England and Wales are listed in Annex C to this practice direction.

Central Body

9.1

The Taking of Evidence Regulation stipulates that each Regulation State must nominate a Central Body responsible for—

(a) supplying information to courts;

(b) seeking solutions to any difficulties which may arise in respect of a request; and

(c) forwarding, in exceptional cases, at the request of a requesting court, a request to the competent court.

9.2

The United Kingdom has nominated the Senior Master, Queen's Bench Division, to be the Central Body for England and Wales.

9.3

The Senior Master, as Central Body, has been designated responsible for taking decisions on requests pursuant to Article 17 of the Regulation. Article 17 allows a court to submit a request to the Central Body or a designated competent authority in another Regulation State to take evidence directly in that State.

Evidence to be taken in another Regulation State for use in England and Wales

10.1
Where a person wishes to take a deposition from a person in another Regulation State, the court where the proceedings are taking place may order the issue of a request to the designated court in the Regulation State (Rule 34.23(2)). The form of request is prescribed as Form A in the Taking of Evidence Regulation.

10.2
An application to the court for an order under rule 34.23(2) should be made by application notice in accordance with Part 23.

10.3
Rule 34.23(3) provides that the party applying for the order must file a draft form of request in the prescribed form. Where completion of the form requires attachments or documents to accompany the form, these must also be filed.

10.4
If the court grants an order under rule 34.23 (2), it will send the form of request directly to the designated court.

10.5
Where the taking of evidence requires the use of an expert, the designated court may require a deposit in advance towards the costs of that expert. The party who obtained the order is responsible for the payment of any such deposit which should be deposited with the court for onward transmission. Under the provisions of the Taking of Evidence Regulation, the designated court is not required to execute the request until such payment is received.

10.6
Article 17 permits the court where proceedings are taking place to take evidence directly from a deponent in another Regulation State if the conditions of the article are satisfied. Direct taking of evidence can only take place if evidence is given voluntarily without the need for coercive measures. Rule 34.23(5) provides for the court to make an order for the submission of a request to take evidence directly. The form of request is Form I annexed to the Taking of Evidence Regulation and rule 34.23(6) makes provision for a draft of this form to be filed by the party seeking the order. An application for an order under rule 34.23(5) should be by application notice in accordance with Part 23.

10.7
Attention is drawn to the provisions of rule 23.10 (application to vary or discharge an order made without notice).

Evidence to be taken in England and Wales for use in another Regulation State

11.1
Where a designated court in England and Wales receives a request to take evidence from a court in a Regulation State, the court will send the request to the Treasury Solicitor.

11.2
On receipt of the request, the Treasury Solicitor may, with the consent of the Treasury, apply for an order under rule 34.24.

11.3
An application to the court for an order must be accompanied by the Form of request to take evidence and any accompanying documents, translated if required under paragraph 11.4.

11.4
The United Kingdom has indicated that, in addition to English, it will accept French as a language in which documents may be submitted. Where the form or request and any accompanying documents are received in French they will be translated into English by the Treasury Solicitor.

11.5

The order for the deponent to attend and be examined together with the evidence on which the order was made must be served on the deponent.

11.6

Arrangements for the examination to take place at a specified time and place shall be made by the Treasury Solicitor and approved by the court.

11.7

The court shall send details of the arrangements for the examination to such of

(a) the parties and, if any, their representatives; or

(b) the representatives of the foreign court,

who have indicated, in accordance with the Taking of Evidence Regulation, that they wish to be present at the examination.

11.8

The provisions of paragraph 4.3 to 4.12 apply to the depositions referred to in this paragraph.

Annex A Draft Letter of Request (where the Taking of Evidence Regulation does not apply)

To the Competent Judicial Authority of in the of

I [*name*] Senior Master of the Queen's Bench Division of the Senior Courts of England and Wales respectfully request the assistance of your court with regard to the following matters.

1

A claim is now pending in the Division of the High Court of Justice in England and Wales entitled as follows [*set out full title and claim number*] in which [*name*] of [*address*] is the claimant and [*name*] of [*address*] is the defendant.

2

The names and addresses of the representatives or agents of [*set out names and addresses of representatives of the parties*].

3

The claim by the claimant is for:-

(a) [*set out the nature of the claim*]

(b) [*the relief sought, and*]

(c) [*a summary of the facts*.]

4

It is necessary for the purposes of justice and for the due determination of the matters in dispute between the parties that you cause the following witnesses, who are resident within your jurisdiction, to be examined. The names and addresses of the witnesses are as follows:

5

The witnesses should be examined on oath or if that is not possible within your laws or is impossible of performance by reason of the internal practice and procedure of your court or by reason of practical difficulties, they should be examined in accordance with whatever procedure your laws provide for in these matters.

6

Either/

The witnesses should be examined in accordance with the list of questions annexed hereto.

Or/

The witnesses should be examined regarding [*set out full details of evidence sought*]

N.B. Where the witness is required to produce documents, these should be clearly identified.

7
I would ask that you cause me, or the agents of the parties (if appointed), to be informed of the date and place where the examination is to take place.

8
Finally, I request that you will cause the evidence of the said witnesses to be reduced into writing and all documents produced on such examinations to be duly marked for identification and that you will further be pleased to authenticate such examinations by the seal of your court or in such other way as is in accordance with your procedure and return the written evidence and documents produced to me addressed as follows:

Senior Master of the Queen's Bench Division
Royal Courts of Justice
Strand
London WC2A 2LL
England

PART 35 EXPERTS AND ASSESSORS

35.1 Duty to restrict expert evidence

Expert evidence shall be restricted to that which is reasonably required to resolve the proceedings.

35.2 Interpretation and definitions

(1) A reference to an 'expert' in this Part is a reference to a person who has been instructed to give or prepare expert evidence for the purpose of proceedings.

(2) 'Single joint expert' means an expert instructed to prepare a report for the court on behalf of two or more of the parties (including the claimant) to the proceedings.

35.3 Experts—overriding duty to the court

(1) It is the duty of experts to help the court on matters within their expertise.

(2) This duty overrides any obligation to the person from whom experts have received instructions or by whom they are paid.

35.4 Court's power to restrict expert evidence

(1) No party may call an expert or put in evidence an expert's report without the court's permission.

(2) When parties apply for permission they must provide an estimate of the costs of the proposed expert evidence and—

(a) the field in which expert evidence is required and the issues which the expert evidence will address; and

(b) where practicable, the name of the proposed expert.

(3) If permission is granted it shall be in relation only to the expert named or the field identified under paragraph (2). The order granting permission may specify the issues which the expert evidence should address.

(3A) Where a claim has been allocated to the small claims track or the fast track, if permission is given for expert evidence, it will normally be given for evidence from only one expert on a particular issue.

(Paragraph 7 of Practice Direction 35 sets out some of the circumstances the court will consider when deciding whether expert evidence should be given by a single joint expert.)

(4) The court may limit the amount of a party's expert's fees and expenses that may be recovered from any other party.

35.5 General requirement for expert evidence to be given in a written report

(1) Expert evidence is to be given in a written report unless the court directs otherwise.

(2) If a claim is on the small claims track or the fast track, the court will not direct an expert to attend a hearing unless it is necessary to do so in the interests of justice.

35.6 Written questions to experts

(1) A party may put written questions about an expert's report (which must be proportionate) to—

(a) an expert instructed by another party; or

(b) a single joint expert appointed under rule 35.7.

(2) Written questions under paragraph (1)—

(a) may be put once only;

(b) must be put within 28 days of service of the expert's report; and

(c) must be for the purpose only of clarification of the report,

unless in any case—

(i) the court gives permission; or

(ii) the other party agrees.

(3) An expert's answers to questions put in accordance with paragraph (1) shall be treated as part of the expert's report.

(4) Where—

(a) a party has put a written question to an expert instructed by another party; and

(b) the expert does not answer that question,

the court may make one or both of the following orders in relation to the party who instructed the expert—

(i) that the party may not rely on the evidence of that expert; or

(ii) that the party may not recover the fees and expenses of that expert from any other party.

35.7 Court's power to direct that evidence is to be given by a single joint expert

(1) Where two or more parties wish to submit expert evidence on a particular issue, the court may direct that the evidence on that issue is to be given by a single joint expert.

(2) Where the parties who wish to submit the evidence ('the relevant parties') cannot agree who should be the single joint expert, the court may—

(a) select the expert from a list prepared or identified by the relevant parties; or

(b) direct that the expert be selected in such other manner as the court may direct.

35.8 Instructions to a single joint expert

(1) Where the court gives a direction under rule 35.7 for a single joint expert to be used, any relevant party may give instructions to the expert.

(2) When a party gives instructions to the expert that party must, at the same time, send a copy to the other relevant parties.

(3) The court may give directions about—

(a) the payment of the expert's fees and expenses; and

(b) any inspection, examination or experiments which the expert wishes to carry out.

(4) The court may, before an expert is instructed—

(a) limit the amount that can be paid by way of fees and expenses to the expert; and

(b) direct that some or all of the relevant parties pay that amount into court.

(5) Unless the court otherwise directs, the relevant parties are jointly and severally liable for the payment of the expert's fees and expenses.

35.9 Power of court to direct a party to provide information

Where a party has access to information which is not reasonably available to another party, the court may direct the party who has access to the information to—

(a) prepare and file a document recording the information; and

(b) serve a copy of that document on the other party.

35.10 Contents of report

(1) An expert's report must comply with the requirements set out in Practice Direction 35.

(2) At the end of an expert's report there must be a statement that the expert understands and has complied with their duty to the court.

(3) The expert's report must state the substance of all material instructions, whether written or oral, on the basis of which the report was written.

(4) The instructions referred to in paragraph (3) shall not be privileged against disclosure but the court will not, in relation to those instructions—

(a) order disclosure of any specific document; or

(b) permit any questioning in court, other than by the party who instructed the expert,

unless it is satisfied that there are reasonable grounds to consider the statement of instructions given under paragraph (3) to be inaccurate or incomplete.

35.11 Use by one party of expert's report disclosed by another

Where a party has disclosed an expert's report, any party may use that expert's report as evidence at the trial.

35.12 Discussions between experts

(1) The court may, at any stage, direct a discussion between experts for the purpose of requiring the experts to—

(a) identify and discuss the expert issues in the proceedings; and

(b) where possible, reach an agreed opinion on those issues.

(2) The court may specify the issues which the experts must discuss.

(3) The court may direct that following a discussion between the experts they must prepare a statement for the court setting out those issues on which—

(a) they agree; and

(b) they disagree, with a summary of their reasons for disagreeing.

(4) The content of the discussion between the experts shall not be referred to at the trial unless the parties agree.

(5) Where experts reach agreement on an issue during their discussions, the agreement shall not bind the parties unless the parties expressly agree to be bound by the agreement.

35.13 Consequence of failure to disclose expert's report

A party who fails to disclose an expert's report may not use the report at the trial or call the expert to give evidence orally unless the court gives permission.

35.14 Expert's right to ask court for directions

(1) Experts may file written requests for directions for the purpose of assisting them in carrying out their functions.

(2) Experts must, unless the court orders otherwise, provide copies of the proposed requests for directions under paragraph (1)—

(a) to the party instructing them, at least 7 days before they file the requests; and

(b) to all other parties, at least 4 days before they file them.

(3) The court, when it gives directions, may also direct that a party be served with a copy of the directions.

35.15 Assessors

(1) This rule applies where the court appoints one or more persons under section 70 of the Senior Courts Act 1981 or section 63 of the County Courts Act 1984 as an assessor.

(2) An assessor will assist the court in dealing with a matter in which the assessor has skill and experience.

(3) An assessor will take such part in the proceedings as the court may direct and in particular the court may direct an assessor to—

(a) prepare a report for the court on any matter at issue in the proceedings; and

(b) attend the whole or any part of the trial to advise the court on any such matter.

(4) If an assessor prepares a report for the court before the trial has begun—

(a) the court will send a copy to each of the parties; and

(b) the parties may use it at trial.

(5) The remuneration to be paid to an assessor is to be determined by the court and will form part of the costs of the proceedings.

(6) The court may order any party to deposit in the court office a specified sum in respect of an assessor's fees and, where it does so, the assessor will not be asked to act until the sum has been deposited.

(7) Paragraphs (5) and (6) do not apply where the remuneration of the assessor is to be paid out of money provided by Parliament.

PRACTICE DIRECTION

EXPERTS AND ASSESSORS

This Practice Direction supplements CPR Part 35

Introduction

1

Part 35 is intended to limit the use of oral expert evidence to that which is reasonably required. In addition, where possible, matters requiring expert evidence should be dealt with by only one expert. Experts and those instructing them are expected to have regard to the guidance contained in the Protocol for the Instruction of Experts to give Evidence in Civil Claims 2014 at www.judiciary.gov.uk. (Further guidance on experts is contained in Annex C to the Practice Direction (Pre-Action Conduct)).

Expert Evidence—General Requirements

2.1

Expert evidence should be the independent product of the expert uninfluenced by the pressures of litigation.

2.2

Experts should assist the court by providing objective, unbiased opinions on matters within their expertise, and should not assume the role of an advocate.

2.3

Experts should consider all material facts, including those which might detract from their opinions.

2.4

Experts should make it clear—

(a) when a question or issue falls outside their expertise; and

(b) when they are not able to reach a definite opinion, for example because they have insufficient information.

2.5

If, after producing a report, an expert's view changes on any material matter, such change of view should be communicated to all the parties without delay, and when appropriate to the court.

2.6

(1) In a soft tissue injury claim, where permission is given for a fixed cost medical report, the first report must be obtained from an accredited medical expert selected via the MedCo Portal (website at: www.medco.org.uk).

(2) The cost of obtaining a further report from an expert not listed in rule 35.4(3C)(a) to (d) is not subject to rules 45.19(2A)(b) or 45.29I(2A)(b), but the use of that expert and the cost must be justified.

(3) 'Accredited medical expert', 'fixed cost medical report', 'MedCo', and 'soft tissue injury claim' have the same meaning as in paragraph 1.1(A1), (10A), (12A) and (16A), respectively, of the RTA Protocol.

Form and Content of an Expert's Report

3.1

An expert's report should be addressed to the court and not to the party from whom the expert has received instructions.

3.2

An expert's report must:

(1) give details of the expert's qualifications;

(2) give details of any literature or other material which has been relied on in making the report;

(3) contain a statement setting out the substance of all facts and instructions which are material to the opinions expressed in the report or upon which those opinions are based;

(4) make clear which of the facts stated in the report are within the expert's own knowledge;

(5) say who carried out any examination, measurement, test or experiment which the expert has used for the report, give the qualifications of that person, and say whether or not the test or experiment has been carried out under the expert's supervision;

(6) where there is a range of opinion on the matters dealt with in the report—

(a) summarise the range of opinions; and

(b) give reasons for the expert's own opinion;

(7) contain a summary of the conclusions reached;

(8) if the expert is not able to give an opinion without qualification, state the qualification; and

(9) contain a statement that the expert—

(a) understands their duty to the court, and has complied with that duty; and

(b) is aware of the requirements of Part 35, this practice direction and the Protocol for Instruction of Experts to give Evidence in Civil Claims.

3.3

An expert's report must be verified by a statement of truth in the following form—

I confirm that I have made clear which facts and matters referred to in this report are within my own knowledge and which are not. Those that are within my own knowledge I confirm to be true. The opinions I have expressed represent my true and complete professional opinions on the matters to which they refer.

(Part 22 deals with statements of truth. Rule 32.14 sets out the consequences of verifying a document containing a false statement without an honest belief in its truth.)

Information

4

Under rule 35.9 the court may direct a party with access to information, which is not reasonably available to another party to serve on that other party a document, which records the information. The document served must include sufficient details of all the facts, tests, experiments and assumptions which underlie any part of the information to enable the party on whom it is served to make, or to obtain, a proper interpretation of the information and an assessment of its significance.

Instructions

5

Cross-examination of experts on the contents of their instructions will not be allowed unless the court permits it (or unless the party who gave the instructions consents). Before it gives permission the court must be satisfied that there are reasonable grounds to consider that the statement in the report of the substance of the instructions is inaccurate or incomplete. If the court is so satisfied, it will allow the cross-examination where it appears to be in the interests of justice.

Questions to Experts

6.1
Where a party sends a written question or questions under rule 35.6 direct to an expert, a copy of the questions must, at the same time, be sent to the other party or parties.

6.2
The party or parties instructing the expert must pay any fees charged by that expert for answering questions put under rule 35.6. This does not affect any decision of the court as to the party who is ultimately to bear the expert's fees.

Single joint expert

7
When considering whether to give permission for the parties to rely on expert evidence and whether that evidence should be from a single joint expert the court will take into account all the circumstances in particular, whether:

(a) it is proportionate to have separate experts for each party on a particular issue with reference to—
  (i) the amount in dispute;
  (ii) the importance to the parties; and
  (iii) the complexity of the issue;
(b) the instruction of a single joint expert is likely to assist the parties and the court to resolve the issue more speedily and in a more cost-effective way than separately instructed experts;
(c) expert evidence is to be given on the issue of liability, causation or quantum;
(d) the expert evidence falls within a substantially established area of knowledge which is unlikely to be in dispute or there is likely to be a range of expert opinion;
(e) a party has already instructed an expert on the issue in question and whether or not that was done in compliance with any practice direction or relevant pre-action protocol;
(f) questions put in accordance with rule 35.6 are likely to remove the need for the other party to instruct an expert if one party has already instructed an expert;
(g) questions put to a single joint expert may not conclusively deal with all issues that may require testing prior to trial;
(h) a conference may be required with the legal representatives, experts and other witnesses which may make instruction of a single joint expert impractical; and
(i) a claim to privilege makes the instruction of any expert as a single joint expert inappropriate.

Orders

8
Where an order requires an act to be done by an expert, or otherwise affects an expert, the party instructing that expert must serve a copy of the order on the expert. The claimant must serve the order on a single joint expert.

Discussions between experts

9.1
Unless directed by the court discussions between experts are not mandatory. Parties must consider, with their experts, at an early stage, whether there is likely to be any useful purpose in holding an experts' discussion and if so when.

9.2
The purpose of discussions between experts is not for experts to settle cases but to agree and narrow issues and in particular to identify:

(i) the extent of the agreement between them;

(ii) the points of and short reasons for any disagreement;
(iii) action, if any, which may be taken to resolve any outstanding points of disagreement; and
(iv) any further material issues not raised and the extent to which these issues are agreed.

9.3
Where the experts are to meet, the parties must discuss and if possible agree whether an agenda is necessary, and if so attempt to agree one that helps the experts to focus on the issues which need to be discussed. The agenda must not be in the form of leading questions or hostile in tone.

9.4
Unless ordered by the court, or agreed by all parties, and the experts, neither the parties nor their legal representatives may attend experts discussions.

9.5
If the legal representatives do attend—
(i) they should not normally intervene in the discussion, except to answer questions put to them by the experts or to advise on the law; and
(ii) the experts may if they so wish hold part of their discussions in the absence of the legal representatives.

9.6
A statement must be prepared by the experts dealing with paragraphs 9.2(i)–(iv) above. Individual copies of the statements must be signed by the experts at the conclusion of the discussion, or as soon thereafter as practicable, and in any event within 7 days. Copies of the statements must be provided to the parties no later than 14 days after signing.

9.7
Experts must give their own opinions to assist the court and do not require the authority of the parties to sign a joint statement.

9.8
If an expert significantly alters an opinion, the joint statement must include a note or addendum by that expert explaining the change of opinion.

Assessors

10.1
An assessor may be appointed to assist the court under rule 35.15. Not less than 21 days before making any such appointment, the court will notify each party in writing of the name of the proposed assessor, of the matter in respect of which the assistance of the assessor will be sought and of the qualifications of the assessor to give that assistance.

10.2
Where any person has been proposed for appointment as an assessor, any party may object to that person either personally or in respect of that person's qualification.

10.3
Any such objection must be made in writing and filed with the court within 7 days of receipt of the notification referred to in paragraph 10.1 and will be taken into account by the court in deciding whether or not to make the appointment.

10.4
Copies of any report prepared by the assessor will be sent to each of the parties but the assessor will not give oral evidence or be open to cross-examination or questioning.

Concurrent expert evidence

11.1

At any stage in the proceedings the court may direct that some or all of the experts from like disciplines shall give their evidence concurrently. The following procedure shall then apply.

11.2

The court may direct that the parties agree an agenda for the taking of concurrent evidence, based upon the areas of disagreement identified in the experts' joint statements made pursuant to rule 35.12.

11.3

At the appropriate time the relevant experts will each take the oath or affirm. Unless the court orders otherwise, the experts will then address the items on the agenda in the manner set out in paragraph 11.4.

11.4

In relation to each issue on the agenda, and subject to the judge's discretion to modify the procedure—

(1) the judge may initiate the discussion by asking the experts, in turn, for their views. Once an expert has expressed a view the judge may ask questions about it. At one or more appropriate stages when questioning a particular expert, the judge may invite the other expert to comment or to ask that expert's own questions of the first expert;

(2) after the process set out in (1) has been completed for all the experts, the parties' representatives may ask questions of them. While such questioning may be designed to test the correctness of an expert's view, or seek clarification of it, it should not cover ground which has been fully explored already. In general a full cross-examination or re-examination is neither necessary nor appropriate; and

(3) after the process set out in (2) has been completed, the judge may summarise the experts' different positions on the issue and ask them to confirm or correct that summary.

ANNEX

Protocol for the Instruction of Experts to give Evidence in Civil Claims

Index